COGNITIVE
DEVELOPMENT

COGNITIVE DEVELOPMENT

Melinda Y. Small
Bowdoin College

Under the General Editorship of

Jerome Kagan
Harvard University

Harcourt Brace Jovanovich, Publishers
San Diego New York Chicago Austin Washington, D.C.
London Sydney Tokyo Toronto

Preface

The study of cognitive development has been influenced by two theoretical orientations: Piaget's theory and information-processing models. *Cognitive Development* has been organized to demonstrate that these two approaches complement each other. Piaget presents a truly developmental theory of cognition that describes developmental changes from birth to adulthood. However, much of recent research has been dominated by information-processing models of specific cognitive structures and processes. Typically, these models are not developmental or are limited in developmental scope. Nonetheless, they have contributed to our understanding of cognition and have raised developmental questions.

In this textbook, I have attempted to demonstrate the importance of both approaches to our understanding of cognitive development. Piaget provides us with a broad integrative model of development that focuses on cognitive structures. The information-processing models have focused on cognitive processes and have thus extended or modified our knowledge of cognition. As we learn more about the relationship between structure and process, we can look forward to developmental models that incorporate both the structural and processing features of cognition.

The first eight chapters of the textbook are organized around four developmental periods: infancy, early childhood, late childhood, and adolescence. These periods approximate the age spans of Piaget's four stages of cognitive development. Each chapter emphasizes the cognitive changes of structure and process that are particularly prevalent during each period. The last two chapters are my attempt to demonstrate how the various developmental changes in cognition discussed in earlier chapters relate to two topics fundamental to development: problem solving and social cognition.

Although the primary purpose of this book is to convey to the reader our knowledge of cognitive development, a secondary and closely related purpose is to demonstrate how psychologists study cognitive development and how the field has developed. I have tried to do this by emphasizing the interplay of theory and methodology in how research questions are generated and how findings are interpreted. The book describes many of the theoretical positions

v

that have stimulated research as well as key studies that have been designed to test these theories. Where appropriate, I have also presented alternative interpretations of research. All of this has been done in the hope that readers will gain some appreciation of how the field itself develops as psychologists analyze their theories, methods, and findings.

I wrote the textbook with the needs of both undergraduate and beginning graduate students in mind. And because students have varied backgrounds, I have not assumed an extensive or common background in psychology. I have included necessary background information and concrete examples throughout the text to elaborate the developmental research.

I have found that many, if not most, undergraduates do not have the knowledge of deductive logic necessary for appreciating the research on the development of reasoning. Indeed, this book began as a manuscript on deductive reasoning for my undergraduate class on cognitive development. My students needed to learn something about a deductive logic, and they needed to work on example problems. Thus, throughout the chapters I have assumed that the reader needs background information or, at least, needs to be reminded about it. Furthermore, I hope that many readers will use this book as a first step to a deeper study of cognitive development. To further this possibility, I have used a wide variety of references and illustrations, trusting that some of these will inspire readers to extend their study.

I owe many thanks, first to Nancy S. Johnson for her dedicated and extensive commentary on all aspects of the manuscript, and then to Shirley Schuster and Donna Trout for patiently turning my handwriting into a readable manuscript. I thank the staff of the Hawthorne-Longfellow Library, especially Laura McCourt, Sydnae Steinhart, John Ladley, Leanne Pander, and Guy Saldanha, for making so many resources available to me. Many students read and commented on various chapters of early versions of the manuscript, and I thank them for their thoughtful comments. I also thank the following reviewers for their valuable suggestions and comments: Jeffrey Fagen, St. John's University; George Holden, University of Texas; Jerome Kagan, Harvard University; Bradford Pillow, University of Pittsburgh; Ruth B. Pitt; and Amanda Walley, University of Toronto. Finally, I thank my husband, Ray Rutan, for his continous support.

Melinda Y. Small

Contents

vii

Copyrights and Acknowledgements and Illustration Credits

1

Introduction

COGNITION ◀

The study of cognition is the study of the knowledge we possess, the organization of this knowledge, and the processes we have available to us for using this knowledge in the everyday activities of attention, learning, memory, comprehension, and problem solving. As an example, consider the act of reading and comprehending this paragraph. To comprehend each word you must recognize the word and recall its meaning, which is stored in long-term memory. Your understanding of each sentence also depends upon your knowledge about the English language and how it is structured. As you read this passage, your prior knowledge about psychology may also affect your comprehension. If you have had a prior course in cognition, this brief introduction may bring to mind other activities that you know are related to cognition, for example, categorization and perception. Although it may not always seem the case, your knowledge base is a huge one. The ideas that come to your mind as you read are not a random sample of your past learning, but are related in some way to the ideas expressed in the text. Psychologists need to understand how knowledge is organized to understand your comprehension of the text. Finally, as you read this passage, you are engaging in a number of additional processes. These include attending to the material, encoding the information in the passage, retrieving related information from memory, and modifying your knowledge base as a function of the information gained in the passage. This diversity of human cognitive skills makes the study of cognition a complex and challenging enterprise.

During the past century psychology has been dominated first by *Freudian theory*, with its emphasis on the emotions and motivations of nonrational thought, and then by *Behaviorism*, which denied thought altogether, instead offering a form of human engineering for the modification of behavior. Today cognitive scientists attempt to understand the knowledge structures and the operations of the mind that guide, for example, language comprehension and reasoning, functions that are so often taken for granted by each of us, yet which govern so many of our daily accomplishments (Gardner, 1980). Unlike Freudian theory, *cognitive theories* attempt to model the thought processes of goal-directed behavior, processes which may or may not be open to consciousness.

Implicit or explicit in most theories of cognition is the assumption that the individual is actively seeking information, constructing hypotheses about reality, and testing these hypotheses. This assumption is in direct contrast to that of the Behaviorist tradition which dominated American experimental psychology before the 1960s. The Behaviorists (for example, Skinner, Watson) assumed a passive individual whose behavior was modified by the stimulus consequences of the behavior. They assumed that behavior was a function of associations between stimuli (S-S) and/or stimuli and responses (S-R). According to the Behaviorists, these associations were learned through the principles of classical and operant conditioning. Thus, an individual's behavior was controlled by the stimulus conditions of the environment and a few general principles of learning that shaped all human behavior. This is a very different view than that of cognitive psychologists who assume that individuals are problem-solving, goal-oriented, and active participants in the modification of their behavior.

The *study of cognitive development* is the study of the changes in cognitive structures and processes that occur with age. Do infants perceive and know the world and their experiences in it as do adults? Clearly not. The issue for the psychologist investigating cognitive development is to specify the knowledge structures and processes of the infant and to trace the developmental changes in these structures and processes. Furthermore, the developmentalist seeks to determine the mechanisms that cause these developmental changes.

METHODS OF STUDY

How can we investigate these mental structures and processes? Just as the electron is not visible to the physicist, so mental structures and processes are not visible to the cognitive psychologist. The psychologist, however, can observe behavior and from these observations attempt to draw inferences about cognition. This is a very different use of behavior than that of the Behaviorists. The Behaviorists studied behavior for its own sake and rejected speculations about the nature of mental events; the cognitive psychologist is not studying behavior per se but using it to make inferences about mental structures and processes. Throughout this book there is an emphasis on the methods used to answer questions about cognitive development. As you will see, the inferences that can be drawn from any given study are clearly dependent on how the question is posed, the nature of the question (see Kessen, 1960; Wohlwill, 1973, for extended discussions of this issue), and the method used to investigate the issue. If, for example, the question is a descriptive one that asks what changes occur in a given behavior or capability as a function of age then either the cross-sectional method or the longitudinal method is appropriate. In the *cross-sectional method* children of different ages are tested and comparisons are made between the age groups to determine if there are differences in performance. In the *longitudinal method* the same children are observed at different ages. This method is particularly valuable when there are individual differences in the timing of a developmental change in behavior and the investigator is concerned with the rate of change. In such a situation the averaged scores of children in a cross-sectional study may not adequately reflect the rate of change. A longitudinal study would not only indicate the change but the individual differences in the timing of the change (compare, Diamond, 1985).

If the goal of the research is to explore explanations for developmental changes then the *experimental method* is required. This method is designed to answer questions that are testing specific hypotheses. As researchers in cognitive development have identified major developmental trends in a variety of cognitive skills, hypotheses have been offered to explain why the changes occur. The experimental method is used to test such hypotheses.

There are many variations of these three methods. Which variation is used in a given study will depend upon a number of factors, including the research question, the relative costs in time and money, and the theoretical orientation of the researcher.

THEORY

Theories are the constructions of scientists who desire to explain the phenomena they study. Theorizing is an attempt by the scientist to make some order of the multitudinous observations of a discipline. It is an attempt to abstract the general principles that are the basis for the observed environmental events. A *theory* is a set of assumptions about the basic concepts that underlie the phenomena of interest and the relationships that exist between these concepts. For example, the assumptions of quantum theory include concepts such as quarks and charms and how these concepts are related to each other. Theories make it possible for the scientist to derive predictions about what should happen in a given situation if a given theory is "correct." But any number of theories can be constructed for a given set of facts. Indeed, theory construction is analogous to story construction. Suppose that you have the following facts:

1. Andy and Mitch are on the front lawn exchanging a tennis ball.
2. Suddenly, Mitch takes the ball and runs off.
3. Henrietta comes out the door and scolds Andy.

Make up a story to explain this set of facts and ask a few friends to do the same. Consider the assumptions of each story and the differences in these assumptions. How can you choose between these interpretations of the observations? As it stands you cannot, except possibly on the grounds of aesthetics or originality. There is no reason to argue that one story is more correct than another. Scientists start at the same point, but they are not satisfied to stop at this stage; rather, they want to find ways to eliminate some of the alternative theories or stories. Ideally, scientific theories are stated with enough precision to make it possible to derive predictions for what should happen in a new situation. Theories are then tested by setting up the situations and observing the similarity between the predictions of each theory under consideration and the outcome of the test situation.

According to the assumptions of your story, what will be the next event? Now suppose the next event is:

4. Henrietta hands Andy a leash.

How must you modify your story to incorporate this additional fact?

As theories are tested, some predictions are not supported. When this happens, theories are often modified enough to accommodate the new observations (see Kuhn, 1970). Theories in any science evolve as new data are collected, new methods are developed, and alternative hypotheses are proposed. Research methods and the interpretation of data are intimately tied to theoretical perspectives. This book, therefore, emphasizes the role of theory in cognitive development research: how theories are modified as research continues, and how theories influence the types of questions that are asked about cognition.

In the following chapters we will consider the strengths and weaknesses of many theories, for there is no one "correct" grand theory of cognitive development. Just as the theories of physical events have continued to develop during the past 600 years, so the cognitive psychologist can look forward to an extended future of theory development.

▶ THEORIES OF COGNITIVE DEVELOPMENT

Two theoretical orientations have dominated the research on cognitive development: Piaget's and information processing. Both are described generally here and are elaborated on throughout the following chapters. Ten to fifteen years ago research on cognitive development was founded either on Piaget's theory or on information-processing theories. There was little cross talk between the two camps. Current research, however, is often influenced by theoretical formulations that incorporate elements of both Piagetian and information-processing theories (for example, Siegler, 1978; Case, 1985). The organization of this book is intended to reflect the contributions of both Piaget's theory and information-processing theories to our understanding of cognitive development.

JEAN PIAGET

Jean Piaget, the Swiss psychologist, wrote extensively on cognitive development for over half a century before his death in 1980. Although his work had relatively little influence upon research in this country prior to Flavell's book on the subject in 1963, it has had a profound influence since then and is the most comprehensive and coherent theory of cognitive development. The theory has a broad scope which covers the age range from birth to the end of adolescence and many content areas, such as memory for objects, causality, imitation, and logic. Piaget's theory can best be described as a *structural theory*; that is, the emphasis is on the organization of the child's knowledge rather than the processes for the acquisition and application of the knowledge. According to Piaget, a child's cognitive structure is composed of a set of schemes which are abstractions of his behavior or thought patterns. Initially, *schemes* are patterns of action. Even newborns exhibit organized behavior. Schemes are these organized patterns of infant action. Although each act of, for example, sucking can differ in details, there are regularities common to all sucking behavior. Schemes are these regularities. Schemes make it possible for an infant to generalize a behavior pattern, such as sucking, to new objects. With experience the schemes change and become more abstract rules about what operations can be performed on what things; in adolescence the "things" become thoughts themselves.

Piaget acknowledges the role of both innate structures and the environment in the development of cognitive structures and stresses the interaction of the two factors; his emphasis, however, is on experience. But Piaget's emphasis on the role of experience is not like that of the learning theorists of the Behaviorist tradition, who assume a passive role for children as perceptual experiences are imposed upon them. Rather, Piaget assumes that children play an active role and construct their own reality. At any given time children have a set of schemes about the nature of the world and in any new situation use these schemes to direct their actions. As children act on their environment, they observe the transformations that occur as a consequence. For example, the young infant dropping a cup from the high chair will observe certain types of changes in the orientation and position of that cup. If these transformations do not conform to the schemes of the child's knowledge base, modification of the schemes may occur.

Piaget assumes that two biological functions, adaptation and organization, affect the development of cognitive structures. These invariant functions are seen as common to all biological systems and, unlike the cognitive structures, they do not change with age and experience. *Adaptation* has two component functions: accommodation and assimilation. All actions and thoughts involve both of these processes. *Assimilation* is the individual's effort to deal with the environment by incorporating it into already existing schemes for thought or action. For example, the young infant has an early scheme for blanket grasping. When attempts are first made to grasp a rattle, the infant is attempting to assimilate the rattle to the blanket grasping scheme. This will not be successful, but eventually through trial and error the infant will adjust the grasping scheme to the characteristics of the rattle. *Accommodation* is this process of modification of an existing scheme to the characteristics of a particular object or event. As the child's experiences broaden, accommodation and assimilation constantly interact in this manner to promote the development of cognitive structures. The second function, *organization,* serves to organize schemes into increasingly complex relations with each other. Piaget assumed that there is a hereditary tendency to integrate the psychological structures, schemes, into higher-order systems or structures. This integration results in the coordination of schemes. For example, the individual sucking, grasping, and looking schemes of young infants are eventually organized into an action pattern that integrates the three into a "look-grasp-suck" scheme. For Piaget, cognitive development occurs because there is conflict between the children's representation of the world (schemes) and the consequences of their application of these schemes in the environment. Through the processes of adaptation and organization of the schemes, children actively work to construct cognitive structures that are better representations of their world.

Piaget's theory is a stage theory in which he assumes that cognitive structures pass through four major qualitative stages. These stages occur in the following invariant order.

1. The first, *sensorimotor,* covers the period of infancy from birth to 18 to 24 months. During this period the infants' knowledge is in the form of action schemes. They know how to act on objects.

2. It is not until the second stage, *preoperations,* from two to seven or eight years, that children have mental representations of objects, independent of actions on the objects. It is during this period that children first have the cognitive structures necessary for knowing that objects exist even when they are not within sight, touch, or hearing.

3. *Concrete operations,* the third stage, lasts until 11 or 12 and is characterized by the development of a system of mental operations for operating on objects. Children not only can think about objects but also can think about manipulating objects.

4. During the final stage, *formal operations,* adolescents have acquired the cognitive structures that make it possible to think about thoughts themselves. They are no longer restricted to reflecting about concrete objects, but can now mentally manipulate nontangible propositions that may or may not represent the state of the concrete environment.

Thus, Piaget assumes that cognitive development is marked by four stages that are characterized by major qualitative changes in the nature of the cognitive structures. Although recent research does not always support Piaget's assumption that there are stage-like changes in cognition (Brainerd, 1978; Flavell, 1982), there is evidence for invariant sequences of cognitive development (Flavell, 1982). Therefore, this book uses Piaget's four stages of cognitive development as a heuristic device to organize the extensive research on cognitive development. The cognitive structures of each of Piaget's stages and related research are discussed in detail in subsequent chapters.

THE INFORMATION-PROCESSING APPROACH

The information-processing approach to cognition assumes that the mind is a system for storing and processing information. Three factors led to the demise of Behaviorism in the 1960s and the rise of the information-processing theories (Anderson, 1985). The first factor was a seminal book by Broadbent in 1958 which brought together two influences: information theory of the communication sciences and the human factors research on human skills and performance. In his book Broadbent reported a program of research on selective attention and a theory to explain the fact that an individual does not encode all available stimulus information. The Behaviorists used stimulus consequences and S-R associations to explain behavior, but had not addressed the problem of the selective and limited attention capacities of the organism. Broadbent's book made clear the importance of this weakness in Behaviorist theories.

The second factor was Chomsky's (1957) work on linguistic theory in which he described the syntactic knowledge that an adult must possess to comprehend language. Also, Chomsky's review in 1959 of Skinner's *Verbal Behavior* (1957) presented a critique of Skinner's stimulus-response explanation of language acquisition that made clear the limitations of Behaviorism for explaining language and the importance of knowledge structures for understanding language behavior.

The third factor was from computer science. The first commercial computer was available in 1950, and programs were written to perform a variety of tasks. The knowledge structures and processes for handling information used in these programs were recognized as useful analogies for the study of mental structures and processes. Although some information-processing theories are computer programs that are designed to carry out specific cognitive functions, the greater influence of computer science on cognitive psychology has been indirect. Psychologists have adopted many concepts from computer science and "observing how we could analyze the intelligent behavior of a machine has largely liberated us from our inhibitions and misconceptions about analyzing our own intelligence" (Anderson, 1985, p. 8).

Information processing can best be viewed as an approach to theorizing about cognition. There are many information-processing theories. For the most part, these theories have focused on adult (that is, college students) cognition. When the information-processing approach has been used to address developmental questions, the theories have focused on a limited aspect and/or age range of cognitive development (for example, memory or transitive inference).

There is no information-processing model of cognitive development that in any way approaches the comprehensive scope of Piaget's theory.

Adult models of cognition vary in scope, the problems addressed, and whether stated as a specific computer program, but all information-processing theories have several basic assumptions in common (Howard, 1983). First, it is assumed that humans process environmental information in a series of stages between the occurrence of a stimulus and the production of a response and that each of these stages takes some amount of time. Second, during these processing stages, the information is transformed. For example, information that is initially in a visual code is transformed into a verbal one. Third, at some point in the system, there is a limited capacity—there is a limit on the amount of processing that occurs at one time (Howard, 1983).

A simplified model, as illustrated in Figure 1-1, indicates the five major components of information processing: sensory registers, short-term memory, long-term memory, central processor, and response system. Information flows from the environment to the sensory system and from there the coded information activates certain aspects of permanent memory. These activated memories are then part of working memory, which is assumed to have a limited capacity. Overseeing the processing of the information is the central processor, which deals with goals and the plans for reaching the goals. The fifth component, the response system, controls all output, as varied as singing and tree climbing.

Each of the three memory systems—sensory registers, working memory, and long-term memory—is assumed to have specific characteristics in terms of its capacity, the cause of forgetting, and how the information is represented. As specified in Table 1-1, for example, the capacity of the sensory registers is large, subject to decay (that is, over time the representation deteriorates), and the representation is similar to the external stimulus. Thus, information presented visually is coded in a large-capacity register in a visual code that is similar to the actual stimuli presented.

Working memory, however, has a small capacity. The information is presented in a variety of codes and susceptible primarily to interference; the activation of new information replaces old information. Long-term memory has an unlimited capacity with several types of representation of the information, including semantic, verbal, and visual. Forgetting is a function of retrieval failures. Information is not lost from long-term memory; rather, forgetting is a failure to retrieve the information stored in a long-term memory (Howard, 1983).

Figure 1-1 represents a limited view of the complexity of the relationships between the major components and the variety of processes that are involved. For example, we see that the central processor and working memory function together to activate and monitor the plans and subgoals of the system. The model also indicates the range of information that is held in permanent memory which is or is not activated, depending upon the environmental situation.

Although the model depicted in Figure 1-1 portrays the control processes

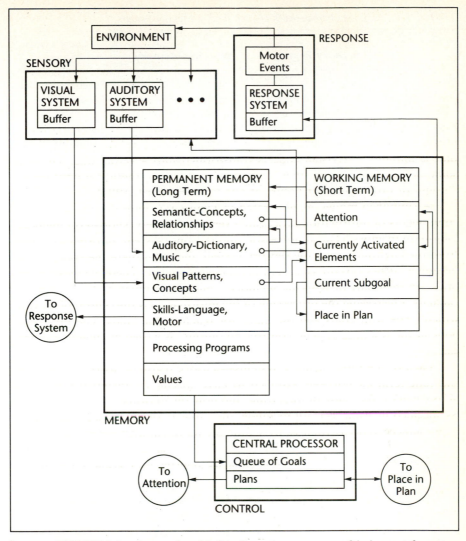

FIGURE 1-1 *A general model of the five major components of the human information-processing system. (From Dodd & White, 1980.)*

of the central processor as separate from long-term memory, these are actually stored as procedures in long-term memory. Thus, long-term memory contains both *declarative knowledge,* or a diverse set of facts (I know that the gravity of the moon is less than the gravity of the earth, I know that I know how to play tennis, and so on) and, *procedural knowledge,* or "how-to" knowledge (I know how to walk, I know how to play tennis, and so on).

Finally, it is assumed that the knowledge stored in long-term memory is organized. Clearly, our behavior indicates that there must be *some* form of

TABLE 1-1 *Assumed Characteristics of Each Kind of Memory System*

	Sensory Registers	Working Memory	Long-Term Memory
Capacity	Large	Small	Functionally infinite
Cause of Forgetting	Primarily decay, but also interference	Primarily interference, but also decay	Retrieval failures
Kind of Representation	Closely tied to form of external stimulus	Flexible, probably including verbal, visual, and semantic	Semantic, verbal, and visual

Source: Howard, 1983. Reprinted with permission of Macmillan Publishing Co. from Cognitive Psychology *by D. V. Howard. Copyright © 1983 by Darlene V. Howard.*

organization. When I get in the driver's seat of a car, I carry out the procedures for driving a car, not for walking. All information-processing theories assume some form of structure for the knowledge in long-term memory. The theories differ, however, in the nature of the organization. We will return to this issue when we discuss concept acquisition.

▶ ISSUES IN DEVELOPMENT AND COGNITION

THE NATURE OF KNOWLEDGE REPRESENTATION

All theories of human knowledge must deal with questions of how knowledge is mentally represented, a key problem for any theory of cognition. Assumptions about how knowledge is represented have important implications not only for what types of knowledge we acquire from our experiences, but also for how we access this knowledge and, thus, how this knowledge relates to our daily cognitive tasks. To illustrate, the lexicon of a language can be represented in an alphabetical dictionary. This form of representation means it is relatively easy to access words that begin with a particular letter; it is very difficult to find the words that end with that letter. Thus, throughout the book there is an emphasis on the nature of mental representation. The following general overview serves to introduce this issue.

Consider first Behaviorist learning theory. The Behaviorists assume that knowledge is represented in the association between a stimulus and a response. As an analogy consider the behavior of my dog, Xing (a Tibetian mastiff). She has been trained to guard sheep, and is very shy of humans. If a stranger approaches, she barks and circles backwards, putting herself between the stranger and the sheep. She does "know" me, however, since, when I drive up, she does not bark and greets me when I get out of the car.

The Behaviorists would explain this behavior in terms of S–R connections (Stimulus–Response). That is, a complex of stimuli, my visual image, my voice, my smell, the sound of my car, has been associated with a greeting response because such behavior has been reinforced in the past with attention and food.

This is not a cognitive theory, since the theory does not assume that mental representations mediate the stimuli and the responses. Again, an analogy may be helpful. When I am gone does my dog "think" about me? Does she have a knowledge structure that represents me independent of my presence? That is, does she have the declarative knowledge that I exist even when I am not present? I think about Xing even when she is not physically present. When I remember in the middle of my day at the office that it is time for Xing to have her rabies shot, I access a representation of Xing that is independent of her presence. Does Xing think about me in my absence? This is a difficult question to answer about a nonverbal organism; we will confront this problem in the chapters on infancy.

The Behaviorists assumed that all behavior could be explained in terms of S–R associations. But as the S–R analysis was extended to explain children's discrimination learning (Spiker, 1963) and the acquisition of language (Skinner, 1957), the S–R connections became cumbersome and included mediating non-physical stimuli and responses (see, for example, Kendler, 1960). And, as our brief historical review indicates, psychologists were beginning to recognize the implications of other forms of knowledge representations, such as those evident in Chomsky's linguistic theory and in information theory.

Chomsky's linguistic theory assumes mental representation of knowledge. He assumes that our knowledge of language, knowledge that makes it possible for us to comprehend and produce meaningful sentences, is represented by a set of abstract rules for transforming ideas into sentences. Chomsky's theory assumes that the expression of these ideas in language is generated from rules of syntax that are possessed by all human language users (see Chomsky, 1980).

The information-processing theories have been concerned with the representation of the knowledge base (stored knowledge) as well as the processes that operate on that knowledge base. The assumptions of these theories have varied considerably, but they do have a few common themes. First, most assume that declarative knowledge is represented in the form of propositions, knowledge structures that specify relations between concepts. This assumption is directly influenced by the work in computer programming and means that concepts, not words or images, are used to represent knowledge. Although not all cognitive psychologists accept this as the only form of representation (see Shephard & Metzler, 1971), it is assumed by most to be a primary form of representation (see Anderson, 1976). Theories differ, however, in their assumptions about how propositional information is organized (see Collins & Quillan, 1969; Meyer, 1970; Smith, Shoben & Rips, 1974).

Additionally, all theories make assumptions about the nature of the processes that operate on the knowledge base and the relative importance of these processes in the model. These processes are the procedural knowledge that we use to perform various cognitive activities. Some theories, for example, assume a relatively small knowledge base and use powerful computational processes to solve problems. As an example, imagine alternative models for multiplication (Mandler, 1983). At one extreme would be a model that includes a vast store of knowledge about numbers including a multiplication table up through one hundred. When asked to multiply 56 times 78, this program would search for these two numbers and the answer stored with them. At the other extreme would be a program that has a minimal amount of number knowledge stored but includes the operations necessary for multiplying any numbers. Both of these programs will generate the correct answer, but in very different ways. Of course, models somewhere in the middle of these two extremes are possible. Indeed, my introspection about my own multiplication skills and my early training suggests that I have a knowledge base that includes a multiplication table for numbers up to 10 and rules or operations for multiplying numbers greater than 10. My children, however, were taught the new math in the 1960s. This math emphasized operations and not number facts, and they seem to use a more limited multiplication table data base and to be more dependent on operations for solving all multiplication problems. Thus, each information-processing theory makes assumptions about the nature of the knowledge structure and the processes that operate on knowledge.

Piaget's theory assumes that there are qualitative changes in the representation of knowledge. As children develop through their four stages, the knowledge structures become increasingly sophisticated. Indeed, as we will discover in the next chapter, Piaget assumes that representation in the sensorimotor stage is not mental; it is in the form of sensorimotor schemes, which are similar in some respects to the stimulus–response associations of the learning theorists. Or, put into information-processing terms, infants have procedural knowledge, but not declarative knowledge (see Mandler, 1984a, for a discussion of this issue). Infants know how to act on objects, but they do not know about objects or that they know how to act on objects.

Piaget represents the knowledge structure of the later stages of cognitive development as increasingly sophisticated forms of symbolic representation. For Piaget, thinking involves the activation and manipulation of these symbols (Mandler, 1984a). In the final stage, formal operations, Piaget represents the adolescent's cognitive structures as a version of symbolic logic that is similar to that used by logicians.

THE COMPETENCE-PERFORMANCE DISTINCTION

Implicit in the above discussion of representation is another issue, the competence-performance distinction. Cognitive development has two interrelated aspects: a competence component and a performance component (see Flavell & Wohlwill, 1969, for an extended discussion). The *competence component* represents the knowledge, the rules and mental operations on these rules, that are prerequisites for cognitive activities. Such competence can be represented in two ways—formal and psychological—and both are used in models of cognitive development. Competence can be expressed as a formal, logical representation of knowledge for a given sphere of action. For example, Chomsky's linguistic theory is a formal competence model of language and Piaget's theory is a competence model of cognition in general. Formal competence models are possible for any number of domains, but all are characterized by abstract representations of knowledge for that domain. These formal representations of competence need not, however, be the same as the psychological representations of competence. When a young child learns to ride a bicycle this accomplishment reflects a knowledge of the relations between objects, trajectories, and the redistribution of weight that is necessary to maintain balance. In principle, these relations could be formally represented as mathematical functions. However, it does not necessarily follow that psychological representation of the knowledge necessary for bike riding is in the form of these mathematical functions. Models that attempt to depict psychological competence make assumptions about the nature of knowledge as it is mentally represented.

Competence models or theories do not make assumptions about the psychological processes that affect the performance of a real child or adult. That is, Chomsky's theory does not specify how an adult speaker produces grammatical statements, but rather what the speaker must know in order to produce such statements. Competence models are not directly concerned with individual differences or situational/task demands that may affect cognitive activities.

The *performance component* of cognitive development identifies those factors that determine how competence is expressed and how it may be constrained. Again, an analogy may be helpful. I know the rules of croquet and I know many strategies for playing the game. This knowledge of croquet is my croquet competence. But my performance in any given game depends upon a number of factors, some not specific to croquet. These include such conditions as energy level, concentration, desire to win, manual skills, whether I recognize when to use a specific strategy, and my ability to plan ahead to take advantage of the rules and strategies of the game.

My croquet competence can be inferred from my playing behavior, but no one game will adequately portray my competence. Thus, competence must be abstracted from multiple observations of my play. Clearly, my performance is dependent upon my competence, but to understand my performance many other factors must also be identified and evaluated.

Similarly, an understanding of cognitive development requires the recognition of the importance of both the competence and performance components of cognition. Without a competence model to specify the nature of competencies that have the potential for expression, we cannot understand cognitive development. Although it is possible to write competence models of cognition, such models do not aid us in our understanding of the conditions that do and do not foster the application of the competence. Therefore, cognitive psychologists must also consider the role of performance factors in development.

MATURATION AND EXPERIENCE

Although there is nothing to indicate that the nature of human development has changed in the last 300–400 years, our conception of human development certainly has changed. In the period prior to the 1700s, scientists and educators generally accepted the preformation position that at conception the individual was completely formed in miniature. For these preformationists, growth and development was simply the simultaneous enlargement of the several body parts. Even the invention of the microscope did not immediately destroy this view. Scientists so strongly held this conviction that they reported seeing tiny horses in the semen of the horses; Hartesoeker (c. 1694) envisioned a small man within a human spermatozoan (Hunt, 1961).

Eventually, the doctrine of predetermined development replaced the theory of preformation. The biological work that destroyed preformationism indicated that there were qualitative and universal changes during embryonic development. These embryonic transformations were assumed to be predetermined at conception. An individual's development was an unfolding that was prescribed and unalterable. Although this maturational position was the dominant view of human development during the late eighteenth and nineteenth centuries, not all philosophers were in agreement.

Indeed, John Locke (1632–1704) took the position that the child comes into the world with a mind that is a blank slate. This view influenced John Watson and the Behaviorists in the 1930s to such an extent that Watson took an extreme environmentalist position asserting that, aside from the few reflexes at birth, experience completely determined the development of the individual.

The extreme positions of the nativists and environmentalists generated research programs in the 1930s, but as methodology improved and adequate data were collected, it became increasingly clear that more complex models were necessary (Hebb, 1958). Based on earlier work by Gottlieb (1981), Aslin and his colleagues (Aslin & Pisoni, 1980; Aslin, Pisoni & Jusczyk, 1983) have distinguished the following four types of developmental theories.

1. The *maturational theories* assume that experience has no effect on development and that developmental changes are a function of the unfolding of a predetermined developmental schedule. The other three types (illustrated in Figure 1-2) assume that experience has some effect on development.

2. The *universal theories* assume that a capacity is fully developed at birth, but that relevant experience is necessary to maintain that capacity. A failure to receive such experience results in a loss or attenuation of capacity.

3. *Attunement theories* assume that the capacity is not fully developed at birth and that depending on the nature of the experience it has no effect, facilitates, or attenuates the capacity.

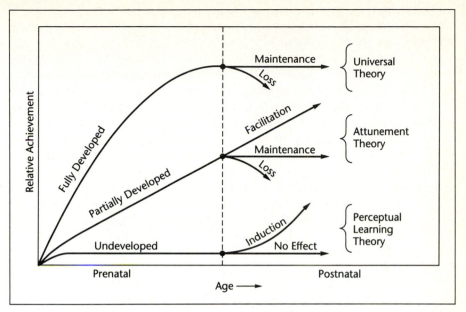

FIGURE 1-2 *Effects of early experience on development as explained by the following three developmental theories: universal, attunement, and perceptual learning.* (From Aslin, Pisoni & Jusczyk, 1983. Modified from Gottlieb, 1981.)

4. Finally, *perceptual learning theories* assume that the capacity is not present at birth and only develops with the appropriate experience.

Biological and behavioral research with animals indicates that the type of theory that best explains development depends upon the specific capacity under consideration. That is, no one type of theory appears adequate to explain the myriad of developmental changes evident in a species.

What of human development? Although the potential importance of the environment is generally recognized, no contemporary theorist takes a hardcore environmentalist interpretation of cognitive development. Indeed, such a position is logically flawed since an extreme environmental view would not be able to explain how development gets started. At the minimum, nature must provide the organism with capabilities to process environmental information and with some initial set of responses. Controversies pivot around the question of what capabilities are present at birth and how these develop.

Piaget has taken an interactionist position on the nature-nurture issue. The infant is born with a set of reflexes, a sensory system, and the two functional invariants, organization and adaptation. Through interaction with the objects and events of the environment, the sensorimotor schemes underlying early infant behavior are modified. As these interactions continue in a normal environment, the cognitive structures of the four stages universally develop in a fixed sequence. Thus, the consequences of interaction with the environment are dependent upon the present state of the child's cognitive structures: ". . . the human organism is born with the capacity to acquire sensorimotor and higher ('cognitive') structures. However, the only way to acquire these structures is by way of experiencing the concrete world, that is, living a human life" (Furth, 1974, p. 59). For Piaget the important aspects of the environment that promote cognitive change are the ones that are common experiences, experiences that are universal to the species, for example, cups fall when they are dropped. This differs importantly from the Behaviorist's emphasis on experience, which was an emphasis on the particular experience of the individual. Piaget's theory focuses on what knowledge is abstracted from the ordinary experiences of children. He assumes that these universal experiences with objects and people result in the development of the same cognitive structures for all children (Furth, 1974).

Further, Piaget assumes that children are motivated to interact with their environment; they have a need to use their schemes, which often means generalizing a scheme to new objects. Additionally, experience interacts with knowledge structures in such a way as to reorganize the knowledge structures themselves. Development is not simply an increasingly larger set of S–R associations.

Although the role of experience in cognitive development is generally acknowledged by contemporary psychologists, for the most part the issue has not been directly addressed. In part this may be a recognition of the complexity of the alternative environmental influences as illustrated in Figure 1-2, and the fact that the animal data suggest that no one general interpretation is adequate to explain the development of the organism.

In part, however, this failure to address the issue may be a recognition of the difficulties of studying the effects of environmental manipulation on human development. One major difficulty, of course, is the practical problem of doing such research. What manipulations should be made and for how long? But the more prohibitive difficulty is the ethical one.

In animal research there are two approaches to the study of environmental effects on development. One is to deprive young animals of early experiences that are assumed to be important in development. For obvious ethical reasons, these types of studies are not done with humans. Our limited knowledge of deprivation experiences comes from the individual cases of atypical rearing conditions. But these instances can be difficult to interpret since it is not always clear whether neurophysiological and/or physical changes have occurred before or during the abnormal upbringing.

The second approach is to use enrichment conditions. In this case the infant animal is exposed to environmental situations over and above the normal rearing conditions. (Note that in most animal studies the normal laboratory rearing conditions are deprived conditions relative to the normal rearing conditions in nature.) There have been a number of enrichment studies with human infants and children, including numerous enrichment studies of the development of Piaget's cognitive stages, especially concrete operations. But all enrichment studies have problems of interpretation. If there is no effect for the enrichment program relative to the performance of a control group, no interpretation is possible. That is, such a result does not mean that training has no effect on the specific cognitive skill under study. Rather, the only interpretation is that with these children, at this time, in this place, and with these specific training conditions, the children do not benefit. This is, of course, the problem of the interpretation of the null hypothesis.

What interpretation can be given for a significant positive enrichment effect? Since most of such studies have investigated relatively short-term effects, it is not clear when training has any persistent effects on development. Furthermore, the interpretations of long- or short-term effects are complicated by the fact that it is not possible to know if the training procedures imitate the conditions of everyday experience. That is, the training may facilitate cognitive change, but this does not mean that that type of experience is necessary for such a change; other daily experiences may also result in the cognitive change (see Flavell, 1985; Wohlwill, 1973, for a discussion of this issue).

MECHANISMS OF COGNITIVE DEVELOPMENT

For the developmental psychologist there are two key questions: What changes occur? How do the changes occur? This book focuses on the first question because the vast majority of the cognitive development research has concentrated on what changes in cognition occur with development. This emphasis is appropriate since it would be impossible to answer the second question without answering the first.

This is not to say that theoretical positions have not been taken on the mechanisms for development. Piaget proposed a general mechanism for developmental changes. If there is a conflict or contradiction between children's present knowledge structures and their immediate experiences, disequilibrium occurs, and they work to return to a state of equilibrium. This is done through the process of adaptation. Thus, Piaget assumes basic biological functions to explain developmental changes, functions that are not amenable to experimental test.

Traditional learning theory also assumes a general mechanism for change; it assumes that the principles of learning apply in all situations. Although this is not a cognitive theory, it has become evident to many cognitive psychologists that some form of learning must be incorporated into information-processing theories. Indeed, some theorists do incorporate learning assumptions (see, for example, Anderson, 1976). These assumptions are intended to explain how new knowledge is acquired. But such learning theories do not address the question of developmental change (see Wohlwill, 1973, for a discussion of this issue). Developmental changes in cognition can imply not only changes in the content of the knowledge base, but also in the cognitive structures, changes in how the knowledge is organized.

► ## SUMMARY

The study of cognitive development is the study of the development of knowledge structures and processes. Since these structures and processes cannot be directly observed, they are inferred from the behavior of infants and children. Several methods, including cross-sectional, longitudinal, and experimental, are used to draw inferences and to test theories of cognitive development.

Two types of theories, Piaget's and information processing, have dominated the research in cognitive development. Piaget's theory is a comprehensive one that emphasizes the development, from infancy to adolescence, of qualitative changes in the knowledge structures. There is no one information-processing theory; rather, there are many, all of which make the common assumptions that the mind is a system for storing and processing information and that information is processed in a series of stages that transform and manipulate the information. Information-processing models of cognitive development have been narrow in scope and often have not been developmental. They have served, however, to stress the importance of cognitive processes, as well as cognitive structures, for our understanding of cognitive development.

Four issues are basic to the study of cognitive development. First, is the nature of knowledge representation. Any model or theory of cognitive development must make assumptions about how knowledge is mentally represented. This includes assumptions about the nature of the basic components of knowledge representation as well as the organization of these components. Second, we make a distinction between the performance that is observable and the cognitive competence that is inferred from behavior. This distinction reminds us that a number of factors, in addition to cognitive competence, contribute to performance. As we seek to trace the development of cognitive competence we must be aware of these other factors that can affect the behaviors we observe. Third, all developmentalists have a concern with the relative influences of experience and maturation on developmental change. Although this issue is not always directly confronted, we will see that this issue has influenced some models of cognitive development. Related to this is the fourth issue, how developmental change occurs. Although Piaget has taken a position on this issue, information-processing models have had less to say about the mechanism of cognitive change.

2

Infancy: Sensorimotor and Perceptual Development

SENSORIMOTOR DEVELOPMENT ◀

Infancy is generally defined as the first one and one-half to two years of life and is characterized by extensive changes in physical growth, motor skills, cognitive skills, and social-emotional responsivity. The neonate is born with a set of reflexes (see, for example, Barclay, 1985). These are involuntary behavior patterns that are elicited by specific stimulations. Some of these, such as the rooting and sucking reflexes, are important in finding and ingesting food. Other reflexes, such as blinking and grasping, appear to have protective value; others control the position of the infant.

Most newborn reflexes are controlled by the lower brain centers, particularly the brain stem and the spinal cord. By three or four months of age, the majority of these reflexes disappear and are replaced by voluntary actions. Indeed, it is often a sign of cortical damage if they do not disappear, since it is generally acknowledged that as the cortex of the brain matures it inhibits, or overrides, many involuntary reflexes.

Cognition, however, is not about reflexes, but rather about the structure of knowledge and the processes for the acquisition of knowledge. Thus, our concern will be about what knowledge infants have, how this knowledge is acquired, and how the knowledge is represented. Clearly, an important step in understanding cognitive development is to determine the sensory and perceptual skills of the infant; we need to know how newborns are linked to the world if we are to trace the development of their cognitive skills.

Over a period of several years in the 1920s and 1930s, Piaget made extensive observations of his three children. On the basis of these observations, Piaget (1952b; 1954) argued that thought arises from action. Newborns arrive with a set of reflexes. Through an infant's interaction with the objects of the environment, the sensorimotor schemes that underly behavior are modified and coordinated. For Piaget sensorimotor schemes are relatively stable systems for acting on the environment. However, each infant's act differs in some detail; no two actions are identical. For example, the newborn does not suck the nipple in exactly the same way every time. Piaget's sensorimotor schemes are abstractions of those features that are common to a set of actions. The sucking schema describes the infant's regular way of behaving when the lips are stimulated (Ginsburg & Opper, 1988). As the infant acts on objects in the environment, the sensorimotor schemes are modified and organized into higher-order relations with each other. Thus, for Piaget the changes that occur in the relative complexity of the sensorimotor schemes are a function of the infant's motor activity. The infant's knowledge of the world is represented only in these sensorimotor schemes. That is, the infant knows what to *do* with a given object; in information-processing terms the infant's knowledge is *procedural*. Only at the end of this sensorimotor stage does the infant begin to have mental representation or *declarative* knowledge (Mandler, 1984a).

Piaget assumes that development in the sensorimotor stage progresses through a series of six substages which describe the invariant order of the developmental changes in six content areas: general activity, imitation, and the concepts of object, time, space, and causality. Two of these, general activity and object concept, are illustrated in Table 2-1. Although ages are specified with each substage, it is important to realize that Piaget's theory is about stages of development, not the age norms of a given stage. Thus, children can progress through the stages at different rates; there will be individual differences in the ages of the children at a given stage of development.

In the first substage of general activity, newborns begin with a set of innate reflexes that are modified during this period to the individual characteristics of the stimulus. In the second substage, infants begin to make primary circular reactions; their random movements prove pleasurable or interesting and they attempt to repeat these actions for their own sake. These are *primary circular reactions* because the repetition is centered on the infants' own actions. During this stage intercoordination of the schemes begins to develop. Infants, for example, coordinate the look and grasp schemes. By the third stage, infants are attentive to the consequences of their actions. Actions that occurred by chance are repeated to produce the consequences; these are *secondary circular reactions*. The repetitive activity is now focused on the environment. As we will see in Chapter 3, infants this age will kick their feet vigorously when kicking produces the movement of a mobile overhead.

In the fourth substage, the action patterns are coordinated and become

TABLE 2-1 *Characteristics of Development During the Sensorimotor Period*

Stage	General Activity	Object Concept
1. Reflex 0–1 month	Reflex activity; learns to accommodate this activity to differences in size, shape, and position.	No differentiation of self from other objects; infant's world is limited to self and own actions.
2. First action patterns 1–4 months Primary Circular Reactions	Random movements produce interesting results; infant attempts to rediscover and repeat the action pattern.	Develops ability to follow a moving object with eyes. Passive when object disappears.
3. Reproduction 4–8 months Secondary Circular Reactions	Acts initiated by chance can now be repeated purposefully. Such goal-directed activity initiated only after chance discovery of the connection between activity (for example, kicking) and the consequence (for example, movement of mobile).	Anticipates the landing place of dropped objects; able to recognize partially visible objects and will search for partly hidden objects.
4. Means-end coordination of secondary reactions 8–12 months	Coordinates familiar actions into larger pattern. For example, the striking action is used to eliminate a barrier (means) so that an object can be grasped (goal).	Will search for completely hidden objects, but will not search in new location when object displaced to second location.
5. Experimentation 12–18 months Tertiary Circular Reactions	Varies action pattern to produce different results. Appears to be actively seeking novelty as she, for example, drops different objects on the floor from different positions.	Searches for objects after displacement, but only if the displacement is visible.
6. Representation 18–24 months	Beginning of thinking before action. Prior to this, actions have been based on immediate sensory experience. Now evidence that has mental image that is beyond the immediate experience.	Searches for hidden objects after invisible displacement. A mental image of the object makes it possible to coordinate activity of search even when child does not see the object hidden.

more goal directed. The secondary circular reactions are used to produce new results. For example, a hitting action is used not only to produce sounds but also to remove an obstacle. In the fifth substage, as the schemes are applied to different objects, infants experiment and discover how the consequences can vary depending upon the schemes applied and the nature of the object. These *tertiary circular reactions* are forms of experimental actions. Infants may sit in their high chairs dropping various objects to the floor and delighting in the diverse consequences.

Finally, in the last substage of sensorimotor development, infants show evidence of thinking before acting. It is then that a mental representation of an object is available even when the object is not present. That is, prior to the sixth substage, the infants' knowledge about the world is represented by what action to make to a given sensory input. If a rattle is presented, then the infant has sensorimotor schemes that represent what to do with that rattle, but in the absence of the rattle the infant cannot represent the object and past experience independently of sensorimotor schemes for action with the object. But when infants have *object permanence,* they know that an object exists even when it is not in sight. They act to search for an object that is not in sight. This indicates an ability to maintain a mental representation of the object and an ability to use that information to govern a planned action. Thus, for Piaget, infants are not cognitive until the sixth substage of the sensorimotor stage. We will return to the research on the development of object permanence and implications for knowledge representation in Chapter 3.

Piaget's theory does not consider the sensory capacities of infants independent of the sensorimotor schemes. Indeed, at the time of his research the methodology was not available for investigating such questions. More recently, a number of researchers have attempted to assess the basic sensory capacities of newborns and the development of these capacities during the first year. These capacities will, of course, affect the nature of the environmental information that is available to infants. There are studies of the other senses (for example, Engen & Lipsitt, 1965; Spears & Hohle, 1967), but the emphasis here will be on vision and audition.

▶ PERCEPTION

Psychologists typically make distinctions among sensation, perception, and cognition. An analogy may best illustrate each. When I look up on a starry evening, my visual sense detects the presence of light rays. To study *sensation* is to study the ability of organisms to detect the stimulation of the senses and to make discriminations between different levels and types of stimulation. Not all energy changes in the environment can be detected by a given organism; humans, for example, need special equipment to detect the high-frequency sound waves that bats use for navigating and locating their prey. In this chapter we consider the basic sensory capacities of young infants for vision and audition. The data indicate that even newborns have the ability to see and hear stimulation, at least stimulation that is close and moderately intense. This research, however, tells us little about how infants organize and interpret the stimulation.

Adults do not experience endless streams of sensation. Perceptual processes such as interpretation, comparison, classification, and organization transform sensory information into our perceptual experiences of objects in space. *Perception* is the study of how sensory stimulation is organized and interpreted. Perceptual systems search for structure or regularities in the environment. As I scan the stars, I may recognize the Big Dipper. That is, I see a specific set of stars as a distinct set with a particular internal organization. Theories of perception attempt to explain how sensory stimulation comes to be organized and thus meaningful for the individual. Some types of organization clearly depend upon training. Try to recall your first attempts to locate and identify a constellation. Most likely you had to be shown where to look and which stars are part of the constellation and which are not. Thus, some perceptual learning is culturally bound. The Chinese, for example, organize the stars into very different constellations. As will be evident, other perceptions, such as the perception of depth, may be closely tied to the maturation of the organism.

As indicated in Chapter 1, cognition involves more than perception. Perception focuses on the stimulus information available in the here and now and the use of stored information to interpret this sensory information. *Cognition* focuses on the relatively independent role of stored information in thinking. For example, an astronomer's knowledge of the heavens makes it possible to predict the location of constellations such as the Big Dipper without reference to specific perceptual information. It should be evident that sensation, perception, and cognition are closely linked. For this reason, our review of cognitive development begins with the sensory and perceptual capacities of infants, particularly vision and audition, which have been the focus of infant as well as developmental research.

TOP-DOWN AND BOTTOM-UP ANALYSES OF PERCEPTION

Perception is influenced not only by the data available through the senses but also by the cognitions that guide our interpretation of this stimulation. A *bottom-up analysis* of perception proceeds from the elements of the stimulation to the rules for organizing the elements into a whole. A *top-down analysis* focuses on how our cognitions affect our perceptions. As an example, look at the picture in Figure 2-1. What do you see? Notice that your perception is not immediate and that in this case, unless you are familiar with this picture, it may take some time for you to organize the information. Suppose I tell you that it is a picture of a cow; can you see it?

FIGURE 2-1 *What do you see? Do you see a cow? If not, try the picture on a few friends until someone sees the cow. Ask that person to show you how the black and white elements are organized to represent a cow. (From Adams, 1974.)*

CHAPTER 2 / INFANCY: SENSORIMOTOR

Our perceptions depend on both bottom-up and top-down processes. The balance between the two will depend upon the particular situation. The perception of the cow was facilitated when you knew what the figure was supposed to depict; this knowledge gave you some idea of how to organize the elements of the picture. Nevertheless, if you expected to see a complete cow, you may still have had difficulty organizing the information.

METHODS OF STUDY

Three principal methods have been used to explore the characteristics of infant sensation and perception: the visual preference test, the habituation-dishabituation paradigm, and the operant-conditioning paradigm. These are not the only methods available (see Maurer, 1975, for a review of methods used to study infants' visual perception), but they are the ones that stimulated the early research efforts. Other methodologies will be discussed when they are particularly relevant to the research on a specific developmental issue.

VISUAL PREFERENCE TEST   The majority of infant perceptual studies have investigated vision. Undoubtedly, one reason for this emphasis rests with the effectiveness of the visual preference test with infants, as indicated by the work of Berlyne (1958) and Fantz (1958; 1961). These experiments found that infants look at some visual stimuli longer than others. Pairs of visual stimuli were presented to the infant, and the orientation of the infant's visual fixation was determined by observing which pattern was reflected on the infant's cornea (see Figure 2-2). The fact that young infants do fixate some visual stimuli longer than others has been used to define infant visual preferences. This technique can be used to draw inferences about the discriminative abilities of infants. That is, if infants spend reliably more time looking at one stimulus than another, we can infer that they can discriminate between the two stimuli. The reverse is not the case, however. The fact that infants do not look longer at one member of a pair does not necessarily imply that they cannot see the difference between the two; rather, they may simply not have a preference for either one and therefore may divide their time equally between the two stimuli. It should be noted that "preference" does not necessarily mean a voluntary choice or selection; some preferences may reflect an involuntary, or automatic, attraction to certain types of stimuli.

HABITUATION-DISHABITUATION PARADIGM   It is a common finding in studies of adults and animals that the repetition of a specific stimulus leads to a decrease in the magnitude of the responses that occur to the onset of that stimulus (Sokolov, 1960; 1963; Thompson & Spencer, 1966). When this decrement is not a function of peripheral factors, such as sensory adaptation or fatigue, it is called *habituation*. Habituation has been demonstrated in human infants with several response measures, including cardiac response, visual fixation,

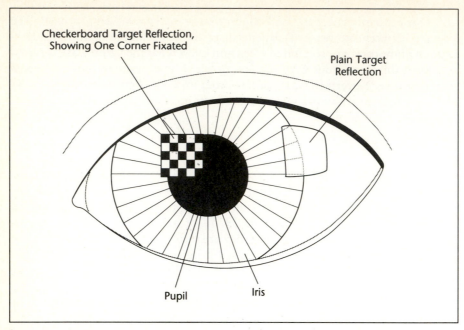

Checkerboard Target Reflection,
Showing One Corner Fixated

Plain Target
Reflection

Pupil   Iris

▶ **FIGURE 2-2** *Schematic drawing of infant's eye as seen in the test chamber by the experimenter when checked and plain squares are exposed. This illustrates the limiting condition for satisfying the criterion of fixation; more generally the target reflection would overlap the pupil to a greater degree.* (From Fantz, 1965.)

and sucking rate. Many researchers, although not all, attribute habituation to cortical mechanisms rather than peripheral mechanisms such as changes at the retina (see Bartoshuk, 1962; Sokolov, 1960; Thompson & Spencer, 1966).

When a change in stimulation following the habituation of a response results in an increase of the response, it is called *dishabituation*. If an infant's response to a specific stimulus habituates with repetition of the stimulus and dishabituates when a new stimulus is presented, we can infer that the infant can discriminate between the two stimuli. Failure to dishabituate does not, however, indicate an inability to discriminate. The dishabituation stimulus is presented after the habituation stimulus. Therefore, at the minimum, dishabituation of a response requires both memory for the habituation stimulus and discrimination of the dishabituation stimulus from the memory of the habituation stimulus (see Bornstein, 1985, for a discussion of this method).

OPERANT-CONDITIONING PARADIGM   A third procedure for studying infant perception is operant conditioning. In this case the infant is trained to make a response (for example, a head turn) in the presence of a specific stimulus. This is done by presenting the stimulus and rewarding the response when it occurs in the presence of the stimulus. For example, a tone may be presented to one side of the infant. If the infant's head turns in the appropriate direction, a visual reinforcer is given, such as a moving toy. Two techniques can be used with operant conditioning. One technique is *discrimination learning*. In this technique the infant is trained to make different responses (for example, turning the head in opposite directions) to different stimuli. If the infant can learn to make these differential responses, then we can infer the ability to discriminate between the two stimuli.

The other technique is the *generalization test*. Extensive research indicates that when tested with stimuli that vary in similarity to the original training stimulus, the strength of an organism's response to these test stimuli is a function of the similarity between the training stimulus and the generalization stimuli. Thus, the generalization test can be used to assess the perception of similarity and differences by infants.

Operant conditioning is time consuming and often difficult to establish with young infants. But it does provide information that is not available with the other two procedures and is particularly effective with older infants.

▶ VISION

The gross anatomy of the eye is depicted in Figure 2-3. As evidenced in this figure, all structures are present at birth. The issue is whether they actually function at birth and, if so, the extent to which their functions approximate those of the adult (see, for example, Goldstein, 1984, for an introduction to sensation and perception).

PATTERN DETECTION

Critical to an acquisition of visual information is the ability to detect patterns of light and dark. You are able to read this page because your visual system is capable of distinguishing between the dark marks and the light background. Two factors affect pattern detection: acuity and contrast sensitivity. *Acuity* is a measure of the ability to resolve a black line against a white background and is a direct function of the size of pattern elements. The most common technique for measuring the acuity of children and adults is the Snellen Chart which has rows of letters that vary in size. There are individual differences in adult acuity, but the norm is 20/20 (Snellen notation). An individual with 20/20 acuity can see and verbally identify, from 20 feet, the smallest row of letters on the chart that most people can resolve at 20 feet.

What of young infants? Typically, infant acuity is assessed by presenting stripes of different widths and determining the narrowest detectable width; widths are represented in *spatial frequency,* the number of stripes per unit area. For example, in Figure 2-4 the two patterns are the same overall size,

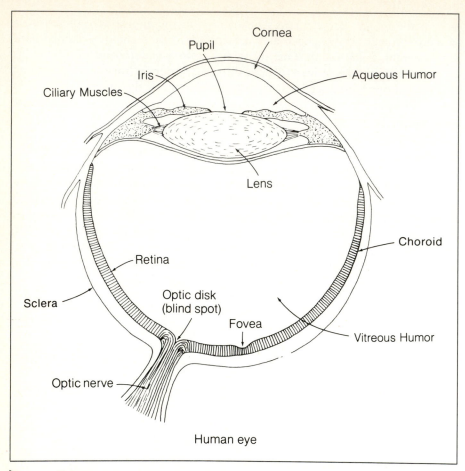

Cornea

Pupil

Iris

Ciliary Muscles

Aqueous Humor

Lens

Choroid

Retina

Sclera

Optic disk
(blind spot)

Fovea

Vitreous Humor

Optic nerve

Human eye

▶ **FIGURE 2-3** *Anatomy of the eye. When light strikes the cornea, it is refracted, or bent, toward the lens, which is adjustable and further refracts the light toward the retina at the back of the eyeball, with central targets focused on the fovea. The rods and cones of the retina transform the light into electrical activity, which is transferred along the optic nerve to the visual cortex, located at the back of the brain.*

but the one on the right has a higher spatial frequency than the one on the left.

Several methodologies have been used to assess the highest spatial frequency detectable by infants (see Aslin, 1987). To illustrate, using a version of the preference test, Lewis, Maurer, and Kay (1978) presented newborns with single lines of varying widths on some trials and a blank field on others. The newborns did not fixate the smallest line presented longer than the blank field, but did look significantly longer at the line that was comparable to an acuity of 20/150 (see also Cornell & McDonnell, 1986). As an approximate demonstration, hold Figure 2-4 nine inches from your eyes. The newborns in

CHAPTER 2 / INFANCY: SENSORIMOTOR

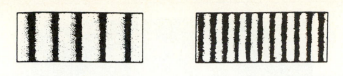

► **FIGURE 2-4** *Gratings with low and high spatial frequencies used to determine infant acuity.* (From Banks & Salapatek, 1981.)

this study did fixate a line with the spatial frequency of the left grating, but not one with that of the right grating.

These findings should be viewed with caution since we know that infant acuity estimates vary with the measurement technique and stimulus patterns used. We do not know whether 20/150 is a good estimate of infant visual acuity in the "real world" environment. In general, however, researchers agree that newborn acuity is relatively poor compared to normal adult acuity and improves considerably in the first few months (Banks & Salapatek, 1983).

Acuity is one determinant of an adult's ability to detect patterns. Another determinant of pattern detection is our sensitivity to the contrast of the elements of a pattern. In a high-contrast situation, the dark elements are very dark (black) and the light elements are very light (white); with low contrast, the darkest and lightest elements are both gradations of gray—there is less difference in brightness between the extremes. Dusk, for example, is a time of low contrast. Playing baseball at this time can be difficult because both the ball and the sky appear gray.

Contrast sensitivity is the "smallest amount of contrast required to detect the presence of a grating" (Aslin, 1987, p. 18), and is manipulated by varying the intensity of dark bars on a light background. In adults, the ability to detect contrast, represented by the *contrast sensitivity function* (CSF), is a function of both the amount of contrast and the spatial frequency of the gratings used to test contrast sensitivity. Figure 2-5 (top) illustrates a grating in which the spatial frequency increases from left to right and the contrast increases from top to bottom. The bottom half of the figure shows the typical CSF of an adult, indicating maximal sensitivity to contrast differences for the intermediate spatial frequencies, a gradual decline in sensitivity for the low spatial frequencies and a rapid decline in sensitivity for the high spatial frequencies. For very high spatial frequencies (for example, acuity levels equivalent to 20/10 Snellen notation), most adults cannot detect the gratings, regardless of the degree of contrast between the lines and the background. Thus, pattern detection is not only a function of the spatial frequency and the ability to resolve a given spatial frequency (acuity), but also of the amount of contrast and our sensitivity to differences in contrast.

Figure 2-5 also represents assessments of the development of the CSF between one and three months (see, for example, Banks & Salapatek, 1981).

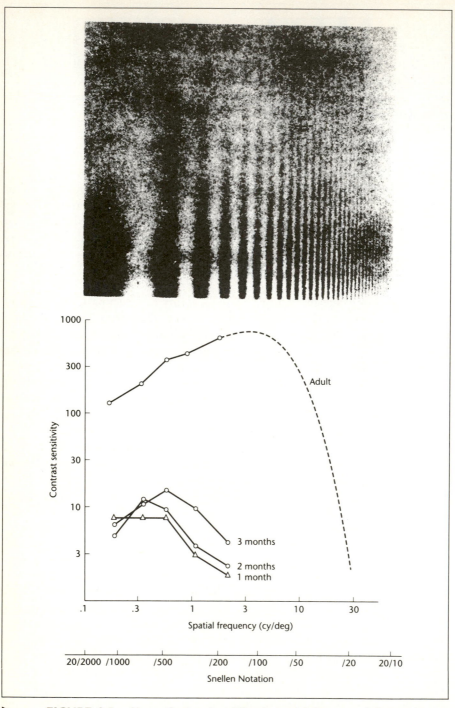

► **FIGURE 2-5** *Above: Grating that differs in spatial frequency (left to right) and contrast (top to bottom).* (From Banks & Salapatek, 1981.) *Below: The contrast sensitivity function for an average adult and for young infants.* (From Goldstein, 1984.)

These functions demonstrate three aspects of infant pattern detection. First, not surprisingly, sensitivity to high spatial frequency patterns (acuity) improves during the first few months. Second, overall contrast sensitivity also improves during these months. Third, the adult dropoff in contrast sensitivity for low spatial frequency gratings (for example, large stripes) is not evident in the youngest infants. Taken together these findings indicate that young infants detect a relatively narrow range of patterns and that detectability improves substantially during the first few months.

ADJUSTMENTS OF THE OCULOMOTOR SYSTEM

Objects of interest or importance in our environment are not always centrally located or at the optimal distance for resolution. The oculomotor system is capable of assessing visual information and making motor responses that optimize the quality of the information available at the retina. As in the case of acuity and contrast sensitivity, the data indicate that the newborn oculomotor system has limitations and that it approaches adult capabilities in the first few months (see Aslin, 1987, for a review).

PERIPHERAL VISION   Tests of acuity and contrast sensitivity indicate the ability of the system to detect targets that are centrally fixated on the fovea. Adult vision, however, is also affected by peripheral vision up to 70 degrees to either side of a central target (McBurney & Collings, 1984). In fact, coach John McKay claimed that O. J. Simpson's excellent peripheral vision made it possible for him to know where players were located on the field and therefore contributed to his greatness as a running back.

Our eyes move continually, but not randomly. Where we look next is influenced by an awareness of information in the periphery of the visual field. Since peripheral vision plays a role in directing eye movements and the scanning of the visual field, it is particularly valuable to know the extent to which infants can pick up information in their peripheral vision. To answer this question, investigators have presented a stimulus centrally; when the infant fixates this central stimulus, a peripheral target is presented at various distances from the center. Eye movements to the peripheral target indicate that it has been detected. Taken together (Harris & MacFarlane, 1974; Lewis, Maurer & Kay, 1978; MacFarlane, Harris & Barnes, 1976) these data indicate that newborns can detect targets up to 30 degrees from the center and that by six to seven weeks the infants can detect targets as far as 45 degrees from the center. Furthermore, the effective visual field continues to expand up to 50–60 degrees through the first five months, which approximates the visual field of adults (de Schonen, McKenzie, Maury & Bresson, 1978).

ACCOMMODATION   In the normal young adult, the image of a visual target is focused on the retina by the lens. As the distance of a target varies, the lens of the eye bulges or flattens to keep a clear image on the retina at distances from 10 cm to infinity. These changes in the shape of the lens occur by involuntary contraction and relaxation of the ciliary muscles (see Figure 2-3). When the ciliary muscle is relaxed, the lens is relatively flat and far objects are in focus. When the muscle is contracted, near objects are brought into focus. This change in the state of the ciliary muscles and the concomitant change in the shape of the lens that is contingent upon changes in the distance of a visual target is called the *accommodation response*. In this manner we keep objects in focus. This response is analogous to the adjustment made with the length of the camera lens to bring a specific object into focus.

The measurement of accommodation is related to the visual acuity of the infant (Hershenson, 1967). If the infant does not distinguish the target from the background, the accommodation response will not occur because, from the infant's point of view, there is nothing upon which to focus. Recognizing this problem Banks (1980) investigated the accommodation response while maximizing the resolution of the target. His data show that one-month-olds do make some accommodation responses and by three months the response is well-developed and quite accurate (see Banks & Salapatek, 1983, for a review). As the visual acuity of infants develops, the visual system is better able to assess the clarity of the retinal image and make the appropriate accommodation response.

THE RELATION BETWEEN ACUITY, ACCOMMODATION, AND CONVERGENCE   In adults convergent and divergent eye movements serve to maintain a clear image of an object on the fovea of each eye. That is, as an object moves toward us or away from us our eyes converge or diverge to keep the image of the object on the fovea of each eye. But this does not guarantee a clear image unless an appropriate accommodation response is made by each eye as the object approaches and withdraws from us. Thus, these two visual-motor systems are coordinated in adults to maintain a clear retinal image. This coordination of the convergence and accommodation responses occurs by two months of age (Aslin & Jackson, 1979). However, this is the youngest age that has been tested, so we do not yet know when this coordination initially occurs. Since the accommodation response does not occur unless the visual system detects that there is a target in the visual field and that the target is not in focus, the accommodation response is tied to the acuity of an individual. We have seen that there is considerable development in visual acuity during the first three months; thus, considering the relationship between the accommodation response and acuity we might expect that the accommodation-convergence relationship develops during the first three months of life.

COLOR DISCRIMINATION

The retina consists of two types of sensors: rods and cones. The *rods* function at low light intensities and produce colorless sensations; the *cones* begin to function at higher intensities and produce color sensations. Only cones are located at the center of the retina (fovea). Both rods and cones, however, are present outside this area. At birth the fovea is not fully developed and it matures for a few months after birth (Banks & Salapatek, 1983). This fact undoubtedly has contributed to the belief that newborns do not discriminate colors.

Taken together, several studies (see, for example, Bornstein, 1976; Oster, 1975; Schaller, 1975), using different techniques and limited sets of hues, indicate that infants over three months can discriminate red, green, blue, and yellow. There is, however, a developmental change in the discriminability of blue. Adams and Maurer (1983) tested newborns using the preference test and found evidence that newborns can discriminate green, yellow, and red hues from grey, but not blue from grey. This is an example of a situation in which psychologists are willing to assume an inability from negative results. That is, the fact that under comparable conditions, the infants did discriminate the grey from three colors but not from blue leads to the inference that they can discriminate some, but not all, colors.

DEPTH PERCEPTION

Adults perceive the world as three-dimensional. Several factors contribute to our perception of depth. One of these, *binocular disparity,* occurs because we have two eyes that are separated. As a consequence, when we fixate an object, two slightly different images appear on each retina (as illustrated in Figure 2-6). These different views of an object result in *stereopsis,* the three-dimensional perception of space. Indeed, stereoscopic viewers and 3-D movies are designed on this principle. If you look carefully at the pictures that are opposite each other on the discs used with stereoscopic viewers, you will see that they are similar but not identical.

Do infants see three dimensions? Aslin and his colleagues (Aslin, Shea, Dumais & Fox, 1979; Fox, Aslin, Shea & Dumais, 1980) investigated stereopsis in young infants using a technique that does not provide any *monocular cues* (cues available from one eye, such as accommodation) for depth perception. They generated a random element display of 60,000 red and green dots which appeared as individual dots moving randomly. When a red filter was placed in front of one eye and a green one in front of the other, each eye received a slightly different image of a rectangle. Under these conditions adults report seeing a rectangle that is in front of or behind the random dot field. A similar type of effect can be achieved if you turn your TV set to a channel that is just producing visual noise ("snow") and put a dark lens from sunglasses in front of one eye, but not the other. The TV noise will now appear to have two streams of "snow," one moving in front of the other.

Infants ranging in age from two and one-half to four and one-half months were presented a random element display in which it was possible to move a rectangular region defining a stereoscopic field across the random element field.

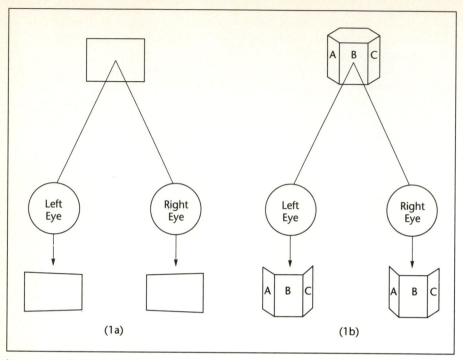

▶ *FIGURE 2-6* *An illustration of binocular disparity in which each retina receives a slightly different image, resulting in our three-dimensional perception of the world around us. (From Aslin, Shea, Dumais & Fox, 1979.)*

At this age infants will follow moving objects with their eyes. This tracking response was used to determine if infants perceive the stereoscopic region as separate from the rest of the visual field.

The youngest infants in this study did not follow the rectangle as it moved, but the three-and-one-half- and four-and-one-half-month-old infants did. What conclusion can be drawn from these findings? Do infants older than three months have stereopsis; that is, do they see three dimensions on the basis of binocular disparity cues? There is no way that psychologists can directly know what others see, rather they can only infer perception and this requires careful attempts to eliminate alternative inferences. It is possible, for example, that the older infants detect the retinal disparity of the images, but do not perceive the third dimension, depth.

Aslin and his colleagues pursued this problem by manipulating the disparity of the two retinal images to determine if four-month-olds respond to the degree of retinal disparity in a manner similar to adults. These infants did not follow the rectangle when the disparity between the retinal images was very large; they did, however, for the middle levels of disparity. Adults report comparable effects when they are judging depth perception. That is, they do not perceive depth if the retinal disparity is very large but do at middle levels of disparity. This similarity in response for both infants and adults, along with comparable findings with the visual preference procedure (see Held, Birch & Gwiazda, 1980), suggest that infants become sensitive to binocular disparity around four months of age and further supports the inference that infants have depth perception by four months of age. Indeed, Granrud (1986) has demonstrated that, as sensitivity to binocular disparity develops, there is a concomitant improvement in depth perception.

SUMMARY OF BASIC VISUAL CAPACITIES

The research on the visual capacities of the infant appears to have two trends. First, the newborn has a variety of visual skills. Thus, as we have seen, the newborn discriminates some colors and has a level of acuity and accommodation that indicates the ability to detect some object detail at near distances. Furthermore, newborns have peripheral vision for targets that are approximately 25 degrees from an initial fixation point, which means that they do not need to be directly looking at an object to detect it. At birth, the most mature aspect of the visual systems appears to be sensitivity to movement, including motion in the periphery (Bronson, 1974). This review of the basic visual capacities indicates that the newborn's visual world is not the same as an adult's, but that it should not be characterized as a "blooming, buzzing confusion" (James, 1890, p. 488).

The second trend indicates that within the first four or five months of life there is considerable development and integration of the visual capacities. Within this time period acuity, contrast sensitivity, accommodation, and convergence develop, as does color sensitivity to the blue wavelengths; a number of response measures also indicate the development of depth perception during this period (see von Hofsten, 1986). Knowledge of infant visual limitations and development have proven important in the design of studies to explore the higher-level perceptual skills of young infants. That is, if we want to ask, for example, questions about how young infants organize visual information we must be sure to design visual materials that are within their sensory capacities.

The several changes observed in infant visual capacities have led, of course, to speculations about the nature of the developmental changes, both in terms of behavioral and neurophysiological changes. In particular, three different neurophysiological models have been proposed by Bronson (1974), Maurer and Lewis (1979), and Haith (1980) and are reviewed by Banks and Salapatek (1983). Each model has its strengths and weaknesses. One common problem for these neurophysiological models of development is that we have little knowledge about the relationships between cortical and perceptual functions in adults, much less in infants. This means that modelers often have to rely on animal research, especially research with the cat. Unfortunately, there are enough differences in the visual systems of cats and humans to create doubt about the appropriateness of the extrapolation from the animal research to explanations of human development.

With or without neurophysiological models of perceptual development, research must pursue the development of the functions of the perceptual systems. Indeed, it is often the models of perceptual function that guide the anatomical/physiological research (Banks & Salapatek, 1983). Functional models can help to narrow the set of neurophysiological areas that may be involved in a given phenomenon. Although we know considerably more about the visual capacities of infants than we did 20 years ago, we have yet to explore systematically the development of these functions or the factors that affect this development.

ATTENTION

Adults are not aware of all the sensory stimulation that impinges upon them. As you read this, your attention is directed toward the words on the page and perhaps other aspects of your environment, such as a radio playing. But chances are slim that you are aware of the feel of your clothes on your skin—until your attention is drawn to that sensation. Put in information-processing terms, the several sensory registers (see Chapter 1, Figure 1-1) are all receiving input, but only some of this information is processed further into working memory and we are only aware of the information in working memory. In adults, attention may be directed by top-down processes as well as bottom-up processes. If I have the goal (top-down) of learning the material in a chapter, then my attention will be directed to the words on the page. Bottom-up processes may also direct my attention. If the radio playing down the hall is particularly loud, that noise may attract my attention. Our attention has a limited capacity. We cannot attend to all things simultaneously; rather, in one way or another, we select aspects of our environment for attention. What of young infants? Do they have selective attention? If so, what directs this attention and how does it develop?

The visual preference paradigm has been used to study infant visual attention. Fantz (1958) demonstrated that young infants look longer at patterned stimuli than at homogenous stimuli and that they look longer at some patterns than at others. For example, Fantz (1963) compared the fixation times of young infants for six stimuli: schematic face, bull's eye, newsprint, solid red, solid yellow, and solid white. The schematic face was fixated longer than the other stimuli, and the three unpatterned colors had the shortest fixation times. Other studies have confirmed, at several ages, the conclusion that patterned stimuli are fixated longer than solids (see, for example, McCall & Kagan, 1967; Stechler, 1964).

Given that neonates discriminate patterns, what dimensions control infant preferences for particular patterns? Since we know that infant visual preferences are influenced by brightness (Hershenson, 1964) and also by movement (see Ames & Silfen, 1965), the research designed to answer this question has attempted to control for brightness and has usually used stationary stimuli.

With such controls in place, many kinds of patterned stimuli have been used to determine the stimulus dimension(s) that underlie infant preferences. For example, *complexity,* in some studies defined as the number of squares in a checkerboard pattern, is related to visual fixation time. Brennan, Ames, and Moore (1966) presented checkerboards containing 4, 64, and 576 squares to 3-, 8-, and 14-week-old infants. The youngest infants looked longest at the least complex checkerboard. The 8-week-olds looked longest at the stimulus of medium complexity; the 14-week-olds fixated the most complex checkerboard more than the other stimuli. Thus, within the first weeks, the attentional preference of infants changes from least to most complex for this set of stimuli.

But very few patterned stimuli are composed of checkerboards, and this definition of complexity does nothing to help us predict infant attention to other types of patterns. Indeed, as the variety of patterned stimuli under investigation increased, so did the number of dimensions that predict the preferences of young infants (see Banks & Salapatek, 1981; 1983, for reviews). Yet each dimension only predicts behavior for a limited subset of patterns. For example, Fantz, Fagan, and Miranda (1975) found that both the size and the number of the elements in a pattern influenced newborn preferences. When the size of the elements was held constant, the infants preferred to look at the pattern with the most elements; when the number was held constant, the infants preferred the display with the largest elements. Thus, the two dimensions are independent determinants of infant attention. But if these two are held constant, other dimensions such as the symmetry, shape, or orientation of the elements can be varied. Thus, a large number of dimensions, not all of which have been specified, would be necessary to make predictions about infant visual preferences for a possible pattern. Ideally, however, we seek a single, more general dimension that can explain the findings to date and has the potential for deriving predictions about any conceivable pattern. Banks and Salapatek (1981; 1983) have proposed a model of visual preference that is a function of pattern detectability and appears applicable to all types of patterned stimuli.

As we have seen, the detection of patterns is related to the contrast sensitivity function. Banks and Salapatek (1981) assume that visual patterns are filtered by the contrast sensitivity function and that infants prefer to look at patterns that contain the greatest contrast once filtered by the infant CSF. Or put another way, "young infants seem to prefer the stimulus that is most 'visible' " (Dannemiller & Stephens, 1988, p. 211). As we have seen, contrast sensitivity improves substantially during the first few months of infancy. Thus, as the visual system matures, infant preferences should change and the preferences should be predictable from the CSF of a given age.

Predictions derived from this model of visual preferences have adequately described the performance of infants in several studies by other experimenters (see, for example, Banks & Salapatek, 1981; Gayl, Roberts & Werner, 1983; Slater, Earle, Morison & Rose, 1985). Further research will be necessary to determine how well this model describes infant preferences for various types of patterns, but in principle the CSF can be applied to any visual pattern. This interpretation of early visual attention is a bottom-up analysis that assumes that attention is a function of the characteristics of the patterns relative to the ability of infants to detect patterns at a given age. Banks and Salapatek (1983), however, do not claim that their model can account for the development of preferences beyond the first few months (see Dannemiller & Stephens, 1988).

Research indicates that as the infant matures, visual attention is increasingly influenced by top-down processes. That is, attention is not simply a function of stimulus characteristics, such as complexity. For example, the familiarity of a patterned stimulus will affect an infant's attention. If infants are familiarized with a particular stimulus and then given a preference test with the familiar stimulus and a novel stimulus, they typically attend to one of the stimuli more than the other. Some of this research supports Hunt's (1963) hypothesis that infants under two months of age attend to the familiar stimulus whereas older infants prefer to look at the novel stimulus. But other data suggest that age is not the important variable; rather, infant attention is determined by how familiar the infant is with the stimulus before the preference test (Rose, Gottfried, Melloy-Carminar & Bridger, 1982). This hypothesis assumes that at all ages infants look at the familiarization stimulus if they are not completely familiar with it, and the novel one when they are fully familiar with the original stimulus.

Hunter, Ames, and Koopman (1983) offer an integration of these positions. They assume that it takes longer to become familiar with complex stimuli than with simple ones. Furthermore, they assume that, as previously demonstrated, there are developmental changes in stimulus complexity. That is, a stimulus that is complex for a younger infant may be a simple one for an older one. Finally, they assume that the familiarized stimulus is fixated if it is not completely familiar; when it is familiar, the infant attends to the novel stimulus.

The assumptions of this hypothesis lead to the prediction that attention will depend upon both the relative complexity of the stimulus and the extent of familiarity, an interplay of top-down and bottom-up influences. Hunter and his colleagues offer data that support their hypothesis. But considerably more research will be necessary to determine the extent to which this hypothesis explains infant attention to familiar and novel stimuli (compare Kaplan & Werner, 1986) and how this hypothesis might relate to Banks and Salapatek's model of attention.

In summary, young infants, including newborns, selectively attend to visual patterned stimuli. A number of stimulus dimensions appear to determine infant attention. One, pattern detectability, which is a function of acuity and contrast sensitivity, appears to be the most influential in the first two or three months (see also Pipp & Haith, 1984). Infant visual attention is also influenced by past experience with specific stimuli. When infants are particularly familiar with a visual pattern, they attend to a novel pattern more than the familiar one. But they will continue to attend to a pattern that is not entirely familiar.

WHAT INFORMATION DO INFANTS EXTRACT FROM PATTERNED STIMULI?

The fact that young infants are differentially attentive to patterns does not tell us anything about where they look within the patterns and what information they derive from the patterns. Or, to put it another way, the attention data do not indicate whether young infants see the patterns as adults do. We address this issue throughout the remainder of this section on visual perception.

Our first problem is to determine which features of a pattern receive more attention and whether infants see an entire pattern. When adults look at a pattern, object, or scene, they make two quick, *saccadic,* or ballistic, eye movements across the stimulus every second (on the average), and they fixate some features more often than others. Infants also make saccadic eye movements, which raises the questions: How do infants scan patterns? Can their eye movements tell us something about pattern perception?

Salapatek and Kessen (1966) made the initial attempt to answer these questions. They used the *visual scanning paradigm* which entails making video recordings of corneal reflections of the pattern relative to the pupil and determining the infant's fixations of the elements of the pattern (see Haith, 1980, for a description of the methodology). Kessen, Salapatek, and Haith (1972) compared the eye movements of newborns for horizontal and vertical edges. This study indicated that there was greater scanning across a vertical contour than a horizontal one and that both contours were scanned more than the comparable positions in a homogenous field. This tendency to scan across a vertical contour more than a horizontal one has been replicated and may reflect the fact that more muscles are required for the vertical movements necessary to scan a horizontal contour than for horizontal movements across a vertical contour (Haith, 1980).

In the initial study of infant visual scanning, Salapatek and Kessen (1966) studied newborns' scanning of a triangle. The eye movement tracings indicated that the newborns did scan the pattern, but that the scanning was constrained to one portion or feature of the contour. Although a second study (Salapatek & Kessen, 1973) indicated that newborns will sometimes scan more extensively, several studies indicate that the extent to which a figure is scanned increases with age. For example, Salapatek and Miller (Salapatek, 1975) presented five different stimuli to one- and two-month-olds. Results indicate that the two-month-olds scan more of the figures than the one-month-olds. When compound stimuli were presented to infants, the two-month-olds were more likely to scan the internal element of the compound stimulus than the one-month-olds. Thus, with age there is more extensive scanning of patterns, including the internal elements of a pattern (see Figure 2-7).

In summary, we know that newborns scan across edges or contours and that they are more likely to do this with vertical contours than horizontal ones. When a stimulus is more complex, newborns tend to scan a single feature; but under some circumstances, which are not yet understood, they will engage in

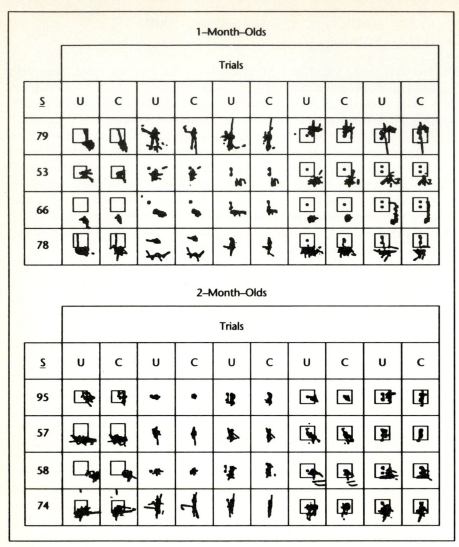

FIGURE 2-7 *Scanning patterns of 1-month-olds and 2-month-olds when presented simple and compound stimuli. With age there is more extensive scanning of patterns, including internal elements, as evidenced here. (From Salapatek, 1975.)*

more extensive scanning. Within the first three months the extent of the scanning increases such that more features of a pattern are scanned and features that are internal to the pattern are scanned as well as those that are external.

The scanning research suggests that newborns do not process the internal elements of a pattern, but this research does not tell us, for example, what information is taken in with each fixation, how information from two or more fixations is organized and represented, or how visual information guides the eye movements themselves (see Bronson, 1982, for the beginning of a program of research to answer some of these questions).

PATTERN DISCRIMINATION   Neonates can, under some circumstances, detect patterns. The next question is whether they can discriminate between patterns. As is so apparent in eyewitness testimony, it is one thing to know that something is there and quite another to distinguish this thing from others. The scanning data suggests that neonates do not always scan the internal elements of a figure and, thus, one line of research has assessed the ability of young infants to discriminate between figures that have comparable *external features* but different *internal features*.

These investigations indicate a developmental trend. Newborns do not discriminate between figures that have the same external features but different internal figures, infants over two months are regularly able to make these discriminations, and one-month-olds discriminate the internal figures under limited circumstances described below.

Milewski (1976) used the habituation-dishabituation paradigm to investigate pattern discrimination in one- and four-month-olds. The infants were presented the figures illustrated in Figure 2-8. The one-month-olds did not show any evidence of dishabituation when only the internal element was changed (condition I); they did, however, show dishabituation when the external element was changed and when both elements were changed (conditions E and I-E, respectively). In contrast, the four-month-olds showed dishabituation when only the internal element was changed (the I condition) as well as in the other two experimental conditions (E and I-E). Thus, it appears that younger infants do not see or process the internal features of a complex stimulus, but that older infants are deriving the information in the internal as well as the external features.

A prerequisite of this research paradigm is, of course, attention to the figures. Yet, we have seen that infant attention is sensitive to the characteristics of stimuli (for example, size of the figure). In a second study, Milewski (1976) demonstrated that the failure of younger infants to discriminate the internal elements of his compound figures cannot be attributed to an inability to resolve the smaller figures. When these figures were presented alone one-month-olds did discriminate between them. Further, in a third study, Milewski found that the internal location of the smaller element was a determining factor in pattern discrimination. One-month-olds were habituated to one of the external figures and then tested for dishabituation with the smaller figure inside the external figure or placed adjacent to it. The response patterns indicated that the infants distinguished between the habituation stimulus and the test pattern with the adjacent smaller element but not between the training stimulus and the figure with the smaller element placed inside the original figure. These findings support the scanning data indicating that the internal elements of compound figures do not attract the visual attention of infants younger than two months of age.

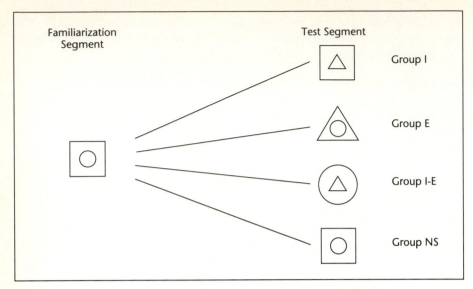

Familiarization Segment

Test Segment

Group I

Group E

Group I-E

Group NS

▶ **FIGURE 2-8** *Shown the above patterns, one-month-olds did not see or process the internal features of complex patterns, whereas four-month-olds perceived both the internal and external features.* (From Milewski, 1976.)

But we also have seen that infant attention is influenced by several stimulus characteristics (such as complexity). The internal figures in the Milewski study are relatively simple and may not, therefore, have the optimal characteristics for eliciting attention from one-month-olds. Indeed, Ganon and Swartz (1980) have demonstrated that one-month-olds do discriminate between complex patterns if the internal figures are salient (bull's eye and checkerboard). In addition, Bushnell (1979) has shown that moving internal elements will also be discriminated by one-month-olds. Thus, it would appear that if the internal elements of a complex pattern have stimulus characteristics that are particularly salient for one-month-olds they can process information that is embedded within a complex figure.

The one study assessing newborn discrimination of internal elements suggests that they do not attend to salient elements. Bushnell, Gerry, and Burt (1983) presented the Ganon and Swartz figures, illustrated in Figure 2-9, to newborns using the *differential visual tracking paradigm*. In this paradigm the infant is presented with a stimulus to one side. When the infant fixates the stimulus, it is moved in front of the infant and to the other side. Bushnell and her colleagues found that the newborns would follow the two patterned figures (bull's eye and checkerboard) further than the two unpatterned stimuli (square and triangle) if these figures were not bounded by an external element (top row of Figure 2-9). There was no such difference in following for the bounded figures. This indicates that the infants can discriminate between the two sets of figures, but that they do not do so when they are internal to a larger figure. We do not yet know whether moving internal elements would induce newborns

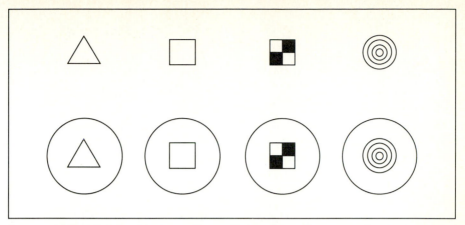

FIGURE 2-9 *Newborn infants will discriminate the patterned and nonpatterned figures in the top row, but will not discriminate between patterned or nonpatterned figures when they are internal to a larger figure (bottom row). (From Bushnell, Gerry & Burt, 1983.)*

to attend to and discriminate complex patterns (see Antell, Caron & Myers, 1985). Maurer (1983), however, has demonstrated that newborns and one-month-olds will scan the internal features of a high-contrast schematic face, but it is not yet known whether neonates can discriminate between such stimuli based on differences only in their internal features.

Taken together, the evidence suggests that by two or three months of age, infants can discriminate complex figures that differ only in the internal elements. Prior to this age, infants' attention is limited to the external contours of figures unless the internal elements are particularly salient. We do not yet know, however, whether there are stimulus characteristics that are salient enough to attract newborn attention to internal elements, characteristics that also are discriminable by such young infants.

PRINCIPLES OF ORGANIZATION   By four months of age infants are processing the information of fairly complex patterns. But adult perception of visual patterns involves more than just seeing all of the elements in a pattern. Adult perception is structured; the elements or features of the pattern are organized in some manner. Look again at the picture of the cow in Figure 2-1. The many black and white features of that picture are organized now in such a way that some are seen as part of the cow and others are not. Some features are seen as related and depicting the object (cow); others are seen as unrelated and part of the background. The complex pattern is segmented into parts and the parts have a structured relationship.

It is difficult to organize our perceptions of some patterns without knowing what to look for. You probably had that experience the first time you saw the cow or the first time you used a microscope. But some forms of perceptual organization appear to be more immediate. For example, the figure on the left in Figure 2-10 is seen to consist of the two parts that are illustrated on the

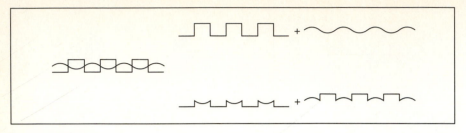

top right. Why don't we see this figure as composed of the two parts represented on the bottom right? The Gestalt theorists (for example, Koffka, 1935) of the 1920s and 1930s tried to explain such phenomena by proposing a theory of perception that emphasized the importance of segmentation of visual patterns and the organization of these features or segments. Parts of a whole are seen to go together if the parts are similar, have proximity to each other, share common fate, display good continuation, and form a simple and symmetrical shape. For example, the *principle of good continuation* specifies that straight or smoothly curving lines are seen as belonging together, that "lines tend to be seen in such a way as to follow the smoothest path" (Goldstein, 1984, p. 171). This principle describes our segmentation of Figure 2-10.

Several other principles are illustrated in Figure 2-11. Consider the pattern on the lower left. It is an array of dots and squares all equidistant from each other, yet because of the similarity of the elements in the columns we see the pattern as one of pairs of columns of dots and squares; if the pattern is rotated, we now see pairs of rows.

Theorists have taken different positions on the origins of these principles of organization. Some, like the Gestaltists, (for example, Kohler, 1947) have argued that they are innate and that they represent a basic tendency for us to "perceive the simplest, most regular configurations" (Kellman & Spelke, 1983, p. 484). Others have taken an empiricist position and emphasized the role of experience in the acquisition of the principles (for example, Piaget, 1954; Hochberg, 1981; Rock, 1977). A few of these principles have been investigated with infants in an effort to address this issue, but before considering these studies we need to consider how such research must be done (see, for example, Bornstein, Ferdinandsen & Gross, 1981; Kellman & Spelke, 1983).

We have seen that many lower-order variables affect the performance of infants in visual research. These variables include such factors as the brightness of the stimuli, the size and the number of elements, pattern detectability, presence of internal details, and so forth. Thus, if we want to determine whether the principle of proximity, for example, influences infant pattern perception, we must be sure that all of these known factors are controlled in the stimuli and, as these lower-order variables are more accurately specified, we must

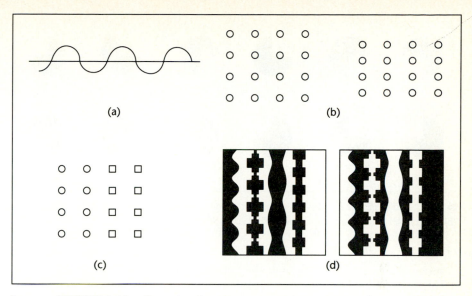

FIGURE 2-11 *Examples of various principles of organization: (A) good continuation, (B) proximity, (C) similarity, (D) symmetry. (Modified from Banks & Salapatek, 1983.)*

reassess the previous literature on the perception of the higher-order variables. With these precautions in mind, we consider two Gestalt principles; symmetry and good continuation.

It is a common finding that children and adults prefer figures with *symmetry,* or balanced proportions; that they process them more efficiently; and that they remember them better (Bornstein, 1984). In a series of studies, Bornstein and his colleagues (Bornstein, Ferdinandsen & Gross, 1981; Bornstein & Krinsky, 1985; Fisher, Ferdinandsen & Bornstein, 1981) have demonstrated that vertically symmetrical patterns are special for four-month-olds. Using figures that were composed of the same elements and were equivalent in perimeter, contour, and area, they found that, although there were no preference differences, infants habituated more quickly and completely to vertically symmetrical patterns than to patterns with vertical orientations, horizontal symmetry, oblique symmetry, or asymmetry. Furthermore, infants this age discriminate vertically symmetrical patterns from vertically oriented asymmetrical patterns composed of the same elements. Taken together, these data suggest that four-month-olds perceive vertically symmetrical patterns as organized wholes and that it is easier for them to process patterns that have vertical symmetry (see also, Humphrey, Humphrey, Muir & Dodwell, 1986).

The principle of good continuation is assumed to influence our perceptions of many types of visual stimuli. For example, adults perceive the subjective contours of a square in the arrangement of elements at left in Figure 2-12. The angles of each element are subjectively continued as straight lines that connect each angle and, thus, form a square. In contrast, the other two patterns in

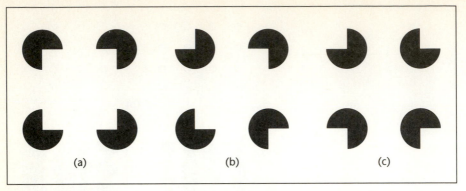

▶ **FIGURE 2-12**   *Do you perceive the subjective contours of a square in pattern (a), (b), or (c)?* (From Bertenthal, Campos & Haith, 1980.)

Figure 2-12 do not, even though the patterns have the same elements. Using a habituation-dishabituation experimental design, Bertenthal, Campos, and Haith (1980) controlled for the known lower-order variables and found that seven-month-olds discriminated subjective contours of the square in Figure 2-12, even after a brief viewing of the figure. The five-month-olds, however, did not show such perception except under lengthy viewing conditions.

Spelke and her colleagues (Kellman & Spelke, 1981; 1983; Schmidt & Spelke, 1984) used very different stimuli to assess the role of the principle of good continuation in the perception of four-month-olds. To illustrate, Kellman and Spelke (1983) used the three-dimensional stimuli depicted in Figure 2-13. The occlusion (experimental) group saw the display on the left with the rod occluded by the block; the two control groups saw the two right-most displays. All infants were tested with the two test displays. Although each control group preferred to look at the rod of the test display that differed from the rod used during the habituation period, the occlusion group did not respond differentially to the test displays. If they had perceived the rod as continuous during the habituation phase, then they should have dishabituated to the test stimulus that was a broken rod, but not to the complete rod. No such difference occurred. These findings make it impossible to know what the infants perceive in the occlusion condition and give no evidence that they perceive the visible parts of the part as continued. Although Spelke and her colleagues investigated the perception of several types of stimuli (for example, a photograph of a face occluded by a three-dimensional block), there was no evidence that the principle of good continuation influences the pattern perception of four-month-olds (Spelke, 1985).

When, however, Kellman and Spelke (1983) tested infants with a rod that, during habituation, moved back and forth behind the block, they found that four-month-olds perceived the moving, but occluded, rod as a complete rod. Thus, in the static conditions good continuation and the surface similarity of the occluded rod did not structure the perceptions of the young infants; but

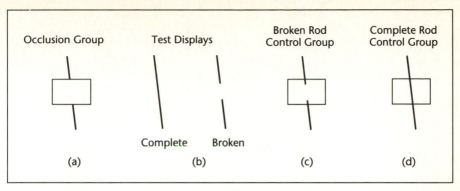

Occlusion Group   Test Displays

Broken Rod   Complete Rod
Control Group   Control Group

Complete   Broken

(a)   (b)   (c)   (d)

▶ **FIGURE 2-13** *A test of the principle of good continuation for four-month-olds. The occlusion group was shown figure (a), the two control groups figures (c) and (d), and all infants were tested with figure (b). (From Kellman & Spelke, 1981.)*

when occluded parts moved together, even dissimilar ones, the parts were perceived as parts of the same object (Kellman & Spelke, 1983). This finding serves to further confirm the importance of motion information in the visual perception of young infants. Furthermore, Kellman, Gleitman, and Spelke (1987) have demonstrated that infants detect the real motion of objects, not simply the retinal changes that occur with movement. Four-month-olds were habituated in one of two conditions that were comparable to those of Kellman and Spelke (1983). In the stationary display condition [(a) in Figure 2-14] the infant was moved before a stationary display of a rod behind an occluding screen. In the moving display condition, the infant and the rod moved as indicated in (b) of Figure 2-14.

When the infants were tested for dishabituation to a complete or broken rod, there was no dishabituation after training with the stationary display. There was, however, dishabituation to the broken rod when the rod was moved during the habituation trials. Taken together with the Kellman and Spelke (1983) findings, the results indicate that young infants perceive unity of an occluded object when the object moves. Thus, whether they are stationary or moving, young infants can pick up the information that indicates the movement of an object. Perception of the unity of an object depends on the detection of real motion, not the optical changes in the retinal projections that occur with motion.

In summary, the limited research on the development of the Gestalt principles suggests that vertical symmetry may organize visual perception by three to four months of age and that good continuation is functional at seven months, at least with some types of stimuli. But it is not clear when principles like proximity and similarity begin to play a role. Furthermore, the fact that common movement influences the perception of young infants even when good continuation and similarity of surface does not suggests that, contrary to the Gestalt principles, young infants do not have a general tendency to organize

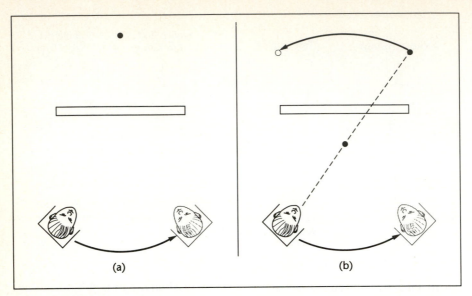

▶ **FIGURE 2-14** *Display conditions in the experiment. Panel a: Observer movement condition. Panel b: Conjoint movement condition. (Top views of the object and observer positions at one extreme of movement are shown, with positions at the other extreme shown by dotted figures.) (From Kellman, Gleitman & Spelke, 1987.)*

their perceptions into the simplest figures. Rather, they appear to organize their visual experiences as events in a three-dimensional world. The Gestalt laws of organization generally ignore the importance of depth and movement information for our perceptual organization of the three-dimensional world (see Goldstein, 1984). Nor do they consider the influence of familiarity and meaning, which we know affects adult perceptions (Helson, 1933). Extensive research is necessary to determine how the Gestalt principles relate to the development of perception and the other factors that influence infant perception.

IS THE HUMAN FACE A SPECIAL PATTERN?   Some theorists have speculated that human infants are better able to perceptually organize the configuration of the human face than any other visual pattern (for example, Fantz, 1961). How might we decide whether the configuration of the human face has a special status for infants? There are three ways in which the facial stimulus could be special. First, discrimination of and preference for the facial stimulus might occur early in life, before extensive exposure to the face. Second, the development of preference and/or discrimination of the face might follow a different course of development than other stimuli. Third, the recognition of the differences between faces and the features of faces might occur earlier than for other types of stimuli (Yin, 1978).

Although early studies indicated that even newborns have a preference

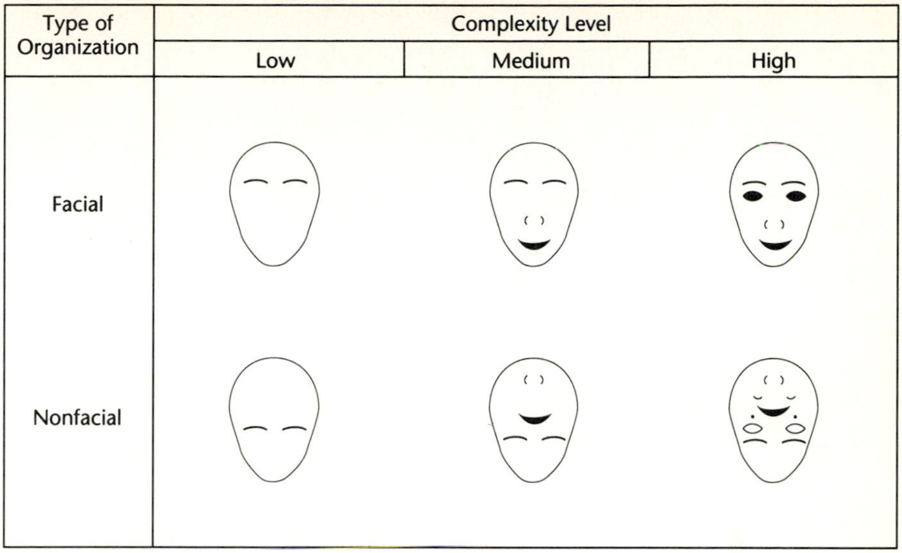

Type of Organization	Complexity Level		
	Low	Medium	High
Facial			
Nonfacial			

▶ **FIGURE 2-15** *Stimulus patterns representing three levels of complexity and two types of organization. (From Haaf & Brown, 1976.)*

for facial configurations (see, for example, Fantz, 1961), subsequent work that controlled for the lower-order variables (for example, amount of contrast, symmetry) that affect attention have not replicated this finding (see, for example, Fantz, 1965). More recently, Haaf and his colleagues (Haaf, 1977; Haaf & Bell, 1967; Haaf & Brown, 1976) have shown that when complexity (the number of features) is manipulated independently of facial configuration (the arrangement of the features) discrimination of facial configuration begins to emerge around 10 weeks of age. This is best demonstrated in the Haaf and Brown (1976) study, in which there were three levels of complexity for the facial and nonfacial stimuli, each differing in the number of elements (see Figure 2-15). At each level of complexity, the facial stimuli differed from the nonfacial stimuli only in similarity to the configuration of the human face; there were no differences in symmetry. As is evident in Figure 2-16, the 10-week-old infants were affected by complexity, and a preference for the facial configuration, although not a significant one, is evident for the high-complexity face. By 15 weeks of age this preference is significant. In addition, studies that have derived pattern preference predictions from stimulus energy models such as the contrast sensitivity model of Banks and Salapatek (1981) accurately predict the visual preferences of neonates and six-week-olds, but not the preference of two- and three-month-olds for facelike patterns (Dannemiller & Stephens, 1988; Kleiner & Banks, 1987).

These findings suggest that by two and one-half months of age there is something about the configuration of the human face that attracts infant attention. The design of these studies does not make it possible, however, to

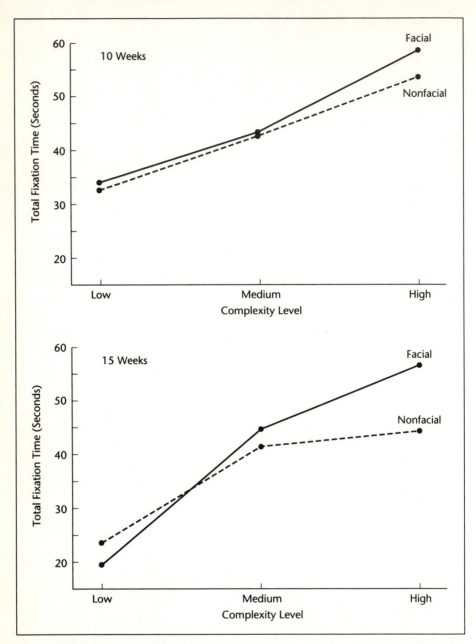

▶ **FIGURE 2-16** *Fixation times for 10-week-old infants (top). Fixation times for 15-week-old infants (bottom). (From Haaf & Brown, 1976.)*

CHAPTER 2 / INFANCY: SENSORIMOTOR

determine what that is. For example, the high-complexity face of the Haaf and Brown (1976) study differs from the other two levels of complexity not only in the number of features but also in the specific features represented (that is, the eyes). When young infants look longer at the high-complexity facial configuration it may not be the complete configuration that attract their attention but rather a specific feature, such as the eyes.

In an attempt to determine when infants discriminate the configuration of the human face rather than specific features, Caron, Caron, Caldwell and Weiss (1973) used a variation of the habituation paradigm with four- and five-month-olds. During the habituation phase different groups of infants were shown one of the 16 distorted face stimuli illustrated in Figure 2-17; the regular face was shown during the test trials. The control group saw the regular face in both phases. If a feature or a relation between features is discriminated in the perception of the human face, then the extent to which there is a difference between the distorted face and the regular one should be reflected in the looking times of the experimental group relative to those of the control group. That is, the experimental groups are seeing two different stimuli. If the two stimuli are discriminated, then there should be an increase in responding to the regular face, relative to the control group.

For example, consider the distorted face at the top of the first column; it differs from the regular face because the eyes are missing. If infants include the eyes in their perceptions of the face, then when the regular face is presented after habituation to the distorted face, this difference will be detected and reflected in longer looking times relative to the control group. This is just the way the four-month-olds performed, suggesting that they do process the eyes of the regular face. But they did not discriminate the distorted face that is missing the nose and mouth (top of second column) from the regular face. This suggests that infants this age do not process the nose and mouth in a regular face.

Taken together the 16 comparisons indicate that for four-month-olds "(a) the eyes are a more salient feature of the face than the nose-mouth; (b) the two eyes are perceived as a structured unit, localized in the upper half of the head and paired in the horizontal axis; (c) the head (including hair and face contour) is more prominent than the inner face pattern; and (d) the property of 'faceness', that is, the invariant configuration of eyes, nose, and mouth, is not perceptually organized. At five months of age three significant developmental changes have occurred: (a) the mouth has become as salient as the eyes; (b) the head no longer predominates over the interior face; and (c) the face configuration has emerged as a distinct visual entity" (Caron, Caron, Caldwell & Weiss, 1973, p. 396). These and related findings (see Fagan, 1972) lead to the conclusion that infants under five months do not respond to the entire facial configuration; rather, high-contrast areas like the eyes and hairline dominate perception.

The research on infant perception of the human face does not suggest an innate attraction to faces for young infants. Discrimination of the face does

REGULAR
FACE

EYE
DISTORTIONS
No Eyes

Low. Eyes

Vert. Eyes

Scr. Eyes

Single Scr. Eye

NOSE-MOUTH
DISTORTIONS
No N-M

Raised N-M

Horiz. N-M

Scr. N-M

INNER-FACE
DISTORTIONS
Scr. Sym. Face

Scr. Asym. Face

Inv. Inner Face

HEAD
DISTORTIONS
Bald Head

Inv. Head

HEAD AND FACE
DISTORTIONS
Inv. Bald Head

Inv. Reg. Face

▶ **FIGURE 2-17** *The distorted-face stimuli (each repeatedly exposed to a different treatment group) and the intact schematic face (shown to all treatment groups during retention and to control groups during both repetition and retention). (From Caron, Caron, Caldwell & Weiss, 1973.)*

not occur early, without prior experience. Nor is there evidence that the development of the discrimination of the face follows a special course (see, for example, Kleiner, 1987). The face is special, however, in that it has many of the characteristics that attract infant attention. It has vertical symmetry, features of high contrast (for example, hair line and eyes), and moving parts (eyes and mouth). Infants do not have innate mechanisms for discriminating and attending to the human face, but they do have lower-order visual preferences (high contrast, movement) that serve to attract early attention to the face. Further, the face is special because it is probably the visual pattern in the environment of the young infant most frequently attended to, and may therefore play an important role in early perceptual learning. Indeed, three-month-old infants are able to discriminate a picture of their mother's face from that of a stranger (Barrera & Maurer, 1981). Thus, before infants are responsive to the entire facial configuration, they are capable of recognizing something specific to their own mother's face. This means that by this age infants have some type of memory for their mother's face. In Chapter 3 we take up the topic of infant memory.

PERCEPTUAL EXPECTATIONS

As adults we not only experience individual perceptual events, but also recognize that such events are embedded in sequences of events. Our perceptual experiences usually are not random events, rather there are regularities that relate events to each other. These regularities lead us to have expectations for future events, expectations that prepare us for action. When a traffic light before me changes from red to green, I expect the cross traffic to stop and the cars in front of the light to start moving. Preschool children also recognize the regularities of their experiences and come to have expectations about familiar events and games. Recently, Haith (1988) and his colleagues have begun to explore the development of visual expectations in early infancy. Their research indicates that three-and-one-half-month-old infants do acquire expectations and these expectations govern their actions.

In these studies infants were presented regular and irregular series of pictures that were presented to the left or right of center. The question was whether infants would anticipate the position of the next slide by looking in that direction before the slide was presented or whether expectation of a picture in a specific location would facilitate the looking response by decreasing the time to look once the picture was presented. In one condition the regular series presented pictures that alternated between the left and right locations. Compared to an irregular series, the infants seeing the regular series were more likely to anticipate the location of the next picture and the looking response had a shorter reaction time. Furthermore, the infants also derived expectations for 2/1 and 3/1 regularities in which pictures were presented 2 or 3 times to one side before the position was changed.

Haith's research demonstrates that even when young infants have no control over their environment, they can detect perceptual regularities, derive expectations from these regularities and that such expectations "constitute a foundation for the coordination of the baby's own behavior with dynamic events" (Haith, 1988, p. 4). Thus, by three to four months of age infants are able to obtain the type of perceptual information that prepares them to be future oriented and to act on their expectations.

OBJECT PERCEPTION

THE PERCEPTUAL CONSTANCIES   Adults usually see an object as *constant,* that is, an object is seen as the same object despite changes in the distance, illumination or orientation of the object. Such perceptual constancy occurs despite substantial variations in the image projected on the retina. As an object moves away from the eye, for example, the retinal image decreases in size. Yet, the adult sees the object as the same size. Similarly, as the orientation of the object changes, the shape of the retinal image varies. Nevertheless, the shape of the object is seen as constant. Such size and shape constancy makes it possible to identify objects under a variety of circumstances (see Bartley, 1969, for a comprehensive discussion of visual perceptual constancies). Although there are many types of visual constancies, two—size and shape—have been investigated with young infants (see Day & McKenzie, 1977, for a review).

Many theorists, in the empiricist tradition, have assumed that perceptual constancies are learned or constructed from our experiences. Helmholtz (1890/1962), for example, argued that with experience a child sees an object at many distances and in a variety of orientations, with concomitant changes in the retinal images. With this knowledge it is possible for the child to infer the size and shape of an object when a familiar retinal image occurs. Helmholtz's position, in effect, assumes that constancy is learned for each individual object and thus implies that constancy does not occur with new objects.

Since constancy does occur even with objects never seen previously, another explanation is that the child learns general relationships between changes in distance and orientation and the concomitant changes in the retinal image. Knowledge of these general relations would then make it possible for the child to predict the actual size and shape of unfamiliar objects. Both of these theories assume that substantial learning occurs, with the child coordinating retinal information and distance and orientation cues to estimate real size and shape (Brunswik, 1956).

In a variation of the empiricist position, Piaget (1952b) assumed that size constancy develops after the coordination of vision and prehension, at about six months of age. As the sensorimotor schemes that coordinate these two senses develop, the variable information that occurs through vision is adjusted to the constant information about size that occurs with touch.

Taking a nativist position, Gibson (1966) argued that the information necessary for the perceptual constancies is given in the environment. The child does not need to learn to coordinate distance and size or shape cues or to coordinate visual and tactile cues to perceive constancy. Rather, perception is direct, not indirect. The child must detect the information that is available. When objects move in space, for example, there are continuous transformations that are invariant; an object of a given size and shape generates a family of transformations that are unique to that specific object. Gibson assumed that the perceptual systems of the human are designed to detect these invariants in our environment. For example, in the case of shape constancy, a rectangular door projects a variety of trapezoidal retinal images except when we look at it straight on, yet we perceive it as a rectangle. How do we know the shape of this object, regardless of perspective? Gibson answers that, "Although the changing angles and proportions of the set of trapezoidal projections are a fact, the unchanging relations among the four angles and the invariant proportions over the set are another fact, equally important, and they uniquely specify the rectangular surface" (Gibson, 1979, pp. 10–11). Thus, Gibson assumes that the young infant detects the invariants of the environment rather than constructs them through experience.

SIZE CONSTANCY   Bower (1966b) used an operant conditioning procedure to investigate the size constancy of six- to eight-week-old infants. In this procedure a head-turning response was conditioned to a white cube, 30 cm on each side, presented at a distance of one meter. After the response was firmly established to this stimulus, three new stimuli, as well as the original stimulus, were presented in a generalization test phase, illustrated in Figure 2-18. Test-stimulus 1 was a 30 cm cube presented at 3 meters; Test-stimulus 2 was a 90 cm cube presented at one meter; and Test-stimulus 3 was a 90 cm cube presented at three meters. During the generalization test the infants made 98 responses to the original stimulus; 58 to Test 1, which was the same actual size as the original stimulus; 54 to Test 2, which was the same distance as the original stimulus; and 22 responses to Test 3, which differed in the actual size and the distance relative to the original stimulus, but had a retinal image that was the same size. The fact that the infants responded to Tests 1 and 2 more often than Test 3 indicates that the infants: (a) can recognize the actual size of an object (Test 1) even when the distance and the size of the retinal image have changed, and (b) can recognize when an object is presented at the same distance (Test 2) even though the actual size and the retinal size of the object differ from the original. Thus, the infants discriminate the actual size of the object as well as the true distance of an object and do not perceive the original object on the basis of the size of the retinal image. These data indicate the occurrence of size constancy and contradict the empiricist position which would predict the most responding for Test 3 since it is the same retinal size as the training stimulus.

Although subsequent research has not confirmed Bower's report of size constancy by one and one-half to two months of age (see Day, 1987, for a

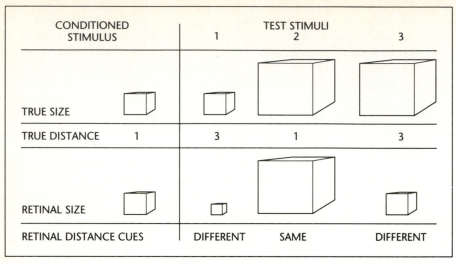

CONDITIONED STIMULUS	TEST STIMULI 1	2	3
TRUE SIZE			
TRUE DISTANCE	1	3	1	3
RETINAL SIZE			
RETINAL DISTANCE CUES	DIFFERENT	SAME	DIFFERENT

▶ **FIGURE 2-18** *The conditioned stimulus and the test stimuli of the size constancy study. The chart shows how test stimuli were related to the conditioned stimulus in various respects. (From Bower, 1966b.)*

review), using the habituation paradigm, Day and McKenzie (1981) demon-strated size constancy by eighteen-week-old infants. The infants discriminated between two different size objects that were moved toward and away from them. Thus, despite the continual changes in retinal image size and the fact that at some distances both objects produced retinal images of the same size, the infants perceived the differences in real size of the two objects. Taken together the research indicates size constancy by four to five months of age, and perhaps earlier. We have yet to trace, however, the early development of size constancy or how it relates to the development of distance perception (Day, 1987).

SHAPE CONSTANCY   In a second set of studies, Bower conditioned the head-turning response to a rectangle presented at a 45-degree angle to the infants' eyes (Bower, 1966a). The projected retinal shape of this stimulus would be trapezoidal. The test stimuli were the original stimulus, the same rectangle placed at right angles to the line of sight (retinal shape is rectangular), a trapezoid at right angles to the line of sight that projected the same retinal image as the original stimulus (a trapezoid), and this trapezoid at the 45-degree angle (to test for generalization on the basis of orientation) (illustrated in Figure 2-19). The test stimulus of the same rectangle elicited nearly as many responses as the original stimulus. The amount of responding was considerably less and equivalent for the two trapezoids. The data thus indicate that two-month-olds do not respond to the retinal shape of a stimulus as expected from the empiricist position; rather, they respond to the actual shape of the stimulus, an indication of shape constancy.

Stimulus	Real Shape	Orientation	Retinal Shape
1	Same	Different	Different
2	Different	Different	Same
3	Different	Same	Different

▶ **FIGURE 2-19** *Test stimuli in the shape constancy experiment differed from the conditioned stimulus as shown in the table. (From Bower, 1966b.) From "The Visual World of Infants," by T. G. R. Bower. Copyright © 1966 by Scientific American, Inc. All rights reserved.*

Subsequent research has confirmed shape constancy by three months of age (see Cook, 1987, for a review). Caron, Caron, and Carlson (1979) used the habituation paradigm to investigate shape constancy in 12-week-olds. The infants were shown either a square or a trapezoid at different slants (60, 40, 20, −20, and −40 degrees from the frontal plane). After habituation of the visual fixation response occurred, half the infants were presented the original shape with a frontal plane orientation (0 degree slant) and the other half were presented the other shape (novel) at the 0 degree slant. The infants who were presented the novel stimulus had significantly greater dishabituation of the fixation response than the infants who saw the same shape in the habituation and dishabituation phases. Thus, the infants were able to recognize the real (objective) shape of the original stimulus despite the fact that they never experienced during habituation the retinal shape that was projected when it was presented. This study and others (see Kellman, 1984) suggest that motion information may be particularly important in the early perception of shape constancy.

Using both the conditioning and habituation methodology, it has been established that by two to three months of age infants have shape constancy and by four to five months size constancy (see also Bornstein, Krinsky & Benasich, 1986). The absence of studies with younger infants makes it impossible to rule out the effects of early experience on the development of these constancies. Demonstration of size or shape constancy with newborns would be necessary to reject a learning interpretation of these perceptual constancies (compare Granrud, Haake & Yonas, 1985). However, a failure to demonstrate such constancies with newborns does not reflect on nativist explanations such as Gibson's, since the emergence of perceptual constancies may be dependent upon physiological maturation. With the data now available Gibson's position appears particularly strong. Learning interpretations would need to assume very rapid learning in the early months to explain the shape constancy data. Further, Piaget's position is weakened since shape constancy, at least, occurs before infants have had much experience handling the visual objects of their environment, and before the visual and prehension sensorimotor schemes are coordinated. However, we will need to know more about the development of perceptual processes and the nature of the stimulus information that underlies size and shape constancy before we will have adequate models of the development of the perceptual constancies.

PERCEPTION OF INVARIANTS   The occurrence of perceptual constancies at a relatively young age lends some support to Gibson's assumption that the perceptual systems are designed to detect the *invariants,* those aspects of the visual information that are unchanging. That is, in the flow of changing sensory information (for example, changing cues for distance, changing retinal size or shape), young infants detect the patterns of information that denote the unchanging size or shape of an object.

A few studies have directly assessed young infants' ability to detect invariant relations. For example, Antell, Caron, and Myers (1985) have demonstrated that newborns are sensitive to an invariant identity-nonidentity relation. As illustrated in Figure 2-20, infants were habituated to the successive presentation of two stimuli that had identical or nonidentical arrangements of elements. All infants saw the same stimulus elements; the only difference between conditions was the relation between the two elements of each stimulus. If infants can detect this relation (that is, "same" or "different") then the fixation response should recover when the relation is changed. This was the case. Infants in the experimental conditions (SD, DS) dishabituated when the relation between the elements was changed during the test phase. No such response recovery occurred when the relation remained unchanged in the control conditions (C). Newborns not only discriminate between two visual stimuli that differ in lower-order characteristics, such as amount of contrast (see Bushnell *et al.,* 1983), but also discriminate the higher-order relations of same/different.

In a series of experiments, Gibson and her colleagues (Walker, Owsley, Megaw-Nyce, Gibson & Bahrick, 1980) have demonstrated that infants as young as three months detect the invariant properties that specify the rigidity and elasticity of objects. For example, during a habituation phase infants were presented a round piece of foam rubber with two different deforming motions that are possible with elastic objects (these were selected from the three illustrated in Figure 2-21, "ripple," "fold" around horizontal axis, or "fold" around vertical axis). Following habituation, one-third of the infants saw the object presented with the third deforming motion and one-third saw the rigid motion of the object illustrated in Figure 2-21. The infants in the control group continued to see the two deforming motions that were presented during the habituation phase. Only the rigid motion group showed a significant increase in visual fixation during the dishabituation phase.

These findings lead to the inference that during the habituation trials with the two deforming motions the infants perceived the common characteristics of deforming motions and therefore dishabituated to a rigid motion. They did not dishabituate to a third type of deforming motion, however, since it con-

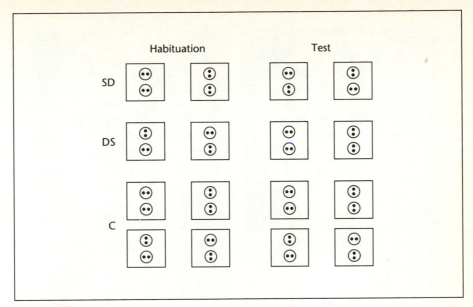

FIGURE 2-20 *The stimuli presented to the experimental and control groups. Within conditions, infants received successive exposure to each of the two stimuli in that condition. (SD = habituation to identical elements, recovery to nonidentical elements; DS = habituation to nonidentical elements, recovery to identical elements; C = control.) (From Antell, Caron & Myers, 1985.)*

tinued to convey the information that is common to deforming motions. It should be noted that such an inference would not be appropriate if only one type of deforming motion was used during habituation. In that case, the comparison between the deforming motion and a rigid one would only indicate whether the infants discriminate two different motions, not whether they perceive the invariance of the deforming motions.

In summary, we have a few demonstrations of the detection of perceptual invariants by young infants. We know nothing, however, about the development of this ability, the types of invariants that are detectable, or the factors that may constrain the detection of invariants. For example, newborns detect same/different relations between elements that vary only in one feature (that is, horizontal vs vertical arrangement of the dots). Are they capable of detecting this same relation when the elements are more variable, when there are more differences between the elements, and, thus, greater demand on information-processing capabilities?

THE PERCEPTION OF OBJECTS AS SEPARATE ENTITIES Adults perceive objects; the world is structured into "manipulatable units with internal coherence and external boundaries" (von Hofsten & Spelke, 1985, p. 198). What of young infants? Do they see objects as separate entities? Spelke (1985) and her col-

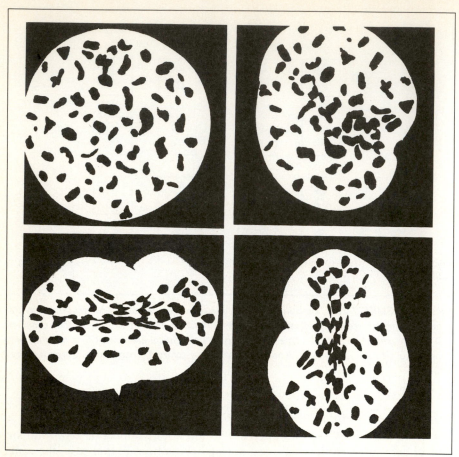

▶ **FIGURE 2-21** *Snapshots of the object displayed during a cycle of each of the four motions: rigid motion around horizontal axis (top left); "ripple" deformation (top right); "fold" around horizontal axis (bottom left); and "fold" around vertical axis (bottom right). (From Walker, Owsley, Megan-Nyce, Gibson & Bahrick, 1980.)*

leagues have investigated this question. Their evidence indicates that three-month-olds do perceive objects as unitary and distinct from a background and that infants this age expect an object to retain its unity as it moves.

Spelke and Born (see Spelke, 1985) presented a large cylindrical object suspended before a uniform background (see Figure 2-22). After the object was stationary for 30 seconds, it was moved forward in two ways. In one condition, depicted in the lower left of Figure 2-22, the whole object moved forward. When objects move forward from a background, the background remains unchanged, the object has a larger projected image, and the texture of the object becomes less dense. In the second condition, half the object remained in place as represented on the right side of the lower right drawing of Figure 2-22. The other half of the object moved forward with a section of

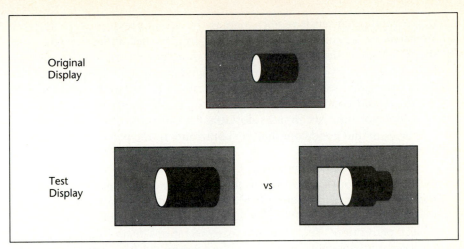

Original
Display

Test
Display

vs

▶ **FIGURE 2-22** *Displays used in an experiment on perception of the unity and per-sistence of suspended objects. The object and background surface were in the position depicted in the upper drawing during the stationary periods. During the object movement and the broken movement periods, the surfaces moved from that position to one of the two positions depicted in the lower drawings.* (From Spelke, 1985.)

the background. When a figure and its adjacent background move forward the texture density of both the background and the figure becomes less dense. In other words, the left side of the object moved forward as if the whole display, object against a background, was moving forward. If infants expect an object to move as a whole, then they should be surprised or puzzled when it moves in parts. This indeed was the response of the infants. Observers who did not know the stimulus conditions judged video tapes of the infants' responses. More surprise was indicated when only part of the object moved. Two subsequent experiments confirmed these findings.

In a second series of experiments, Spelke and her associates sought to determine how infants perceive adjacent objects. Six-month-olds saw a display of two adjacent objects (a cube and a cylinder) that differed on several dimensions. In one condition, the objects were both moved forward together; in the other, only the cube moved forward. The infants were judged to be more surprised when one object moved alone. This result suggests that the infants perceived the two adjacent objects as a single unit, if we are willing to assume that adults would not find one of the test displays more "surprising" than another.

Spelke's data indicate that three-month-olds expect objects to maintain unity as they move. This leads to the inference that by this age infants perceive objects as separate entities; three-dimensional objects are seen as separate from their adjacent backgrounds. This, of course, is a given of adult perception. But as will be evident in Chapter 3, considerable controversy has surrounded the early development of object perception. Spelke's data further suggest, however, that infant object perception depends on the detection of the spatial separation of surfaces and is not sensitive to changes in the color or texture of the surfaces as predicted by Gestalt theory. These data confirm her finding (Kellman & Spelke, 1983) that surface information does not contribute to the perception of occluded objects by young infants. Indeed, taken together, the data indicate that two principles—common movement of object parts (see also Kellman & Short, 1987) and connected surfaces—determine object perception by three-month-olds. Not until six months do Gestalt principles such as similarity of surface or form and good continuation contribute to the perception of objects (Quinn & Eimas, 1986).

Spelke's work raises important questions about how to explain infant object perception (Spelke, 1988). On the one hand, the empiricist and Gestalt approaches appear inadequate. On the other hand, Gibson's theory has its own weakness (see Spelke, 1988). We have seen that object motion is important for object perception. Yet, contrary to expectations from Gibson's theory, object perception does not depend upon the perception of the optical invariants that are produced by motions. Infants discriminate between their own motion and the motion of objects, even when the optical information for the two situations is comparable (Kellman, Gleitman & Spelke, 1987).

▶ AUDITION

The gross anatomy of the human ear is depicted in Figure 2-23. At birth the major structures of the auditory system appear to be adult-like (Aslin, Pisoni & Jusczyk, 1983). Indeed, anatomical and electrophysiological data indicate that the inner ear begins to function around the fifth or sixth fetal month (Bredberg, 1985). There are a number of early studies indicating that newborns as well as fetuses are responsive to a variety of auditory stimuli. Unfortunately, these early studies were relatively unsystematic, and the responses investigated (for example, blinking, kicking, general movement) were not objectively recorded. More recently, conditioning, high-amplitude sucking, and electrophysiological measurements have been used to study auditory development.

The *high-amplitude sucking (HAS) paradigm* is a combination of the habituation-dishabituation and operant-conditioning paradigms that has proven particularly valuable with young infants. Infants will suck on a tube if sounds or visual patterns are presented contingent on a specific rate of nonnutritive sucking (Siqueland & DeLucia, 1969; Eimas, Siqueland, Jusczyk & Vigorito, 1971). This sucking response eventually habituates if the reinforcer remains constant. When the sucking response habituates to a given sound, infants in the experimental condition are presented another sound, one which varies in some specified manner from the first. If these infants increase their rate of sucking to the new stimulus and the infants in a control condition who continue to hear the original sound do not, then it can be inferred that the infants in the experimental condition can discriminate between the two sounds.

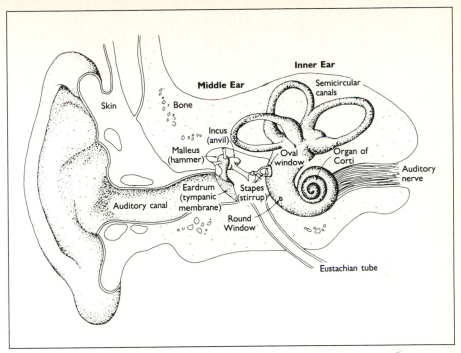

Inner Ear

Semicircular canals

Skin

Middle Ear

Bone

Incus (anvil)

Malleus (hammer)

Oval window

Organ of Corti

Auditory nerve

Eardrum (tympanic membrane)

Stapes (stirrup)

Auditory canal

Round Window

Eustachian tube

▶ **FIGURE 2-23** *When sound waves reach the eardrum (tympanic membrane), it begins to vibrate. The vibrations of the eardrum in turn initiate the vibration of the three bones (malleus, incus, and stapes) of the middle ear. As the last bone (stapes) of the middle ear vibrates, it moves against a membrane (oval window) of the inner ear (cochlea). The inner ear is filled with fluid and receptor cells are located on its basilar membrane. When the oval window vibrates, the fluid moves and the receptor cells of the basilar membrane are stimulated. The resulting nerve impulses are transmitted via the auditory nerve to the brain.*

DETECTION THRESHOLD

Sound waves differ on two physical dimensions: the *amplitude* (loudness) of the wave, expressed in decibels (db), and the *frequency* (pitch) of the wave cycles, expressed in hertz (Hz). In Figure 2-24 the loudness of some familiar sounds is compared to the decibel scale. *Threshold* (decibels = 0–15) is the minimal level of loudness at which an individual first reports hearing a sound. The question of concern here is whether the newborn hears all the sounds that a normal young adult hears. This is a difficult issue because, unlike vision, in which we can determine what infants are looking at, there is no natural response that indicates what an infant is listening to.

Generally, the studies of newborn auditory sensitivity indicate loudness thresholds between 50 db (normal conversation) and 90 db (heavy city traffic) (Schneider, Trehub & Bull, 1979). The variability in the thresholds established in these studies is indicative of a recurring problem in infant research. An infant may fail to make a response to a particular stimulus either because the infant

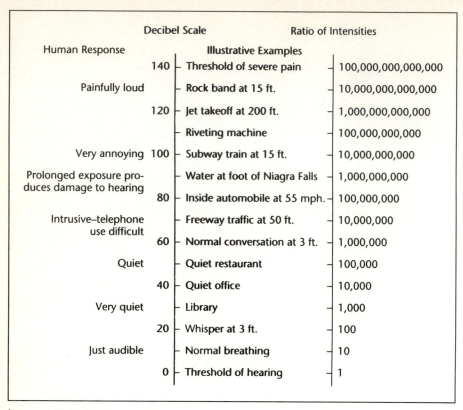

	Decibel Scale		Ratio of Intensities
Human Response		**Illustrative Examples**	
	140	Threshold of severe pain	100,000,000,000,000
Painfully loud		Rock band at 15 ft.	10,000,000,000,000
	120	Jet takeoff at 200 ft.	1,000,000,000,000
		Riveting machine	100,000,000,000
Very annoying	100	Subway train at 15 ft.	10,000,000,000
Prolonged exposure pro-duces damage to hearing		Water at foot of Niagra Falls	1,000,000,000
	80	Inside automobile at 55 mph.	100,000,000
Intrusive–telephone use difficult		Freeway traffic at 50 ft.	10,000,000
	60	Normal conversation at 3 ft.	1,000,000
Quiet		Quiet restaurant	100,000
	40	Quiet office	10,000
Very quiet		Library	1,000
	20	Whisper at 3 ft.	100
Just audible		Normal breathing	10
	0	Threshold of hearing	1

▶ **FIGURE 2-24** *Hearing: The loudness of several familiar sounds. (From Kimble, Garmezy, & Zigler, 1974.)*

does not perceive the stimulus, or because the stimulus does not elicit the particular response under investigation. Tentatively, these studies suggest that the newborn can hear sounds in the range of normal conversation and perhaps even quieter sounds. Studies using electrophysiological measures at the auditory cortex and the brainstem generally indicate lower thresholds, but not below 40 db (see Schneider, Trehub & Bull, 1979; Aslin, 1987, for reviews).

There is little research between the neonate period and five to six months, and what is available is difficult to interpret (Schneider *et al.*, 1979). Trehub, Schneider, and Endman (1980), however, used a head-turning response in two developmental studies of six- to 24-month-olds. In this conditioning paradigm infants sat in front of two speakers and were trained to turn their heads in the direction of the source of the sound. When a tone was presented at a speaker and the infants turned their heads in that direction, four seconds of visual reinforcement (an active toy) was presented. After the infants were conditioned to turn their heads to a sound, tones of varying intensity were presented to determine if the infants made a head-turning response. Since adult loudness thresholds vary with the frequency of the tone, Schneider and his colleagues manipulated both frequency (200–10,000 Hz) and intensity. Each frequency was presented several times at each of several different intensities.

Their results indicate that infants from six to 24 months of age had comparable thresholds at 10,000 Hz and that this threshold was 15 db higher than the adults. But at 19,000 Hz the difference was much smaller and the 24-month-olds were similar to the adults. The six-month-olds had higher thresholds than the older infants at the lower frequencies, by 5 to 8 db. Subsequent studies (for example, Sinnott, Pisoni & Aslin, 1983) have confirmed that infant thresholds are similar to those of adults at the higher frequencies and that infants have higher thresholds than adults at the low frequencies.

How can we account for the differences in sensitivity between infants and adults? A look at the structure of the ear (see Figure 2-23) suggests a number of mechanisms that might lead to developmental changes. For example, the auditory canal, which is much smaller in infants, is known to affect auditory sensitivity. Similarly, comparisons of infant and adult middle ear systems indicate reduced stiffness of the middle ear elements of the infant, which may affect sensitivity. Developmental changes may also occur at the neural level, perhaps in the brainstem pathways (Berg & Smith, 1983). The fact that auditory sensitivity continues to improve into adolescence suggests that factors such as these may involve growth over relatively long periods of time (Roche, Siervogel & Himes, 1978).

DISCRIMINATION

The research on absolute thresholds tells us something about the ability of infants to detect sound. The next question is whether infants can discriminate between sounds. In the natural environment we must detect sounds against a noisy background. Thus, basic to auditory perception is an ability to discriminate between sound intensities, which is particularly important in speech perception since subtle intensity differences signal syllable stress. Adults can detect intensity differences of 1 to 2 db. Several studies (see Aslin, 1987, for a review) indicate that six- to nine-month-olds detect minimal intensity differences of 3 to 12 db, suggesting that they have a capability significant for speech perception. Unfortunately, the operant head-turn paradigm is difficult to use with infants younger than six months; we, therefore, know nothing about intensity discrimination in the first few months.

Similarly, it appears that by six months of age infants are capable of frequency discriminations that approach those of adults. Adults can discriminate 0.5–1 percent frequency differences (for example, 10 Hz difference at 1000 Hz). Six- to nine-month-olds are capable of discriminating two percent differences. Thus, at the loudness of normal conversation six-month-olds are capable of intensity and frequency discriminations that are prerequisites for speech perception (see Aslin, 1987, for a review).

SOUND LOCALIZATION

Adults are able to locate the source of sounds because they have two ears. If a sound originates from one side of the head, there are discrepancies between the two ears in the intensity of the auditory wave and the timing of the phases of the wave. The integration of this information from both ears makes localization possible. When a sound originates from a source equidistant from both ears, for example, straight ahead, overhead, or behind, it is difficult to locate the exact source of a sound without moving the head, since there are no such discrepancies.

Studies with animals indicate that sound localization involves the auditory cortex and that more complex neural mechanisms are implicated in sound localization than in frequency or intensity discrimination (see Clifton, Morrongiello, Kulig & Dowd, 1981 for a review). For this reason, developmental changes in the ability to locate sound are assumed to reflect cortical development.

Muir and Field (1979) presented rattle sounds through speakers at a 90-degree angle to the newborn's left-right midline. Under these conditions, the newborns turned toward the sound 74 percent of the time. Other studies have confirmed the finding that newborns reliably orientate to lateral sounds (for example, Clifton, Morrongiello, Kulig & Dowd, 1981), but developmental studies (Field, Muir, Pilon, Sinclair & Dodwell, 1980; Muir, Abraham, Forbes & Harris, 1979) demonstrate that by two months of age there is a decrease in the sound localization response, which does not reliably occur again until four months of age (see Muir, 1985, for a recent review). Although both learning and maturational explanations have been offered for this somewhat unusual developmental change, longitudinal research comparing the performance of identical triplets and unrelated infants supports a maturational explanation since the timing of the changes in sound localization was more similar for the identical triplets than for the unrelated infants (Benson & Anderson-Beckman, 1981). Indeed, several researchers (Clifton, Morrongiello, Kulig & Dowd, 1981; Muir *et al.*, 1979; Muir, 1985) suggest that the U-shaped function relating age and sound localization reflects shifts to new levels of cognitive organization, with the newborn response a reflexive one and the response of the four- to five-month-olds a voluntary one under intentional control.

EARLY VOICE PREFERENCES

There is increasing evidence that young infants recognize and prefer some speech sounds over others (see, for example, DeCasper & Fifer, 1980; DeCasper & Prescott, 1984; Mehler, Bertoncini, Barriere & Jassik-Gerschenfeld, 1978; Spence & DeCasper, 1987). Newborns, for example, prefer the sound of their mothers' voice over the voices of other females and they prefer female voices in general to male voices (DeCasper & Prescott, 1984). Indeed, it is not until two weeks of age or later that infants appear to discriminate and prefer their fathers' voice to other male voices.

This early preference for the maternal voice led DeCasper and Spence (1986) to speculate that this preference is founded upon prenatal experience. Intrauterine measurements indicate that the noises of the cardiovascular system are relatively loud; but these measurements also indicate that the mother's voice is even louder, unlike an external voice such as the father's. Of course, one way to test the effect of prenatal experience on voice preferences is to deprive a group of fetuses of any experience of their mother's voice and then compare their newborn preferences to the appropriate control condition. Clearly, this approach is not ethically acceptable. However, DeCasper and Spence speculated that if given enough experience with specific speech patterns, the newborn may prefer these familiar sounds. To test this possibility, a group of mothers were asked to read aloud regularly specific passages from children's books for a few weeks before the birth of the infant. These infants were then tested as newborns for their preferences for these passages relative to comparable passages that were not read during the prenatal period. The newborns preferred to hear the familiar passage that had been recited during the prenatal period; there were no such preferences for the novel passages.

This preference was determined by conditioning the sucking response. First, a baseline level of sucking on a nonnutritive nipple was established for each infant. Then, one story (for example, the familiar one) was presented contingent on a sucking rate that was lower than the baseline rate; the presentation of a second story (for example, a novel one) was contingent on a high sucking rate. The relationship between stories and sucking rate was reversed for half of the neonates.

If the infants prefer to hear a familiar story, then their sucking rate should be the one that produces the familiar story rather than the rate that produces the novel story. This was the case. Furthermore, the design of the study made it possible for DeCasper and Spence to argue that the newborns preferred something about the auditory characteristics of the familiar story, not simply the characteristics of the mother's voice. The mothers recorded three stories for use in later testing before they began reading the story selected for daily reading aloud. This means that the mothers did not know in advance which story would be used with their infant and that therefore this knowledge could not be reflected in the recordings that were used during the test phase. In addition, half the infants were tested with recordings that were made by another infant's mother. These infants preferred the familiar story to the same extent as those who were tested with their mothers' recording. Finally, a group of naive newborns who were not familiarized were tested with the same materials in the same manner and did not prefer any of the stories.

This review of infant audition has raised as many questions as it has answered. We do know that newborns can hear sounds in the frequency range of human speech and that they are sensitive enough to detect normal speech levels. Newborns are attentive to sound and make responses to locate it in space. As yet we know relatively little about the development of auditory skills, but recently researchers have begun to explore more of these capabilities (see Bundy, Colombo & Singer, 1982; Clarkson & Clifton, 1985; Trehub, 1987; Trehub, Thorpe & Morrongiello, 1987). Although we do not have direct evidence of newborn auditory skills, the preference data indicate that they have capabilities that make them sensitive to variations in speech sounds. Indeed, a large body of research has investigated the ability of infants to discriminate speech sounds; these findings are summarized in Chapter 3. Finally, the effect of early experience on neonatal preferences for speech sounds raises many questions about how early experience may affect the development of speech perception and language development as well and questions about how early experience affects auditory capabilities and preferences in general.

▶ PERCEPTION AND INTERSENSORY RELATIONS

Our knowledge about the environment originates not only from our individual sense modalities but also from the integration of information from two or more senses. This coordination of the senses leads us, for example, to have expectations about the hardness of an object that we see. It means that we perceive unified events or objects, for example, a quiet, small fuzzy puppy in front of us. Furthermore, when we receive information in one sense modality, we are likely to seek more information in other modalities (Spelke, 1976).

HOW DOES INTEGRATION OF SENSORY INFORMATION DEVELOP?

Essentially two positions have been taken on the development of intermodal integration of perceptual information. One assumes that the several sensory systems are separate initially and that integration develops. The other assumes that there is a unity of the senses at birth and that with development the senses become differentiated.

Piaget (1952b) assumed that initially there is no coordination of the senses. The neonate starts with reflexes that are specific to each sense modality. As the reflexes are modified and exercised in Stage 2, the infant experiences situations in which two of these early schemes are activated simultaneously. For example, the *tonic neck reflex* (fencer) puts the infant in a position in which his eyes are oriented toward one outstretched hand. When that hand grasps an object, there is a good probability that the object will also be seen (Bushnell, 1981). Through these chance concurrent expressions of the Stage 2 schemes, the infant learns that an object that is grasped can also be looked at. The infant then learns to anticipate the feel of an object by the look of it and to anticipate the look of an object by its feel. These coordinations continue to develop throughout the first six months of life. Piaget assumed that coordination of pairs of senses developed in the first three months and that coordination among three of them was acquired during the next three months (see Butterworth, 1981; 1983).

Piaget's theory is a *constructive theory,* that is, our knowledge of the world is dependent upon our actions upon it. We cannot know, for example, the spatial arrangement of our world simply by sensing visual or auditory information. Such knowledge is constructed through our active interaction with objects in space. These experiences make it possible to coordinate information from various senses (for example, to coordinate vision with touch) and thus to construct our knowledge of the world. We come to know the objective world as the several separate senses are coordinated through extended experiences with objects in space.

Gibson (1950; 1966; 1979) proposed a *nativist theory,* in which the environment contains the necessary information for our percepts and in which perception is the process of extracting information from the environment, not constructing it through multiple experiences. In other words, Gibson assumed that human perceptual systems are active information-seeking systems designed to directly pick up information from the environment without mediating mental processes such as memory and inference. Just as the structure of the human hand with its opposing thumb makes possible fine manipulations of objects, so the structure of the perceptual systems makes it possible to know the nature of the objective world. Further, Gibson assumed that humans are given perceptual systems that are coordinated and that these coordinated systems are designed to know that there are three-dimensional objects around us in a three-dimensional space. Gibson argued that the coordinated senses are sensitive to the *amodal properties* of the several senses, that is the properties that are common to two or more sense modalities. Such amodal properties include intensity, movement, shape, duration, number, location, and texture. For example, information about the location of an object can be specified by vision, audition, touch, or smell; information about shape and texture can be specified by both vision and touch.

Gibson's theory is not a developmental one, but Bower (1974), in keeping with Gibson's assumptions, proposed that at birth there is a primitive unity of the senses. The infant processes the amodal properties of objects, but does not distinguish between seeing, hearing, or feeling this information. Development is the differentiation of the several senses. Directly or indirectly, Gibson's theory has stimulated a growing body of infant research on the coordination of the senses and the perception of amodal properties.

VISUAL-AUDITORY COORDINATION

We have already reviewed research that indicates that newborn eye and head movements are influenced by the location of sounds. Mendelson and his colleagues (Haith, 1978; Mendelson & Haith, 1976; Mendelson, 1979) have asserted that newborn visual and auditory senses are coordinated to process the amodal property of location. Newborns have different patterns of eye movements when sound is presented with a formless visual field than when there is no sound with the formless field. When there is a formless visual field without sound, the newborn's eyes actively scan the field. Mendelson (1979) argues that the visual system is built to "'search' for scannable forms" (p. 336). When sound is presented with a formless visual field, newborns scan with smaller eye movements, have more oculomotor control, and scan in the direction of the sound. These researchers argue that when a sound is presented in a formless visual field the scanning eye movements of the newborn are attempts to find visual information in conjunction with the sound.

These findings indicate that the eye movements of newborns are spatially coordinated with the location of a sound. This suggests some coordination at birth of the visual-auditory systems (Crassini & Broerse, 1980), but it is not yet clear whether the searching eye movements that occur with sound affect how visual information is processed. At the very least, however, these eye movements may "facilitate the detection of intermodal equivalences, since sounds are usually accompanied by sights" (Butterworth, 1981, p. 54). The spatial organization of vision and audition at birth may ensure that amodal properties are detected in the infant's world. We do not, however, have any developmental data relating this early coordination to later coordination of visual and auditory information.

MATCHING AUDITORY AND VISUAL AMODAL INFORMATION A number of studies have concentrated on the ability of infants to match amodal visual and auditory information. For the most part, these studies have not been developmental and have focused on the cross-modal matching of four- to seven-month-olds (see Rose & Ruff, 1987, for a review). Many of these studies used a matching paradigm introduced by Spelke (1976) in which two visual events are presented simultaneously and a sound track that matches one of these with respect to an amodal property (for example, temporal patterning) is presented between these. If an infant visually explores the visual presentation that matches the sound more than the one that does not, it is assumed that the infant perceives the match.

These studies demonstrate that infants this age do detect sight-sound correspondences in, for example, rhythm (Mendelson & Ferland, 1982), tempo (Spelke, 1979), substance (Bahrick, 1983), number (Starkey, Spelke & Gelman, 1983), and speech (Kuhl & Meltzoff, 1982). They also raise questions about the stimulus bases for the correspondences (Rose & Ruff, 1987). To illustrate, consider a set of studies demonstrating the detection of numerical correspondence (Starkey *et al.*, 1983). In the first experiment six- to eight-month-olds were presented two visual displays: one with two objects, the other with three objects. As illustrated in Figure 2-25, the nature and location of the objects varied from trial to trial.

On each trial, simultaneous with the visual presentation, two or three drumbeats were sounded (1.33 beats per second). In this experiment and a

TRIAL	POSITION		OBJECTS		DRUM BEATS (No.)
	Left	Right	Left	Right	
1	1 / 2	1 / 2 / 3	1) Memo Pad 1) Comb	1) Bell Pepper 2) Animal Horn 3) Scissors	2
2	1 / 2	1 2 3	1) Ribbon 2) Pipe	1) Coin Purse 2) Ring Box 3) Feather	2
3	1 / 2	1 / 3 2	1) Orange Case 2) Pine Burr	1) Dark Brown Cloth 2) Egg Beater 3) Wooden Carving A	2
4	1 / 2	1 / 2 3	1) Wooden Bowl 2) Lemon	1) Glass-Holder 2) Red Yarn 3) Blue Yoyo	2
5	1 2	1 2 3	1) Key 2) Black Disc	1) Cork Screw 2) Jar Lid 3) Glasses Case	3
6	1 2	1 2 3	1) Wig 2) Drain Plug	1) Strap 2) Flute 3) Tea Steeper	3
7	1 2	1 / 2 3	1) Water Glass 2) Figurine	1) Hair Dryer Cap 2) Metal Cylinder 3) Wooden Carving B	3
8	2 / 1	3 / 1 2	1) Candle 2) Black Case	1) Pillow 2) Orange 3) Vase	3
9	1 / 3 2	1 / 2	1) Memo Pad 2) Comb 3) Scraper	1) Bell Pepper 2) Animal Horn	2
10	1 / 2 / 3	1 2	1) Ribbon 2) Pipe 3) Yellow Rubber Glove	1) Coin Purse 2) Ring Box	2
11	1 / 3 2	1 / 2	1) Orange Case 2) Pine Burr 3) Toy Animal	1) Dark Brown Cloth 2) Egg Beater	2
12	1 / 2 / 3	1 / 2	1) Wooden Bowl 2) Lemon 3) Blue Sponge	1) Glass-Holder 2) Red Yarn	2
13	1 2 3	1 2	1) Key 2) Black Disc 3) Unpainted Wooden Block	1) Cork Screw 2) Jar Lid	3
14	3 / 1 2	1 2	1) Wig 2) Drain Plug 3) Pink Case	1) Strap 2) Flute	3
15	1 2 3	1 / 2	1) Water Glass 2) Figurine 3) Wooden Mushroom	1) Hair Dryer Cap 2) Metal Cylinder	3
16	2 / 1 / 3	1 2	1) Candle 2) Black Case 3) Pink Cup	1) Pillow 2) Orange	3

FIGURE 2-25 The order of displays given to one infant. As illustrated above, the number and type of objects varied as did the drumbeats. However, results concluded that infants preferred the visual display that matched the number of drumbeats. (From Starkey, Spelke & Gelman, 1983.)

replication of it, the infants looked longer at the visual display that matched the drumbeats in number. Can we conclude that the infants detected the correspondence of number? The timing of the drumbeats leaves open the possibility that the infants are detecting temporal correspondence. That is, the duration of the three-drumbeat sequence was longer than the two beat sequence. If we assume that it takes longer to scan three objects than two objects, then there is a temporal correspondence between the time to scan the objects and the duration of the drumbeats.

In a third experiment the durations of the two- and three-beat sequences were equated. Nevertheless, the infants made numerical matches suggesting that the infants are detecting cross-modal numerical correspondences (but, see Moore, Benenson, Reznick, Peterson & Kagan, 1987). Rose and Ruff (1987), however, offer an alternative basis for the matching behavior. As the objects were presented, the overall size of the visual display is confounded with numerosity. Thus, the infants may be detecting an intensity correspondence between the amount of visual stimulation and the amount of auditory stimulation rather than a numerical correspondence.

In summary, it appears that some form of visual-auditory coordination occurs for newborn detection of location. Further, we have evidence that four- to seven-month-olds detect the auditory-visual correspondences of several amodal properties. But we know nothing about the development of these cross-modal matches or whether these matches are based on more basic stimulus properties than presently assumed.

VISUAL-TACTILE COORDINATION

Two types of visual-tactile coordination have been investigated: *manual* and *oral*. In an early study of visual-tactile (manual) correspondence, Bower, Broughton, and Moore (1970) argued that neonates perceive the equivalence of visual and tactual *locations*. In their study they observed the reaching response of infants to visual objects presented in five different positions and reported that 70 percent of the arm extensions were to the appropriate visual location. Bower *et al.* reasoned that such responses show that for these infants seeing something indicates something touchable in the same location.

Unfortunately, this study had only five subjects and suffered from methodological weaknesses. For example, there was no control condition in which arm extensions were measured when no visual object was present. Such a control condition is necessary to rule out the alternative interpretation that the arm extensions observed occur spontaneously, independent of the presence of visual objects. Nor did Bower *et al.* specify any objective criteria for classifying arm movements as extensions toward an object.

Since then, studies with improved methodologies have been unable to replicate the Bower *et al.* finding that newborns reach for what they see (see Bushnell, 1981, for a review; compare von Hofsten, 1982). Nor is there any evidence that newborns look toward their hands when they touch something. Research on visual-tactile (manual) coordination indicates that there is a gradual development of coordination during the first few months. On the basis of her review of the literature, Bushnell (1981), taking a position similar to Piaget's, argues that the visual and tactile senses are not coordinated at birth for location and that such coordination grows out of some of the neonate reflexes (for example, tonic-neck reflex). She further argues that by about three months of age, infants have had enough experience with a few particular objects for them to have equated visual and tactile space for these objects. Infants this age reach at the sight of their own hands or dangling toys. During the next three months, this visual-tactile equivalence generalizes to other objects.

Bushnell also considered the development of the integration of the visual and tactile senses for *perceptual features* of objects, such as size, shape, and texture. She argues that this integration does not occur until the period when the infants are performing reaching responses consistently to seen objects, at about five to six months of age. The infant comes to know the cross-modal equivalences of object features through the manipulations that follow the grasping of the seen objects.

It may be premature, however, to attribute the development of visual-tactile (manual) coordination to experience. The relatively late development of visual-manual correspondences may reflect not the influence of experience, but the relatively slow maturation of the manual-tactile system. Correspondences will not be evident until the manual-tactile system has matured enough to process adequate tactile information (Rose & Ruff, 1987). This cannot be resolved until we have extensive and systematic research on intramodal as well as intermodal perceptual development. To illustrate, a recent study (Streri & Spelke, 1988) has demonstrated that through manual movement four-month-olds can discriminate between rigidly movable rings and independently movable rings. Furthermore, this discrimination transferred to the visual mode. In the intramodal study the infants were habituated to a pair of wooden rings that were connected by a rigid rod or to a pair of comparable rings that were connected by an elastic band. The rings were presented one in each hand, with a cloth preventing the infants from seeing the objects. Thus, in one condition the two rings moved rigidly together; when one ring was moved, the other also moved in a comparable manner. In the other condition the two rings moved independently of each other. After habituation the infants manipulated the novel sets of rings longer than the familiar ones; and, when the dishabituation test was with a visual presentation of the rings moving, the infants tended to look longer at the novel object.

These studies demonstrate that infants can use the motion information that they produce through their activity to discriminate between objects; and, that when such intramodal discrimination occurs, it transfers to the visual mode. Thus, as in the case for visual perception, motion information is important in the tactile-manual perception of objects. Further, these findings suggest that this information is abstract enough that infants can recognize the same objects visually. Thus before infants have had much experience handling seen objects, they can make haptic discriminations; and the information derived from manual exploration can be matched to the information derived from visual exploration of the same objects.

Two studies further suggest the significance of intramodal development and indicate a different developmental course for the detection of visual-tactile (oral) correspondence of perceptual features. Meltzoff and Borton (1979) tested 29-day-old infants in the visual preference paradigm using two different pacifiers—one smooth and one very bumpy. Initially one of the two pacifiers was inserted in the infant's mouth for 90 seconds, followed by a visual presentation of both pacifiers. The visual fixation responses of the infants indicated that the preferred object was the one that had been presented to the mouth, and this was the case in two separate experiments. Such a preference indicates that the tactile information of the first phase was available in the visual test.

Gibson and Walker (1984) present further evidence of visual-tactile (oral) coordination by one-month-olds in a study of the perception of the amodal property of substance (rigidity vs elasticity). This property of an object can be conveyed tactually since rigid objects have a different feel than elastic ones, which can be squeezed. Substance can also be conveyed visually. An elastic object when squeezed has different transformations of shape than a rigid object that is rotated in space.

Gibson and Walker presented a rigid or elastic object of the same size and shape in the mouth of the infants for 60 seconds, followed by a visual preference test. During the test phase, two objects (similar, but not identical to the training stimulus) were presented simultaneously. The rigid object was rotated about the horizontal and vertical axes; the other was squeezed and released in a rhythmical motion that approximated the movement of the rigid object.

For both types of objects, the infants looked longer at the novel object. That is, infants who mouthed the rigid object preferred to look at the elastic object, and those trained with the elastic object preferred to look at the rigid object. These findings support the inference that infants this age can detect information about substance and that visual and tactile-oral information about substance is coordinated.

It is not clear why the infants in the Meltzoff and Borton studies preferred the familiar stimulus and those in the Gibson and Walker study preferred the novel one. We have seen, however, that stimulus familiarity affects preferences. Nevertheless, the fact that there was a preference indicates that they could discriminate between the two visual stimuli. Also the fact that their preferences were determined by their prior oral training indicates that the preference behavior does not simply represent a visual preference for a specific object.

Thus, both studies of visual-tactile (oral) coordination find evidence for the coordination of object feature information at one month of age, which is much earlier than is evident in the visual-tactile (manual) research. This difference in development may reflect the role of the cephalocaudal and proxi-

---

modistal principles of growth and motor control. Further research will be necessary to discover the developmental course of visual-tactile (oral) coordination (see Rose, Gottfried & Bridger, 1981) and the role of early experience in this coordination.

PROPRIOCEPTIVE-VISUAL COORDINATION

Meltzoff (1981; but see Hayes & Watson, 1981) has argued that the imitation of facial expressions by young infants is another indicant of the ability of young infants to detect the correspondence of information from two perceptual modalities: vision and proprioception. The *proprioceptive sensors* are the internal sensors of the body that indicate where parts of the body are in space and make possible such activities as tying a knot with your hands behind your back. In a series of experiments with infants ranging in age from 12 to 21 days old, Meltzoff and Moore (1977) demonstrated that infants this age will imitate at least four different adult facial expressions, three of which are illustrated in Figure 2-26. Furthermore, infants this age can make the imitations even when the response is delayed a few seconds. The response was delayed by putting a pacifier in the infant's mouth during exposure to the adult expression and then removing it after the expression was finished. The infants made the imitation response after the pacifier was removed.

How is it that young infants make such imitative responses? Piaget proposed six substages in the development of imitation during the sensorimotor period. In the first substage there is no imitation. What he calls *pseudo-imitation* is evident in the second substage. By this he means that infants do imitate the actions of an adult, but only those actions that the infant makes first. True imitation begins in the third substage, but is limited to imitation with body parts that can be seen by the infant. For example, the infant can imitate hand gestures but cannot imitate facial expressions until the fourth substage, which occurs around eight months of age.

An alternative explanation is that during the first month of life infants learn to make facial imitations. That is, either through reinforcement of mouth opening responses or matching responses by an adult, the infant learns to make specific facial expressions in the presence of similar adult facial expressions.

Both the Piagetian and learning interpretations of infant imitation of facial expressions would have difficulty explaining such imitations by newborns. Meltzoff and Moore (1983a) offer evidence that newborns do imitate adult facial expressions. This study was done with 40 newborns ranging in age from 42 minutes old to 72 hours old who saw two expressions, mouth opening and tongue protrusion. Each expression was seen for four minutes; the order of the two expressions was counterbalanced. The results showed that the newborns produced significantly more mouth opening responses to the mouth-opening model than to the tongue-protrusion model and more tongue protrusions in the presence of the tongue-protrusion model than the mouth-opening

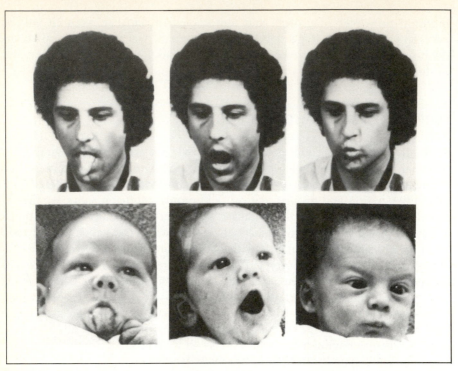

▶ **FIGURE 2-26** *Sample photographs from videotape recordings of two- to three-week-old infants imitating (a) tongue protrusion, (b) mouth opening, and (c) lip protrusion demonstrated by an adult experimenter. (From Meltzoff & Moore, 1977.)*

model. This *differential* responding cannot be explained in terms of random oral responses or arousal responses in the presence of a moving human face.

Meltzoff and Moore (1983b) argue that early imitation occurs because infants map visually and proprioceptively perceived body transformations on to each other and that the visual and motor representations of body movement are amodal. This view and the data on which it is founded differ substantially from Piaget's findings. Since several studies have failed to demonstrate imitation in young infants (see Over, 1987, for a review; see also Reissland 1988 for positive results), we have yet to determine the circumstances that do and do not elicit imitation responses by young infants. Indeed, neonate imitations may be constrained by their limited ability to detect visual patterns.

Finally, in a series of experiments using a visual preference test, Bahrick and Watson (1985) have demonstrated that five-month-olds can detect the proprioceptive-visual correspondence of their leg movements. Two video displays were presented simultaneously; one was an "on-line" production of the infant's current leg movements (which were hidden from view), the other was a recording of a peer's leg movements. In three experiments, infants preferred to look at the display of the peer's leg movements, the leg movements that did not match their own ongoing activity. No such preference was evident in a comparable study with three-month-olds. It is not yet clear whether this finding reflects a failure at this age to detect the visual-proprioceptive correspondence or the absence of a preference for noncorrespondence.

In summary, the research on intersensory coordination has demonstrated that by four to five months of age infants are capable of detecting several types of visual-auditory, visual-manual, and visual-proprioceptive correspondences. We know nothing, however, about the development of these perceptual coordinations. The limited newborn data indicate that at birth the auditory-visual and visual-proprioceptive systems are coordinated for at least some types of information (that is, location and facial expression), which lends support to Gibson's nativist position and Bower's assumption of a primitive integration of neonatal senses (Bower, 1974; Butterworth, 1981).

However, the fact that there is no evidence of visual-tactile (manual) integration prior to three months of age emphasizes the need to consider the development of each type of sensory integration as a separate issue that may have its own developmental course. Further, we need studies of intramodal as well as intermodal development before we can begin to sort out the relative effects of experience and maturation on the development of sensory integration. Thus, for example, the relatively late development of visual-tactile (manual) coordination may reflect not the importance of experience as assumed by Piaget, but the relatively late maturation of tactile-manual perception. Or, conversely, the relatively early visual-tactile (oral) integration could reflect the effects of early experience rather than an innate visual-oral coordination. That is, the awake young infant has a high probability of observing the nipple before and/or after the oral-tactile experience. A month of such coordinated experience may contribute to the development of visual-oral sensory integration. If so, we will need models for the process of integration during the first weeks.

Although we do not yet have the data necessary to determine how sensory integration develops, we do know that in the first month of life infants are capable of some intersensory coordination. None of these involve the tactile-manual system, however. Thus, newborns make visual searches in the location of a sound. Yet they do not seek visual information where they feel objects. Similarly, neonates visually recognize objects that they have mouthed, but a comparable sensory integration for handled objects does not occur until months later. By the middle of their first year, infants are capable of many types of intersensory coordinations, coordinations that are basic to the perception of unitary, multimodal objects and events.

▶ ## SUMMARY

Although Piaget assumes that infants do not have cognitive structures until the end of the infancy period, his extensive research on development during the sensorimotor period has emphasized the importance of infancy for understanding the beginnings of cognition. Piaget sees these beginnings in the activities of the young infant in relation to the environment. The actions that develop from the newborn reflexes are represented by the sensorimotor schemes, and they eventually lead to the mental representations that mark the end of the sensorimotor stage.

Piaget's theoretical emphasis on the importance of action (and/or the unavailability of appropriate methods) meant that he did not directly assess the development of sensory capacities of the infant. Rather, the sensory capabilities were important to the extent that they elicited actions by infants. Many researchers, however, have attempted to understand the development of vision and audition, independent of motor consequences.

This research indicates that the newborn's visual and auditory systems do not function at the level of an adult's, but that newborns are prepared to gather visual and auditory information that is at close range and within normal levels of intensity. Contrary to Piaget's assumptions, some intersensory coordination is evident in newborns, but there may be important qualitative changes in all forms of intersensory integration during infancy.

Neonatal awareness of adult facial expressions and imitation of them is an important beginning form of social interaction. Whether it is reflexive or not, it does mean that newborn attention is attracted to the human face and that newborns are responsive to the human face in a way that can be recognized by the caregiver.

Within the first four to five months, the sensory and perceptual capacities of the infant develop extensively, and these changes occur during the same period when numerous reflexes drop out and are replaced by voluntary actions. Thus, it appears that the human infant comes into the world prepared with sensory capacities and motor responses for gathering information and making contact with adults. These capabilities develop rapidly in the first few months as the central nervous system matures.

3

Infancy: Memory, Categorization, and Object Permanence

Memory processes are at the heart of most theories of cognition. Indeed, all information-processing models of cognition assume a major role for memory (see, for example, Figure 1-1 in Chapter 1). For a moment, imagine yourself without a memory. You would be unable to recognize these letters, let alone understand the message. Each experience would be new and unique with no relationship to prior experiences. You would have no knowledge base with which to organize and provide meaning to your experiences. Nor would you have any knowledge of your past.

The term "memory" has been used in a variety of ways. "Broadly defined, *memory* is demonstrated when any type of past environmental information affects the organism's current behavior" (Olson & Strauss, 1984, p. 32, italics added). Thus, for some theorists learning implies memory (for example, Bolles, 1976; Fagen & Rovee-Collier, 1982). In order for an organism to learn to make a specific response in a given context, the organism must in some way remember the consequences of that response on previous training trials and the context in which the response was learned. This is a very general use of the term memory.

The sensorimotor circular reactions of Piaget's third substage are examples of learned behavior; infants repeat responses that have led to interesting consequences. But such learning, which is displayed by many young animals, does not imply cognitive capacity. There is nothing about these learned responses that requires the assumption of mental representations that can be accessed independent of the stimulus context of the learning situation. Rather, the assumption of stimulus–response associations is sufficient to explain such learned behaviors. Or, to put this in information-processing terms, these behaviors reflect the acquisition of procedural knowledge. For example, in the presence of a mobile, infants can learn procedures for making it move. The study of memory, in this case, would be the study of the ability of infants to retain this procedural knowledge over periods of time.

Other theorists, particularly cognitive psychologists, have made a distinction between this general form of memory and a more restrictive definition which requires mental representation (that is, declarative knowledge). Thus, Piaget differentiated between *memory in the wide sense,* which includes the acquisition of skills and adaptive responses (perceptual and motor procedures) and *memory in the narrow sense* which "is the ability to consciously reflect on a specific incident in one's personal past" (Schacter & Moscovitch, 1984, p. 173). As an analogy, consider my dog Xing. She knows how to get water when the bowl is empty: she sits by the bowl and stares at me, and she retains this knowledge over long periods of time. The other day she returned to the house after being away for three months and "remembered" what to do when she found the bowl empty. But this evidence of "memory" does not imply that she has a mental representation of her past behavior and its consequences. That is, her behavior does not imply that she *knows* that in the past she has gotten water in this manner (see Mandler, 1983; 1984a, for extended discussion of this distinction). Xing's behavior illustrates the more general definition of memory, since she has demonstrated procedural knowledge.

Memory in the narrow sense assumes *declarative knowledge,* or conscious representation of knowledge. But it should be recognized that declarative knowledge may or may not include an awareness of "pastness." For example, I know the meaning of "amenable" and if you ask me I can access this knowledge. I do not, however, know when or where I learned the meaning. Here the focus is on the distinction between memory in the broad sense and memory in the narrow sense (conscious representations with an awareness of pastness), since this distinction is of particular relevance for our understanding of infant memory.

WHY IS THE DISTINCTION BETWEEN THESE TWO USES OF MEMORY IMPORTANT?

First, the two definitions have different implications. The narrower definition requires an awareness or consciousness of the past, which the more general use of the term does not. Thus, we must recognize that when psychologists use the word memory, they do not always mean the same thing.

Second, the general use of the term does not make it possible to distinguish memory from learning and perception. Lockhart (1984), for example, argues that if we are to understand the development of memory, we must distinguish between memory and learning. Indeed, much of the adult research on memory is about memory in the narrow sense, but as we will see, it is less clear whether most of the research on infant memory is about memory in the narrow sense.

Therefore, we must be cautious about how we interpret the relevance of the infant research for our understanding of the development of memory in the narrow sense.

Third, the two types of memory may follow very different developmental courses. Without making clear the distinction, it would be difficult to identify such differences in development. For example, the development of awareness of one's past may have important implications for how one attempts to remember most events and what strategies are used to comprehend present events.

An individual's memory depends upon a number of processes. My memory for an event or object will depend upon the nature of my perceptual systems. That is, not all of the physical energy in our environment is transformed into a code (encoded) by the human nervous system. None of us, for example, can perceive ultraviolet light, although other animals can. Furthermore, our perceptions will depend upon the focus of our attention. A consideration of the model in Figure 1-1 of Chapter 1 will indicate other factors that can affect memory, including the control processes that involve goals, plans, and strategies and the knowledge base itself (long-term memory).

Developmental changes in any of these factors will affect the content of memory. We have seen that neonates, for example, scan contours, but that they do not use this strategy systematically and, therefore, are not likely to perceive a visual pattern in its entirety. Thus, the content of infant memories will be limited by the perceptual processes. As perceptual processes and other processes for handling information develop, we can expect concomitant changes in an infant's memories and the effect that this knowledge base has on the acquisition of further information.

In this chapter we will explore the development of memory during infancy, but our conclusions will be limited by the procedures that are available. Studies of memory in adults and older children can make use of verbal behavior, and such behavior allows subjects to tell us whether or not they are aware of the pastness of a given memory. Thus, we can explicitly study memory in the narrow sense. Unfortunately, we have limited techniques for asking questions of prelinguistic infants, and so it is difficult to tell whether their responses reflect memory in the general sense or in the narrow sense.

▶ VISUAL RECOGNITION MEMORY

Recognition memory in adults occurs when a stimulus is judged to be the same as one that is familiar from past experiences. If I walk into a restaurant and spot a face across the room that is familiar, I am judging that I have seen that face before. I may not be able to put a name to the face or remember where I saw the face before, but I do know that I have seen the face. Thus in *recognition memory* I may not *recall* the name that goes with the face or remember how and in what situation I came to be familiar with the face; I simply judge that the face I see now is one that I have seen before.

Many theorists (for example, Kintsch, 1970) assume that recognition memory requires fewer mental processes than recall. In *recognition* a stimulus is physically present and a *judgment* must be made about whether the memory representation of a previous stimulus matches the perceptual representation of the object/event before the subject. In *recall* a physical stimulus is not present; in some way, possible representations of the to-be-remembered item must be self-generated and then tested against memory representations (Werner & Perlmutter, 1979). What do I do when I cannot recall the name of the familiar face in the restaurant? I may attempt to reconstruct where I saw the person. Was it recently? No. A college classmate? As I generate these possibilities I test them for accuracy and continue to narrow the alternatives. Depending on my persistence and the particular representations that I generate, I may or may not recall the name of the familiar person.

Adult visual recognition memory is impressive. Standing, Conezio, and Haber (1970), for example, presented 2,500 pictures to college students and found 90 percent correct recognition. A number of studies with children (see Brown & Scott, 1971) indicate that even preschoolers have remarkable visual recognition memories although the level of accuracy will depend upon several factors, which we will consider in Chapter 7.

Infants cannot give verbal responses to specify their awareness of pastness. As a consequence, most researchers have used the habituation-dishabituation paradigm or the paired-comparison paradigm to investigate infant recognition memory. Researchers using the habituation-dishabituation paradigm have adopted Sokolov's (1963) model of habituation, which assumes that when a particular stimulus is presented repeatedly, a *schema,* or memory model for that stimulus, gradually develops. This representation of the stimulus is stored in memory and compared to current visual input. If the input matches the schema, responses are inhibited to that stimulus. If, however, the current visual input is sufficiently different from the memory model, then the infant continues to look at the novel stimulus. Thus, the Sokolov model assumes that a schema is developing during habituation and that dishabituation of a response indicates that the comparison stimulus does not match the memory that has developed.

There are several variations of the habituation-dishabituation paradigm (see Cohen & Gelber, 1975; Olson & Sherman, 1983, for critical analyses of these), each of which has its advantages and disadvantages. For our purposes, however, the factors important for assuming a demonstration of memory are (a) habituation of a response to one stimulus and (b) dishabituation of the response to a novel stimulus, provided it can be demonstrated that the increased response to the novel stimulus is not simply a function of a preference for that particular stimulus. That is, we have seen that a number of variables will contribute to infant visual attention, for example, brightness, and complexity. These preferences must be controlled for in one way or another if recognition memory is to be inferred from the dishabituation of a response (Sophian, 1980).

A second paradigm, the paired-comparison procedure, is also used to study infant visual recognition memory. The paired-comparison paradigm is a variation of the habituation paradigm and the preference test. In the familiarization phase, the infant is presented with a pair of identical stimuli. In the test phase the original stimulus is now paired with a novel one; these stimuli are presented equally often to each side. The rationale is that if a memory for the original stimulus develops then on the test phase the infant will prefer to look at the novel stimulus and that such a preference indicates that the infant recognizes the familiar stimulus. In fact, a preference for either stimulus would indicate that the infant recognizes the original stimulus (see Rose, Gottfried, Melloy-Carminar & Bridger, 1982, for related data). Again, this is with the proviso that the initial preferences are assessed and controlled.

DEVELOPMENTAL FINDINGS

Our first question about infant recognition memory is about acquisition. Are there developmental changes in the acquisition of memory models for visual stimuli? Our review of infant pattern perception indicated a number of instances in which infants one month of age and older showed signs of recognizing visual stimuli. What of newborns? Are they capable of visual recognition memory? Few studies, unfortunately, have addressed this issue, and several have not found evidence of memory (see Werner & Perlmutter, 1979, for a review). But as indicated earlier, a failure to demonstrate a particular phenomenon is difficult to interpret (see Sophian, 1980, for a critical discussion). For example, we have seen that there are developmental changes in how stimuli are encoded. As described in Chapter 2, three-month-olds (Caron *et al.*, 1973) in the habituation-dishabituation paradigm did not discriminate between a facial configuration without a nose and mouth and a regular facial configuration. This indicates that infants this age do not encode the noses and mouths of a facial configuration. Does this mean that infants this age are incapable of visual recognition memory? Clearly not. Infants the same age do encode the eyes of a facial configuration and demonstrate visual recognition memory. The perceptual processes are closely linked to memory content and the study of memory.

Nevertheless, there is some evidence that newborns can recognize visual stimuli. In a series of studies Friedman and his colleagues (Friedman, 1972) used the habituation paradigm and found dishabituation responses indicating recognition memory for 2×2 and 12×12 checkerboard patterns. But relatively few of the infants who began in the studies completed the testing phase or showed the dishabituation response. A number of factors that affect newborn performance may account for the failure of so many infants. For example, it is generally recognized that learning is most likely to occur when the subject is in an alert and awake state. Yet, newborns spend very little of their time in this state; and when they are in this state it only lasts for about 10 minutes (Clifton & Nelson, 1976).

Recently, Slater and his colleagues (Slater, Morrison & Rose, 1983; 1984) have demonstrated newborn recognition memory for both simple and complex stimuli in the paired-comparison paradigm. Their research indicates that the details of the familiarization procedure will affect the performance of newborns (for example, they need large stimuli and long familiarization periods). Taken together, these data suggest that under ideal conditions newborns do acquire memories for some visual patterns (see also Antell, Caron & Myers, 1985). Despite the limited occurrence of habituation and recovery in newborns, the data indicate "that the newborn infant is already equipped not only to recognize repetitive stimulation but to inhibit attending behavior and selectively to attend to new stimuli or new stimulus components" (Horowitz, 1974, p. 3). Indeed, Olson and Sherman (1983) speculate that there is an innate predisposition for visual recognition memory that is only constrained by perceptual processes. Thus, during the first month or so of life, infants are capable of acquiring visual information, but opportunities for such learning are limited by the immature visual system and the infrequency of the alert, awake state.

Most of the work on visual recognition memory has focused on the performance of three-month-olds. For the most part, this emphasis occurs for practical reasons. By this age, infants are awake for long stretches of time, mothers feel comfortable about traveling with the infants to laboratories, and the infants are attentive to a variety of visual stimuli. Indeed, research demonstrates that infants this age acquire memories for a variety of social (for example, facial expression) and nonsocial (for example, shape) stimuli (for reviews see Werner & Perlmutter, 1979; Olson & Sherman, 1983). Thus, there is extensive evidence that by three months of age infants have immediate recognition memory for many types of visual patterns. But, again, even at older ages, memory depends upon the nature of the stimuli and the conditions for the acquisition of the information.

FACTORS THAT FACILITATE RECOGNITION   Several studies have demonstrated that if infants see two different stimuli simultaneously during the habituation phase, recognition is improved (see, for example, Fagan, 1978; Ruff, 1978). In a series of studies, Fagan familiarized seven-month-olds with pairs of stimuli that differed in some detail. For example, a facial target stimulus was presented with a photo of the same face taken from another angle; an abstract target was a square composed of several elements, and the comparison stimulus had the elements arranged in another manner. Essentially, Fagan found that immediate memory for a target stimulus was better when a comparison stimulus was presented during habituation than when the target stimulus was presented alone. How this comparison stimulus facilitates recognition is not clear. Fagan (1978) has suggested that such comparison stimuli encourage infants to go beyond encoding elementary features such as brightness and size and to direct attention to the nature of the elements and the relations between them (compare Antell, Caron & Myers, 1985). Perhaps the opportunity for comparison heightens attention to the similarities and differences of the two stimuli, which would promote the encoding of stimulus aspects that are relevant on the test trials (Bushnell & Roder, 1985). Further research will be necessary to determine how comparison stimuli facilitate recognition and how comparison processes develop during infancy.

A number of variables affect adult memory. Cornell and his colleagues (Cornell, 1980; Cornell & Bergstrom, 1983) have investigated two of these—*distributed study* and the *serial position effect*—with infants and found suggestive similarities between adult and infant memory processes. It is a common finding that adults and children remember more if the items to be remembered are given repeated presentations (see, for example, Hintzman, 1976; Rea & Modigliani, 1987). But the repetitions are more effective if they are distributed rather than massed (Melton, 1970). That is, if the repetition of each item occurs immediately after itself, the repetition does relatively little to improve memory; often there is no improvement over a single presentation of the item. If, however, the repetitions are spaced, with other activities or other to-be-remembered items interspersed between the repetitions of each item, memory is improved. Cornell (1980) sought to determine if such distributed presentations would facilitate the delayed recognition memory of five- to six-month-olds. Each infant was familiarized with the massed presentation of a stimulus and the distributed presentation of another stimulus. The stimuli were presented on four separate trials with the trials three seconds apart in the massed condition and one minute apart in the distributed condition. The infants were then tested for recognition after retention intervals of five seconds, one minute, five minutes, and one hour. In the immediate recognition test (five seconds), the infants fixated the novel stimulus after both massed and distributed presentations. Thus, the infants remembered the original stimulus with either type of presentation. On the delayed recognition tests, however, only those stimuli presented with distributed trials were recognized; there was no evidence of memory in the massed condition.

Another factor that has a powerful effect on adult memory is the *serial position effect,* the position of an item within a series of to-be-remembered items. When given such a series, adults will remember items presented at the beginning and end of the list better than those presented in the middle of the list. Cornell and Bergstrom (1983) presented three different pictures of female faces in a fixed order to seven-month-olds for four trials. Recognition was tested after five-second, one-minute, and five-minute retention intervals. There was no evidence of recognition memory for the middle stimulus at any of the retention intervals including the immediate one. The stimuli presented in the first and last serial position were recognized in the immediate test and the one-minute delayed test. Only the first stimulus was recognized in the five-minute retention test.

Adults recognize visual stimuli after extended delays between the familiariza-tion phase and a test phase. Bahrick, Bahrick, and Wittlinger (1975), for example, demonstrated that we can recognize photos of our high school class-mates even after 50 years, and several studies (for example, Brown & Cam-pione, 1972; Brown & Scott, 1971; Entwisle & Huggins, 1973; von Wright, 1973) have shown that preschoolers and young children will recognize 75–85 percent of visual items that are tested after one- to four-week delays.

We have seen that even newborns recognize visual patterns when im-mediately tested for recognition. How long do infants retain this information? Are there developmental changes in the retention capacity of infants? There are no studies of delayed recognition memory with infants under four to five months of age. Studies with five- to six-month-olds indicate, however, that the retention of infants this age is robust. Fagan (1973), using the paired-com-parison procedure, in four separate studies found that infants this age have retentive capacities ranging from three hours to two weeks and that the extent of the retention depends upon the nature of the stimuli tested. A variety of stimuli were presented with several different delay intervals. He found rec-ognition memory for patterned stimuli after delays of 48 hours; photographs of faces were retained for two weeks.

But, using similar stimuli with six- and nine-month-olds, Rose (1981) found that six-month-olds remembered faces only after a brief delay and that there was no evidence of recognition of multidimensional stimuli after a delay of 150 seconds. The nine-month-olds, however, showed recognition of the faces and the multidimensional stimuli with the delay test.

Why the apparent discrepancy between these two studies? Rose's proce-dure differed from Fagan's in an important way. During the familiarization phase, Fagan presented the stimuli for two minutes; his observations of the infants indicated that they actually fixated the stimuli for an average of 40 to 60 seconds. Rose, however, terminated the familiarization stimuli after each infant had fixated them for 5 to 20 seconds (depending on the particular pattern). It would appear that the retention capacity of infants is tied to the time available for encoding the information. We have already seen that at a given age the time necessary to encode a stimulus depends upon the complexity of the stimulus (for example, Fagan, 1974). We also have seen that for a given stimulus younger infants need more time to encode the stimulus. Thus, the demonstrated development in retention may be a function of how much has been acquired rather than of some change in the ability to retain information once it is acquired (Werner & Perlmutter, 1979). This supposition conforms with adult research which indicates that retention is a function of presentation time (see Potter & Levy, 1969).

Further, the fact that face stimuli were retained for longer periods in the Fagan study suggests the potential importance of prior experience in the ac-quisition and/or retention of visual information. That is, infants have extensive experience with human faces and by five months of age have a general schema for the human face. Such a general schema may facilitate the encoding of a particular face and thus the retention of the information.

Although it is possible that young infants have declarative knowledge about their world, there is nothing in the infant visual recognition research to suggest memory processes in the narrower sense. Rather, the findings can be explained more parsimoniously as evidence of procedural knowledge: knowledge of how to look at objects and how to organize visual information. Since developmental changes in the retention of this knowledge are affected by the development of perceptual processes (see, for example, Ruff, 1984), some researchers have argued that there is little change in memory processes (see Olson, 1976). That is, it is assumed that developmental changes in the acquisition of visual information, not changes in how information is retained once it is acquired, are critical to the development of recognition memory. Although the relevance of perceptual processes is clear, it should be noted that developmental changes in retention processes have not been ruled out. To investigate retention or memory, independent of acquisition, it is necessary to assess retention when acquisition is comparable at each age tested. This has not been done and is difficult to do.

Furthermore, the fact that the retention of visual information is robust during infancy and that several variables (for example, distributed practice) appear to affect both infant and adult memory in comparable ways, has suggested to some that the recognition process is an innate given. Others, however, have argued for caution in the comparison of infant and adult recognition memory because the methodologies differ in a potentially important respect, expressed awareness of pastness. Since we do not have the methodology to assess whether young infants know that a familiarized stimulus was seen in the past, this issue will not be easily resolved.

▶ MEMORY FOR CONDITIONED RESPONSES

Infant recognition memory is also evident in the operant-conditioning paradigm. The fact that young infants can learn to make a conditioned response to a specific stimulus indicates not only that they can learn the response, but also that they remember the stimulus conditions for making the response. Undoubtedly, the most extensive program of research of infants' memory for conditioned responses has been conducted by Rovee-Collier and her associates. Using the *conjugate reinforcement paradigm,* which is a variation of operant conditioning, Rovee and Rovee (1969) demonstrated that three-month-olds would learn to kick their feet in order to move a wooden mobile (reinforcer) that was overhead. In this procedure, the reinforcement (mobile) is always in sight, but the extent to which it moves and makes noise is directly related to the extent of the foot movements of the infants. The experimental and control groups both had a sequence of baseline, conditioning, and extinction sessions. In the baseline session all infants were in their cribs with the mobile overhead; leg movements did not affect the mobile. During the conditioning session, the experimental subjects had a ribbon that was attached to the mobile tied to their left foot. Each leg movement moved the mobile, and the intensity of the leg movement affected the extent of the mobile movement. The infants in the control condition received noncontingent reinforcement. The mobile was moved by the experimenter, independent of the infants' leg movements, with the same speed and frequency that the experimental infants produced. The extinction sessions were the same as the baseline session. Conditioning is judged to be evident when, relative to the control group, the experimental subjects kick more during the extinction test than during their baseline session.

RETENTION OF THE CONJUGATE FOOT-KICK RESPONSE

Rovee-Collier and her colleagues (Fagen & Rovee-Collier, 1982) have investigated the retention of conditioned responses. Typically, in the *retention paradigm* used by Rovee-Collier, infants are conditioned in two or three training sessions that are separated by 24 hours. Each session consists of three phases as illustrated in Figure 3-1. In the first phase of the first training session (baseline) the operant level of the kicking response in the presence of a still mobile is determined. This phase is followed after one minute by a nine-minute training period (conditioning) in which the mobile is connected to the foot of the infant; thus, mobile movement is contingent upon leg movement. A three-minute immediate retention test follows one minute after the training phase. During this test the mobile is again presented without movement. Twenty-four hours later a second training session occurs with a long-term retention test at the beginning and subsequent training and retention phases. The third session occurs at different intervals depending upon the purpose of the study. Typically, retention of the conditioned response is measured by the ratio (L/I) of the rate of responding in the long-term test (L) to the rate of responding for the immediate test of the previous session (I). A ratio of one or more indicates that the infant is responding at least at the same rate on the delayed test as in the immediate retention test of the preceding session. Ratios of less than one are assumed to indicate some forgetting. No retention is assumed when the long-term test rate is not significantly different from the baseline rate.

Sullivan, Rovee-Collier, and Tynes (1979) tested three-month-olds in this manner; different groups of infants were tested for long-term retention after delays of two, three, four, five, six, eight, and fourteen days. The data indicate a forgetting function that declines gradually over time as illustrated by the solid line in Figure 3-2. By 14 days there is no evidence of retention. In addition, developmental comparisons (Earley, Griesler & Rovee-Collier, 1985) indicate that two-month-olds can be conditioned in this paradigm and that immediate retention is comparable to that of three-month-olds. But memory for the con-

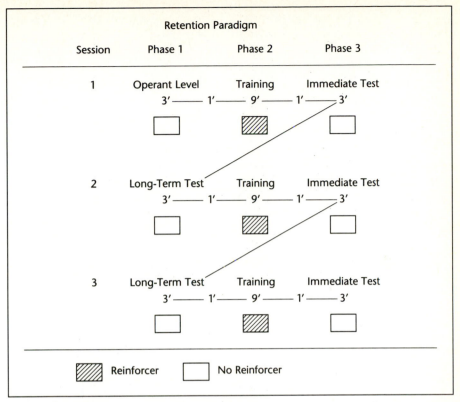

FIGURE 3-1 *The experimental design for investigating the retention of conditioned responses by infants. (From Rovee-Collier, 1979.)*

ditioned response over longer retention periods is not as robust. Thus, as shown in Figure 3-2, eight-week-olds demonstrate significant memory for the conditioned response with delays of up to three days, but not with longer delays. It should be noted that as in the case of the habituation paradigm, it is not possible to determine whether this developmental effect reflects changes in perceptual processes and/or retention per se.

REACTIVATION   Rovee-Collier and her collaborators have demonstrated that infant forgetting can be alleviated if the infants are "reminded" about the learning situation prior to the long-term retention test. Using a variation of the reactivation procedure used in animal research (Campbell & Jaynes, 1966; Spear, 1976), this research indicates that 8- and 12-week-old infants retain the conditioned response for periods longer than indicated in Figure 3-2 if their memory is reactivated prior to the retention test (a similar effect has been demonstrated for recognition, Cornell, 1979). Typically, in the reactivation procedure the infants in the experimental condition are shown the reinforcer,

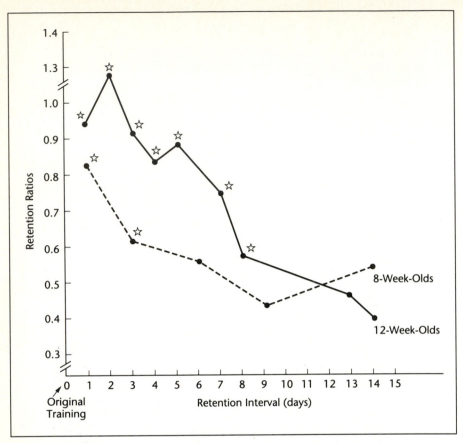

FIGURE 3-2 *A ratio of 1.00 indicates "perfect" retention, and ratios that indicate performance during the long-term test that are above the pretraining baseline rate are starred. Each point represents independent groups of infants tested following training. (From Earley, Griesler & Rovee-Collier, 1985.)*

the moving mobile, for three minutes 24 hours prior to the long-term retention test. Note that the reinforcer is presented noncontingent on the infants' behavior and the infant is in an infant seat that makes leg kicks difficult. The control group, that in this case has been conditioned, does not see the mobile prior to the retention test.

This research demonstrates two important things. First, three-month-olds show evidence of retention of the response after 14- and 28-day retention intervals, if they have the reactivation procedure 24 hours prior to the test (Rovee-Collier, 1979; Rovee-Collier & Fagen, 1981; Sullivan 1982). As discussed earlier, these are retention intervals for which they do not show retention without reactivation (see Figure 3-2). Furthermore, the control subjects in these reactivation studies did not retain the responses at these delays. Thus, the reactivation procedure is effective even when there is no evidence of memory on a long-term retention test.

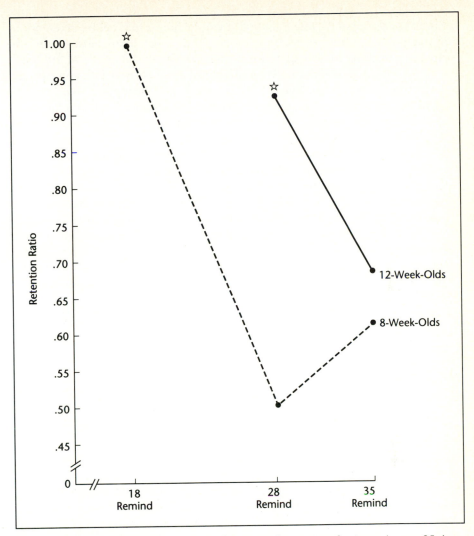

► **FIGURE 3-3** *Retention ratios of reactivated memories after intervals up to 35 days. Starred points indicate retention ratios that are above pretraining baseline rates. (From Earley, Griesler & Rovee-Collier, 1985.)*

Second, the retention of two-month-olds also is facilitated by reactivation (Davis & Rovee-Collier, 1983), but the effectiveness of the procedure is less for the younger infants. As illustrated in Figure 3-3, two-month-olds showed reactivated memories after an 18-day retention interval, but not after 28 days; three-month-olds, however, did have reactivated memory after 28 days. Reactivation was not effective for either age group after the 35-day retention interval (Earley, Griesler & Rovee-Collier, 1985).

Thus, this reactivation research suggests that infant memory is not effectively assessed by a single retention test. It would appear that failure of retention may represent a *failure to retrieve* information rather than a loss of the information. Similar failures of retrieval are evident in children's and adults' attempts to recall information. Although initial attempts may fail, appropriate cues can facilitate retrieval of the information. For example, if the familiar face in the restaurant is someone from my years at summer camp and the topic of canoeing comes up at dinner, it may function as a retrieval cue for the name of the familiar person.

The reactivation procedure serves to activate retrieval cues for the conditioned response. This means that learned responses may continue to be retrievable if the infant has periodic, appropriate reminders, even when the infant is not reconditioned. Indeed, Lucas (1979; Rovee-Collier, Sullivan, Enright, Lucas & Fagen, 1980) investigated the relative effectiveness of reactivation with three-month-olds. The infants in the reactivation conditions were presented the reminder 13 days after the original training and tested for retention 3, 6, 9, or 15 days later. As is evident in Figure 3-4, the forgetting curve for the reactivation condition is similar to the forgetting curve after the original training. This indicates that the effectiveness of the reactivation procedure for memory retrieval is comparable to the effectiveness of the original training. Whether reactivation is as effective as retraining has not yet been explored.

WHAT DO INFANTS REMEMBER? Given that young infants can retain information about conditioned responses over relatively long periods of time and that they are sensitive to reminders about the conditioning situation, what is the nature of the memory that infants have for the learning situation? In order to address this issue we need to analyze the nature of operant conditioning.

The traditional analysis of the foot-kick operant conditioning paradigm would be that the static mobile serves as a *discriminative stimulus*. That is, the infant is learning that in the presence of a specific stimulus, a given response—in this case, a foot kick—is reinforced. Although most studies of infant conjugate operant conditioning have not been concerned with demonstrating the discriminative nature of conditioning, Fagen, Yengo, Rovee-Collier, and Enright (1981) did demonstrate that three-month-olds can learn such a discrimination. Infants were shown two distinctive mobiles. The foot-kick response was reinforced in the presence of one mobile, but not the other; the response rate increased only in the presence of the reinforced mobile.

Thus, when infants learn a conditioned response, they are clearly learning something about the characteristics of the discriminative stimulus. Infants are also learning the characteristics of the reinforcer. That is, with repeated exposure to the moving mobile, the infant is learning about the characteristics of that mobile. Finally, the learning takes place in a specific setting or context. This can include the state of the infant, the surroundings, and so on. Extensive adult research indicates that adult memories are influenced by changes in context (for example, Smith, Glenberg & Bjork, 1978). An extreme demon-

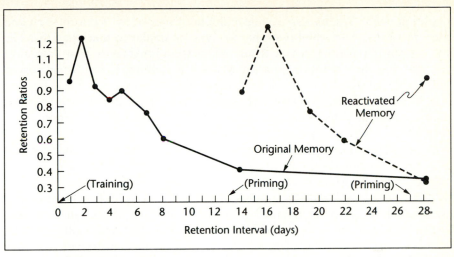

FIGURE 3-4 *As evidenced in this figure, the forgetting curve for reactivated memory is similar to the forgetting curve for original memory. (From Fagen & Rovee-Collier, 1983.)*

stration is a study in which university students learned word lists either sitting on a dock at the water's edge (D) or with scuba gear 20 feet under water (W). Those tested for recall in the same situation as they learned the list (DD and WW) recalled more words than those tested in a different context (that is, DW and WD) (Godden & Baddeley, 1975).

Rovee-Collier and her colleagues have investigated the nature of the information that is acquired in the foot-kick paradigm, in particular, what it is that infants learn about the discriminative stimulus, that is, the nonmoving mobile. Twenty-four hour retention tests indicate that both 8- and 12-week-old infants have memories for the specific details of the mobile. This is demonstrated in studies in which zero to five of the mobile elements are changed on the retention test. Infants of both ages did not respond above chance levels if two or more of the original mobile elements were changed (Earley, Griesler & Rovee-Collier, 1985). Thus, infant memories include information about the specific details of the discriminative stimulus.

Retention tests with a completely different mobile and delays up to 96 hours indicated that the performance of three-month-olds continued to be depressed at these retention intervals when the test mobile differed from the training mobile. But on a 96-hour retention test the performance of the infants was above chance and comparable to those infants tested with the original mobile at the same retention interval (Rovee-Collier & Fagen, 1981).

How can we interpret this finding? It is generally recognized that adults and children encode two types of information: specific visual details and general or prototypic features. Furthermore, adult research suggests that the general features are retrievable for longer periods of time than are the specific details (Hasher & Griffin, 1978). It would appear from the Rovee-Collier and Fagen data that young infants also encode and retain both types of information and that the relative retrievability of the two types is similar to that of adults. The infants can retrieve the specific detail information for three to four days after training, but the general feature information is retrievable for periods up to about eight days.

What can the reactivation procedure tell us about infant memory? For the most part, the effective reminder has proven to be a replica of the reinforcer, that is, the training mobile in motion. For example, Rovee-Collier and her colleagues have not found reactivation effects for the training mobile when it is not moving (the discriminative stimulus) or for a moving mobile that has two or more elements changed from the original (Rovee-Collier & Fagen, 1981). Furthermore, the effectiveness of the reminder is context bound. That is, the reminder must be presented in the same context as the original training, that is, in the infant's crib in the same room (Hayne & Rovee-Collier, 1985). Interestingly, however, not all cues present during training will serve as effective reminders (Rovee-Collier, Griesler & Earley, 1985). Further research will be necessary to determine why some cues are more effective reminders of conditioned responses. Rovee-Collier and Fagen (1981) have argued that, to be effective, reactivation cues must be identical to those noticed during the original training. Further, they have some evidence that infants pay more attention to the mobile when it is moving during reinforcement, which might explain the failure of the static mobile to function as a reminder.

Finally, the effectiveness of a reminder is time dependent. Evidently, it takes time for the attributes of the reminder to serve as retrieval cues. Infants were tested for retention either 1/4, 1, 8, 24, or 72 hours after the reactivation treatment (Fagen & Rovee-Collier, 1983). Retention was an increasing monotonic function of delay between reactivation and retention test. Whether retention continues to improve with reactivation delays greater than 72 hours is yet to be determined. Why the delayed effectiveness of reactivation? The common explanation is that the memory for a specific event/object is composed of the many attributes of the event/object. When reminder cues are similar to these memory attributes, the memory attributes are activated. Activation takes time, however. Thus, as time passes, the number of activated attributes increases. If enough memory attributes are active, the memory becomes accessible and the conditioned response is produced (Spear, 1978).

This research reveals the complexity of memory even in three-month-olds. On the one hand, we see that infants learn and retain not only the specific details of a learning situation, but also the general characteristics of the situation. As time passes, the behavior of the infant is increasingly under the control of the general characteristics of the learning situation, which suggests that the specific details are no longer retrievable. On the other hand, only the more specific details of training function as effective reminders after these details are no longer accessible. Retrieval is facilitated by those reminder cues that are similar to the specific characteristics of the training situation.

Rovee-Collier (Rovee-Collier, Patterson & Hayne, 1985), has argued that reminder specificity has particular benefits for the infant. Behavior that is appropriate in one setting may not be appropriate in another. Imagine what would happen if infant memories were activated whenever general characteristics of the original learning situation occurred. The conditioned response would occur in settings that often would be inappropriate, reinforcement would not occur, and the response would be extinguished. Reminder specificity reactivates infant memories for learned responses in very specific situations, but protects the infant from making responses in situations where there is not enough appropriate contextual information to warrant such a response, thus guarding infant memories from extinction.

Although the retention of conditioned responses does not tell us anything about an infant's awareness of the past, it does indicate how past experiences affect the infant's behavior and something about the nature of infant recognition memory. Thus, we have seen that infants encode and recognize information for specific details, that retrieval of this information becomes difficult as time passes, and that when specific details are not readily accessible the more general characteristics are retrievable.

The limited developmental research (two- and three-month-olds) indicate that the younger infants do not retain information about the learning context as long as the older infants. Does this suggest a developmental change in the ability of infants to retain information? We cannot know from the present research. The younger infants may not encode the perceptual attributes of the discriminative stimulus, reinforcer, and so on, in the way that the older infants do. Thus, the difference in memory may reflect a difference in the encoding of the information, not in the retention of the information. Additionally, developmental differences in the effectiveness of reactivation procedures may also reflect differences in the original encoding processes rather than differences in retrieval processes. This issue is yet to be addressed.

Even when a discriminative stimulus no longer elicits the conditioned response, other characteristics of the learning context (for example, the reinforcer) can remind infants about the learning situation such that the discriminative stimulus once more elicits the response. This means that retraining is not necessary to renew a forgotten response. It further indicates that the memory for a learned response is not unitary. Rather, the memory is a composite of the several attributes of the learning situation. When enough of these attributes are accessible, the memory of the learning context is retrieved and the conditioned response occurs.

Taking the recognition and conditioning research together, we have evidence that recognition memory exists from birth and that the development of perceptual processes plays a significant role in the retention of visual information. Further, retrieval is an important process for infant recognition memory. Recognition is not simply a question of matching a physical stimulus with a unitary memory model. Recognition occurs when enough of several attributes can be retrieved, but the accessibility of the specific details and the general characteristics of a visual stimulus run different time courses. Thus, the research indicates that infant memory is not a simple phenomenon. Further, it appears to have several similarities to animal and adult memory, which suggests a continuity of memory processes that needs further investigation, a continuity independent of the awareness issue.

Finally, the fact that reactivation effects occur for visual fixation (Cornell, 1979) as well as conditioned responses suggests the significance of infant recognition memory for the development of an infant's exploration and manipulation of his world. When young infants recognize a stimulus, they explore it less than an unfamiliar one. Visual recognition memory serves to promote exploration of the visual world. When infants do not remember, a reminder can facilitate retrieval of the forgotten information. Thus, young infants are not doomed to repeated relearnings of prior, but inaccessible memories. Visual exploration is freed from continuous processing of the same information. Similarly, when infants discover the interesting consequences of their behaviors and then forget the circumstances that are critical for these consequences, retraining is not necessary; a brief reminder can serve to reinstate the response.

▶ ## CATEGORIZATION

Much of adult perception rests on the categorization of objects or events. Different stimuli are in some way treated in an equivalent manner (for example, grouped together, given the same name). Categorization is an important process because it reduces the amount of information that must be managed; individual objects and events are grouped and treated interchangeably. Such categorization is basic to adult cognition and language. Imagine trying to tell a friend what happened during your day without using categorized events or objects. You could not describe the simplest event. If we did not categorize our experiences, each would be novel and unrelated to any other.

One powerful basis of categorization is perceptual similarity. Recent research has attempted to determine if preverbal infants have the ability to categorize their perceptual experiences and, if so, on what basis they establish these categories. Categorization can take several forms. For instance, the perceptual constancies described in Chapter 2 demonstrate that we treat the sensory changes generated as an object moves through space as equivalent. Despite changes in the retinal image and distance cues, we perceive a set of sensory variations as representing the same object and this type of categorization (for example, size and shape constancy) is apparent by four to seven months of age. In this chapter the emphasis is on the two types of categorization that are significant in language and conceptual development: categorical perception and the categorization of discriminable, multidimensional stimuli.

CATEGORICAL PERCEPTION

One type of categorization research examines the nature of our perceptions as changes are made along a physical dimension. We perceive changes on some physical dimensions as a continuum of change. For example, if light intensity is varied from dim to bright, adults perceive a steady change in brightness. Other physical dimensions, however, are perceived as partitioned into *categorical perceptions,* or categories. Adult research, using a variety of response measures, indicates that adults perceive color as a discontinuous psychological dimension (Bornstein & Korda, 1984; 1985). To illustrate, if the wavelength of light is gradually changed from 400 nm to 700 nm, adults perceive a few broad categories of color (such as blue, green, yellow, red) and they generally agree where these qualitative changes in color occur on the continuous physical dimension of wavelength. This is not to say that adults do not discriminate between colors in a given category; clearly, they do. It is easier, however, for them to make discriminations across the categorical boundaries than within the categories. And this is the case whether their language does or does not label the several color categories (Heider, 1972; Heider & Oliver, 1972). This fact and related physiological data (Marler, Zoloth & Dooling, 1981) suggest that categorical perception of color is physiological in origin, rather than learned (Bornstein, 1973).

If categorization of colors is physiologically based, we might expect young infants to respond in a manner similar to that of adults. In two separate experiments (Bornstein, Kessen & Weiskopf, 1976a, b), Bornstein habituated three- and four-month-olds to a single wavelength. On the test trials two wavelengths equidistant from the original stimulus were presented. One of these was within the adult color category; that is, if the original was a blue stimulus with a wavelength of 480 nm, the test was another blue stimulus with a wavelength of 450 nm. The other test stimulus crossed the color boundary, for example, a green test stimulus with a wavelength of 510 nm. Dishabituation occurred to the wavelength of a different category, but not when the wavelength was the same adult category as the habituation wavelength. This finding suggests that infants categorize colors as adults do. Methodological issues, however, have made it unclear whether the infant findings are contaminated by color preferences (Banks & Salapatek, 1983). As techniques are refined, this issue needs to be resolved and developmental changes in the categorical perception of color explored.

CATEGORICAL SPEECH PERCEPTION　　Most of the research relevant to infant categorical perception has concentrated on human speech sounds. This emphasis recognizes the predominance of human speech in the auditory environment of young infants and stems from two sources: theoretical and methodological. Noam Chomsky's (1957; 1965) linguistic theory revolutionized the field of linguistics and strongly influenced developmental psycholinguists (for example,

McNeill, 1966). As indicated in Chapter 1, Chomsky's theory focuses on the "rules" of syntax that are necessary to produce and understand language. Chomsky believes that these rules reflect innate constraints on the mental processes of humans. As such, we would expect to see an orderly development of language skills. Clearly, as any first-year language student will attest, one basic and early component of language acquisition is the ability to distinguish the sounds of language. Therefore, research interest has centered on the ability of young infants to discriminate speech sounds.

This theoretical concern with the development of language occurred when techniques were available to analyze the characteristics of speech sounds and to produce synthetic speech for the study of adult speech perception. Using these techniques, Liberman and his colleagues at Haskins Laboratories had amassed a body of data and in 1967 proposed a theory of adult speech perception (Liberman, Cooper, Shankweiler & Studdert-Kennedy, 1967). At the same time, a method was developed that could be used to study infant auditory perception; this method, often called the high-amplitude sucking (HAS) paradigm, was described in Chapter 2 (but see Kuhl, 1985, for recent alternative methodologies).

Before considering the development of speech perception, it is necessary to understand the nature of speech sounds. Human speech sounds are complex patterns of sound waves that vary in frequency, amplitude, and duration. This is best illustrated with a *spectogram,* an electronic visual reproduction of a sound. In Figure 3-5 the spectographic representations of /ba/ and /pa/ are presented. The Y-axis represents the frequencies that are produced. Looking at the representation of /ba/, three bands of frequencies are evident, two near 1 KHz and one at about 2.5 KHz. The X-axis represents time, and we can see that the frequencies produced for a given sound change over time. For example, the three bands of sounds for /ba/ start at lower frequencies and then rapidly change to higher ones. The darkness of the markings represents the intensity of the sound. Thus at any one time, several frequencies are produced with varying intensities and the combination of frequencies can change over time.

Each speech sound has bands of dominant frequencies which are referred to as *formants* and are numbered from the lowest frequency up. *Steady-state formants* remain the same during the production of a sound, such as the first formant of /pa/; *transitional formants* may rise or dip, such as all three formants of /ba/ and the second formant of /pa/. Typically, we need only the first two or three formants to recognize a word or phoneme; the others make the sound seem more "natural."

Speech sounds, however, vary acoustically from one speaker to another and even from one occasion to another for the same speaker. Different accents produce different sound frequencies and high- and low-pitched male and female voices also differ in the sound frequencies that are produced. Speech perception requires the ability to recognize the commonalities of sound patterns despite variations in frequency, duration, and intensity.

Within each language there are distinctive sounds that are combined to

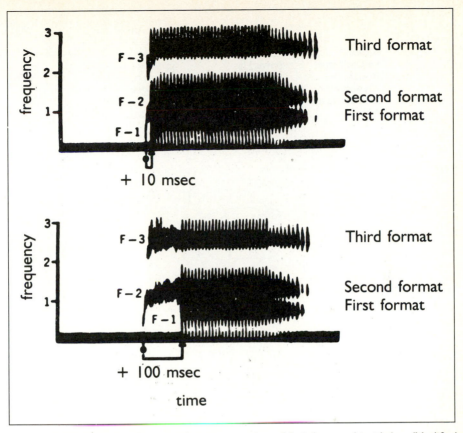

FIGURE 3-5 *Spectographic representations of /ba/ above, and /pa/ below. (Modified from Eimas, Siqueland, Jusczyk, & Vigorito, 1971.)*

form the syllables of the language. These sounds, called *phonemes,* are the smallest units of the language. Although they are not meaningful by themselves, they do signal changes in meaning. For example, in English the change of the first phoneme from /p/ to /b/ changes the word /pin/ to /bin/.

Each phoneme can be described as a combination of distinctive features that make it possible to define the similarities and differences between pairs of phonemes. Since the invariant *acoustic* characteristics of a given phoneme have proven difficult to characterize (see Liberman, 1970, for a discussion of the complexities), most systems defining the distinctive features of human speech use features of the *production* of the sounds (for example, whether the vocal cords are vibrated or not) rather than the acoustic characteristics of the sounds (for example, how formants change in frequency over time). These systems vary, but most include a distinction between two major classes of sounds, vowels and consonants, and use features that are similar to those illustrated in Figure 3-6.

For example, some consonants are distinguished from each other on the

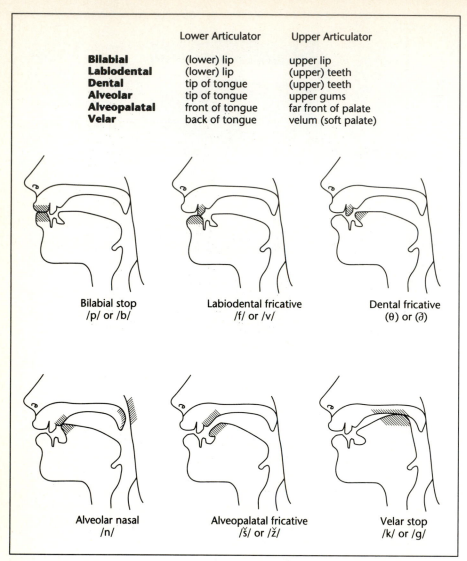

	Lower Articulator	Upper Articulator
Bilabial	(lower) lip	upper lip
Labiodental	(lower) lip	(upper) teeth
Dental	tip of tongue	(upper) teeth
Alveolar	tip of tongue	upper gums
Alveopalatal	front of tongue	far front of palate
Velar	back of tongue	velum (soft palate)

Bilabial stop
/p/ or /b/

Labiodental fricative
/f/ or /v/

Dental fricative
(θ) or (ð)

Alveolar nasal
/n/

Alveopalatal fricative
/š/ or /ž/

Velar stop
/k/ or /g/

▶ **FIGURE 3-6** *Six different points of articulation occur in English: bilabial stop, la-biodental fricative, dental fricative, alveolar nasal, alveopalatal fricative, and velar stop. (Modified from Gleason, 1961.)*

basis of the timing of the vibration of the vocal cords. If the vocal cords pulsate as soon as the air stream is released from the lungs, the sound is *voiced* (as in the /b/ of /ba/). Delayed vibration of the cords is termed *voiceless* (as in the /p/ of /pa/). If you place your fingers on your vocal cords and alternate saying /ba/ and /pa/, you can feel the vibration of the vocal cords and that the onset of the vibration is delayed in /pa/ relative to /ba/. Consonants also are distinguished in terms of the *place of articulation*. All consonants in English are produced by a closure or a narrowing in the mouth. This closure or narrowing occurs when two parts of the mouth (articulators) come together. For example, in /b/ and /p/ the closure is made by bringing the lips together (*bilabial*); in /d/ and /t/, the closure is made by placing the tongue against the upper gums, near the back of the front teeth (*alveolar*).

The *manner of articulation* also varies for English consonants. If the passage of the air through the mouth is completely terminated, the sound is a *stop* (for example, /b/ in /ba/, /t/ in /ta/). When the air is forced through a narrowing of the mouth the result is a *fricative* consonant (for example, /f/ in /fa/, /z/ in /za/). A *nasal* consonant is one in which air is prevented from passing through the mouth and passes only through the nasal cavity (for example, /m/ in /ma/, /n/ in /na/. Thus, any pair of consonants can be compared in terms of the number and type of features that differ. For example, /b/ and /p/ are both bilabial stop consonants that differ on only one feature—voicing; /b/ and /d/ are both voiced stop consonants and differ only in place of articulation. If you produce a number of these sounds, you will have a better appreciation of the different features and how they vary.

THE DEVELOPMENT OF SPEECH PERCEPTION

Although not all the distinctive features of English have been studied, several studies with infants between two and four months of age have demonstrated that infants this age can discriminate between items that differ by only one feature in each of the following classes of phonemes: stop consonants that differ in voicing (/b/ vs /p/) and place of articulation (/b/ vs /d/), fricative consonants, (/s/ vs /z/), glides (/w/ vs /y/), and liquids (/l/ vs /r/) (see Eimas, 1975; 1985; and Trehub, 1979, for reviews). Thus young infants are capable of at least some of the sound distinctions that are necessary for the perception of English phonemes.

Adult perception of many phonemes (especially consonants) is categorical (see Maurer & Lewis, 1979, for a review; see Hary & Massaro, 1982, for an alternative view; see Repp, 1982, for a review of the temporal and spectral dimensions of speech). This means that adults perceive speech sounds as sets or categories of sounds rather than as a continuum of gradually changing sounds. Thus, despite the speech variability evident from speaker to speaker, adults treat sets of speech sounds as equivalent. This has been demonstrated with synthetic speech, which makes it possible to manipulate the physical characteristics (for example, frequency and timing) of the formants of sounds independently and continuously. For example, the spectograms in Figure 3-5 indicate that /pa/ and /ba/ differ only in voicing, which is represented by *voice onset time* (VOT), the timing of the onset of the first formant relative to the onset of the second formant. Using synthetic speech, the time between the onset of the first and second formants can be varied physically and system-atically to determine the speech perception of adults, that is, how adults label the sounds and whether or not they can discriminate between physically different sounds to which they give the same label. For example, when adult speakers of English are presented a series of synthetic sounds that vary in terms of VOT, they label the sounds as belonging to two distinct categories. The stimuli that have VOTs ranging from 0 to +30 msec (the second formant precedes the first by 0 to 30 sec) are labeled /b/ by adults; those from +30 msec to +150 msec are labeled /p/. In addition, the discriminability of the sounds within a category (for example, 0 vs +20 msec) is much poorer than the discriminability of sounds that belong to different categories (for example, +20 vs +40 msec), even when the magnitude of the physical difference is the same (for example, a 20 msec difference in VOT) (Lisker & Abramson, 1970).

This relationship between the two tasks is represented in Figure 3-7. When the timing of the onset of voicing is varied, adults identify and label the sounds as members of two categories, /b/ and /p/, as represented by the solid line. For example, when presented a sound with no difference in VOT (VOT = 0 in Figure 3-7), adults identify it as /b/ as indicated by the solid line. But sounds with +30 msec VOT or more are identified as /p/. In a discrimination task (represented by the dotted line) in which they must judge whether two sounds are the same or different, they do not hear differences in VOT that fall within a phonemic category, but readily hear the differences at the boundary of the categories where the labels change from /b/ to /p/. Taken together, these two sets of findings have been used to specify the occurrence of categorical speech perception.

Eimas and his colleagues have used synthetic speech to determine if young infants perceive speech sounds categorically. Such categorical perception would greatly reduce the information-processing demands of acquiring language. Eimas, Siqueland, Jusczyk, and Vigorito (1971) presented pairs of sounds that differed by 20 msec of VOT to one- and four-month-olds. The first member of the pair was presented contingent on a high-amplitude sucking response. When this response habituated, a novel sound was presented in the two experimental conditions. In one condition the first sound came from one adult phonemic category, /ba/ (+20 msec), and the second sound was from a different category, /pa/ (+40 msec). In the second experimental condition the second sound came from the same adult category as the first, for example, /ba/ (−20 msec) versus /ba/ (0 msec). A third group, the control condition, heard the same sound, for example, /ba/ (+20 msec), throughout the experiment.

For infants in the "different" category condition, who heard a second sound that was from a different adult category, there was a substantial increase in responding when the sound was changed. Such an increase in responding did not occur in the "same" category condition or in the control condition. Thus the four-month-olds and even the one-month-olds had better discrimination of a VOT change (20 msec) between adult phonemic categories than a comparable physical change within an adult phonemic category. Subsequent research by Eimas and his colleagues has demonstrated categorical perception

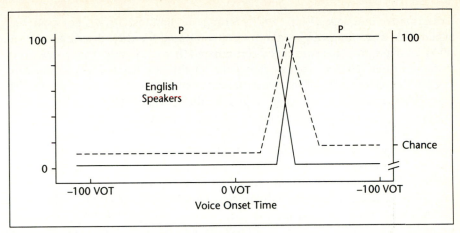

FIGURE 3-7 *Idealized version of results of identification and discrimination tests. Identification is shown by solid lines; discrimination functions are superimposed using dashed lines. (From Strange & Jenkins, 1978.)*

for stop consonants differing in place of articulation, for example /da/ versus /ga/; for nasals, /ma/ versus /na/; and for liquids, /la/ versus /ra/ (Eimas, 1974, 1975; Eimas & Miller, 1978).

Although not all possible comparisons have been made, this research supports the inference that young infants perceive speech sounds in a manner that is comparable to that of adults. These initial findings indicating the similarities of infant and adult speech perception led some researchers (for example, Eimas & Miller, 1978) to argue that humans have an innate ability that is specialized to process speech. Recent animal research, however, shows that some animals (such as chinchillas) perceive some aspects of human speech categorically. In addition, some nonspeech sounds are perceived categorically by animals and adults (see Kuhl, 1979, for a review). More recently, theorists (for example, Eilers & Oller, 1985; Jusczyk, 1981) have argued that early infant speech perception is a function of general auditory mechanisms, but that as the infant has experience trying to attach meaning to speech, linguistic mechanisms develop for speech perception.

Thus, at an early age, because of the nature of the auditory system, infants perceive human speech sounds categorically, particularly consonants (but see Burnham, Earnshaw & Quinn, 1987); the many possible variations along a dimension such as VOT are not readily distinguished and are perceived as broad categories of sound. Such categorical perception clearly reduces the amount of information infants must process as they begin to acquire their native language.

Cross-cultural comparisons of adult speech perception indicate that language experience also influences the perception of phonemic categories. The discriminative capabilities of adults are closely tied to the phonemes present in the native language (Kuhl, 1979; Strange & Jenkins, 1978). For example, when Thai and American speakers were compared for their discrimination of VOT changes, the Thai speakers discriminated three categories that correspond with the three Thai phonemes that vary on this dimension. The Americans discriminated only the two categories that correspond to the two English phonemes (Abramson & Lisker, 1970). Similar cultural differences have been found with other phonetic features (see Burnham, Earnshaw & Quinn, 1987).

How might we understand the role of experience in the development of speech perception? Ideally, cross-cultural studies using identical methods and stimuli with both adults and infants would give us a picture of the developmental changes in the different languages. Unfortunately, there are few such studies. There are, however, individual studies of VOT contrasts with young infants from Spanish, English, Kikuyu, Hindu, and Salish language environments (Eimas, 1975; Lasky, Syrdal-Lasky & Klein, 1975; Streeter, 1976; Werker, Gilbert, Humphrey & Tees, 1981; Werker & Tees, 1984). Taken together, these studies suggest that infants initially perceive categorical boundaries that may not be evident in their native language. For example, there are three categories of VOT contrasts. One category is one in which the first formant precedes the second formant by 25 msec or more. The second category includes those sounds in which the formants are simultaneous or one formant precedes the other by 25 msec or less (−25 msec to +25 msec). The third category includes all sounds in which the second formant precedes the first by 25 msec or more (Pisoni, 1977; but see Aslin, Pisoni, Hennessy & Perey, 1981, for an alternative).

In the case of VOT contrasts, at least, it would appear that young infants have the ability to discriminate a universal set of phonetic categories and that this ability is modified as a function of specific language experience. In Chapter 1 we considered four possible models of the effects of early experience on development (Aslin, Pisoni & Jusczyk, 1983; see Figure 1-2 in Chapter 1):

1. *maturation,* which assumes that the ability is fully developed at birth and that experience has no effect on the ability;
2. *universal,* which assumes full development at birth and that appropriate experience is necessary to maintain the ability;
3. *attunement,* which assumes partial development at birth and that specific appropriate experience can facilitate development; and
4. *perceptual learning,* which assumes that an ability is undeveloped at birth and develops with appropriate experience.

In a review of the developmental and cross-cultural studies of early speech perception, Burnham, Earnshaw, and Quinn (1987) argue that the evidence to date supports an attunement model of the development of speech perception. Both the maturation and universal models assume that an ability is fully developed at birth. Young infants do not, however, make all the categorical discriminations that are evident in adult speech perception. Nonetheless, as we have seen, a simple perceptual learning model is ruled out by the finding that young infants are capable of some categorical discriminations. In support of the attunement model, Burnham and his colleagues cite evidence to indicate that "specific linguistic experience enhances, realigns, or sharpens the boundaries between categories" (Burnham *et al.*, 1987, p. 247). *Enhancement* occurs when the stimuli in the region of the boundary between the two categories become more discriminable. To illustrate, one- to four-month-olds discriminate some fricatives (for example, [ʃ] vs [s], as in ship and sip, respectively) but do not discriminate others (for example, [f] vs [θ], as in fought and thought, respectively). Yet, this discrimination occurs for 12- to 14-month-olds, and with 6-month-olds after extensive training. Similarly, with linguistic experience some categorical contrasts are *sharpened* (the boundary width between two categories becomes narrower) and others are *realigned* (the categorical boundaries shift along the dimension).

Thus, infants appear to have an auditory system that is prepared to make categorical discriminations that are relevant to speech perception (for example, Eimas, 1985). With linguistic experience, the categorizations are further developed and refined (for example, Werker & Lalonde, 1988). This effect of linguistic experience undoubtedly reflects the language learner's attention to the meaningful language contrasts (Burnham *et al.*, 1987). As children acquire a first language, we might expect that some speech discriminations will be more difficult, requiring more experience, than others that more closely approximate the early categorical discriminations (for example, Eilers & Oller, 1985). We have seen that the phonemes of a language differ from one language to another. If all infants begin with a universal set of categorical discriminations we might expect that the infants will first discriminate the phonemes of their native language that approximate the innate discriminations. Phonemic discriminations that differ from the universal discriminations should require more experience with the language and, therefore, occur later in development.

CATEGORIZATION OF MULTIDIMENSIONAL STIMULI

Categorical perception is the categorization of stimuli that vary along a single dimension; this categorization appears to reflect, in part at least, physiologically based limitations in our ability to discriminate stimuli within a category (for example, VOT). Most adult categorizations, however, occur with objects and events that are multidimensional and discriminable. For example, boats vary in size, color, and shape, yet we group these, often highly discriminable, objects together. Despite the many differences between objects, we categorize some together. The perceptual commonality between members of a category can range from relatively simple ones, such as the differences in shape that distinguishes square objects from round objects, to complex perceptual patterns, such as the pattern of attributes that distinguishes a Boeing 737 from a DC9.

The challenge for the cognitive psychologist is to discover the types of information that specify category membership and to develop theories that specify the cognitive processes that are fundamental to categorization. These issues have been the focus of extensive research with adults and verbal children and are the topic of Chapter 5. Here we concentrate on the early development of this type of categorization and the factors that affect the preverbal infant's categorization of the visual world.

Several studies have demonstrated that infants categorize shape (Ruff, 1978), human faces (for example, Cohen & Strauss, 1979), toy animals (Cohen & Caputo, 1978) and fruit (McClusky & Linn, 1977). Most of this research has used the habituation-dishabituation paradigm or its variation, the paired-comparison procedure, to determine whether infants will treat discriminable multidimensional objects that are members of an adult category as equivalent. In the habituation-dishabituation paradigm this question is addressed by first habituating infants to two or more exemplars of an adult category, exemplars that differ from each other but also have the commonalities of the adult category. The infants are then tested for dishabituation to a novel exemplar from the same category or a novel exemplar from a novel category. Dishabituation to the exemplar from the novel category indicates, of course, that the infant discriminates this stimulus from the habituation stimuli. Failure to dishabituate to the novel exemplar of the habituation category is an indication of categorization—the test stimulus is treated as equivalent to the habituation stimuli.

To illustrate, in one of the few developmental studies, Cohen and Strauss (1979) investigated the ability of 18-, 24-, and 30-week-old infants to categorize the human face. The infants were habituated in one of three conditions. In Condition 1 the infants repeatedly saw the same picture, a female face in a side orientation. The infants in Condition 2 saw the same female face in four different orientations, each with three different expressions (smile, frown, and surprise). The infants of Condition 3 saw four different females modeling the four orientations and three expressions of Condition 2.

Although it was evident in Condition 1 that all ages could discriminate the habituation stimulus from the test stimulus of the same face, only the 30-week-olds showed evidence of categorization. This was evident in Condition 2 where there was dishabituation to the novel face, but no dishabituation to the same face in a different orientation. The younger infants in Condition 2 dishabituated to both the novel face and the habituation face in a different orientation and expression. Thus, exemplars of the same face with different expressions and orientations were categorized together by 30-week-old infants but not by the younger infants. In Condition 3, the oldest infants did not dishabituate to either test stimulus. With habituation to a variety of female faces, infants this age have formed the category "female face" since they did not differentially respond to a novel female face. Importantly, this failure to respond does not reflect fatigue since the last stimulus presented was a checkerboard; and, in all conditions at all ages, dishabituation occurred for this stimulus.

As is often the case with early studies, the Cohen and Strauss study raises as many questions as it answers. First, members of adult categories have different types of perceptual similarities. Members of some categories (for example, square) seem to have a perceptual similarity that is simple and immediate, but other categories have similarity relations that are complex and may require extended perceptual experience (for example, DC9s). The failure of infants under seven months to categorize in the Cohen and Strauss study may not reflect an inability to categorize, but an inability to categorize the human face. The human face has a relatively complex organization and, as we have seen, infants do not process the complete structure of the face until five months of age. Consider, for example, what is required to categorize the face in Condition 2. A face is seen in 12 different poses (3 expressions × 4 orientations). From this diverse experience, the infant must process and retain the information that makes it possible to recognize this face in yet another pose. Although adults readily do this, it is difficult to specify how we do it. Somehow, we ignore information that is irrelevant (for example, orientation and expression) to the structure relations that define the category and "discover" the commonalities of the several exemplars of a category (length of nose, distance between eyes). Thus, one issue raised by the Cohen and Strauss findings is the relationship between the development of infant categorization and the nature of the structural relations between members of a category.

A second issue, closely related to the first, addresses the development of those processes (that is, categorization processes) that determine categorical membership. Some of these, such as encoding and retention processes, are apparent in infant recognition memory. But the categorization of discriminable, multidimensional stimuli must also involve comparison processes that ignore differences and discover commonalities. The problem is to specify how this is done to reveal the nature of the knowledge and the processes that are the foundation of infant categories.

CATEGORY STRUCTURE   Adult categories vary in structure; all categories do not manifest the same pattern of similarities and differences between members. Recognizing the apparent diversity of adult categories, some psychologists have focused on the extent to which infant categories reflect structures that are comparable to those of adults. This research demonstrates that by three months of age infants categorize objects that have a *feature* or a *prototype* in common. In one of the few conditioning studies of categorization, Hayne and her colleagues (Hayne, Rovee-Collier & Perris, 1987) used the Rovee-Collier conjugate reinforcement paradigm and trained infants in the experimental condition with a different-colored mobile in each of the training sessions. The elements of the mobile (colored blocks), however, had a common feature (a "2" or an "A") painted on them. Infants in the control condition saw a mobile with a constant color as well as a constant character.

The infants did not differ on the immediate retention test of the third session, but retention tests 24 hours later indicated that the control subjects

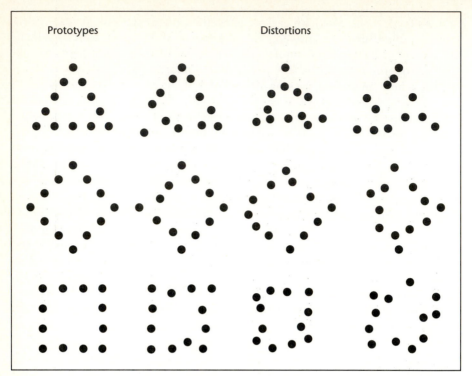

Prototypes   Distortions

FIGURE 3-8 *From top to bottom, the prototypical triangle, diamond, and square; and from left to right, examples of distortions of each. (From Bomba & Siqueland, 1983.)*

did not kick above baseline level if the mobile was changed in any way (that is, color, character, or both color and character). Similarly, the experimental subjects kicked at baseline level if the character was changed; they continued to kick, above baseline, however, if the color changed and the character remained constant. Thus, the experimental subjects treated a test mobile as equivalent to the training mobile if it had the feature (that is, the character) that was common to the training mobiles. This finding demonstrates that with extensive training, three-month-olds can categorize objects that share a common feature yet differ on a salient dimension.

Several investigators have examined the ability of young infants to categorize exemplars derived from a prototype (see Quinn & Eimas, 1986, for a review). To illustrate, Bomba and Siqueland (1983) used three standard forms (triangle, diamond, and square) to derive the set of dot patterns illustrated in Figure 3-8. That is, three categories of three exemplars each were constructed from distortions of the prototypes. Or, to put it another way, the three exemplars of each category had in common whatever similarity occurred because they were distortions of the same prototype.

Bomba and Siqueland (1983) first established that three- to four-month-olds do not have visual preferences for the prototypes or their distortions. Then, groups of infants were habituated to one set of distortion forms. If infants perceive the three distorted forms as members of a category, then on a preference test the prototype for these forms should be less novel than a prototype for a novel set of distorted forms and the infants should look longer at the novel prototype. This was the behavior of the infants; they preferred the novel prototype to the one from the familiarized category. Thus, the previously unseen prototype is perceived as a member of the familiarized category. In another experiment, these researchers established that infants this age can discriminate the distorted forms from each other and from their prototype. These two findings together support the inference that, like adults (see Posner & Keele, 1968; 1970), three-month-olds can categorize discernible exemplars that do not appear to share any one feature, but do have a prototype in common.

Many adult categories have a *correlated attribute structure* in which two or more features are correlated. Birds, for example, have wings and feathers. Recent findings suggest a developmental shift from processing features independently to processing correlations between features (Younger & Cohen, 1985; 1986). To illustrate, in one study four-, seven-, and ten-month-olds were presented drawings of imaginary animals that varied with respect to three attributes (body, tail, and feet). As illustrated in Tables 3-1 and 3-2, each of these had three different values.

During habituation the infants were presented with a set of four animal pictures in which two attributes were correlated and the third was not. One such combination is illustrated in Table 3-2. The "a" (body) and "b" (tail) attributes of Set A are correlated—that is, the giraffe (1) body occurs with a feathered tail (1) and the cow (2) body occurs with a fluffy (2) tail and the "c" attribute (feet) varies between either clubbed (1) or webbed (2). In essence, the four animals represent two exemplars from each of two contrasting categories that have a correlated attribute structure (that is, Stimuli 1 and 2 vs Stimuli 3 and 4).

Following the habituation trials, three test stimuli were presented (see Table 3-2). One was completely novel, with different values for each of the attributes (for example, 333). If the infants have a memory for the attributes of the habituation stimuli then they should dishabituate to this test stimulus. A second test animal was a novel composite of the attribute values of the habituation stimuli; the "a" and "b" attributes were uncorrelated (for example, 211). If infants detect not only the attributes of the habituation stimuli but also the correlation between two of them, they should dishabituate to this stimulus since it is a novel combination of attributes that does not maintain the correlational structure. The third test stimulus maintained the correlation and was one of the familiarized animals (for example, 222).

The four-month-olds only dishabituated to the novel animal, which indicates that these infants detected the familiar attributes of the habituation animals, but not the correlation between the two attributes. The 10-month-

TABLE 3-1 *Stimulus Dimension Values*

Dimension Values	Body (a)	Tail (b)	Feet (c)
1	Giraffe	Feathered	Webbed
2	Cow	Fluffy	Club
3	Elephant	Horse	Hoofed

Source: Younger & Cohen, 1986. © The Society for Research in Child Development, Inc.

olds, however, dishabituated to both the novel and the uncorrelated test animals, supporting the inference that they did detect the correlation of the attributes. This and a related study indicated that the 7-month-olds were in a transition in which they could detect correlated attributes, if other attributes (for example, "c") did not vary independently.

In summary, categorization is an early infant skill that is evident by three months of age for some types of discriminable, multidimensional stimuli at least. From an early age, infants not only recognize differences between objects but also similarities. We cannot know from the research, however, whether infant categorization represents category learning or category recognition (Olson, 1984). On the one hand, it seems unlikely that the relatively brief presentations in most habituation studies are sufficient for infants to acquire new categories. Rather, the infants may come to the experiment with such categories; the results reflect their recognition of these categories. On the other hand, the extensive training provided in the Rovee-Collier conditioning study may be adequate enough for infants to learn a new category. At this point we do not have research that differentiates between these two possibilities. Nevertheless, this distinction is an important one because it raises questions about how prior knowledge of perceptual categories affects performance in categorization tasks. That is, developmental differences in categorization may reflect differences in the ability of infants to learn a category with a given structure and/or differences in infants' prior acquisition of similar perceptual categories.

During the first year, as perceptual processes develop, infants become more sensitive to the internal organization of objects that can define various adult categories. However, we have just begun to explore the types of perceptual similarities that might underlie infant categorization. The failure of the younger infants in the Younger and Cohen studies to categorize on the basis of correlated attributes may not, for example, indicate a failure in their ability to recognize correlated attributes, but a failure to do so with those stimuli. Our review of perceptual development has illustrated that some aspects of experience are more salient for young infants than others. Thus, for example, young infants may be more sensitive to the correlated attributes of three-dimensional, moving, noisy objects than two-dimensional line drawings of imaginary animals.

TABLE 3-2 *Habituation and Test Stimuli Represented in Abstract Notation*

| | Habituation Stimuli | | | | | |
| | Set A | | | Set B | | |
Stimulus	a	b	c	a	b	c
1	1	1	1	1	2	1
2	1	1	2	1	2	2
3	2	2	1	2	1	1
4	2	2	2	2	1	2

| | Test Stimuli | | | | | |
| | Set A | | | Set B | | |
	a	b	c	a	b	c
Correlated	2	2	2	2	1	1
Uncorrelated	2	1	1	2	2	2
Novel	3	3	3	3	3	3

Source: Modified from Younger & Cohen, 1985, 1986.

THE PROCESS OF CATEGORIZATION   Given that young infants categorize multi-dimensional stimuli, the next question is how this categorization is accomplished. Developmentalists have looked to adult models of categorization for potential models of infant categorization (for example, Quinn & Eimas, 1986; Sherman, 1985). Some researchers of adult categorization assume that adults abstract or derive a summary representation of the familiar exemplars of a category. For some theorists this summary is a prototype that is an average of the exemplar information. Novel exemplars that are similar to the proto-typical representation of a category are treated as members of that category. Other models (see Smith & Medin, 1981, for a discussion) assume that categories are represented, not by a prototype, but by the familiar exemplars themselves. Novel exemplars are categorized (treated as equivalent) when they are similar enough to the familiar exemplars. We return to this issue in Chapter 5 since most of the relevant research has involved older children, not infants (but see Strauss, 1979).

▶ ## OBJECT PERMANENCE

Piaget's theory assumes a major change in cognitive development during the last half of the second year (18–24 months). As adults we believe that objects are separate entities that are permanent in nature and that have an existence that is independent of our actions. When I walk out of my office into another room, I know that my books continue to exist even though I cannot see them. But Piaget assumes that humans do not start life with this knowledge. Rather, young infants are unable to distinguish themselves and their actions from the objects and persons of their environment. The development of object permanence occurs during the sensorimotor period as the infant develops increasingly sophisticated schemes for actions. The object concept occurs at the end of the second year when infants know that objects have form, solidity, and depth, when infants know that these objects exist independent of the observer in a three-dimensional space that includes the observer. It is then that infants have mental representations for the objects and persons of their world.

The *object concept* is sometimes referred to as *identity-existence constancy* (see, for example, Day & McKenzie, 1977). This constancy, however, differs from the two perceptual constancies that we considered in Chapter 2. The perceptual constancies, such as size and shape constancy, involve the organization of stimulus information that is before the individual. This is not the case with the identity-existence constancy in which memory, as well as perceptual information, plays a role. I have a mental representation of the books that are in my office, representations that include information such as location, color, authors, topics, and titles. I do not need to see the books to know that they exist and to remember some of their characteristics.

Thus, in Piaget's theory the development of object permanence implies important changes in perceptual and memory capacities. The infant now knows the characteristics of objects and space and can mentally represent the objects in space. For Piaget the development of object permanence is the beginning of cognition. Until this point, the infant's knowledge is sensorimotor and does not include mental, symbolic representation.

Piaget assumed that at birth the infant has no impression of space; the infant perceives light and has reflexes (such as the pupillary reflex) that occur to light. The young infant exists in a flat, two-dimensional space; objects are perceived as "pictures" that come and go as separate experiences that are not connected or organized in time. Objects are indistinguishable from the sensory impressions that occur with the actions of the infants (for example, looking, listening, touching); there is no objective world, no world of objects separate from the self.

Piaget proposed six stages in the development of object permanence; these stages parallel the stages of general activity described in Chapter 2 (see Figure 2-1). These stages are defined by the manual search behavior of infants in a series of hidden objects tasks. In Stages 1 and 2 (0–4 months), Piaget sees nothing in the behavior of infants to indicate that they see objects as existing independently of the infants' actions and perceptions. When objects, for example, move out of sight infants this age do not search for the object that has disappeared. I have two consecutive pictures of my daughter at three months of age. In the first one she is holding a rattle before her with a smile on her face. In the second she stares ahead with a blank look and the rattle lies on the mattress two inches from her right ear. Piaget argues that the accomplishments of this period do not require the assumption of the object concept. For example, recognition of objects during this period does not mean that the infant recognizes these objects as separate entities; rather, such recognition is simply a match of the present stimulation and established sensorimotor schemes.

In Stage 3 (4–8 months) infants will search for and uncover objects that are partially covered, but will not search for objects that are completely hidden. Thus, if objects are shown and placed before infants, they will reach for them. Similarly, if objects are shown and then partially covered by a cloth infants will reach for and grasp the objects. But infants do not reach, uncover, and grasp objects that are completely covered. Furthermore, this failure to uncover the object is not due to motor difficulties (Bower & Wishart, 1972).

Although infants do not have the object concept at this stage, they are making actions that are modifications of earlier behaviors and these actions are precursors to the development of object concept. For example, infants in this stage have learned to anticipate the visual trajectory of moving objects, to cover their own faces in the game of peekaboo, and to recognize partial objects.

The fourth stage (8–12 months) is the most provocative of the six stages of object permanence. Here infants make errors that are puzzling. Infants in this stage now uncover and retrieve objects that are completely hidden, but they make what is called the $A\overline{B}$ error. When infants see an object hidden in location A, they will uncover the object on the first trial and successive trials in this location. But if the object is again displayed and then hidden at location B, infants will search for the object at location A. This error occurs despite the fact that they see the object being hidden at location B. Why do such errors occur? It was this type of error that led Piaget to his basic assumption that the object concept does not exist until later in development. According to Piaget, the $A\overline{B}$ error occurs because the infant still does not have the object concept. In the prior stages, the object is represented by the actions that the infant makes on the object. In Stage 4, the object is still partially defined by the actions made on the object at a particular location. Thus, the object is known as "actions in a certain location." When the location of the object is changed to B, the infant searches in location A because the object is defined by certain actions in location A.

In Stage 5 (12–18 months) the $A\overline{B}$ error disappears and infants are capable of locating objects that are invisibly hidden. That is, infants this age can find an object hidden at location A after they see the object covered by a hand or cup and moved under a cover at Location A. But it is not until Stage 6 (18–24 months) that infants attain object permanence as defined by Piaget. It is not until then that infants can find an object that has been invisibly hidden in a second location, B. If an object inside the hand is moved under one cloth and then under another, the infant will search in one place and if the object is not found will search in other locations, including the hand, until it is found. The infant knows that the object exists somewhere and continues to search for it until it is located.

Since Piaget's description of the development of manual search behavior, several studies have replicated Piaget's findings (for example, Uzgiris & Hunt, 1975; Wishart & Bower, 1984). Psychologists do not question the developmental changes in behavior that occur on Piaget's search tasks. However, they do question Piaget's interpretation of the data (see Schuberth, 1983; Wishart & Bower, 1984, for reviews). Many of the alternative explanations have been attempts to identify performance factors that affect behavior in the search tasks. These approaches have tended to deemphasize the object concept issue and have concentrated instead on the role of spatial knowledge, memory, or perceptual processes in the $A\overline{B}$ error. Most of these explanations are task specific and do not attempt to deal with the development of responses to hidden objects across the entire sensorimotor period (but see Luger, Wishart & Bower, 1984; Wishart & Bower, 1984).

For example, one of the nicest demonstrations of the importance of the development of memory capacity on the incidence of the $A\overline{B}$ error is a longitudinal study by Diamond (1985). In this study of the effect of memory on the $A\overline{B}$ error, 25 infants were tested biweekly over a period of six months. The testing began when the infants first searched for a hidden object and continued until the age of one year. During these sessions, the infants were given multiple tests of the $A\overline{B}$ error. This was done by reversing the location of the hidden object three to four times in a session. That is, after the first AAB trials, the object was hidden at B and the test for the $A\overline{B}$ error was at location A, and so forth.

Diamond wanted to determine how a delay between when the experimenter hid an object and when the infant was allowed to reach for it affected the occurrence of the $A\overline{B}$ error. The reaching responses were delayed on each trial by having the mother, who was holding the infant, gently restrain the infant from moving toward the object, preventing the infant from making a bodily orientation toward the object. Furthermore, the experimenter counted aloud to distract the infant from visual fixation of the location of the object.

Three types of behavior patterns were tabulated: (a) accurate performance in which the infant consistently reached for the hidden object regardless of its location; (b) the $A\overline{B}$ error which means the infant searched correctly on the first two trials (for example, AA), but continued to search in that location when the location was changed to B; and (c) the infant searched at A, but made random responses when the location was changed to B.

During each test session the delay that produced the $A\overline{B}$ error was determined for each individual infant by adjusting the delays according to the performance of the infant. For example, if an infant was making the $A\overline{B}$ error with a given delay, the delay was increased by two to three seconds until a delay was identified, at which the infant performed randomly. Similarly, if an infant was making the $A\overline{B}$ error at a given delay, the delay was decreased by two to three seconds until the infant no longer made the AB̄ error, but was performing accurately on the B test trials. Thus, in each test session the delay interval that would result in the AB̄ error was determined.

Diamond's findings are depicted in Figure 3-9. The solid line moving from left to right represents the average delay at each age that resulted in the AB̄ error. These data indicate that, as the infants got older, increasingly longer delays were necessary to produce the AB̄ error. Or, to put it another way, during this period the occurrence of the AB̄ error is a function of the infant's memory capacity, a capacity that increases during the period between seven and one-half and twelve months of age.

The vertical lines represent the range of the delays that produced the AB̄ error at each age tested. The length of these lines makes it abundantly clear that there are large individual differences. Although the majority of the infants, for example, did not make AB̄ errors with delays less than 10–12 seconds at 12 months of age, three infants were making AB̄ errors with delays of 5 to 8 seconds.

The longitudinal design of this study made it evident that the AB̄ error occurs for all infants and persists for several months. This is not always evident in cross-sectional studies of the AB̄ error. If groups of infants are tested at different ages with one delay condition, that delay will be too long for some infants and too short for others. Thus, it will appear that at any age many infants do not make the AB̄ error. This is not the case, of course, as the longitudinal data clearly indicate. Diamond's longitudinal design also makes it evident that the tolerance of delay increases with age, going from an average of only 2 seconds at seven and one-half months to over 10 seconds at twelve months.

What do these data tell us about the development of memory and its relationship to the AB̄ error? First, it is clear that whether an infant between seven and one-half and twelve months makes the AB̄ error will depend upon the length of the delay between the hiding of the object and the opportunity to respond. So, for example, at ten months of age only one infant was making the AB̄ error if there was no delay, and 13 infants were not making the AB̄ error (accurate performance as defined above) unless the delay was 10 seconds or greater. Thus, any account of this stage in the development of object concept must consider the effects of the development of memory capacity on performance in the Stage 4 search task.

Second, there are individual differences in the development of memory capacity. Thus, at any given age the delay that results in the AB̄ error varies from one individual to another. But it is important to note that the pattern of development appears consistent across individuals. That is, at any given age a decrease of 2 to 3 seconds from the delay that produces AB̄ errors will result in accurate performance and a comparable increase will lead to random performance.

But memory cannot fully explain the AB error. A study of Wishart and Bower (1984) demonstrated that the AB̄ error occurs even when the object is

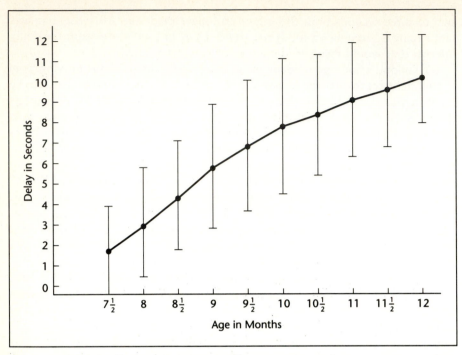

▶ **FIGURE 3-9** *Delay at which the A͞B error occurs by age. (From Diamond, 1985.)*

in sight on a platform. Diamond (1985) argues that a second factor is also at work. Success on the two A trials strengthens the tendency to reach for the object at location A. She argues that A͞B errors can occur even with "infants who 'know' where the toy is (they either can see it or remember where it is hidden) because of a failure to resist the 'habit' to repeat the old, successful response" (p. 880).

Thus, Diamond sees the A͞B error as a "failure of a memory-based intention to override habit" (p. 881). Infants have learned to look for the object at A and may persist in this habit and make the A͞B error even if they know where the object is. "Improved performance on A͞B with age, therefore, indicates the development of the ability to use stored information to guide behavior in the face of an acquired tendency to do otherwise. This achievement depends on both recall memory and the ability to resist or inhibit prepotent response tendencies" (p. 882).

Diamond's research reminds us that performance factors and individual differences in the development of these capacities can affect behavior in Piaget's object permanence tasks. But these data tells us little about the competencies that underlie the behavior. Do infants between six and twelve months have the object concept? It is not possible to answer that question from Diamond's data, but her data do indicate that with limited memory demands, many infants this age do not make the A͞B error.

THE COMPETENCE-PERFORMANCE ISSUE REVISITED   Diamond's work also highlights the problems of the developmental theorist. First, the theorist can only observe behavior and behavior seldom if ever directly reflects the competencies of the infant. Second, the developmentalist must infer knowledge structures from such behavior. This is doubly difficult because these competencies may be changing and there may be individual differences in the rate of these developmental changes. Third, there are also performance factors that must be identified and these too may develop and change at different rates.

If you dwell on this problem for awhile it may become evident that more than one combination of competence-performance assumptions may adequately explain a given set of observations. For example, from his observations of the AB error Piaget assumed a limited competence (no object concept) and therefore concerned himself little with the effect of performance factors. Another theorist may assume a competence that includes the object concept, but further assume that specific performance factors detract from performance in a given task (for example, manual search).

Taking this approach, Baillargeon (Baillargeon, Spelke & Wasserman, 1985; Baillargeon, 1986) developed a task that does not make the performance demands of the search tasks. The manual search task not only requires the ability to inhibit a previous action pattern, but also the ability to coordinate two separate actions (that is, one action on the occluder and one action on the object). Thus, failure on Piaget's task may reflect the inability of young infants to perform such an action sequence (Baillargeon et al., 1985). To deal with this problem, Baillargeon and her colleagues introduced a task that does not require manual search.

Initially, five-month-olds were habituated to a screen moving through a 180-degree arc on a flat surface. After habituation, a box was placed behind the screen and the infants were shown a possible and an impossible event. In the possible event (A in Figure 3-10) "the screen moved until it reached the occluded box, stopped, and then returned to its initial position. In the impossible event [B in Figure 3-10], the screen moved until it reached the occluded box and then kept on going as though the box were no longer there. The screen completed a full 180-degree arc before it reversed direction and returned to its initial position, revealing the box standing intact in the same location as before" (Baillargeon, Spelke & Wasserman, 1985, p. 195).

Baillargeon and her colleagues reasoned that if the infants understood that the box continued to exist after it was occluded and that the screen could not move through the space occupied by the box, then the impossible event should be novel and/or surprising and as such attract prolonged attention. If, however, the infants did not have this knowledge, then the impossible event is more similar to the habituation training than the possible event. Therefore, the novel event is the possible event and, thus, should attract more attention.

On the test trials, the infants looked significantly longer at the impossible event. Furthermore, a control experiment demonstrated that infants this age do not prefer to look at a 180-degree rotation of the screen, as opposed to a 120-degree rotation. These findings indicate that, in contrast to Piaget's po-

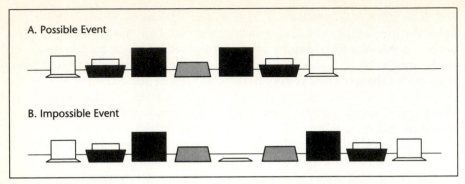

A. Possible Event

B. Impossible Event

▶ **FIGURE 3-10** *Schematic representation of the possible and impossible test events.* (From Baillargeon, Spelke & Wasserman, 1985.)

sition, five-month-olds know that an object exists as as solid three-dimensional entity in a specific location, even when it is occluded. Further, they know that an object (such as the screen) cannot move through space that is occupied by another object (such as the box).

In a second set of experiments with six- and eight-month-olds, Baillargeon (1986) demonstrated that infants know that objects exist continuously in space as well as time. The infants in Experiment 1 were first habituated to the event depicted at the top of Figure 3-11. "Directly before them was a small screen; to the left of the screen was a long inclined ramp. The infants watched the following event: the screen was raised (so the infants could see there was nothing behind it) and then lowered, and a toy car was pushed onto the inclined ramp; the car rolled down the ramp and across the display box, disappearing at one end of the screen, reappearing at the other end, and finally exiting the display box to the right" (p. 27).

This habituation phase was followed by two test events, one possible, the other impossible. In both of these tests the box was revealed when the screen was raised. In the possible event the box was behind the tracks; in the impossible event the box was on the track. After the screen was lowered, the car rolled down the track behind the screen and out the other side of the screen. The second experiment differed from the first only in the fact that the box was placed in front of the tracks in the possible event test.

Both sets of results showed that the infants looked longer at the impossible event than the possible event. These results suggest that infants know (a) that a stationary object continues as a stationary and substantial entity in a specific spatial location, (b) that a moving object continues to exist and follows its trajectory when it is occluded, and (c) that a solid object cannot move through space occupied by another solid object. In Chapter 2 we saw that four-month-olds perceive objects as separate entities. In this research it is evident that, by five to six months of age, infants' knowledge of objects goes beyond perceptual information. Contrary to Piaget's position, infants this age have an object

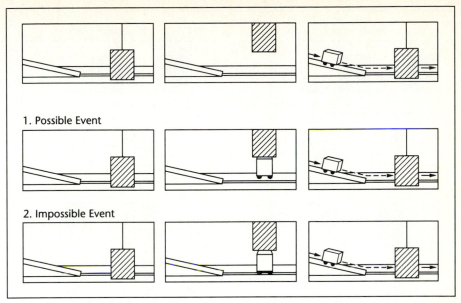

1. Possible Event

2. Impossible Event

▶ **FIGURE 3-11** *Schematic representation of the habituation (top panel) and test events (middle and bottom panels).* (From Baillargeon, 1986.)

concept that is comparable in several respects to an adult's understanding of the characteristics of objects.

Piaget's search tasks require not only knowledge that a hidden object exists but also the ability to represent its location (where it should or might be) (Harris, 1983). Recently, Baillargeon and Graber (1988) have demonstrated that by eight months of age infants not only have the ability to represent mentally a hidden object but that they also can remember its last location. In this study seven- and eight-month-olds saw two types of events (see Figure 3-12). "At the start of each event, the infants saw an object standing on one of two identical placemats located on either side of the infants' midline. After three seconds, identical screens were slid in front of the placemats, hiding the object from the infants' view. Next, a human hand, wearing a long silver glove and a bracelet of jingle bells, entered the apparatus through an opening in the right wall and 'tiptoed' back and forth in the area between the right wall and the right screen. After frolicking in this fashion for 15 seconds, the hand reached behind the right screen and came out holding the object, shaking it gently until the end of the trial. The only difference between the two test events was in the location of the object at the start of the trial. In one event (possible event), the object stood on the right placemat; in the other (impossible event), the object stood on the left placemat, and thus should not have been retrieved from behind the right screen" (Baillargeon & Graber, 1988, p. 504).

This study and a second one that counterbalanced the location of the

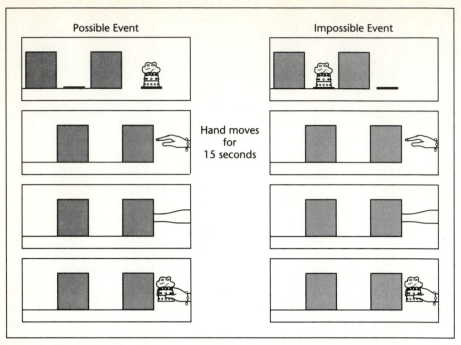

▶ **FIGURE 3-12** *In this study, infants saw an object placed behind a placemat, and then retrieved from behind the "correct" placemat (possible event) and from behind the "incorrect" placemat (impossible event). This study indicates that infants older than eight months of age are able to remember the location of an object despite a 15-second delay. (From Baillargeon & Graber, 1988.)*

object indicated that older infants ($\overline{X}$ = eight months) but not younger ones ($\overline{X}$ = seven months, ten days) looked longer at the impossible event than the possible event. Thus, these infants could remember the location of the object during a 15-second delay. These findings suggest that infants' poor performance in Piaget's search task is not attributable to memory failure. Rather, Baillargeon and Graber argue that the error in the search task "reflect difficulties in the interaction of memory and action" (p. 509). The search task not only requires representation of the location of the hidden object but also the coordination of a search response with this memory. They suggest that with short delays infants can use this memory to plan a search response (as evident in the Diamond study). But with longer delays this memory is "superseded by other information (such as where the infants reached on their last successful trial) or lost altogether" (p. 509).

Taken together, the data suggest that five- to six-month-olds do know that a hidden object exists. Further, by eight months infants can remember the last location of a hidden object. The integration of this knowledge with action does not occur, however, until near the end of the second year. Further research is needed to explore the development of the relations between action and cognition.

▶ MEMORY AND REPRESENTATION

As discussed earlier, Piaget did not assume the occurrence of mental representation until object permanence was achieved. It is then that infants infer that a hidden object is in another location because they "know" that the object exists even when it is not perceptually available. They have a representation that can be accessed without the perceptual experience of the object.

Our review of visual recognition memory and the retention of conditioned responses indicates that at an early age infants are capable of perceptual learning and that learned perceptions are retained for extended periods of time. Similarly, young infants can learn to make specific responses in a given situation and remember what to do in that situation. But these memories do not require the assumption of mental representation. Recognition memory is dependent upon the presence of perceptual information and conditioned responses occur in the presence of specific stimulus conditions.

Piaget's stringent definition of object permanence leaves little doubt for most cognitive psychologists that such behavior involves mental representation. Rather, the issue has been whether mental representation occurs at an earlier age, but is not evident in the search behavior of infants because of the performance demands of the tasks.

As we have seen, the search tasks underestimate infants' knowledge of objects. In the Baillargeon studies an object was occluded for a few seconds yet the behavior of the five- and six-month-olds indicated that they maintained a representation of the object during this period. By eight months of age infants remember the location of hidden objects. These findings do not conform to Piaget's assumption that mental representation is the outcome of an extended period of sensorimotor development, but do complement research indicating that by the end of the first year infants can recall the location of familiar objects.

In a study of language comprehension, Huttenlocher (1974) asked infants "Where is _____?" questions about familiar objects and persons. Although the sample was small, Huttenlocher's data indicate a developmental progression in which infants first are able to locate objects in sight. This is followed by the ability to locate objects that are out of sight in permanent locations. Finally, the infants could locate objects in temporary locations at the beginning of the second year.

Ashmead and Perlmutter (1980) used diaries of mothers' observations of their infants' behavior to investigate infant recall. Although this method does have problems of interpretation, their findings confirm those of Huttenlocher. The data further suggest that representation develops in a social context before it does with physical objects. The diaries indicated that seven-month-olds look for objects in permanent locations. For example, infants this age will seek cereal in a cupboard or potatoes in a bin. Should this memory be attributed to representation? Probably not, since the infants have extended experience with the actions necessary to find an object in a permanent location.

Although not frequent in the seven-month-olds, by nine months of age infants were seeking animate things—people and pets—in temporary locations. So, for example, some infants sought a parent in the bedroom if one parent was not yet up. The search for inanimate objects in a temporary location develops later; it is most frequent in the reports describing the behavior of 11-month-olds. In order to locate an object in a temporary location, infants must know that the object exists somewhere and also remember where it was located last. They cannot rely upon a learned action sequence to locate the object, as might be the case for objects in permanent locations. Rather, it is assumed that when infants locate objects in temporary locations, they have a mental representation of the object and its last known location. Thus, by one year of age infants are not only capable of mentally representing an object, but also capable of locating it in familiar surroundings.

If the development of mental representation is not the result of sensori-motor development, the problem then becomes one of specifying how mental representation does develop (Mandler, 1983; Spelke, 1986). Furthermore, studies indicating the early development of the object concept suggest that we must also determine how action comes under the control of and is coordinated with cognition (Baillargeon & Graber, 1988).

▶ ## SUMMARY

In this chapter a distinction was made between two meanings of memory. The more general meaning of memory does not imply declarative knowledge, but rather the retention of procedural knowledge, knowledge that is evident early in the visual recognition memory and conditioned responses of young infants. Although infant visual recognition memory is constrained by the developmental status of perceptual processes, the infant data are suggestive of a continuity with adult memory processes. For example, two factors, distributed practice and serial position, that influence adult memory also affect infant recognition memory. Furthermore, as in the case of adults, infants retain information for the general characteristics of a stimulus longer than the specific details of a stimulus.

Research using the conjugate reinforcement paradigm indicates developmental improvement in the retention of a conditioned kicking response, but for both two- and three-month-olds a forgotten conditioned response is reactivated if a reminder is presented sometime before the retention test. Reactivation is time dependent and the effective reminder must be similar to the conjugate reinforcer and the learning context.

Categorization is critical to the organization of environmental information. Categorical perception occurs when continuous variations along a physical dimension are perceived as partitioned categories. Most infant research has focused on the categorical perception of speech sounds. Adults perceive variations in speech as phonemic categories. Young infants also perceive phonemic categories. Further, we have evidence that infants have in common a universal set of phonemic categories and that these categories are modified with language experience.

A second type of categorization occurs when we treat sets of multidimensional, yet discriminable, stimuli as equivalent. Despite obvious differences between stimuli we discover similarities. Infant research indicates that young infants can categorize stimuli on the basis of a common feature or a common prototype. The limited research suggests a developmental change in the ability of infants to categorize stimuli that have correlated attributes in common.

Piaget assumed that memory in the narrower sense, memory that required mental representation, did not develop until object permanence occurred at the end of the second year. Although cognitive psychologists generally agree that the development of object permanence implicates the development of mental representation, subsequent research indicates that performance factors such as memory demands and response habits can conceal memory in the narrower sense. Tasks that do not require manual search indicate that infants as young as five months of age know that an object continues to exist when it is occluded. In the third quarter of the first year they know that occluded objects continue to exist in space and time and even remember the specific location of a hidden object. These findings confirm observations that infants this age remember the temporary location of familiar objects.

4

Early Childhood:
Communication and
the Beginnings
of Language

All children of normal intelligence learn a language within the first few years of life. By the time children enter school, they can produce and comprehend a language that was acquired without special training and without awareness of the complexities of the language. Indeed, except for students of linguistics and those learning a second language, most of us take for granted our daily use of language, with no appreciation of the vast implicit knowledge that underlies our verbal behavior. Just as we walk and run without awareness of how the muscles and nerves are regulated and organized, so we speak and comprehend without awareness of how such skills are possible.

The study of language and its development has important implications for our understanding of the human mind. Since the primary purpose of language is to communicate information from one person to another, the structure and function of language must reflect the ideas, processing capacities, and social/communication conventions of a speaker. The purpose of this chapter is to consider in general the nature of language and the cognitive skills that are evident when preschoolers acquire language.

▶ ## THE UNIVERSALS OF LANGUAGE

The primary function of language is communication. Although the term *communication* has been used in a broader sense, here it is defined as a social act in which one individual intends to convey information to another individual. The information is transmitted by a signal system; such signal systems include gestures, music, flags, and, of course, language. Language has several characteristics that distinguish it from the other forms of communication; these language universals are evident in all of the 5,500 natural languages of humans (see Hockett, 1960).

The first, and certainly the most obvious, universal is that language involves the vocal-auditory channel. As a consequence of the physics of sound the signal fades rapidly. Thus, a listener must be able to process transitory auditory signals. Furthermore, the design of the human auditory-vocal system is such that, for the most part, listeners are able to produce what they hear. This differs from many forms of animal communication in which one individual is receptive to a signal but cannot produce it himself. In addition, the auditory-vocal system provides feedback. Speakers are able to hear themselves as well as others. These two features taken together mean that speakers of a language can monitor and reproduce the sound that they utter. (Although the visual-manual systems found in the sign language of the deaf do not use the vocal-auditory channel, they do possess the remaining universals discussed here.)

Second, language is symbolic. The sounds of a language represent meanings. The signals produced are not by-products of other activities, but are produced to convey the speaker's thoughts to the listener. When my dog pants, I know that she is hot since I know that panting is an activity dogs use to control body temperature. But this information is a side effect of the dog's activity; the panting sound itself does not carry the meaning "hot." In contrast, I can use the word "hot" to mean that the stove is hot, the weather is hot, and so on. The word is not a side effect of my own hotness. The word represents or stands for a concept.

Third, the symbols of language are arbitrary. Words are arbitrary because there is nothing in the physical characteristics of words that relates them to specific concepts. Thus, different languages use different sounds to symbolize a given concept: "white" in English, "blanc" in French, and "bai" in Chinese. In contrast, many airport and road signs use nonarbitrary symbols to represent the locations of telephones, food, gasoline, and toilets.

Fourth, language uses rule-governed structures. We do not create sentences by randomly combining sounds. Rather, each of us uses particular language forms or structures, which are also known by other members of our language culture. This common structure makes it possible for speakers to convey ideas through speech sounds. For example, consider the following string of words: The boy girl cheerful happily the kissed. The words are all common English words. You comprehend each of the words, yet the overall arrangement of the words does not convey any well-organized idea; it does not indicate how the "boy" and "girl" are related to the action, "kiss." In contrast, the following string of words conveys information about what the "girl" did to the "boy," how she felt about doing it, and the boy's disposition: The girl happily kissed the cheerful boy.

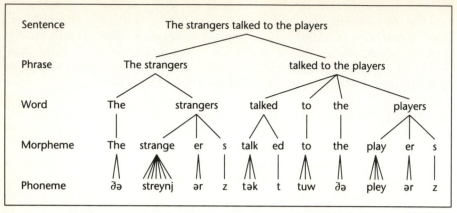

		The strangers talked to the players					
Sentence							
Phrase	The strangers		talked to the players				
Word	The	strangers	talked	to	the		players
Morpheme	The	strange er s	talk ed	to	the	play er s	
Phoneme	ðə	streynj ər z	tək t	tuw	ðə	pley ər z	

FIGURE 4-1 *As depicted above, language is organized as a hierarchy. We communicate via sentences, which are composed of phrases, which in turn are composed of words. Words are combinations of morphemes, which are combinations of phonemes. (From Gleitman & Gleitman, 1987.)*

Furthermore, language rules are organized as a hierarchy of structures (see Figure 4-1). At the top of the hierarchy are the rules of discourse. Most of our everyday use of language does not stop after one sentence. Rather, we engage in conversation, stories, and so on, that involve an organized succession of sentences. Thus, discourse is composed of sentences. Sentences, in turn, are composed of phrases, which are composed of words. Words are combinations of morphemes, which are combinations of phonemes (Gleitman & Gleitman, 1987).

Fifth, language imposes categorization at a variety of levels. The rules of language are rules about categories. For example, in English the many possible speech sounds are organized as 37 distinct phonemic categories. Similarly, words are categorized by syntactic function into grammatical classes (such as noun and verb). Such categories and the rules for their combination make it possible to generate a wide variety of patterns from a limited set of categories.

Sixth, language is productive. This means that language is creative; there is an infinite number of grammatical sentences in any given language. Although we seldom create new words, we do create and understand new sentences whenever we use language. Consider this last sentence. You could go through this book and many others without finding a repetition of this same sentence (Slobin, 1979). Thus, we are continually producing and understanding new sentences. Such productivity means that we do not learn a language by memorizing a set of sentences.

Seventh, language has the capacity for displacement. Speakers are able to make reference to other times and locations than the present. My dog has a few signals for her needs, but these are immediate needs. I have yet to come home and have my dog signal that her water bowl was empty half the day.

Similarly, although the primates have a variety of communicative signals, there is, to date, no evidence that their signals are used to refer to remote objects or events.

Finally, individuals learn many aspects of language through cultural transmission. Indeed, the arbitrariness of the symbols of language requires that the conventions for symbolization must be passed from one generation to the next.

► ## THREE DIMENSIONS OF LANGUAGE

Language has three interrelated dimensions: semantics, syntax, and pragmatics (Bloom & Lahey, 1978). *Semantics* is the linguistic representation of our general knowledge about objects, events, and the relations between objects and events; it is the meaning, the thoughts, that language symbolizes. The expression of meaning is accomplished through the *syntax* of the language. The syntactic rules of a language specify the linguistic units of the language and rules for combining these units to connect sound with meaning. The *pragmatic* aspect of language specifies how language is used.

There are two aspects of language use. First, language has two types of functions: interpersonal and intrapersonal. The *interpersonal functions* include the communicative functions such as conveying information and requesting information. The *intrapersonal functions* have received relatively less attention. But it is evident that adults often talk to themselves when trying to solve problems or learn new material. Indeed recently some educators have recognized the value of writing as a problem-solving strategy in science and mathematics (Lindvall, Tamburino & Robinson, 1982).

Second, how language is used depends upon the context. A particular communicative function can take several forms; the form used depends upon the context of the utterance, including the characteristics of the participants (Bloom & Lahey, 1978). For example, students use a different form of address with their professors than they do with their peers; mothers do not speak to young children in the same way that they speak to older children and adults (see Newport, Gleitman & Gleitman, 1977).

Adult language involves a complex interplay of the semantic, syntactic, and pragmatic dimensions. Although it is possible and often necessary to consider these components individually, all three interact whenever adults produce or comprehend language. Thus, as children acquire language they develop a competence that includes knowledge about how to use language effectively as well as the linguistic knowledge necessary to produce well-formed, meaningful utterances. The goals of the developmental psycholinguist are to specify the character of these components in children's language and to trace the development and interaction of the three dimensions of language.

► COGNITIVE PREREQUISITES FOR THE USE OF LANGUAGE

The effective use of language presupposes several cognitive skills. All of these cognitive capacities are evident in children's nonverbal behavior either before the onset of language or during the development of language.

KNOWLEDGE OF OBJECTS AND EVENTS

All languages convey information about objects (animate and inanimate), events, and the relation between objects and events. We saw in Chapters 2 and 3 that prelinguistic children have some knowledge of objects and events. For example, by four or five months of age infants perceive objects as separate, three-dimensional entities. They are also sensitive to a variety of differences and similarities among events, such as the difference between the transformations of elastic objects and rigid objects and the pattern of changes in the attributes of mobiles. Furthermore, our review of the development of object permanence indicated the growing sophistication of the infant during the first two years, not only in knowledge about the continued existence of unseen objects, but also in memory for these objects and the ability to use such memory to direct activity. There is no doubt that children come to language with some knowledge of their world. With the development of language, psychologists can use children's productions and comprehension to further explore their knowledge of objects and events.

THE ABILITY TO ANALYZE A WHOLE INTO ITS PARTS

Each level of the hierarchical structure of language is composed of constituent parts. The use of language requires the ability to analyze units into their constituents. This does not mean, however, that there is a conscious awareness of such analyses. Earlier we presented evidence that young infants are able to recognize phonemes as distinct parts even when they are embedded in other speech sounds. When children acquire language, they are capable of part–whole analyses for many different types of "wholes."

THE ABILITY TO FORM CATEGORIES

Closely related to part–whole analysis is categorization. The constituents of language are categories. We have already described evidence that young infants do categorize speech sounds. Furthermore, we have evidence that within the first year infants' categorizations are different enough to include facial patterns as well as the number of objects in an array. When children acquire language they not only categorize on the basis of perceptual features (phonemes) but also on the basis of function in a sentence (for example, grammatical classes).

THE ABILITY TO LEARN AND MANIPULATE SYMBOLS

The use of language requires children to learn and manipulate a set of arbitrary symbols. By the time children reach kindergarten age, they have acquired an extensive set of symbols. As we will see, children's words do not always symbolize the same concepts as those of adults. But they are conventional enough for family and strangers to comprehend many of the expressions of preschoolers.

The ability of young children to use symbols to express their thoughts further indicates the development of mental representations for a variety of concepts. As indicated in Chapter 3, psychologists differ in when they are willing to attribute mental representation to children prior to language production. The very earliest words children use often seem to be tied to specific action sequences and thus appear to function as parts of procedures rather than symbolic representations. When words are no longer restricted to specific contexts, but are used to symbolize unseen objects or planned actions, we have evidence that speech productions symbolize the child's mental representations, representations that are accessed independent of specific perceptual events or action sequences. The child now has declarative knowledge about objects, events, and relations.

THE ABILITY TO USE LANGUAGE AS A TOOL

Language is usually used as a means for accomplishing one's goals. That is, language is directed toward others as an instrument for fulfilling the many communicative functions that are possible with language. As we will see, young children, even before language production, have learned to use adults to accomplish their goals. With the development of language, children acquire a more powerful and refined tool for reaching their goals.

THE ABILITY TO UNDERSTAND AND PRODUCE SEQUENCES OF ACTIONS

Young children's play indicates that they can sequence actions both in symbolic play and in a variety of games. Similarly, language requires the sequencing of speech productions and the ability to understand the sequences produced by others. Environmental events can involve the simultaneous presence of objects and actions. Yet children must be able to sequence their speech production in a conventional manner in order to convey their thoughts about events. We will see that young children do sequence their actions, including vocalizations, in games like "peek-a-boo" before they begin to produce sequences of words.

THE INTENTION TO COMMUNICATE

The use of language implies the intention to communicate and requires that children learn such conventions of communication as turn-taking. *Communication* is defined as an act in which one individual intends to convey a message to another individual. This definition of communication makes a distinction between a sender intending meaning and a listener inferring meaning (Chalkley, 1982). Thus, when a mother infers that a crying neonate is hungry, there is no communication since there is no evidence that the infant intends to convey information to the mother. Indeed, the cry of a hungry infant is reflexive and occurs whether a listener is present or not. The intention to communicate, however, is evident in children's gestures before they begin to use language.

▶ ## METHODS OF STUDY

Both linguists and psychologists study language. But they do so from different points of view and with different methods. *Linguists* concentrate on describing the formal characteristics of language. That is, linguists seek to specify the abstract grammatical structures that underlie the production and comprehension of language. To put the matter in terms of competence and performance, linguists have the goal of describing the competence that must underlie a language system. They do this by using observations of naturally occurring language and intuitions about language. These *intuitions* are judgments about the characteristics of sentences, including judgments about the grammaticality of specific sentences (Gleitman & Gleitman, 1987; Howard, 1983). The linguist attempts to identify those characteristics of language that distinguish grammatical sentences from nongrammatical sentences.

The *psycholinguist*, or psychologist interested in language, has a goal that differs from that of the linguist. The psycholinguist attempts to understand how humans use language. Thus, unlike the linguist, the psycholinguist wants to understand the acts of speaking and comprehending language. To do this the psychologist must not only understand the form of language and the functions of communication, but also the processes that are involved in these acts. The psycholinguist wants to understand the performance of the language user and therefore must consider competence as well as the processes that affect production and comprehension of language. Furthermore, *developmental psycholinguists* seek to determine how language is acquired. They must not only identify variables that influence language production and comprehension but also assess the extent to which the linguists' models of adult language do and do not reflect the developing structures of children's language.

Although the methods of study have varied with the specific questions and the age of the subjects, young speakers have most frequently been studied by observing their speech *production*. Two techniques have been used to study the speech production of young children. One method is to observe periodically the spontaneous utterances of children. This technique requires some method for interpreting what children *know* from what they produce (Bloom, 1970). Recently, videotapes of the observations have been used to record the nonverbal context as an aid to interpretation.

One of the psycholinguist's goals is to trace the semantic and syntactic development of children's language. But children's beginning language is limited and does not have forms that directly and independently indicate semantic and syntactic relations. Suppose a child says, "Mommy sock." From this information we know something about the topic of the utterance, but we do not know what the utterance means. That is, the child may simply be labeling two different objects that are in view. Or the utterance may express an actor + object-of-action relation as in, "Mommy is putting on a sock." Another possibility is that the child is expressing the possessor + object-of-possession relation as in, "There is mommy's sock." In order to interpret young children's utterances, psycholinguists use not only the word order of the utterances but also the context of the utterances, the situation in which the utterance occurs, to interpret children's productions. For example, if a child reaches in a laundry basket, pulls out one of her mother's socks, and says, "Mommy sock," the context supports the inference that the child is making a comment about a possessor + object-of-possession relation (Bloom, 1970).

The other method used to study speech production is to *elicit* utterances from the child. There are several tasks for eliciting such utterances, but all of them require that the child be able to comprehend instructions. In this procedure no interpretation of the child's knowledge of language is possible if the child does not perform. For example, if a child fails to describe a picture when requested to do so, the failure "may stem from an inability to produce the description, to understand what the picture is about, or to recognize that the task at hand is picture description" (Tartter, 1986, p. 334). Indeed, production data in general have the disadvantage that production depends upon a number of competence and performance factors. Therefore, it is difficult to determine the reason for the failure to observe a certain type of production. This, of course, is not a problem specific to the study of language, but one that warrants emphasis.

There are also a variety of methods for studying language *comprehension*. Some of these, such as asking the child to explain a sentence, require the child to produce language. Others require the child to act out requests. Tests of comprehension have the advantage that specific types of language skills can be tested, but they have the disadvantage that the cooperation of the child is required and it is often difficult to determine when a young child is and is not cooperating. Thus, failure to perform is again difficult to interpret (Limber, 1976). Furthermore, we have evidence that nonverbal context as well as the form and content of a test sentence can affect young children's comprehension of sentences (Clark, 1973). Therefore, it is necessary to control and/or specify the influences of nonlinguistic variables in order to interpret children's comprehension performance appropriately.

Although all children of normal intelligence acquire language, they do so at somewhat different rates, as will be evident in subsequent illustrations. This means that if we wish to study developmental changes in language, age comparisons can be misleading because children of a given age may be in different places in their language development. A common method for dealing with this problem is to use *mean length of utterance* (MLU) as a measure of linguistic development (see Klee & Fitzgerald, 1985). Although the average number of words in a child's utterances can be used in this measure, a more useful measure is the *average number of meaningful elements* (morphemes). Thus, the utterance, "I lifted heavy boxes" has six morphemes: "I," "lift," "-ed" (which conveys the meaning of action in the past), "heavy," "box," "-es" (which carries the meaning of plural) (Dale, 1976).

Finally, it should be noted that most studies of early language study spontaneous production, often across some longitudinal period. In order to identify the consistencies of syntax, semantics, and pragmatics in a child's language, independent of specific vocabulary words, it is necessary to collect a large corpus or body of productions. Indeed, corpora of 10,000 or more utterances have been analyzed for individual children. The analysis of such data requires extensive research effort, and, as one consequence, most investigations of early language involve few children, usually from two to six. The advantage of such an approach is that extensive developmental data are available for individual children. The disadvantage, of course, is that the developmental course of a few children may not represent general principles of language development. This problem is reduced when several studies investigate the same phenomena and confirm each other's findings.

▶ PRELINGUISTIC COMMUNICATION AND THE EMERGENCE OF ONE-WORD UTTERANCES

Young children communicate with others before they begin to produce language. As indicated earlier in this chapter, communication is used here to specify that the speaker intends to convey a message to the listener. Although there are differences of opinion about how to define intention (see, for example, Harding, 1984; Scoville, 1984), most developmental psycholinguists assume the narrower definition in the investigation of infant communication (for example, Bruner, 1983; Bates, 1979).

How can we know that prelinguistic children intend to communicate?

Adults have a variety of ways to indicate the intention to communicate. These often involve verbal behaviors such as using the name of the individual who is being addressed or terms like "hey," "excuse me," and "hello." And of course we can ask the speaker, "Are you talking to me?" Obviously, prelinguistic children cannot use these techniques to convey intention to communicate. But there are some visible signs that have been used to define *operationally* young children's intention to communicate. These are signals that children make in an effort to get the attention of other individuals; such signals include looking, touching or grasping, or using a vocalization (such as, "uh-uh"). Once children have established attention of the other, they then direct attention to the content of the message, such as pointing at a desired toy. Thus, children must be able to coordinate an action for getting attention with an action for conveying a message. To illustrate, Sugarman-Bell (1978) provides the example of a child who looks at the adult, continues to look at the adult until the adult looks at her, points at a desired toy in the adult's lap, and then pulls the toy while looking at the adult.

THE DEVELOPMENT OF THE INTENT TO COMMUNICATE

Most infants begin intentional communication between eight and ten months of age. It is then that infants combine gestures or vocalizations for getting an adult's attention with gestures to indicate the content of the intended message. Prior to this time, however, mothers do interpret their infants' behavior as expressing needs (see, for example, Vedeler, 1987) and these interpretations change in nature as infants develop. For example, when infants are approximately six to seven months of age, mothers change their interpretation of crying from an expression of physical needs to an expression of psychological needs (Pratt as cited in Bruner, 1983). And by eight months of age, infants' crying becomes socialized. "It takes the form of a much more ritualized cry: less persistent, more punctuated by pauses during which the child checks on uptake by the mother or by other adults. Acoustically as well, his cries also become more 'conventional,' his initial 'flat' sound spectrum being replaced by cries with a more pronounced fundamental frequency" (Bruner, 1983, p. 92). Thus crying, which is initially reflexive, takes on an intentional communicative function around the same time that infants begin to use gestures to communicate.

Harding (1983, 1984) argues that the development of the intent to communicate is guided by cognitive development, particularly means–end skill (as described by Piaget), and mother–infant interaction. As illustrated in Figure 4-2, Harding proposes a model in which an infant's development from Stage 3 to Stage 5 of sensorimotor development results in changes in the infant's communicative behavior and the mother's reaction to the behaviors. Thus, in Stage 3, the infant has disassociated cause from effect and uses procedures to

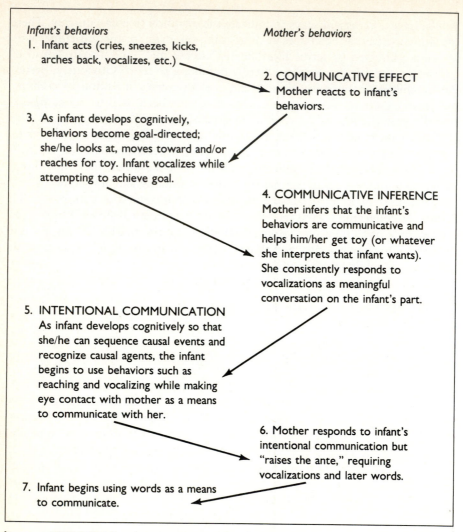

Infant's behaviors

1. Infant acts (cries, sneezes, kicks, arches back, vocalizes, etc.)

3. As infant develops cognitively, behaviors become goal-directed; she/he looks at, moves toward and/or reaches for toy. Infant vocalizes while attempting to achieve goal.

5. INTENTIONAL COMMUNICATION
As infant develops cognitively so that she/he can sequence causal events and recognize causal agents, the infant begins to use behaviors such as reaching and vocalizing while making eye contact with mother as a means to communicate with her.

7. Infant begins using words as a means to communicate.

Mother's behaviors

2. COMMUNICATIVE EFFECT
Mother reacts to infant's behaviors.

4. COMMUNICATIVE INFERENCE
Mother infers that the infant's behaviors are communicative and helps him/her get toy (or whatever she interprets that infant wants). She consistently responds to vocalizations as meaningful conversation on the infant's part.

6. Mother responds to infant's intentional communication but "raises the ante," requiring vocalizations and later words.

▶ **FIGURE 4-2** *A proposed description of the developmental sequence of prelinguistic communication. (From Harding, 1983.)*

achieve a goal or effect. These procedures are global, uncoordinated activities that are not specific instrumental attempts to achieve the goal or to signal what is wanted. That is, shrieking is not an activity that in and of itself can bring a toy into the infant's hand or indicate that a particular toy is desired. But mothers use the context of the infant's activity to infer and satisfy the infant's goal.

In Stage 4 infants use instrumental behaviors to achieve their goals (for example, reaching for a desired toy). Their behaviors are directed toward specific objects *or* toward their mothers (compare, Sugarman, 1984). These mothers continue to interpret the children's behaviors as goal directed, but interpret a more limited set of behaviors as communicative, behaviors such as eye contact, vocalization, and reaching.

In Stage 5 infants convey the intention to communicate by combining attention to the mother with attention to the desired goal. Communication with their mothers has become a subgoal that is instrumental in reaching the infants' end goal. Children are no longer dependent upon or limited by their own action capabilities for meeting their desires. Harding further reports that during this period mothers become increasingly restrictive about which infant behaviors they consider communicative. For example, behaviors such as crying, shrieking, and fake cough were interpreted as communicative behaviors at six months, but only more conventional vocalizations, with or without associated actions, were judged communicative at ten months of age.

Thus, before infants use instrumental actions to achieve their goals, mothers interpret their infants' behaviors and function as instruments to achieve their infants' goals. Furthermore, mothers appear sensitive to infants' developing cognitive skills and modify their interpretation with more restrictive requirements for a behavior to qualify as communicative. The forces that promote these changes have yet to be specified. That is, infant behaviors may change because mothers expect more of them and are not, therefore, responsive to the earlier forms of behavior. As a consequence, infant behaviors are modified. Another possibility, of course, is that infants mature independently of their mothers' responses to their behavior. A more complex possibility is that as infants mature and their communicative behaviors change, they use their mothers' responses to their behavior to determine which behaviors are appropriate for communicative functions.

EARLY PARENT–INFANT INTERACTIONS   Important in the development of communication is the mutual give-and-take of parent–infant interactions. Adults maintain communication with each other through eye contact, facial expressions, gestures, and turn-taking exchanges. In this process each communicating partner is influenced by the behavior of the other. We have behaviors that we use to maintain a conversation and others that signal the end of a conversation. The role of these signals is probably most evident when they fail. To illustrate, I have an acquaintance who has not learned that an essential feature of conversations is turn taking. Rather, he engages in monologues that seldom end unless you interrupt him.

Most of us, however, have learned the importance of turn taking. Furthermore, we have evidence that infants as young as three months are sensitive to turn taking. Bloom, Russell, and Wassenberg (1987) analyzed the vocalizations of three-month-olds in two conditions. In the *contingent condition* an adult responded with social interaction (simultaneously she smiled, touched the abdomen lightly, and said "Hi [baby's name]"), but only after each vocalization of the infant. In the *random condition* the adult responded on a prearranged schedule that was not responsive to the infants' vocalizations but did have the same time intervals and the same manner as the infants in the contingent condition.

Adult observers were asked to assess the quality of the infants' vocalizations. These analyses indicated that the infants in the contingent condition produced a greater proportion of speech-like syllabic sounds. If the adult engaged in turn-taking behavior, the infant produced more sounds that had speech-like characteristics. Furthermore, in a second study that replicated the first except that the adult made a "tsk, tsk" sound rather than talking to the baby, Bloom (1988) found that in the contingent condition there was no increase in the syllabic sounds produced by the infants. The two studies taken together indicate that young infants are responsive to turn-taking only if it occurs in conjunction with adult speech. It is important to note that the adult observers who perceived the differences in the infant vocalizations were not interacting with the infants nor aware of the vocalization conditions. While we do not have the relevant data, we can wonder whether this sensitivity of adults to the quality of infant vocalizations influences adult responses to infants. We might speculate that when infant vocalizations are perceived as speech-like, adults are more likely to continue an interaction with an infant (Bloom, Russell & Wassenberg, 1987).

Although we do not yet know how the characteristics of infant vocalizations affect adult reactions, we do know that mothers use consistent sound patterns with young infants to express their communicative intentions. Stern, Spieker, and MacKain (1982) observed mothers as they interacted with their infants at two, four, and six months of age. The analyses indicated that the mothers used rising-pitch contours when the infants were not visually attending and the mothers wanted eye contact. *Rising-pitch contours* are represented by phrases such as, "Wanna go shopping, huh?", where the pitch gradually rises to the end of the phrase. When the infants were gazing and smiling at the mothers, the mothers used sinusoidal and bell-shaped contours to maintain the infants' gaze. *Sinusoidal* and *bell-shaped contours* are represented by phrases such as "Catch them hurry up" and "Come on" where the pitch rises and falls. The mothers also used specific pitch contours for specific types of sentences; for example, yes–no questions had rise contours.

Thus, by three months of age, infants are sensitive to at least one adult signal of communicative intent, turn taking, and they respond with vocalizations that may foster the social interaction. Furthermore, adults are using other consistent patterns of sound to signal specific communicative intents. We might wonder when infants recognize these other communicative efforts and respond with behaviors that are responsive to the specific intents. Nevertheless, the research indicates that, by the time infants are three months of age, infants and adults alike engage in behaviors that appear to promote the social interactions of communication.

WHAT COMMUNICATIVE FUNCTIONS DO PRELINGUISTIC CHILDREN EXPRESS?

Adults not only intend to communicate when they use language, but also intend "to accomplish a specific type of communication" (Chalkley, 1982, p. 80). For example, we can make statements that function to greet someone, inform someone, or even lie to someone. In fact, the philosopher Austin (1962) identified at least 1,000 different communicative functions and this list probably is not an exhaustive one.

Chalkley (1982) reexamined the data of several studies to assess which communicative functions were evident in the protocols of preverbal children. Her review indicated that requests were predominant in the preverbal child's communications. These include requests for objects and actions, as well as requests for help, sympathy, and repetition. Another common preverbal function was "reference," in which the child focused another's attention on an object or action. The infants also communicated emotion, both positive and negative, and a variety of social functions such as greeting and making offers.

THE DEVELOPMENT OF REQUESTS   Bruner (1983) traced the early development of three types of requests: requests for objects, invitations to take a role in play, and requests for supportive action. The two children studied began to make requests for nearby objects around eight months. Before this, the infants produced vocalizations that were interpreted by their mothers as general expressions of need, but at eight months the infants began to indicate what they wanted. Requests for near objects were the dominant form of requests between 8 and 12 months.

The early requests were made with arm extension toward the desired object. The reach appears real with the body bent forward, the hand opening and closing, and the child making effortful noises. But these efforts were not real because the children did not grab objects that were within their reach. In a few months the gesture and vocalization became more stylized, more conventional; the reach was not effortful, the hand was open and extended in the direction of the object, and the vocalization was more distinctive, "huhmm" for one child and "heaah" for the other.

As the children became more mobile and developed memories for objects and their locations, requests for distant and absent objects became more frequent and nouns were substituted for the stylized request vocalization. For example, at 16 months, Richard requested a book on a shelf by combining the reach gesture with "ghuk" (his word for "book"). Around 21 months of age Richard initiated a request with the noun rather than the gesture and shortly after the gesture dropped out altogether.

Invitations to join in play began around 13–14 months and increased in frequency during the next year. The requested activities included reading a book, looking out the window together, and a variety of games. Requests for supportive action are attempts by the child to get assistance for goal-directed actions such as getting a box open or bringing a chair indoors. These requests were particularly frequent at 18–19 months, suggesting that the child has a greater appreciation for the varieties of roles that the adult can play as an instrument in the child's activities. An adult not only can fetch the desired objects but also can assist with incomplete tasks. For example, at 15 months Jonathan has this exchange with his mother (Bruner, 1983, p. 108):

▶ Jonathan: (Holds music box; looks at box; then at mother.)

Mother: (Chatting with observer.)

Jonathan: Mm.

Mother: (Continues talking with observer.)

Jonathan: (Looks at box; tries to wind it; turns to mother.) Hmmm. (Tries to wind box; looks at mother; crawls to mother.) Eeh, eega, hmmm. (Holds box out to mother.)

Mother: (Reaches toward box.)

Jonathan: (Withdraws box; demonstrates attempt to wind; hands box to mother.) Here.

Mother: Do you want mummy to turn it for you? Look. (Demonstrates how to wind.)

Jonathan: (Looks at observer; then watches mother winding. As soon as music starts, Jonathan reaches and takes back the box, turning away without acknowledgment.)

To make requests for supportive action, the child must have some knowledge of means–end relations. Initially, these efforts to communicate depend heavily upon the mother's interpretations, but over the next few months the children showed increased sophistication in putting together a plan for requested assistance and tying together appropriate utterances. In the example above, Jonathan knows that music (end) is produced by winding the music box (means) and must relate this knowledge about the music box to a sequence of gestures to attract attention and solicit help in his goal-directed actions. In this example, Jonathan uses gestures, such as the attempt to wind the box, that are specific to the goal at hand. Later, of course, children substitute specific words for these gestures to convey their intent. Deaf children without a language model (that is, deaf children of hearing parents who do not sign), however, continue to elaborate their gestural systems in the effort to communicate, presumably to communicate more precisely and efficiently (Goldin-Meadow, 1985).

FAILURES TO COMMUNICATE   Mothers do not always understand a child's communicative intentions. What happens when a child's message is not comprehended? Message failures at the beginning of the development of intentional communication (8 to 12 months of age), are most likely to result in the child giving up the communicative effort or resorting to crying or whining (Harding & Golinkoff, 1979). But in the next few months (12 to 18 months) infants begin to engage in communicative exchanges in which they negotiate failed messages. These negotiations include repetition of the original gestures/vocalizations or modifications (repairs) of the communicative behaviors. Consider, for example, this exchange (Golinkoff, 1983, pp. 58–59):

▶ 1. Jordan: (Vocalizes repeatedly until his mother turns around.)
2. Mother: (Turns around to look at him.)
3. Jordan: (Points to one of the objects on the counter.)
4. Mother: Do you want this? (Holds up milk container.)
5. Jordan: (Shakes his head "no.")
(Vocalizes, continues to point.)
6. Mother: Do you want this? (Holds up jelly jar.)
7. Jordan: (Shakes head "no.")
(Continues to point.)
8, 9, 10, & 11: (Two more offer–rejection pairs.)
12. Mother: This? (Picks up sponge.)
13. Jordan: (Leans back in highchair, puts arms down, tension leaves body.)
14. Mother: (Hands Jordan sponge.)

In this episode the child not only formulates an intention but maintains it over several failures to reach his goal. Further, he repairs his communicative behavior with a head shake in addition to his original vocalization and pointing gesture. It would appear that when messages fail infants must find new means to communicate and achieve their goals (Golinkoff, 1983).

When messages fail in adult communication, the speaker responds in accordance with the perceived nature of the misunderstanding. Wilcox and Webster (1980) present evidence that children with mean lengths of utterances (MLUs) between 1.10 and 1.58 (17 to 24 months of age) are responsive to two different types of message failure. In this study an experimenter used two types of feedback to indicate failure to comprehend a child's requests. In one condition the experimenter responded, "What?" (with rising intonation), which indicates to adults that a request is not accurately perceived. In the second condition the experimenter misunderstood the intent of the request by treating it as a declarative statement. When the child, for example, requested a ball, the experimenter responded, "Yes, I see it" or "Yes, I have it."

The children made differential responses to these two types of communicative failure. They were more likely to make repetitions in the "What?" than in the misunderstood condition and more likely to make repairs of their requests in the misunderstood condition than in the "What?" condition. Thus, children this age are sensitive to different types of communication failure and use different techniques to negotiate the failed request.

THE DEVELOPMENT OF REFERENCE   When preverbal children make a request, they are attempting to satisfy an immediate need or goal. They have learned to use a signal to another as a means to achieve their goals. A variety of animals also are capable of signaling requests. For example, my dog sits in front of me and gently offers her right paw when she wants attention. This signal is never used for food or water and she never uses it with anyone except me or my husband. She has a very routinized pattern of gestures that she uses to achieve a specific goal. Language, however, has a communicative function, *reference,* or the sharing of information, that is not evident in animal communication but is one of the functions of preverbal children's communication (see Terrace, 1985, for a review of the chimpanzee research). As an analogy, consider my dog again. She has a signal that she uses when her waterbowl is empty, and whenever I fill the bowl she immediately drinks. Thus, her signal is always a request; she has yet to signal that her waterbowl is empty simply for the sake of conveying that information to me. Preverbal children do, however, make reference to objects and events simply to inform another about some aspect of the environment, to indicate that some feature has been noticed. Unlike the request function, the referential function achieves no other goal than to share information.

The reference function requires the joint attention of two individuals (Bruner, 1983). Early joint attention develops around two months of age when eye-to-eye contact is established between mother and infant. Mothers use this attention to present objects, often with vocal comments, in their infants' line of sight. The infants then direct their attention to the object. Mothers and babies develop stable patterns of give and take in the next few months. During these episodes infants spontaneously switch attention between the object and their mothers, and this visual attention is accompanied by vocal and/or other behaviors (Bruner, 1975; Gray, 1978). By 8 to 10 months of age, an infant will follow a mother's line of gaze when she looks away from the infant. Around a year of age, infants use pointing, often with vocalizations, to direct attention to objects. This pointing behavior is used to draw attention to objects of interest, rather than to request the objects. Furthermore, mothers are more likely to name the indicated objects when infants point than when they use other gestures (such as, open-handed reaches) (Masur, 1981). Indeed, the development of early vocabulary (at 21 months) is positively correlated with the mother's naming of objects during episodes of joint attention (Tomasello & Farrar, 1986).

During the next year, mothers and infants engage in a variety of activities that emphasize the reference function. Mothers indicate and name objects, ask "What's that?" questions about pictures in books, and ask infants to locate and name objects. Similarly, infants point out and label objects or request labels for objects of interest. Thus, a variety of social interactions engage mother and infant in activities that direct each other's attention to topics of interest.

Although considerable research has demonstrated the development of reference in prelinguistic mother–child interactions, there is nothing in prelinguistic communication that explains how children come to know that gestures and words can refer to objects. Indeed, Macnamara (1982) has argued that referring is a cognitive given of humans. Although both young children and chimps use the open, extended hand to request objects, only children spontaneously use pointing gestures to direct the attention of others (Terrace, 1985). Just as the human perceptual system organizes visual input as three-dimensional entities in space, so humans "know" that sounds and/or gestures can stand for objects (Huttenlocher & Smiley, 1987). Indeed, deaf children who have not learned American Sign Language have been observed to "invent" their own gesture systems to make reference to the objects and events of their environment (Goldin-Meadow, 1985). Even without a conventional language model, children develop structured gesture systems that make reference to their environment and resemble language in many respects.

Although mother–infant interactions and the development of prelinguistic communication do not explain how children know that objects and events can be referred to, these precursors nevertheless may be important in language and cognitive development (Messer, 1983). These early interactions, for example, may encourage an infant's attention to linguistic information from the parent (Shatz, 1985). Intensive longitudinal studies will be necessary to explore the relations between the quality and quantity of mother–child interaction and individual differences in language skills (compare, Newport, Gleitman & Gleitman, 1977; Lieven, 1982; Tomasello & Farrar, 1986; Whitehurst, Falco, Lonigan, Fischel, DeBaryshe, Valdez-Menchaca & Caulfield, 1988).

In summary, prelinguistic children express a variety of communicative functions with gestures and vocalizations. Such communication indicates that young children can use signals to indicate a number of functions, that they can coordinate their gestures and vocalizations to elicit the attention of another and to solicit the participation of adults. Furthermore, during this period the use of sound progresses from reactive through directive to informative, and the sounds increasingly approximate the adult conventions (Howe, 1981). Thus, by the time that language is evident, young children are already engaged in communication. The development of prelinguistic communication closely follows Piaget's descriptions of the development of goal-directed behavior in general. What is unclear, however, is how the development of prelinguistic communication and cognitive development during infancy relates to the acquisition of language (compare, Golinkoff, 1983; Shatz, 1985). That is, children must have certain communicative knowledge to use language. But this does not mean that such communicative competence is sufficient for language acquisition. As discussed earlier, the intention to communicate is just one of the prerequisites of language development. Although some animals show evidence of communicative intent, this ability is not enough to ensure the development of language.

PRODUCTION   Children differ considerably in the timing of the onset of the first words. Indeed, it is not easy to determine when the first words occur because they often do not match adult words. Some of these first words appear to develop out of stylized vocalizations that are made during gesture and play routines (Bates, Bretherton, Shore & McNew, 1983; Bruner, 1983). For example, Bates and her colleagues report that Carlotta initially used the sound, "bam," at a regular point in a game of knocking over blocks. The sound, "bam," was simply part of a series of actions. Several weeks later, however, Carlotta used the sound in a different manner: "Carlotta was seated among her toys momentarily silent and empty-handed. She looked up, said the word, 'bam,' and after a brief hesitation turned to pound on her toy piano" (Bates *et al.,* 1983, p. 64). The sound now appears actually to stand for, or symbolize, the sound that will result from pounding the piano.

Most infants' first 50 words name objects (51 percent; for example, "ball"), specific people or pets (14 percent; for example, "mommy"), and actions (14 percent; for example, "give," "bye-bye"). Less common are modifiers (9 percent; for example, "red," "mine") and personal-social words (8 percent; for example, "no," "yes," "please"). Function words such as "what," "the," and "for" are quite rare (4 percent). These first words primarily name objects that change (for example, move, make noise), objects that the child can act on (for example, shoes, but not diaper), and actions that the child can make (for example, run, jump) (Nelson, 1973).

In general, the first words of a young child name familiar and salient objects and activities. Children's early words do not, however, necessarily refer to the same class of objects or events as they do when used by adults. This discrepancy in the use of words is even evident in the lexicon of older children and adults. We all have had the experience of thinking that we know the meaning of a word and then discovering that our meaning does not match the conventional meaning. Indeed, one challenge for students of science is to ensure that the meaning they assign to specific words matches that intended in the discipline.

Logically, a child's word meaning might relate to adults' word meanings in several possible ways (Reich, 1986) as illustrated in Figure 4-3. One possibility is that a child's use of a word may be *identical* with that of adults'. This means that any instance of an adult concept is named in the same way by the child. Although this is fairly rare with beginning words, it is most frequent with proper names of family, friends, and pets. A second possibility is a *mismatch*. The child uses an adult word, but there is no overlap between the adult meaning and the child's meaning. For example, Reich's (1986) son called the TV set "TV Guide," but denied that the guide was a "TV Guide" or the set was called a "TV."

Another possible relation is *underextension*. The child may use a word in a narrower sense that adults. Reich (1976) gives an example of his son's

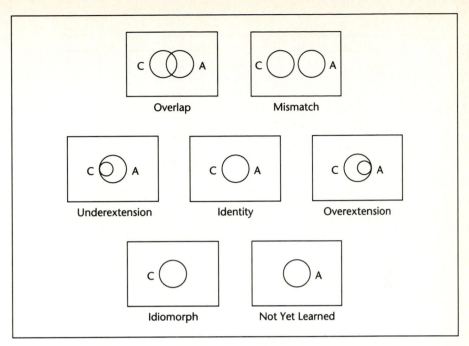

▶ **FIGURE 4-3**   *Seven possible relations of the child's word meaning to that of the adult.* (From Reich, 1986.)

underextension in the comprehension of "shoes" at eight months of age (see Figure 4-4). When asked, "Where's the shoes?", he would crawl to his mother's closet and play with her shoes but only with her shoes and only when the shoes were in the closet. When the shoes were placed at location X or he was placed in front of his father's shoes (location Z), he would still crawl to the shoes in his mother's closet. Gradually the meaning of "shoes" expanded. First, it involved the shoes in his father's closet, then also the shoes on the floor if no one was in them, and finally, shoes even when they were being worn.

At the other extreme, *overextension* occurs when a child has a broader meaning for a word than adults do. An example is a child's use of the word "moon" to refer not only to the real moon in all its phases, but also to a ball of spinach, half of a Cheerio, a slice of lemon, and a shiny leaf (Bowerman, 1978). Another possibility is *overlap,* in which the word is overextended in some ways and underextended in others. An example is a two-year-old who uses "muffin" to refer to blueberries and blueberry muffins, but not for any other muffins (Dale, 1976). Finally, a child may use an *idiomorph,* a word that does not appear to refer to any adult concept; and, of course, there are adult words which children simply have not yet learned at all. As children have more experience with their language, their comprehension and use of words is modified and comes to match the conventions of the culture more

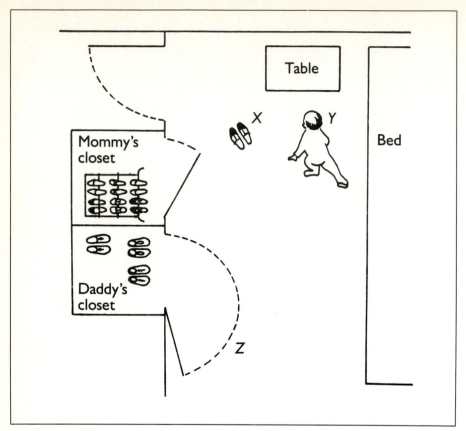

▶ **FIGURE 4-4** *An example of* underextension. *The infant (Y) when asked, "Where's the shoes?", would crawl to his mother's closet and play only with her shoes while they were in her closet. The infant would not react to her shoes if they had been placed in positions X or Z. (From Reich, 1986.)*

closely. During this process, communication can and does occur, as long as there is some degree of correspondence.

Although the majority of children's first words name objects, initially the most frequently used words are *non-nomial words* that do not name objects or events (Gopnik & Meltzoff, 1986a,b). Gopnik (1982) investigated children's use of non-nomial expressions such as "gone," "there," "oh dear," and "down." In her longitudinal study of nine children under two years of age, the children were videotaped periodically in their homes and the context for the production of each expression was compared. If a child used the same expression in different contexts, it was assumed that the word symbolized a concept that was general to each of these contexts.

Gopnik found that "gone" and the locative expressions, "down," "up," "in," "out," "on," and "off" were used early and produced when the *child* tried to achieve some result. That is, "gone" was used when the child tried to or did make an object disappear. This use occurred before it was used to comment on disappearances that the child did not cause. Similarly, "down" and the other locative expressions were first used when the child made objects move, before it was used to comment on spatial relationships and movements that the child did not cause.

Gopnik sees a common factor in the children's use of the non-nomial expressions that she investigated. None are used for specific objects, people, or actions; rather, initially they are used to comment on the child's plans. By *plan* Gopnik means "an action or a series of actions that are performed in order to bring about a certain event." Initially, terms like "gone" comment on the child's own plans; later they are extended to other events or relationships.

In summary, Bruner's (1983) work indicates that by one year of age children use a combination of gestures and sounds to communicate their needs. Initially, the sounds used are variable and function as part of the action sequence rather than as symbols. The sounds themselves gradually become stylized and consistent for individual children. With continued input from adults in these communicative interactions, the infant learns to produce sounds that approach the convention of the native language (for example, "ghuk" for "book"). These sounds do not, however, necessarily symbolize adult concepts, but each child does come to know that certain sounds can be used to represent specific objects and events. Furthermore, all children come to know that almost any object or event can be symbolized with words and that each word represents some object, event, or relationship.

COMPREHENSION   The few studies that have investigated early language comprehension indicate that prelinguistic children and those producing one-word utterances can comprehend considerably more than they can produce (see, for example, Benedict, 1979; Huttenlocher, 1974; Sachs & Truswell, 1978). Huttenlocher (1974), for example, tested four children periodically between the ages of 10 months and 18 months. In each of these home visits she tested those object and action words that the mother thought the child comprehended. The children tested by Huttenlocher all understood words that they did not produce.

As indicated in Chapter 3, Huttenlocher found that the children initially comprehended object words referring to seen objects. Evidence suggests that when children can respond appropriately to requests to retrieve unseen objects in temporary locations, they can comprehend arbitrary symbols *and* mentally represent the objects that they symbolize.

Furthermore, there is evidence that at least some action words symbolize rather abstract actions. For example, at 10 months Wendy, one of the children in Huttenlocher's study, produced four words: "hi," "see," "mommy," and "daddy." She also understood at least four other words—one object word ("cookie") and three action words ("bye-bye," "bang-bang," and "peek-a-boo"). Huttenlocher describes the test of "peek-a-boo" as follows (1974, p. 342):

> During the session Mommy puts on the floor near Wendy a diaper, a cookie, a pretzel and a stainless steel mixing bowl with a spoon in it. A bunny book, milk truck with bottles, and her bottle have already been put there. She says to Wendy, "Make peek-a-boo." Wendy promptly picks up the diaper, puts it over her face, and peeks out smiling. Through the session I say the same thing three other times with the same prompt response. A little later Wendy again has many things around. Now, however, the diaper is not in view. I say, "Make peek-a-boo." She looks around, sees no diaper, and looks puzzled. Then with a smile she picks up the bowl and hides, peeking around the side and breaking into laughter as she does so.

This episode not only demonstrates that Wendy comprehended peek-a-boo but also that her representation of the action was not tied to a single object (diaper) or even single type of object (material to drape on the head). Rather, the peek-a-boo action was represented by the more abstract understanding of the sequence of disappearance and reappearance (Bruner, 1983).

The four children tested by Huttenlocher differed substantially in their development of language comprehension. At 17 months, for example, Wendy did not indicate any comprehension of more than one word at a time. Kristen, however, at 14 months did not produce any words, but could comprehend contrasts such as "your shoe/your nose" and "mommy's shoe/mommy's nose." Craig began comprehending such contrasts shortly after a new sister arrived at 17 months. But this comprehension was limited to "your bottle/your diaper" and "baby's bottle/baby's diaper." This limitation is demonstrated when Craig is asked, "Where is your shoe?", and points to his shoe, but also points at his shoe when asked "Where is Mommy's shoe?" Thus, Craig does not yet have a general comprehension of possession. At this age, Craig produces only two words, "uh-uh" and "di," but he can comprehend commands that have up to three contrasting terms, such as "Give (show) Mommy (me) the baby's (your) bottle."

Huttenlocher's work not only demonstrates that children can comprehend words well before they are produced, but also that children can integrate the meaning of two or three words. Furthermore, Sachs and Truswell (1978) have demonstrated that children in the one-word stage can integrate the meaning of two-word commands that do not express familiar events. In their investigation the children were given novel commands such as "tickle book," "smell truck," and "kiss ball." The words were all familiar; the relations expressed in the commands were not. Thus, even when words are combined to convey unusual relations, young children are capable of inferring the intended meaning. This ability to integrate the meanings of words is an important precursor to the discovery that syntax (for example, word order) has an effect on the meaning of a message (Sachs & Truswell, 1978).

Further research is needed to determine the causes for the asymmetry in the development of comprehension and production of words. Although linguists tend to view linguistic competence as unitary, the processes of comprehension and production may demand different sets of linguistic knowledge. The discrepancy between comprehension and production in language acquisition, a discrepancy that is also evident when adults learn a second language, may reflect the fact that, initially, these two linguistic competences are not coordinated. But such coordination is necessary for speakers to communicate. Indeed, Clark & Hecht (1983) have proposed that the mismatch between children's comprehension of language and their perception of their own production is one factor that motivates children to modify their language production. Clark (1982) argues that to detect mismatches of language comprehension and production, children use a standard of comparison that is "provided by their representations in memory for the adult pronunciation of words and phrases, rather than by any representations for their own pronunciations" (p. 172). Clark illustrates this assertion with what she calls the *fis* phenomenon:

▶ 1. . . . a child called his inflated plastic fish a "fis." In imitation of the child's pronunciation, the observer said: "This is your 'fis'?" "No," said the child, "my 'fis.' " He continued to reject the adult's imitation until he was told, "That is your fish." "Yes," he said, "my 'fis' " (Berko & Brown, 1960, p. 531).

2. Father: Say "jump."
Child: Dup.
Father: No, jump
Child: Dup.
Father: No, "jummmp."
Child: Only Daddy can say dup! (Smith, 1973, p. 10).

This, and other evidence (see, for example, Dodd, 1975) suggest that representations based on adult pronunciations take priority over the child's own representations of pronunciation and can, therefore, provide the standard for comparison of discrepancies between comprehension and production (Clark, 1982).

▶ ## THE ACQUISITION OF WORD MEANING

Young children come to language acquisition with nonlinguistic knowledge, the knowledge that their thoughts and those of others can be symbolized in sound, and the desire to communicate their thoughts. As children learn language, they must discover the means for expressing their thoughts with the symbol system of a given language. We have seen that children have begun to assign meanings to words by the one-word period. By the time children are six years of age, they know 13,000 different words, or 7,800 basic root words (Miller, 1977; Templin, 1957). This is an impressive feat that raises a number of related and complex issues.

We make a distinction between *conceptual* knowledge and *semantic* knowledge. Concepts are our organizations of the world; we categorize the objects and events of our experience, and concepts are the mental representations that underlie our categorizations. (The nature of these representations is the topic of Chapter 5.) Semantic knowledge is the knowledge that we have that makes it possible to relate sentences to our world knowledge. This includes knowledge of individual word meanings as well as how the meaning of a sentence is determined both by the meaning of the individual words and the structure of the sentence.

Although it is common to state that words refer to objects and events, except for proper names, they actually symbolize categories of objects and events. That is, the word "dog" is a label for a class of animals, not a single instance of a dog. The nonverbal behavior of young infants indicates that they categorize their perceptual experience in a variety of ways. When language develops, the naming response can be used to investigate the nature of the categories for which children have labels.

The acquisition of word meaning has been approached from three perspectives—linguistic, philosophical, and psychological—that are yet to be integrated (Miller, 1978). As one consequence of this diversity of perspectives, there is not, as yet, a common theoretical approach to the acquisition of word meaning (see Blewitt, 1982, for a review). However, all agree that the major challenge for the child is what Clark (1973, 1977) called the *mapping problem*. Children must map linguistic knowledge to their nonlinguistic or conceptual knowledge. A problem exists because the two types of knowledge—linguistic and nonlinguistic—do not have a one-to-one correspondence (Rice & Kemper, 1984). Although there is presumed to be considerable overlap of nonlinguistic knowledge and linguistic knowledge, there is nonlinguistic knowledge that is not expressible in language (for example, how to ride a bicycle) and linguistic knowledge that is not tied to nonlinguistic meaning (for example, in English we say "untie" and "unfold" but not "uncapture" and "uncome)." There is no obvious conceptual distinction that corresponds to this linguistic distinction [Bowerman, 1982]). Even when conceptual and linguistic knowledge do overlap, the relation is not always a straightforward one. For example, all humans are capable of many color discriminations. Yet the Dani language has only two color words (Heider, 1970). When a child learns Dani he must determine which of his many color discriminations are mapped onto each term; he must learn a many (colors)-to-one (word) correspondence.

In other cases, a child may have a salient category (for example, "dogs that run free") that does not have a simple label in the language. I am partial to a group of dogs that are "large, long-haired with bear-like heads" (for example, Great Pyrenees, Newfoundlands, and Tibetan Mastiffs). In English, seven words are needed to label this category of dogs. Young children will be unable to label such a concept until they learn enough language to combine the appropriate words. Here a child must learn a one (concept)-to-many (words) correspondence.

Furthermore, language makes linguistic distinctions for conceptual distinctions that may not be salient or explicit for a young child. In Japanese, for example, two different words are used to distinguish between "taking off something that perches on the surface of the body" (for example, eyeglasses) and "taking off something that envelops a body part" (for example, a glove). The English language, however, uses the same verbs ("take off" or "remove") for this conceptual distinction. Thus, as children learn language, they are not only learning how to express their conceptual knowledge within a semantic system, but also conceptual distinctions and conventions that are specific to the language itself.

During the preschool years, the development of children's conceptual knowledge is extensive. Some of these thoughts may be difficult or impossible to express in a language (for example, the exact spatial relations of their mothers' facial features or how lambs look when they run); some of these may be expressible in single words (for example, the fact that the pet dog is called "Curly"); and certainly many thoughts require the combination of two or more words (for example, "I am holding my Teddy bear"), in which case children must learn not only which words represent individual concepts, but also how to combine the words to express the relations between concepts. As they do so, their conceptual development continues and becomes inextricably linked to their linguistic knowledge. At some point, for example, someone may tell the child that small stuffed bear-like toy animals are called "Teddy" after Teddy Roosevelt, the 26th president of the United States. Thus, the child's knowledge of "Teddy bears" is modified to include knowledge about Teddy Roosevelt, knowledge that could only be acquired through language.

Most theorists (for example, E.V. Clark, 1983; Nelson, 1985) agree that conceptual development and the acquisition of word meaning interact such that either one may precede the other and may guide the acquisition of the other. Clearly, words are meaningless if they do not map onto some aspect of our conceptual knowledge, but children also can discover the limits that define a concept by determining the limits of the use of a word (Bloom & Lahey, 1978; Olson, 1977). We do not yet, however, have a model for this interplay in early word acquisition. Nor do we have a general method for assessing independently the development of concepts and words in a given domain (see Rice, 1980 for a discussion), which would be necessary to trace the interaction of conceptual and semantic knowledge (but see Mervis, 1985; Smith, 1984; Soja, 1986).

PRINCIPLES THAT CONSTRAIN THE ACQUISITION OF WORD MEANING

Consider for a moment the child's task of deciphering word meaning. Suppose the mother points to a large, black dog lying on a rug in front of a window and says "Xiong." How can the child determine the meaning of this word? There are many possibilities; in fact, there are an "indefinite number of logically possible hypotheses that are consistent (with the mother's behavior)" (Markman, 1987, p. 255). To illustrate a few of these, "Xiong" could mean "dog," "large," "black," "furry," "furry and black," "animal," "dog on a rug" and so forth.

We know that young children acquire words rapidly. Indeed, one diary indicates that in a three-week period around 16 months of age one child acquired 111 new words. Approximately 50 percent of this child's first 300 words had extensions in the first week of use that were comparable to those of adults (Dromi, 1987). Thus, young children are learning many new words, and they are doing this with considerable accuracy. How is this possible when there are so many potential meanings for each word?

Several lines of investigation suggest that at least two principles constrain children's hypotheses about the possible meaning of new words (Clark, 1987, 1988; Markman, 1987). The principle of taxonomic category specifies that when someone points to an object and labels it, children assume that the new word refers to a category of objects. That is, this principle specifies that words refer to whole objects, not their components or attributes (Clark, 1988). The second constraint is the principle of contrast, which is the assumption that objects have only one label (Clark, 1987; Markman, 1987). Thus, with these two constraints some of the possible hypotheses about the meaning of a new word can be eliminated.

THE PRINCIPLE OF TAXONOMIC CATEGORY   As will be evident in Chapter 5, young children organize much of their world in terms of *thematic relations,* or how objects relate to each other and to events. This attention to thematic relations is important because understanding the world requires knowledge of the ways that objects interact (Markman, 1987). Yet, children readily learn words, such as "dog" and "ball," which label object categories, not thematic relations.

Markman and Hutchinson (1984) have demonstrated that early word acquisition is facilitated because young children make the implicit assumption that new words label object categories. In their first study, three-year-olds were shown first a target picture and then two other pictures. They were asked to select the picture that was the same as the target. One of the choice pictures was from the same category as the target picture; the other had a thematic relation (see Table 4-1 for the materials used in this study).

In one condition (the no-word condition) the experimenter pointed to the target and told the child, "Look carefully now. See this?" Then she presented the two choice pictures and told the child to "find another one that is the same as this." The second condition (the novel-word condition) was the same except that the child was told that a puppet talked in puppet talk and the puppet then named the target picture and said, for example, "See this? It is a 'sud.' Find another 'sud' that is the same as this 'sud.' "

In the no-word condition, the children made the taxonomic choice 59 percent of the time. In the novel-word condition, however, this selection oc-

TABLE 4-1 *Pictures Used to Test Word Acquisition*

Standard Object	Taxonomic Choice	Thematic Choice
Police car	Car	Policeman
Tennis shoe	High-heeled shoe	Foot
Dog	Dog	Dog food
Straightbacked chair	Easy chair	Man in sitting position
Crib	Crib	Baby
Birthday cake	Chocolate cake	Birthday present
Blue jay	Duck	Nest
Outside door	Swinging door	Key
Male football player	Man	Football
Male child in swimsuit	Female child in overalls	Swimming pool

Source: Markman, 1987.

curred 83 percent of the time. Thus, when children "think they are learning a new word they look for categorical relationships between objects and suppress the tendency to look for thematic relations" (Markman, 1987, pp. 260–261). Similar effects were demonstrated when children learned unfamiliar words for unfamiliar objects. Despite their early attention to thematic relations, young children assume that novel words label taxonomic categories rather than thematic relations.

We might wonder for a moment why language is organized the way that it is, why the word meanings do not more closely reflect the prevalence of spatial, temporal, and causal relations in our understanding of the world.

> The most important reason may be that if a language had single nouns which refer exclusively to pairs of thematically related objects, it would be at great cost. The enormous expressive power of language would be lost. The expressive power of language derives from its ability to convey new relations through combinations of words. There are a potentially infinite number of thematic relations that one might want to express. The many thematic relations can easily be described through combinations of words—for example, sentences and phrases. If single words referred only to thematic relations, however, there would be an extraordinary proliferation of words, probably more than humans could learn. One would need separate words for a baby and its bottle, a baby and its crib, a baby and its mother, a baby and its diaper, and so on. Thus, the combinatorial power of language would be wasted. This, then, may be the major reason why nouns refer primarily to taxonomic categories, rather than to thematically related objects (Markman, 1987, p. 268).

Somehow, then, young children make an assumption about the nature of language that does not reflect their interest in thematic relations yet is completely appropriate and facilitates their acquisition of word meaning.

THE PRINCIPLE OF CONTRAST   Clark (1987) has argued that contrast is inherent in the nature of language (see Clark, 1988; Gathercole, 1987, for criticisms and discussions of this principle). This principle states that "any difference in *form* in a language marks a difference in *meaning*" (Clark, 1987, p. 2). Clark demonstrates the relevance of this principle for understanding mature language. For example, this principle means that there are no true synonyms. Although two terms may be interchangeable in many contexts, there are contexts in which they are not, and this failure of interchangeability reveals often subtle contrasts in meaning.

Although the principle of contrast has several implications for understanding the nature of language in general, the focus here is on the implications of this principle for understanding word acquisition. Clark has derived three predictions from the principle of contrast. First, children assume that words contrast in meaning. Second, children give priority to known words. Third, children assign novel words that they hear to gaps in their lexicon.

Heibeck and Markman (1987) present data that lends support to the assumption that the principle of contrast guides children's acquisition of word meaning. In one study, two-, three-, and four-year-olds were given a task in which a familiar color, shape, or texture term was contrasted with an unfamiliar term of the same domain. "Each child was asked to help the experimenter by retrieving one of two items that had been placed on a chair in the corner of the room. For example, in the color condition, one child might hear, 'Oh, there's something that you could do to help me. Do you see those two books on the chair in the corner? Could you bring me the chartreuse one, not the red one, the chartreuse one?' " (p. 1023). The familiar and unfamiliar terms for each domain are presented in Table 4-2.

After 10 minutes of casual conversation, the children were tested with three tasks: production, hyponym, and comprehension. The *production* task determined whether the child could produce the new term. For example, in the color condition the child was shown three familiar colors and three unfamiliar colors and asked to name each one. The *hyponym* task was used to assess whether the child knew the domain of the new word. The experimenter presented, for example, a new book with a familiar color (for example, blue) and said, "See this book? It's not chartreuse because it's _____." If the child answered with a color term, it was assumed that the child realized that chartreuse is a color term. In the *comprehension* task, the child was shown "an array of objects representing three unfamiliar and three familiar domain terms and the target term. For this task a child in the color condition would hear, "Can you show me a blue one? Can you show me a chartreuse one?" This was repeated for each term represented in the array (p. 1024).

The results for the comprehension task indicated that the children performed above chance and that there were no age differences. The two-year-olds comprehended as many new words as the older children. There were differences, however, in how well the children learned the different domains,

TABLE 4-2   *Familiar and Unfamiliar Terms*

	Color	Shape	Texture
Unfamiliar	amaranth	hexagon	coarse
	beige	octagon	fibrous
	bice	oval	fleecy
	burgundy	parallelogram	granular
	chartreuse	pentagon	nubbly
	maroon	rectangle	woven
	turquoise	trapezoid	
Familiar	black	round	fuzzy
	blue	square	rough
	brown	triangle	smooth
	green		soft
	orange		
	red		
	white		
	yellow		

Source: Heibeck and Markman, 1987. © The Society for Research in Child Development, Inc.

with all ages comprehending more shape words than color words and more color words than texture words.

In the hyponym task, similar domain differences were evident. All children selected a contrasting shape in the shape condition, but only 56 percent did so in the texture condition. Furthermore, there were age differences with fewer two-year-olds making domain-appropriate selections in the color and texture conditions. Domain, but not age, also had a significant effect in the production task.

Taken together, two studies indicate that children are indeed capable of fast-mapping word meanings. From one exposure to a new term that had been contrasted to a familiar term, the children learned enough to constrain the potential meaning of the new term. Additionally, a second study demonstrated that the linguistic contrast need not be explicit. Fast-mapping was evident in an implicit condition in which the children heard, for example, "Bring me the chartreuse one, not the other one."

The fact that it was easier to learn new terms in some domains (for example, shape) than in others (for example, texture) raises important questions about what conditions, other than contrast, do and do not facilitate the acquisition of word meaning. This issue is yet to be resolved.

The Heibeck and Markman (1987) work supports Clark's assumption that from an early age children assume that words contrast in meaning. Another study supports Clark's prediction that children assign novel words to gaps in their lexicon. Dockrell (1981, cited by Clark, 1987) demonstrated that young children associate unfamiliar words with unfamiliar objects. Three- and four-year-olds were presented with, for example, a set of animals. Three of these were familiar (cow, pig, and sheep); one was unfamiliar (tapir). When they heard a novel word (gombe) they assumed that the novel word labeled the novel animal. Similar effects have been demonstrated with two-year-olds (Golinkoff, Hirsh-Pasek, Baduini & Lavallee, 1985). Furthermore, Golinkoff and her colleagues demonstrated that two-year-old children extended the novel word to a new exemplar from the same category and preferred *not* to use a second novel term for the novel object that they had labeled with the first novel term. Thus, they assumed that two novel terms contrasted in meaning, that they were not synonymous (Clark, 1987).

The principle of contrast means that "children with similar input . . . may differ in the course they follow in organizing their lexicon. Consider their acquisition of terms for animals. Child A acquires the term 'dog' as his first term at a point when his vocabulary totals 20 words. Child B acquires the same term, 'dog,' as her fifth term for an animal (following cat, horse, cow, and rabbit), at a point where her vocabulary totals 150 words. The set of contrasts within the domain for animals for these two children is very different. Child A contrasts 'dog' as the sole animal term with his other 20 words drawn from several domains. Child B contrasts 'dog' with each of four other animal terms, and with the rest of her vocabulary, some five times larger than A's. In the lexicon, different points of acquisition for the same expression may lead to different lexical organizations from child to child. The general point in acquisition is this: 'What's already been acquired affects what gets acquired next' " (Clark, 1987, p. 23).

During the three to four years before children enter school, their lexicons expand rapidly. With the acquisition of words, children acquire an important means for accessing their nonlinguistic knowledge. That is, preschoolers have the capacity to mentally represent spatially and temporally distant objects and events, and words are effective retrieval cues for this information. For example, when children comprehend the question, "Where is Teddy bear?," a retrieval cue has been provided for their knowledge about "Teddy" and its location. Furthermore, children's lexical and conceptual knowledge grows into a complex relationship in which language promotes the acquisition of concepts, and the development of conceptual knowledge leads children to search for the appropriate symbols to express this knowledge.

From an early age children are capable of fast-mapping words to meaning. This mapping is facilitated by two principles that serve to constrain the process of word acquisition. First, children assume that novel words refer to taxonomic categories, not thematic relations or object attributes. Second, children assume that novel words contrast in meaning with familiar terms. They assume that novel terms refer to unfamiliar objects, not to familiar objects that already have labels.

Around the second year, children begin to produce two-word utterances. Many developmental psycholinguists have focused on these productions to determine whether they reflect an underlying linguistic structure. If no such structure existed, we would expect these two-word combinations to be random pairings of the child's one-word vocabulary. This is not the case; regularities of word order are apparent. Developmental psycholinguists seek to determine the nature of the rules that govern children's early "sentences" and how these rules come to match the adults' rules. Such a mission eventually requires a complete and generally accepted adult grammar. Linguists are probably a long way from reaching this goal. As a consequence, there are several alternative grammars of adult language. No one of these is generally accepted; but linguists and psychologists do agree about two points that are relevant for our purposes. One is that syntactic rules involve hierarchical structures. The other is that adult syntax requires an analysis in terms of abstract grammatical categories such as "noun" and "verb."

THE HIERARCHICAL STRUCTURE OF GRAMMAR

For generations linguists have recognized that language has a hierarchical structure, not simply a left-to-right linear structure. This structure can be represented in *phrase structure* grammar, a model similar to that most of us were taught in school. Consider this sentence: They are visiting firemen. Upon reflection you will recognize this sentence is an ambiguous one; it has two possible meanings, yet there is only one string of words. How are you able to distinguish these two meanings? Underlying the string of words are two possible phrase structures. In each there is a noun phrase and a verb phrase, but the structure of the verb phrase differs for the two interpretations, as illustrated in Figure 4-5 (Slobin, 1979). In one case "visiting" is an adjective that modifies the noun "firemen." In the other case "visiting" is a verb describing the action of the noun "they."

Phrase structure grammars recognize that some words in a sentence are more closely related than others. The sentence in Figure 4-5 is ambiguous because it not clear whether "visiting" should go with "firemen" or with "are." But now consider a simple, unambiguous sentence: The boy hit the ball. The words "the ball" appear to go together in a way that "hit the" does not. Rather, the word "hit" appears to relate to the unit "the ball" which can be represented by the single word "it." As illustrated in the top half of Figure 4-6, the words of the sentence can be combined into increasingly larger and more abstract units, with "the boy" represented by "he" and "hit it" by "acted" (Slobin, 1979).

Thus, phrase structure grammars divide a sentence into constituents or

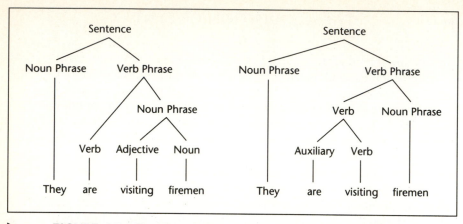

▶ **FIGURE 4-5** *The phrase structure grammar of the sentence, "They are visiting firemen," is ambiguous, allowing two different interpretations of the sentence's meaning: (they) ([are] [visiting firemen]) and (they) ([are visiting] [firemen]). (From Slobin, 1979.)*

parts at several levels. As illustrated in the bottom half of Figure 4-6, the first division is into a noun phrase (NP) and verb phrase (VP). The noun phrase is further divided into an article (the) and a noun (boy). The verbal phrase constituents are verb (hit) and noun phrase, which has the constituents article (the) and noun (ball). Phrase structure grammars, then, assume a finite set of rules for dividing or rewriting sentences into constituent phrases (for example, S → NP + VP). There are, in turn, rewrite rules for phrases (for example, NP → article + adj + noun) with the final level of constituents consisting of word classes, such as noun, verb, and adjective. The final rewrite is from word class to specific word.

Phrase structure grammars have their limitations (Slobin, 1979). As a consequence, many theorists have argued that each sentence is represented at two levels: a surface phrase structure, which is closely related to the specific string of words, and a deep structure, which is related to the underlying meaning of a sentence. For example, transformational grammars assume that the deep structure of the sentence, "Read this sentence" includes the "understood" subject, "you." The rule that transforms the deep structure into the surface structure of that sentence deletes the underlying subject of the sentence.

THE NATURE OF LINGUISTIC CATEGORIES

Although linguists agree that language structure is hierarchical, they differ in their assumptions about the nature of the basic constituents of deep structure. Some linguists (for example, Chomsky, 1957) assume that these constituents are syntactic, for example, noun and verb phrases. Others (for example, Fillmore, 1968) assume that the basic constituents also include semantic relations

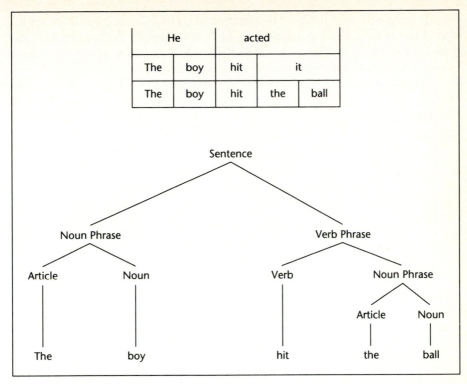

▶ **FIGURE 4-6** *The phrase structure grammar in the sentence, "The boy hit the ball," leaves this sentence unambiguous. As depicted in the top half of this figure, the words can be combined into larger and more abstract units. (Modified from Slobin, 1979.)*

such as agent (the animator–instigator of action), instrument (inanimate force or object which causes the action), and object (the object acted upon). Both types of theory have influenced how psycholinguists have described children's grammars and their assumptions about how language is acquired (see, for example, Bloom, 1970; Braine, 1976; Brown, 1973).

CHILDREN'S GRAMMARS

There are three questions of grammar that we can ask about children's early language. Are linguistic categories evident? If so, what kinds of categories (for example, syntactic or semantic) are used? Are these categories organized in a hierarchical, rather than linear, structure? The early regularities in children's two-word utterances suggest that the answer to the first two questions is that linguistic categories do underlie early productions and that these categories are semantic. This is not to say, however, that there are not individual differences (see Bowerman, 1982; Nelson, 1981). Indeed, some early language is word specific (Braine, 1976). For example, the child Craig (page 146) understood the specific word combinations of "your bottle," "baby's bottle," and "your shoe," but not "Mommy's shoe." Therefore, he did not have the general semantic categories of "possessor" and "possessed."

Although semantic relations can be categorized in a variety of ways (see Howe, 1981, for critical comment), for our purposes the following relationships illustrate the general types of semantic relations that have been inferred from children's two-word utterances (Brown, 1973):

agent + action	Teddy fall
action + object	kick ball
agent + object	baby cookie
action + locative	sit chair
object + locative	birdie tree
possessor + possessed	Daddy chair
attribute + object	red truck
demonstrative + object	here Mommy

In English such semantic relations are indicated syntactically by either word order (for example, John chased Mary vs. Mary chased John), inflections (for example, 's for possession), or prepositions (for example, "The sweater is 'on' the chair" where "on" indicates a locative relation). Because very young children rarely use either inflections or prepositions, if only formal characteristics are used to analyze children's first sentences, then many of these semantic relations would not be evident in their speech. However, some sentences that have the same form on the surface appear to represent very different semantic relations or meanings when one also considers the specific context in which they are spoken. For example, "Daddy car" may indicate agent + object in one context and possessor + possessed in another context (deVilliers & deVilliers, 1982). Within a few months, however, children are expressing combinations of these semantic relations with inflections and the more constrained word orders that occur with longer utterances. For instance, "Teddy fall roof" expresses the relation agent + action + locative. The semantic relations underlying the two-word utterances are now combined with appropriate word order for the three words.

Thus, young children do not begin language imitating adult utterances, rather they express their thoughts using simple rules for semantic relations. Within a few months, the rules become more complex, increasingly reflecting the inflections, prepositions, and word order of their language. With these more complicated forms comes the expression of more complicated thoughts. For example, at 18 months, Eve produces utterances such as "open my toy box" and "head." At 27 months she says, "I put them in the refrigerator to freeze" and "An I want to take off my hat" (deVilliers & deVilliers, 1979).

Children begin language with knowledge about semantic categories (for example, agent, object, and action). But the structure of mature language also includes syntactic categories. These syntactic categories (such as noun and verb) do not directly relate to semantic categories; there is no simple relation between a given semantic category and a particular syntactic category. To illustrate this point, consider these sentences: "The boy chased the girl" and "The girl chased the boy." In both sentences "boy" is a noun and thus subject to the same syntactic rules (for example, pluralization is indicated by adding "-s"). Yet, in the first sentence, "boy" is the agent, and in the second sentence it is the object. The grammatical categories such as noun and verb can only be defined by the syntax of the language. It is our knowledge of syntax that makes it possible to recognize that "boy" is a noun in both sentences. Developmental psycholinguists seek to determine how children break the linguistic code of the adult system; if grammatical categories are defined by syntactical rules and the syntactical rules specify relations between grammatical categories, how can a child break into the system? Although the answer to this question is not immediately evident, we do know that by three years of age children have such categories as noun, verb, and adjective (see Maratsos, 1983, for a review).

In answer to the third question about the organization of early language into either a hierarchical or linear structure, psycholinguists do not agree as to when hierarchical structure first appears in children's language (Peters, 1986). We do have, however, evidence of hierarchical structure in the language of preschool children. Around three or four years of age the very simple sentences of the two year old are expanded into sentences that include noun phrases and verb phrases (see, for example, Bloom, Lahey, Hood, Lifter & Fiess, 1980; Braine, 1987). Probably the most straightforward demonstration of a child's understanding of phrase structure occurs in children's answers to "what" questions. For example, when children are asked "What are you looking for?" and answer "The blue book," their answer reveals an understanding that "what" in the question is a substitute for a noun phrase, "the blue book." Similarly, when children this age answer "What are you doing?" with a verb phrase such as "Playing the fiddle," they exhibit an understanding that "what-do" in the question replaces a verb phrase (deVilliers & deVilliers, 1978).

Furthermore, at this age children are producing complex sentences in which "one sentence (the 'embedded sentence') is subordinated to—i.e., serves as a constituent in—the other ('matrix sentence')" (Bowerman, 1979, p. 285). For example, in "I don't want you read that book" the embedded sentence "you read that book" is the object of the matrix sentence "I don't want. . . ." Between two and four children begin to produce several types of complex sentences that indicate an underlying hierarchical structure (Bowerman, 1979).

Children's knowledge of hierarchical structure is also evident in their ability to appropriately combine morphemes (see Figure 4-1). For example, in English most plural nouns are composed of a word plus a suffix ("-s" or "-es"). In a classic study, Berko (1958) demonstrated that three- and four-year-olds correctly pluralize nonsense words. The children were shown a novel creature and told, "This is a 'wug.' " They were then shown a picture with two of the creatures and asked to complete the sentence, "Now there are two _____." The fact that the children correctly responded with "wugs" indicated that the children had analyzed plural nouns into their constituents and abstracted the pluralization rule.

Indeed, after children derive such rules they may overgeneralize the rule to create novel forms that are not present in adult speech (Brown, Cazden & Bellugi-Klima, 1969). For example, in English the past tense of regular verbs is formed by adding "-ed." Irregular verbs, however, do not have such a pattern: "go" changes to "went" and "do" to "did." Irregular verbs are common in children's early language, and early on they have memorized the correct past tense for each of these verbs and a few regular verbs. Later, however, children learn the general rule governing the past tense for regular verbs and then begin to overgeneralize this ending to irregular verbs: "go" to "goed" and "do" to "doed." These new errors, which could not be imitations of adult speech, nicely demonstrate that the children have analyzed the constituents of regular verbs, constructed a rule about the past tense form, and attempted to impose this newly discovered organization even on irregular verbs.

Thus, we have evidence that preschoolers have accomplished part–whole analyses of sentences (that is, noun phrases, prepositional phrases) as well as the syntactic categories (nouns, verbs). This is not to say that the hierarchical structure of children's syntax does not become more complex, but it serves to illustrate that children are sensitive to the hierarchical structure of language rather early in their language acquisition.

THE RELATION BETWEEN COGNITION AND LANGUAGE

The question here is how cognition contributes to the acquisition of language. To address this question, we must make a distinction between necessary and sufficient conditions for language acquisition. Clearly, the cognitive prerequisites described at the beginning of this chapter are necessary for language acquisition. The fundamental issue is what conditions are sufficient for language acquisition. Although psycholinguists and psychologists do not agree about these conditions (see, for example, Chomsky 1965; Cromer, 1979; Schlesinger, 1977), they do agree for several reasons that a strict learning interpretation will not explain acquisition (Chomsky, 1959). These reasons include the fact that language is species specific; only humans naturally acquire language. Furthermore, children learn language in a relatively short period of time; and, to a large extent, the process of acquisition appears uniform and insensitive to variations in the language environment. Indeed, the language environment of the young child does not appear to have the characteristics necessary for the acquisition of language. Children hear strings of sounds; yet, they acquire rules about the hierarchical structure of language, about syntactic categories, and about rules for relating categories. The language of adults does not specify which sounds belong to which syntactic categories. Nor do adults use positive or negative reinforcement to shape the children's grammar. Parents often correct the truth value of children's utterances, but seldom correct the form of the utterance (Brown, Cazden & Bellugi-Klima, 1969).

Although psycholinguists do not have a comprehensive theory of acquisition, most contemporary models of language acquisition agree on three features of acquisition. First, children are sensitive to regularities or orderly patterns in language. Their observations of regularities lead children to formulate and test hypotheses about language. This is not, however, necessarily a conscious process for the young child. Second, the nature of these hypotheses is constrained by innate characteristics of humans. In principle an infinite number of hypotheses could be generated about language (for example, "pay attention to the second word" or "words starting with 'th' are more important"). Under these circumstances, discovering the correct hypotheses could take a lifetime. Thus, all models assume some innate constraints on the acquisition process. The models differ, however, in whether these constraints are specific to language (see, for example, Chomsky, 1965; Erreich, Valian, & Winzemer, 1980) or whether they are more general cognitive constraints (see, for example, Schlesinger, 1977). Third, linguistic experience is used to confirm or disconfirm hypotheses. On the basis of their observations of others' language behavior and responses to their own language behaviors, children maintain or modify their working hypotheses about the characteristics of language.

Some linguists have argued that language acquisition is unrelated to cognitive development. Chomsky (1957, 1959), for example, argued that humans are born with knowledge of language universals. That is, the child knows in advance that language has a hierarchical structure and that grammar "must have a set of phonological rules for characterizing sound patterns, and a set of semantic rules for dealing with meaning, linked by a set of syntactic rules dealing with word arrangement" (Aitchison, 1977, p. 95).

Chomsky thus assumed that humans are born with *a language acquisition device* (LAD), or mechanisms and knowledge specialized for acquiring language. The environment plays a very limited role, triggering this innate ability to acquire language. Children simply have to discover which language is to be acquired. As have many linguists, Chomsky treated language as a system that is autonomous of other aspects of human development (Elliot, 1981). Chomsky, having rejected the learning interpretation of the Behaviorists, saw no environmental mechanisms for the acquisition of language and offered a nativistic explanation instead.

Others, particularly cognitive psychologists, have argued that cognition determines language acquisition. For example, Piaget's position on language development differs substantially from that of Chomsky's (compare, Piatelli-Palmarini, 1980). Piaget argued that language acquisition depends upon cognitive prerequisites. During the sensorimotor stage, the child's actions in his physical environment culminate in the ability to use signs to stand for objects and in the capacity to mentally represent objects and events. When these two developments are achieved at the end of the sensorimotor period, they can then function together and language is possible. Piaget did not, however, specify the exact role of the cognitive prerequisites in the acquisition of language.

A number of theorists have attempted to specify the influences of cognitive development on language acquisition (see Cromer, 1979, for review). Although a large number of studies indicate parallels between cognitive development and language acquisition, the findings do not support the position that cognition determines language acquisition for two reasons. First, these are correlational studies; therefore, causal interpretations are not appropriate. For example, the fact that there is a correlation between short-term memory capacity and the development of language does not mean that the development of short-term memory causes language acquisition. Indeed, in this case we might argue the opposite. Children have increased capacity to hold information in short-term memory because of the development of more sophisticated linguistic structures, which facilitate *chunking*.

Second, the fact that children have certain cognitions does not mean that these cognitions are enough for language to develop. Cognitive development may be *necessary* for language acquisition, but this does not mean that it is *sufficient* for language acquisition. Clearly, for example, children must have the ability to process auditory information. This does not mean that such an ability is sufficient for language to develop.

A CRITICAL PERIOD FOR LANGUAGE ACQUISITION   Some theorists (for example, Lenneberg, 1967) have assumed that there is a *critical period* for language acquisition. For example, on the basis of indirect evidence Lenneberg (1967) argued that if language is acquired sometime between early infancy and puberty, it is acquired normally, with full fluency. After this critical period, language is acquired with difficulty and without complete success. Until recently, the evidence has been indirect because direct evidence would require isolating children from language experience and then introducing them to a language environment at different ages. Obviously, this is not ethically acceptable.

Recently, however, Newport and her colleagues (Newport, 1986; Newport & Supalla, in press) have assessed the language capabilities of deaf adults who have acquired their primary language, American Sign Language (ASL), at varying ages. If a deaf child is born into a family that uses ASL, that child is exposed to language from an early age. But most deaf children are born into families of hearing parents who do not use ASL. For these children their first experience of ASL occurs when they attend a residential school where the other children use ASL as their everyday language; this first experience can occur at varying ages.

Assessments of ASL skills indicate that the most proficient deaf adults are those who learned ASL at an early age from signing parents. The next proficient were those who acquired ASL between four to six years of age. Those adults who acquired ASL after the age of 12 were the least proficient.

These findings lend support to the assumption that there is a critical period for language acquisition. This assumption can take two forms, however (Johnson & Newport, 1989):

Version One: The Exercise Hypothesis
Early in life, humans have a superior capacity for acquiring languages. If the capacity is not exercised during this time, it will disappear or decline

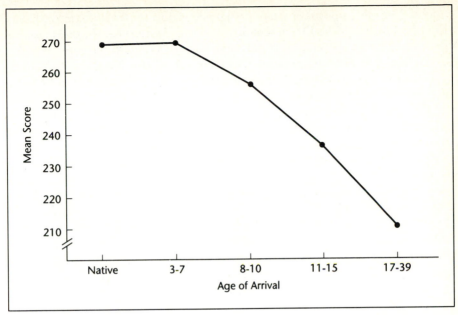

FIGURE 4-7 *The relationship between age of arrival in the United States and total percent correct on the test of English grammar. (From Johnson & Newport, 1989.)*

with maturation. If the capacity is exercised, however, further language learning abilities will remain intact throughout life.

Version Two: The Maturational State Hypothesis
Early in life, humans have a superior capacity for acquiring languages. This capacity disappears or declines with maturation.

To test the implications of these two hypotheses, Johnson and Newport (1989) assessed the English language skills of native Chinese and Korean college students and faculty who had come to this country at different ages. These data indicate that if they were first immersed in English between three and seven years of age their English was equivalent to that of native speakers. After this age, as illustrated in Figure 4-7, there was a steady decline in performance. These data, thus, support the Maturational State Hypothesis.

Taken together, the ASL research and the second language findings suggest that, contrary to Lenneberg's proposal, there is not an abrupt decline at puberty in language acquisition capabilities. Rather, from an early age and up to puberty, there is a steady decline in capability. This suggests a gradual maturational change that has its effect on language acquisition. The next problem is to specify the nature of the maturational change.

MATURATIONAL CONSTRAINTS ON LANGUAGE LEARNING The maturational change in language acquisition occurs as children become more capable in other cognitive domains. In most cognitive domains, children are less capable than adults. Yet, the opposite is true of language acquisition. How can we resolve this seeming paradox? One possibility is that language acquisition is independent of cognitive development and that our special language capability (our LAD) declines with age, independent of cognitive development. Thus, those constraints that make language acquisition possible are intact at an early age, but decay or deteriorate with age.

Newport (1986) has proposed an alternative type of explanation in which she suggests that it is the cognitive limitations of the young child that impose the constraints that facilitate language acquisition. That is, young children have perceptual and memory limitations that serve to constrain the language input that children process. In support of this supposition, Newport presents evidence that early and late learners of ASL make different types of errors as they acquire the language. Late learners are more likely to make holistic errors; early learners make component (morpheme) errors. This suggests to Newport that late learners analyze ASL as holistic structures; they are capable of processing whole signs and do so. The younger learners, unable to process whole signs, are acquiring the components (morphemes) of the signs. Since ASL has a morphological structure (see, for example, Meier, 1987), this gives the advantage to young learners. Whatever the eventual resolution of this issue, the maturational changes in language acquisition indicate "that some significant internal constraints are required to account for why children, and only children, uniformly succeed in learning language" (Newport, 1986, p. 14).

Although psycholinguists and developmental psychologists have yet to resolve the relations between language and cognition in general (for reviews, see Cromer, 1979; Rice, 1980), we do see specific indications that, early in the acquisition of language, the interplay of nonlinguistic and linguistic knowledge and strategies is not a simple one. Three of these interactions are illustrated here.

THE EFFECT OF NONLINGUISTIC KNOWLEDGE ON LANGUAGE COMPREHENSION

Young children have gained nonlinguistic knowledge about their world prior to the acquisition of language and we have some evidence that this knowledge affects their efforts at language comprehension. The few studies that have attempted to identify the strategies that young children use to comprehend sentences (for example, Chapman & Kohn, 1978; Strohner & Nelson, 1974) indicate that two- and three-year olds are likely to use a *probable event strategy* to interpret active and passive sentences. Children this age correctly interpret sentences such as "The girl feeds the baby" and "The baby is fed by the girl," but misinterpret "The baby feeds the girl" and "The girl is fed by the baby." Thus, there is no evidence that children this age use the rules for active or passive sentences in comprehension. Rather, they rely upon their knowledge of familiar situations to interpret sentences with familiar words.

By three years of age children also use a *word order strategy* as evident in their interpretation of semantically reversible sentences, such as "The girl follows the boy" and "The boy follows the girl." These are sentences for which the probable event strategies would not lead to a choice between the two possible interpretations. Children this age use an *actor-action-object strategy* in which the first noun in the sentence is interpreted as the actor and the second as the object. Children using such a strategy should correctly interpret active reversible sentences (for example, "The girl follows the boy") but misinterpret passives (for example, "The boy is followed by the girl"). This is the case for three-year-olds (Strohner & Nelson, 1974). The use of this strategy for active sentences is further influenced by the animacy of the nouns, with animate nouns (for example, kitty) in the first position more likely to be interpreted as actors than inanimate nouns (for example, door) (Chapman & Kohn, 1978). This may well reflect the children's experience that animate objects are more likely to act than inanimate objects. By five years of age children are, for the most part, relying on syntactic information to interpret active and passive sentences; errors still occur, however, for sentences that state improbable events in the passive voice, for example, "The bear was caught by the mouse."

Although there are individual differences in the strategies that young children use to comprehend sentences (Bridges, 1980; Chapman & Kohn, 1978), the earliest comprehension strategies are influenced more by context, including the child's knowledge about objects and events, than by syntactic structure (see Clark, 1980). Over the next few years, however, syntax increasingly influences the child's interpretation of sentences.

Even for adults, language comprehension demonstrates the interplay of syntax, semantics, linguistic context, nonlinguistic context, and general knowledge in the process of comprehension (see, for example, Flores d'Arcais & Schreuder, 1983). Language comprehension is viewed as an interactive process in which both top-down and bottom-up processes contribute information. Clearly, bottom-up processes that access phonological, lexical, and syntactic information are necessary components of adult comprehension. But just as clearly, top-down processes, which specify the linguistic and nonlinguistic context as well as relevant general knowledge, play a role. This is perhaps most evident when a sentence is metaphorical or ambiguous, as illustrated nicely by the following excerpt from an Erma Bombeck article (H. Clark, 1983, p. 298):

> We thought we were onto a steam iron yesterday, but we were too late. Steam irons never have any trouble finding roommates. She could pick her own pad and not even have to share a bathroom. Stereos are a dime a dozen. Everyone's got their own systems. We've just had a streak of bad luck. First, our Mr. Coffee flunked out of school and went back home. When we replaced her, our electric typewriter got married and split, and we got stuck with a girl who said she was getting a leather coat, but she just said that to get the room.

Without context and knowledge about college roommates, phrases such as "stereos are a dime a dozen" and "our electric typewriter got married" cannot be interpreted appropriately.

What information do children use in comprehension? Bottom-up processes are evident in the early language comprehension of children. Phonological and lexical analyses must be executed for children to comprehend individual words. But given these bottom-up processes, young children also use their knowledge of the nonverbal world (top-down) to interpret how the meanings of the individual words are related. Only gradually during the preschool years do we see evidence that children use syntactic analysis to comprehend sentences. Yet, even when they have the syntactic knowledge, knowledge of the world can override the syntactic analysis.

Lempert and Kinsbourne (1983) argue that young children differ from older children and adults in the extent to which salient perceptual features of the nonverbal context control comprehension. Thus, even when there is evidence that young children have acquired a linguistic rule, a conflicting nonverbal context that attracts attention may dominate the child's interpretation of a sentence. (In Chapter 6 this conflict between "rules" and responses based on current perceptions is evident in preoperational children's attempts to solve the tasks Piaget used to assess the development of concrete operations.) The fact that five-year-olds comprehend passive sentences except when they involve improbable events is a case that illustrates the point. Young children's comprehension and production are often influenced by the perceptual events of the here and now. That is, young children usually talk about those aspects of their immediate environment that attract their attention. Similarly, they understand sentences in terms of what attracts their attention in the nonverbal context and their nonlinguistic knowledge of such structures. Thus, the context can be both supportive and misleading depending upon the relation between the context and the intention of the speaker.

As adults we usually are not aware that, initially, the nonverbal context of the listener can be very different from that of the speaker. We have learned to use all information available to us in an interactive comprehension process. As an example, consider a recent telephone conversation that I had one morning:

▶ Melinda: "Hello."
Caller: "Melinda?"
Melinda: "Yes."
Caller: "It's Harry. You're up."

My immediate nonverbal context indicated that indeed I was standing and I was awake. But why would anyone call me to tell me that? And who was Harry? Harry knew me well enough to call me by my first name. Yet, I have no friends or students who are named Harry. As I searched my memory for someone named "Harry" the connection between "Harry" and "up" came to me. I had left my computer for repair a few days earlier. Harry was not commenting on my state; he was commenting on the state of my computer.

If we recognize that the nonverbal context of speaker and listener do not always match when conversation begins, and that young children are dominated by what attracts them and do not make the adjustments evident in the above example, then we might understand why young children's comprehension of sentence structure may or may not match the syntactic knowledge evident in their production. Productions are about children's thoughts. When they learn linguistic rules, they use them to express their thoughts; there are no conflicts between attention and linguistic expression. But if young children's nonverbal contexts do not match that of the speakers', the salient features of the context may dominate the interpretation, even when they know the linguistic rules.

As children mature they are less dominated by the immediate situation and increasingly able to select their own strategies for comprehension. In the above example, I actively sought to remember Harry and rejected my immediate nonverbal context as a strategy for interpreting, "You're up." To fully know, or represent, the meaning intended by a speaker, the listener must be able to represent the context to which the speaker's utterance refers. But this context is not a given; it is a frame of reference that is constructed (Bridges, Sinha & Walkerdine, 1981). Young children have yet to acquire the skills and strategies that make it possible to access information that is not readily available or to integrate information from the many available sources.

EFFECTS OF LANGUAGE ON CATEGORIZATION

As children learn linguistic rules, they are capable of using these rules to categorize novel words and the objects they represent. Preschoolers come to know that different types of grammatical classes correspond to different kinds of concepts. For example, children as young as 17 months can use sentence structure to distinguish between proper names and object names (Katz, Baker & Macnamara, 1974; Macnamara, 1982). In one study children were shown pairs of dolls that were identical except for hair color or pairs of blocks that differed only in color. Half the children were trained with a nonsense object name. For example, one object of the pair was labeled by saying: "Look what I've brought you. This is a 'zav.' " On subsequent training trials, the same object was referred to as "the 'zav.' " In English, of course, the articles "a" and "the" before a word indicate a word that refers to a category of objects. In the proper name condition the object was named without the article: "Look what I've brought you. This is 'Zav.' "

After the name training, the children were tested by requests to perform a variety of actions with the named object. For example, the pair of objects were placed before the children who were then asked to show the named object to their mothers. Those children who were trained with the pair of dolls in the proper name condition more often chose the specific object that had been named during training. This was not the case with the object name training; these children equally often chose either doll. Such a finding suggests that the linguistic form of the name training led the children in the proper name condition to identify the nonsense syllable as a proper name for a specific doll, whereas children in the common noun condition inferred that "zav" was a category label.

The results for the block pairs indicate, however, that the children's use of syntactic information depended upon the nature of the objects named. The children in the proper name condition did not select the named block more often than the other block. This effect was demonstrated in two separate experiments with 17- and 22-month-old girls. Thus, the children made use of the linguistic evidence with dolls but not with blocks. Macnamara argues that their prior experience with dolls and blocks has led them to distinguish between two types of object classes, those in which individuality of the objects is salient (for example, people) and those in which it is not. Having learned this distinction, children use the linguistic form for proper names only with the class of objects (dolls) for which individuality of objects is salient, and this appears to be the case for unfamiliar objects (animal-like toys) as well as familiar ones (Gelman & Taylor, 1984).

At least by four years of age (the youngest age tested) children can use syntactic form to distinguish the grammatical categories of verb, mass noun, and count noun (Brown, 1957). In English, verbs are signaled by syntactic forms such as the "-ing" in "The dog is runn*ing*." Mass nouns such as "snow," "milk," and "clay" are nouns that do not have a characteristic form or size and are used in the singular with "any" and "some" in sentences like "Do you have *any milk?*" and 'I want *some clay.*' Count nouns, however, refer to individual objects and the singular form is preceded by "a" or "the" as in, "I want *a book*" and "Have you seen *the key?*" Brown (1957) demonstrated that four-year-olds can use these syntactic cues for grammatical categories to determine the referents of novel words. For example, when asked to show a picture of "sibbing," the children selected an action picture, rather than a picture of an object. Thus, the children are using syntactic knowledge to determine word class and then using the word class of a novel word to determine the appropriate referent in the given nonlinguistic context.

In summary, as children learn the syntactical rules of language they are able to use this knowledge and their knowledge of the correlations between conceptual distinctions and linguistic classes to infer the referents of novel words. Although adult grammatical classes are not perfectly correlated with conceptual distinctions, young children appear capable of using imperfect correlations to map the linguistic code to their nonlinguistic knowledge.

Furthermore, young children's knowledge of conceptual distinctions will guide their use of newly acquired linguistic knowledge. Thus, we saw that two-year-olds will only use the proper name distinction with object classes in which individuality is salient. Further research will be necessary to determine whether this relationship between conceptual knowledge and emerging linguistic knowledge is a common pattern as children acquire new linguistic distinctions during the several years of language acquisition.

RELATIONS BETWEEN SENSORIMOTOR DEVELOPMENT AND THE CONTENT OF EARLY WORDS

Gopnik and her colleagues (1982; Gopnik & Meltzoff, 1984, 1986a,b) have demonstrated that certain kinds of meanings develop at about the same time that children solve specific related problems (Gopnik & Meltzoff, 1986a,b). In particular, they have demonstrated positive correlations between children's performance on the object permanence task and their use of disappearance words such as "gone." Similarly, they have demonstrated a comparable relation between the understanding of means–ends and the use of words to indicate success (for example, "there") and failure (for example, "uh-oh").

In one of these studies, Gopnik and Meltzoff (1986a) followed 19 children longitudinally until they acquired both disappearance and success/failure words. At the same time the children were tested periodically with variations of Piaget's object permanence and means–ends tasks. The data indicate positive correlations between the development of object permanence and the use of disappearance words. Similarly, there was a correlation between means–ends performance and the occurrence of success/failure words. It is important to note that these relations were specific. Performance on the object-concept task was not related to the use of success/failure words; nor was the use of disappearance words positively correlated with means–ends performance.

Thus, we have evidence that early in language development the content or meaning of children's frequent one-word utterances is related to their emerging conceptual knowledge. Furthermore, Gopnik and Meltzoff (1986a) present some evidence to suggest that cognitive and semantic changes occur concurrently. At this point, however, we can only speculate how each might serve to influence and facilitate the other. We do know that the content of children's early speech is related to their conceptual development. Young children talk about the "conceptual problems" that they are working on. Since the development of object permanence and means–ends skill have extended periods of development, we might look for an interplay between this conceptual development and the acquisition of words that label these conceptual achievements. But one thing should be emphasized: the correlations between cognitive development and language development do not mean that cognitive development is sufficient for language development. Indeed, we have evidence that dogs are capable of object permanence (Pasnak, Kurkjian & Triana, 1988). This does not imply that dogs are, therefore, capable of communicating this knowledge.

LANGUAGE AND THOUGHT

There is no simple relation between language and cognition. Although cognitive capacities, processes, operations, and concepts such as object permanence may be necessary for language to develop, there is, as yet, no evidence that cognitive competencies strongly determine language.

However, it is obvious to all of us that as language develops it is inextricably linked to thought. This is not to say that language is thought. We can cite many examples and studies to refute this position (see Howard, 1983, Chapter 7). Yet much of our education and consequent acquisition of knowledge is based upon language. As I sit here writing, I am aware that I am formulating and evaluating my thoughts verbally as internal speech.

THE INTRAPERSONAL FUNCTION OF LANGUAGE   The emphasis in this chapter has been on the interpersonal functions of language. Yet, we know that there are times when we use language without the intention of communicating to another. In an attempt to specify how culture comes to influence children's cognitive development and to regulate their behavior, the Soviet psychologist Vygotsky (1934/1962), proposed a developmental model of the relationship between speech and thought. Vygotsky argued that thought and speech have different origins in ontogenetic development. There is a preintellectual stage of early speech development when a child's utterances are not meaningful. Similarly, there is a prelinguistic stage of thought when a child's thoughts are not expressed in speech. In the early years, these two lines of development proceed independently, but during the preschool years thought and speech gradually become interdependent; thoughts are verbalized as inner speech and speech becomes meaningful.

Vygotsky sought to specify how the thoughts that control our behavior develop. As adults we all have had the experience of verbally thinking through our actions before acting. When I play croquet, there are times when my next shot is not immediately obvious. At these times I step back to consider the positions of the balls and to think through the several options open to me. As I assess each possibility, I silently verbalize the consequences of each potential move and eventually make a decision that directs my behavior. Vygotsky sought to understand how such verbal thinking or inner speech develops. Vygotsky saw the origins of the development of inner speech and voluntary action in the early social interactions of adults and children. Adults use language to manipulate and control children's behavior. At first, voluntary actions occur when a child performs in response to an adult command. As we have seen, infants are attentive to adult speech. At an early age adult speech can attract a child's attention to a specific object. For example, at eight months of age, Reich's son shifted his attention and crawled to his mother's closet when asked, "Where's the shoes?"

Vygotsky argued that as children acquire language they begin to make overt spoken commands to themselves. Thus, they use "private speech" to control their own behavior. Language is used "as an instrument of thought, . . . as a tool to plan, guide and monitor problem-solving activity" (Frauenglass & Diaz, 1985, p. 357). Gradually, this speech is internalized. The speech becomes covert; the child instructs himself through inner speech. Inner speech is difficult to define since it is unobservable, but Vygotsky asserted that inner speech is abbreviated and comes closest to what we experience as silent verbal thought. Thus, Vygotsky assumed that with the internalization of speech verbal thinking develops; one type of thought, thus, becomes verbal in form.

Vygotsky's theory has stimulated several lines of research. Here we consider one of these: the nature of young children's private speech. In Chapter 9 we further consider Vygotsky's theory and its implications for the development of problem-solving skills.

THE DEVELOPMENT OF PRIVATE SPEECH   Vygotsky's theory predicts a developmental increase in the appearance of private speech and then a decline as inner speech replaces private speech. The several studies attempting to verify this inverted U relationship between age and the incidence of private speech suggest that the developmental pattern is more complex (see Fuson, 1979, for a review). Taken together, this research suggests that two-year-olds produce a high level of private speech, that following this there is a decline followed by another high level between four and five years of age. Finally, there is a decline in private speech through the elementary school years. The complexity of these findings probably reflects, in part at least, the effects of differences in methodology. These studies differed in the settings for assessing private speech, how private speech is defined, and the nature of the task before the child. For example, task difficulty should affect the incidence of private speech, with private speech more likely if a task is difficult for a child (Vygotsky, 1962).

We do know, however, that when young children are alone they do talk to themselves. In a now-classic study, Weir (1962) recorded the presleep talk of her two-year-old son. This work and subsequent research (see, for example, Kuczaj, 1983) indicate that children this age engage in language play in which they practice linguistic forms. During this play, children make several types of modifications including substitutions such as the following (Britton, 1970):

> but I don't be sick like this
> but I don't be sick in bed
> but I don't be sick on the bed

They also use forms of discourse such as the following (Kuczaj, 1983):

> He's in trunk. He's in back. Miss Piggy in back. I put Miss Piggy in back. I put bunny rabbit in back. I put Miss Piggy in trunk. I put Miss Piggy in trunk first, first. I put Miss Piggy in back. Put bunny rabbit in the . . . back.

Overt language play in the crib appears to drop out by three years of age as does overt practice in general by four years of age (Kuczaj, 1983). Thus, overt language play and practice is most prevalent during the time that language acquisition is at its height, when, presumably, language is most difficult for the child. The frequency of overt private speech declines as children acquire more and more knowledge of language. Now, presumably, when language play and practice occur, it is in the covert form of inner speech. For example, as I prepared to write the previous sentence, I did not say the sentence aloud first. I was aware, however, of thinking about what I wanted to say and verbally practicing the form the sentence would take on paper.

Further, Nelson (1984) has demonstrated that a two-year-old's private talk before sleep may serve as a means for reviewing daily experiences. In this study, Nelson recorded the presleep dialogues between Emily and a parent, as well as Emily's presleep monologues. Although the earliest monologues (21–22 months of age) freely intermix the past, present, and future and have the feel of stream of consciousness, by 23 months of age Emily was reviewing rather accurately an event that occurred earlier in the day. (In the following excerpt, Tanta is Emily's name for the babysitter and Mormor is her name for her grandmother [p. 121]):

> 23;8 When Mormor make pretty mommy had a help my slept and mommy came and mommy said "get up time go home." [Emily imitates Mommy's call.] Then my slept and to wake Mormor coming. Then get up time go home. Time to go home. Yesterday did that. Now Emmy sleeping in regular bed. Yesterday my slept in Tantas house and mommy woke me and Emmy go "time a go *home*." Then Daddy bring P water* up. And yesterday Daddy and Mommy and Mormor and Daddy bring me in my regular bed. Actually Mommy got me. [True] Daddy and Mommy threw my kitten in and Mommy Daddy make my bed. Threw threw mommy kitten in. Bring my, bring bring . . . I sleeping Tanta house. Mommy come and woke me up and call me "Time go home!" Woke(?) and mommy said time bring P water. Then mommy-daddy put me in the bed in my regular bed. Actually, actually Mommy did it.
>
> *Perrier Water

In the preceding monologue Emily is recalling what happened earlier in the day when she slept at the babysitter's. "Yesterday" serves to indicate the past.

Around 24 months Emily begins to make plans and to speculate about possibilities. For example, in the following monologue she considers the possible causes, intentions, or goals that would explain why Daddy is running (p. 124):

> 23;6 That the daddy. Coming up and running downstairs. And running and running and running downstairs. Daddy running and running down here get some dinner. I don't know. Maybe Daddy getting food for muffins. *Maybe.* I don't know what Daddy getting downstairs. Maybe Daddy getting some books or getting blanket. I don't know what Daddy doing. Maybe getting some books.

Emily's monologues also make a connection with the presleep dialogue with her father. Emily has been told "that after nap they would go to Childworld and buy an intercom so that they could hear the baby when he cried in other parts of the house. This explanation was repeated three times at Emily's insistence" (p. 116). In the monologue Emily cannot remember "intercom" but substitutes for the word what she remembers about it. Then she elaborates on her trip to Childworld by including the purchase of an infant seat (p. 117):

> 23;15 Daddy says buy diapers for Stevie and Emmy and buy something for Stephen plug in and say a-h-h [imitating his cry] and put in . . . on Saturday go Childworld buy diaper for Emmy and diaper for the baby and then buy something for the Emmy and see for that baby plug in and that diapers for anybody, and buy moon that day, at Childworld and buy coats and maybe Childworld 'cause that one at broken at Tanta's. The one that's broken here . . . the infant seat. . . .

Thus, in her presleep private talk we see Emily reconstructing past events, speculating on present events, and planning future events. In all these Emily uses her prior knowledge and information gained through language to solve problems. As Emily overtly works on these problems, the information gained through language is internalized. With acquisition of language, Emily has the means for reviewing and transforming her experiences. With language she can differentiate past, present, and future, explore possibilities, and distinguish the general from the specific. Through language Emily acquires knowledge and with her own overt speech she transforms the information and makes it her own (Nelson, 1984).

Central to Vygotsky's model of private speech is the assertion that private speech has different functions than social speech. In particular, private speech has a self-regulatory function that is not evident in social speech. To test this possibility, Furrow (1984) compared the social and private utterances of 23- to 25-month-olds as they played in the presence of an experimenter. Twelve categories of speech function were coded during the play sessions; these are described as follows (Furrow, 1984):

1. Instrumental: An utterance refers to the child's wants, and/or an utterance is whined—for example, "I want it."
2. Regulatory: An utterance refers to an event that might be immediately carried out; another person is the specified agent, or there is no agent and the child does not perform the action herself—for example, "Go there."
3. Self-regulatory: An utterance refers to an event that might be immediately carried out; the child is the stated agent or there is no agent and the child performs the action herself—for example, "I put that there."
4. Attentional: An utterance refers to a sensory event that is ongoing or might be immediately carried out—for example, "Look."
5. Interactional: Utterance content is a conventional greeting—for example, "Hi."
6. Expressive: Utterance content is an evaluative opinion, an expression of an internal state, or a stock phrase that expresses feeling—for example, "I love you."
7. Referential: An utterance refers to a present object or a present event that does not involve the child—for example, "That."

8. Describing own activity: An utterance refers to an ongoing or just completed event in which the child was involved—for example, "Putting it."

9. Question: Utterance intonation contour resembles adult rising question intonation and/or an utterance is syntactically a question—for example, "What that?"

10. Imaginary: An utterance is sung, is word play, or represents a transformation of real objects or events, whether present or not—for example, "That hat" (said of block on head).

11. Informative: An utterance refers to a nonpresent object or event—for example, "Daddy at work."

12. Incomprehensible: An utterance is inaudible or incomprehensible.

The results indicated that the children were more likely to describe their own activity and to make self-regulatory utterances when they were engaged in private speech. Informative, regulatory, and attentional utterances were more likely, however, when the child was making social contact with the experimenter. Although this research suggests that differentiation of private speech from social speech occurs at an earlier age than expected from Vygotsky's model (p. 134), the findings do support his assertion that, unlike social speech, private speech has a self-regulatory function.

We do not have a clear picture of the development of private speech during the preschool years, but a recent longitudinal study indicates that, as expected during the early elementary school years, private speech declines as speech is internalized. In this study, Bivens and Berk (1988) observed children from first through third grade as they worked at their seats on math problems. Relying on earlier attempts to identify private speech (for example, Kohlberg, Yaeger & Hjertholm, 1968), these researchers coded the children's utterances into nine categories that specified three levels of private speech (Bivens & Berk, 1988):

1. Level 1: Self-stimulating, task-irrelevant private speech
   a) Word play and repetition
   b) Task-irrelevant affect expression
   c) Comments to absent, imaginary, or nonhuman objects
2. Level 2: Task-relevant externalized private speech
   a) Describing one's own activity and self-guiding comments
   b) Task-relevant, self-answered questions
   c) Reading aloud and sounding out words
   d) Task-relevant affect expression (e.g., "I did it!")
3. Level 3: Task-relevant external manifestations of inner speech
   a) Inaudible muttering: remarks involving clear mouthing of words which cannot be heard.
   b) Lip and tongue movement: no clear mouthing of words, just lip and tongue movements.

The results indicated that in each grade private speech occurred during 60 percent of the observation intervals. Although the percentage of private

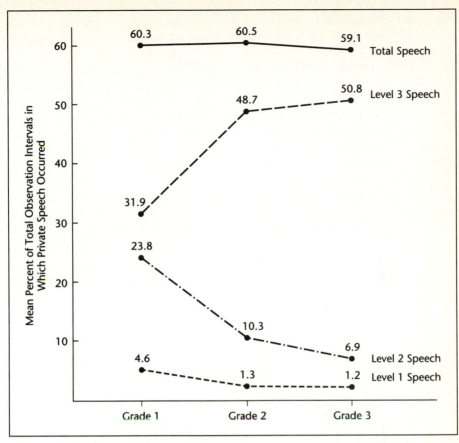

60.3   60.5   59.1   Total Speech

50.8 Level 3 Speech

48.7

31.9

23.8

10.3

6.9 Level 2 Speech

4.6   1.3   1.2 Level 1 Speech

60

50

40

30

20

10

Mean Percent of Total Observation Intervals in
Which Private Speech Occurred

Grade 1   Grade 2   Grade 3

▶ **FIGURE 4-8**   *Level 1 task-irrelevant speech decreases with age. Level 2 private speech decreases at the same time Level 3 inner speech increases with age. (From Bivens and Berk, 1988.)*

speech did not change during the three years, as expected from Vygotsky's model, the type of private speech did change. As indicated in Figure 4-8, Level 1 task-irrelevant speech decreased with age. Level 3 internalized speech, however, increased with age. And as illustrated, the large decrease in Level 2 private speech occurs at the same time that there is a dramatic increase in Level 3 inner speech.

Vygotsky assumed that as private speech develops it serves to control the child's own behavior. Although other studies (see, for example, Goodman, 1981) and the Bivens and Berk findings do suggest a relationship between the development of private speech and other task-related behaviors, such as attention and self-control of behavior, it is not clear that the development of private speech brings attention and behavior under control. Rather, there may be a *more* complex relationship between private speech, attention, and self-regulation (Bivens & Berk, 1988). Resolution of this issue must await further research.

Finally, private speech may serve more than a self-regulatory function for initiating behavior. Meacham (1979), for example, has proposed that young children tend to forget anticipated goals and that verbalizations "may play a role in remembering the goals of motor activities and consequently in testing or evaluating the outcome of those motor activities relative to intended goals . . ." (p. 257). Meacham proposes that, initially, young children use verbalizations to describe the outcome of their motor activity. Later in development, however, verbalizations precede the motor activity and are used to describe the anticipated goals of the activity. Such verbalizations of anticipated goals can then serve to facilitate memory for the goals, evaluation of outcomes, and subsequent corrections in behavior. If Meacham is correct, then we have further reason to believe that private speech plays an important role in the development of children's ability to think through a problem, to assess their progress, and to adjust their behavior (see Kendall & Braswell, 1985, for a review of the research on training impulsive children to use self-verbalizations).

In summary, when children acquire language they acquire a powerful cognitive tool. Language is an effective retrieval cue for accessing mental representations. Children are no longer dependent upon the potential retrieval cues of the perceptual "here and now" to access their knowledge. Their thoughts can be directed to past and future events, as well as to real and imaginary objects.

Language, of course, is also a means for children to express their thoughts and to share information. Through verbal exchanges, children test the appropriateness of their conceptual distinctions and modify them when necessary. The child who approaches a wolf at the zoo, calls it "doggie," and is corrected by a parent, learns that, perceptual similarities aside, some "dog-like" animals are not treated like dogs, are not called "doggie," and are not petted. Furthermore, with the acquisition of language children are no longer dependent upon their own personal experiences for the acquisition of knowledge. The traditions and history of the culture can be transmitted through language. Increasingly, their knowledge of the world, both physical and social, is mediated by language.

Further, with the acquisition of language children have acquired a means for directing, assessing, and regulating their own behaviors. When private speech is internalized, thoughts can be formulated as verbal propositions. In this form thought has all the flexibility and creativity of language itself. Children can consider the possible and the impossible, the future and the past, the general and the specific. They can instruct themselves, reprimand themselves, and reward themselves. Communicative functions that initially were restricted to interpersonal communication become intrapersonal as well.

SUMMARY

Early in the preschool years, children begin to acquire a language. This accomplishment entails several prerequisite cognitive skills. These include knowledge of objects and events, the ability to organize a whole into its parts, the ability to form categories, the ability to learn and manipulate symbols, the ability to use language as a tool, the ability to understand and produce sequences of actions, and the intention to communicate with others.

Before language develops, around 8 to 10 months of age, children are expressing their intents to communicate through gestures and vocalizations. In particular, children begin to make requests in which they gain the attention of another and then indicate their desires. At the same time they make references to objects and events simply to inform another. Both of these communicative functions appear to develop out of early infant–mother interactions.

When children begin to produce words, the meanings of their words do not always match the adult meanings, and comprehension typically precedes production. Although we do not have an adequate model of how word meanings are acquired, we do know that young children are capable of fast-mapping and that the acquisition process is constrained by two principles: the principle of taxonomic category and the principle of contrast.

Around two years of age, children begin to produce two-word utterances. Underlying these utterances are simple rules of semantic relations. In the later preschool years it becomes evident that children's language has a hierarchical structure of syntactic rules that relate grammatical categories.

Although we do not have a model of how cognitive development relates to language acquisition, we do know that language acquisition is most effective in the younger years when cognitive skills are not fully developed. It is not clear whether the maturational constraints on language acquisition represent changes in a language acquisition device or general constraints imposed by cognitive limitations.

As children acquire language, conceptual development is interlinked with linguistic knowledge. Young children, for example, use nonlinguistic context to comprehend language, and linguistic knowledge influences how children categorize objects and events. Further, the earliest words appear to express their developing sensorimotor knowledge of object permanence and means–ends relations.

Young children not only use language for communicative, interpersonal functions, but also for intrapersonal functions. When alone they overtly practice language forms, review the day's activities, and plan future activities. Young children also appear to use overt private speech to regulate their own activities. With development this overt private speech becomes internalized as inner speech, which appears to guide our plans and activities.

5

Early Childhood: The Representation of Knowledge about Events, Concepts, and Theories

During the preschool years, children not only acquire knowledge about language, but also expand their knowledge about the physical and social world, a process that persists through adulthood. In this chapter we consider various ways of characterizing the nature of this knowledge and its organization. This issue has more than one approach. Until recently, developmental psychologists have concentrated on the form or the mode of knowledge representation. They have recognized the possibility of three types of knowledge: *sensorimotor, imaginal,* and *conceptual.* Further, many have postulated that each of these has a different mode of representation. Thus, for example, my knowledge of how to ride a bike or to walk is represented in some type of motor code, and my ability to bring to mind a familiar tune or a specific painting is dependent upon some type of imaginal code. But we also have abstract, conceptual knowledge that cannot be represented in a sensorimotor or imaginal code. Consider abstract concepts such as "liberty." Many people may report that they have an image associated with the concept of "liberty," such as the Statue of Liberty, but this image cannot be the concept itself since the image does not include the type of information that would make it possible to distinguish between instances of liberty and nonliberty. Therefore, most cognitive psychologists, in an effort at parsimony, assume that concepts are represented in the form of *amodal propositions*. That is, my representation of a concept is a set of descriptive propositions that in some way characterize the members of the category. These propositions are abstract, however, and may or may not be readily visualized or verbalized.

Many psychologists assume that concepts are the elementary or basic units of knowledge for humans and have, therefore, sought to determine the nature of our concepts. It is these mental representations that not only symbolize my past experience, but also guide my extensions of my concepts. That is, concepts not only represent my own experience with specific instances of a concept, but also carry information that makes it possible to recognize new, unfamiliar instances of a concept. Thus, my concept for "table" guides my decision about whether a novel object is or is not a table, regardless of obvious perceptual variations in color, size, material, and style. Concepts also guide our inferences about new instances of concepts. For example, when I am told that the small sapling before me is a peach tree, I infer that this object has a certain genetic makeup and that eventually it will have the characteristics that define the category "peach tree."

Concepts are not isolated units of information; rather, they relate to each other in a variety of complex ways. For example, to know the concepts "dog," "cat," and "banana" is to know that cat and dog are more closely related than dog and banana or cat and banana. Similarly, to know the concepts "dog" and "cat" is to know how these concepts contrast with each other. Furthermore, our knowledge of conceptual relations can guide our inferences about new concepts. To learn that "pangolins" are "mammals" leads to the inference that pangolins are warm-blooded vertebrates that nurse their young. Without perceptual experience I would not recognize a pangolin, but I would know the relation of the "pangolin" concept to the "mammal" concept and that those characteristics that are true of mammals are also true of pangolins.

Finally, we have extensive knowledge about events. We know the component activities of familiar events and how the activities relate to each other. Students, for example, come to the first day of a class with certain expectations about what will happen in the next hour. Some activities are considered more likely than others. What student would not be surprised if the instructor served champagne and caviar and then asked the class to take the final exam for the course?

► THE REPRESENTATIONAL-DEVELOPMENT HYPOTHESIS

Some theorists (for example, Bruner, Olver & Greenfield, 1966; Piaget & Inhelder, 1971; Werner, 1948) have proposed a developmental change in the mode of knowledge representation. Although there are variations in details, the common assumption is that, initially, knowledge is represented in an enactive or *motoric mode*. For example, as we have seen, Piaget assumes that during the first year and one-half an infant's knowledge of the world is limited to a *sensorimotor mode of representation*. Later, according to the variations of the representational-development hypothesis, an imaginal or *ikonic mode of representation* develops. Still later a *conceptual form of representation* develops. This is not to say that each new mode of representation supplants earlier modes; rather, each new mode of representation is a more powerful means for representing knowledge. To illustrate, no one has learned to play squash by watching someone else or by verbal instruction. The knowledge is acquired through repeated motor efforts. But with an imaginal mode of representation we are capable of representing perceptual experiences, independent of our own actions. If we have seen it played, we can imagine a game, even if we never have played. With some form of conceptual representation, we are also capable of representing abstract knowledge. With only enactive and imaginal knowledge I could play and imagine a game, but I would not be able to give verbal instructions in strategy and technique or specify how squash is and is not similar to tennis.

In Chapter 3 we reviewed the infant research on the development of sensorimotor intelligence and, particularly, object permanence, which marked for Piaget the development of imaginal representation. Here we focus on the assumption that, prior to the development of conceptual representation, children are limited to ikonic or imaginal representations. In a review of the relevant research, Kosslyn (1978) has argued that the evidence is inconclusive for two reasons. First, the theorists who proposed versions of the representational-development hypothesis used the hypothesis to explain their data. That is, their research was not an attempt to test the hypothesis; rather the hypothesis was an assumption that they made to explain their observations. As such, it is one of many possible assumptions. For example, Bruner considers the behavior of children in a variety of perceptual tasks in which the performance of young children differs from that of older children and adults. He explains these changes by assuming the later development of conceptual representation. Yet the data do not demand such an assumption. For example, the developmental change in performance may instead reflect changes in children's ability to deal with task demands or even changes in the nature of conceptual representation itself rather than a change in the mode of the representation.

Second, when investigators attempted to test the representational-development hypothesis directly (see Kosslyn, 1978, 1980, for a review), another problem was confronted. As formulated, the several versions of the hypothesis are not specific enough to be tested. The nature of imaginal representation is not specified, nor how conceptual representations differ from imaginal representations. Thus, predictions cannot be derived from the hypothesis that would distinguish between imaginal and conceptual representations.

Kosslyn (1978) offers a variation of the representational-development hypothesis that is more specific about the nature of visual imagery. His research has demonstrated that in a verification task about the properties of familiar animals (for example, "Do cats have heads?") nine-year-olds and adults respond more quickly with high associates (for example, "Cats have claws.") than weak associates (for example, "Cats have heads."). Such findings support the assumption that this knowledge is represented in the form of abstract propositions rather than as images. However, if instructed to form images before responding, both age groups are faster to respond for larger parts (for example, head) than small parts (for example, claws), which would be expected if the information is represented in the form of images that preserve the perceptual characteristics of the attributes. In contrast, six-year-olds did not differ for the two types of instructions. In both conditions the younger children responded faster to the large, low-association parts. These data suggest that, unlike older children, the six-year-olds rely upon imagery, even without special instructions. These data and related findings with other tasks led Kosslyn to propose that propositional representation is dominant for adults, although they are capable of imaginal representation. In his version of the representational-development hypothesis, Kosslyn does not take a position on whether young children are capable of conceptual representation. Rather, the hypothesis asserts that young children are more likely to rely on imaginal representations.

Although Kosslyn offers data that support the assumption that young children rely on imagery more than adults, another interpretation is possible (Farah & Kosslyn, 1982). The young children could be accessing a propositional representation, but one that is organized by the size of the part rather than the level of association between parts and the animal. That is, at all ages the information about the animals is represented in a propositional, rather than imaginal, form, but the organization of this information changes with age.

This alternative interpretation exhibits the importance of structure and process in the representation of knowledge. That is, using the computer analogy, *structure* specifies the nature and organization of the representation of knowledge. But the system must have a *process* for extracting the information from this structure. As an illustration, suppose that a data file contains a list of numbers and when you request this list, the computer produces it in numerical order. Can you assume that the structure of the list as represented in the computer is numerical? Not unless you know the process used to extract the information in the file. The same output would occur if the numbers were arranged randomly in the file and the machine searched the file looking for the lowest number, the next lowest, and so forth. Thus, "structures and processes cannot be studied individually, in isolation from one another. The only way to detect a structure . . . is if some process operates on it. Similarly, the only way that a process can be observed is when it is operating on some structure" (Farah & Kosslyn, 1982, p. 128). We are always observing a structure-process pair (Newell, 1972). Therefore, we cannot expect that a single experiment or experimental procedure will be an adequate test between alternative structure-process pairs. Rather, the experimental strategy must be one of *converging operations*. More than one experimental operation or procedure must be used so that "a structure can be observed in different experiments in which it is operated on by different processes. Characteristics that are observed in all processing contexts can then most parsimoniously be assumed to belong to the structure, not the various processes" (Farah & Kosslyn, 1982, p. 129). Further developmental work with a variety of tasks will be necessary to determine whether young children really do rely more on imagery representations than older children.

In summary, a representational-development hypothesis has been offered by several theorists. However, these earlier hypotheses were not specific enough to be tested directly. Kosslyn has offered a modified version in which there is a developmental change in the reliance on imaginal representations relative to descriptive propositional representations. Kosslyn presents data to support this version, but further research will be necessary to eliminate alternative explanations of these data. There is no doubt that children's knowledge increases in sophistication, that they are increasingly capable of representing abstract knowledge. It is not clear, however, whether this development is preceded by a qualitative change in the mode of knowledge representation (see Carey, 1985a, for a discussion).

▶ SCRIPTS AND THE REPRESENTATION OF EVENTS

From birth, adults engage infants in a variety of daily routines. These events have a temporal sequence of activities that are organized to accomplish a specific goal. For example, a child's bathing routine has a succession of activities that minimally includes undressing, getting wet, soaping, rinsing, drying off, and dressing. As young children come to anticipate their roles in these frequent routines, we might ask what type of knowledge young children have about daily events.

If we look to the adult research and theories of event representations, we find evidence that adults abstract from familiar events a generalized representation that takes the form of a *script* (Schank & Abelson, 1977), or conceptual representation of an ordered sequence of activities. The generalized structure of scripts has slots for information about the actions, actors, and props of an event. These slots are filled by generic representations rather than representations of specific experiences. Thus, the script for going to a restaurant has slots for actions such as ordering, eating, and paying, and for actors such as waiters, and for props such as menus.

Furthermore, our scripts have sub-scripts that are variations on the main script. For example, the fast food restaurant script has the slot for payment in a different temporal position than does the general restaurant script. Similarly, the actor slot for a host or hostess, which is optional in the general script, is not optional in the gourmet restaurant script; when this slot is filled, it involves particular actions that occur in a specific place in the temporal sequence of the event.

Our generalized representations of events guide our behavior and our expectations about the behavior of others in familiar situations. Thus, when I enter a new gourmet restaurant, I do not need a sign to inform me to "Wait to be seated." I expect the slot for a host or hostess to be filled. My script for such restaurants will guide me through the evening. Similarly, when I read the following excerpt I recognize the significance of the forgotten reading glasses even though no mention was made of a menu and the difficulty John will have reading it without his glasses (Abelson, 1981, p. 715):

> John was feeling very hungry as he entered the restaurant. He settled himself at a table and noticed that the waiter was nearby. Suddenly, however, he realized that he'd forgotten his reading glasses.

THE DEVELOPMENT OF CHILDREN'S SCRIPTS

A number of studies have demonstrated that adults organize their knowledge about events in a manner that is similar to scripts (see Slackman, Hudson & Fivush, 1986). What of young children? Do they represent the familiar events of their experience in a general form that is comparable to the scripts of adults? An alternative is that young preschoolers have not yet derived general representations, that their representations of eating at a restaurant are episodic, specific to personal experiences. What of the temporal order represented in scripts? Some theorists (for example, Fraisse, 1963; Piaget, 1969) have argued that preschoolers are not capable of representing temporal sequences. Rather, they assert that children's memories are composed of disordered elements (Fraisse, 1963).

Nelson and her colleagues (for a review see Nelson, 1986) have sought to understand the nature of young children's event knowledge. To do this they have asked children general questions such as, "Can you tell me what happens when you have lunch at the day-care center?" Children as young as three can answer questions of this type. This is not to say that their answers are exact copies of their knowledge of events. A young child's verbalizations may not adequately represent all that he knows about events, but if they are consistent we can infer some minimum level of knowledge.

Children as young as three years of age do have scripts, which Nelson refers to as *general event representations* (GERs). Such GERs have been inferred from the fact that preschoolers' descriptions of familiar events do specify the elements and order of the actual events, and the descriptions are consistent from one test session to another. Furthermore, the major events, including the goal, are specified using general terms. Consider the following protocols (Nelson & Gruendel, 1986, p. 27):

Making Cookies
Well, you bake them and eat them. (3:1)

My mommy puts chocolate chips inside the cookies. Then ya put 'em in the oven . . . Then we take them out, put them on the table and eat them. (4:5)

Add three cups of butter . . . add three lumps of butter . . . two cups of sugar, one cup of flour. Mix it up . . . knead it. Get it in a pan, put it in the oven. Bake it . . . set it up to 30. Take it out and it'll be cookies. (6:9)

First, you need a bowl, a bowl, and you need about two eggs and chocolate chips and an egg-beater! And then you gotta crack the egg open and put it in a bowl and ya gotta get the chips and mix it together. And put it in a stove for about 5 or 10 minutes, and then you have cookies. Then ya eat them! (8:8)

The three-year-olds describe the critical actions in the appropriate temporal sequence and there is no indication that the children are describing specific episodes. Thus, by three years of age, children have general representations of the temporal sequences of actions. Furthermore, the children can access this temporal information from either direction, that is, first to last or last to first. This is evident in the types of *temporal repairs,* or adjustments, that children make when they leave out an element in their description. Even three-year-olds will use terms such as "but first" and "before" to indicate an element that comes earlier in the temporal sequence of an event.

With age and/or familiarity, children's scripts become more elaborate. In the excerpt, the three-year-old describes two major actions for making cookies: baking and eating. The four-year-old has added taking the cookies out of the oven and putting them on the table before eating them. The eight-year-old is almost giving a recipe for chocolate chip cookies. What is noteworthy is that the change with age is not one of generality, but one of elaboration. The three-year-old describes in general terms just as the eight-year-old does. This generality is evident in the use of the impersonal "you" and "we" with timeless verb forms such as "you eat" and "we take them out."

The distinction between general descriptions of events and descriptions of specific episodes is also evident when preschoolers are asked general questions such as "What happens when you have a snack at camp?", versus specific questions such as, "What happened when you had a snack at camp yesterday?" Preschoolers use the present tense ("we eat") for the general question but the past tense for the specific question ("we ate"). Indeed, preschoolers have more difficulty answering the specific question than the general one (Hudson, 1986). They have difficulty accessing particular episodes (what happened yesterday) for routine events, events that have general representations. This is not to say that young children do not have episodic memories; Hudson (1986) has reported that even after a year kindergarteners remember an unusual event (for example, a class trip to an archeology exhibit). But young children have more difficulty accessing their episodic memories than their GERs. Many potential retrieval cues are not effective (for example, "yesterday"). To appreciate the issue, try to answer the question, "What did you have for dinner four nights ago?" Chances are that you will have to reconstruct at least part of that day to find a cue that gets you to the correct answer. The effort to reconstruct the day takes time and concentration.

Alternatively, children, and perhaps adults, may have a different interpretation of the specific questions, an interpretation that differs from the one intended by the experimenter. When asked, "What happened when you had a snack at camp yesterday?", the children may interpret this as, "What *out of the ordinary* happened when. . . ?" This alternative recognizes the possibility that children have learned that such questions are usually used in a pragmatic context that intends the latter interpretation (Snow, 1987). Until this alternative explanation is eliminated, we cannot know whether the findings reflect difficulties in accessing episodic memories.

THE ACQUISITION OF GENERAL EVENT REPRESENTATIONS The developmental increase in the elaboration of children's GERs may reflect an increase in familiarity with particular events or the role of cognitive development in general. In an attempt to examine the effect of familiarity on children's scripts, Fivush (1984; Fivush & Slackman, 1986) tested a group of kindergarten children on four different occasions: the second day of school and in the second, fourth, and tenth weeks of school. To assure that the repeated testing did not affect the children's scripts, their performance was compared to a group of children who were only tested in the tenth week.

Even after only one day's experience in school, the children's scripts were stated in general terms with a high level of agreement about the acts reported and the temporal sequence of the acts. Going to school was not a novel event for these children, since most had attended nursery school; but their scripts on the second day of kindergarten indicated that they had general representations specific to the events of the kindergarten. They mentioned acts that were specific to kindergarten (for example, putting belongings in a locker) and did not include preschool activities (for example, show and tell).

Thus, after one experience with the kindergarten routine, children had acquired a general representation of the temporal sequence of activities, and this GER was distinct from the GER for their preschool routine. This finding confirms experimental research indicating that under some circumstances young children can learn novel temporal sequences of actions after one presentation (Brown, 1976). It also raises the question of how children's prior experience and expectations are related to the acquisition of new GERs.

Four types of changes were evident in the children's scripts as they gained familiarity with the classroom routine. First, the scripts became more elaborate. On the second day of school, the children mentioned an average of seven acts. By the tenth week the scripts contained an average of 12 acts and this number did not differ from that of the control group. Importantly, the acts added to the scripts were appropriately incorporated into the temporal sequence of the day's activities.

Second, the temporal organization of the scripts became more complex. The children's use of conditional statements, specifying the timing and sequential dependencies of events, increased in frequency during the ten weeks (X = .40 and 2.26 for second day and tenth week, respectively). These statements indicate the condition or state that must be present for an event to occur. For example consider the statements, "If it's time for meeting, go sit on the blue line" (Michael, Week 4). "And then, if I have time, I do art project" (Tiffany, Week 10). Both of these specify that a particular action will occur if a given condition is met. The probability of an action depends upon the presence of other related activities. Such conditional statements suggest that the children have some understanding of causality; the occurrence of one activity is related to the presence of another activity (Fivush & Slackman, 1986). We return to this issue in Chapter 6.

Third, a *hierarchical organization* becomes evident. The well-organized GERs for the activities of the school routine have subordinated collections of possible actions for each type of activity and the children report more possible actions with increasing experience. For example, when asked about "minigym" at Week 2, Ayana responds, "We go, and run around and play." At Week 10 she responds, "Play a lot. And Wilfred chases us. Sometimes we play house. Sometimes I play by myself." Thus, with experience, the component actions of the GER can come to exemplify a larger collection of possible activities (Fivush & Slackman, 1986).

Finally, the GERs become more abstract. Although from the beginning the GERs are general, they become less concrete over time. By Week 10 the children mention more activities, but include fewer details; a single label is used to represent the many possible actions for that activity. As an example, consider the changes in one child's description of what happens when she first enters the classroom in the morning (from Fivush & Slackman, 1986, p. 88):

> "We play with the blocks over there, and the puppet thing over there, or we could paint." (Week 2)

> "We can play." (Week 10)

THE USE OF RELATIONAL TERMS   The scripts of preschoolers indicate that children this age correctly use relational terms such as "before," "after," "because," "so," "if," "or," and "but" at an earlier age than many psychologists have assumed (for reviews, see French, 1986; French & Nelson, 1985). The development of such terms has been of interest because they express relationships between propositions; they are linguistic terms for describing logical relationships. These relations, such as temporal sequence, causality, and disjunction, were reported by Piaget (1969) to be unavailable to children until the onset of concrete operations.

Yet the work by French and Nelson (1985) demonstrates that preschoolers accurately use these terms to describe relationships between activities in familiar events. Why the discrepancy between their work and that of others?

Typically, the research indicating the rather late development of these terms has used comprehension tasks. French and Nelson's analysis of the discrepancy is similar to the one offered in Chapter 4 for the differences in the task demands of language production and language comprehension.

When young children describe a familiar event, they have a mental representation and must find the appropriate linguistic means for expressing the relations of the GER. But when their linguistic knowledge is tested in a comprehension task, they may not already have the appropriate mental representation for the sequence of events that are described. Therefore, they are confronted with the task of constructing a representation of the statements used in the comprehension task and also determining how the terms that specify the relations between propositions relate to the representation they are attempting to form.

As a partial test of this possibility, Carni and French (1984) read two types of stories to three- and four-year-olds. One set of stories described familiar activities that have an invariant temporal order in the real world. For example:

> Jane and her mother went to the grocery store one day. They got a shopping cart. Then Jane sat in the little seat. Her mother pushed the cart around the store and they put food in it. Then they paid for the food. Then they carried the groceries home. (p. 397)

Another set of stories described familiar activities that have an arbitrary order. For example:

> One day Jane's aunt came to visit. They played with Jane's new doll. Then they colored in coloring books. Jane's aunt made pancakes and they ate them. Then they sang songs. Then they walked around outside. (p. 397)

As the stories were read, pictures depicting each sentence were placed before the child in the order that they were read. After each story the child was asked either a "before" question (such as, "What happened before the [third activity]?") or an "after" question (such as, "What happened after the [third activity]?"). The children indicated their response by pointing at or labeling one of the pictured activities.

The three-year-olds did not perform above chance for the arbitrary sequence stories. That is, despite the fact that pictures were placed in order before the child and remained there during the test question, the younger children could not take advantage of this temporal cue and indicate which events came before or after a specific target activity. These same children could identify before and after events in the invariant sequence and they did not differ from the four-year-olds in this respect, although the performance of the four-year-olds was comparable on the two types of stories. Thus, three-year-olds can comprehend before and after when the events are familiar, have an invariant temporal sequence and, presumably, the children have GERs for the events depicted in the story. Although children this age do not have a comprehension of before and after that is basic enough for all tasks, they do have an understanding of these terms that they can apply when they have mental representations of the events. As a consequence, Carni and French (1984) argue that it is not lexical knowledge that develops, but the cognitive skills necessary for the application of this knowledge.

THE ROLE OF GERS IN CHILDREN'S COGNITION   Nelson and her associates (for example, Hudson & Nelson, 1983; Nelson & Gruendel, 1979) have argued that the GERs of young children can influence their performance in related activities. That is, Nelson assumes that GERs for familiar events can set a cognitive context for young children and support comprehension, memory, and conversation efforts. For instance, it is a common finding that the conversations of young preschoolers are better described as simultaneous monologues than dialogues. This speech has been described as *egocentric* (Piaget, 1926, 1962) or noncommunicative. In the following example, two three-and-one-half-year-old boys are taking turns, but the content of each boy's speech is related only to his own utterances, not to that of the other boy's (Kohlberg, Yaeger & Hjertholm, 1968, p. 693):

▶ Brian: I'm playing with this.
David: A what's, a what's.
Brian: Oh nuts, oh nuts.
David: Doodoodoo, round, round up in the sky. Do you like to ride in a (toy) helicopter?
Brian: Ok. I want to play in the sandbox.
David: Much fun. Do you want to ride in the helicopter?
Brian: I'm going outside.

Now consider a conversation between two four-year-olds in which the children are pretending to make dinner plans in a telephone conversation (Nelson & Gruendel, 1979, p. 76):

▶ Gay: Hi.
Daniel: Hi.
Gay: How are you?
Daniel: Fine.
Gay: Who am I speaking to?
Daniel: Daniel. This is your daddy. I need to speak to you.
Gay: All right.
Daniel: When I come home tonight, we're gonna have . . . peanut butter and jelly sandwich, uh, at dinner time.
Gay: Uhmmm. Where's we going at dinnertime?

Daniel: No where. But we're just gonna have dinner at 11 o'clock.

Gay: Well, I made a plan of going out tonight.

Daniel: Well, that's what we're gonna do.

Gay: We're going out.

Daniel: The plan, it's gonna be, that's gonna be, we're going to Mc-Donald's.

Gay: Yeah, we're going to McDonald's. And, ah, ah, ah, what they have for dinner tonight is hamburger.

Daniel: Hamburger is coming. OK, well, goodbye.

Gay: Bye.

Nelson and Gruendel (1979) argue that when preschoolers share knowledge about a topic, when they have a GER in common, they can use this knowledge to sustain a dialogue. If children have a shared script, they are more likely to have conversations that are dialogues rather than egocentric speech. With a common script, young children are better able to share topics and maintain cooperative pretend play (Nelson & Seidman, 1984). Thus, the children in the second example know the roles to take in the dinner planning activity. They know that dinner can be at home or out, that going out can be going to McDonald's, and that at McDonald's the menu will include hamburgers. With this shared knowledge, they complete the dinner planning event by agreeing on where and what they will eat. Young children, of course, will have had less experience than older children and therefore fewer GERs. Thus, the likelihood of having shared knowledge in a conversation will be less for young children than for older children.

There is also evidence that GERs will influence young children's comprehension and memory for stories that are based on familiar events (Hudson & Nelson, 1983; McCartney & Nelson, 1981; Mistry & Lange, 1985; Wimmer, 1979). For instance, Mistry and Lange (1985) presented five- and ten-year-olds with two types of stories about familiar events: *strong-script stories* in which the temporal sequence of events is invariant (for example, grocery shopping) and *weak-script stories* in which the sequence of activities is arbitrary in the real world (for example, a park visit). Strong scripts involve expectations about events and the sequence of these events. Weak scripts, however, have more variable temporal information. Mistry and Lange reasoned that the integrated structure of the strong-script stories would facilitate the comprehension and recall of these stories relative to less-organized, weak-script stories.

As expected, children of both ages remembered more of the events mentioned in the strong-script stories than the weak-script stories. These findings indicate the importance of the thematic relations of GERs in young children's comprehension and memory of events and objects of scripted stories (but see Lucariello & Rifkin, 1986, for a discussion of the organization of event categories).

WHAT DO SCRIPTS TELL US ABOUT YOUNG CHILDREN'S REPRESENTATIONS OF KNOWLEDGE?

Nelson's work demonstrates that young children have general knowledge about the common events of their experiences. The question, however, is whether their script-like descriptions of events directly reflect the cognitive structures, the mental representations, that underlie this event knowledge. Although Nelson assumes that they do, we have seen often enough that the demands of a given task may or may not reflect children's knowledge representations. Extensive research using converging operations will be necessary to determine the knowledge structures that underlie event knowledge. To illustrate this point, consider the computer analogy offered on page 181 of this chapter. A computer may output a list of numbers in numerical order; this does not necessarily mean, however, that the list is stored in this form. Indeed, adult research has demonstrated that, although event sequences are temporal, linear sequences, some events of a script are more central than others (see Abelson, 1981). For example, ordering and eating are more central to the restaurant script than discussing the menu or lifting the fork, which are subordinate to the first two. Thus, adult knowledge structures are not directly evident in their temporal descriptions of event sequences. Rather, they are characterized by part–whole relations as well as temporal relations (Barsalou & Sewell, 1985). Whether children's knowledge structures for events have such part–whole relations is yet to be determined.

Nelson's work also raises two questions about the development of event representations. First, her work demonstrates that children as young as three have representations for temporal sequences. Nelson and Gruendel (1981) have taken the position that young children's earliest representations of events include information about the components of the event as well as information about the temporal order of events. Others, however, have argued that the event representations of very young children involve the components but not temporal order (for example, O'Connell & Gerard, 1985). In two studies, Bauer and her colleagues (Bauer & Mandler, 1987; Bauer & Shore, 1987) have demonstrated that infants between 16 and 23 months do represent the temporal order of events of familiar as well as novel event sequences. Furthermore, the children remembered the temporal order of familiar event sequences (for example, for "Give doll a bath": take off doll's pajamas, put doll in tub, and wash doll). They also remembered novel sequences that had causal or enabling relations (for example, for "Make a rattle": put the ball in the larger cup, cover it with the smaller cup, shake it). But they had a more difficult time remembering novel-arbitrary sequences (for example, "Go for a train ride": put the cars together, put them on the track, and put the driver in the car). Thus, if the events are familiar or are organized by causal relations, young children do encode and remember temporal order relations, even after one experience of the event sequence.

Nelson's work raises a second issue. Young children's GERs indicate that they segment the continuous stream of daily activities into events and that, in turn, these are segmented into slots or categories of actions, actors, and props. We saw evidence of comparable segmentations in the semantic relations expressed early in children's language. How is it that young children accomplish such segmentations? Although this issue has not been directly confronted, many psychologists have sought to investigate the development of children's categorizations and the conceptual representations that underlie these categories since these are viewed as the primary segments of children's knowledge.

Nelson and her colleagues (Lucariello & Nelson, 1985; Lucariello & Rifkin, 1986) have taken the position that a child's knowledge is initially organized as the representation of events and that with experience the slot-filler categories are formed for each script. Fivush (1987) has argued that two types of categories, functional and thematic, originate in children's event representations. The *functional categories* are categories that arise from the functional substitutability of objects in scripts. Furthermore, there are two types of substitutability. *Alternatives* are objects that substitute for each other in different instantiations of a given script. For example, the lunch script has a category of "things you eat for lunch" and on different occasions different items represent this category. Thus, on one day this may be peanut butter, on another bologna. There are also objects that are *contiguous* in time and space and serve a common function in a given script. For instance, the getting dressed in the morning routine involves clothes, such as pants and a sweater, that do not substitute for each other but serve the same function in the instantiation of a given script. Although Lucariello and Nelson (1985) present tangential evidence to support the early development of functional categories, extensive research will be needed to determine whether and how knowledge of functional categories derives from knowledge of familiar events.

Thematic categories are categories of objects that occur in the same routine. Objects in these categories are both temporally and spatially linked and are perceptually and functionally diverse. A highchair and a spoon are very different perceptually and they have different purposes. They are, however, common to the eating routines.

Mandler, Fivush, and Reznick (1987) have demonstrated that children as young as 14 months of age are sensitive to thematic categories. In this study 14- and 20-month-olds were presented with eight items—four common to the kitchen (pan, spoon, cup, and plate) and four common to the bathroom (toothbrush, soap, toothpaste, and comb)—and encouraged to play with them. Although children this age do not spontaneously group objects together, they do sequentially touch similar objects (Sugarman, 1981). The children's behavior indicated that 60 percent of the 14-month-olds sequentially touched objects from the same category. This behavior cannot simply reflect knowledge about the actions associated with particular objects. No actions were common to the objects of each category. Rather, the children are grouping objects on the basis of the more abstract commonalities of spatial-temporal relations (Fivush, 1987).

In summary, children have general representations of their experiences by three years of age. With familiarity, children's knowledge of events becomes more elaborate, more abstract, develops a hierarchical organization, and indicates a knowledge of temporal organization and causal relations. In addition, we are beginning to have evidence that knowledge of events is influential in the young child's conversations and comprehension and memory of stories. Young children, however, appear to be more bound to the cognitive context of their knowledge than older children. If the task or problem at hand is similar enough to the script knowledge, preschoolers bring to a situation the GER that can facilitate their performance. But they do not appear flexible in the application of this knowledge (see, for example, Hudson & Nelson, 1983). As an analogy, we have seen evidence that perceptual context can dominate a young child's comprehension of a situation. Similarly, the GER research suggests that a young child's script knowledge can set a cognitive context that guides and, perhaps, dominates behavior. Older children, however, appear more flexible in their application of script knowledge.

Further research is necessary to determine the nature of the mental representations that underlie children's knowledge of events, how children operate on these mental representations, and how conceptual development relates to the acquisition of GERs.

▶ ## CONCEPTUAL DEVELOPMENT

For generations, philosophers and, more recently, psychologists have attempted to specify the structure of concepts. An understanding of the structure of concepts tells us something about the basic components of our knowledge structures. In the structure of concepts is the information that makes the generalization of concepts possible. Knowledge gained from experience with some "tables" makes it possible to generalize to all tables. Furthermore, knowledge of concept structures can tell us something about the type of information humans extract from their experience. From our specific experiences with individual concept instances, we create our representations of the concepts themselves. Thus, to understand the nature of children's concepts is to understand how children organize their experiences.

In this section we will consider three models of the structure of concepts that have influenced adult as well as developmental research. At the outset we should make clear that each of these models has its strengths and weaknesses (see Farah & Kosslyn, 1982, for a review). Furthermore, most of the research has been limited to concrete concepts, in particular those that can be represented visually (compare, Hampton, 1981). Extensive research will be necessary to determine whether abstract concepts (such as, liberty, promise, cooperation) have an internal structure that is similar to the more perceptually based concepts (compare, Honeck, Kibler & Sugar, 1985).

THE CRITERIAL FEATURE MODEL

The classical view of concept structure assumes that our concepts are specified by a set of features that characterize all the members of a category. This view assumes that every concept has a set of necessary and sufficient features that define the concept (Smith & Medin, 1981). For example, "square" has the following features: closed figure, four sides, sides equal in length, and equal angles. These four features are *necessary* and jointly *sufficient* for defining square. As a consequence of the use of necessary and sufficient features, this model assumes that membership in a category is all-or-none; all members are equivalent exemplars of the concept.

Implicit in this model of concept structure is the assumption that we analyze objects and events into features. Our concepts are, thus, sets of the features that we abstract from specific experiences. This model of concepts further assumes that the process for determining the *extension* of a concept, which objects or events are instances of a concept, is based upon the abstraction of the features of the novel object or event. If all the criterial features of a particular concept are present, then the novel item is judged to be a member of the category. When I confront a novel painting, I abstract the features of that painting; if it has the set of criterial features that define Rembrandt's style, I judge it to be a Rembrandt.

Central to this model is the process of abstraction of features. But notice that the criterial features of even a simple concept such as "square" are themselves concepts (for example, "four," "side," and "equal"). Thus, the criterial feature model assumes that the features of a concept are themselves concepts and that all concepts can ultimately be decomposed into a set of unanalyzable basic features that are mental givens (see, for example, Armstrong, Gleitman & Gleitman, 1983, for a discussion). To date, however, this set of basic categories or features has not been identified.

A large body of experimental research (Gholson, 1980) has determined that young children can solve problems that require the abstraction of a criterial perceptual feature (for example, "square") from multidimensional stimuli (for example, "large red square", "small green square"). For example, using an imitation task Smith (1984) has demonstrated that two-year-olds have concepts for specific colors and sizes. In this task Smith used a follow-the-leader procedure in which there were three participants: two experimenters and the child. On each trial each participant had before her three objects that differed in size and color. The first experimenter would select one object (for example, a red 5-inch flower) from her set (which also included a yellow 3-inch flower and a blue 1-inch flower) and say, "I take this one." The second experimenter would then take a red 1-inch flower from her set (which also included a yellow 5-inch flower and a blue 3-inch flower) and say, "I take this one." If the child also picked the red object from her set (which included a yellow 1-inch flower, a red 3-inch flower, and a blue 5-inch flower) then it was assumed that the child understood that the experimenters' selections were the same color, although they differed in size. Thus, the child could compare the objects in terms of attributes on separate dimensions.

Although the two-year-olds performed at a lower level than the older children, the children at all ages were able to follow the experimenters' lead and select an object that matched the color or size attribute. These data corroborate research cited in Chapter 3 that 10-month-olds categorize visual stimuli on the basis of perceptual features. Thus, at an early age children can abstract simple perceptual concepts from multidimensional stimuli that are presented in a restricted situation.

Unfortunately, we know relatively little about how these experimental findings relate to the nature of children's early concepts. First, the research demonstrates that young children can *identify* simple perceptual concepts, but this research does not tell us anything about how these concepts are initially *acquired* or whether, for example, the concept "square" has a criterial feature structure. Second, it has been argued on both theoretical and empirical grounds that many concepts cannot be accurately defined by a list of features (see Smith & Medin, 1981, for a discussion of this issue). Although mathematical and logical concepts are defined by a specific list of criterial features, it has proven difficult to define many natural categories with such lists. Thus, a prime number is a number that cannot be divided by any other number except itself and one. But try to define dog with a list of attributes. Is there a list that would mean that all dogs are included in the category? Does your list include "mammal," "furrycoat," "four-legged"? These do not distinguish dogs from cats, nor does "size" or "color." Barking does, but at least one dog, the Basenji, does not bark. Rosch (1975) has argued that it is impossible to specify a criterial list for the natural categories that are first named by children; rather, many such concepts are ill-defined.

FAMILY RESEMBLANCE

Rosch and her colleagues (Rosch & Mervis, 1975) have argued that the structure of natural concepts (categories of natural objects as opposed to mathematical and logical concepts) is one of *family resemblance*. That is, each member of a category has some features in common with other members of the category, but no set of features is held in common by all members of the category. Rather, the concept is specified by a set of *characteristic* (but not criterial) features. As an analogy, the Smith brothers in Figure 5-1 share several family features: brown hair, large ears, large nose, moustache, beard, and eyeglasses. Each brother, however, possesses a different set of these characteristic family features (Gleitman and Gleitman, 1987). To explain how such concepts might be mentally represented, two main types of models have been proposed: prototype models and exemplar models.

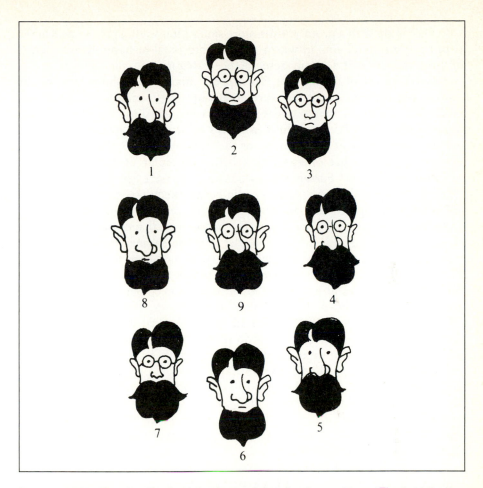

▶ **FIGURE 5-1** *The Smith brothers and their family resemblance. The Smith brothers are related through family resemblance, though no two brothers share all features. The one who has the greatest number of the family attributes is the most prototypical. In the example, it is Brother 9, who has all the family features: brown hair, large ears, large nose, moustache, and eyeglasses. (From Gleitman & Gleitman, 1987.)*

PROTOTYPE MODELS   *Prototype models* assume that the concept is represented by a summary representation (prototype) of the characteristic features. Thus, for example, the prototype for the Smith family would include the five characteristic features. The prototypes of a concept bear the greatest family resemblance to the members of their own category and have the least overlap with other categories (Rosch & Mervis, 1975).

This model assumes that the extension of a concept is determined by the similarity of the novel object to the prototype. The more features an object has in common with a prototype the more similar it is to that prototype. Unlike criterial feature concepts in which membership is all-or-none, Rosch asserts that the members of a family resemblance category will vary in how representative they are of the concept. To support this, she has shown that adults can make judgments about the representativeness of members of natural categories. For example, when college students were asked to rate members of a category for "the extent to which instances of semantic categories represent their idea or image of the meaning of the category name" (Rosch, 1975, p. 197), they agreed that orange was a better exemplar of "fruit" than was "coconut" or "olive." Furthermore, when students were asked to list the attributes of each member of a category, the better exemplars of a category had more attributes (perceptual and functional) in common than the less representative members of the category. The most typical members of the fruit category had 16 features in common; the least typical members did not have any attributes in common with each other (Rosch & Mervis, 1975).

Although the rating data have been taken as evidence for the prototype structure of concepts, it has been shown that the exemplars of concepts that are clearly defined by criterial features also vary in typicality (Armstrong, Gleitman & Gleitman, 1983). When adults were asked to rate the typicality of exemplars of concepts such as "odd number" and "prime number," they had no difficulty doing so and were consistent in these ratings (for example, "3" was the most typical odd number). Thus, it would appear that ratings of the prototypicality of exemplars are not direct indicators of the structure of concepts. Rather, adults have more than one type of *category knowledge;* they have knowledge structures that define category membership as well as knowledge of the representativeness of exemplars (see Armstrong, Gleitman & Gleitman, 1983, for a discussion).

We do, however, have experimental evidence that adults and children can acquire concepts that have a prototype structure and that the prototype is abstracted from the exemplars of the concept (for example, Posnansky & Neumann, 1976; Posner & Keele, 1968; Reed, 1972). For example, Posner and Keele (1968) used a random dot pattern as a prototype, from which a computer generated dot patterns that were distortions of the prototype. As illustrated in Figure 5-2, subjects learned to categorize three such sets of distorted dot patterns (the prototypes were not included in the acquisition sets). After these categories were learned, they were given a recognition test for the dot patterns they had seen. This test included old exemplars, new exemplars, and the prototypes. The subjects not only recognized the old exemplars, but also thought that the prototypes were old exemplars. When college students learned to categorize the dot patterns, they also acquired the prototypes of the categories and were unable to distinguish these prototypes from the familiar distortions of the prototypes. Thus, it is assumed that each category is mentally represented by the prototype of the category.

Rosch argues that some natural concepts are more basic than others. The members of these *basic-level categories* have more within-category similarity

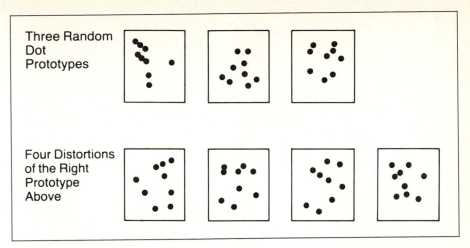

▶ **FIGURE 5-2** *Sample stimuli from Posner and Keele's (1968) study of the acquisition of prototypes.* (After Posner, 1973. Reprinted by permission of the author.)

to each other and more between-category discriminability than concepts at superordinate or subordinate levels. Thus, basic-level categories are more differentiated from each other than categories at other levels (but see Medin, 1983, for a criticism). In the limited taxonomy of Figure 5-3, "dog" and "bird" are basic-level categories. The members of the "dog" category are similar in many ways, which is also the case for the members of the "bird" category, and there is very little similarity between the members of the two categories. Now consider the subordinate categories. Members of the Tibetan mastiff class have many similarities, but they also share many of these features with other categories (for example, Newfoundland, German shepherd) at the same level. At the superordinate level, members of the "animal" category may have few common attributes. For example, dogs and birds are members of the "animal" category and have relatively little in common.

Rosch assumes that the basic-level categories are fundamental and carry the most information because members of basic categories have correlated attributes. For example, creatures with feathers are more likely to have wings and to be able to fly than creatures with fur. At this level, unlike the subordinate level, such correlations distinguish one category from another and thus Rosch argues that basic-level concepts are acquired first. In a variety of experimental tasks, Rosch and her colleagues (Rosch, Mervis, Gray, Johnson & Boyes-Braem, 1976) have demonstrated that, for adults, the primary level of categorization of natural objects is at the basic level. Furthermore, they present evidence that young children first categorize and label natural objects at the basic level. In one experiment, children ranging in age from 3 through 11 years were asked to group pictures of animals (cats, dogs, butterflies, and fish) and vehicles (train, car, motorcycle, and airplane). The children were shown triads of pictures and asked to indicate the "two that are alike, that are the same

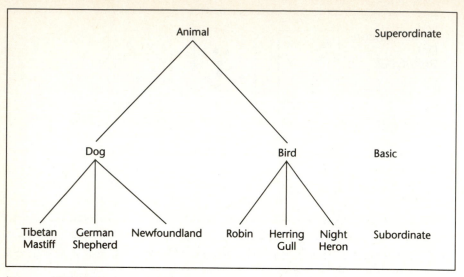

▶ **FIGURE 5-3** *Some natural concepts may be more basic than others. For example, members of basic-level categories may have more within-category similarity to each other and more between-category discriminability than concepts at superordinate or subordinate levels.*

kind of things." Half the triads were structured at the basic level with two of the pictures from the same basic-level category (for example, two different dogs) and the third from the other superordinate category (for example, a car). The superordinate triads had two pictures from the same superordinate category, but not the same basic-level category (for example, a train and a car). The third member of the triad was from another superordinate category (for example, a cat). Even the three-year-olds grouped objects by basic-level categories (99 percent correct), but it was not until four years of age that the children grouped at the superordinate level (55 percent correct for the three-year-olds versus 96 percent correct for the four-year-olds). Thus, it appears that in a natural category taxonomy, one level—the basic level—is more primary than the other levels (compare, Lucariello, 1983).

Mandler and Bauer (1988), however, have data to indicate that young children's first conceptual categories may not be the basic-level categories of adults. In earlier work it was common for basic-level and superordinate categories to be confounded. That is, the basic-level comparisons were chosen from different superordinate categories (for example, dogs vs cars). Thus, it may be that superordinate differences are contributing to children's performance. In their first experiment, Mandler and Bauer (1988) demonstrated that children as young as 12 months of age distinguish between basic-level categories, if the categories are from different superordinate categories. In this study 12- 15- and 20-month-olds were tested in object-manipulation tasks. The basic-level task contrasted four toy dogs (poodle, collie, bloodhound, and bulldog) with four toy cars (Volkswagen bus, sportscar, sedan, and station wagon). The superordinate task involved four animals (horse, spider, chicken, and fish) and four vehicles (airplane, motorcycle, truck, and train engine). In each task the objects were placed randomly in front of the child. Sequential touching was significantly above chance at all ages for the basic-level categories; only the 20-month-olds indicated categorization of the superordinate categories.

In a second experiment 16- and 20-month-olds were tested with basic-level categories from the same superordinate category (for example, dogs vs horses) as well as from different superordinate categories (for example, dogs vs cars). At both ages sequential touching indicated categorization of the basic-level, different-superordinate categories, but not the basic-level, same-superordinate categories.

Taken together, these data indicate that young children's categories are not adult basic-level categories. Young children distinguish between basic-level categories from different superordinate categories, but do not distinguish between basic-level categories from the same superordinate category. Thus, they are using information that is relevant to superordinate distinctions. Their categories are more global than basic-level categories, but at the same time their categories do not reflect the subclass distinctions and hierarchical structure of adult superordinate categories. Although further work will be necessary to determine the generality of Mandler and Bauer's findings, their data suggest that early conceptual categories are neither basic nor superordinate categories of adults. Furthermore, taken with the fact that young children also have thematic categories, the data suggest that the categorical responses of young children do not simply reflect responses to perceptual similarity.

EXEMPLAR MODELS   A second type of concept structure for family resemblance concepts assumes that concepts are represented by *exemplar models,* or specific exemplars of the concept rather than abstractions of the exemplars. Both the criterial feature and prototype models assume that concept structure is derived by the abstraction of features. Exemplar models assume no such abstraction process. Indeed, one of the appealing aspects of such models is that they do not assume the abstraction of features. Suppose that I see a Rembrandt painting for the first time. What features do I abstract to represent this painting? There are many possible features including the innumerable higher-order relations. How do I know which features are relevant of Rembrandt's style? Nothing can guarantee that I will abstract the characteristic features of a Rembrandt painting. At some later date, when I see another Rembrandt, I can only know it as a Rembrandt if my initial representation includes the characteristic features of Rembrandt's style.

Exemplar models assume that my concept of Rembrandt's style is a representation of exemplars and that when I see another Rembrandt I compare the similarity of the novel painting to previously seen exemplars of Rembrandt paintings. Thus, I have not lost information that may be potentially relevant for the representation of Rembrandt's style. The major challenge for exemplar models is to specify the basis for similarity judgments. On what basis are exemplars grouped together? Further there is the problem of storage. Are all exemplars stored? If not, on what basis are some exemplars stored and not others?

Exemplar models have received some support in the adult research (see, for example, Brooks, 1978; Kemler Nelson, 1984). Although there are no developmental comparisons of prototype and exemplar concept structures, one study does indicate that young children remember more exemplar-specific information than adults. Boswell and Green (1982) presented preschoolers with a concept acquisition task in which the children learned to classify and name five abstract shapes for each of two categories. After the acquisition phase and an interpolated task, the children's concepts were assessed by two transfer conditions. In one condition (remember), the children were instructed to name those shapes that had been presented during acquisition. In the other condition (categorize) the children were instructed to name the old shapes as well as new family members of each category. In both conditions, the children were shown the original ten shapes, the two prototypes, new shapes derived from each prototype (new family members), and unrelated shapes (strangers).

Comparison to adult performance indicated that adults categorized the prototypes in *both* test conditions. Thus, even when instructed to name only the old figures, 95 percent of the time they also categorized the prototypes as old figures. This, of course, supports the assumption that during acquisition adults are sensitive to the commonalities among the figures and derive prototypes. These findings contrast with those for the preschoolers, who correctly categorized (90 percent) the prototypes in the categorization condition, but only categorized the prototypes 37 percent of the time if they were instructed to name just the old figures. Taken together, these data corroborate the supposition that young children may derive prototypes, and that they also retain exemplar-specific information.

This is not to say that adults do not retain exemplar information. Indeed, they are likely to do so immediately after acquisition (see, for example, Robbins, Barresi, Compton, Furst, Russo & Smith, 1978). But the Boswell and Green data suggest the possibility that there are developmental differences in the attention strategies used during acquisition, with young children more attentive to the characteristics of individual figures and adults seeking categorical information in the figures (Boswell & Green, 1982). Thus, young children may only derive a prototype as a byproduct of their attempts to categorize each figure, whereas adults may actively search for information that underlies the categories.

Related to this possibility is yet another question: How are prototypes acquired? One possibility, and probably the most popular one, is that they are derived during training. That is, characteristic features are abstracted during the acquisition phase. However, another possibility is that prototypes are the result of the decay of the detailed knowledge of specific exemplars (Robbins et al., 1978). Robbins and his colleagues (1978) have presented evidence that adults engage in both types of concept formation, depending upon task demands. The developmental implications of differences in attentional strategies and different processes for the acquisition of prototypes have yet to be explored.

PERCEPTUAL DEVELOPMENT AND THE ACQUISITION OF CONCEPTS

Since most of the developmental research on the nature of concept structures has concentrated on concepts that have visual exemplars, theories of visual perceptual development have to some extent influenced our notions of conceptual development. Several theorists (for example, Gibson, 1969; Werner, 1948) have proposed a *differentiation hypothesis,* which specifies that initially young children perceive objects as undifferentiated wholes. Only later in development do they analyze these wholes and perceive the differentiated dimensions or features of objects. As an analogy, when a person approaches me, I see a human body. This is a holistic impression that is not analyzed into the many parts that comprise the body; I do not perceive a set of body parts approaching me. I can, of course, analyze the parts of the body and undoubtedly tailors do this readily, but my first impression is a holistic one.

Smith and Kemler (1977, 1978) have offered a refinement of the differentiation hypothesis that is linked to adult research on the perception of stimulus dimensions. Garner (1974), using a set of converging operations, demonstrated that adults perceive some dimensions as separable from each other (for example, size and brightness) and others as integral (for example, length and height of rectangles). For example, when asked to classify objects into sets, adults will match objects on the basis of identity of features if the dimensions of the objects are separable. If, however, the dimensions are integral, adults categorize objects on the basis of overall similarity.

In their version of the differentiation hypothesis, Smith and Kemler (1977, 1978) demonstrated that young children perceive dimensions that are separable for adults as integral dimensions. Smith and Kemler (1977) presented kindergarten, second, and fifth grade children with sets of stimuli (size and brightness varied) in which overall similarity and feature identity were manipulated independently. They found that the kindergarten and second grade children were more likely to make overall similarity classifications rather than dimensional ones; the opposite was true of the fifth graders.

A strong version of the differentiation hypothesis, and the one implied in the earlier versions of the hypothesis, assumes that the perception of young children is restricted to holistic processing. But as we saw earlier in this chapter, children as young as two years of age are capable of abstracting perceptual features from multidimensional objects (see, for example, Smith, 1984), particularly when a good overall similarity solution is not available (Smith, 1979, 1983). Thus, research supports a weaker version of the hypothesis, which specifies that young children are more likely than older children to prefer or rely on overall similarity than feature abstraction.

Although young children are capable of feature analyses (Kemler & Smith, 1979; Kemler, 1983), their primary mode of perception is holistic, without analysis into individual dimensions, even for separable dimensions. The implications of this perceptual trend for the development of concept acquisition have been investigated by Kemler Nelson (1984). She reasoned that if young children are particularly sensitive to holistic similarity, they should acquire categories based on family resemblance more readily than those with a criterial feature structure. To test this possibility, kindergarten and fifth grade children were given a concept learning task in which the categories had either a family resemblance structure in which each member had a different combination of three of the four characteristic features (hair style, nose shape, ear size, and moustache type; see Figure 5-4 for representative stimuli) or a criterial feature structure in which all members had one of the features (for example, one type of moustache) in common. Although children of both ages readily learned the family resemblance categories (83 percent at each age) and the fifth graders learned the criterial feature categories (75 percent), the kindergarteners had greater difficulty learning the criterial feature categories (42 percent solved the problem). Thus, we have further evidence that young children are less likely to abstract criterial features from objects and that, as a consequence, they are less likely to acquire concepts that have a criterial feature structure.

Adult research suggests that this developmental difference in the abstraction of criterial features may reflect a change in information-processing strategies rather than a change in representation capabilities. For example, Kemler Nelson (1984) demonstrated that adults are less likely to acquire the criterial feature structure of a category if they are not making an intentional attempt to categorize. College students were presented the six faces in the top half of Figure 5-4 in one of two conditions. Students in the *intentional* learning condition were instructed to learn to categorize the faces as those of doctors or policemen. The same faces were shown with the appropriate uniforms in the *incidental* learning condition, but the students were asked to judge which faces fit their stereotypes for each occupation. Students in this condition saw each face consistently paired with an occupation, but had no instructions to categorize the faces.

After acquisition, each group of students was asked to categorize the faces, including the two test stimuli. If subjects derived a criterial feature structure for the categories during acquisition, then the top face of the test stimuli is a doctor and the bottom one a policeman, based upon the nose. The opposite assignment, however, would be expected on the basis of overall similarity or family resemblance. Although half the students in the intentional condition classified the test faces on the basis of the criterial feature, only 20 percent did so in the incidental condition. Such findings suggest that the analytical approach to processing information is more likely when individuals are intending to discover rules of classification (see, however, Kemler Nelson, 1988; Ward, 1988; Ward & Scott, 1987, for discussions of the issues). Indeed, adults will even attempt to discover attribute rules for the classification of integral stimuli

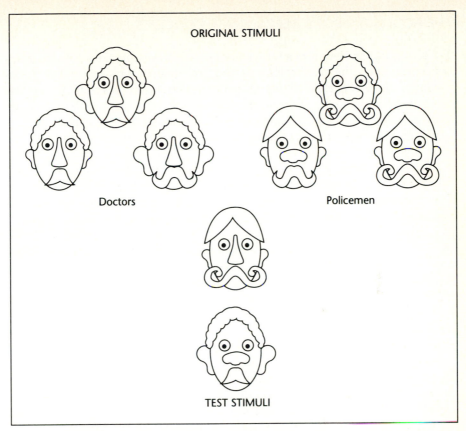

ORIGINAL STIMULI

Doctors

Policemen

TEST STIMULI

▶ **FIGURE 5-4**   *Examples of stimuli used in the concept-learning study to determine how we analyze and categorize information. Students in the intentional learning group were asked to learn to categorize the above faces as those of doctors or policemen. Students in the incidental learning condition were shown the same faces in doctor and policeman uniforms, but were asked to judge which faces fit their stereotypes for each occupation. (From Kemler Nelson, 1984.)*

(Kemler & Smith, 1979). Thus, there may be a developmental change in information-processing strategies, with older children more likely to make self-conscious, intentional efforts to discover features and the rules that relate them.

Although perceptual knowledge is an important aspect of some concepts, conceptual knowledge is more than knowing the perceptual characteristics of the members of a category. My concept of "dog" is more than the perceptual knowledge that makes it possible to distinguish dogs from other objects. I know that dogs are animate, that they are domesticated mammals, and that there are many different breeds. In Chapter 3 we considered evidence that infants can categorize perceptual entities. Here we are concerned not only with categorization, but also with conceptual knowledge, knowledge that is often abstract and goes beyond the immediate perceptual information.

For the most part, experimental research on the development of concepts has concentrated on the classification of concrete objects. This research suggests the importance of correlated perceptual features in the acquisition of concepts. Yet young children do acquire superordinate categories in which the members possess many perceptual features that are irrelevant to the category and in which there is relatively little perceptual similarity among the members of the category.

How do young children acquire such concepts? Clearly, one important means of acquisition for adults and older children is through verbal instruction. For example, in principle it is possible to give a nonverbal demonstration of "mammal," but most students learn this concept from a verbal description of the criterial features that define the concept. Horton and Markman (1980) have shown that young children can benefit from linguistic information about superordinate concepts. Preschool, kindergarten, and first grade children were presented with either a basic-level concept acquisition task in which there was a high level of perceptual similarity between members of each class of novel animals or a superordinate category task in which there was less perceptual similarity between members of each category (see Figure 5-5). Half the children in each condition were given verbal descriptions of the criterial features as the animals were presented. As is evident in Figure 5-6, at all ages the basic-level categories were easier to learn than the superordinate categories, and descriptions of the criterial features did not affect the acquisition of the basic-level categories. Linguistic information, however, did facilitate the acquisition of the superordinate categories by the kindergarten and first grade children. Although the preschoolers understood the linguistic descriptions (for example, "horns on top of its head and a tail made of feathers") and could sort animals on the basis of these features, the preschool children were unable to use this information in the acquisition of the superordinate categories.

These data suggest that the perceptual similarity of the exemplars of the basic-level concepts is enough for the acquisition of such concepts, but that the perceptual diversity of the members of the superordinate categories requires further emphasis of the relevant features. One important form of emphasis is linguistic. But to compare a list of criterial features to each exemplar may require a systematic comparison that is beyond the capabilities of preschoolers (Horton & Markman, 1980).

This is not to say that preschoolers cannot acquire superordinate concepts; we have seen that they do. Nor do most superordinate concepts have criterial perceptual attributes (Melkman, Tversky & Baratz, 1981). Rather, how young children acquire superordinate categories will depend upon the nature of the defining or characteristic features of the concept and their experiences with the exemplars. Thus a child who observes his mother using a variety of "tools" around the house may discover the functional similarity of these objects. Or some categories (for example, animal) may be acquired when a child recognizes

BASIC LEVEL: SALAMANDERS

Exemplars

Distractors

SUPERORDINATE LEVEL: UNGULATES

Exemplars

Distractors

▶ **FIGURE 5-5** *Examples of exemplars and distractors of the basic-level category, "salamanders," and the superordinate-level category, "ungulates." In this study of preschoolers, kindergartners, and first graders, half the children were given verbal descriptions of the criterial features for each category and half the children were not. (From Horton & Markman, 1980.)*

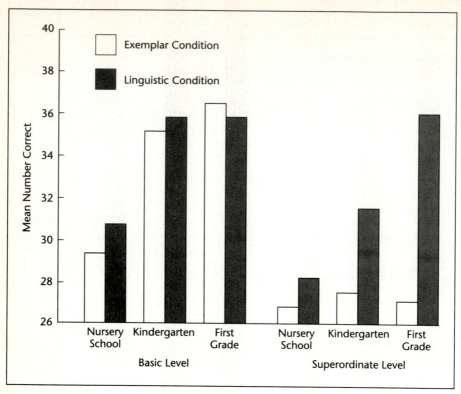

▶ **FIGURE 5-6** *Category level X grade X linguistic vs exemplar condition interaction. As is more likely evidenced above, kindergarten and first grade children were more likely to learn the superordinate categories if there was linguistic information, whereas preschoolers were not. (From Horton & Markman, 1980.)*

the behavioral/functional similarity (for example, it moves, eats) between perceptually divergent objects (Nelson, 1973). Clearly, however, as children acquire vocabularies and develop the processing and strategic skills necessary for integrating information, linguistic information will play an important role in the acquisition of abstract concepts (see, for example, DeBaryshe & Whitehurst, 1986).

Furthermore, we have evidence that parents label objects in ways that distinguish between basic-level and superordinate categories. One reason that young children may have difficulty acquiring superordinate concepts is that the principle of contrast, discussed in Chapter 4, would work against learning two different terms for the same object. Since basic-level terms and concepts are learned earliest, the principle of contrast would make it difficult for a child to accept a second, superordinate label for an object that already has a basic-level label. Callanan (1985), however, has demonstrated that, when introducing superordinate terms, parents use strategies that distinguish between superordinate and basic-level categories. First, they are more likely to point to groups of objects when using superordinate labels. Basic-level terms are introduced by pointing to a single object and labeling it; superordinate terms are introduced by pointing to a group of objects and labeling with phrases such as, "These are machines." Additionally, parents use basic-level terms with inclusion statements to label superordinate categories (for example, "A bus is a vehicle"). Thus, parents use children's knowledge of basic-level concepts and terms to introduce labels for superordinate categories.

THE CHARACTERISTIC-TO-CRITERIAL SHIFT IN CONCEPT STRUCTURE

A few studies have shown that young children's definitions of some words are first dominated by perceptual, characteristic features of the concept and then are modified to include more abstract, criterial features (see, for example, Keil & Batterman, 1984; Landau, 1982). These studies indicate a *characteristic-to-criterial shift* in children's definition of words such as "island," "grandmother," and "menu." For example, a perceptual and characteristic, but not a criterial, feature of "grandmother" is "old." Keil and Batterman (1984) presented kindergarten, second, and fourth grade children with pairs of stories relevant to 17 words. One member of the pair described the characteristic features of the concept without the criterial feature. For example:

> This man your daddy's age loves you and your parents and loves to visit and bring presents, but he is not related to your parents at all. He's not your mommy or daddy's brother or sister or anything like that. Could that be an uncle? (p. 277)

The other member of the pair described the criterial feature with noncharacteristic features of the concept. For example:

> Suppose your mommy has all sorts of brothers, some very old and some very, very young. One of your mommy's brothers is so young he's only two years old. Could that be an uncle? (p. 227)

Analyses of children's responses to these two types of stories showed that 13 of the terms demonstrated the characteristic-to-criterial shift. But the shift occurred at different ages for different words. For example, the shift occurred earlier for "lie" and "robber" than "uncle" and "museum." Thus, the shift does not appear to indicate a general developmental change in how children define concepts (Keil, 1986). Rather, Keil and Batterman have proposed that the shift occurs as children acquire more knowledge about a concept. Unfamiliar concepts are represented by exemplar-based representations that are specific to the child's own limited experience. As more knowledge is acquired, the representation comes to include criterial features that are abstract rather than perceptual.

CATEGORICAL INFERENCES

When adults learn that a novel object is a member of a particular category, they readily infer that this member possesses the features that characterize the category, including features that are not apparent. Do young children make comparable inferences? Do young children go beyond perceptual appearances and draw inferences about the nonapparent properties of natural objects? In an effort to address these issues, Gelman and Markman (1986b) presented three- and four-year-olds with a series of pictures of natural objects. As each target picture (for example, small brown snake) was presented, the object was labeled and the child was told a novel fact about the object (for example, "See this snake? This snake lays eggs."). In the presence of the target picture, four test pictures were presented, one at a time. Each was labeled, and the child was asked whether the animal had the property of the target picture. One test picture was the same category and had an appearance similar to that of the target (for example, another small brown snake); another was the same category but with a different appearance (for example, a large gray cobra). The third type was a different category but similar in appearance to the target (for example, a small brown worm); the fourth was a different category and appearance (for example, a cow).

The important comparison is between the two test conditions that pit appearance and category against each other. There were no developmental differences; for all 10 targets, children of both ages were more likely to attribute the target property to those objects that were the same category, although differing in appearance (64 percent), than to those that were similar in appearance but did not belong to the same category (29 percent).

Thus, young preschoolers readily infer new properties on the basis of category information (see also Gelman & Markman, 1987). Young children go beyond their limited experiences with a novel exemplar; they assume that category membership is special information that implies common, nonapparent properties. One study, however, indicates that, although preschoolers readily infer new properties on the basis of category membership, they are less likely to infer category membership on the basis of property information (Gelman, Collman & Maccoby, 1986). That is, to know that two objects have the same, nonapparent property does not lead young children to infer that the two objects are members of the same category. The contrast in the findings suggests that category membership has a special meaning for young children that guides their organization of novel experiences.

Given that young children do make categorical inferences, the question then is, "What constrains such inferences?" Consider for a moment what would happen if children's inferences were not constrained. Children would make all kinds of inappropriate inferences. To illustrate, suppose I point to one of my dogs and tell you that she eats brussel sprouts. Would you infer that all my dogs or that all dogs in general eat brussel sprouts? Now contrast this with the statement that one of my dogs eats cooked chicken. Chances are that your inferences would be more constrained for the brussel sprouts than for the chicken. In this case your knowledge about the taste of chicken and brussel sprouts as well as your knowledge of dogs' diets undoubtedly determines the nature of your categorical inferences. What of young children? Are their categorical inferences constrained? If so, on what basis?

Gelman (1988) has demonstrated that two types of variables seem to constrain children's categorical inferences. The first variable reflects the difference in *content* between natural kind categories and artifact categories. *Natural kind categories* are categories of objects that occur naturally in our world (for example, sheep, gold). These categories are distinguished by the richness of their correlated features, many of which are not obvious (for example, DNA structure). This richness of features means we still have much to learn about natural kind categories. Indeed, the business of science is to identify these features (Gelman & Markman, 1986a).

Artifact categories, however, do not have the same richness of correlated features. Nor are there many unobservable features. Rather, the important commonality of members of artifact categories is function (see Richards, 1988, for a discussion of the potential relevance of 'function' for categorization). Wheelbarrows have one or two wheels and are made of metal, wood, or plastic. There is no correlation between the number of wheels and the material from which a wheelbarrow is constructed. All wheelbarrows, however, have the same function. If children distinguish between these two types of categories, we might expect that inferences are more constrained for artifact categories than natural kind categories.

The second variable, category homogeneity, recognizes that some categories are more homogenous than others. That is, on the surface members of some categories are more similar to each other than members of other categories. This leads to the possibility that categorical inferences are constrained by category homogeneity, that children are more likely to make categorical inferences for homogenous categories (that is, subordinate categories) than for more inclusive but less homogenous categories (that is, superordinate categories).

In a series of studies with preschool and second grade children, Gelman (1988) has demonstrated that preschoolers' inferences are constrained by category homogeneity. Thus, as expected, the most inferences occurred for subordinate categories, with basic-level and superordinate categories following the predicted pattern. By second grade, the children's inferences also were constrained by category content. The older children were more likely, in general, to draw inferences for natural kind categories than artifact categories. Furthermore, the older children were more likely to generalize properties that were appropriate for natural kinds (for example, properties inside the object) to natural kind categories than to artifact categories. And the reverse was true for properties that were appropriate for artifact categories (for example, properties that specified the function of the object).

Thus, between the ages of four and one-half and eight there is a developmental shift. The younger children rely on domain-general strategies to draw categorized inferences. The content of the categories does not constrain their inferences; rather, the domain-general characteristic of category homogeneity determines their categorical inferences. Within a few years, however, children use domain-specific knowledge about properties and domain differences to further constrain their inferences. As children acquire knowledge about biological categories, for example, they use their knowledge about the differences between natural kind and artifact categories to constrain their inferences. In a later section we specifically consider how domain-specific knowledge relates to conceptual development. Here the important point is that preschoolers have general strategies for constraining inductive inferences and that, as children acquire content-specific knowledge, they also use this knowledge to constrain their inferences. By second grade, inductive inferences are sensitive to the nature of the category, the domain, and the property being taught (Gelman, 1988).

In summary, a number of concept structures and processes for the judgment of category extension have been proposed. Although adult research has eliminated some of the proffered alternatives, it also has demonstrated how responsive adults are to a medley of concept structures. Thus, we know that adults do acquire criterial feature concepts. Indeed, many of the concepts in formal education are of this type. But we also know that adults acquire family resemblance concepts, both natural and artificial. Although the structure of family resemblance concepts and the process for determining the extension of such concepts are not well understood, we do know that task demands will influence how adults form concepts.

A developmental perspective on the acquisition of concepts further underscores the complexity of the problem (see, for example, Andrews, 1988). Experimental research indicates that young children are capable of acquiring simple criterial feature concepts. Similarly, we have evidence that young children can acquire concepts that are structured around prototypes. Furthermore, under some circumstances at least, prototype concepts are easier to acquire than criterial feature concepts. Perceptual and memory research suggests that this difference in acquisition may, in part, reflect developmental changes in children's attention to exemplar information, attention to overall similarity, and ability to test strategically hypotheses about criterial features.

In general, the research to date does not support the position that young children are incapable of forming the same types of conceptual representations as adults. Rather, children appear to differ in their strategies for extracting information from their experiences. These strategies and the resultant information that they make accessible determine what types of concept structures children acquire and how readily they are acquired.

When young children compare objects on the basis of overall similarity, they are limited in the types of comparisons that are possible. If, however, criterial features are abstracted, it is possible to consider two stimuli (for example, a male baby and a man) the same according to one criterion (sex) and different according to another (age) (Kemler, 1983). Although young children appear less flexible in their representations of concepts, they may be particularly well equipped to acquire natural categories since many of these have a family resemblance structure. Indeed, if young children sought to categorize their world in terms of criterial features, the acquisition of family resemblance concepts would be retarded (Medin, 1983). That is, if a child attempts to organize the instances of a family resemblance category with hypotheses about criterial features, eventually all of these hypotheses would be disconfirmed.

Taken together, the research indicates that no one of the three conceptual structures we have considered adequately describes conceptual development. In recognition of this fact, some "theorists have converged on the view that conceptual understanding derives from multiple forms of representation" (Richards & Goldfarb, 1986, p. 184). In the future, we can look forward to the development and evaluation of more comprehensive models of children's representations of conceptual knowledge (compare, Richards & Goldfarb, 1986).

▶ CONCEPT RELATIONS

Concepts are not isolated units of information. Most psychologists assume that our knowledge is represented by a network of relationships (for example, Anderson, 1976). Adult models of conceptual organization have made different assumptions about which conceptual relations are the basis for the organizations, yet little research or theory has specifically addressed the implications of the differences among the several types of conceptual relations (Markman, 1981). Nevertheless, we know that adults distinguish among at least five families of concept relations: contrasts, case relations, similars, part–whole, and class inclusion (Chaffin & Herrmann, 1984). The *contrast relations* included several types of antonyms as well as contrasts that were similar to antonyms (for example, popular-shy). The *case relations* were comparable to the semantic relations described in Chapter 4 (for example, action-instrument and agent-object). The *similars* (for example, tower-tall) reflected various types of similarity of meaning. *Part–whole* expressed relationships in which one member was a part of the other (for example, engine-car), and finally the *class inclusion* relationship was one in which one concept was a subordinate or subclass of the other, (for example, oak-tree).

What of young children? How are their concepts organized? Do different types of relations develop in the same way? Most of the research on the development of concept relations has addressed two types of relations: class inclusion and part–whole. Children's beginning language, however, does indicate that young children can organize their world in terms of case relations (for example, actors, actions, and objects). How this knowledge is represented in conceptual organization has yet to be determined. Since little research has focused directly on young children's knowledge of the contrasts and similarities of conceptual meanings (compare, Nelson, 1985), the emphasis here is on class inclusion and part—whole relations.

CLASS INCLUSION

Much of the developmental research on concept relations reflects Piaget's (Inhelder & Piaget, 1964) emphasis on class inclusion relations. Many natural categories are hierarchically organized with subordinate classes as subsets of superordinate classes. That is, the superordinate classes include two or more subclasses. Such taxonomic organizations are evident in the relations of classes such as "cat," "dog," and "animal" as well as scientific concepts such as "operant conditioning," "classical conditioning," and "learning."

Piaget's work indicated that children do not perform appropriately on a class inclusion task until the onset of concrete operations, around seven or eight years of age. In this task the child is shown, for example, four roses and two daisies and asked whether there are more roses or more flowers. Prior to concrete operations, the typical response is that there are more roses, even when children know that both roses and daisies are flowers. Piaget's findings have fostered a large body of research that we return to in Chapter 6.

Other tasks, however, have demonstrated that under some circumstances preschool children do express a knowledge of taxonomic relations (see Huttenlocher & Lui, 1979, for a review). It is a common finding that adults' knowledge of taxonomic relations is reflected in their performance in memory tasks. For example, in a free recall task in which a list of words includes several representations from a given taxonomic category (for example, apple, pear, orange, and chair, sofa, table), adults will cluster the words from the same categories in their recall of the list. Thus, they recognize that apple, pear, and orange are members of the superordinate category, "fruit," and use their knowledge of this class inclusion relation to facilitate recall.

Under some circumstances, preschoolers also show evidence of clustering in a free recall task (see, for example, Rossi & Wittrock, 1971). Even two-year-olds remember a pair of words better if they are members of the same taxonomic class than if the pair is from two different classes (Goldberg, Perlmutter & Myers, 1974). A number of such studies with a variety of memory tasks have demonstrated that preschoolers have some knowledge of taxonomic relations for nouns and the objects they represent (Huttenlocher & Lui, 1979). Yet such data do not demonstrate that young children have knowledge of class inclusion relations themselves, which was Piaget's issue (Markman & Callanan 1984). That is, these data indicate that young children have knowledge of the similarity relations that are involved in hierarchical classifications (for example, unlike "bananas," "dogs" and "cats" are "animate"). This does not mean, however, that they have the concept of the class inclusion relationship and all that it implies (for example, "dog" and "cat" are subclasses of "animal" and therefore there must be fewer "dogs" than "animals").

The fact that preschoolers do have knowledge of the similarity relations of taxonomic categories does not mean that preschoolers always use such knowledge. Indeed, task demands will affect how children respond. For example, in word association tests young children are more likely to respond with a thematically (functionally) related word (for example, "boy" in response to "good"), whereas older children and adults tend to give associates from the same grammatical class (for example, "bad" in response to "good"). This developmental shift from *syntagmatic responding* to *paradigmatic responding* typically occurs around eight years of age and has been offered as evidence for developmental changes in conceptual organization (Nelson, 1977). That is, younger children are seen as organizing their knowledge on the basis of how things relate in the real world, whereas older children have a more abstract organization based on relations such as grammatical class, class inclusion, and similarity of meaning.

Several studies (for example, Scott, Greenfield & Urbano, 1985; Smiley and Brown, 1979), however, have demonstrated that the syntagmatic-paradigmatic shift may not represent a conceptual reorganization, but a change in the preferred mode of responding as a function of task demands. Smiley and Brown (1979) presented children and adults ranging in age from preschool to elderly with a series of picture triads. One picture was the standard (for example, sheep); the other two had either a thematic (for example, sheep-wool) or a taxonomic (for example, sheep-goat) relation to the standard. Subjects were asked to select the picture that went "best" with the standard. As illustrated in Table 5-1, young children were more likely to choose the picture that represented a thematic relation. But notice that the elderly adults, unlike the older children and the college students, also chose the thematic relation. Are there two reorganizations of conceptual knowledge?

This seems unlikely. Indeed, Smiley and Brown asked the subjects to justify a relation between each picture and the standard. (This verbal justification task was too difficult for preschoolers.) As evident in Table 5-2, at all ages subjects were equally able to state a relation for their preferred and nonpreferred relations. That is, even though the first graders overwhelmingly selected the pictures that represented thematic relations they were just as capable of specifying taxonomic similarity relations as thematic relations. Thus, the syntagmatic-paradigmatic shift does not represent a change in how concepts are organized, but in which type of concept relation dominates in a given task when a choice must be made between the two (Scott, Greenfield & Urbano, 1985). This preference may well be sensitive to both the extent and recency of formal education (Smiley & Brown, 1979). Studies have demonstrated that young children will use the nonpreferred taxonomic relation after rather limited training or modeling of that mode of responding (Smiley & Brown, 1979; Sharps & Gollin, 1985). This change in preference, however, is rather short-lived at this age (Smiley & Brown, 1979).

Formal education, of course, emphasizes the logical relations of classes and therefore may strengthen children's taxonomic relations (Kareev, 1982). Indeed, earlier we saw that as children acquire knowledge their concepts are

TABLE 5-1 *The Number of Subjects Classified as Preferring Thematic or Taxonomic Relations*

	Classification	
Age	Taxonomic	Thematic
Preschool	1	13
First grade	2	14
Fifth grade	17	3
College adults	15	1
Elderly adults	4	14

Note: N = 20 per group. Missing entries reflect subjects who did not show a preference.
Source: Smiley and Brown, 1979.

modified; in particular, they are specified less by characteristic, perceptual features and more by abstract, often criterial features. Many abstract concepts are difficult to learn except through language. Thus, it would appear that, with education, children become more aware of the abstract features that specify taxonomic relations and, therefore, more likely to recognize and use such relations to solve problems (Chi, 1985b).

In summary, although there are developmental changes in the extent to which children have knowledge of the similarity relations that are inherent in taxonomic classifications and in how they use this knowledge, there is little evidence that there is a fundamental change in the organization of our mental representation of concepts. Whether young children use their knowledge of similarity relations depends upon the demands of a task and the salience of these relations in a given context. With acquisition of related knowledge and the language skills necessary to acquire abstract concepts, children learn more similarity relations and the salience of these relations is heightened, if only temporarily, by specific training and/or formal education.

PART–WHOLE RELATIONS

We have already seen that young preschoolers have representations for at least one type of part–whole relation, the actor, action, and object slots of GERs. Markman (1981) has demonstrated that preschoolers also have knowledge of the part–whole relations of collections. *Collections* are object classes in which members (parts) are related to each other by a specific temporal and/or spatial relation. For example, a "forest" is a collection of individual "trees." The part–whole relations of collections are relations between individual members of classes and, thus, differ from taxonomic relations, which are relations between classes. To illustrate, the class of oaks is part of the class of trees. But no individual "oak" is part of any individual "tree." In contrast, the class of

TABLE 5-2 *The Proportion of Adequately Justified Responses for Both the Preferred and Nonpreferred Relations*

		Relation	
Age	N[a]	Preferred	Nonpreferred
First grade	16	0.90	0.87
Fifth grade	20	0.93	0.97
College	16	1.00	1.00
Elderly	18	1.00	0.83

[a]Justification for those subjects showing a clear preference.
Source: Smiley and Brown, 1979.

"oaks" is not a part of the class of "forest." Rather, an individual "oak" can be a part of an individual "forest."

Preschoolers can use the part–whole relations of collections to solve problems, including a version of Piaget's class inclusion task, and their knowledge of the part–whole relations of collections is comparable to their knowledge of the part–whole relation of objects (Markman & Seibert, 1976). For example, in the class inclusion version of the task children were told:

> Here are kindergarten children. These are the boys and these are the girls and these are the children. Who would have a bigger birthday party, someone who invited the boys or someone who invited the children? (p. 568)

The collection version changed kindergarten children to kindergarten class:

> Here is the kindergarten class. These are the boys and these are the girls and this is the class. Who would have a bigger birthday party, someone who invited the boys or someone who invited the class? (p. 568)

Young children made the usual error on the class inclusion version of the task, but solved the collection version. In the object condition the children were shown a picture (for example, a butterfly) and asked, "Who would have more to color, someone who colored the wings or someone who colored the butterfly?" Children this age had no difficulty recognizing that the whole butterfly is greater than one of its parts, and their performance in the collection condition was comparable to that in the object condition.

Thus, at an early age children understand the part–whole relations of collections of objects as well as part–whole relations of objects (Macnamara, 1982). Furthermore, this tendency to organize relations between objects as collections is evident in young children's labeling of familiar objects. When children (two to three years of age) first acquire superordinate terms, they often treat them as labels for collections rather than classes (Callanan & Markman, 1982). If children this age consider a superordinate term (for example, "toy") to be a collection term rather than a class term, they should be unwilling to acknowledge that a single object (for example, doll or ball) is a toy. That is, just as a single tree is not a forest so a doll is not a toy. Indeed, children tested with sets of familiar objects made significantly more errors on a singular question, "Is this a toy?" (21 percent), than the plural question, "Are these toys?" (11 percent).

In summary, young preschoolers have representations for the part–whole relations of objects, collections, and events, and these representations appear more frequent than representations of taxonomic relations. Although pre-schoolers are capable of representing the similarity relations that are intrinsic to taxonomic hierarchies, this difference in the development of concept relations may reflect the fact that superordinate classes are often defined by abstract, criterial features that are grounded in extensive knowledge. Additionally, the difference may reflect the fact that superordinate terms are often used in a context in which concrete spatial-temporal relations promote a collection interpretation and thus delay the acquisition of the taxonomic relations. Indeed, "toy" may be a particularly instructive example since the use of this word often seems to imply a collection, as in "Pick up your toys."

► CONCEPTS AND DOMAIN-SPECIFIC KNOWLEDGE

Children's concepts are neither isolated nor static units of knowledge. As children acquire knowledge, conceptual relations become increasingly complex and concepts are modified. In a developmental study of children's "animal" and "living thing" concepts, Carey (1985b) has demonstrated that conceptual change can be linked to the acquisition of related domain-specific (for example, biological) knowledge.

Although young children distinguish between living and nonliving things, they do not understand "living thing" in the same way as older children and adults (Carey, 1985b; Keil, 1983). This is evident in children's extension of the concept which differs from that of adults'. For example, young children who exclude inanimate objects (for example, clouds) from the category "living things," also exclude plants from the category. These children make a distinction between animals and plants, but have not yet merged these two concepts into a single higher-order category, "living things" (Carey, 1985b).

Young children, however, do have the same extension as adults for the concept "animal"; preschoolers distinguish between instances of animals and nonanimals in a way that is comparable to that of adults. But during the period between four years and ten years of age, the concept itself changes as children acquire biological knowledge. Indeed, Carey (1985b) argues that the preschooler's concept of "animal" is embedded in a psychological theory of human intentions and behavior and that with the acquisition of biological knowledge, the concept is modified and eventually becomes a biological concept in a biological theory.

Most adults have an intuitive theory of biological knowledge that defines animals by a few biological functions such as "things that eat, breathe, and have offspring." Although this intuitive theory does not match the expert system of the professional biologist who, for example, distinguishes between plants and animals by the presence or absence of cell walls, it is based upon extensive biological knowledge and generally serves well to distinguish animals from nonanimals. Thus, the concept "animal" is embedded in a complex of biological knowledge.

Clearly, young children have considerably less biological knowledge than older children and adults. For example, preschoolers know little about the internal organs of the human body and do not distinguish these parts and their functions from structures and functions of the whole body. Thus, they believe that just as the body is made of bones, skins, and food, so the brain is similarly constructed. Furthermore, the function of the various internal organs are understood as human behavior (for example, the heart is for love) (Crider, 1981). Nevertheless, preschoolers do have an "animal" concept. Carey (1985b) has sought to determine the nature of the preschool concept and to chart the development of the concept as children acquire biological knowledge. In this effort, Carey distinguished between the types of changes that can occur when an individual acquires knowledge in some domain.

Certainly as individuals shift from novice to expert status in some knowledge domain, they acquire new information. However, many investigators have argued that the novice-to-expert shift also can involve a *restructuring of knowledge*. This restructuring can take two forms. In the weaker sense, this means that experts have different representations of the relations between concepts and that these relations can lead to new superordinate categories. For example, young children have "animal" and "plant" concepts and at some point in their development these concepts become subordinate to a higher-order concept, "living thing," that represents those aspects that animals and plants have in common.

The stronger version of restructuring involves all that the weaker version does as well as changes in the core concepts themselves (Carey, 1985b). The concept itself changes (for example, animal takes on new meaning). Carey asserts that the two types of restructuring have different implications for research on the acquisition of knowledge. A weak version would focus on the nature of the expert system and what the novice system lacks in particular relations and higher-order concepts. The strong version in addition must consider the nature of the novice system, which may be a highly structured conceptual system but one with different core concepts than the expert system.

To make an assessment of children's "animal" concept relative to their biological knowledge, Carey (1985b) showed children and adults pictures of animals (for example, people, aardvark, worm), plants (for example, orchid) and inanimate objects (for example, clouds) and asked whether each of these objects had six animal properties. Three of these properties are common to all animals (eats, sleeps, has babies); the other three (has a heart, has bones, thinks) are not common to all animals.

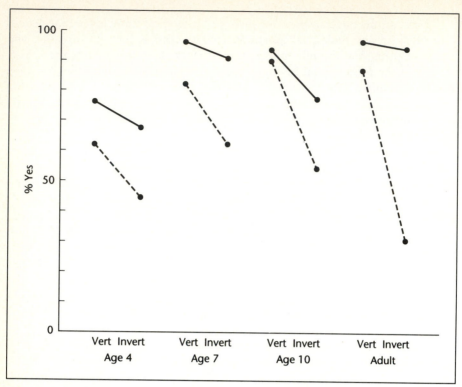

FIGURE 5-7 *Attribution of animal properties to vertebrates (aardvark, dodo) and to invertebrates (stinkoo, worm). ●——● eats, sleeps, has babies: ●---● has a heart, has bones, thinks. (From Carey, 1985b.)*

The youngest children (four-year-olds) did not recognize that some properties are common to all animals and instead attributed both types of properties to the animals on the basis of the similarity of the animal to people. This is evident in the vertebrate-invertebrate comparison depicted in Figure 5-7. The four-year-olds do not attribute the common properties to all vertebrates, and the attribution of these properties decreases for invertebrates as it does for the second set of properties. With development, however, we see that the common properties are attributed more often until adults do not distinguish between vertebrate and invertebrate. At the same time the attribution of the second set of properties is increasingly restricted to vertebrates.

In another study subjects were introduced to an unfamiliar internal organ, omentum, and then given an exemplar of an animal that had an omentum. This exemplar was either people, dogs, or bees. Following this they were tested for their attribution of this property to other animals. When taught with people, all ages projected the property to dogs, as evident in Figure 5-8. The pattern of projection was very different, however, when taught on dogs and tested with people. The adults had a symmetrical pattern of projection as did the

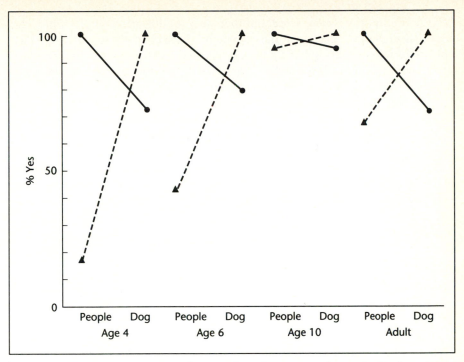

> **FIGURE 5-8** *Projection from people to dogs compared to projection from dogs to people.* ●——● *taught on people;* ▲---▲ *taught on dogs.* (From Carey, 1985b.)

ten-year-olds. The four-year-olds, however, were unwilling to attribute the property to people if they were trained that dogs had the property.

Recognizing the biological similarity of people and dogs, older children and adults project an attribute equally in either direction. The young children, not having this biological knowledge, project "people" attributes to other animals, but do not project "animal" attributes to people. On the basis of these and related data, Carey (1985b) argues that, although young children and adults have the same extension for "animal," the concept has different meanings. For adults and older children "animal" is a biological concept that is tied to their knowledge of biological structures and functions. The four-year-olds' concept, however, is a "psychological" one, grounded not in biological knowledge, but in the child's understanding of the intentions and behaviors of people (children's "psychological" understanding will be discussed in Chapter 10). Thus, as children acquire biological knowledge, the common biological characteristics of animals and plants are acquired and the "animal" concept is modified. When this occurs, the biological commonality of animal and plant is acquired, and the category "living things" is understood in an adult manner.

In summary, Carey's findings suggest that at least some concepts are restructured in the strong sense and that such modifications occur when children acquire knowledge about the domain in which the concepts are embedded. Just as early physicists defined and organized core concepts in ways that differ from modern physics (Wiser & Carey, 1983), so young children may have different, not simply deficient, core concepts (compare, Keil, 1983).

The data further raise the possibility that the characteristic-to-criterial shift in conceptual structure and the development of taxonomic relations may, in part, at least, represent not simply the acquisition of abstract, defining features but also the acquisition of a body of knowledge that makes these features meaningful. Specific concepts and conceptual relations do not develop in isolation, rather there is a little understood and intricate interplay of influences within knowledge networks (compare, Keil, 1987; Gelman, 1987).

▶   SUMMARY

This chapter considered the nature of children's representations of knowledge. Although some theorists have argued that there is a developmental change in the mode of representation, there is no conclusive evidence of a developmental change in the mode or form of knowledge representations. There is some suggestive evidence that younger children may rely more on imagery representations than conceptual representations, but further work is necessary to examine this possibility.

Young preschoolers have general event representations or scripts for familiar events. Even after a single experience they have scripts that represent the actors, props, and temporal sequence of actions of the event. As they become more familiar with an event the scripts become more elaborate and more abstract, a hierarchical organization develops, and the temporal organization becomes more complex. Young children's scripts indicate that they can use and understand relational terms at an earlier age then previously suggested. Further, when they have a relevant script their conversations are more mature and memory for stories is facilitated.

Three models of concept structure were considered: criterial feature, prototype, and exemplar. We have evidence that children are capable of learning concepts with any one of these structures. However, young children's information-processing strategies appear to make it easier for them to learn concepts with family resemblance structures (that is, prototype or exemplar). Although basic-level categories are generally acquired before subordinate and superordinate, children's early concepts do not match the basic-level concepts of adults. Rather, their early concepts are more global, including information that is relevant to the superordinate category as well as the basic-level category. As children acquire more abstract knowledge many of their concepts shift from a characteristic feature structure to a criterial feature structure. From a young age children make inferences based on category membership. If they know that a novel object belongs to a given category they infer that the novel object has the nonapparent properties that are common to that category. Preschoolers, however, do constrain their inferences. They are less likely to make inferences for heterogenous categories (superordinate) than homogeneous categories (subordinate). During the early school years children also begin to constrain their inferences on the basis of the content of the concept and the nature of the property. Thus, inferences about artifacts are more restricted and generally limited to functional properties. Inferences about natural kind concepts are more likely to be about properties inside the object.

Concepts are not isolated knowledge representations. Rather, they have various types of relations to each other and are embedded in theories. Two types of concept relations, class inclusion and part–whole, have been the focus of developmental research. Although young children do not understand the logic of class inclusion as studied by Piaget, they do have knowledge of the similarity relations of taxonomic categories. The syntagmatic to paradigmatic shift that occurs around eight years of age indicates, however, that younger children, unlike older children, often prefer to respond in terms of thematic relations rather than taxonomic relations. Preschoolers have knowledge of part–whole relations as evident in their knowledge of events, collections, and objects. Finally, as children acquire knowledge in a given domain (for example, biology) the basic concepts (for example, animal) of the domain can change in meaning.

6

Middle Childhood: Concrete Operations and the Development of Higher-Order Concepts

Piaget's theory of cognitive development assumes that a second major change in the nature of cognition occurs around seven to eight years of age, when children enter the stage of concrete operations. This aspect of his theory has proven particularly controversial and, as a consequence, has stimulated an extensive body of research. In this chapter we examine this controversy and the implications of recent research for our understanding of cognitive development during early and middle childhood.

As discussed earlier, Piaget defined the onset of the preoperational stage with the development of the child's capacity to mentally represent objects, a capability that is reflected, for example, in the development of the object permanence concept and the onset of symbolic play. The stage of concrete operations is defined by the development of the ability to operate on and systematically manipulate these mental representations. Piaget assumed that the mental operations of the concrete operations period develop from the child's overt actions on objects. With repetition, the child's actions are internalized as mental representations of the actions. During the preoperational stage, children are capable of mental representations of their perceptual experiences, but these representations are static; Piaget uses the term *figurative knowledge* to characterize these representations. The knowledge structures of preoperational children do not include mental operations that can transform these mental representations of experience in systematic ways. As a consequence, preoperational children are limited in their comprehension of object transformations. With the development of concrete operations, children have operative knowledge, knowledge that is founded upon an understanding of object invariance and transformations (Piaget, 1970). The child is now capable of the mental operations that are necessary for the development of several higher-order concepts, such as conservation, classification, and seriation (Inhelder & Piaget, 1964).

The higher-order concepts that derive from the system of mental operations that define the stage of concrete operations can be viewed as conceptual invariants. Just as perceptual psychologists have sought to specify the invariants (for example, size and shape constancy) of our perceptual systems, so Piaget sought to specify the invariants of cognition. In Chapter 5 we reviewed research that sought to specify the internal structure of individual concrete concepts, how children represent the categories of their experiences. Piaget's goal was quite different. He sought to trace the development of higher-order concepts that involve relations between concrete concepts, relations such as "equal to," "not equal to," "greater than," "less than," "is a subset of," and "is a superordinate of." These are higher-order concepts that are general and abstract enough to pervade much of our thinking.

In this chapter we consider Piaget's position on the development of several of these concepts and the rejoinder of subsequent research. Central to Piaget's position is the assumption that there are qualitative, stage-like changes in the cognitive structures that underlie the development of these concepts. Much of the ensuing research has been critical of this position and has stressed the information-processing demands of Piaget's tasks, arguing that adequate performance, by Piaget's criteria, requires skills that are independent of the mental operations assumed by Piaget. Taken together, the research suggests the intricate relationship between knowledge structures and cognitive processes in the development of the higher-order concepts of concrete operations. As researchers have attempted to test Piaget's claims, they have discovered that Piaget's tasks are not direct measures of cognitive structure. Rather, the tasks also involve information-processing skills that include language, memory, and perceptual processes. But as researchers have modified Piaget's tasks to control for information-processing demands, the tasks have often been changed in ways that permit children to succeed using simpler solutions than those that were of interest to Piaget.

▶ THE CONSERVATION CONCEPTS

Probably the most familiar of Piaget's concepts are the *conservation concepts*. When my favorite piece of pottery ends up on the floor in pieces, I know that it will never be the same; at best it will be a patched piece of pottery. But I also know, despite the traumatic change in its appearance, that the pieces before me have the same total mass, weight, and volume as the original (Donaldson, 1982). I know this invariance despite the commanding physical change. According to Piaget, the conservation concepts that *conserve,* or maintain, such quantitative relationships (for example, number, length, mass) between objects when irrelevant properties change do not develop until seven or eight years of age.

Prior to the onset of concrete operations, the thinking of preoperational children is dominated by perceptual features; preoperational children center their attention on one detail and cannot execute the mental operations that would integrate the information from other aspects of an event. As a classical illustration of the limitations of the preoperational child, consider the responses of Nadine, age five (from Bringuier, 1980):

> —When's your birthday?
> —I don't know.
> —Have you been five a long time?
> —Yes.
> —Look, we're going to play games. Tell me what this is. What is it? I know you've used them before—they're little checkers. What color are they?
> —Some are green and some are red.
> —Green and red. Which are prettier?
> —The red ones.
> —The red ones. So I'll be green. Watch what I'm going to do. I'm putting my green checkers like this. There. You see? I'm lining them up. Now you take the little red checkers and put them below mine. Like I did. There, very good. Now tell me, what do you think? Are there just as many red pieces as green ones? What do you think? More red ones? (Nadine hesitates.) If you look at the greens and then at the red, are there more greens than reds?
> —They're both the same.
> —All right. They're the same. How did you know?
> —There aren't more greens or reds.
> —There aren't more greens or red! Fine. Now watch what I'm going to do. (She spreads out the red checkers.) Now, tell me if there's the same number of greens and reds. No? Which has more?
> —The reds.
> —There are more reds. Why?
> —Because you changed them.
> —I changed them, yes. But how do you know there are more reds?
> —Because the greens are closer together.
> —But Nadine, suppose we counted them. If we counted them with a finger, how many would there be? Would there be the same number of reds and greens, or would they be different?
> —They'd be the same!
> —And if you count them, what do you get?
> —There's the same number.
> —That's good. Now we're going to change the greens. What have we got now?

—The reds are closer together than the greens.

—Yes, and if we counted them, would there be more reds? Or more greens? Or would they be the same?

—No.

—What would we get?

—Because the greens are spread out more and the reds are closer together.

—Yes. So, what do we have? More greens, or more reds, or the same of each?

—More greens.

—More greens this time. What do we have to do to make them the same again?

—Have to put them like they were before.

—Have to put them like they were before. Like that, they're alike now. Okay, now we'll play with something else.

According to Piaget, Nadine's performance in this task indicates that she does not have the concept of *number conservation,* which specifies the invariance of the abstract property, number, despite changes in perceptual features such as length. Nadine attends to the length of the transformed array but does not consider that this array is also less dense; she cannot decenter her attention from the one perceptual feature. Even though Nadine counts the objects and pronounces that they are the same number, she is captured by the perceptual display. Only with the development of concrete operations is the child able to recognize the relation between length and density in this task.

Two abstract rules of reversibility are central to the cognitive structures of concrete operations. The reversibility rule of *inversion* or *negation* specifies that any mental operation can be negated. Any mental operation carried out in one direction can be inverted by carrying it out in the other direction. To use a common example, the operation of $2 + 3 = 5$ can be inverted to $5 - 3 = 2$ to return to the original quantity. Or in the number conservation task described above, the mental operation of returning the chips to their original location would negate the spreading action. The second rule of reversibility, *reciprocity* or *compensation,* specifies that for every mental operation there is a different, but reciprocal operation, that compensates for the effects of the original operation. Using arithmetic as an analogy, division is the reciprocal operation of multiplication. Or to illustrate with the number conservation task, the decrease in the density of the row that is spread out compensates for its increased length.

Piaget's conservation tasks are tests of a child's knowledge of the invariant discontinuous (for example, number; number conservation is considered in detail in a later section) and continuous (for example, liquid quantity, weight) quantitative relationships of objects. All the conservation tasks have three phases. First, the child is shown two objects or arrays that are either equivalent or nonequivalent in quantity. Second, one of the objects is transformed in appearance, but not in the relevant quantity. Third, the child judges whether there was a quantitative change and justifies the decision. A child's justification is of particular importance because in the justifications of concrete operational children Piaget saw evidence of the two rules of reversibility that are central to his theory and provide, for him, evidence that the child really *understands* the relationship, and is not simply making a correct response without understanding the basis for it.

Piaget reported a *horizontal decalage* in the development of conservation. That is, children do not acquire the several types of conservation concepts at the same time. Rather, there is an invariant sequence in which number precedes quantity (liquid and substance) followed by weight and then volume, which does not occur until 11 or 12 years of age, at the end of concrete operations. Although Piaget's theory itself provides no explanation for the horizontal decalage, replication studies (for example, Uzgiris, 1964) support this developmental sequence.

TASK DEMANDS AND PERFORMANCE

Essentially, investigators are in agreement about the development of children's performance in the conservation tasks; they are not, however, in agreement about how to interpret the data. Piaget assumed that performance on the conservation tasks directly reflects the development of a child's logical and conceptual competencies (see, for example, Gelman, 1972; Miller, 1978). One of the major criticisms of Piaget's tasks is that they not only require knowledge of conservation but also linguistic and attentional skills that are difficult for young children. For example, the conservation tasks use words such as "more," "less," "as much as," "same," and "different," and we know that young children have difficulty with such relational terms (see, for example, Donaldson & Wales, 1970; Siegel, McCabe, Brand & Matthews, 1978). Furthermore, nonverbal assessments of conservation have demonstrated that young children sometimes succeed on nonverbal tasks when they do not pass the verbal version (see, for example, Wheldall & Poborca, 1980).

Piaget took the position that a child's attention and verbal comprehension are a direct consequence of her knowledge structures. Others, however, have argued that, to some extent, these and other cognitive processes develop independently of conceptual knowledge and that, therefore, variations in the linguistic and nonlinguistic context of conservation tasks will influence young children's performance. To illustrate, in the standard conservation task the child is asked the same question about equivalence twice, once before the transformation and then again after the transformation. Rose and Blank (1974) reasoned that the repetition of the question may suggest to the child that the second question is about the changes made by the experimenter and calls for a change in judgment. To test this possibility they compared the performance of first graders in the standard task with a group who were questioned once, after the transformation. Twice as many errors were made in the standard task as in the one-question task. Furthermore, children who had the one-question task first were less likely to make errors in the standard task. Such findings suggest that the children are using their pragmatic knowledge about conventions of questioning to interpret the demands of the experimental task (see also Siegal, Waters & Dinwiddy, 1988). That is, the fact that the experimenter makes a very deliberate action that produces a salient perceptual change and that young children try to make sense of the situation not by words alone but by the whole interaction, the words-in-context, would lead young children to reach a different interpretation of the second question (Donaldson, 1982). In support of this view, McGarrigle and Donaldson (1975) found that more four- to six-year-olds conserved numbers when a "naughty" teddy bear moved the objects than when the teacher rearranged the objects. Thus, if the transformation is seen as accidental, the action is not seen as relevant to the question and young children can correctly solve the problem.

These and similar findings demonstrate that modifications in the conservation tasks can improve the performance of young children, suggesting that the standard conservation tasks underestimate young children's abilities. But they raise another issue: What are the modified tasks testing? At some point in development, all children readily succeed in the standard conservation tasks. What is the difference between these children and younger children who need contextual support in order to produce correct responses? Piaget, committed to a stage model, took the position that the difference was the ability to think about relations such as "equal to" and "not equal to" independent of specific objects or context. It is only then that a child conserves quantity and knows in the abstract that those transformations used in conservation tasks have no relevance to the quantitative relations of objects. For Piaget, knowledge of conservation is either explicit or nonexistent.

Many researchers, however, have argued that young children do have knowledge of equality and unequality as evidenced by their performance in the several modifications of the conservation tasks. But, according to this position, whether this knowledge is expressed in a child's performance depends upon the demands of the task (see, for example, Gelman, 1979). We saw an analogous situation in the development of preschooler's comprehension of active and passive sentences. Even when we have evidence that they understand active and passive syntax, young children fail to comprehend passive sentences that conflict with their knowledge of object relations. Thus, the argument is that even young children have knowledge of conservation but that there are developmental changes that occur in the *expression* of this knowledge.

A potential problem with this argument is that correct performance in a modified version of the conservation task may sometimes occur without an understanding of the principles of conservation. To illustrate this point, consider a study by Murray and Armstrong (1978) that investigated the development of conservation of numerical equivalence. In this task subjects were shown two glass jars, one with 50 red beads, the other with 50 blue beads. The experimenter then removed six red beads from the first jar and mixed them with the blue beads in the second jar. Subjects were asked to imagine that, without looking, the experimenter then randomly removed six beads from the second jar and placed them in the first jar. They were then asked two questions. The first question asked whether there were the same number of red beads in the red bead jar as blue beads in the blue bead jar, or a different number, or whether they didn't know one way or the other. The second question asked "if, after the transformation was performed many times the number of red beads in the red bead jar would always, sometimes, or never equal the number of blue beads in the blue bead jar" (p. 258).

Although most second- and third-graders answered the first question correctly (96 percent correct—that is, that there were the same number of red beads in the red bead jar as blue beads in the blue bead jar), the older students were not likely to answer correctly (5 percent correct, ninth and eleventh graders; 20 percent correct, college students). If the reader doubts that the number of red beads in the red jar will equal the number of blue beads in the blue jar, consider the following algebraic proof "in which n = number of beads in each jar initially, x and y a particular number of beads moved from one jar to another, R = red beads, and B = blue beads. . . . Given: $nB = nR$; then first part of transformation yields $nR - xR = nB + xR$; then the second part yields $nR - xR + yB + (x - y)R = nB + xR - yB - (x - y)R$. The result of collapsing and simplifying terms from the second part yields $(n - y)R + yB = (n - y)B + yR$" (p. 256).

Should we assume that young children have knowledge of this conservation and college students do not? Answers to the second question suggested that this was not the case. Students were not all solving the problem in the same manner. Only 39 percent of the youngest children who answered the first question correctly realized that the number of red beads in the first jar would always equal the number of blue beads in the second jar. All the college students, however, who solved the problem realized that equivalence would always be the case. Such findings suggest we will need careful analyses of the conservation-type tasks to understand the meaning of correct responses.

In summary, Piaget assumed that during the preoperational stage a child's actions come to be mentally represented as operations. With the development of these mental operations, the child has the requisite knowledge structures for the higher-order conservation concepts that specify the invariant quantitative relationships of objects.

This aspect of Piaget's work has prompted extensive research and a recognition that, even when young children have certain knowledge, the expression of this knowledge is sensitive to the immediate context and the child's interpretation of that context. Certainly, at some point in development, children have little knowledge of conservation. But, contrary to Piaget's position, there appears to be a long transition period in which the relationship between knowledge structures and cognitive processes is a complex, interactive one. Extensive research with converging operations will be necessary to explore the development of conservation concepts during this period. As we saw in Chapter 5, knowledge structures and cognitive processes cannot be studied individually. Any task involves both structure and process (Farah & Kosslyn, 1982).

Furthermore, the fact that the several conservation concepts do not develop at the same time suggests that the development of the specific conservation concepts is embedded in the development of a child's knowledge of the individual quantitative domains (for example, number, weight, or volume) in a more complicated way than Piaget's theory would suggest. For this reason, some researchers have developed new tasks to explore the development of the quantitative concepts themselves. We consider one such program of research in the next section.

► ## NUMBER CONCEPTS

Although few adults have the sophisticated number concepts of mathematicians, we all have a knowledge of numbers that is perhaps taken for granted but evident in our daily activities. Our knowledge of number concepts is most obvious in our counting behavior. When adults count, they use a procedure for generating a numerical representation of a set of items. Numbers, however, are not things that we perceive in the world; they are abstract symbols that we impose on the objects and events of our experience (Gelman, 1982). Moreover, the counting process requires the coordination of the following five principles (Gelman & Gallistel, 1978).

1. The *one–one principle* specifies that each item in a set must be matched with a distinct number name. To do this, a set of distinct number names must be generated. Furthermore, it is necessary to keep in mind two categories: the items that have already been counted and those that are yet to be counted.

2. The *stable-order principle* specifies that the number names must be used in a constant order on each occasion. Imagine a counting system in which the members of one set are counted as "1, 2" and the members of a second set as "2, 1." Such a system follows the one–one principle but not the stable-order principle, which specifies that the number names must have the same order for each count. Without the coordination of these two principles, we cannot compare the number of items in the two sets.

3. The *cardinal principle* specifies that the last number in a count is special because it indicates how many items are in a set. These three principles are basic to the counting procedure.

4. The *abstraction principle* stipulates that the counting procedure can be applied to any set of discrete objects, real or imagined. In principle, I could count any type or combination of objects. Thus, I could count all the houses and boats in my present view. Why I might do this is, of course, another issue.

5. Finally, the *order-irrelevance principle* indicates that it does not matter in what order the items themselves are counted. The order in which I number the objects does not in any way affect the ultimate number of items in the set. The number names are not labels for specific objects.

THE DEVELOPMENT OF COUNTING

Do young children have any knowledge of these counting principles? Although preschoolers do engage in counting behavior, many psychologists have assumed that children this age count by rote and so their counting provides no evidence about number concepts (for example, Piaget, 1952a). Recently, however, Gelman has presented a body of research to support her argument that preschoolers' counting indicates that they do have some knowledge of numbers (Gelman, 1982; Gelman & Gallistel, 1978; Gelman & Meck, 1983).

Children as young as two and one-half years of age will count spontaneously, and their counting behavior suggests that it is guided by the one–one and stable-order principles. At this age counting is limited to two or three items, but 80 percent of count sequences have one number word for each item. These number lists, however, can be idiosyncratic (for example, two, six; one, four, three) and can even include letter sequences (for example A, B). But more than half the children this age were consistent in their application of their nonconventional number lists. For instance, a child who counted three items with the sequence, "one, two, six," would use the same number sequence when counting four items, such as "one, two, six, ten." Such data support the inference that the children are adhering to the stable-order principle in their counting. Indeed, the fact that some young children use stable, but nonconventional lists suggests that they have implicit knowledge of the one–one and stable-order principles before they acquire the conventional language-specific means of counting.

Young preschoolers' counting is limited to small sets, but Gelman and Meck (1983) have demonstrated that three-year-olds also adhere to the one–one, stable-order, and cardinal principles when asked to judge the counting behavior of a puppet that made counts of large (for example, 12 and 20) sets. The children watched a puppet count and were able to indicate when the puppet did and did not count correctly. Thus, when the performance demands of counting are reduced, young children can apply the three basic how-to-count principles to sets that they cannot yet count themselves.

During the preschool years, children learn the conventional list of number names and are increasingly able to apply these names to large sets of items. Thus, with age, preschoolers use the one–one, stable-order, and cardinal principles to count ever larger sets. Furthermore, Gelman and Gallistel (1978) present evidence that three- to five-year-olds have some knowledge of the abstraction principle. When given heterogenous and homogenous sets of objects, preschoolers count them in an equivalent manner, which suggests that the specific content of a set does not affect the counting behavior. Anything is countable. Finally, when children this age were asked to start their count with a different item than on the last count, they were often willing to change the order in which they counted the objects in an array and when questioned knew that any object can have any number. This is not to say that a pre-schooler's knowledge of the order-irrelevance principle is the same as that of an adult's (Baroody, 1984), but Gelman's research does support the contention that young preschoolers have knowledge of the three how-to-count principles and that older preschoolers also appreciate the notion that numbers can be applied to any set of objects.

OTHER NUMBER KNOWLEDGE

A variety of tasks have been used to assess children's knowledge of other number concepts. Some of these have directly assessed children's understanding of concepts such as addition and subtraction and suggest that preschoolers do know that addition increases the size of a set and that subtraction decreases set size (see, for example, Gelman, 1982; Siegler & Robinson, 1982). Yet there is a considerable body of research demonstrating preschoolers' limitations. Undoubtedly, the most notable shortcoming is their failure on Piaget's number conservation problem, a finding that has been replicated many times. In this task children are initially shown two sets of objects that are aligned with each other and equal in number. After the child agrees that the two sets have the same number, the experimenter transforms the display by spreading out one set of objects. The child is again asked whether the number of objects is the same or different. Before the age of 5 or 6, children report that the longer row has more objects. Piaget argues that preoperational children make this error because they do not understand one-to-one correspondence between sets of objects and are, therefore, influenced by irrelevant perceptual aspects of the display.

Yet, as we have seen, counting involves one-to-one correspondence since each item in a set is matched with a specific number name. Increasingly, it has become clear that how or whether young children express their competence depends upon the demands of a task. Gelman (1982) has taken the argument further by making the distinction between implicit and explicit knowledge (see Rozin, 1976, for a general discussion of this issue). *Implicit knowledge* is knowledge that guides behavior but cannot be directly accessed. In Chapter 4 we saw that preschoolers have implicit linguistic knowledge, knowledge that makes it possible for them to produce and comprehend language. Yet children this age do not know that they have such knowledge, much less anything about the nature of this linguistic knowledge. That is, they do not have *explicit knowledge* about language. Gelman (1982) argues that preschoolers have im-plicit, but not explicit, knowledge about numbers. Thus, although counting behavior indicates they have implicit knowledge of the one–one principle, they do not directly access this knowledge in the number conservation task. They are not aware of, and therefore not able to think about, the one–one principle itself.

In an effort to demonstrate this point, Gelman (1982) gave three-and four-year-olds pretraining in which they counted pairs of small (3 or 4 objects) equal or unequal sets, gave the cardinal number of each set after it was covered, and, following transformation (lengthening or shortening) of one array, made judgments of equality/inequality. After this training, the children were given the standard number conservation problems. In two separate studies, Gelman found that with this training the children solved these problems for both large (8, 10) and small sets (4, 5). Importantly, their justifications indicated that they did not have to count the displays to solve the problem. Thus, Gelman asserts that counting training and comparison of specific cardinal values made knowledge of the one-to-one correspondence explicit for such displays. When given the conservation problems, these children can access the fact that initially there was one-to-one correspondence between the objects of the two sets, that the transformation did not change this fact, and that, therefore, the correspondence still held. Their verbal justifications indicated aspects of this reasoning.

Gelman's data are important because she finds number conservation after pretraining that is not lengthy (5–7 minutes) nor specific to the conservation task. That is, it is difficult to argue that Gelman's limited pretraining procedure changed the children's basic reasoning about numbers. Further, it is important to note that Gelman did not give explicit training in the principle of one-to-one correspondence. Rather, the children counted in order to make judgments about cardinal equivalence. Since the principle of one-to-one correspondence is a component of counting, Gelman argues that the implicit ability to use the principle was made explicit by the pretraining procedure. Although preschoolers have numerical competence, it "is a competence that is fragile, that can be on-again, off-again, that is used only in restricted settings, that does not generalize readily" (Gelman, 1982, p. 218). Cognitive development involves, in part at least, children's increased ability to access their competence; it involves implicit knowledge becoming explicit.

THE DISTINCTION BETWEEN IMPLICIT AND EXPLICIT KNOWLEDGE

Children have knowledge that they are not conscious of and cannot express. Such implicit knowledge can affect behavior but it does so without the child's awareness that such knowledge exists or that it is affecting behavior. Language is probably the easiest domain for demonstrating the distinction between implicit and explicit knowledge. All children learn a language and, as we have seen, from early age a hierarchical structure of linguistic knowledge underlies language behavior. That is, the regularities of young children's language production indicate that these productions conform to certain rules, rules that guide, in some way, the child's speech. This knowledge is implicit because even as we observe children's language to be rule governed, there is nothing in their behavior to indicate that they are aware of these rules, that they consciously use these rules to direct their behavior. Some problems can be solved with implicit knowledge; communication is one such problem. Now consider the problem $2X + 5 = 10X; X = ?$ Most of us have learned rules for such problems, and this knowledge is explicit. As we carry out the operations for solving the problem we are aware of the rules that we use to solve the problem. In this case it is difficult, if not impossible, to solve the problem without explicit knowledge of the necessary rules.

Thus, some problems require explicit knowledge, others can be solved with implicit knowledge. Piaget's emphasis was on the development of explicit knowledge. For Piaget, to understand number conservation is to know explicitly that number does not change unless objects are added or subtracted, to know that all other types of transformations are irrelevant to the conservation of number. A child must not only respond correctly, but also be able to offer justifications that indicate explicit knowledge of the reasons for conservation.

More recently psychologists have recognized that children may have more knowledge than is evident in Piaget's concrete operations tasks. They have sought to understand the development of implicit knowledge. Unlike explicit knowledge, implicit knowledge is knowledge with limited access (Rozin, 1976). Implicit knowledge is tied to specific and narrow contexts. Part of the process of cognitive development, and the acquisition of knowledge in general, is making explicit knowledge that is implicit (Rozin, 1976). Young children have many unconnected, limited access capacities. With development these capacities become connected to each other and more generally accessible. Returning to language again, we have seen that all children learn to talk without special tutoring. At an early age they discriminate phonemic categories and have a set of rules for analyzing, articulating, and combining phonemes. They have an implicit system of phonological knowledge that makes comprehending and producing speech possible. Contrast this with learning to read English. Written English is a phonetic language. The graphemes of the written language stand for the phonemes of the spoken language. Yet most children require special tutoring to learn to read and many find it difficult. Why this difference between talking and reading? Reading a phonetic written language requires that children gain access to their complex system of phonological knowledge and connect this knowledge to visual input. What is implicit must become explicit (Rozin, 1976).

The problem for psychology is to formulate an "understanding of the circumstances under which unaccessible (knowledge) can be made accessible" (Rozin, 1976, p. 254). Gelman (1982) argues that pretraining makes the children's implicit knowledge of one-to-one correspondence explicit. Clearly, after pretraining the children were able to solve the conservation task with adequate justification, but we do not know what type of change in knowledge representation or cognitive processes occurs when knowledge changes from implicit to explicit. Although the distinction between implicit and explicit knowledge has an intuitive appeal, we will need precise models that specify the difference between implicit and explicit knowledge in a given domain (compare, Greeno, Riley & Gelman, 1984). Only with such models can we know what it means for implicit knowledge to become explicit.

To illustrate the point further consider the distinction between procedural and declarative knowledge. In Chapter 3 we distinguished between these two types of knowledge representation, one as the representation of procedures for "knowing how" and the other as representation of facts for "knowing that" (Mandler, 1983). The problem for psychologists is to clarify how the nature of representation relates to the accessibility of knowledge. The distinction between implicit and explicit knowledge does not appear independent of the procedural/declarative distinction. On the one hand, procedural knowledge appears to be less generally accessible than declarative knowledge (Mandler, 1983, pp. 423–24):

> Perceptual processing seems to be largely procedural in nature; we usually do not use "facts" to recognize something. . . . We have all seen hundreds of thousands of faces, but without artistic training few of us "know" the proportions of the human face. We use this information over and over again during the course of recognizing, but do not have a stored list telling us that the eyes, ears, nose, and mouth are all in the lower two thirds of the face or that the eyes and ears both appear at approximately the same height. . . . This knowledge is context bound and seems to be used only within a single recognition procedure.

On the other hand, differences in accessibility seem to imply differences in representation. As knowledge becomes less context bound and more generally accessible there must be changes in how this knowledge is represented. Although the procedural/declarative and implicit/explicit distinctions have proven useful for psychologists, we are at a point where further progress requires more exact specification of the meaning of these distinctions and their implications for knowledge representation.

In summary, preschoolers' counting behavior indicates that children this age have knowledge of several principles relevant to counting and number concepts in general. Whether preschoolers express this competence in numerical reasoning problems depends upon the demands of the task and whether these tasks require explicit knowledge of these principles. Preschoolers rely upon perceptual cues and need help in ignoring irrelevant perceptual information. Indeed, an important aspect of cognitive development is the children's increasing ability to access their competencies. Knowing "what competency to access when" is an important competence, and one that is not well-developed in preschoolers. This is not to say that children do not acquire new numerical competencies (see, for example, Ginsburg, 1983). At this point, however, we know little about the development of explicit knowledge or how the development of new competencies relates to the development of explicit number knowledge (see, however, Gelman, Meck & Merkin, 1986; Greeno, Riley & Gelman, 1984). Moreover, we know nothing about the relation between infants' perception of numerical categories (see, for example, Strauss & Curtis, 1981) and the number concepts of two- to three-year-olds (see Harris, 1985, for a discussion).

▶   # CLASSES AND RELATIONS

Two of Piaget's concrete operational tasks appear to address directly children's knowledge of the logic of object classes and relations. Both of these tasks—class inclusion and transitive inference—have been investigated extensively. As in the case of conservation research, the emphasis of this research has been on the task demands that affect performance rather than on the development of children's understanding of the relations of class inclusion (for example, "subordinate to") and transitive inference (for example, "greater than").

CLASS INCLUSION

In the taxonomic, hierarchical relations of *class inclusion,* one class is a subset of another class. This means, as illustrated in Figure 6-1, that all the members of subordinate classes, A_1 (for example, dogs), and A_2 (for example, cats) are members of a superordinate class, A (for example, animals).

The class inclusion relationship is an asymmetrical one; all members of Class A_1 are members of class A, but not all members of class A are members of class A_1. All dogs are animals; only some animals are dogs.

In one of Piaget's class inclusion tasks, the child is shown several objects from two subsets (for example, four roses and two daisies) of a superordinate class (flowers). The child is then asked whether there are more roses or more flowers. To this question, the preoperational child responds that there are more roses. Piaget argues that the child compares the two subclasses (four roses vs two daisies) because the preoperational child cannot think about the two subclasses and also maintain the totality of the superordinate class. Without reversible thought, the preoperational child cannot simultaneously decompose A into A_1 and A_2 and also combine A_1 and A_2 to form A (Inhelder & Piaget, 1964).

Piaget reports that children understand the logic of class inclusion around seven or eight years of age, near the beginning of concrete operations. For the most part, replication studies do not support this relationship between age and class inclusion (see Winer, 1980, for a review). Indeed, these studies indicate an extended range for the onset of class inclusion comprehension. We have evidence that children younger than the age of concrete operations pass vari-

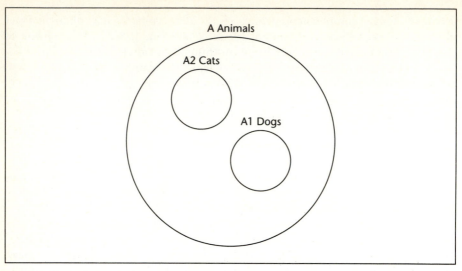

FIGURE 6-1 *In this illustration of class inclusion, all members of the subordinate classes AI (Dogs) and A2 (Cats) are members of the superordinate class A (Animals).*

ations of the class inclusion task (see, for example, McGarrigle, Grieve & Hughes, 1978; Siegel, McCabe, Brand & Matthews, 1978) and that children considerably older than seven or eight have difficulty with the standard task (see, for example, Carson & Abrahamson, 1976).

As might be expected, a number of variables affect children's performance. But no one of them accounts for all of the variability in children's performance in the class inclusion task (Winer, 1980). Indeed, attempts to model the necessary component skills of the class inclusion task suggest that there are several factors that can contribute to a child's performance on the task (Klahr & Wallace, 1972; Trabasso, Isen, Dolecki, McLanahan, Riley & Tucker, 1978). For example, using an information-processing analysis of the class inclusion task, Trabasso and his colleagues propose eight component processes that a child must successfully execute:

1. mentally representing the physical display;
2. interpreting the question as a request to compare two quantities;
3. finding a referent for the subset (for example, roses);
4. determining the number of objects in the subset;
5. finding a referent for the superordinate class;
6. determining the number of objects in the superordinate class;
7. comparing the two quantities; and
8. responding.

Trabasso demonstrates that many variables can affect a child's successful execution of one or more of these skills and further argues that logical competence cannot be assessed independently of the "perceptual, semantic, referential, quantification, comparison, and decision processes" (p. 151) that the task requires for successful solution.

In this analysis Trabasso assumes that children count the objects in each set before making quantitative comparisons. The class inclusion relation, however, is not about that type of inductive quantitative comparison. To illustrate, if I tell you that "quarks and charms are subatomic particles" and you understand this statement, then you know that there are more subatomic particles than either quarks or charms. And you know this because if you understand the statement you know that quarks and charms are subsets of the class, subatomic particles, and one of the deductive implications of the set–subset (class inclusion) relation is that the inclusive set (for example, subatomic particles) must have more members than any of the subsets.

As evident in Trabasso's work, many researchers have focused on performance factors rather than the logical aspect of the class inclusion task. As a consequence, it is not clear which modifications of the class inclusion task require a child to understand the relations of class inclusion and which do not. To illustrate this point, consider a study by McGarrigle and his colleagues (1978). Children were shown an array of four cows in a lying position, three black and one white. Among others, they were asked two questions. Are there more black cows or more cows? Are there more black cows or more sleeping cows? Five- and six-year-olds made the usual errors on the first question, but significantly more correct responses on the second question. Clearly, performance changed with modifications in the task but does this variation require knowledge of the class inclusion relationship? The adjective "sleeping" may heighten the salience of the "sleeping cows" set, encourage specific quantification of the two comparison sets, and, therefore, lead to a correct response. But this performance does not necessitate that the child understand the class inclusion relationship. One can count the sleeping cows and count the black cows and compare those two quantities without understanding that, since all of the black cows are sleeping (in the McGarrigle *et al.* [1978] display), there *must* be more sleeping cows.

We have seen in Chapter 5 that children of preoperational age have some knowledge of hierarchical relationships (for example, dog, animal). Piaget did not, however, use his class inclusion task to study the development of such relationships, but rather the development of the understanding of the logical implications of class inclusion (Smith, 1982). For this reason, Piaget relied heavily on a child's verbal justifications to assess this understanding. When a child can provide logical justifications for his responses, he has *explicit* knowledge of these logical implications, explicit knowledge of the concept of class inclusion.

As is the case for all tasks, performance on the class inclusion task is not a direct measure of logical competence, and a number of factors interact to influence children's assumptions about the task and their consequent performances. Since most of the subsequent research has investigated the many cognitive processes that affect performance and has not focused on the logic of class inclusion relations, we know little about the development of implicit or explicit knowledge of the class inclusion concept. Furthermore, appropriate methodologies have not been developed to assess this issue (Markman, 1984). Gelman's research on the development of number concepts, however, offers a model for the type of converging operations that are necessary to address the question.

TRANSITIVE INFERENCE

If a penny is smaller than a nickel and a dime is smaller than a penny, it is logically appropriate to draw the transitive inference that a dime is smaller than a nickel. *Transitive inference* tasks can take several forms, but all involve "a chain of reasoning in which the relation between two objects in an array that are not explicitly linked is inferred from the relations between two pairs of objects that are explicitly linked" (Sternberg, 1980, p. 340). The reasoning of transitive inference requires knowledge of asymmetrical relational concepts such as "greater than" or "less than." For example, if Xiong is bigger than Xing and Xiong is smaller than Curly, then it follows that Curly is the biggest, Xiong is mid-sized, and Xing is the smallest. This conclusion follows when we understand the logic that if B (for example, Xiong) is smaller than C (for example, Curly), then C is bigger than B, and the possibility that B can be smaller than one object, C, and greater than another object, A (for example, Xing).

In an attempt to trace the development of children's understanding of the quantitative relations that underlie the reasoning of transitive inference, Piaget developed a variety of seriation tasks. For example, in one of these problems, children are asked to order a randomly arranged set of graduated sticks from shortest to longest. Four- and five-year-olds have difficulty with this problem; some divide the sticks into a collection of small sticks and large sticks, others make a few isolated correct comparisons, and others arrange the tops of the sticks in a step-like fashion without attending to the length of the sticks. By five to six years of age, children can put the sticks in an ordered array, but it is done in a trial-and-error fashion.

Concrete operational children, however, systematically produce the ordered array and appear guided by a plan. Furthermore, when given another set of sticks, they can correctly insert each of these into the original series of sticks. To do this, a child must realize that the new stick can, at the same time, be both shorter than and longer than; the child must coordinate these two inverse relations (Ginsburg & Opper, 1988). At this age children also begin to solve the transitive inference problems, which require not only knowledge of the seriation relations, but also the ability to coordinate the relations mentally.

One version of Piaget's transitive inference task uses three sticks that differ in length, although the differences are barely perceptible. Two pairs of sticks are presented to children and the relationships are stated: "'Stick A' is longer than 'Stick B,' 'Stick C' is shorter than 'Stick B.'" The children are then asked whether Stick A or Stick C is longer. If the judgments of the children are appropriate and if the children can adequately verbalize the reasons for their judgments, they are capable of transitive inferences, according to Piaget's criteria. Piaget assumes that with the facts, $A > B$ and $C < B$, concrete operational children can deduce that $A > C$. The ability of the children to make this deduction implies that they possess the logic of *reversibility of relations,* if $C < B$, then $B > C$, and that the facts, $A > B$, $B > C$, indicate a seriated, quantitative relationship (for example, $A > B > C$).

Critics of Piaget's task have argued that factors (particularly language and memory abilities) other than reasoning can affect performance on the task (Braine, 1959, 1962). Thus, children younger than seven may fail Piaget's transitive inference task not because they are incapable of the requisite logic, but because the memory demand is too great for young children or because the language skills necessary to understand the problem or explain the answer are not developed enough.

Subsequent research has attempted to eliminate these factors in the assessment of transitive inference (Brainerd, 1978). Trabasso and his colleagues (Riley & Trabasso, 1974; Trabasso, Riley & Wilson, 1975), for example, used extensive training to ensure that the child had encoded and remembered each of the premises prior to the test for transitive inference. To determine that the child did indeed remember the original premises, recall of these premises was tested at the time of the transitive inference test. Furthermore, the children were trained with the relations stated in both directions (for example, "A is shorter than B" and "B is longer than A").

From 16 sets of data with children ranging in age from four to seven years of age, Trabasso found a strong correlation between memory for the original premises and performance on the transitive inference test ($r = .87$). That is, those children who performed well on the test of the training pairs were more likely to make a correct response on the inference test. Furthermore, within this age range, performance on the inference test was between 78 and 92 percent correct (Riley & Trabasso, 1971).

Trabasso's data, as well as other related research (for example, Siegel, 1971a, b), indicate that the comprehension of the premises as well as the memory for the original premises will influence performance on the transitive inference task. As a consequence, some investigators have attributed the developmental change in transitive reasoning to a change in the understanding of and memory for the premises, rather than a developmental change in reasoning per se (but see Breslow, 1981; Brainerd & Kingma, 1984). Here again we seem to have a situation in which Piaget was asking one question and subsequent investigators have posed another. Piaget was concerned with the development of children's *spontaneous* knowledge of the inverse relations (that is, if $A > B$, then $B < A$). In Trabasso's research, however, children are extensively trained until they have memorized each premise (A > B) and its inverse (B < A). Thus, in Trabasso's task, unlike Piaget's, inverse relations are specified and emphasized. To further illustrate this issue, we next consider Trabasso's research on the representation of information in a transitive inference task.

Trabasso and Riley (Riley, 1976; Trabasso, 1975; Trabasso & Riley, 1975) proposed an information-processing model of transitive inference which assumes that children mentally represent the premises as a single linear array (for example, A > B > C). They reason that if the information in the premises is retained as separate propositions (for example, A > B; B > C), then the response latencies for questions that involve comparisons of terms presented in a single premise (for example, "Is B > A?") should be faster than for those involving two or more premises (for example, "Is C > A?"). In the former case, accessing a single proposition makes a response possible; in the latter case more than one premise must be accessed and the information in two premises must be compared to make a response. However, if the information in the premises is represented as a single spatial array, the individual need only compare two terms on the array. Those items that are farther apart in the array should be easier to discriminate and therefore have faster response times.

Thus, the two models of representation lead to opposite predictions for response latencies, with a *distance effect* of faster responses for comparison of distant items predicted for the spatial representation and the reverse prediction for the two separate propositions representation. Research with subjects from six years to college age indicated a distance effect for the response latencies and thus suggested that from six years on the information in the premises is combined in a single representation.

Trabasso and his colleagues argue that children younger than the age of concrete operations can reason logically and that this occurs when they have all the premise information available and can therefore represent it in a single array. That is, the premises are represented in a single spatial array because the children use the logic of transitive relations to construct the array. Nosbush, Oakes, and Breslow (1983), however, did not find evidence for such a representation by young children when the premises were trained without cues to the seriation of the terms of the premises. They compared the performance of five- to six-year-olds trained with a random order of presentation of the premises to a group who were trained as in the Trabasso, Riley, and Wilson (1975) study, in which the premises were presented in a seriated order during training. The children in the ordered training condition performed as in the Trabasso *et al.* study; their performance on the inference test was nearly perfect and there was some evidence of a distance effect. The children trained in the random condition, however, had difficulty learning the premises, and those who did learn them answered only 63 percent of the inference questions correctly, suggesting that they had difficulty integrating the information in the transitive inference task. There was no evidence of a distance effect. Thus, the type of premise training was related to the level of performance on the inference task.

These findings suggest that the evidence of transitive inference in young children may be more a function of a particular type of training that results in a specific type of mental representation than transitive reasoning (see, for example, Chapman & Lindenberger, 1988). That is, the transitive reasoning of young children evident in Trabasso's findings may be a function of the children learning to put premise information in an order, rather than as a consequence of the children's understanding of reversibility, that is, "the understanding that an object 'B' may be larger than 'A' and smaller than 'C'" (Breslow, 1981, p. 327; see Halford & Kelly, 1984, for related data). We appear, therefore, to have another example of a modification of Piaget's task that improves performance but in which the modified task may no longer require the type of knowledge that was of interest to Piaget.

In summary, the research on class inclusion and transitive inference illustrates three important issues. First, Piaget was asking different questions than many of his critics. In their efforts to demonstrate the several cognitive competencies that can affect children's performance, critics have not centered on Piaget's questions. Second, as a consequence, subsequent research has focused on the development of the nonlogical competencies. Third, eventually all children find Piaget's class inclusion and transitive inference tasks easy. Yet we know little about the transitional period that precedes this. Indeed, we might expect that the distinction between implicit and explicit knowledge is a relevant one during this period.

▶   ## THE APPEARANCE-REALITY DISTINCTION

One of the most pervasive conceptual distinctions that adults make is the distinction between appearance and reality. When a student tells me that he knew more than he wrote on the exam, he is reminding me of his distinction. Mystery writers play with the distinction; psychologists confront the distinction as they attempt to infer competence from performance. Adults have extensive and explicit knowledge that things may not be what they seem.

Knowledge of this distinction appears to have a gradual and prolonged period of development (Flavell, Green & Flavell, 1986). Piaget took the position that preoperational children tend to *center* on the perceptually salient (phenomenism) aspects of their experience. They think about appearance rather than reality. This is illustrated by their behavior in the perspective-taking task. In the standard version children sit at a table before a display of three cones ("mountains") that vary in size (see Figure 6-2). The children are asked to replicate what they see with a second set of cones. The children are then asked to demonstrate what the experimenter or a doll, seated at a different side of the table, sees (Piaget & Inhelder, 1956). Piaget reported that preschool children could not take the perspective of another and that this capability did not begin to emerge until six to nine years of age.

Flavell and his colleagues (Flavell, Flavell & Green, 1983; Flavell, Zhang,

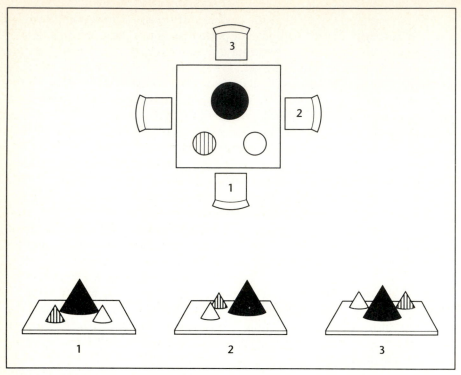

▶ **FIGURE 6-2** *A depiction of the three mountains problem. The child is asked to identify what a doll (or another person) would see while seated in each of the three numbered locations.* (From Phillips, 1975.)

Zou, Dong & Qi, 1983; Flavell, Green & Flavell, 1986) have determined that young children not only make errors of *phenomenism* (reporting perceptual appearance when reality is requested) but also errors of *intellectual realism* (reporting reality when appearances are requested). Such intellectual realism is evident in young children's drawings. When asked to draw exactly what they see, they will also draw what they know is there, although hidden from sight. Thus, it appears that the young child's thoughts can be captured by either cognitively or perceptually salient information.

In an attempt to explore the development of children's knowledge of the distinction between appearance and reality, Flavell and his colleagues conducted a number of studies with subjects ranging in age from three years to college. A variety of tasks were used in these investigations but the following task is one of the simplest (appearing) of these. After pretraining to assure that the children understood the phrases, "what it looks like" and "what it really and truly is," children were shown objects (for example, a glass of milk) with and without color filters (for example, blue) in front of them.

Approximately half of the three-year-olds tested were unable to correctly answer the appearance and reality questions in this and similar tasks (Flavell, Green & Flavell, 1986). Their responding was not random, however. In some situations they relied upon appearance to answer both questions (phenomenism) and at other times they answered both questions in terms of reality (intellectual realism). Furthermore, some appearance-reality distinctions were easier than others. For example, most three-year-olds solved the problem that involved disguising a clown doll to look like a ghost. Yet most said that an imitation rock made of soft, sponge-like material really was a rock. By five years of age, however, children readily made the distinction between appearance and reality in these tasks.

The failure of many three-year-olds to make a distinction between appearance and reality raises a problem of interpretation. By now we have seen many situations in which task demands can serve to conceal the competence in question and, thus, competence is underestimated. Flavell and his colleagues used three research strategies to address this issue (Flavell, 1986). First, they made cross-cultural comparisons to assess the generality of their findings. Despite language and cultural differences, the performance of Chinese three- to five-year-olds indicated comparable error patterns, age changes, and levels of performance to that of American children (Flavell, Zhang, Zou, Dong & Qi, 1983). Second, efforts to train three-year-olds on specific appearance-reality distinctions (real vs apparent color) did not improve their performance (Flavell, Green & Flavell, 1986). Finally, they modified the original tasks in order to make them easier (from an adult point of view) and found no improvement in the performance of three-year-olds (Flavell, Green & Flavell, 1986). Until someone demonstrates that there are task demands that conceal young children's knowledge of the appearance-reality distinction, the converging operations used by Flavell indicate that most three-year-olds have limited knowledge of the distinction, that their knowledge is not general nor accessible in all situations.

How can we explain the failure of young children to honor the distinction between appearance and reality? In the spirit of Piaget's (Piaget & Inhelder, 1969) interpretation of young children's performance on perspective-taking tasks, Flavell and his colleagues (Flavell, *et al.*, 1986) have offered the hypothesis that young children do not yet know that something can simultaneously have more than one representation. This does not mean that young preschoolers are incapable of representing an object in more than one way. That this is possible is illustrated by the three-year-olds who said that the color of milk was blue as they looked through the blue filter, but also stated that the color would be white when the filter was removed. The young child is capable of mental representations of appearances and mental representations of reality, but he cannot represent both at the same time. The representation of an object can change, but the same object cannot have more than one representation at a time. When confronted with contradictory or mutually exclusive properties for the same object (for example, white and also blue), they resolve the contradiction by relying on one or the other representation of the object.

As children come to know more about the nature of mental representations and the subjectivity of mental representations, they come to resolve the apparent contradictions of multiple representations in their recognition of the distinction between representations of reality and representations of appearance. In support of this interpretation, Flavell (1986) reports high positive correlations between performance on his appearance-reality tasks and the perspective-taking (appearance-appearance) task, both of which appear to require simultaneous, but contradictory representations. That is, the perspective-taking task (Figure 6-2) requires children to recognize that a given display can have different appearances. Similarly, the appearance-reality tasks require children to recognize that there can be a reality that differs from appearance. The fact that the appearance-appearance and appearance-reality distinctions develop together suggests to Flavell (Flavell, Green & Flavell, 1986) that a common ability, dual coding, underlies these distinctions.

Further, Flavell has argued "that dual coding in pretend-play situations may help mediate dual coding in appearance-reality (and appearance-appearance) situations . . ." (Flavell, Green & Flavell, 1986; p. 63). From an early age (around one year) children engage in pretend play. Young children have extensive practice in pretend play and develop the ability to differentiate between what is pretend and what is real. This was most graphic to me when my just-turned-three nephew and I were riding with his mother to a shopping mall. As we drove along, Matthew and I discussed what we were going to buy at the mall. Matt informed me he was going to buy a pocketbook. When I inquired where his money was, he further informed me that it was in the (imaginary) pocketbook he was holding. In the discussion that followed, I learned that the pocketbook was beige and had many things inside it. Upon reaching the mall, I started to get out of the car and reminded Matt to bring his money for the new pocketbook. Matt looked seriously at me, handed me his beige pocketbook, told me to shop for him and that he had been pretending. Matt knew he was pretending—perhaps he wasn't quite sure about me.

In support of the supposition that the appearance-reality and appearance-appearance distinctions develop out of pretend play, Flavell, Flavell, and Green (1987) have demonstrated that young children are capable of making the pretend-real distinction before they make the appearance-reality distinction. Thus, "it is possible that gradually coming to understand the pretend-real distinction through play . . . helps the child understand the conceptually similar appearance-reality and appearance-appearance . . . distinctions" (Flavell, Flavell & Green, 1987; p. 822).

Flavell and his colleagues have demonstrated that our knowledge of the appearance-reality distinction continues to develop throughout the elementary and high school years. Several types of tasks proved to be particularly demanding for six- and seven-year-olds. For example, in one task subjects were shown pairs of objects and were asked to judge which member of a pair had a greater discrepancy between its appearance and its reality. That is, subjects were required to judge the degree of discrepancy between an object's appearance and reality, make relative comparisons between two objects with respect to this discrepancy, and then justify their choice. The stimuli included pairs such as (a) a real piece of candy and a magnet that looked like a piece of candy and (b) a realistic-looking fake rock and a fake-looking fake water faucet.

Making such comparisons proved difficult for first graders. Often children this age based their choices on characteristics other than the appearance-reality discrepancy, characteristics such as color, function, and the reality of the object (for example, choosing the real piece of candy because it was real and rejecting the magnet that looked like candy because it was fake). The choices of sixth graders were more similar to those of the college students. These two ages differed, however, in the abstractness of their justifications. Sixth graders gave adequate concrete comparisons between the specific appearances and realities of the objects (for example, "This looks like a rock but really is a sponge."), but did not offer more abstract explanations that referred in general terms to deception, reality, and appearance (for example, "This doesn't look like what it really is."). Knowledge of the appearance-reality distinction is highly accessible for college students. They can reflect on and readily communicate their knowledge of this distinction and even use this knowledge to create new examples of the reality-appearance discrepancy (Flavell, Green & Flavell, 1986).

In summary, Flavell and his colleagues have documented a prolonged developmental change in our understanding of the reality-appearance distinction. Three-year-olds have some knowledge of the difference between the reality and the appearance of certain objects, at least in tasks involving simple and, perhaps, familiar transformations (for example, putting on a costume). During the preschool years this knowledge becomes more general, with an increasing awareness that things are not always as they appear. Extensive research will be necessary to determine the extent to which developmental changes during the preschool years reflect a general conceptual change, one that underlies developmental changes in perspective taking (Flavell, Green & Flavell, 1986), conservation (Braine & Shanks, 1965a; 1965b), or children's understanding of pretense (Flavell, et al., 1987), all of which appear to require an understanding of reality and appearance. Finally, the fact that three-year-olds were able to make the appearance-reality distinction for some objects suggests that familiarity with specific objects and the acquisition of domain-specific knowledge may contribute to the developmental changes in the appearance-reality distinction. Number knowledge, for example, is a domain in which young children can distinguish between appearance and reality, at least when conditions encourage a child to focus on reality despite misleading appearances.

▶ ## CAUSALITY

Adults and preschoolers alike perceive their experiences as temporal sequences of segmented units or events. In addition, adults perceive causal relations between some of these events. Causal relations package events together in asymmetrical and necessary relations. That is, of two events, one (cause) is perceived to produce the other (effect); the effect, however, does not produce the cause. This relation is a necessary one because the occurrence of the effect is dependent upon the occurrence of the causal event. Heat, for example, is necessary to make cookies. In fact, the object cookie does not occur unless heat is applied in a specific way to the cookie batter.

The scripts of preschoolers suggest that children this age have some concept of causality. They use terms, such as "because," "if . . . then," that adults use when describing cause-effect relations. Yet these data do not make it clear whether children recognize the necessary relations between a cause and an effect or whether they are expressing the fact that two events always occur in a specific temporal relation. Recently, a number of investigators have examined the development of the concept of causality. But before describing these data, we must consider the nature of the adult concept of causality.

Our conceptualization of causality is a complex one that has engaged philosophers for generations. For the most part, philosophers have taken a *normative* approach to causality. They have attempted to specify the conditions that *should* define a cause and effect relation; to date there is no philosophical consensus on the normative meaning of causality. Adults, however, do make judgments of causality. Psychologists have taken a *descriptive* approach to the problem and have identified several rules that underlie these judgments, at least in Western cultures.

Adults make causal judgments about events that involve both animate and inanimate objects. In Chapter 10 we explore the development of causal attribution for social events; here we focus on causal relations between inanimate objects. Basic to our conceptualization of these causal relations is the assumption of *determinism* (Bullock, Gelman & Baillargeon, 1982). Adults assume that physical changes have causes. I may not know why my car will not start, but I do assume a cause for its failure to start.

Adults use several rules or principles to determine a cause (Bullock, Gelman & Baillargeon, 1982; Shultz, Fisher, Pratt & Rulf, 1986). The *principle of temporal priority* stipulates that a cause cannot follow its effect; causes either precede or are coincident with effects. You would think me a little peculiar if I told you that my car would not start this morning because it rained very hard after I tried to start it. The *principle of mechanism* indicates that there is some mechanism by which a cause has its effect. This mechanism may be a direct link, as in the case of a cue ball hitting another ball and moving the second ball. Or there may be an intermediary mechanism as in the case of the light switch, which closes an electric circuit, which in turn supplies electricity to a light bulb. The *principle of temporal contiguity* specifies that the cause and effect occur close together in time. Similarly, the *principle of spatial contiguity* specifies that the events occur close together in space. The *similarity principle* stipulates that the properties of the cause are similar to the properties of the effect. For example, the intensity of an effect would vary proportionately with the intensity of the cause (Shultz & Ravinsky, 1977). Finally, the *principle of covariation* indicates that the cause and effect have a systematic relationship and that the cause is the event that covaries most consistently with the effect. As we will see in a later section, these principles do not all have equal importance for adults' concept of causality.

THE DEVELOPMENT OF CAUSAL REASONING

Recent studies of causality have focused on preschoolers' implicit knowledge of the principles of causality and their ability to use different types of stimulus information to make judgments of causality. In general, these data indicate that by three years of age children have implicit knowledge about causality. That is, they act in a manner that is consistent with the assumption that there are cause-and-effect relations (see, for example, Bullock, Gelman & Baillargeon, 1982). The data also suggest, however, that there are differences between three-year-olds and older preschoolers in how the several principles relate to their conception of causality.

THE ASSUMPTION OF DETERMINISM Experimental and anecdotal evidence suggests that young children do assume that events are determined (see Shultz and Kestenbaum, 1985, for a review). Consider the example of a very verbal two-year-old (Bullock, 1985, p. 186):

> The child was at the swimming pool and he had been told to stay in the shallow end. However, while his mother was turned away, the boy walked to the deep end of the pool, watched for a bit, and then jumped in. Because he could not swim, he flailed about and sank. The lifeguard jumped in and fished him out. After the boy sputtered a bit, he was pronounced safe. His mother, though, was concerned, especially after her explicit instructions to stay in the shallow end because he could not swim. She asked him why he had done such a silly (not to mention forbidden) thing. The boy replied, "Well, Mom, I watched, I saw that none of the people in the shallow end could swim, and all of the people in the deep end could. I thought that if I jumped into the deep end then I could swim too!"

Clearly the boy assumed that the ability to swim had a cause. However, without knowledge of the relevant mechanisms, which would require extended observations, he relied upon spatial and temporal contiguity cues to infer the cause of swimming.

Similarly, in the laboratory, when preschoolers were shown an event in which there was no obvious causal mechanism (for example, a jack-in-the-box jumps up without any antecedent event) and were queried about it, they made responses suggesting that they believed the event was determined. These responses included accusing the experimenter of playing a trick, complaining that they had no way to determine the cause, and claiming that something, unknown to them, had caused the event. Furthermore, the four- and five-year-olds offered possible causal mechanisms such as wire, buttons, and switches (Bullock, Gelman & Baillargeon, 1982). Three-year-olds, however, were less willing to speculate about the cause of the event. Whether this represents a difference in verbal skills, or in the assumption of a causal mechanism cannot be determined. Most investigators, however, accept determinism as a basic assumption of even very young children (Bullock, 1985).

THE PRINCIPLE OF PRIORITY   Bullock and Gelman (1979) have demonstrated that preschoolers attribute causation to antecedent events and that they will do so even when the antecedent event is not spatially contiguous with the subsequent event. In this study, the children first were shown the apparatus illustrated at the top of Figure 6-3. A steel ball was dropped into one runway (A), a puppet jumped up from the middle section two seconds later (B), and then a steel ball was dropped into the other runway (A'). After seeing this sequence twice, the children were asked what had happened. They were then shown the same sequence two more times. On these trials the children were asked to indicate the ball that had made the puppet pop out. Seventy-five percent of the three-year-olds and all of the five-year-olds chose the first event as the cause.

In the second phase the children were shown two sequences: A-B and A'-B, in which it was demonstrated that event B could occur after the drop of either ball—that is, after each ball was dropped the puppet appeared. They were then shown a sequence like the one in the first phase, ball drop (A), puppet up (B), ball drop (A'), and were asked to make a causal judgment. The majority of the children attributed the cause of the puppet jumping up to the antecedent event (A), although the three-year-olds were less consistent in their choice than the four- and five-year-olds.

Finally, in the third phase the children were presented the apparatus as shown at the bottom of the figure. One runway was placed two inches from the center section. When asked whether a ball dropped in the separated runway would make the puppet jump up, approximately half of the children at each age thought not, thus the children performed at chance level, indicating their sensitivity to spatial contiguity. They were then shown the event sequence with one ball dropped in the separated runway, the puppet jumping up, and the other ball dropped in the contiguous runway (C-D-C') and asked what happened. Spatial contiguity is pitted against temporal precedence. After seeing the sequence with the separated runway, the children selected the antecedent event (C), whether separated spatially or not. These data indicate that preschoolers are sensitive to both the priority and spatial contiguity principles and that when temporal priority and spatial contiguity are in conflict, the temporal order of events dominates their judgment of causality.

For adults the principle of priority is a general one that cannot be violated. What of young children? Does the priority principle dominate all other cues of causation? Although the Bullock and Gelman (1979) findings demonstrate that the children chose the antecedent event as the cause, their familiarity with the specific event rather than a general principle may have guided their judgement of causality. To test this possibility Sophian and Huber (1984) pitted specific learned cause-effect relations against temporal priority cues. Three- and five-year-olds learned a novel cause-effect relation. For example, a par-

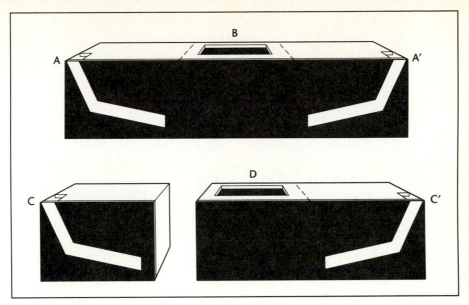

▶ **FIGURE 6-3** A study of the principle of priority. In phases one and two (top) preschoolers were able to correctly attribute causation (the puppet's appearance in the middle section)
to the antecedent event (ball placement into runway A). In phase three (bottom) preschoolers
were shown the following event sequence: a ball dropped into runway C, the puppet's appearance
(middle, D), and a ball dropped into runway, C. They attributed causation to the antecedent event
(C) whether separated spatially or not. (From Bullock and Gelman, 1979.)

ticular stuffed figure was always present when a toy animal did a trick; the
animal never did its trick when a second, similar stuffed figure was present.
After the children learned these cause-effect relations they were tested in a
conflict situation in which the figure trained as the cause was presented after
the animal did its trick and the other figure was presented first. When asked
what made the animal do its trick, the three-year-olds chose the subsequent
(trained) figure as often as the antecedent figure. The five-year-olds, however,
relied on the temporal order more than the trained knowledge in their causal
judgments.

Thus, it would appear that for young preschoolers (three-year-olds) the
principle of priority does not have a necessity that overrides all other cues of
causation. Rather, the causal judgments of this age are also influenced by other
causal cues, in particular knowledge about specific event relations. During the
preschool years, however, the principle of priority develops into a general one
that dominates specific cues of causation.

THE PRINCIPLE OF MECHANISM   A few studies have investigated the development
of the assumption that physical events are determined by other physical events
and that mechanisms are necessary for an antecedent event to cause an effect
(Bullock, Gelman & Baillargeon, 1982; Shultz, 1982). Baillargeon, Gelman,

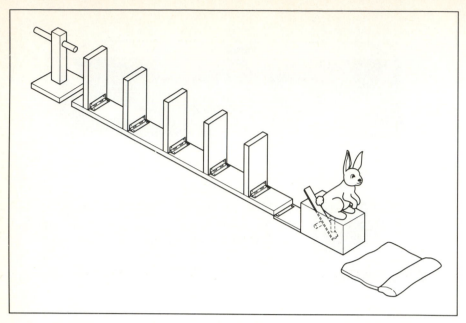

▶ **FIGURE 6-4** *The Fred-the-rabbit apparatus, used to test children's understanding of the principle of mechanism. In this experiment, children were shown a mechanism (rod), which initiated a series of events that resulted in the movement of the rabbit. Children were then asked to make predictions of the rabbits movement when various modifications were made to the mechanism. (From Bullock, Gelman & Baillargeon, 1982).*

and Meck (1981; Bullock, Gelman & Baillargeon, 1982) showed three- and four-year-old children an apparatus in which the movement of a rod at one end initiated a series of events that resulted in an effect three feet away (see Figure 6-4 for an illustration of the apparatus). After a demonstration of the apparatus, the children made predictions about the effects of modifications to the apparatus. These modifications were either irrelevant ones that would not affect the final effect, such as using a rod of a different color, or relevant ones that would change the final effect, such as a rod that was too short. The children observed 23 different modifications and were asked to make predictions for each one. As evident in Table 6-1, even the three-year-olds used information about mechanism to reason about event sequences, with 80 percent or more of the predictions correct for the relevant and irrelevant conditions.

Thus, young preschoolers can recognize specific mechanisms of causation. But we also have evidence that three-year-olds may not assume that a causal mechanism is a necessity (Bullock, 1985). When four- and five-year-olds do not know the mechanism that causes an event, they will invent specific mechanisms. Three-year-olds do not appear to assume that there must be a causal mechanism; young preschoolers appear to find information about mechanism relevant, but not necessary (Bullock, 1985). Although further research is needed, the available data support the hypothesis that, as in the case of the principle

TABLE 6-1 *Mean Percentage of Correct Predictions following Modifications to an Event Sequence*

		Source of Modification	
Modification Type	Age (years)	Initial Event	Intermediary Event
Relevant	3	81	78
	4	87	85
Irrelevant	3	88	96
	4	100	100

Source: Bullock, Gelman, and Baillargeon, 1982.

of priority, the principle of mechanism is just one component of causation for young preschoolers. Unlike older preschoolers, a general principle of mechanism does not pervade three-year-olds' conception of causation. Indeed, the generality of the mechanism principle may depend upon young children learning more about how events work (Bullock, 1985; Schultz, 1982).

THE PRINCIPLE OF COVARIATION   It would appear that from an early age we assume that physical events are caused and that we seek causal mechanisms in events that have temporal precedence. In our daily activities, however, cause-effect relations are embedded in a complex stream of simultaneous and successive events. For any event a multitude of potential causes precede it. Nevertheless, even when they do not know the mechanisms, adults infer specific cause and effect relations. These causal inferences are based upon multiple observations in which two events, cause and effect, covary. As an example, our understanding of the link between smoking and lung cancer derives from numerous observations in which scientists and physicians repeatedly found that smokers were more likely than nonsmokers to have lung cancer. The recognition of this covariation then led researchers to seek the causal mechanisms that coupled the two events.

What of young children? Do they assume causal relations in covarying events? In an attempt to address this question, Shultz and Mendelson (1975) presented children with the sequence of events: AX, B, AX, ABX, B, ABX, where $\overline{AB}$ indicates that A and B occurred simultaneously. Thus the A event was a consistent covariant of the X event; the B event was an inconsistent covariant. The children were asked the following questions: If A is present, will X happen? If B is present, will X happen? What makes X happen? How do you make X happen using either A or B? Even though the three- and four-year-olds were less likely to do so than the two older groups (6- to 7-year-olds and 9- to 11-year-olds), all ages chose the consistent covariant as the cause of the X event.

Philosophers make distinctions between two types of covarying events: necessary and sufficient (see, for example, Skyrms, 1975). The *necessary condition* is one that is always present in the presence of a given event but can also occur in the absence of the effect. When the cause does not happen, the event does not happen. For example, oxygen is necessary for combustion, but oxygen is often present without combustion. A *sufficient condition* is one that always is accompanied by a given event, but the event can occur without the sufficient condition. When the cause happens, the event also happens (Black, 1946). For example, fire is a sufficient condition since heat, the effect, is always present. But heat can occur without a fire (as in sunshine). These two types of conditions can be combined, resulting in a *necessary and sufficient condition*. In this case, if the condition is present the effect always occurs, and it only occurs if the condition is present. Thus covariation of events has three different types of relations.

Some philosophers of science assert that only the necessary and sufficient condition is an actual cause. Yet cause as commonly used can refer to any one of the three types of covariation (Bindra, Clarke & Shultz, 1980). *Cause,* meaning necessary condition, is used most often when the goal is to remove an undesirable event. To eliminate such an occurrence, we need to find some necessary condition and eliminate that condition. We smother a fire to eliminate oxygen. Cause in the sense of a sufficient condition is used most often when we want to produce a desired event. When we're cold we use fire to heat ourselves. In some situations, cause is used to mean the necessary and sufficient condition(s), as in when a fire chief is asked to determine the cause of a particular fire (Copi, 1972).

Siegler (1976) sought to determine whether children perceive cause-effect relations in the different types of covariation. Five- and eight-year-olds were presented with three pieces of apparatus: a computer with several lights that flashed on and off in a preprogrammed cycle; a card programmer, which had a slot for a computer card; and a box with a light on top of it. The children were told that the light bulb would come on and they were to decide what made the light go on—the computer or the card programmer. The children then experienced one of four conditions in which neither the presence or absence of the computer lights was consistently associated with the illumination of the light bulb. In the necessary and sufficient condition a card was inserted into the card programmer six times and the light bulb flashed on immediately after each insertion. In the necessary-only condition the card was inserted twelve times and the bulb flashed after six of those insertions. In the sufficient-only condition the children saw the card inserted three times. The light flashed six times; three of these were immediately after the card insertions. In the fourth neither necessary or sufficient condition, the occurrence of the six light flashes was not related to the card insertions.

When the children were asked, "What do you think made the light go on? Was it always the computer or always the card programmer or sometimes one and sometimes the other?" (Siegler, 1976, p. 1060), children in the necessary and sufficient condition selected the card programmer and this was true for both age groups. The five-year-olds in the necessary-only and sufficient-only conditions also were more likely to select the card programmer; the eight-year-olds tended to split their votes for the causal agent in necessary condition and to select a "sometimes one/sometimes the other" choice in the sufficient condition. In the neither necessary or sufficient condition, children of both ages split their choices between the three possibilities. Thus, children show a developmental change in the judgment of causality as a function of the nature of the covariation. The younger children attribute a causal connection on the basis of the temporal precedence in the three covariation conditions. The older children, however, demand more consistency in the regularity before they will attribute a causal connection.

THE PRINCIPLE OF SIMILARITY   Children will use the similarity of events in their causal judgments, especially when they do not have other relevant (for example, spatial or temporal) information. For example, when liquid from two potential causes (for example, blue dropper bottle (X) or pink dropper bottle (Y) was simultaneously put in clear liquid and the liquid then turned color, blue (x) or pink (y), children between six and twelve years of age were more likely to attribute the cause of the color change to the bottle that was similar in color to the liquid.

When, however, the similarity principle was put in conflict with the principle of temporal contiguity (for example, X-Yx) or the principle of covariation (for example, Xy, Y, XYy) the older children, but not the six-year-olds, tended to give up the principle of similarity and make their judgments significantly more often on the basis of temporal contiguity and consistency of covariation (Shultz & Ravinsky, 1977).

THE SELECTION AND APPLICATION OF CAUSAL PRINCIPLES

Our concept of causality is not a simple one. Rather, it is a theory of physical events that embraces several principles. Two of these, mechanisms and temporal priority, appear to be general enough to override the other principles, at least by five years of age. These principles are also general in the sense that they do not identify specific causes. That is, the principle of mechanism does not stipulate the causal mechanism of a given physical change, rather it specifies that there is a causal mechanism. Similarly, the principle of temporal priority does not indicate which of many prior events is a cause; it specifies that the cause is a prior event. Thus, when children and adults do not have specific knowledge about the cause of an event, they assume that there is a causal mechanism and that this cause occurred prior to the event. With these constraints on the perception of cause-effect relations, we use several principles to guide our judgments of causation.

But none of these principles guarantees that the cause of an event will be identified correctly. Causes are not always structurally similar to their effects (for example, bacteria and pneumonia). Nor is a cause always contiguous in time (for example, conception and birth) or space (for example, tides and phases of the moon) with its effect. And all psychology students learn that the covariation (correlation) of events does not always signal a cause-effect relation. Thus, the principles that guide our perception of causality, that organize our experience into cause-effect relations, are heuristic principles that constrain our causal inferences, rather than rules that guarantee the correct identification of a cause. (We return to a discussion of other heuristic principles in Chapter 8.)

Furthermore, in any given situation, information relevant to one or more of the principles can be lacking or in conflict. With several principles available and information varying from one situation to another, causal judgments require some type of selective process for the application of the causal principles to a specific situation (Shultz, Fisher, Pratt & Rulf, 1986). Although we know little about such a process, we might expect to discover developmental changes in the process. Our limited evidence of developmental changes in the application of the similarity principle and the use of covariation information suggests such a possibility. In addition, we know that context-specific knowledge plays a role in our assessment of causality (Einhorn & Hogarth, 1986). Thus, further understanding of the development of causal reasoning awaits the systematic exploration of many variables.

In summary, we have evidence that even preschoolers have, at least, implicit knowledge of the adult principles of causality. But we also have evidence that the preschool concept is not the adult concept of causality. Although three-year-olds appear to have some appreciation of mechanism and temporal priority, at this age neither of these principles seems to be necessary. During the preschool years, children have increasing access to these principles and make more general application of them (Bullock, 1985). Young children assume causal mechanisms and by four years of age will seek such mechanisms in novel situations. Furthermore, there are developmental changes in how young children judge the relevance of covariation for the attribution of causality.

Our limited research on the development of causality after the preschool years (for example, Shultz, 1982) and our knowledge of the complexity of adult causality (for example, Koslowski & Okagaki, 1986) indicate that causality is a complex interplay of many factors including content-specific knowledge about causal mechanisms and processes for selecting and applying the principles that are basic to causal inference.

Finally, the fact that children as young as three have some conception of causality raises questions about the origins of causality. When and how does causality begin to develop? Recently, Leslie and Keeble (1987) have presented evidence that six-month-olds perceive causal relations in visual events. These findings suggest the possibility that the beginnings of causality are early in development and that these beginnings arise out of basic perceptual processes. Further research will be necessary to replicate these findings and to trace the development of causality from infancy to preschool age.

EN d

SUMMARY

The focus of this chapter was on the development of concrete operations and higher-order concepts such as conservation, class inclusion, numbers, transitive inference, and causality. Piaget assumed that the onset of the concrete operational stage around seven or eight years of age signaled the beginning of a child's ability to use the mental operations of inversion and reciprocity to think about object relations. With the development of these mental operations a child has the requisite cognitive skills for the development of the higher-order concepts.

Subsequent research has focused on Piaget's concrete-operational tasks and the extent to which performance on these tasks adequately represents children's cognitive competencies. Although researchers generally agree on the developmental course of concrete operations, many have argued that the tasks make demands that go beyond the cognitive competencies assumed by Piaget. Often when task demands are modified the performance of young children does improve. For example, we saw that extensive training with the premises of the transitive inference task led even preschoolers to make the appropriate response on the inference test.

Although performance does improve with modification of Piaget's tasks, it is not always clear that the modified tasks are measuring the same competencies that Piaget sought to assess. Piaget was concerned with the development of explicit knowledge, as evident by his requirement that children be able to verbally justify their responses.

Work on the development of children's number knowledge indicates that before preschoolers can solve the number conservation task they do have implicit knowledge of several principles that are relevant to counting. Thus, their counting behavior indicates that they have knowledge of the one–one, stable-order, and cardinal principles. Further, if this knowledge is made explicit during pretraining young children can solve the number conservation task.

Flavell and his colleagues have demonstrated that preschoolers have a limited comprehension of the distinction between appearance and reality. As in the case of Piaget's perspective-taking task, young children have difficulty maintaining simultaneously two mental representations of an object or visual display. There is some evidence that the ability to represent dual codes develops through pretend play. During pretend play young children know the parts they are playing and at the same time maintain their own identities. Pretend play precedes the development of the reality-appearance distinction.

Although young children do not have an adult conception of causality their conception has many principles in common with that of adults. Three- and four-year-olds assume that some mechanism causes an effect. Further they assume that a cause must temporally precede the effect. As children develop, their understanding of principles, such as similarity and covariation, changes, as does their coordination of the several principles of causality.

7

Middle Childhood: The Development of Processes for Learning, Memory, and Comprehension

The emphasis in the previous two chapters was on the development of knowledge structures—on the representation of knowledge in long-term or permanent memory. The emphasis in this chapter is on the development of the processes that we use to learn and remember information. During their school years children are faced with a variety of learning, reading, and writing tasks that require directed efforts to comprehend and remember information. In this chapter we consider the research that has attempted to specify the nature of children's information-processing skills and, particularly, the development of these skills during early and middle childhood, a period when we see substantial growth in these skills.

Much of this research has been influenced by information-processing models of adult cognition. Look again at Figure 1-1 in Chapter 1. This general model specifies the basic components of memory and their relations. The individual boxes represent different types of knowledge structures, which are assumed to have different forms of representation. The depiction, however, is not intended to imply that different knowledge representations are in separable compartments or modules somewhere (Waldrop, 1988a, b). Rather, the boxes represent differences in functional characteristics. This model is a generic one; there are many information-processing theories that differ in specific assumptions and emphases. But all models assume that there are information-transforming processes (represented by the lines connecting the boxes), that the execution of the processes takes time, and that somewhere in the system there is a limited capacity for processing information. In this chapter we emphasize those processes, models, and issues that have influenced developmental research and theory on learning, memory, and comprehension.

► # ATTENTION

All models of adult information processing recognize that our capacity to attend to information is limited. We cannot process all information available to us at a given moment. Moreover, laboratory work indicates that college students are sensitive to this limitation and are able to direct and maintain their attention according to the demands of a task (for example, Moray, 1959; Neisser & Becklen, 1975). That is, in any given situation there are numerous external and internal stimuli that can be the focus of attention; yet, many, if not most, of these may be irrelevant to the task at hand. College students can often effectively attend to the information that is relevant to a task. At times attention does drift from the intended task, but for the most part college students can focus and control their attention.

Children do not appear to have the same control over their attention. Developmental research clearly demonstrates that young children are less likely to maintain selective attention to relevant information (see Lane & Pearson, 1982, for a review). Although the detrimental effect of irrelevant information on younger children's performance has been demonstrated in several experimental paradigms, it is most straightforwardly evident in the *speeded classification task* (for example, Well, Lorch & Anderson, 1980). For example, Strutt, Anderson, and Well (1975) asked subjects to sort a deck of cards as quickly as possible on the basis of the figures depicted on each card. In the zero-irrelevant dimensions condition the figures differed only on the relevant dimension used for sorting (for example, form: circle vs square). In conditions with one- and two-irrelevant dimensions, the figures also differed on one or two other dimensions that were not relevant to the sorting (for example, presence of a horizontal or vertical line in the figure, presence of a star just above or below the figure). The effect of irrelevant dimensions on sorting speed was determined by subtracting the speed of the sort in the zero-irrelevant dimension condition from the speed of the other two conditions. As evident in Figure 7-1, the irrelevant information interfered with performance at all ages; but, the interference effect was substantial for the six-year-olds, declined dramatically between six and nine, and then continued to decline more slowly until adulthood.

Although it is generally agreed that selective attention improves with age, the sources of this change are not clear (Hagen & Wilson, 1982; Jeffrey, 1982;

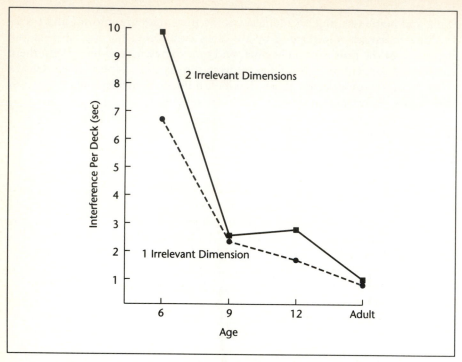

► **FIGURE 7-1**   *Mean amount of interference per deck as a function of age and the number of irrelevant dimensions. As is evident here, irrelevant information interfered with sorting ability at all ages. The interference effect was substantial for six-year-olds, declined dramatically between six and nine, and continued to decline into adulthood. (From Strutt, Anderson & Well, 1975.)*

Lane & Pearson, 1982, 1983; Odom, 1982). One possibility is that young children have more trouble separating the relevant dimension of a figure from the other aspects of the figure. As we saw in Chapter 5, younger children often process visual figures as wholes rather than analyzing them into distinct dimensions. Thus, when instructed to attend to a single visual dimension, younger children may have more difficulty isolating this dimension from the whole. This cannot be the entire answer, however. Developmental changes in selective attention are not limited to tasks that require visual analysis. Young children also are more distracted by a competing message when required to listen selectively (see, for example, Doyle, 1973), and they are less selective in deploying their attention when they must perform two tasks simultaneously (see, for example, Lane, 1979; Schiff & Knopf, 1985).

   With development, children not only are more attentive to information that an experimenter specifies as task relevant, but also are more flexible in the allocation of attention, adjusting the selectivity of their attention to task demands (Hale, 1979; Hagen & Hale, 1973). Hale and his colleagues, for example, found that when children are not directed to attend to specific information, older children attend to more potentially relevant information than younger children (see, Hale, 1979, for a review). Using a *component selection*

CHAPTER 7 / MIDDLE CHILDHOOD: PROCESSES

task, these researchers (for example, Hale & Taweel, 1974) presented children with a row of colored shapes and asked them to learn the spatial position of each of these stimuli. The colors and shapes of these stimuli were redundant; therefore, the children could solve this problem by attending to either a single component (color or shape) or both components of the stimuli. In a test phase, the basis of learning was determined by presenting each stimulus component one at a time (for example, a colorless shape or a colored card) and asking for its appropriate location.

If a child learns the positions of the stimuli by attending to one or the other component, then the test scores for one dimension should be above chance and the other at chance. Attention to both components of the stimuli, however, can be inferred from above-chance performance on both types of components. Several studies using this paradigm and a variety of stimuli reveal that between the ages of four and eight performance was near perfect for one dimension (dominant) and that there was a developmental increase in performance for the nondominant dimension (see Hale, 1979, for a review). That is, most children tend to solve the problem by attending to one dimension (such as, shape), but attention to the redundant dimension (such as, color) increases with age. Furthermore, if instructed to use the nondominant component (color) to solve the problem, older children will increase their attention to that dimension and decrease it to the dominant component (shape) (Hale, Taweel, Green & Flaugher, 1978). Under the same conditions, however, younger children do not decrease their attention to the dominant dimension as they increase their attention to the nondominant dimension (see Figure 7-2).

Taken together, the data indicate a developmental increase in the flexibility of attention deployment. Older children are better able to direct their attention as a function of task demands. When left to their own devices, their attention is less restricted to the dominant or salient dimensions of the available information. When instructed to direct their attention, they are more focused and more likely to ignore salient but irrelevant information. Thus, as voluntary attention develops, children's attention is increasingly evoked and maintained by the goals and plans of the child rather than by the physical characteristics of stimuli (Zaporozhets & Elkonin, 1971).

Children's performance in other tasks we have considered, for example, the conservation and class-inclusion tasks, suggests a similar developmental change in attention deployment. And since the acquisition of knowledge requires attention (see, for example, Nissen & Bullemer, 1987), we can expect the development of attention-deployment skills to have an important role in children's learning and memory (see, for example, Brown, 1982). As children develop, for example, they become more aware of the role of psychological factors, such as motivation and capacity limits, in the maintenance of attention (Miller & Bigi, 1979; Pillow, 1988). As will be evident later in this chapter, children become increasingly knowledgeable about the factors that influence their ability to acquire and retain information. The goal for future research is to understand how attention-deployment skills develop and to identify those factors that determine the use of these skills. Adults and older children may

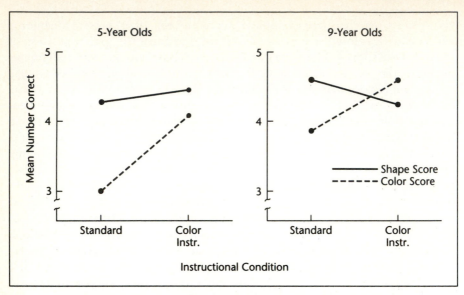

▶ **FIGURE 7-2** *Mean correct responses to shapes and colors in test phase for each Age × Instruction subgroup. Younger children (left) do not decrease their attention to the dominant dimension as they increase their attention to the undominant dimension, whereas older children do (right). (From Hale, Taweel, Green & Flaegher, 1978.)*

either be more selective or less selective, depending upon the situation (Ackerman, 1986). The challenge now is to specify how situations serve to encourage or discourage selective attention and why young children differ from adults in these situations (see Day, 1980; Hagen & Wilson, 1982; Jeffrey, 1982; Lane & Pearson, 1982, 1983; Odom, 1982).

▶ ## LEARNING AND MEMORY

Information-processing models make a theoretical distinction among three types of processes that are particularly relevant to learning and memory: encoding, storage, and retrieval. *Encoding processes* transform a physical stimulus into a mental representation or code. Reading this sentence involves an encoding process that transforms the visual patterns into semantic representations. *Storage processes* preserve mental representations either temporarily or permanently. It is one thing to identify the words of a sentence, it is another to have a stored representation of the words that is independent of their physical presence. *Retrieval processes* function to retrieve information from our stored representations. As evident in Chapters 5 and 6, we have vast amounts of stored knowledge, only a small part of which plays a role in our behavior at a given time. It is the retrieval processes that bring specific information into operation.

A TETRAHEDRAL MODEL OF LEARNING AND MEMORY

During the past 25 years, extensive research on memory and its development has served to underscore the complexity of human memory. Memory is not a unitary package of information that can be described with a few general laws (Jenkins, 1979). Rather, memory is dynamic and is determined by four types of variables: the characteristics of the learner, the criterial tasks, the nature of the materials, and the learning activities. A tetrahedral model, as illustrated in Figure 7-3, has been used to represent these variables and their interrelationships (Bransford, 1979; Brown, Bransford, Ferrara & Campione, 1983; Jenkins, 1979). It is only within the context of these variables and their interactions that we can begin to understand the nature of human memory.

Learners come to a situation with many characteristics that affect memory. These include such diverse factors as the learner's knowledge, motivation, and physical state. If, for example, learners know that attention is necessary for learning and they also have the goal of learning, they may engage in activities that maintain attention. As this example makes clear, the memory variables are interdependent and interact to determine memory.

The demands of a criterial task also will affect the process of remembering. For example, recall tasks require different retrieval processes than recognition memory tasks, thus placing different demands on learners. Young children often do much better on recognition memory tasks than on recall tasks (see, for example, Brown & Campione, 1972). Thus, we cannot talk about the development of children's memory in general terms, but must consider the nature of the criterial task used to assess memory. Furthermore, memory in a specific type of task is influenced by the other variables of the tetrahedron. Consider a study by Mandler and Robinson (1978) in which first, third, and fifth graders were presented with two types of pictures of scenes. Organized scenes depicted a set of objects as they are usually arranged in the real world (for example, a kitchen scene with stove, refrigerator, sink). Unorganized scenes depicted the same objects as the organized scenes, but arranged in a random way. Recognition of the unorganized scenes was comparable for all ages; recognition of the organized scenes, however, improved with age. This difference appears to reflect developmental changes in children's knowledge of familiar scenes. Just as general knowledge structures, such as scripts, influence our memory for familiar social events, so general knowledge structures influence our memory for the spatial arrangement of objects in the real world. As children acquire this knowledge, it facilitates the encoding and storage of organized scenes. Thus, at the very least, the development of recognition memory reflects the relationship between the nature of the materials and the knowledge children bring to the materials.

Similarly, the nature of the materials contributes to and interacts with other variables to determine our memories. For example, it is common finding that the familiarity of materials can influence our memories (see, for example, Underwood & Schulz, 1960). Typically, I remember more of an article on

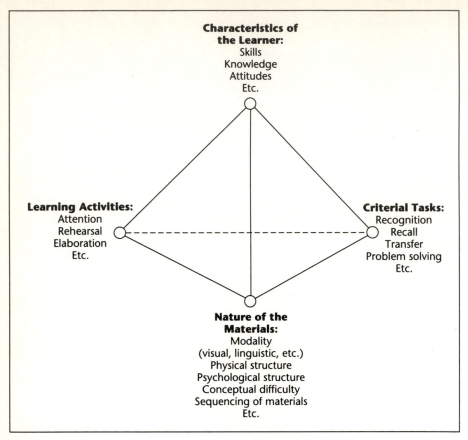

Characteristics of
the Learner:
Skills
Knowledge
Attitudes
Etc.

Learning Activities:
Attention
Rehearsal
Elaboration
Etc.

Criterial Tasks:
Recognition
Recall
Transfer
Problem solving
Etc.

Nature of the
Materials:
Modality
(visual, linguistic, etc.)
Physical structure
Psychological structure
Conceptual difficulty
Sequencing of materials
Etc.

▶ **FIGURE 7-3** As depicted in this tetrahedral model, learning and memory are determined by four types of variables: the characteristics of the learner, the criterial tasks, the nature of the materials, and the learning activities. (From Bransford, 1979.)

psychology than on chemistry. This difference undoubtedly reflects differences in my interest in the two topics and, thus, the amount of attention I direct to each. Furthermore, I bring more background knowledge to a psychology article, which makes new information easier to understand and remember.

The learners' activities also influence what information is encoded and stored. The acquisition of knowledge, for example, requires at least some attention to the information. Sleeping students do not learn from a textbook lying next to them.

In summary, we will not find general laws of memory that are "applicable to any subjects, to all learning activities, to all classes of materials, and to all types of criterial tasks" (Jenkins, 1979, p. 443). The four variables of the tetrahedral model of learning and memory cannot be considered in isolation; rather, they interact in powerful ways to determine what is learned and what is remembered. Learning and memory are two sides of the same coin.

METHODS OF STUDY

Research on memory development has emphasized deliberate forms of remembering, using tasks in which subjects are aware of what they remember and/or their attempts to remember. For example, in a recognition memory task, subjects are asked to judge whether a given stimulus is familiar to them, whether they are aware of a personal experience with that stimulus. The demands of this task, as indicated earlier (see Chapter 3), differ from those of the infant recognition memory tasks in which memory is inferred from the effects of prior experience on behavior. The infant may or may not know that she saw the familiar stimulus. Similarly, recall tasks often require deliberate and conscious efforts to remember information that was experienced in a specific context.

Although paradigms have been developed to study adult memory without awareness (for example, Jacoby & Witherspoon, 1982), to date the developmental research has focused on tasks in which children are instructed to make efforts to remember (but see Anooshian, 1987, for a developmental study of memory without awareness). Furthermore, most research on memory development has focused on recall, in part because there is an impressive and extended developmental improvement in recall. For example, in a digit-span task in which subjects are presented a series of numbers for immediate serial recall, college students typically recall eight digits; three-year-olds, however, recall about three digits (Chi, 1978). This chapter focuses on the development of children's ability to learn and recall information intentionally.

Most of the research on the development of children's deliberate efforts to learn and remember have used tasks that require memories for information that is associated with a particular time and/or place. Earlier we made a distinction between procedural knowledge and declarative knowledge; some investigators make a further distinction between two types of declarative knowledge: semantic and episodic memory (for example, Tulving, 1972, 1984). This distinction has had several variations (for a discussion, see Nelson & Brown, 1978; Tulving, 1985), but here *semantic memory* consists of the knowledge structures discussed in Chapters 5 and 6, which are our knowledge of concepts and their relations, our knowledge of words and language, and our general knowledge of the world. *Episodic memory,* however, is memory for specific, personally experienced events and includes information about the temporal and spatial context of the event. This distinction between the kinds of information that define semantic and episodic memory is evident in our use of the verb "know" when referring to our general knowledge of the world and the verb "remember" for our recollections of personal experiences (Tulving, 1984). Not all psychologists agree, however, that these differences in type of memory content require the assumption of two distinct memory systems (for example, Jacoby & Witherspoon, 1982; McKoon & Ratcliff, 1979), and, indeed, it should be evident that the two are not independent (see, for example, Hannigan, Shelton, Franks & Bransford, 1980). It is through particular experiences (episodic memory) that we acquire and modify our general knowledge (semantic memory) (Tulving, 1972).

Although any memory task requires both episodic and semantic memory, much of the experimental research on memory development emphasizes episodic aspects of memory. When, for example, children perform in the digit-span task, we are not investigating their semantic memory, their knowledge of numbers, but their episodic memory, their ability to remember which particular numbers were presented in the list. Of course, this task does involve semantic memory. The identification of the experimenter's words or the visual patterns on a screen requires the activation of the children's knowledge of numbers; they cannot know which numbers they just heard unless they can identify them. Although memory tasks like the digit span are often used to investigate memory development independent of the concomitant development of semantic knowledge, as will become evident, several factors, including the development of semantic knowledge, interact to affect children's acquisition and memory of information.

WORKING MEMORY

Most information-processing theories make a distinction between a long-term memory and a short-term memory system (but see Craik & Lockhart, 1972). This distinction is used to accommodate the data that we have a limited capacity for handling information and that retention of information sometimes has a short duration. The nature of the short-term memory system, however, is a controversial issue (see Dempster, 1985, for a discussion); as a consequence, there are several different conceptions of the short-term memory system, as well as variations in terminology. Here we will use *working memory* to refer to the theoretical conceptualization of the short-term memory system that has been adopted by many developmental psychologists and *short-term memory* to refer to performance on tasks that test for memory relatively soon after acquisition. These tasks are assumed to implicate working memory, but, in most cases, involve both working memory and permanent memory.

Working memory represents the information that we are attending to at a given time, including information from the sensory stores and permanent memory. It is a temporary mechanism for coordinating and processing information from our internal and external environments and is characterized by two important limits. First, working memory has a limited storage capacity. In adults this limitation is characterized as 7 ± 2 chunks of information (Miller, 1956). That is, adults can only think about (attend to) approximately seven pieces of information at one time. Second, the activation of information in working memory has a short duration unless specific efforts are made to maintain attention to the information. One strategy for maintaining information in working memory is maintenance rehearsal, a process by which information in working memory is continually attended to in a serial fashion. Such rehearsal is under a subject's conscious control and takes time (Chi, 1976).

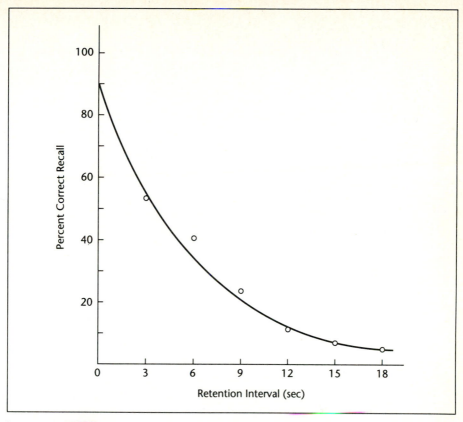

▶ **FIGURE 7-4** *The importance of rehearsal as demonstrated by the Brown-Peterson paradigm. Subjects were presented with three items and then given an interim task which prevented rehearsal. As evidenced here, under these conditions recall declined rapidly, even with retention intervals of 18 seconds or less.* (From Howard, 1983.)

The importance of rehearsal for maintaining information in working memory has been demonstrated in the Brown-Peterson paradigm (Brown, 1958; Peterson & Peterson, 1959). In this task subjects are presented with three items (for example, letters) and then given an interim task that prevents rehearsal (for example, counting backwards by threes from 361). Under these conditions, as is evident in Figure 7-4, recall declines rapidly, even with retention intervals of 18 seconds or less.

Adult research indicates that working memory has two functions. One function is to maintain attention to information that is needed to solve a problem (Craik & Watkins, 1973). As a result, working memory plays a role in reasoning and verbal comprehension (Baddeley & Hitch, 1974). To illustrate this, compare your efforts to solve mentally the following three arithmetic problems: $4 \times 7 = ?$, $47 \times 23 = ?$, and $472 \times 356 = ?$ The mental effort and operations required to answer the first problem are easily within the capacity of working memory, but most of us would find that the third problem

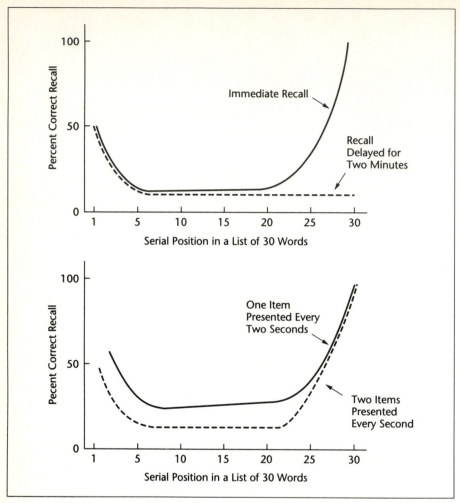

FIGURE 7-5 *The top drawing shows how percent correct recall should be affected by requiring subjects to delay recall (dotted line) for two minutes during which they count backward by threes. Such a delay should influence only working memory and, hence, the recency portion of the curve. The bottom drawing shows how recall should be affected by varying the rate of presentation. This should influence only long-term memory, so slow presentation (the solid line) should be better than fast presentation (the dotted line), but only for the primacy and central regions of the curve. (From Howard, 1983.)*

required attention to more operations and information than we can maintain in working memory.

A second function of working memory is to transfer information to permanent memory. The acquisition of new associations requires attention to the new information (see, for example, Nissen & Bullemer, 1987). In order for information to be stored in permanent memory, it must be operated on (recoded) when it is in working memory. As we will see, these operations are varied; but as a consequence of transfer to permanent memory, adult performance on short-term memory tasks reflects recall both from working memory and from permanent memory. If, for example, subjects are given a free recall task in which items are recalled immediately after presentation and can be recalled in any order, adults' performance indicates a *serial position effect* (see Figure 7-5). Recall is best for items presented at the beginning of the list (*primacy effect*) and at the end of the list (*recency effect*). Numerous investigations with a variety of manipulations have demonstrated that the primacy effect represents recall of items from permanent memory and that the recency effect reflects recall from working memory (see Howard, 1983, for a discussion). To illustrate, if recall is delayed, it should affect recall from working memory, but not permanent memory. Thus, delayed recall should reduce the recency effect but not the primacy effect, which is the case. Similarly, a faster rate of presentation should interfere with recoding and transfer of information to permanent memory, but should not influence working memory. Thus, as depicted in Figure 7-5, this manipulation should depress the primacy effect and have no effect on recency. This is the case for adults. Most memory tasks do not exclusively assess working memory, because adults will transfer some of the information to permanent memory, if the conditions permit.

Extensive research on the developmental changes in children's recall has established changes not only in total recall, but also in children's ability to maintain information in working memory and to transfer information from working memory to permanent memory. For example, the fact that young children are less likely than older children to show a primacy effect (see, for example, Ornstein, Naus & Liberty, 1975), suggests that young children have difficulty transferring information to permanent memory.

In their efforts to understand why such developmental changes occur, investigators have focused on the development of five types of learning and memory variables: mnemonic strategies for remembering, metamemory (knowledge about memory), content knowledge, the automation of memory processes, and maturational changes in memory processes. As would be expected from the tetrahedral model, however, these variables have interacting effects on the development of memory that researchers are just beginning to explore.

THE DEVELOPMENT OF MNEMONIC STRATEGIES

Adults spontaneously use a variety of strategies that facilitate recall. Although there are differences in the definition of *strategy* (see, for example, Paris, Newman & Jacobs, 1985; Pressley, Forrest-Pressley, Elliott-Faust & Miller, 1985), here it is used to mean "a selected action performed for the purpose of achieving a particular goal" (Paris *et al.*, 1985, p. 85). Thus, *mnemonic strategies* are "courses of action which are deliberately instigated for the purpose of remembering" (Brown, 1975, p. 110). These procedures include such methods as rehearsal, clustering or categorization, and imagery (see Kosslyn, 1980, for a discussion of imagery).

Rehearsal, as we have seen, is one strategy that adults use to maintain information in working memory. A variety of techniques demonstrate that the majority of young children do not spontaneously engage in rehearsal until around five years of age (see, for example, Daehler, Horowitz, Wynns & Flavell, 1969; see Ornstein & Naus, 1978, for a review). Furthermore, when rehearsal occurs, children's memory performance improves. For example, the recall of six-year-olds who do not rehearse spontaneously and are induced to rehearse is comparable to that of six-year-olds who do rehearse spontaneously. However, young children who are trained to rehearse do not always apply this strategy when it is appropriate (see, for example, Keeny, Cannizzio & Flavell, 1967). Furthermore, young spontaneous rehearsers do not use the same types of rehearsal procedure as older children and adults. It is not until sixth grade that most children spontaneously use a cumulative rehearsal strategy in which each new and unrelated item is rehearsed in a set of two or more previously presented items; before this children spontaneously rehearse words singly, as illustrated in Table 7-1.

Rehearsal not only maintains information in working memory (Craik & Watkins, 1973), but also provides an opportunity for subjects to perform elaborative processes on the information, processes that are important in the permanent storage of information. Elaborative strategies serve to integrate associations or images with the to-be-remembered information. That is, it is not rehearsal per se that transfers information to permanent memory, but operations on the information that establish relationships between it and existing information in permanent memory. These operations occur as we maintain attention to the information during the rehearsal process (Craik & Lockhart, 1972).

To give one illustration, in free recall tasks, college students tend to organize the words and recall related items together. When such *clustering* occurs, there is a concomitant increase in recall (compare, Frankel & Rollins, 1982). That is, recall of randomly ordered lists of related words (for example, four animals, four kinds of clothing, four kinds of furniture, and four color names) is superior to recall of an unrelated list, and the words in the related list are clustered into categories during recall.

Extensive research indicates that young children are less likely to use elaborative strategies (Zaporozhets & Elkonin, 1971; Naus & Ornstein, 1983) and that during the school years there is a tremendous increase in the quality and variety of children's mnemonic strategies (Hagen, Jongeward & Kail, 1975). Initially, elaborative strategies are used only under optimal conditions, with structured tasks and materials that promote an elaborative strategy. For example, if related words are presented adjacently, clustering of the related words is more likely at the time of recall. With age, children become more active in initiating the use of strategies and use them across a wider range of tasks and conditions. Since the deliberate use of mnemonic strategies has a substantial effect on memory performance, many investigators have assumed that memory development is a function of developmental changes in the use of mnemonic strategies.

TABLE 7-1 *Typical Rehearsal Protocols (Unrelated Words)*

Word Presented	Rehearsal Sets	
	Eighth Grade Subject	**Third Grade Subject**
1. Yard	Yard, yard, yard	Yard, yard, yard, yard, yard
2. Cat	Cat, yard, yard, cat	Cat, cat, cat, yard
3. Man	Man, cat, yard, man, yard, cat	Man, man, man, man, man
4. Desk	Desk, man, yard, cat, man, desk, cat, yard	Desk, desk, desk, desk

Source: Ornstein et al., 1975. © The Society for Research in Child Development, Inc.

Given that indeed there are developmental increases in the deliberate use of mnemonic strategies, the question then is to explain how this change occurs. This is really two questions: How are specific strategies learned? and How do children learn when to use a particular strategy? Most of the research relevant to the first question has focused on training children to use specific elaborative strategies (see, for example, Pressley, Heisel, McCormick & Nakamura, 1982). This research indicates that children can be trained to use specific strategies. We know, however, that children do acquire some mnemonic strategies without directed training. We return to this question in the section on the acquisition of metamemory.

The second question recognizes that even when children are capable of executing a mnemonic strategy they do not always do so spontaneously. To use a strategy deliberately, children must not only be able to execute the strategy but also must know that the strategy would be useful in a given situation. This requires that the children know something about the nature of memory and their own memory capabilities in that situation. Thus, developmental changes in the use of mnemonic strategies may reflect, in part at least, the development of children's knowledge about memory itself, or metamemory (Flavell, 1971).

THE DEVELOPMENT OF METAMEMORY

Although investigators have not always agreed upon the definition of *metamemory* (Cavanaugh & Perlmutter, 1982; Wellman, 1983), here the term refers to the factual knowledge that children have about memory tasks, processes, and strategies, as well as their knowledge of the current states of their own memory, including its contents and limits (Wellman, 1983). Thus, metamemory is domain-specific knowledge about memory. In an attempt to understand how the acquisition of knowledge about memory influences children's memory performance, we focus on three issues: the nature of children's metamemory, how this knowledge relates to memory performance, and how metamemory is acquired.

Flavell and his colleagues (for example, Flavell & Wellman, 1977) have identified two types of memory knowledge: sensitivity and variables. *Sensitivity* is the knowledge that a particular situation requires specific efforts to remember. Some situations require specific efforts to remember whereas others do not. All of us, young children and adults alike, learn and remember many things incidentally. When I watch a film, for example, I do so for entertainment and rarely make efforts to remember specifics of the film. Yet, I have no difficulty describing the plot of the film to a friend the next day or next week. If, however, I had to write a review of the film, I might very well make additional efforts to ensure my recall of specific details.

Even preschoolers know that some situations require efforts to remember. For example, Weissberg and Paris (1986) tested the recall of three- to six-year-old children in two types of situations: games and lessons. In one game situation the children were asked to pretend that they were shopping. The experimenter read them a five-item shopping list of what they were to buy, and after a short delay the children used play money to purchase the items at a pretend store. In the lesson conditions the same children were given standard instructions to remember the words that they heard.

At all ages recall was higher in the lesson conditions than the play conditions. Although there were developmental increases in the incidence of rehearsal, half of the three-year-olds rehearsed in the lesson conditions (vs 12 percent in the play conditions), and children at all ages rehearsed more often in the lesson conditions than the play conditions. Thus, young preschoolers have some sensitivity to the need for efforts to remember and are capable of spontaneous rehearsal. Their failure to rehearse in the play situations may reflect a failure to recognize the need for efforts in such a situation or the distraction of the game activities, which prevented them from initiating and/or executing the rehearsal (compare, Istomina, 1975; Mistry & Rogoff, 1987).

The other type of memory knowledge, *variables,* is knowledge about three aspects of a situation—person, task, and strategy—that can affect memory. *Knowledge of person variables* is knowledge about those aspects of the self or other humans that can influence performance in that situation. *Knowledge of task variables* is knowledge of those characteristics of a task that are relevant to memory performance. *Knowledge of strategy variables* is knowledge of the mnemonic strategies that can facilitate memory. Thus, metamemory is knowledge about the variables of the tetrahedral model (Figure 7-3) that are known to affect learning and memory.

A number of studies have demonstrated developmental changes in children's comprehension of these variables (for example, Kreutzer, Leonard & Flavell, 1975; Wellman, 1977). Young preschoolers typically know that more items are harder to remember than a few items and that a distracting noise can interfere with remembering. Furthermore, most three-year-olds know that some variables (for example, a person's weight, hair color, and clothes) are irrelevant to memory performance (Wellman, 1977). Three- to five-year-olds know that some person variables, such as fatigue and mood, affect how easily information is acquired (Hayes, Scott, Chemelski & Johnson, 1987). In addition, five-year-olds understand that "the variables of age (adults remember better than young children), help (that splitting the memory load with a friend is easier than doing it alone), drawing (that drawing a representation of the to-be-remembered items aids retrieval), time (that long study time facilitates recall), and cues (that external related cues facilitate retrieval) are all relevant to memory" (Wellman, 1985, p. 183). By the time that children are in the first grade, they know about many person, task, and strategy variables, and this knowledge continues to grow during the elementary school years (Flavell & Wellman, 1977).

But adult knowledge of memory is not simply a collection of facts about isolated variables. Rather, it can best be understood as a theory of memory in which various facts, concepts, and beliefs are interwoven. To illustrate, when I have a small class of students (12 or less), I can usually learn their names simply by asking their names and then using their names frequently in the first few classes. In larger classes, however, I use additional strategies, including imagery, to remember names. Thus, knowledge of both task variables (number of students) and strategy variables (naming, rehearsal, and imagery) are weighed in my attempts to remember.

Recent research has demonstrated that young children also integrate information about memory variables and, importantly, that there are developmental differences in how the variables are combined. Wellman, Collins, and Glieberman (1981) presented nine memory situations to students ranging from preschool to college age. These situations represented all possible combinations of three levels of numbered items (4, 8, and 12 items) and three levels of effort (no, little, and a lot of effort) by an imaginary learner. The students were asked to predict how many items would be remembered in each situation. Their responses indicated that, at all ages, students integrated knowledge about the two variables: both number of items and effort influenced the predictions. But the young children emphasized effort more than the number of items; this emphasis decreased with age.

Such findings suggest that even when young children have knowledge of specific variables, they may have different conceptions of how these variables are interrelated. In Chapter 5 we saw a similar situation in the development of children's biological knowledge (Carey, 1985b). Thus, not only are there developmental changes in children's knowledge of individual facts about memory variables but also developmental changes in how they relate to each other, presumably within a more general theory of memory and cognition (Wellman, 1985).

THE RELATION BETWEEN MEMORY PERFORMANCE AND METAMEMORY   Although the original impetus for the investigation of metamemory was to explain memory development, many studies have failed to demonstrate high positive correlations between performance and metamemory. For example, a common negative finding is that a child asserts the importance of a mnemonic strategy (for example, organization) and then fails to use the strategy in a memory task. It is not clear, however, how to interpret these findings because we do not have an adequate conception of how knowledge of memory variables relates to the application of that knowledge in a given memory task (Wellman, 1983). For example, I know that imagery is a powerful mnemonic strategy, but I do not always use this strategy.

Furthermore, most investigations of the metamemory/memory performance relation have assessed knowledge of a single memory variable relative to performance in a single task. Yet, as we have seen, children have integrated systems of knowledge and young children place a premium on effort. If this factor is more heavily weighted than the memory strategy assessed (for example, organization), then a child may very well rely on effort in a memory task rather than use an organization strategy. Before we can derive predictions for performance in a given situation, we must know more about a child's system of memory knowledge, how that knowledge is accessed, and how that knowledge is weighed relative to other factors.

Although investigations of the relations between children's knowledge of strategies and memory performance generally show a weak relationship at best, the results are more positive in studies of the relation between performance and children's knowledge of their own memory states (see, Schneider, 1985, for a review). Indeed, several studies suggest that, when requested, even young children can monitor their state of knowledge and that they will allocate efforts to remember on the basis of these assessments (see Schneider, 1985; Wellman, 1985). Wellman (1977), for example, has demonstrated that a "feeling-of-knowing" is related to the efforts of kindergarteners to retrieve information. The children were shown pictures of concrete objects and asked to name them. Those pictures that they could not name were presented again, and the children were asked whether they thought they knew each one's name anyway even if they could not remember it. Following this, these pictures were presented two more times as children were asked questions about each object (for example, "What if I told you a lot of names, could you pick out the right name for this picture?"); no requests, however, were made for names. During these presentations, the children's responses were scored for spontaneous efforts to retrieve the names of the objects, efforts such as attempts to name (for example, "fun . . . fum" for "funnel"), retrieval-related cues (for example, references to the function of the object, "doctors use it"), requests for time to retrieve (for example, "I know it, let me see. . . ."), questions on retrieval (for example, "What *is* that?"), affirming that retrieval is possible (for example, "I know that name."), and release from effort to retrieve ("That's what it was."). The children were more likely to make efforts of retrieval for those objects they thought they knew than for the ones they thought they did not know.

There is also suggestive evidence that metamemory plays a role in the acquisition of elaborative strategies, particularly the transfer of trained strategies to new tasks (Pressley, Borkowski & O'Sullivan, 1985). To illustrate, Kurtz, Reid, Borkowski & Cavanaugh (1982) queried second graders about their knowledge of an elaborative strategy for associating unrelated items in a paired-associate task, as well as about several aspects of their general knowledge of memory. After this assessment, the experimental subjects were trained to use the elaborative strategy in a paired-associate task. One week later these children, and control subjects who did not receive strategy training, were given a paired-associate task and a transfer task that required learning associations for sets of three pictures. As might be expected, strategy training affected performance; the experimental subjects used the elaborative strategy and outperformed the control subjects on both tasks. More importantly, the use of the strategy by the experimental subjects was positively correlated with their metamemory. That is, those experimental subjects who knew more about the nature of memory were more likely to use the newly acquired strategy in the transfer tasks. Such data suggest the potential importance of children's general knowledge about memory in their decisions to use a specific strategy in a given situation. Furthermore, we have experimental evidence that when children understand the value of a mnemonic strategy for their own performance, they are more likely to use the strategy (Paris, Newman & McVey, 1982; Pressley, Ross, Levin & Ghatala, 1984). That is, when children were not only taught a mnemonic strategy, but also given feedback that emphasized the usefulness of the strategy, they were more likely to use the strategy.

Thus, we have some evidence of a relation between children's metamemory and their behavior in a memory task. These findings, however, highlight how little we know about children's integration of their system of memory knowledge. At this point, for example, we know nothing about how children's knowledge of memory variables relates to their abilities to monitor their own memory contents. Furthermore, we know little about how the development of metamemory relates to more general aspects of the development of planning and problem-solving abilities that will influence children's abilities to access and apply their knowledge of memory.

THE ACQUISITION OF METAMEMORY   Knowing that the use of mnemonic strategies increases with age and is influenced by children's knowledge about memory, raises yet another question: How do children acquire knowledge about memory, including mnemonic strategies? Flavell (1981) has proposed that in the course of normal development children have metacognitive experiences that lead to the acquisition of memory knowledge. Such experiences are most likely to occur when we have to think, speak, or act in new and unaccustomed ways (for example, when trying to solve a novel problem), when we are not in a highly emotional state and have the time and resources to think about our cognition, and when we can reflect upon new cognitive demands before us. The fact that cross-cultural research demonstrates a positive relationship between the use of mnemonic strategies (for example, clustering) and amount of education, independent of age, suggests that the demands of schooling may be particularly important for the generation of metacognitive experiences (see, for example, Sharp, Cole & Lave, 1979; see Rogoff, 1981, and Wagner, 1981, for reviews). "Schools emphasize retention as an explicit goal and provide students with diverse test-like experiences" (Kail, 1984, p. 174), experiences that can provide feedback about the efficacy of mnemonic strategies (see, for example, Zivian & Darjes, 1983).

Flavell's position not only offers a possible explanation for the acquisition of strategy knowledge, but also the possibility that, with development, metacognitive experiences increase in frequency. Demands for deliberate retention probably increase as a child progresses through school. Furthermore, children and adults may have more attentional and/or memorial resources available for such experiences than younger children. Although there is little research relevant to this issue, Pressley and his colleagues (Pressley, Levin & Ghatala, 1984) present preliminary evidence that children gain less knowledge than adults from the experience of using different strategies and that the knowledge that they gain from the metacognitive experience has less influence on their subsequent efforts to remember.

THE DEVELOPMENT OF CONTENT KNOWLEDGE

Although mnemonic strategies undoubtedly contribute to memory development, these strategies cannot be the only source of memory development since developmental differences in memory performance occur even when recall is unexpected and, presumably, deliberate efforts to remember are not made (see, for example, Geis & Hall, 1976; Lindberg, 1980). This is readily demonstrated in an *incidental learning task*. Lindberg (1980), for example, presented 6, 12, and 22-year-old students with 24-item lists of unrelated words and asked them to make one of four types of responses to each word: (a) physical—to say whether a male or female voice produced the word, (b) acoustic—to produce a rhyming word, (c) semantic—to define the word, and (d) imagery—to imagine the looks of the object named. After this task, subjects had an unexpected recall test.

As evident in Figure 7-6, the recall of the youngest children in the imagery and semantic conditions was substantially poorer than that of the older children and adults, even though deliberate efforts to remember were unlikely to be playing a role. Such differences in performance may be due to the substantial changes that occur in children's domain-specific knowledge. With the development of the knowledge base, children have richer conceptual representations that can facilitate, without mnemonic strategies, the organization and retrieval of to-be-remembered items. To illustrate, consider a child who is presented a list of words that includes "dog" and "honey." If the child has acquired the conceptual relations between "dog" and "animal" and between "honey" and "bear," as well as "bear" and "animal," these connections may be automatically activated during encoding and thus may serve as retrieval cues at the time of retrieval. That is, retrieving "dog" serves as a retrieval cue for "honey" through the "dog-animal-bear-honey" conceptual relations.

Chi (1976, 1978) effectively demonstrated the influence of content knowledge on memory in a study that compared the performance of ten-year-olds

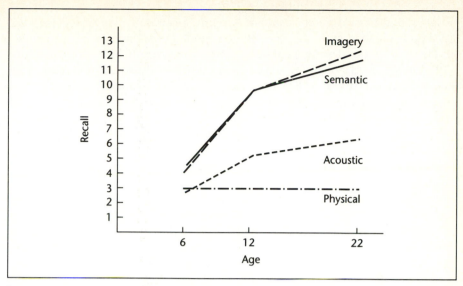

▶ **FIGURE 7-6** *In this incidental learning task, students aged 6, 12, and 22 years were presented with 24-item lists of unrelated words and asked to make one of four types of responses: physical, acoustic, semantic, and imagery. As is evident here, the youngest children scored lower in the imagery and semantic conditions than the older children and adults. (From Lindberg, 1980.)*

and adults on two tasks: digit-span and recall of the positions of chess pieces on a board. Recall on the digit-span task showed the usual developmental trend. The children, however, remembered the positions of the chess pieces significantly better than the adults. Critical to this developmental reversal is the fact that the children were chess players and the adults were not. Just as important is the fact that this difference in memory for the position of the chess pieces occurred only if the pieces were placed on the board in arrangements that approximated normal play, not when they were arranged randomly. When chess pieces are arranged as in a play situation, the pieces have relationships to each other that are meaningful to chess players. Thus, when children have greater domain-specific knowledge than adults, they can remember information related to this content better than adults (see also, Lindberg, 1980).

Demonstrations of the relation between content knowledge (independent of age) and memory performance have led some investigators (for example, Bjorklund, 1985) to argue that early memory development, particularly in the preschool years when deliberate elaborative strategies are not obvious, reflects developmental changes in the richness of conceptual relations and the ease of activating certain types of concepts, not the development of deliberate strategies to organize the to-be-remembered items.

CONTENT KNOWLEDGE AND THE ACQUISITION OF MNEMONIC STRATEGIES As we saw in Chapters 4–6, children acquire extensive knowledge about their world, knowledge that is reflected in the acquisition of lexical and conceptual knowledge about many different content domains. Several investigators have taken the position that even the development and use of mnemonic strategies is influenced by the development of content knowledge (Chi, 1979; Bjorklund, 1985, 1987b). Although few studies have explored this issue, one study (Ornstein & Baker-Ward, 1983) has demonstrated a relation between content knowledge and the use of a specific mnemonic strategy. Third graders were asked to rehearse aloud and recall one of two types of word lists. Although all the words in each list were known to the children, the lists differed in the meaningfulness ("m") of the words. (High meaningful words are words that elicit many conceptual associations relative to low meaningful words.) The quality of the cumulative rehearsal differed substantially for the two types of word lists. In the high "m" condition, students rehearsed more than three items together, compared with less than two items in the low "m" condition. And as might be expected, recall was significantly higher in the high "m" condition than in the low "m" condition. Thus, children this age are capable of the cumulative rehearsal strategy, but whether they use it depends upon their semantic organization of the items.

Such findings suggest a complex interaction between the nature of content knowledge and the use of strategies. This is further illustrated in a study demonstrating that children spontaneously use an organizational strategy with taxonomically related words and then transfer the use of the strategy to a list of unrelated words. Best and Ornstein (1986) asked third and sixth graders to sort and recall three 20-word lists. They were given no instructions on how to sort, but were simply told to sort a set of pictures into two to seven groups so that they would be able to remember the pictures. The children in the uncategorized condition were given three lists of unrelated words to sort and recall. The children in the categorical condition, however, were given a set of highly related words in the first list, moderately related words in the second list, and unrelated words in the third (test) list. As is evident in the scores for the first list in Table 7-2, the type of list had no effect on sixth graders' use of an organizational strategy or on level of recall. The third graders, however, were more likely to cluster (on the basis of their own category sorts) at the time of recall and had higher recall when the words were highly related rather than unrelated. Furthermore, as performance on the third (unrelated) list illustrates, the third graders who had experience with related words and clustered on the first list also used an organizational strategy with the unrelated words of the third list; this was not the case of the children in the uncategorized condition.

These results support the possibility that content knowledge first elicits organizational procedures for highly related content and that the efficacy of such organization promotes the transfer and deliberate use of strategies to other content domains (Borkowski, Levers & Gruenenfelder, 1976; Chi, 1979, 1985; Bjorklund, 1985). That is, when children identify words in a memory list the encoding process not only activates these words/concepts in semantic memory but also activates related concepts. When these conceptual relations

TABLE 7-2 *Mean Recall and Mean Clustering of Third and Sixth Grade Children*

Groups Tested	List 1	List 3 (Test list)
Third Graders		
Categorized Group		
Mean Recall	15.50	11.00
Clustering	.90	.59
Uncategorized Group		
Mean Recall	10.00	7.42
Clustering	.53	.44
Sixth Graders		
Categorized Group		
Mean Recall	15.92	12.92
Clustering	.85	.69
Uncategorized Group		
Mean Recall	16.75	14.92
Clustering	.72	.81

Source: Modified from Best & Ornstein, 1986.

function to facilitate recall, this metacognitive experience serves to encourage the deliberate use of an organizational strategy, even with materials that do not have close conceptual relations.

THE AUTOMATION OF MEMORY PROCESSES

The encoding of word meaning and the consequent activation of related concepts is an automatic process for adults (see, for example, Shaffer & LaBerge, 1979). When you hear a word, you know its meaning whether you want to or not. To illustrate the point, before reading any further, complete the activity described in Figure 7-7.

Undoubtedly, the squares on the left were more difficult than those on the right. This modified version of the Stroop (1935) Effect illustrates that encoding the names of the items is not under your control and that, therefore, the names of the digits interfere with the naming of the number of digits in a square.

Several theorists (for example, Hasher & Zacks, 1979; Schneider & Shiffrin, 1977; Shiffrin & Schneider, 1977) assume that cognitive processes vary along a continuum of automaticity. At one end of the continuum are automatic processes that do not require attention, occur without intention, and interfere minimally with other processes. At the other end are controlled processes that may be conscious, are voluntary, require effort, and will interfere with other effortful processes (Bjorklund, 1985). With extensive practice, processes can become more automatic and once automatic are difficult to regulate or modify.

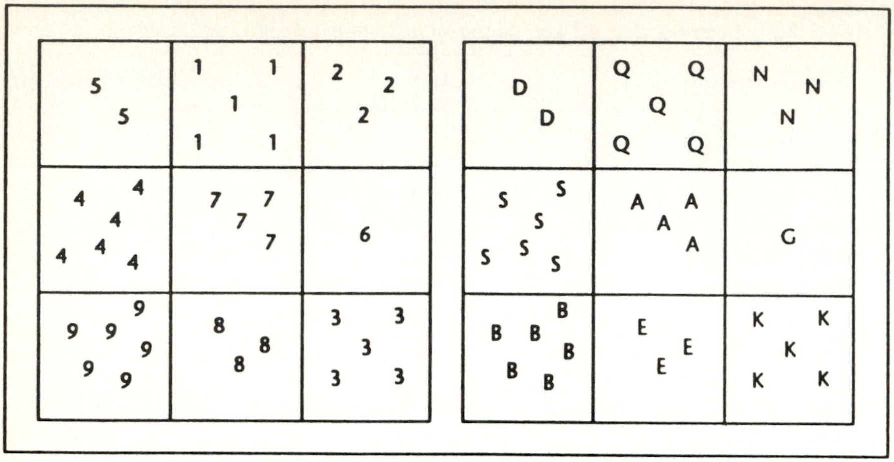

FIGURE 7-7 *Beginning in the upper left corner of the lefthand drawing, call out the number of digits in each square, ignoring the names of the digits themselves (sample stimuli from a modified Stroop task). Next, beginning in the upper left corner of the righthand drawing, call out the number of letters in each square, ignoring the names of the letters themselves (sample stimuli from a control condition for the modified Stroop task). (From Howard, 1983.)*

As processes become more automatic, they require less attention, and less working memory capacity (compare, Norman & Bobrow, 1975).

Thus, many investigators assume that increased automaticity of memory processes contributes to memory development. As children have more experience with processes relevant to memory tasks, the processes become more efficient and require less effort; they require less of working memory's limited capacity and, therefore, free this capacity for the storage of more information and/or the use of controlled processes such as the mnemonic strategies. Children not only acquire richer conceptual networks, but also become more efficient in accessing their conceptual knowledge.

Bjorklund (1985), for example, has argued that the relationship between content knowledge and memory development is mediated by the development of automatic processes for activating individual items (Bjorklund & Bjorklund, 1985) and their associations (Bjorklund & Jacobs, 1985) from semantic memory. This position asserts that it is not physiological maturation per se, but the acquisition of content knowledge that affects the efficiency of cognitive processes such as encoding; and, indeed, there is some research with adults and children that suggests a relationship between content knowledge and speed of processing (for example, Chi & Gallagher, 1982; Roth, 1983).

Furthermore, Case and his colleagues (Case, Kurland & Goldberg, 1982) have demonstrated a relationship between processing efficiency (speed of word recognition) and level of recall. In the first study, children ranging in age from three to six years were tested for recall in a memory span task and for speed of word recognition. In the word recognition task, the children were simply asked to repeat orally presented words as quickly as possible. The time between the presentation of the word and the onset of the child's repetition was the measure of word identification speed. There was a monotonic relation between speed of word identification and memory span; as speed increased, span increased. In an attempt to establish a causal relationship between identification speed and memory span, adults were tested in a similar manner with nonsense words. Memory span for the nonsense words was lower and, importantly, the memory span could be predicted from the speed of processing measure. That is, when adult recognition speed was reduced to that of six-year-olds, their memory span was also equivalent to that of six-year-olds. Such findings suggest that familiarity with the materials affects efficiency of encoding processes which in turn affects memory performance.

Furthermore, one set of studies suggests that developmental changes in the amount of attention required to execute mnemonic strategies may also contribute to the development of memory. Guttentag (1984) found that cumulative rehearsal of a word list required more mental effort for second graders than sixth graders. In the first experiment, the children were required to perform two tasks concurrently. The primary task was cumulative rehearsal aloud, followed by recall. The secondary task was rapid finger tapping. If the memory task involves working memory, then it should interfere with a second task that also requires attention to execute. This was, indeed, the case. The children's rate of tapping was significantly lower in a concurrent condition than in a condition in which the finger tapping was performed alone. But more importantly, the memory task interfered more for the younger children (41 percent decrease in the rate of tapping) than the older children (17 percent decrease). Cumulative rehearsal was less automatic, requiring more working memory capacity for the younger children.

In a second experiment, Guttentag demonstrated that this difference in interference was not simply a developmental difference in the ability to perform two tasks concurrently. When children were instructed to rehearse words singly as they finger tapped, there was evidence of interference but no developmental differences in the amount of interference. Unlike cumulative rehearsal, simple rehearsal did not require more mental effort for the younger children than the older children.

Finally, Guttentag demonstrated that for children in second through fifth grade there was a negative correlation between amount of interference produced by instructed cumulative rehearsal and the set size of spontaneous cumulative rehearsal. That is, the smaller the size of the spontaneous rehearsal set, the less automatic the process of cumulative rehearsal. Taken together, these findings indicate that younger children who do not spontaneously use cumulative rehearsal can, if instructed, do so, but that the effort requires more working memory capacity than for the older children who spontaneously use this strategy.

Such a correlation does not, however, explain why there is a relation between the selection of a strategy and the efficiency of the execution of that strategy. One possibility is that children who spontaneously use a strategy will get more practice with the strategy and, therefore, will execute it more efficiently. Another possibility is that children do not select mnemonic strategies that require excessive effort. When the mental effort required to execute a strategy decreases, children are more likely to select the strategy. Developmental decreases in mental effort to execute a strategy may reflect either the acquisition of content knowledge and the concomitant automaticity of encoding and retrieval processes, or general maturational changes in the efficiency of memory processes, or both.

MATURATIONAL CHANGES IN MEMORY PROCESSES

The fifth approach to the investigation of memory development has argued that there are physical changes in memory capacity and/or processes that are independent of experience. For example, several theorists have assumed that the capacity of working memory increases with maturation (for example, Case 1972, 1974; Pascual-Leone, 1970, 1978). Although these researchers present evidence in support of this assumption, no task is a direct measure of working memory capacity. As a consequence, their findings have alternative interpretations, interpretations that have been supported by a number of converging operations and stress the importance of experiential variables, such as content familiarity. Indeed, some researchers (for example, Dempster, 1985) have begun to doubt whether the capacity hypothesis, as formulated, is even a testable hypothesis.

Another possible structural change is in the speed of activation of information. Several studies suggest developmental changes in the speed of processing (see Chi & Gallagher, 1982, for a review), but the causes are not clear. As we saw in the Case *et al.* study, developmental changes in identification efficiency can be a function of familiarity or practice. Thus, at this point, we do not know whether there is also a maturational change in processing speed that is independent of experience (see Dempster, 1985, for a review).

Another possible source of change is in the rate of deactivation of information from working memory. That is, without rehearsal, information rapidly becomes unavailable. Are there developmental differences in the rate of deactivation? Research has not been directed at this question (see Dempster, 1985, for a discussion of this issue), in part because it is difficult to study. For example, it would be necessary to demonstrate that, at all ages, rehearsal was prevented to the same degree by the distractor task. To date, no study has satisfied this requirement.

We have little evidence of maturational changes in working memory (compare, Chechile & Richman, 1982). We must await the development of appropriate techniques to assess this issue, techniques that in some way eliminate the effects of the many experiential variables that are known to affect the development of memory performance.

In summary, although we know little about maturational changes in working memory, the memory development research demonstrates that at least four types of factors affect children's recall. We have enough evidence to know that these factors do not function independently of each other in the development of memory. Clearly, the deliberate use of mnemonic strategies improves performance, and just as clearly the use of such strategies increases with age. The development of strategy use, however, is related to the development of content knowledge, the automation of processes, and metamemory. We have yet to work out the details of how all of these factors interact during the prolonged period of strategy acquisition.

As is evident in the incidental learning tasks, not all memory development can be attributed to intentional efforts to learn. The knowledge children bring to a situation and how children's encoding processes relate new information to their base knowledge will influence memory for that information. To some extent, developmental changes in memory performance reflect changes in semantic knowledge and the automation of memory processes, which in turn can affect the acquisition and use of mnemonic strategies.

Finally, we can expect factors that guide selective attention to influence the development of children's memory. As children become more flexible in allocating their attention, they can be more responsive to task characteristics and thus better able to encode and store relevant information and ignore irrelevant information. Thus, with development we might expect children to direct attention more effectively to those aspects of a situation that might facilitate later efforts to recall (Ackerman, 1986; Shepp, Barrett & Kolbet, 1987).

RETRIEVAL FROM PERMANENT MEMORY

Permanent memory is our long-term representation of many types of knowledge, knowledge that ranges from procedural knowledge of how to ride a bike to theories of physical and social causality. Although psychologists do not agree on how this knowledge is represented or organized (see Chapters 4–6), they do agree that permanent memory has a large capacity (some might say unlimited) and that the information is highly organized and appears to have more than one type of organization (Howard, 1983, Ch. 6). Most cognitive psychologists also agree that the storage of new information in permanent memory requires attention, the activation of this information in working memory (Howard, 1983, Ch. 4).

What of forgetting? Information in working memory is readily lost if attention to it is not maintained. Permanent memory is assumed to be long lasting, if not permanent. But we are frequently unable to remember something we know we once knew. At one time, although no longer, I could recall the names of the twelve cranial nerves (I do remember that there are twelve). What happened to this knowledge? Although we cannot rule out the possibility that it is no longer in permanent memory, cognitive psychologists have extensive evidence indicating that failure to remember can reflect a failure to retrieve information that is stored in permanent memory rather than permanent memory loss. We have all had the experience of struggling to remember something, a name for example, and having it come to us hours later. Thus, given that information is encoded and stored, the primary issues are how retrieval processes function and why retrieval processes sometimes fail. Psychologists generally agree that retrieval from permanent memory is cued (Howard, 1983, Ch. 5). That is, external stimuli and/or internal thoughts serve to arouse the retrieval process. Sometimes this process is unintentional; for example, in May I noticed a lovely azalea bush and it suggested to me that azaleas would be a good present for my mother. Other times we intentionally use cues to retrieve specific information. Probably no better example is the essay question which, for the student being examined, promotes a search for information that is relevant to the question.

The information retrieved by a given cue depends upon how information was stored and whether storage included the particular cues that are available at the time of retrieval. When I learned the names of the cranial nerves, I was a freshman in college. My failure to remember these may reflect the fact that I do not now have the appropriate cues for retrieval. I do not remember the professor who taught the class. I may have used a mnemonic to learn the nerves, a mnemonic I do not now remember. Thus, my failure to recall the cranial nerves may reflect the fact that I do not have the appropriate cues for retrieval, rather than a loss of information.

The dependence of retrieval on encoding and storage conditions has been demonstrated in a number of adult studies (for example, Tulving & Thomson, 1973) and has been formulated as the *encoding-specificity hypothesis,* which states that "specific encoding operations performed on what is perceived determine what is stored, and what is stored determines what retrieval cues are effective in providing access to what is stored" (Tulving & Thomson, 1973; p. 369). This relationship between encoding and retrieval context was illustrated in Chapter 3 (Godden and Baddeley, 1975).

Thus, if we do not encode information for a particular retrieval context, we may fail to retrieve that information. We cannot always know, however, what the retrieval context will be. The exam question may be worded in a way that does not cue the appropriate information. If, however, information is encoded in a variety of ways and stored with elaborated relationships, it is more likely that relevant cues will be available at the time of retrieval (compare, Baddeley, 1982). As we have seen, however, the nature of children's encoding and storage is influenced by their learning strategies, content knowledge, and selective attention. Further, there is evidence that distinctive or elaborative encoding, which can facilitate retrieval, requires attentional capacity. That is, encoding the meaning of a word is fairly automatic. But the encoding of an elaborative network of associations that incorporates the distinctive context of the occurrence of the word is not automatic. Thus, we might expect developmental changes in the distinctiveness of the cues encoded at the time of acquisition and, therefore, developmental changes in the relative effectiveness of such contextual cues at the time of retrieval (compare, Rabinowitz, Craik & Ackerman, 1982).

► COMPREHENSION AND MEMORY

The research on the development of recall for word lists illustrates the significance of many variables for the development of memory processes. Although children are not usually required to learn and remember lists, for the novice some sets of facts may, indeed, appear to have arbitrary relations (such as, the twelve cranial nerves). Nevertheless, children and adults, both in and out of school, are more frequently engaged in the comprehension of discourse, and their goal is to derive the gist (meaning) of the discourse, rather than to recall the passage verbatim (see, for example, Sachs, 1967). In our discussion of language development, it was evident that comprehension involves both top-down and bottom-up processes. Comprehension demands the concurrent execution of several processes, such as recognizing words and retrieving their meaning, parsing sentences, identifying important ideas, organizing the ideas, and integrating those ideas with prior knowledge (see, for example, Kintsch & van Dijk, 1978). Comprehension can be characterized as a constructive process. Meaning is not inherent in words; rather it is constructed through the interaction of bottom-up and top-down processes. We not only bring reading skills to the comprehension process but also goals, plans, and concepts that influence the process.

Extensive research demonstrates that the knowledge a person brings to discourse influences comprehension and memory. Bartlett (1932), in a now-classic book, argued that knowledge is represented as a set of schemas (or schemata) that are general and organized knowledge structures about the invariants of past experience. The scripts for familiar events discussed in Chapter 5 are one type of schema. Bartlett argued that we use schemas to comprehend prose. Just as a restaurant script guides our behavior and our expectations of the behavior of others in a restaurant, so schemas guide the derivation of meaning from prose.

Bartlett further argued that memory is *reconstructive*. For example, he demonstrated that, as time passes, memory for narratives is characterized by deletions and additions. But the additions and deletions are not random. Rather, the deletions are primarily omissions of details that do not change the meaning of the passage, and the additions are clarifications and elaborations of the meaning. At the time of recall, we reconstruct memories from what we remember of the original material and from the schemas that informed the comprehension process. That means, of course, that memory is a function of comprehension; therefore, what is remembered depends upon the activation of a relevant schema at the time of comprehension. As specified by the encoding-specificity hypothesis, the encoding context influences retrieval of the information. To illustrate this point, read the following passage, and before reading further, close the book, write a title for the passage, and then write all you can recall of the passage (Dooling & Lachman, 1971, p. 217).

> With hocked gems financing him, our hero bravely defied all scornful laughter that tried to prevent his scheme. "Your eyes deceive," he had said. An egg, not a table, correctly typifies this unexplored planet. Now three sturdy sisters sought proof, forging along sometimes through calm vastness, yet more often over turbulent peaks and valleys. Days became weeks, as many doubters spread fearful rumors about the edge. At last, from nowhere, welcome winged creatures appeared signifying momentous success.

In one condition of a study by Dooling & Lachman (1971), college students were given this task. In another condition, students were given the same passage with the title, "Christopher Columbus Discovering America." When tested for recall, students who had the title to organize and give meaning to the passage recalled significantly more than the students who did not have a title and did not, presumably, activate their knowledge of Christopher Columbus. Knowledge of the context enables subjects to perform elaborative encoding operations that make it easier to retrieve the information (Summers, Horton & Diehl, 1985). For example, phrases such as "three sturdy sisters" take on a particular and distinctive meaning as Columbus's three ships, and can be integrated with the meaning of the other phrases. The passage no longer is a string of unfamiliar and seemingly unrelated phrases.

Comparable effects of contextual knowledge on recall have been demonstrated with children, even when the passage, unlike the Christopher Columbus passage, is comprehensible without the context. For example, Brown, Smiley, Day, Townsend, and Lawton (1977) asked children in grades two, four, and six to read an orientation passage that was relevant to the Targa tribe (Targa as Eskimos or Targa as desert Indians) or an irrelevant passage about the Spanish. Those children who read a relevant passage recalled more of the target passage (the adventures of Tor, a member of the Targa tribe) than children in the irrelevant condition, and this was the case at all three ages. Furthermore, analyses of intrusion errors produced during recall indicated that, although the children in the irrelevant condition did not introduce new information relevant to the Spanish passage, approximately half of the intrusion errors of the second graders in the relevant passage conditions were related to the theme of their orienting passage and this proportion increased with age (.64 and .79 for the fourth and seventh graders, respectively) (Brown, et al., 1977).

These findings illustrate two common aspects of the relationships between children's prior knowledge and their comprehension and memory for prose. First, prior knowledge can facilitate children's recall, and in some situations there is little developmental change in the effectiveness of such knowledge.

When developmental differences occur during the middle school years, they often appear to reflect age differences in background knowledge rather than age differences in the application of prior knowledge to the comprehension task. Second, contextual or schematic knowledge will lead to errors in recall that reflect this knowledge, and over time such errors of recall are more likely (see, for example, Landis, 1982). As we forget the details of a passage, we rely on our schematic knowledge to reconstruct the passage.

INFERENCES

Comprehension of discourse requires the semantic integration of sentence information. To construct meaning and establish coherence in discourse we go beyond the information explicit in individual sentences and draw inferences about implicit information that links the explicit statements. Although there are many types of inferences (see, for example, Nicholas & Trabasso, 1980), a broad distinction can be made between deductive and inductive inferences. *Deductive inferences* are those that follow necessarily from the information that is given. For example, the transitive inference is one type of deductive inference. If Bob is taller than Sue and Sue is taller than Henry, then, because of the semantic relations expressed in those two propositions, Bob is taller than Henry must necessarily follow. We saw in Chapter 6 that most children are capable of making transitive inferences by seven or eight years of age. There are several types of deductive inferences, however, and, as will be evident in the next chapter, some of them are difficult even for college students.

Under some circumstances both adults (see, for example, Bransford & Franks, 1971) and children (see, for example, Paris & Carter, 1973; Small & Butterworth, 1981; for a review, see Paris & Lindauer, 1977) spontaneously make deductive inferences and construct mental representations that incorporate these inferences. For example, Paris and Carter (1973) presented seven- and ten-year-olds with sets of three sentences, two of which had an implicit deductive relationship (for example, "The bird is in the cage. The cage is under the table."). After hearing several such sets, the children were given a sentence recognition test. The children had no problem recognizing the original sentences as familiar and new sentences as unfamiliar, except for one type of new sentence. These were sentences that expressed the deductive inferences that followed from the propositions of each set of sentences (for example, "The bird is under the table."). Children of both ages accepted these inferences as old sentences and, thus, did not distinguish between what they heard and what they inferred. Similar results have been reported for adults (see, for example, Bransford & Franks, 1971). Thus, when deductive inferences are easy enough young children readily use such inferences to comprehend prose. As will be evident in the next chapter, however, there are developmental changes in children's ability to reason deductively. There are forms of deductive reasoning that are particularly difficult and, presumably, will have little influence on prose comprehension.

Inductive inferences do not follow entirely from the information given, but rather from additional knowledge that an individual brings to the situation. To illustrate, consider the statement, "The karate champion hit the brick." A common inference is that, as a consequence, the brick broke. We draw this inference on the basis of what we know about karate and karate champions. But, unlike deductive inferences, inductive inferences are not necessarily true: it need not follow that the brick actually did break. Indeed, you probably inferred that the karate champion hit the brick with his (another possible inference) hand or foot. What would happen if a nose or little finger had been used?

In an investigation of children's comprehension of inductive inferences, Hildyard and Olson (1978) determined that children can distinguish between deductive and some types of inductive inferences. Children in grades four and six were presented with pairs of sentences (see Table 7-3 for examples), and asked to judge whether the second sentence was certainly true or whether there was not sufficient information to know whether it was true. At both ages, the children correctly identified 75 percent of the deductive inferences as certainly true. Similarly, the children recognized that there was not enough information to determine the truth of the inductive inferences. The older children, however, were more likely to distinguish between the deductive and the inductive inferences, and to realize that inductive inferences are not necessarily true.

Hildyard and Olson (1978) further distinguished between two types of inductive inferences: enabling and pragmatic. *Enabling inferences* serve to link statements and are essential for coherence. But unlike deductive inferences, the inference is not determined by the information given. Enabling inferences do not follow necessarily from the statements, but rest on the *cooperative principle of conversation* (Grice, 1975), which assumes that the speaker does not deliberately mislead and that, unless otherwise stated, statements have an implicating or causal relationship. For example, consider the following:

John threw the ball through the window.
Mr. Jones came running out of the house.

One enabling inference that links these two statements is:

John broke the window.

Like all inductive inferences, enabling inferences are affected by the content of the statements as demonstrated in the following (Hildyard & Olson, 1978):

John threw the baby through the window.
Mr. Jones came running out of the house.

A possible enabling inference now is:

The house was on fire.

TABLE 7-3 *Examples of the Deductive and Inductive Inferences*

Inferences	Sentences
Deductive	
Comparative (n = 7)	John has more cake than Mary.
	Mary has less cake than John.
Active/passive (n = 12)	The quarterback kicked the football to the forward.
	The football was kicked by the quarterback.
Synonyms (n = 12)	The bomb was dropped over the battleship.
	The bomb was released over the battleship.
Restatement (n = 12)	The bird is inside a cage under the table.
	The bird is under the table.
Implicative (n = 5)	John forgot to bring the truck.
	John did not bring the truck.
Inductive	
Implied causes (n = 8)	John forgot to bring the truck.
	John left the truck at home.
Implied consequences (n = 13)	The quarterback kicked the football to the forward.
	The forward caught the football.
Implied instruments, locations (n = 5)	The bird is inside a cage under the table.
	The bird cage is on the floor.
Elaborations (n = 22)	John has more cake than Mary.
	John ate more cake than Mary.

Source: Hildyard & Olson, 1978. Reprinted with permission of Ablex Publishing Corp.

Pragmatic inferences are also based on world knowledge, but are not essential for interpretation. Rather, they elaborate upon the information in the sentence. Inferences derived from "The karate champion hit the brick" are examples of pragmatic inferences. In a second study, Hildyard and Olson demonstrated that although elementary school children distinguish pragmatic inferences from deductive inferences, they do not distinguish between deductive inferences and enabling inferences. Thus, they appear to assume that inferences that make a story coherent are necessary in the same way as inferences that must follow from the structure of the propositions. Taken together, these findings indicate that children in the late elementary school years have some knowledge of the nature of inferences, that even sixth graders do not distinguish between deductive and enabling inferences, and that the children's understanding of the status of some pragmatic inferences improves during these years. The fact that there were not developmental differences for the deductive inferences probably reflects the particular types of deductive inferences used in the study, as will become evident in Chapter 8.

Children's pragmatic inferences will, of course, depend upon their knowledge base. Even when they have the requisite knowledge, however, young children do not always incorporate pragmatic inferences into their representations of narratives. Paris and Lindauer (1976), for example, presented a list of sentences, half of which made explicit the instrument used to accomplish an action (for example "The truck driver stirred the coffee in his cup with a spoon."), and half of which did not specify the instrument (for example, "The truck driver stirred the coffee in his cup."). At the time of recall, the children were given an instrument as a retrieval cue for each sentence. If an implicit instrument serves as an effective retrieval cue, then, according to the encoding-specificity hypothesis, the instrument must have been encoded at the time of comprehension. A significant Grade × Cue interaction indicated that, unlike the younger children, the fifth graders benefited as much from the cues when the instruments had been implicit as when they had been explicit. These results suggest that at the time of encoding and storage the younger children did not infer an instrument for the action of the sentence; therefore, the instrument did not function as a retrieval cue.

In a second study, first graders were required to act out each sentence as it was presented. Their actions indicated that they inferred appropriate instruments when they were not explicit; and under these conditions, instruments that had been implicit and explicit were equally effective as retrieval cues. Thus, when young children are induced to make inductive inferences, these inferences are reflected in their later memories. The fact that young children may not spontaneously infer relationships raises questions about the conditions that facilitate children's inferential processes and consequent comprehension of prose (see, for example, Schmidt & Paris, 1983). At this point, however, it is unclear how the development of inferential processes for single, isolated sentences is related to the inferential process of normal discourse comprehension, in which the child is attempting to integrate several sentences and, presumably, construct a mental representation of the narrated events.

In an effort to explore these inferential processes of discourse, Ackerman (1986) made a distinction between semantic integration on the basis of common reference and on the basis of enabling or causal inferences. *Referential integration* occurs when it is recognized that two or more sentences have the same referent. For example, in the sentences, "Ray dug a large hole. He planted a Bradford pear tree.", we draw the inference that "he" in the second sentence refers to Ray and that, therefore, Ray both dug a hole and planted a Bradford pear tree. Furthermore, once referential coherence is established, it invites the enabling inference that "Ray planted the Bradford pear tree in the hole that he dug." Children may differ from adults in the ability to draw referential inferences that establish the need for enabling inferences as well as in their ability to make enabling inferences.

In a set of five studies, Ackerman (1986) established that referential and enabling inferences can be empirically distinguished, that referential inferences are necessary but not sufficient for enabling inferences to occur, and that children have more difficulty than adults with both types of inferences. Ackerman presented first grade, fourth grade and college students with six-sentence stories in which the outcome of the story was inconsistent with the original intent. Thus, the subject had to infer the reason for the unexpected outcome. These stories differed in the explicitness of the referential cues.

Taken together, the several studies indicate that, when referential cues are not explicit, younger children are less likely to establish referential coherence. This developmental difference reflects, in part, the information-processing demand of maintaining in working memory, information from one sentence until the occurrence of the second, related sentence. When the two sentences were separated adults were superior to the children, but there were no overall differences in an adjacent condition. Furthermore, children were less likely to draw enabling inferences when there were fewer cues for the inference. Additionally, the data suggest that referential inferences were necessary for drawing enabling inferences. That is, subjects were unlikely to make the plausible inference if they did not recognize the referential inference. Referential inferences, however, were not sufficient for enabling inferences to occur. This is evident in the finding that the plausible inference is not always made when a subject has made a referential inference.

Ackerman's findings serve to highlight the potential role of memory demands, comprehension strategies, and prior knowledge in the development of children's comprehension of prose. When the information load is high (for example, in a separated condition), young children have difficulty maintaining information in working memory, and thus do not semantically integrate information that they do integrate when memory demands are reduced (for example, in an adjacent condition). Indeed, adults also have difficulty integrating information when the relevant information is beyond the capacity of working memory (see, for example, Walker & Meyer, 1980). Thus, the inferential process depends, to some extent, upon the development of working memory and the availability of information in working memory. Further, when information is not in working memory, the comprehender must search long-term memory for related information (Johnson & Smith, 1981). If, for example, a reader realizes that the sentence, "The shirts were hung out on the line," does not specify who did the hanging, the reader may activate a search strategy to retrieve information that clarifies who the actor was. Thus, as children develop strategies for monitoring their comprehension of prose, we might expect that such development will contribute to their inferential processes. We turn to this issue in the last section of this chapter. Finally, although Ackerman did not address this issue, we must recognize that younger children often come to a comprehension task with less relevant prior knowledge, knowledge that could facilitate comprehension in general and drawing inferences in particular.

Ackerman's data suggest that even the youngest children draw referential and enabling inferences when discourse is well-structured. That is, there are linguistic conventions for inviting appropriate referential and enabling inferences (Clark & Clark, 1977; see, for example, Ch. 3). When these conventions are honored, young children do make the appropriate inferences. Young children do not, however, have the resources to derive such inferences when discourse is not structured to facilitate the organization of information. To put it another way, the fact that the young children did draw appropriate inferences in those conditions that approximated the conventions of discourse suggests that the children used knowledge of these conventions to draw inferences. This, of course, implies that young children have some knowledge of discourse structure, knowledge that facilitates comprehension. We turn now to research that has focused on the nature of this knowledge.

SCHEMAS

Cognitive psychologists generally recognize the relevance of prior knowledge for the ability to remember a variety of materials, and many use the term *schema* to denote the general, organized knowledge a person possesses about a particular domain. As a consequence, the term is often vague, meaning nothing more than "prior knowledge" (Brown, 1979; Johnson, 1981). Here it is used in a narrower sense to refer to mental representations of temporal and/or spatial organizations of the part–whole relations of a domain of knowledge (Mandler, 1984b). Some psychologists have sought to specify the particular nature of these temporal/spatial representations (for example, Schank & Abelson, 1977; Mandler & Johnson, 1977). As we saw in Chapter 5, scripts have been proposed to describe our schematic knowledge of familiar event sequences. Further, we have evidence that preschoolers have such scripts and that, with development, children's scripts are elaborated and refined. Similarly, we have evidence that adults have schemas for real-world scenes (see, Mandler, 1984b). Although relatively little is known about the structure of scene schemas, we have evidence that some types of information (for example, spatial relations on the vertical dimension of a picture) are more important than others (for example, the spatial arrangements of the horizontal dimension). Developmental data, including the recognition of organized and unorganized scenes (for example, Mandler & Robinson, 1978), indicate that scene schemas develop during childhood. Similarly, we have evidence for the development of a face schema (see, for example, Kagan, 1971). Although the exact nature of the mental representations of schematic knowledge has not been delineated, we do have evidence that adults have such general spatial/temporal knowledge, that schematic knowledge develops during childhood, and that such knowledge effects the encoding, storage, and retrieval of related information.

STORY SCHEMAS Probably the largest concentration of developmental research has focused on children's schematic knowledge of stories (for example, Mandler & Johnson, 1977; Stein & Glenn, 1979). Children not only understand narratives about specific, familiar events, but also stories about unusual and unfamiliar situations, as evident in their comprehension of fairy tales, folk tales, and fables. This has led some investigators to posit that a general story schema underlies comprehension of stories from the oral tradition and that the schema reflects the regular structures that occur in such stories (for example, Johnson & Mandler, 1980; Mandler & Johnson, 1977; Rumelhart, 1975; Stein & Glenn, 1979; Thorndyke, 1977). *Story grammars* are efforts to identify the regularities of these stories and to write a rule system to describe the regularities. Thus, it is assumed that, despite differences in story content, there is an abstract and invariant underlying structure. In some ways, story grammars are analogous to linguistic grammars. They describe the constituents of the story, the meaningful units, and how these units relate to each other.

Furthermore, it is assumed that, with experience, children derive the regularities of stories and mentally represent these as a *story schema*. Thus, the story schema is a set of expectations about how stories are structured that guides a child's interpretation of a given story. Story grammars differ from scripts in that they are more abstract than scripts, which are tied to specific content (for example, going to a restaurant) (Mandler, 1984b). The goal of story grammar theorists has been twofold. The first goal is to construct story grammars that capture the regularities of stories. The second is to determine how children's comprehension and memory of stories relate to the hypothesized story structure.

Although the specifics of the several story grammars differ, they all assume a hierarchical organization of constituents that are abstract categories of story information. The interrelationships of the constituents are described both in terms of part–whole relations and sequential relations that are either causal or temporal. To illustrate, consider the following story (Johnson, 1983a):

1. *SETTING:* Once there was a monkey named Max, who lived in a zoo.
2. *BEGINNING EVENT:* One day Max fell in a mud puddle and got his shirt all dirty.
3. *SIMPLE REACTION:* Max was very unhappy.
4. *GOAL:* He decided to try to get his shirt cleaned.
5. *ATTEMPT:* Max went to his friend the elephant and said, "Will you wash my shirt off with some water from your trunk?"
6. *OUTCOME EVENT:* The elephant sprayed water on Max's shirt until all the mud was gone.
7. *ENDING EVENT:* On his way home, Max stayed away from the mud puddle.

According to the Johnson and Mandler (1980) story grammar, the major constituents of a story are *setting* and *episode*. The *setting* introduces the protagonist and the time and/or place of the episode or episodes that follow.

An *episode* has a *beginning*, which causes a *development*, which in turn causes an *ending*.

As the rewrite rules for the Max story illustrate in Figure 7-8 the assumptions of story grammars have been influenced by linguistic theory. They differ from many linguistic grammars, however, by incorporating semantic knowledge in the description of the structure of stories. For example, the constituents of story grammars, such as a "goal" or "attempt," are abstract semantic categories, and many of the sequential relations between constituents are causal. Thus, a particular action can only be identified as an "attempt" if a child knows how that action could lead to the desired goal (Johnson, 1983a). Indeed, recent research (for example, Trabasso, Secco & Van Den Broek, 1984; Trabasso & Sperry, 1985) has established the relevance of causal relations in children's comprehension of stories. Some theorists have argued that story comprehension is guided only by general world knowledge and efforts to establish relations between story actions rather than involving abstract knowledge of story structure (for example, Brewer & Lichtenstein, 1981). This issue is yet to be resolved. Nevertheless, story grammars and subsequent theories have provided a powerful tool for assessing developmental changes in children's comprehension and memory for narratives.

It is generally assumed that schematic knowledge can function at three different stages of information processing (compare, Anderson, 1984). Schemas may influence the formulation of hypotheses or *expectations* for future information. As already illustrated, schemas may facilitate *understanding*, as well as *memory* of the discourse or event. These stages are not, of course, independent. Expectations may affect the reader's understanding, which also can affect memory. Story grammar models assume that, to the extent that the structure of stories has been acquired and represented as schematic knowledge, performance will reflect the influences of the story schema on the processing of story information. Thus, "during comprehension of a story . . . the schema provides a basis for predicting what sort of information is likely to come next, for relating new information to what has gone before, and for consolidating information when a given type of unit (for example, the Setting or an Episode) is complete. During retrieval, the schema guides access to stored information and provides a basis for reconstruction when specific information is no longer accessible" (Johnson, 1983a, p. 19).

Expectations of Story Elements   Story grammar models assume that a story schema is used to construct mental representations of a particular story. Thus, expectations derived from the story schema aid in the retrieval of information that is necessary for making inferences to integrate explicit statements of a story (Stein, 1982). A few studies have attempted to assess story expectations directly. Generally, these studies indicate that children do have expectations about the structural elements of a story and that these expectations are consistent across ages, but become more frequent in older children. Whaley (1981), for example, assessed the expectations of third, sixth, and eleventh grade students in two

```
1. Story                    →        Setting and Episode
                                ⎧ a. Beginning CAUSE Development CAUSE Ending ⎫
2. Episode                  →   ⎨                    ⎛ And          ⎞ n,n≥1  ⎬
                                ⎩ b. Episode         ⎝ Then  Episode ⎠        ⎭
3. Beginning                →   ⎧ a. Beginning Event ⎫
                                ⎨ b. Episode         ⎬
                                ⎩                    ⎭
                                ⎧ a. Complex Reaction CAUSE Goal Path          ⎫
4. Development              →   ⎨ b. Simple Reaction CAUSE Action              ⎬
                                ⎩ c. Development (CAUSE Development)^{n,n≥1}    ⎭
5. Complex Reaction        →        Simple Reaction CAUSE Goal
6. Goal Path               →        Attempt CAUSE Outcome
7. Outcome                 →   ⎧ a. Outcome Event ⎫
                                ⎨ b. Episode       ⎬
                                ⎩                  ⎭
8. Ending                  →   ⎧ a. Ending Event ⎫
                                ⎨ b. Episode      ⎬
                                ⎩                 ⎭
```

▶ **FIGURE 7-8** *A set of rules for describing the structure of simple stories. (From Johnson, 1983a.)*

tasks. In the prediction task, the students read incomplete stories and had to predict what could or should happen next. There were five different types of stories that varied in completeness according to the Mandler and Johnson (1977) story grammar. Thus, the setting condition stated only the setting of a story. The other conditions stated: the setting and beginning; setting, beginning, and reaction; setting, beginning, reaction, and attempt; and setting, beginning, reaction, attempt, and outcome. In the macro-cloze task there were again five different types of stories, but each had one story constituent missing. That is, either setting, beginning, reaction, attempt, or outcome had been deleted from the story. Subjects read the stories and had to tell what should or could fit in the blanks left by the deletion.

For both tasks, predictions were derived from the grammar for which constituents should be produced for each story condition. Thus, according to the grammar, if a child reads only a setting, the next structural element should be a beginning. Similarly, if the incomplete story had a setting, beginning, and reaction, the next constituent should be an attempt. Except for the conditions that predicted a reaction production, in both tasks students of all ages produced statements that conformed to the predicted constituents. Furthermore, there was no difference between the sixth and eleventh grade students in their story expectations. The third graders, however, were less consistent than the older students. The findings indicate that children this age do have story expectations that can be predicted from a story grammar and that there are developmental changes in the extent of these expectations, but not in the nature of the underlying schema. The data also indicate, however, that one constituent that is basic to the story grammar, reaction, is unlikely to be produced at any age (see Johnson & Mandler, 1980). Furthermore, performance varied to some extent from one story to another. For example, in the cloze task subjects were less likely to produce an attempt in one story than in the other two stories presented. Thus, children's expectations for information in a story are guided not only by their general knowledge of story structure but also by the specific content of the story.

Memory for Stories   With the development of story grammars, psychologists have tools for assessing the development of prose memory that go beyond assessing recall in terms of the number of words or propositions recalled. A variety of predictions follow from the assumptions of story grammar models (Mandler, 1984b; Johnson, 1983a, b). For example, canonical stories should be easier to comprehend and recall than noncanonical stories. We have seen such an effect in young children's memory for script-like narratives, and a comparable finding occurs for recall of stories, across a wide age range (see, for example, Mandler, 1978; Stein & Glenn, 1979; for a review, see Mandler, 1984b). Furthermore, if comprehension and/or retrieval is guided by the story schema, then recall of noncanonical stories should tend to restore the canonical order of the elements of the story; this is the case for subjects ranging in age from preschool on (see, Mandler, 1984b). Additionally, children and adults should recall the same types of things in stories, despite differences in overall recall. To illustrate, Mandler, Scribner, Cole, and DeForest (1980) compared the story recall of schooled and unschooled children and adults from Liberia and America. As Figure 7-9 demonstrates, all subject populations had the same pattern of recall for the five major constituents of the Mandler and Johnson (1977) story grammar. Thus, despite differences in age and schooling, there is a consistent pattern of story recall.

The fact, however, that so few of the reaction or ending propositions are recalled suggests that the Mandler and Johnson story grammar does not conclusively describe the comprehension and memory process. Indeed, the expectation data described earlier indicated a similar failure of the reaction constituent to influence performance. Taken together, the research suggests that the same schematic knowledge underlies children's and adults' comprehension of stories, at least when the stories are simple enough. However, the nature of this representation is not yet fully understood (compare Johnson & Mandler, 1980; Trabasso, Secco & Van Den Broek, 1984). Additionally, we have suggestive evidence that younger children are not as proficient in their use of this schematic knowledge in the comprehension and/or retrieval process (for example, Mandler & DeForest, 1979).

Part of the development of schema use may reflect developmental changes in the explicitness of schematic knowledge. In Chapter 6, we presented evidence that children have implicit knowledge of numbers, as reflected in their counting behavior. It is not until children have explicit number knowledge, however,

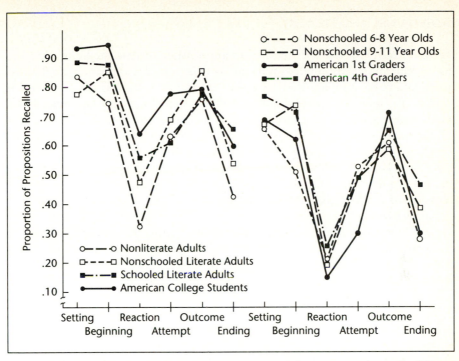

► **FIGURE 7-9**   *Proportion of propositions recalled from story constituents by different populations. The left panel shows data from Liberian adults and American college students. The right panel shows data from Liberian children and American school children. (From Mandler, 1979.)*

(for example, the principle of one–one correspondence) that they succeed in some tasks (for example, number conservation). Similarly, some researchers have suggested that young children automatically use story schemas to comprehend story narratives, as reflected in the story recall of even preschoolers (Johnson, 1983a, b). However, young children may not have the explicit knowledge of story schemas that is required for success in other tasks. For example, although the pattern of recall of story elements is comparable for children and adults, their ratings of the importance of story information is not. Unlike adults, young children do not make consistent importance judgments that reflect the critical constituents of story structure (see, Johnson, 1983a, for a review). Such differences suggest that young children do not have the explicit knowledge of story structure that is necessary for the identification of those propositions of a story that best represent the critical constituents of a story. The challenge now is to specify how the development of explicit knowledge affects the development of children's comprehension of stories, and discourse in general (Garnham, Oakhill & Johnson-Laird, 1982; van Dijk, 1980). Finally, we know little about the acquisition and modification of schemas in general or the story schema specifically (Stein, 1982).

SCHEMA USE AND MEMORY

We have seen that the activation of an appropriate schema facilitates memory for specific information relevant to the schema, and this appears to be the case for a variety of schema including real-world scenes, faces, stories, and familiar events (for a review, see, Mandler, 1984b). Goodman and Golding (1983) have argued that there are two phases of schema activation and that the type of information remembered differs for the two phases. The first phase is *schema confirmation*. During this phase we attend to the information in an effort to select and confirm an appropriate schema. If we have a preliminary hunch or make an early selection, attention may be focused on the information that appears to confirm the schema selected; otherwise, all information receives equal attention.

The second phase is *schema deployment*. During this phase, information consistent with the selected schema does not require much attention, rather attention is directed to unexpected information or information that is inconsistent with the schema. Thus, it is predicted that after schema deployment, memory for consistent information will be confused with schema expectations and, therefore, we should have trouble discriminating what was actually experienced from knowledge represented in the schema. Inconsistent information, however, will not be prone to such confusions.

In most situations there is enough information available for very rapid confirmation of a schema. Thus, most adult research has focused on the second phase, schema deployment, and its implications for memory. Several adult studies with pictures of scenes (for example, Friedman, 1979), faces (Light, Kayra-Stuart & Hollander, 1979), and with scripts (Graesser, Gordon & Sawyer, 1979) confirm the prediction that during schema deployment inconsistent information is remembered better than consistent information. Further, there is some evidence that information inconsistent with a schema receives more encoding effort than consistent information (for example, Friedman, 1979; but see Hashtroudi, Mutter, Cole & Green, 1984). It would appear that schemas prepare us for certain kinds of information. As a consequence less attention is "paid to those things that match the expectations, leaving attentional resources free to devote to the more unusual, and therefore more informative, items" (Mandler, 1984b, p. 105). Although there is some suggestive evidence that younger children may not always focus their attention on information that is inconsistent with their schema (for example, Pace, 1979; Pace & Feagans, 1984), we know little about how deployment of a schema affects children's information processing and subsequent memory.

In an attempt to study schema confirmation, Goodman and Golding (1983) presented subjects with a situation designed to prolong the schema confirmation phase. Subjects had to guess the occupation of an individual on the basis of behavior descriptions that were presented one at a time. Consistent and inconsistent behaviors for four occupations (doctor, grocer, teacher, and firefighter) were determined from the ratings of adults and five-year-olds. These ratings were used to construct three sets of behavior descriptions for each occupation. Each set of 10 descriptions consisted of two role-consistent behaviors (for example, for firefighter, "works with a hose" and "goes to a fire"), three role-inconsistent behaviors from the other three occupations (for example, "checks your throat," "helps kids to read," and "sells food") and five neutral behaviors (for example, "eats dinner").

After hearing one set of descriptions, subjects were asked to guess the occupation; another set was then read, and after a second guess, each subject was informed of the correct occupation and read a third set of descriptions. Two days later, they had an unexpected recognition test for the descriptions. Of particular interest is a comparison of memory for those descriptions presented before a subject knew the correct occupation and those presented after the subject was informed of the occupation. Recognition of the first set of descriptions was comparable for role-consistent and role-inconsistent information for those five-year-olds and adults who did not guess correctly the occupation after the first set of descriptions. But on the third set, when all subjects had been informed of the correct occupation, recognition of the consistent information was poor relative to that for inconsistent information, and this was the case for five-year-olds as well as adults.

These findings lend support to the supposition that activation of schematic knowledge affects the comprehension process in two ways and that what type of information is actively processed and retained depends upon the comprehension phase and how the information relates to the schema. Furthermore, this study suggests that developmental differences in memory for consistent versus inconsistent information may reflect more about developmental differences in the underlying schema or in the phase of comprehension, rather than information processing during the schema deployment phase (compare, Adams & Worden, 1986; Koblinsky & Cruse, 1981; Peeck, Van Den Bosch & Kreupeling, 1982).

COMPREHENSION MONITORING

As we have seen, comprehension is a complex process that is affected by a number of factors, including domain-specific knowledge, schematic knowledge of discourse structure, and information-processing demands. Yet another factor, *comprehension monitoring,* plays an important role in the comprehension process of adults. We not only have the requisite skills for comprehension, but also the ability to monitor the state of our own comprehension. Imagine for a moment a world in which this were not the case. How would you know whether to reread an assigned chapter? How would you determine which questions to ask during a review session? This is not to say that we do not have failures of comprehension monitoring (see, for example, Glenberg, Wilkinson & Epstein, 1982; Epstein, Glenberg & Bradley, 1984). We all have had the experience of reading, believing we understood, and then realizing later

that we did not understand. Nevertheless, adults do monitor their comprehension, and the consequent assessments influence how they proceed in the
comprehension process.

The comprehension-monitoring process has as many levels as the comprehension process itself. Thus, it can range from recognizing, rather automatically, that a word is unfamiliar to assessing whether the conclusions of a
test follow from the logical structure of the argument. Not surprisingly, there
are developmental changes in children's ability to monitor their own comprehension. In a set of studies, Markman (1977, 1979) had third and sixth graders
listen to essays in which there were either implicit or explicit contradictions
of information, contradictions which would make comprehension troublesome
for adults. After each essay, the children were asked questions (such as, "Do
you have any questions?") to probe their awareness of their own comprehension failure. The children failed to recognize the implicit contradictions altogether, and even many sixth graders did not report a problem with the explicit
inconsistencies. Indeed, the third graders failed to recognize the problem, even
after repeating the explicit contradictions aloud. Since these initial studies of
comprehension monitoring, subsequent research has determined that young
children do report problems if the demands of the task are minimized: that is,
if they are instructed to look for specific types of comprehension problems (for
example, Baker, 1984a, b); if the demands on working memory are limited
(for example, Ackerman, 1984a; Pace, 1981); if inferential complexity is minimized (for example, Ackerman, 1984b; Tunmer, Nesdale & Pratt, 1983); if
the setting is familiar (for example, Revelle, Wellman & Karabenick, 1985);
and if the material is familiar (for example, Breen, 1987).

Children's limitations appear to reflect, in part, the failure of children
spontaneously to select and maintain appropriate standards for comprehension
monitoring. Markman and Gorin (1981) demonstrated that, when given
specific instructions, eight- and ten-year-olds can adjust their standard for
comprehension. Children were given passages in which some statements
(falsehoods) contradicted the child's existing knowledge and others (inconsistencies) contradicted information presented earlier in the passage. Those instructed to look for falsehoods were more likely to recognize falsehoods
than inconsistencies and vice versa for those instructed to look for inconsistencies.

Furthermore, under optimal conditions, with specific training and feedback, 5- to 11-year-olds can maintain three standards simultaneously (Baker,
1984a). Baker trained children to look for three types of mistakes: *lexical,* in
which a nonsense word occurred (for example, "Ms. Johnson cooked the
pancakes in a bladmer); *internal inconsistencies,* in which information in two
sentences was contradictory (for example, "He [a rabbit] had dark brown fur
that was as soft as could be. All the other rabbits wished they had his *snow
white fur*"); and *inconsistencies with prior knowledge* (for example, "Jack
always used a baseball bat to chop the wood").

The older children were more successful than the younger children in
identifying all three problems, and by nine years of age, performance was

equivalent for the three types of problems. The younger children, however, had more difficulty recognizing the internal inconsistencies. The detection of an internal inconsistency, of course, is founded on the inferential processes that lead to an interpretation of the discourse that is contradicted in a subsequent statement. Thus, we can expect that those factors that affect the development of inferential processes will also influence the detection of internal inconsistencies, factors such as the demands on working memory and domain-specific knowledge.

In addition, however, another factor appears to play a role. Most studies of comprehension monitoring have focused on children's ability to report discourse inconsistencies (but see Baker, 1985, for a review of other forms of comprehension monitoring). Such a response measure requires that a child remember the detection of the inconsistency until the end of the passage and also be able to verbalize the nature of the inconsistency. A few studies have demonstrated that discourse inconsistencies can affect children's behavior even when they do not report such inconsistencies (for example, Harris, Kruithof, Terwogt & Visser, 1981; Zabrucky & Ratner, 1986). Zabrucky and Ratner (1986) had third and sixth graders read passages in which one sentence was inconsistent with the rest of the passage. Both ages read the anomalous sentence more slowly, but the sixth graders were more likely to look back at this sentence and report the inconsistency. Thus, at some level, young children's behavior is influenced by comprehension difficulties, but this may not result in an awareness of the problem, an awareness that may be necessary for subsequent attempts to rectify comprehension failure.

Clearly, subsequent efforts to comprehend will depend not only on the detection of a comprehension problem, but also on comprehension goals. Consequently, two processes—evaluation and repair—are assumed to follow an awareness of comprehension failure (see, for example, Ackerman, 1984b). In the *evaluation process* the comprehension problem that has been detected is evaluated relative to goals, importance, and the source. In the *repair process,* attempts are made to repair the comprehension failure if the evaluation warrants it.

Preliminary evidence indicates that, even when children are aware of comprehension failures, older children are more likely to make repairs (for example, Ackerman, 1984b) and there may also be developmental differences in the strategies children use to make repairs (for example, Mosenthal, 1979; Schmidt, Schmidt & Tomalis, 1984). Our understanding of the development of comprehension suggests that, initially, children's comprehension processes are automatic and that, as children acquire explicit knowledge about discourse, their comprehension processes come under deliberate, strategic control. Thus, during the elementary and middle school years children become more flexible in the comprehension process and more likely to have the resources necessary for a given task. We saw a similar pattern in the development of children's memory and, as we attempt to model the development of children's comprehension, we can expect to find complex interactive processes that involve the four factors of the tetrahedral model (see Figure 7-3, p. 262).

SUMMARY

This chapter considered the development of information-processing skills, with particular emphasis on attention, learning, memory, and comprehension. All models of information processing assume a limited capacity for attention to information. Younger children are less effective than older children in directing and maintaining their attention, as task demands require.

Children's learning and memory is influenced by four factors: characteristics of the learner, criterial tasks, nature of the materials, and learning activities. The focus of the chapter was on the development of recall which increases substantially during childhood. The development of mnemonic strategies, metamemory, content knowledge, and the automation of memory processes all contribute to the development of recall memory.

Comprehension and memory for prose is facilitated by deductive and inductive processes that integrate the propositions of discourse. Although, under some circumstances, preschoolers do draw inferences in their efforts to comprehend prose, they are not as likely to do so as older children. Furthermore, older children are better able to distinguish between different types of inferences and their implications.

Comprehension of prose is also guided by schematic knowledge. Further, the type of information remembered depends upon the stage of comprehension. As we attempt to determine the appropriate schema for interpreting the information, we are equally likely to remember information that is consistent or inconsistent with the schema. After a schema is deployed, however, it is easier to remember information that is inconsistent with the schema.

Most developmental research has focused on the story schema. Children and adults alike have a story schema which guides their comprehension of narratives. The schema is a general representation of narratives that has a hierarchical organization of constituents such as episode, development, reaction, attempt, and outcome. The schema not only influences expectation for story elements, but also recall of narratives. Young children's knowledge of the story schema appears to be implicit and applied rather automatically.

Critical to comprehension are processes for monitoring our state of comprehension. Even when there is evidence that young children do not comprehend they are less likely than older children to recognize their comprehension failures. With explicit instructions, however, the comprehension monitoring of younger children can be enhanced. Nevertheless, we have some evidence that young children are less likely to make efforts to repair comprehension failures, even when they are aware of the failure.

8

Adolescence:
The Development of
Reasoning

Although the development of reasoning is viewed as a primary aspect of cognitive development (Sternberg, Conway, Ketron & Bernstein, 1981), *reasoning* is a fuzzy concept that is not easily defined (compare, Sternberg, 1986). Generally stated, however, reasoning involves those processes that we use to form and evaluate our ideas of what we believe to be true. "It involves the production and evaluation of arguments, the making of inferences and the drawing of conclusions, the generation and the testing of hypotheses" (Nickerson, 1986, pp. 1–2). Our various experiences provide a basis for our belief in some ideas or facts and our disbelief of others. We come to have beliefs about social stereotypes as well as the best policy for controlling the value of the U.S. dollar. The importance of our beliefs cannot be overstated, because our beliefs often govern our actions (Nickerson, 1986).

Philosophers distinguish between two types of reasoning: deductive and inductive. *Deductive reasoning* is the process of deriving inferences that make explicit what is implicit in the information available to us. For example, the transitive inference discussed in Chapter 6 on page 238 is a type of deductive reasoning. If we know that Matthew is taller than Sebastian, and Seth is shorter than Sebastian, then it must follow that Matthew is taller than Seth. In deductive reasoning, the premises of the argument contain all the information that is relevant for the conclusion. Deductive arguments are either "valid" (correct) or "invalid" (incorrect); they cannot be partly valid. A deductive argument is valid if the premises provide decisive evidence for the conclusion; that is, given the premises, no other contradictory conclusion is possible. Although deductive reasoning can take several forms and the methods for determining the validity of a conclusion vary with the particular form, all valid deductive reasoning is characterized by the fact that if the premises are true, the conclusion also must be true (Skyrms, 1975).

We also come to our beliefs through *inductive reasoning,* or the use of facts to determine the probability that a conclusion is appropriate. Suppose I know nothing about the relative heights of Seth, Matthew, and Sebastian. But suppose that I know that Seth is six and Matthew is eight. On the basis of this knowledge and my knowledge of human growth I may infer that Matthew is taller than Seth. Deductive reasoning is a means of making explicit information that is implicit in sets of propositions; inductive reasoning establishes our beliefs independent of deductive argument. Thus, unlike deductive reasoning, the strength of an inductive argument is not based on logical relations between premises, but on the probability of the correctness of the conclusions, given the available information (Black, 1946).

Next, suppose that Seth is twenty-six and Matthew is twenty-eight. Given this information you should be less willing to draw the inference that Matthew is taller than Seth. Due to the nature of adult heights, the probability that the conclusion is correct is 50 percent. Unlike deductive conclusions, which are either valid or invalid, inductive conclusions vary in their probability that they are correct or appropriate. A strong inductive conclusion is the conclusion that is least likely to be false, relative to other, alternative conclusions.

Another difference between deductive and inductive reasoning is that valid deductive conclusions follow from the premises even if additional information is added. Thus, from

All men are mortal.

Sebastian is a man.

the conclusion "Sebastian is mortal" is valid no matter what else is true about Sebastian—whether he is handsome, an only child, and so on. When an argument has a valid, deductive conclusion, additional information cannot change the validity of that conclusion. But in an inductive argument, the addition of new information *may* change the strength of the conclusion. To the inductive argument above add the premise, "Matthew played center on his college basketball team." Now the conclusion "Matthew is taller than Seth" appears stronger (Copi, 1972). Deductive inferences can be drawn with certainty, but do not go beyond the information in the premises. Inductive inferences extend our knowledge, but also introduce uncertainty (Moore, 1986).

Western philosophers have been particularly concerned with the nature of deductive and inductive reasoning because these processes have played major roles in the development of Western science, a science that is self-critical and self-correcting. Although scientists and philosophers have made efforts to refine and to make explicit the role of deductive and inductive reasoning in their work, we know that such reasoning is not restricted to these endeavors. Deductive and inductive reasoning are evident in our everyday efforts to establish and substantiate our beliefs about the world. In most reasoning situations, deductive and inductive reasoning play interactive roles, but separate analyses will help to clarify some distinctions that have proven important in logic and science.

Piaget (Inhelder & Piaget, 1958) believed that the final stage of cognitive development, formal operations, developed during adolescence. He characterized formal operational reasoning as *hypothetico-deductive,* which means that the individual can generate alternative possibilities (hypotheses), deduce conclusions from these hypotheses, and generate tests for the conclusions. Hypothetico-deductive reasoning involves both inductive and deductive reasoning processes. In recent years, considerable research has attempted to determine the extent to which Piaget's model of formal operations appropriately describes the reasoning skills of adolescence. However, before considering this issue, we consider the research that has limited itself to particular forms of deductive or inductive reasoning. With this background, it will be easier to put Piaget's more comprehensive theory, and the related findings, in perspective.

▶ ## INDUCTIVE REASONING

Inductive reasoning is used "to discover those generalizations which are true of the world in which we actually live" (Black, 1946, p. 279). On the basis of limited experience we come to general conclusions that go beyond our own experiences, that go beyond the information directly available to us. When I put the flame on under a pot of water, I expect that in time the water will boil. This expectation is based on past experiences (which in this case are rather extensive) *and* the assumption (generalization) that, as in the past, future pots of water also will boil if given enough heat.

Unlike deductive reasoning, for which logicians have identified the structure of several types of valid arguments (we consider some of these later in this chapter), there are no formal rules that guarantee the truth of inductive inferences (see, for example, Harman, 1986; Skyrms, 1975). Indeed, inductive reasoning is the creative component of human reasoning; as such it is achieved in a variety of ways with no assurances of correctness. In previous chapters, we discussed several cognitive skills that require inductive processes. Concept acquisition, as discussed in Chapter 5, is an example. On the basis of a few specific experiences, we draw a general conclusion about the meaning of the words we hear or read. It is always possible that we have drawn a wrong inference and that this will become evident with more experience. I know of one graduate student who, from her reading, concluded that "erstwhile" meant "esteemed." Needless to say, a colleague was taken aback when the student referred to him as her "erstwhile colleague." Similarly, we have seen that discourse comprehension requires a variety of inductive inferences. With all the knowledge that is brought to a discourse, the individual arrives at the most probable interpretation of the discourse (Moore, 1986). Of course, causal inference is yet another type of inductive reasoning, and, again, there are no guarantees that a causal inference is correct (Hume, 1777/1963). Indeed, the history of science is a history of changing causal inferences, as new information becomes available (Kuhn, 1970).

As evident in research on the development of concept acquisition, scripts, story schemas, language comprehension, and causal inference, inductive processes are basic to the thinking of young preschoolers. Thus, much of our knowledge about the world rests on inductive processes. In this chapter we focus on two types of inductive reasoning: analogical reasoning and the use of heuristic principles.

ANALOGICAL REASONING

Analogical reasoning is a form of inductive reasoning that extends our knowledge by relating what we do understand to what we do not understand. It is a means of transferring knowledge from a familiar situation to an unfamiliar one (Holyoak, 1984a). Analogical reasoning is so pervasive in our daily affairs that educators and psychologists have long recognized its importance and, as a consequence, often use it as a measure of intellectual ability. Indeed, two aptitude tests, Raven's Progressive Matrices and Miller's Analogies Test, are devoted exclusively to this type of reasoning. Analogical reasoning also has a prominent role in scientific thinking (Lorenz, 1974; Oppenheimer, 1956). For example, cognitive psychologists often use the concepts and relationships of computer systems as an analogy for generating models of thinking. In this case the analogy also goes in the other direction; that is, computer scientists use human performance as an analogy for building useful machines.

Analogies establish higher-order relationships (that is, relationships between relations) between two domains of knowledge and appear to be particularly significant in the acquisition of domain-specific knowledge. The relationships of a familiar domain (base) are mapped onto an unfamiliar, or less familiar, domain (target).

Analogies can take several forms (Capp & Capp, 1965; Freeley, 1966); but, essentially, analogical reasoning is "reasoning based on the assumption that if two things are alike in several important known respects, they will probably be alike in other respects not known or investigated" (Capp & Capp, 1965, p. 128). In Chapter 5 we saw that children are likely to draw the inference that a novel object has a given property if they know that the object belongs to a particular category and members of that category have that property (Gelman & Markman, 1986a). In general, then, if A has C, D, E, F, as well as H, and we know that B has C, D, E, and F, we might reason that B also has H (Moulton, 1966). In its simplest form, an analogy specifies a relationship of equivalence or similarity between two sets of relationships and can be stated as "A is to B as C is to D" (or A:B::C:D). A relationship between elements (A & B) of one domain is used to identify elements (C & D) and their relationships in another domain.

THE DEVELOPMENT OF ANALOGICAL REASONING   Piaget and others (Inhelder & Piaget, 1958; Lunzer, 1965) have argued that children cannot reason with analogies until formal operations. They assert that the analogical relationship is a proportional one and that it is not until adolescence that children can reason with proportions. That is, in the analogy, bird:air::fish:water, the words are related in two directions, bird:air::fish:water and bird:fish::air:water. This structure is assumed to be comparable to mathematical proportions such as $3/4 = 15/20$ and $3/15 = 4/20$ (Levinson & Carpenter, 1974).

Piaget (Piaget, Montanegro & Billeter, 1977) and Sternberg (1977) argue that young children can find first-order relations between the A and B terms and the C and D terms, but that they do not find the necessary higher-order equivalence relation between an A:B relation and a C:D relation. For Piaget the use of higher-order relations requires the reasoning structures of formal operations.

Analogies appear on most intelligence tests for children younger than eleven and performance on the analogy subtest correlates positively with intelligence scores. The analogies used on these tests have another form, one in which the relation between the terms is specified. These "quasi-analogies" take the form, "A bird uses air; a fish uses _____." Thus, the items used in intelligence tests specify the relations but do not maintain the proportional symmetry of the true analogies. That is, when the relation is specified as bird:air:fish: _____, that analogy can be stated also as bird:fish:air: _____. The reverse form of the above, "A bird uses fish, air uses _____," however, does not maintain the analogical relations.

In an attempt to determine the effect of the quasi-analogy form on children's reasoning, Levinson and Carpenter (1974) compared the performance of 9-, 12-, and 15-year-olds on both true and quasi-analogies. There was no significant difference in performance on the two types of analogies for the 12- and 15-year-olds; the 9-year-olds, however, found the quasi-analogies easier than the true analogies. This age difference suggests that the youngest children had difficulty identifying the relevant equivalence relationship in the true analogy. Furthermore, several investigators have demonstrated that the solutions of younger children and poor reasoners are dominated by first-order associative responses (Achenbach, 1970; Gentile, Kessler & Gentile, 1969; Sternberg & Nigro, 1980). Achenbach (1970) tested children in the fifth through the eighth grades on a multiple-choice analogy test in which half the items had a high associate as a foil for the correct answer. For example, the analogy pig:boar::dog:? had a correct response—wolf—as a choice and a frequent associate to dog—cat—as a foil. Children in this age range showed a steady decrease in the errors on the test overall. This improvement in analogical reasoning was due, in part at least, to a decrease in the number of errors for the items that had high associative foils.

Additionally, younger children have more difficulty with abstract relations. Gallagher and Wright (1977) found little developmental change in performance on concrete analogies, such as picture:frame::yard:fence, between fourth and seventh grades. There was, however, an appreciable change over this age range for the abstract analogies, such as food:body::rain:ground, in which the A:B and C:D relations are complex and functional. Indeed, such findings indicate the importance of conceptual knowledge in the development of verbal analogical reasoning. As children acquire knowledge structures that more closely approach those of adults (see, for example, Carey, 1985b), they should be more likely to recognize the abstract relationships of the two domains.

Although the research on verbal analogies indicates developmental changes in analogical reasoning (compare, Sternberg & Nigro, 1980), it is not possible in this research to distinguish changes in conceptual knowledge from changes in the ability to infer analogical relationships given the necessary conceptual knowledge. Most studies have attempted to control for this factor by assessing the familiarity of the terms and using only terms familiar to the youngest children. It is possible, however, that the terms, although familiar to the younger children, do not have the same set of semantic relationships for them. In efforts to eliminate this problem, a few studies have sought to investigate analogical reasoning with familiar, concrete, visual materials (for example, Alexander, Willson, White & Fugua, 1987; Gentner, 1977; White & Alexander, 1986). These studies suggest that some preschoolers are capable of discovering an A:B relation and mapping it onto a C:D relation. For example, Alexander and her colleagues presented four- and five-year-olds with geometric analogies in which blocks differed in size, color, and shape. The children were shown three blocks and were asked to select a fourth block that went with the third block in the same way that the first and second blocks went together.

In two experiments, approximately half of the children at each age performed above chance. Indeed, a few children performed perfectly. The children who performed below chance level were not responding randomly, however. Rather, they had a hierarchy of rules that they used to select a block similar in color and shape to the third block. Thus, all the children appeared to use rules to solve the analogy problems: half used the A:B relationship; the rest used a hierarchical set of rules that ignored the A:B relationship and focused on similarity to the C term. As with the associative responses in verbal analogies, the nonanalogical reasoners are responding on the basis of the similarity of the D term to the C term rather than on the basis of the similarity of a C:D relationship to an A:B relationship.

It would appear that under some circumstances preschoolers can solve analogies; the conditions that limit their performance are not known, however. Adult research on analogical reasoning suggests factors that may affect the development of analogical reasoning. For example, Mulholland and his colleagues (Mulholland, Pellegrino & Glaser, 1980) have demonstrated that adult performance is affected by the number of elements and the number of transformations of elements necessary for the solution of geometric analogies; both the number of errors and latency of the response increased as problems became more complex. Using simpler problems, Stone and Day (1981) demonstrated comparable effects for the solution times of fifth graders, eighth graders, and college students. Furthermore, they found that increased complexity (number of elements and number of transformations) had a greater effect on solution time for the younger subjects. This finding suggests that geometric analogies can require considerable processing effort and that younger children have more difficulty maintaining in working memory the information necessary for solving complex analogy problems (Mulholland *et al.*, 1980).

MODELS OF ANALOGICAL REASONING   For the most part, research on analogical reasoning has concentrated on its use as a measure of intellectual ability, rather than on how such reasoning is done. Recently, however, theorists have tried to determine the processes that play a role in the analogy tasks (for example, Goldman & Pellegrino, 1984; Mulholland *et al.*, 1980; Rumelhart & Abrahamson, 1973; Sternberg, 1977). Sternberg (1977) proposed a model of analogical reasoning which assumes that there are five basic component processes in the typical multiple-choice analogy task. The first process is *encoding,* in which the subject perceives the analogy terms and stores in working memory the general attributes of the analogy terms that may be relevant for the task and the specific value of each of these attributes. For example, consider this Washington and Lincoln analogy: Washington:1::Lincoln:a.10 b.5 (Sternberg, 1977). As illustrated in Table 8-1, each of the five terms is encoded with respect to its attributes (for example, president, portrait on currency, and war hero) and the values of each of these attributes (for example, first president, portrait on one dollar bill, and Revolutionary War hero).

The second process is *inference,* in which the individual discovers the relations between the values of the corresponding attributes of the A and B terms (for example, Washington was the first president and 1 is the first ordinal position) and stores it in working memory. In the third process, *mapping,* the individual attempts to link the first half of the analogy (base) to the second half (target) by discovering relationships between the attributes of the A and C terms (for example, Washington and Lincoln were both presidents, Washington the first, Lincoln the sixteenth). In the fourth process, *application,* the individual applies the relation inferred in the base domain to C and each of the alternative answers (Lincoln → 10; Lincoln → 5) for each of the attributes and finally, in the fifth process, the individual makes a *response.*

Sternberg (1977) has proposed several computer models based on these component processes. In all of the models the processes are executed serially, one immediately after another, and each process consumes real time. The models differ, however, in the sequencing of the component processes and whether they are executed exhaustively or with self-termination. For example, *exhaustive encoding* would mean that the individual encodes the several A and B attributes before inference begins. With *self-terminating encoding,* only one attribute is encoded before going on to the next process, inference; if this particular attribute does not lead to a response, the series starts again with encoding of another attribute.

Sternberg and Rifkin (1979) assessed children's use of the component processes, comparing the Sternberg models with the performance of students

TABLE 8-1 *Attribute-Value list for Analogy Example—Washington: I ::Lincoln:(a. 10, b. 5)*

Process	Analogy term or relation	Relevant attributes and values
Encoding	*Washington*	[(president (first)), (portrait on currency (dollar)), (war hero (Revolutionary))]
	I	[(counting number (one)), (ordinal position (first)), (amount (one unit))]
	Lincoln	[(president (sixteenth)), (portrait on currency (five dollars)), (war hero (Civil))]
	10	[(counting number (ten)), (ordinal position (tenth)), (amount (ten units))]
	5	[(counting number (five)), (ordinal position (fifth)), (amount (five units))]
Inference	*Washington→I*	[(president (ordinal position (first))), (portrait on currency (amount (dollar))), (0)]
Mapping	*Washington→Lincoln*	[(presidents (first, sixteenth)), (portraits on currency (dollar, five dollars)), (war heroes (Revolutionary, Civil))]
Application	*Lincoln→10*	[(0), (0), (0)]
	Lincoln→5	[(0), (portrait on currency (amount (five dollars))), (0)]

Source: Sternberg, 1977. Copyright 1977 by the American Psychological Association. Reprinted by permission.

in the second, fourth, sixth grades, and college level on pictorial analogies using the schematic-picture and people-piece stimuli illustrated in Figure 8-1. The schematic-picture analogies were composed of figures derived from four binary dimensions (hat color, pattern on clothes, footwear, and object carried) that are *separable*. That is, the two values on each of these dimensions can be changed, without affecting the appearance of the other dimensions. The people-picture analogies were composed of four binary dimensions that are *integral* in the drawings (height, weight, color of garments, sex). As illustrated in Figure 8-1, a change in height, for example, also means a change in overall appearance.

Using a complex procedure, Sternberg and Rifkin presented the students with analogies that varied in how many attribute values (1, 2, or 3) changed for the A to B, A to C, and 1 to 2 (answer options) relations. For example, in Figure 8-1 the top A and B figures differ on one value (hat); the A and C figures differ on three values (object carried, footware, and pattern of clothes). Similarly, the two possible answers (1 and 2) differ on three values. They used the solution times for the different types of analogies to estimate the component processes. These estimates were compared to the predictions derived from the different Sternberg models of analogical reasoning.

Their data indicate that, for both types of stimuli, all ages used the encoding, inference, application, and response processes. Encoding, however,

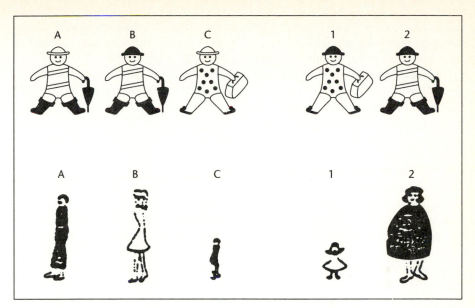

▶ **FIGURE 8-1**   *Schematic-picture analogies (top) and people-piece analogies (bottom). Test results on students in second, fourth, sixth grades, and college level indicate that all ages used encoding, inference, application, and response processes in their analogical reasoning. (From Sternberg & Rifkin 1979.)*

switches from self-terminating to exhaustive at the fourth grade; and the inference process is self-terminating until sixth grade when it switches to exhaustive. The mapping process is not used by the second graders for either type of stimulus; the older students use mapping with the integral stimuli but not with the separable ones. These findings demonstrate the complexity of analogical reasoning, even when prior knowledge is not a factor. Children's strategies are not only sensitive to the nature of the materials, but also change with age. Further research will be necessary to determine the reasons for the changes in children's processing strategies (Goldman, Pellegrino, Parseghian & Sallis, 1982). One possibility, of course, is that strategies change as the functional capacity of working memory increases (Foorman, Sadowski & Basen, 1985; Holzman, Pellegrino & Glaser, 1982). That is, exhaustive processes require greater memory capacity than self-terminating processes. Thus, younger children may use a strategy (self-terminating) that better fits their working memory capacity.

Furthermore, as acknowledged by Sternberg, the models do not address the nature of the encoding process. "Although the models specify in some detail the alternative ways in which attribute information can be combined to arrive at a solution for analogy problems, the models do not specify what the possible attributes are for different types of analogies, nor do they specify how subjects discover these attributes in the first place. A complete model of analogical reasoning would have to specify this further information, something that has not yet been done" (Sternberg, 1977, p. 355).

Indeed, the subjects in the Sternberg and Rifkin (1979) study were explicitly informed of the attributes and values that distinguished the figures and were told to use this information to solve the analogies. The problems were easy enough that the youngest students made errors on only 11 percent of the problems. Thus, the Sternberg and Rifkin analogy task probably underestimates the importance of the encoding process in the solution of analogy problems.

Gitomer and Curtis (1983) present data to indicate that differences in encoding strategies distinguish the performance of high-ability students from low-ability students, especially for difficult analogy problems. In this study college students were presented verbal analogies that varied in difficulty. The analogies were presented in the $A:B::C:D_1, D_2, D_3, D_4$ form (for example, exculpate:incriminate::exonerate:accuse, clear, honor, sentence). Eye movements and fixations were recorded as the subjects attempted to solve each analogy. On the easy problems, both high- and low-ability students were most likely to fixate (and presumably encode) the three analogy terms first and then fixate the answer options before responding, as illustrated in the left frame of Figure 8-2. The high-ability students, however, changed their strategy on the difficult problems. As illustrated in the right frame of Figure 8-2, they were more likely to look back and forth between the A, B, and C terms and the answer options before selecting an answer. This pattern of eye fixation suggests that these students used information in the D terms to reencode the A, B, and C terms when their initial encoding of these terms did not lead to a solution. That is, when problems are difficult and the relevant attributes of the A, B, and C terms are not readily apparent, the students who are most likely to solve these problems are those who use the attributes of the answer options to discover additional attributes of the analogy terms. Although eye fixation patterns do not directly indicate what strategies subjects are using, this study does suggest that cognitive processing strategies for solving analogy problems are affected by the task materials (Grudin, 1980), as well as individual differences (Bethell-Fox, Lohman & Snow, 1984). Such individual differences in the encoding process suggest that there may be comparable developmental changes in the strategies that children use to encode and represent analogy problems.

Although models and investigations of children's performance in standard analogy tests can advance our understanding of the development of reasoning in this type of task, analogical reasoning involves cognitive skills that go beyond those required in such tests (Holyoak, 1984a). In the standard tasks, the two domains are specified and are often equally familiar to the student, who typically needs only to identify a single relevant base relation and then map it onto the target domain. Reasoning by analogy, however, often involves little familiarity with the target domain; it does involve the need to find a base domain to explicate the relations of the target domain, and a system of relations

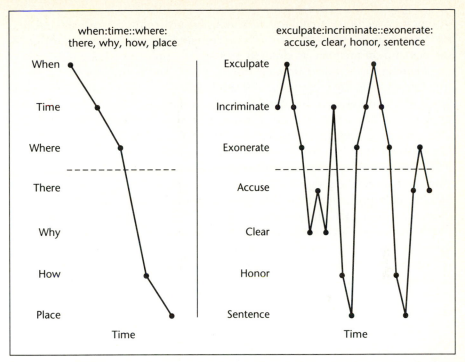

▶ **FIGURE 8-2** *Example of eye fixation pattern for high- and low-ability subjects for easy problems (left frame) and for high-ability subjects for difficult problems (right frame). Test results indicate that the high-ability subjects changed their strategy when attempting to solve the difficult problems. (From Gitomer & Curtis, 1983.)*

in the base domain rather than a single relation. For example, the Rutherford analogy between the solar system and the atom attempts to explain the nature of the atom in terms of the relationships evident in the solar system. A set of relations between the sun and its planets (that is, "distance," "attractive force," "revolves around," and "more massive than") is used to understand nucleus-electron relations within the atom (Gentner, 1983).

In efforts to understand analogical reasoning in the broader sense, Gentner (1983; Gentner & Toupin, 1986) has identified two factors that influence the mapping of relationships from base to target domains. First, the more similar the attributes of the two domains, the easier the mapping. That is, the reasoner finds it easier to map relations between similar objects in the base and target domains than between dissimilar objects. Second, if the relations of the base domain participate in higher-order relations, mapping is facilitated. Such higher-order relations (for example, the causal relation between "distance" and "attractive force") serve to connect and organize the lower-order relations (that is, those that relate objects) of the base domain and can serve to organize the mapping of the lower-order relations to the target domain. Higher-order relations may facilitate analogical reasoning by providing a more general representation of the relations of the base domain, a representation that makes less demand on memory as children attempt to apply their knowledge of the base domain to the target domain.

An experimental investigation of children's mapping of relations from one domain to another indicates the relevance of these two factors in the development of children's analogical reasoning (Gentner & Toupin, 1986). In the Gentner and Toupin task the elements and the lower-order relations of each domain were specified, as well as the mapping from the base domain to the target domain. The problem for the children was to maintain the mapping from the base to the target. Four- to six-year-olds and eight- to ten-year-olds were initially presented with short stories about three characters and were asked to act out each story with toy animals. Two types of stories were presented: systematic and unsystematic. The two were identical except that only the *systematic* stories included a moral that was intended to establish a reason for the actions of the protagonist and thus establish a higher-order relation between the actions (see Figure 8-3 for the two versions of a story).

After learning the given base stories in Figure 8-3 the children were asked to act out the same plot for a different set of three characters (for all children this was the target story of Figure 8-3). Transfer conditions differed, however, in how the characters and their assigned roles related to the original story. As illustrated in Figure 8-3, in condition S/S the characters of the target story were similar to those of the base story (for example, seal vs walrus) and they were to play the same roles. In the D condition the characters were different than the original characters (seal vs lion). In the third condition, S/D, similar characters occur in the transfer story but the roles were changed relative to the original story (for example, the role of the walrus in the original story was played by the penguin rather than the seal in the transfer story).

As expected, at both ages the similarity of the target to the base domain affected the children's transfer of the story actions, with the S/S condition the easiest and the S/D condition most difficult. Thus, when the mappings were easy (S/S condition), even the younger children were almost perfect at transferring (90 percent correct) the actions of one story domain to another set of characters; and this was true for both types of stories—systematic and nonsystematic. The younger children, however, were not sensitive to the presence in the base story of a higher-order relation (that is, the moral) that related the actions of the protagonist. Transfer was comparable for the two types of stories for all three base-target relations (S/S, D, and S/D). In contrast, the older children did benefit from the higher-order relation of the systematic stories. This was particularly evident when mapping was difficult (the S/D condition). This study, however, does not tell us whether the developmental change in the use of a higher-order relation in the base domain reflects developmental differences in knowledge about these relations (for example, the younger children may not have understood the moral) or in the ability to use such higher-order relations to guide the mapping of lower-order relations (Gentner & Toupin, 1986).

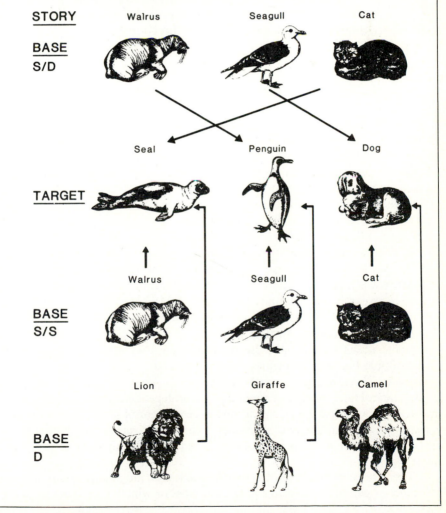

Setting[a]: There once was a very jealous cat who was friends with a walrus. The cat often said to the walrus, "Don't ever play with anyone else but me."

One day the cat went away on a trip and the walrus had no one to play with. But then a seagull came to visit the walrus. He brought a wagon along and said, "Would you like to play with me and my wagon?" The walrus said, "Yes." The seagull and the walrus had a great time pulling each other around in the seagull's wagon.

When the cat came back and found the walrus playing with someone else he got very angry. He shouted, "I'll never play with you again!" The cat was so angry that he jumped into the seagull's wagon. But the wagon began to roll faster down a steep hill. The cat was very scared. The seagull jumped up and chased after the wagon so the cat wouldn't crash. The seagull[b] stopped the runaway wagon and saved the cat's life.

Moral[b]: In the end, the cat realized that being jealous only got him into trouble. It is better to have two friends instead of one.

---

[a] *Setting*, Nonsystematic Version: There once was a very strong cat who was friends with a walrus.

[b] *Moral* is omitted in nonsystematic version.

STORY — Walrus — Seagull — Cat

BASE S/D

TARGET — Seal — Penguin — Dog

BASE S/S — Walrus — Seagull — Cat

BASE D — Lion — Giraffe — Camel

▶ **FIGURE 8-3** *Children aged four to six and eight to ten years were presented systematic and nonsystematic versions of a story. Results indicate the older children benefitted from the higher-order relation of the systematic stories. (From Gentner & Toupin, 1986.)*

In summary, preschoolers appear capable of analogical reasoning if the lower-order relations are concrete and/or familiar (for example, perceptual dimensions or actions), particularly if the domains are similar. Although young children's analogical reasoning is more fragile than that of older children, we have evidence that it plays a role in preschoolers' social modeling (Holyoak & Gordon, 1984), "make-believe" play (Garvey, 1977), and problem-solving behaviors (Holyoak, Junn & Billman, 1984). The limited data suggest the possibility that analogical reasoning may be a basic mechanism of cognitive development that is instrumental in the construction of new and more abstract knowledge structures (Gick & Holyoak, 1983).

When children fail to reason analogically, their responses are dominated by associations or similarities within the target domain. With development, this response tendency decreases and they demonstrate the ability to infer the base domain relations and to map these onto the target. This development reflects, in part at least, changes in domain-specific knowledge, the ability to organize the higher-order relations, and the functional capacity of working memory in the reasoning process.

HEURISTICS AND THE USE OF PROBABILITY INFORMATION

Everyday we make judgments and decisions about objects, people, and events about which we do not have certain knowledge. That is, we make a wide variety of judgments that may involve complex and extensive information, but not the type of information that assures a correct judgment. Although no form of inductive reasoning guarantees "true" or "correct" inferences, philosophers and mathematicians have strategies for maximizing the strength of an inductive inference, some of which involve incorporating statistical or probability information in the judgment process (for example, Black, 1946; Skyrms, 1975). The inferential statistics that psychologists use to draw conclusions from experimental data are sophisticated examples of how statistical information can strengthen our judgments about the meaning of our observations. Nonetheless, extensive research (for example, Kahneman & Tversky, 1972; 1973; Kahneman, Slovic & Tversky, 1982; Tversky & Kahneman, 1974) indicates that in many situations, when statistical information is available and relevant to a judgment, adults fail to make use of it. Instead, they often rely upon a few rather simple heuristic principles, without considering relevant statistical information. These heuristics can be effective, but they also can lead to errors of judgment. Heuristics are general, domain-independent strategies for solving problems. In Chapter 9 we consider the development of several heuristic strategies. Here we consider two heuristics—representativeness and availability—that have been the focus of adult research and raise meaningful developmental questions.

The *representative heuristic* specifies that our judgments about whether an object or person belongs to a particular class or whether an event originates from a given process are based on how representative the object or event is of the class or process. If the object or event is similar in essential features to a general representation of a class or a process, then it is judged to be a member of that class or a consequence of the process. Although this heuristic is certainly valuable for such processes as categorizing objects and events, relating specific events to scripts, and comprehending stories, Tversky and Kahneman have provided extensive evidence that, in some circumstances, this heuristic also can lead to erroneous judgments. As an example, when subjects were asked whether it would be more common to have days with 60 percent or more male births at a hospital with 15 births per day or at one with 45 births per day, or equally common at the two hospitals, most subjects responded that this would be equally likely at the two hospitals. Yet, the law of large numbers specifies that, with a random variable such as sex, deviant sample percentages should be less common with larger samples. In their judgments the students did not recognize the relevance of sample size (that is, 15 vs 45) but relied upon the similarity of the percentage of males in the general population (50 percent) to the target percentage (60 percent), which was the same for the two hospitals (Tversky & Kahneman, 1974).

The dominance of the representativeness heuristic is evident even when it is clear that subjects understand the relevance of the neglected statistical information. Consider another example. Subjects were given descriptions of individuals and asked to judge the probability that each individual engaged in a given occupation. The probabilistic judgments of occupation reflected the stereotypes for each occupation. For example, consider the following description:

> Steve is very shy and withdrawn, invariably helpful, but with little interest
> in people, or in the world of reality. A meek and tidy soul, he has a need
> for order and structure and a passion for detail.

If the description is similar to our stereotype of librarians, we are more likely to judge that Steve is a librarian. But if we also know that Steve is a member of a community in which 75 percent of the men are farmers, this information is relevant for the judgment that he is a farmer. Judgments of college students were not, however, affected by the latter information. Yet, if there was no description of the individual, the students were influenced by the population data and were more likely to judge the nondescript individual to be a farmer than a librarian. Thus, even when college students have knowledge of the relevance of the population base-rates for judgments, they do not always integrate this information into the judgment process. In other words, when subjects are required to make judgments about an individual and information about that individual is pitted against information about the general population, they are more likely to use the information pertinent to the individual when making their judgments, ignoring the potentially relevant population information.

A second principle, the *availability heuristic,* affects our judgments through our knowledge of specific related associations. If there are specific instances or exemplars available, either through retrieval from memory or present in a given situation, that are similar to the object or event to be judged, this information will affect our judgments. For example, when asked to estimate causes of death, students overestimate causes such as homicide and automobile accidents, which are dramatic and overreported in news coverage, and underestimate the underreported causes such as stroke and diabetes (Lichtenstein, Slovic, Fischoff, Layman & Combs, 1978).

In many situations, the availability heuristic is effective, because the availability of associations to specific examples often correctly reflects the size of the population. Are there more Golden Retrievers or Bloodhounds in this country? Undoubtedly, more specific instances of Golden Retrievers come to mind than Bloodhounds when you make this judgment and indeed, availability of these exemplars accurately represents the population. Are there more English words that begin with "k" or more that have "k" as the third letter? When asked this question, college students report that there are more words that begin with "k." This is not the case, but the availability of examples that begin with "k" dominates our judgment. Just as it is easier to locate in a dictionary those words starting with "k" than those that have "k" as a third letter, so it is easier for us to retrieve words beginning with "k."

Many cognitive psychologists see heuristic principles such as availability and representativeness as pervasive in adult thinking. This is not to say, however, that adults cannot use more formal analyses of probability information. Available research suggests that we are more likely to rely on heuristics when under time pressure, with high information loads, and when the outcome is not particularly important to us (see Sherman & Corty, 1984, for a review). Such findings suggest that the application of heuristics may be fairly automatic for adults, but that, depending upon goals, the cognitive effort required, and knowledge of general principles of probability, adults also can deploy deliberate strategies to process statistical information.

The Tversky and Kahneman tasks are difficult for adults. Their tasks require the use of probability knowledge; but, to use probability laws, people have to know the laws, know whether they apply in a given situation, and know how to apply them to that situation (see, for example, Bar-Hillel & Falk, 1982). For example, recent work clearly indicates that recognition and use of statistical information is influenced by content and context (for example, Evans, Brooks & Pollard, 1985; Bar-Hillel, 1980). If, for example, reasoners interpret the base-rate information to have a relevant (for example, Bar-Hillel, 1980) or causal relation (for example, Tversky & Kahneman, 1980) to the required judgment, they are more likely to incorporate the base-rate information into the judgment.

Nisbett and his colleagues (Nisbett, Krantz, Jepson & Kunda, 1983) also have identified several factors that affect the application of probability knowledge. To illustrate, adults are more likely to apply the law of large numbers if the population is heterogeneous rather than homogeneous. That is, if the characteristics of a population are homogeneous, then a small sample from that population is considered as representative of the population as a large sample. If, however, the population is heterogeneous then a large sample is more likely to represent the population. College students were given a questionnaire asking for several judgments about the characteristics of a population, on the basis of the characteristics of 1, 3, or 20 cases sampled from that population. Sample size affected some judgments and not others. For example, if an unknown chemical is green-burning, a one-case sample was judged as representative of that chemical as a 20-case sample, and subjects reported the belief that chemical elements are homogeneous with respect to color. However, obesity was not believed to be a homogeneous characteristic of people, and this is reflected in students' sensitivity to sample size for this judgment; that is, the law of large numbers affected this judgment.

Thus, in a number of studies, Nisbett and his colleagues have established that adults can use probability knowledge, but the application of such *statistical heuristics* is selective, influenced by a number of factors including domain-specific knowledge and cultural conventions about which events require statistical heuristics (for example, lifetime batting averages in baseball recognize that one or two seasons are not necessarily representative of a player's true ability). Both specific content of a judgment problem and the context in which it is presented determine how the available information is interpreted and, thus, whether statistical information is applied to the situation (see also, Fong, Krantz & Nisbett, 1986).

The adult research of inductive heuristics raises important questions about the development of these principles. Apparently, there is no research directly investigating the development of the representativeness or availability heuristics. Thus, we have no idea whether they are general and automatic from an early age or what course of development they follow. As seen in Chapter 6, we do have evidence, however, that young children use heuristic principles to make judgments about causality (for example, temporal precedence). Indeed, one of the principles, similarity, may be a form of the availability or representativeness heuristic. Further, we might wonder how these heuristics relate to children's analogical reasoning.

As the research on the effects of similarity on judgments of causality also makes evident, there are developmental changes in how the similarity principle is weighted relative to other causal principles in the judgment process. We will need to ask questions about how general heuristic principles relate to each other in children's inductive processes and how these heuristics interact with the development of domain-specific knowledge. Obviously, heuristics such as representativeness and availability depend upon access to prior knowledge. Thus, we can expect that the development of these principles might reflect the development of children's knowledge structures. Indeed, Sherman and Corty (1984) have likened the representativeness heuristic to prototype matching and the availability heuristic to exemplar matching. This suggests that issues raised in Chapters 5, 6, and 7 about the development of knowledge structures are relevant to explorations of the development of heuristic principles.

The development of statistical heuristics, of course, depends upon the acquisition of knowledge about chance and the laws of probability. Limited research on this topic indicates that the development of this knowledge is extended and complex (see Lovett, 1985, for a review). Piaget and Inhelder (1975) argued that preoperational children do not distinguish between chance and nonchance events. As concrete operations develop, children acquire a notion of uncertainty, distinguishing between the possible and the deductively necessary or certain. It is not, however, until the final stage of cognitive development, formal operations, that the concept of probability is fully developed.

Subsequent research suggests that Piaget and Inhelder underestimated the knowledge of young children and overestimated that of adolescents (Lovett, 1985). This research is far from systematic and raises more questions than it answers. Nevertheless, the data suggest that when using simple two-alternative random devices, preschoolers have some notion of chance (for example, coin toss) (see, for example, Fischbein, Pampu & Minzat, 1970; Kuzmak & Gelman, 1986); adolescents, however, do not appear to appreciate fully uncertainty in all types of chance situations (Lovett, 1985). As investigators acquire a systematic body of knowledge about the development of the concept of chance and the laws of probability, we will need to determine those factors that constrain the application of this knowledge in children's inductive reasoning.

Basic to cognitive development are the inductive processes that lead children to make generalizations. In previous chapters we have seen that, from their experiences, young children acquire general representations of objects and events, representations that influence their beliefs and expectations, and guide their actions in new situations. In this chapter we have seen that young children are capable of a form of inductive reasoning, analogical reasoning, that requires not only inducing relations between objects or events, but also discovering relations between relations. The fact that analogical reasoning often requires the detection of higher-order relationships has led some psychologists to be pessimistic about the role of analogical reasoning in the early development of children's thinking. Yet, under restricted conditions, when the information-processing demands are not high and the materials are familiar and similar, we find that even preschoolers are capable of analogical reasoning and, as will be evident in Chapter 9, that they can use analogical reasoning to solve problems. Nevertheless, the analogical reasoning of young children is constrained by limitations in relevant domain-specific knowledge and information-processing skills. As children acquire the requisite skills and knowledge, we can expect that they will increasingly engage in analogical reasoning. When asked to do so, children can reason analogically. In everyday situations, however, children are not often asked or instructed to reason analogically. Do young children spontaneously reason with analogies? If so, what factors affect the spontaneous occurrence of analogical reasoning? We return to these issues in Chapter 9.

Research on the availability, representativeness, and statistical heuristics of inductive reasoning has not been developmental. The college work suggests, however, that the availability and representativeness heuristics often dominate inductive reasoning and may, therefore, represent early forms of inductive reasoning. Indeed, theoretical analyses suggest that these heuristics are variations of the inductive processes used in concept acquisition.

Inductive conclusions are by nature, however, probabilistic. The statistical heuristics are principles that recognize the probabilistic nature of inductive reasoning and make use of statistical information to strengthen the probability that an inductive conclusion is correct. We have seen that college students do not always make use of statistical information to enhance their inductive reasoning and that domain-specific knowledge influences their application of statistical heuristics. Thus, even when college students have knowledge of principles such as the law of large numbers, the content or context will determine whether and how they apply the principles in the judgment process. We still have before us the need to explore the development of statistical heuristics and to determine how these principles are coordinated with other heuristics, such as availability and representativeness, that may lead to contradictory conclusions.

► ## DEDUCTIVE REASONING

Many of our beliefs are reached through exchanges with others. Whether it be late night sessions with friends, classroom discussions, or courtroom testimony, we engage in a wide range of interactive discussions and arguments that can influence our beliefs (Girle, 1983). Given that people, including authorities, often profess conflicting positions, how do we assess the quality of such arguments? Our beliefs come not only from direct experience and inductive processes, but also are derived from deductive arguments that can extend and modify our beliefs.

For generations logicians have sought to specify the nature of those arguments that lead to valid conclusions about relations within and between propositions. Although propositions are expressed in language, logicians have discovered that, independent of content, some relations among propositions allow conclusions that are necessarily true if the propositions are true. For example, if we know that "All A are B" and "All B are C," then we know that "All A are C," regardless of the specific content of the terms, "A," "B," and "C." Although the content words of propositions are not relevant to deductive arguments, there are some words that are. As we acquire language, we not only acquire *content words* (for example, dog, animal) but also *function words* (such as "and," "or," "some," "all," "if–then") that serve to specify the relations between content words and between entire propositions. It is the nature of these relations, as stipulated by the meaning of the function words, that determines the validity of deductive inferences. For example, if the first premise in the example just given is changed to "Some *A* are *B*," the conclusion that we can draw is different. The validity of conclusions for the two forms of deductive arguments we consider here, categorical syllogisms and conditional arguments, depends upon the meaning of the function words. As we will see, we cannot take for granted that adults, much less children, comprehend function words in the same way that logicians define them.

Logic and psychology have had a relationship that in many ways approximates that of linguistics and psychology (Falmagne, 1975; Macnamara, 1986). As the linguist focuses on the structure of sentences, the logician's goal is to specify the formal structure of those relations between propositions that lead to a necessary inference or conclusion. Logicians seek to describe an idealized logical competence by formulating a theory that identifies all valid arguments. For generations philosophers believed that the laws of logic were the same as the laws of thought (see, for example, Boole, 1854). As will become evident, this is not the case. Thus, the psychologist seeks to understand how people draw inferences, how they find and use reasons to make decisions, how they establish and confirm their beliefs. In this effort the psychologist must discover how the idealized logic of the logician relates to the daily reasoning of humans. This issue is far from resolved (see, Johnson-Laird, 1983; Macnamara, 1986; Moore, 1986). What is clear, however, is that reasoning is not always logical, nor do formal models of logic tell us *how* people reason (compare, Harman, 1986). The psychologist's problem, then, is to determine the nature of the psychological competence that underlies the reasoning process and how that competence is reflected in performance.

CATEGORICAL SYLLOGISMS

The categorical syllogism is a type of deductive argument that originated with Aristotle and has received extensive study by philosophers for the past 2,000 years. It relates propositions that specify quantitative relations between classes or categories. On the basis of our knowledge of some categorical relations, we seek to determine which other categorical relations must also hold. The simplest form of the syllogism consists of two premises, which state the quantitative relations among three classes, and a conclusion. For example, from the premises:

All Tibetan mastiffs are dogs.

All dogs are mammals.

We can conclude that "All Tibetan mastiffs are mammals." The quantifiers are "all" and "some" in formal logic, but can be terms such as "many," "few," "usually," or "often" in everyday communication (Johnson-Laird, 1975).

Possible sentence types ("moods") that can be used in a syllogism.

Universal, Affirmative (UA)	All *S* are *P*	All artists are beekeepers.
Universal, Negative (UN)	No *S* are *P*	No artists are beekeepers.
Particular, Affirmative (PA)	Some *S* are *P*	Some artists are beekeepers.
Particular, Negative (PN)	Some *S* are not *P*	Some artists are not beekeepers.

Examples of moods of a syllogism.

UA	All *B* are *C*	UN	No *B* are *C*	PA	Some *B* are *C*
UN	No *A* are *B*	PA	Some *A* are *B*	UA	All *A* are *B*
PN	Some *A* are not *C*	UN	No *A* are *C*	PN	Some *A* are not *C*
PN	Some *B* are not *C*	UN	No *B* are *C*	UA	All *B* are *C*
UA	All *A* are *B*	PN	Some *A* are not *B*	PA	Some *A* are *B*
PA	Some *A* are *C*	PA	Some *A* are *C*	UA	All *A* are *C*

▶ ***FIGURE 8-4*** *There are four types of propositions (top) used in a syllogism: universal affirmative (UA); universal negative (UN); particular, affirmative (PA); or particular, negative (PN). There are 64 different moods of the syllogism as a whole (see examples, bottom).*

In order to analyze such arguments, logicians have established conventions for symbolizing the several forms of the categorical syllogism. Each syllogistic argument consists of two premises and a conclusion, as illustrated here.

"All artists are beekeepers."	Major premise
"Some chemists are artists."	Minor premise
Therefore:	
"Some chemists are beekeepers."	Conclusion

One premise, the major premise, expresses a relation between the predicate of the conclusion (beekeepers) and another term (artists). The minor premise expresses a relation between the subject of the conclusion (chemists) and the other term (artists) (Revlis, 1975). There are four types of propositions, called "moods," depending on whether the quantification term is *universal* (U, that is, "all") or *particular* (P, that is, "some") and whether the statement is *negative* (N) or *affirmative* (A), as illustrated in Figure 8-4. There are 64 different moods of the syllogism as a whole since the two premises and the conclusion can take any one of the four moods of a proposition, that is, 4 (major premise) × 4 (minor premise) × 4 (conclusion).

Figure I	**Figure II**
All *beekeepers* are *clowns*.	All *clowns* are *beekeepers*.
All *artists* are *beekeepers*.	All *artists* are *beekeepers*.
All *artists* are *clowns*.	All *artists* are *clowns*.

Figure III	**Figure IV**
All *beekeepers* are *clowns*.	All *clowns* are *beekeepers*.
All *beekeepers* are *artists*.	All *beekeepers* are *artists*.
All *artists* are *clowns*.	All *artists* are *clowns*.

▶ **FIGURE 8-5** *Class terms, such as beekeepers, can occur in one of two orders, resulting in four possible orderings as shown above.*

In addition, the class terms of each premise can occur in one of two orders, which means that there are four possible orderings (called Figures, as in Figure 8-5). As illustrated in Figure 8-5, the common term (for example, beekeepers) can occur either in the first or second position of the major and minor premises. Each of the 64 different moods of the syllogism can occur in each of the four figures which results in 256 different syllogisms.

Of these 256 syllogistic arguments, only 15 have valid conclusions; these are illustrated in Figure 8-6 (Carney & Scheer, 1974; but see Adams, 1984, for a discussion of which arguments are valid). A comparison of the arguments in Figure 8-6 with those presented in Figure 8-4 will establish that none of the arguments in Figure 8-4 are valid. Although logicians typically do not consider another factor, the order of the premises (that is, whether the major or minor premise is presented first), there actually are 516 (2×256) different forms of the syllogism (Johnson-Laird & Steedman, 1978). The order of the premises does not, of course, affect the validity of an argument.

Most adults untrained in formal logic make errors when producing or judging conclusions for syllogistic arguments that are presented in symbolic form, that is, when the categories are not concrete but are represented by symbols such as *A, B,* and *C*. These errors include both failing to accept valid conclusions and accepting invalid conclusions. To illustrate, Erickson (1978) had college students produce conclusions for the four figures of the UA-UA syllogisms. These four syllogisms are shown in Figure 8-7 with the proportion of college students who drew each of the possible conclusions (the valid conclusions are indicated). Notice that there are two valid conclusions for the Figure I syllogism, yet only approximately two percent of the students chose the second one. There are no valid conclusions for Figure II, but only 13 percent of the group recognize this fact. Consideration of the data for the other two Figures indicates a strong tendency for adults to draw invalid conclusions and to fail to draw valid conclusions.

Figure I			
UA	UN	UA	UN
<u>UA</u>	<u>UA</u>	<u>PA</u>	<u>PA</u>
UA	UN	PA	PN
Figure II			
UN	UA	UN	UA
<u>UA</u>	<u>UN</u>	<u>PA</u>	<u>PN</u>
UN	UN	PN	PN
Figure III			
PA	UA	PN	UN
<u>UA</u>	<u>PA</u>	<u>UA</u>	<u>PA</u>
PA	PA	PN	PN
Figure IV			
UA	PA	UN	
<u>UN</u>	<u>UA</u>	<u>PA</u>	
UN	PA	PN	

▶ **FIGURE 8-6** *The fifteen forms of valid categorical syllogisms.* (Modified from Carney & Scheer, 1974.)

MODELS OF SYLLOGISTIC REASONING   What shall we make of the common finding that adults do not always reason according to the logician's ideal? Models of syllogistic reasoning have taken one of two approaches. One approach assumes that adults, at least, are rational and have knowledge of the rules of inference (for example, Henle, 1962). These models assume that errors occur when domain-specific knowledge influences the interpretation of premises, but that general, domain-independent inference rules establish the nature of the relations between the interpreted premises (for example, Braine & Rumain, 1983; Hagert & Waern, 1986). Errors occur not because adults lack the appropriate inferential rules, but because they reason with misinterpretations of the premises. Thus these models assume that a general logical competence underlies syllogistic reasoning. The models differ, however, in their assumptions about the specific nature of the inference rules of that logical competence (see Johnson-Laird & Bara, 1984, for a review).

The other approach assumes that adults are irrational, without knowledge of deductive inference rules. For example, one model (for example, Begg & Denny, 1969; Woodward & Sells, 1935) assumes that the conclusion drawn is based on a general impression of the premises (the *atmosphere effect*). This means that if one of the premises is particular ("some") or contains a negative, the conclusion that is considered valid also is particular or negative. Otherwise, the conclusion takes the form of the affirmative and the general ("all"). This

Premises	Conclusions	Proportion Drawing Conclusion
Figure I	UA (valid)	.93
All B are C	UN	.03
All A are B	PA (valid)	.02
	PN	.0
	None	.02
Figure II	UA	.80
All C are B	UN	.03
All A are B	PA	.05
	PN	.0
	None (valid)	.13
Figure III	UA	.72
All B are C	UN	.02
All B are A	PA (valid)	.20
	PN	.0
	None	.06
Figure IV	UA	.87
All C are B	UN	.03
All B are A	PA (valid)	.05
	PN	.02
	None	.03

▶ **FIGURE 8-7** *Most adults untrained in formal logic make errors when judging conclusions for syllogistic arguments presented in symbolic form. (From Erickson, 1978.)*

atmosphere effect, thus, has no relationship to the logical form of the syllogism itself. Other explanations assume that personal knowledge about the content of the premises determines the conclusion drawn, not an analysis of the form of the argument (for example, Evans, Barston & Pollard, 1983; Pollard, 1982; Revlis, 1975).

Recently, Johnson-Laird (1982) has proposed a third characterization of adult reasoning; he has offered a process model of syllogistic reasoning in which both inductive and deductive processes play a role (Johnson-Laird & Bara, 1984; Johnson-Laird & Steedman, 1978). Unlike the logical competence models (for example, Braine, 1978), this model emphasizes the information-processing aspect of reasoning, rather than knowledge of deductive rules of inference.

The Johnson-Laird model demonstrates that making explicit what is implicit in premises is not easy. It assumes that we comprehend propositions that have class concepts in common by constructing a mental model of the premise information. The construction of this mental model is guided by our semantic knowledge of the function words. There are three stages in this process. The first stage is the interpretation of the premises. Johnson-Laird assumes that we use a few tokens (prototypes) of each class to represent the relation between classes. This representation may or may not be in our conscious awareness. To give a concrete example, the premise "all artists are beekeepers" might be represented as:

artist = beekeeper

artist = beekeeper

(beekeeper)

This indicates that every artist (but two tokens are enough to represent all artists) is also (=) a beekeeper. However, there *may* be beekeepers who are not artists as represented by (beekeeper).

When a second premise is encoded that mentions one of the classes of the first premise, we attempt to modify our initial representation to integrate the information in the two premises. For example, "all beekeepers are clowns" could be integrated as:

artist = beekeeper   = clown

artist = beekeeper   = clown

(beekeeper) = clown

(clown)

This integration process is constrained by the capacity of working memory since the representations of both premises must be maintained simultaneously in order to integrate them. Furthermore, the complexity of the operations required to integrate the premises is affected by the order of the presentations of the premise information. As we saw in Chapter 7, the maintenance of information in working memory requires continual rehearsal or attention to the information, and this is usually done in the serial order of presentation. For example, if the class relations are represented in the order *A-B, B-C,* as the *A-B* representation is maintained there can be an immediate integration of the second premise upon its presentation. However, an order such as *B-A, B-C* increases the load on working memory since as the first premise, *B-A,* is maintained it is necessary to relate the second premise to the first term of the first premise, which would require some type of reordering of the premise representations.

In the second stage of the Johnson-Laird model, a conclusion, relating the *A* and *C* terms, is drawn. That is, on the basis of the integrated mental representation we attempt to specify how the members of the "*A*" class are related to the members of the "*C*" class. In this process there is a tendency to read our mental representation of the *A-C* relation in the direction that the terms are represented. That is, if *A* occurs first in the representation, then we draw an *A-C* conclusion ("All artists are clowns," in our example). If, however, the terms are represented in the opposite order, the conclusions are reversed (for example, "Some clowns are artists") (Johnson-Laird & Steedman, 1978).

As an illustration, consider two syllogisms and the conclusions produced by college students (Johnson-Laird & Steedman, 1978). The premises were in the PA and UA moods and in Figure IV were:

Some *A* are *B*

All *B* are *C*.

There are two valid conclusions for this argument, "Some *A* are *C*" and "Some *C* are *A*." Of 20 subjects, 15 drew the first conclusion and two subjects drew the second conclusion. In Figure I the argument becomes:

All *B* are *A*

Some *C* are *B*.

The same two conclusions are valid, yet performance is reversed. Sixteen students draw the conclusion that "Some *C* are *A*." Only one student drew the conclusion, "Some *A* are *C*." Thus, the figure of the syllogism determines whether an *A-C* or *C-A* conclusion is more likely. Furthermore, the greater the load on working memory, the more difficult it is to draw an inference (see, for example, Johnson-Laird, 1982).

In the third stage of the model, we attempt to construct alternative models of the premise information that would negate or falsify our original conclusion. That is, we attempt to determine if there are any other possible conclusions that would *contradict* our original conclusion. In this we appreciate that an inference is valid if there are no counterexamples to the inference (Johnson-Laird, 1982). For example, consider a syllogism, "All *A* are *B*. Some *B* are *C*." in which the initial mental models is:

$$a = b = c$$
$$a = b \quad (c)$$
$$(b)$$

The conclusion drawn from this representation would be "Some *A* are *C*." But if we try to break the link between *A* and *C*, we may recognize that the *B*s that are *C*s are not necessarily the *B*s that are related to *A*. Therefore, an alternative model is:

$$a = b$$
$$a = b$$
$$(b) = c$$
$$(c)$$

Now, there is no positive link between *A* and *C* and thus the first conclusion is falsified. In this case, because there are no other alternative models, the appropriate conclusion is that this syllogism has no valid conclusion. There may or may not be a link between A and C; it does not necessarily follow that there is or is not (Johnson-Laird & Bara, 1984).

It is this final stage that involves deductive processes. That is, if a conclusion can be derived that contradicts another conclusion, then it necessarily follows that both conclusions cannot be valid. However, if an alternative model yields the same conclusion, it does not necessarily follow that the conclusion *is* valid. There may be yet another alternative model that will yield a contradictory conclusion. Thus, it is the attempt to falsify a conclusion that is a deductive reasoning process that can lead to a necessary conclusion. As will be evident when considering the conditional argument, students do not always attempt to falsify a conclusion. Since each syllogism has a finite set of alternative mental models, if we persist in our attempts to falsify our conclusions, we will eventually come to the correct conclusion. That is, the final testing stage may require extensive efforts at falsification before it is complete, depending upon the number of alternative mental models that are possible for a given syllogism. How many alternatives are generated will depend upon the student's interpretation of the function words, which is the issue of the next section.

The Johnson-Laird model assumes that errors in syllogistic reasoning can occur in any one of the three stages. It is supported by results showing that the reasoning of college students (Johnson-Laird & Bara, 1984) and children (Johnson-Laird, Oakhill & Bull, 1986) is affected by the order of the presentation of the terms (that is, the Figure of a syllogism; see Figure 8-5) and the number of alternative mental models.

In one of the few developmental studies of syllogistic reasoning, Johnson-Laird, *et al.* tested children of 7, 9, and 12 years of age with syllogisms that varied in both the Figure of the syllogism and the number of potential mental models. Although the 7-year-olds found the problems too difficult, there were no significant differences between the 9- and 12-year-olds. For the two older groups, the number of alternative mental models had the expected effect. Although the children correctly solved approximately half the syllogisms with one model (for example, "All *A* are *B*. No *B* are *C*.") they did not solve any of the three-model syllogisms (for example, "Some *A* are *B*. No *B* are *C*."). Additionally, the Figure of the syllogism had the expected effect on the children's performance, with, for example, syllogisms in Figure I (that is, *A-B, B-C*) easier than those in Figure IV (*B-A, B-C*). In Chapter 6 we saw a similar type of effect for children's solution of the transitive inference task. When the premises were presented in the order of the relations, rather than randomly, it was easier for the children to derive an appropriate mental representation of the transitive relation.

The Johnson-Laird model appears to have two particular strengths (but see Ford, 1985). First, it is part of a more comprehensive theory of reasoning (Johnson-Laird, 1983). That is, it includes processes that are relevant both to other forms of deductive reasoning and to language comprehension in general. Thus, it has potential as an integrative theory of reasoning that does not partition reasoning into unrelated types of logical arguments. Second, the model appears to explain data that are not explained by other models. For example, some syllogisms are considerably easier than others. To confirm this for yourself, determine whether there is a valid conclusion for each of the two syllogisms, "All *A* are *B*. No *B* are *C*." and "Some *A* are *B*. No *B* are *C*." Undoubtedly, it was easier for you to determine a valid conclusion for the first syllogism than for the second one.

THE INTERPRETATION OF FUNCTION WORDS   Although most researchers do not agree which theory best describes deductive reasoning, they do agree that interpretation of the function words affects performance (Henle, 1962). That is, adults do not always interpret the function words of the categorical syllogism in the way that logicians do. For example, consider the premise, "All *A* are *B*." How should we represent the relationship between class "*A*" and class "*B*"? As illustrated with Euler diagrams in Figure 8-8, this statement has two possible interpretations: a subset or class inclusion relation and an identity relation. Similarly, two mental models are possible using the Johnson-Laird type of representation:

Identity	*Subset*
a = *b*	*a* = *b*
a = *b*	*a* = *b*

(b)

The situation is more complicated for the proposition "Some *A* are *B*." As illustrated in Figure 8-8, there are four different interpretations because logicians use "some" to mean "at least one and as many as all" (Black, 1946). This, of course, differs from daily use where "some" does not include the possibility of "all" and means "not all but at least one." Logicians recognize that "some" is an indeterminate term that does not specify whether "all members of *A* class are also members of *B* class" (Copi, 1972). This indeterminate meaning of "some" signifies that we may have knowledge about some *A*s, but not about all *A*s. Put another way, "some" represents the situation where we have not observed all *A*s and are unwilling to draw an inductive generalization about all *A*s but know that it is a possibility that all *A*s are like the "some" *A*s that have been observed.

Adults do make errors in the interpretation of function words, and these interpretation errors affect reasoning with categorical syllogisms (for example, Chapman & Chapman, 1959). For example, adults make the *"conversion"* error in which "All *A* are *B*." is also encoded as "All *B* are *A*.", or "Some *A* are not *B*." also is encoded as "Some *B* are not *A*." (see, for example, Newstead & Griggs, 1983). Although, the *identity interpretation* of "All *A* are *B*." implies that "All *B* are *A*.", this need not be the case as evident in the *subset inter-*

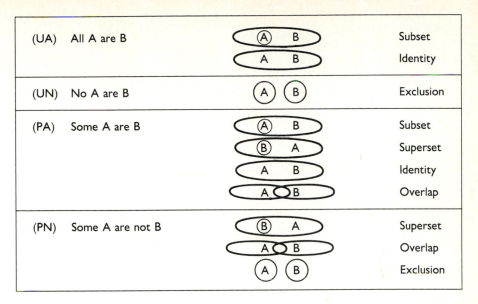

(UA)	All A are B	A B	Subset
		A B	Identity
(UN)	No A are B	A B	Exclusion
(PA)	Some A are B	A B	Subset
		B A	Superset
		A B	Identity
		A B	Overlap
(PN)	Some A are not B	B A	Superset
		A B	Overlap
		A B	Exclusion

▶ **FIGURE 8-8** *Euler diagrams depict the relationships between class "A" and class "B."*

pretation of "All *A* are *B*." Similarly, as evident in the *superset interpretation* of "Some *A* are not *B*.", this proposition need not mean that "Some *B* are not *A*."

Neimark and Chapman (1975) directly investigated children's encoding of premises. Students ranging in age from seventh grade to college were given a set of 24 statements that described the quantitative relations of two classes. Eight of these were the two orders of the four moods of syllogistic premises, UA, UN, PA, and PN. The remainder combined two premises. For each of these statements the students had to choose Euler diagrams that could represent the statement. The students were informed that more than one choice was possible.

As illustrated in Figure 8-9, there was a significant developmental change in the interpretations of the simple propositions. However, at all ages, the universal propositions were easier than the particular propositions. Also, at all ages, the negative universal statement ("No *A* are *B*.") was easier than the affirmative universal ("All *A* are *B*."), but there was not such an effect for negation of the particular proposition. As illustrated in Figure 8-8 the premise (UN) that has only one possible interpretation is easier than the UA premise which has two possible interpretations. Further, for the "particular" premises students did not give the complete, logical interpretation of "some."

Analysis of the errors for the universal propositions (UA, UN) indicates that the most frequent error for the older students was a failure to include both the subset and identity alternatives for the affirmative statement. The younger children made this error, as well as choosing the alternative that reverses the proposition.

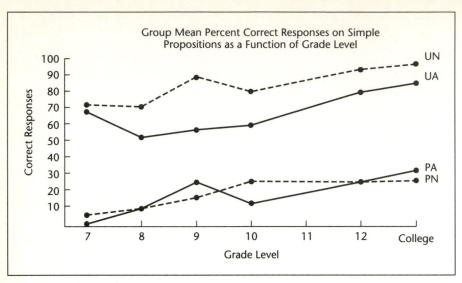

FIGURE 8-9 *Group mean percent correct responses on simple propositions as a function of grade level. As indicated above, there was a significant developmental change in the interpretations of the simple propositions.* (From Neimark & Chapman, 1975.)

The particular, "some," is narrowly defined at all ages. The younger children select the fourth alternative, partial overlap, exclusively. This exclusive use of the partial overlap declines with age as a second alternative is added which expresses the subset relation. The identity interpretation is seldom given even by college students. As might be expected, when asked to represent compound propositions (for example, "All *A* are *B* and some *B* are not *A*."), errors occur because of incomplete or inaccurate encoding of the separate propositions. Thus, premise interpretation appears to play a significant role in the development of syllogistic reasoning.

In summary, the categorical syllogism is a difficult task for adults. The Johnson-Laird model and related research suggest that the information-processing demands of syllogistic reasoning can lead to errors in constructing, manipulating, and evaluating mental models of the syllogistic information. Differences between logical and real-world definitions of terms also lead to difficulties in interpreting premises. The limited developmental research available indicates that these interpretation errors are even more prevalent with children (Caplan, 1981; Neimark & Slotnick, 1970). Nonetheless, the fact that by nine years of age children have a pattern of performance that is comparable to that of adults leads to the preliminary conclusion that by this age children reason with processes for mental representation and manipulation that are similar to those of adults.

EFFECTS OF KNOWLEDGE ABOUT CONTENT TERMS   Most of us do not reason about abstract relations; instead, we reason about specific ideas, about domain-specific knowledge. The question for the psychologist, then, is not only how the form of syllogistic arguments and our interpretation of function words affect our reasoning, but also whether and how the content of propositions influences the reasoning process. Evans and his colleagues have demonstrated that problem content does influence the syllogistic reasoning of college students (Evans, Barston & Pollard, 1983). Subjects were presented sets of categorical syllogisms in two forms, where *H* corresponded to "highly trained dogs," *V* to "vicious," and *P* to "police dogs."

No *H* are *V*	No *H* are *V*
Some P are V	*Some P are V*
Some *P* are not *H* (valid)	Some *H* are not *P* (invalid)

If the reader doubts the difference in validity between the two conclusions, try constructing a "mental model," which is consistent with the premises but contradicts the conclusion, "Some *H* are not *P*." Or consider the Euler circles below; the superset relation between *P* and *V* could result in the following diagram:

No H are V
Some P are V
Some P are not H (valid)

No H are V
Some P are V
Some H are not P (invalid)

If still not convinced, consider an analogous, but concrete, example:

No boys are girls.

Some children are girls.

_____

Some children are not boys (valid).

Some boys are not children (invalid).

Half the conclusions, for each type of syllogism, were propositions that had been rated as believable (for example, "Some highly trained dogs are not police dogs.") by an independent group of students and half had been rated as unbelievable (for example, "Some police dogs are not highly trained."). The syllogisms were presented in prose passages such as the following (Evans, Barston & Pollard, 1983, p. 298):

> "Dogs are used extensively for the purpose of guarding property, guiding the blind and so on. No highly trained dogs are vicious. However, many people believe that their temperament cannot be trusted. The police service use dogs a great deal in their work. Some police dogs are vicious and

although fatal accidents are rare, there is still growing concern over their widespread use."

If the above passage is true, does it follow that: Some highly trained dogs are not police dogs?

Performance in this study clearly indicates that the believability of the conclusion strongly influenced the students' judgments of validity. The students were as likely to accept an invalid conclusion (92 percent) as a valid one (92 percent) if the conclusion was believable, but accepted a valid, "unbelievable" conclusion only 46 percent of the time. These findings indicate that the content of the premises and conclusion can affect reasoning (see also Oakhill & Johnson-Laird, 1985). But the fact that the valid, unbelievable arguments were accepted 46 percent of the time and the invalid, unbelievable ones only 8 percent of the time indicates that the form of the argument also influenced the students' reasoning. Oakhill and Johnson-Laird (1985) have suggested that our knowledge and beliefs can affect "the construction of a model of the premises, the formulation of a conclusion based on it, and the search for models refuting a putative conclusion" (p. 566). For example, if our first integration of the ABC terms leads to a believable conclusion, we may be less likely to try to falsify that conclusion. Moreover, the fact that the Evans *et al.* syllogism was a difficult one by the standards of the Johnson-Laird model raises the possibility that believability plays more of a role in reasoning when information-processing demands are high. Such a possibility has developmental implications that have yet to be explored.

Thus, adult research suggests that subjects often do not restrict their reasoning to the information provided but attempt to relate it to their knowledge of the world. They have difficulty disembedding the logical relations of the premises from the content-specific relations of the premises. Most reasoning situations require attention to content. To reason deductively, we must restrict our attention to the logical form of the premises, suspending our beliefs about the truth of the premises and conclusions, and we must be able to recognize that this is appropriate for the situation. That is, we must learn when and how to eschew our beliefs (Hawkins, Pea, Glick & Scribner, 1984).

Hawkins and his colleagues have demonstrated that even preschoolers can accomplish this feat under some circumstances. Four- and five-year-olds were presented three forms of syllogistic arguments with simplified propositions that did not include "some" or "all" (see Table 8-2 for examples). These arguments were presented with three types of content: fantasy, congruent, and incongruent. *Fantasy* (F) premises expressed information about make-believe creatures (for example, "Every banga is purple."). The *congruent* (C) premises were compatible with the children's practical knowledge (for example, "Rabbits never bite."). The *incongruent* (I) premises were contradictory to their knowledge (for example, "Everything that can fly has wheels."). The researchers reasoned that if children this age do reason deductively they would be more likely to do so with the fantasy materials since these cannot be integrated with

TABLE 8-2 *Construction of Problem Types*

Form	Model	Affirmative example	Negative example
A: Universal	A is B	Every banga is purple.	Bears have big teeth.
	B is C	Purple animals always sneeze at people.	Animals with big teeth can't read books.
	A is C	Do bangas sneeze at people?	Can bears read books?
B: Particular	A has B	Pogs wear blue boots.	Rabbits never bite.
	C is an A	Tom is a pog.	Cuddly is a rabbit.
	C has B	Does Tom wear blue boots?	Does Cuddly bite?
C: Action-Functional	A does B when . . .	Glasses bounce when they fall.	Merds laugh when they're happy.
	B is C	Everything that bounces is made of rubber.	Animals that laugh don't like mushrooms.
	A has C	Are glasses made of rubber?	Do merds like mushrooms?

Source: Hawkins, Pea, Glick, and Scribner, 1984. Copyright 1984 by the American Psychological Association. Reprinted by permission.

their prior knowledge. Further, the children should be more likely to recognize that suspension of prior knowledge is appropriate for the task if their first experiences in the task are with the fantasy materials. Accordingly, the children received one of four orderings of the materials—FIC, IFC, CIF, or random—to test this possibility.

Both the number of correct responses and the justifications that the children gave for these responses indicated that the children could reason deductively with fantasy materials and that this was more likely to occur if these materials were presented first. Furthermore, the children in the FIC condition were more likely to give "logical" justifications in the C and the I conditions as well as the F condition. These results suggest that when conditions encourage and support the suspension of prior knowledge, even preschoolers can solve syllogistic problems. Although the children typically had difficulty with the problems that contradicted their prior knowledge, Dias and Harris (1987) have shown that four- to six-year-olds can reason about propositions that contradict their world knowledge (for example, all cats bark) if the propositions are presented in the context of make-believe play.

Taken together, research indicates that the logician's principles of deductive argument do not adequately describe adult syllogistic reasoning (compare, Harman, 1986). Reasoning is not a process of matching the structure of premises to the formal rules of syllogistic logic (Johnson-Laird *et al.*, 1986). Rather, the reasoning process involves comprehending and mentally representing propositional information, and evaluating conclusions, processes which may tax our information-processing skills and may be influenced by domain-specific knowledge.

The very limited developmental research indicates that children have difficulty interpreting the propositions of syllogistic arguments. When, however, the propositions are simplified and conditions arranged to encourage attention to form rather than content, preschoolers do have some success with syllogistic reasoning. We also have suggestive evidence that children engage in the same reasoning processes as adults, but we still know relatively little about the development of syllogistic reasoning and how it relates to other aspects of cognitive development, such as the functional capacity of working memory, comprehension strategies, domain-specific knowledge, and the development of belief systems.

CONDITIONAL REASONING

Conditional reasoning is a form of deductive reasoning that involves a conditional relationship (that is, "if . . . then") between propositions. To illustrate, suppose that you know that "If a Baldwin apple is picked after a first frost, then it has a good taste." Suppose also that the local orchard is offering Baldwin apples for sale and that there has not been a local frost. What conclusion can you logically draw about the taste of these apples? Although the conditional relationship is not always stated as explicitly as above (that is, as an "if . . . then" statement), it is a prevalent one in everyday reasoning, and a particularly important one in scientific reasoning.

Conditional arguments can take a variety of forms; we will consider only the four simplest forms that are illustrated in Figure 8-10. Each contains one conditional premise of the form "If A then C." and a premise that states either the affirmation or negation of the antecedent (that is, "A" proposition) or the consequent (that is, "C" proposition).

What can we know from the statements of the conditional argument? First, if we know the conditional proposition to be true, we know nothing about the truth or falsity of its component propositions. Consider the proposition, "If the sun shines today, then I will be happy today." ("If S then H."). If we know that "If S then H." is true, we do not know whether "It is sunny today." or whether "I am happy today."

Suppose that the two premises of the first argument in Figure 8-10 are true. What can we say about the conclusion of that argument? Substitute the propositions S ("The sun shines today.") and H ("I will be happy today.") for the As and Cs in the figure. If the two premises are true, then the conclusion must also be true and the argument is a valid one since the conclusion follows necessarily. This form of the argument is called *asserting the antecedent* and is always valid. Consider the second argument. Again assuming that the two premises are true, does the conclusion follow? No, indeed it is possible that I am happy on occasions other than sunny days. For example, I may be happy

1. **Asserting the Antecedent:**	2. **Asserting the Consequence:**
If A then C	If A then C
A	C
C (valid)	A (invalid)
3. **Denying the Antecedent:**	4. **Denying the Consequence:**
If A then C	If A then C
Not A	Not C
Not C (invalid)	Not A (valid)

▶ **FIGURE 8-10** *The four simplest conditional arguments: asserting the antecedent, asserting the consequence, denying the antecedent, and denying the consequence.*

on Fridays no matter what the weather conditions. Conditional arguments in this form are always invalid and this is the fallacy of *asserting the consequence*.

Similar analyses can be made of the other two arguments. Considering the third argument, we have already seen that it is possible for me to be happy on occasions other than a sunny day, thus the third argument, *denying the antecedent,* is another invalid form. The earlier example is of this form: "If Baldwin apples are picked after a frost, then they taste good. The apples were picked before a frost." Although the apples will taste good after the frost, there is no way to know, with the information available, how they will taste before a frost. Finally, the fourth form, *denying the consequence,* is valid. If, indeed, both premises are true, then it follows necessarily that if I am unhappy it is not possible for it to be a sunny day (Black, 1946).

DEVELOPMENT OF CONDITIONAL REASONING   Relatively little research on adult reasoning with the conditional argument has been motivated by theory development (compare, Johnson-Laird, 1975; Johnson-Laird, 1986; Johnson-Laird & Wason, 1970). Rather, the goal has been to determine whether adults actually use the forms of reasoning specified by the logicians (Matlin, 1983). As with categorical syllogisms, considerable evidence indicates that they often do not. Taplin (1971), for example, found that only 45 percent of the college students he tested correctly assessed the validity of the four aguments described above. The students were the most accurate with the valid argument, affirming the antecedent, and the next best with the other valid argument, denying the consequent. The invalid arguments had the most errors, with the students stating that the arguments, asserting the consequence and denying the antecedent, were valid.

Clearly one important determinant of adult conditional reasoning is the encoding process. An interpretation error, *illicit conversion,* occurs when individuals interpret the statement, "If A then C." as also meaning "If C then A."; this is the biconditional interpretation which means "A if and only if C."

This *biconditional interpretation* may be influenced by our daily experiences. In some situations the consequence only occurs when the antecedent occurs. For example, when I was at summer camp we had fish for dinner if it was Friday, and only on Fridays did we have fish. Thus it was equally true that "If we had fish then it was Friday." and "If it was Friday then we had fish."

A number of studies have demonstrated developmental trends in conditional reasoning. As is the case with adults, these studies indicate that children make more errors on the invalid arguments than the valid ones. For example, Roberge (1970) investigated reasoning with children in the fourth, sixth, eighth, and tenth grades. The four arguments were presented with two premises and a conclusion. The children were to judge whether the conclusion had to be true, could not be true, or if it was not possible to tell because there was not enough information.

Performance on the task indicated that the understanding of the two valid arguments reached its peak in eighth grade, with approximately half the children in fourth and sixth grades solving these arguments. But it was not until tenth grade that there was any understanding of the invalid arguments and this occurred for fewer than 20 percent of the students.

Several studies (for example, Bereiter, Hidi & Dimitroff, 1979; Paris, 1973; Sternberg, 1979; Taplin, Staudenmayer & Taddonio, 1974) indicate a developmental change in how children interpret the "if . . . then" relationship. Younger children (second graders) were most likely to make a conjunctive ("and") or biconditional interpretation. Indeed, the biconditional interpretation of "if . . . then" appears comparable to the identity interpretation of "All A are C." "If it is sunny, then I am happy." translates into "All cases in which it is sunny (A) are cases in which I am happy (C)." This interpretation would lead to the type of errors that are common in conditional arguments. The conclusions of both of the invalid arguments are based on the assumption that A and C are identical: "When I am happy, it is sunny." and "When it is not sunny, I am not happy." By the fifth and sixth grades the biconditional interpretation predominates. During the high school years the conditional interpretation begins to appear, with the biconditional interpretation declining in frequency, and this is when the errors decrease for the invalid arguments. But even college students are likely to give a biconditional interpretation.

Rumain, Connell, and Braine (1983) made a distinction between two theories of the biconditional interpretation. One explanation assumes that the biconditional interpretation reflects a defective lexical representation of the meaning of "if . . . then." That is, as in the case for "some" in categorical syllogisms, subjects may have a meaning for "if . . . then" that differs from the logician's. The other explanation assumes that in normal discourse in which Grice's (1975) conversational postulates apply, the conditional invites inferences other than necessary ones (that is, "If A then C." invites "If not A then not C."). For example, the statement, "If you mow the lawn, then I'll give you five dollars." invites the inference, "If you don't mow the lawn, then I won't give you five dollars." Similarly, in the case of Baldwin apples, why would others tell you that they taste good after a frost unless they meant that Baldwin apples do not taste good before a frost?

In a test of these two possibilities, Rumain and her colleagues gave college students and fifth graders conditional arguments in which the conditional premise was a simple "if . . . then" statement and also arguments in which the conditional was expanded to explicitly countermand invited inferences. For example: "If the bottom has N, then the top has X (major premise). But if the bottom doesn't have N, then the top may have X or it may have some other letter. And, if the top has X, then the bottom may have N or it may have some other number (expansion)." If the subjects have a faulty lexical entry, then the expanded premises should contradict this interpretation and cause confusion. If, however, expanded premises serve to suppress invited inferences, then performance should improve relative to the simple premises, especially for the two invalid arguments.

The expanded premises improved performance on the invalid arguments for both adults and children. This finding suggests that by 10 years of age children do have the appropriate lexical entry for the conditional and that failure to recognize the fallacy of the two invalid arguments reflects the occurrence of invited, but not necessary, inferences. Further, the fact that college students typically outperform children on the traditional form of the arguments (without expansions) suggests that, when confronted with these reasoning problems, college students are better able to ignore invited inferences, to suspend comprehension processes that are adaptive for ordinary discourse (Rumain et al, 1983).

In summary, although it is difficult to make direct comparisons between the several developmental studies of conditional reasoning, a few generalizations do appear to be appropriate. First, an argument that affirms the antecedent is easier than any other at all ages and, under some circumstances, even very young children can solve this problem (Kodroff & Roberge, 1975). Second, arguments that deny the consequence are the more difficult valid argument for all the children, and an improvement in performance occurs at a later age than for the argument that affirms the antecedent. Third, the invalid arguments are very difficult for all children, with some improvement around the eighth grade. Fourth, developmental changes in the interpretations of the conditional statement can account for at least some of the development in conditional reasoning. Finally, the biconditional interpretation of the conditional reflects the inability of children to recognize that the invited, inductive inferences that facilitate ordinary conversation are not appropriate for the reasoning required in a conditional argument. This conforms to the finding cited in Chapter 7 that elementary age children have difficulty discriminating between deductive inferences and plausible (enabling) inferences (Hildyard & Olson, 1978).

CONDITIONAL PROPOSITIONS AND THE LOGIC OF HYPOTHESIS TESTING The form of a conditional argument determines the validity of a conclusion, and it also determines how to test the hypothesis that the conditional proposition itself is true. Logically, some information is relevant for testing the hypothesis, and some is not. To illustrate, one common experimental task presents four cards to the subject, as illustrated in Figure 8-11. Subjects are informed that each card has an "A" or "D" on one side and a "2" or "7" on the other side. They are asked which cards should be turned over to determine if the conditional statement, "If there is an A on one side then there is a 2 on the other.", is true (Wason & Johnson-Laird, 1972). Before reading further, try the problem.

Ideally, what information do we need to solve this problem? Let us consider each card. If we turn the "A" card over and find a "2," the hypothesis is confirmed; a "7" would indicate that the hypothesis is false. Thus, this evidence can tell us something about the hypothesis. What would we expect if the hypothesis is true and we turn over the "D" card? The hypothesis says nothing about the relation between "D" and the two numbers. A "2" on the other side might occur since the hypothesis does not say that "2" cannot occur when "A" is not present. Nor does turning over the "2" card give us any information. Again, the hypothesis does not require that "2" occur only with "A." Finally, turning over the "7" will tell us something about the truth of the hypothesis. If "A" is on the other side, the hypothesis is false, because the hypothesis specifies that a "2" occurs whenever there is an "A." Thus, the correct response to this problem is to turn over the "A" and the "7" cards. But this is not the response of most adults (Wason & Johnson-Laird, 1970; 1972). Of 128 college students tested, 46 percent chose "A" and "2," 33 percent "A" alone, 4 percent "A" and "7," the other 17 percent chose one of the five other possible combinations.

Why do these errors occur? Several explanations have been offered. One, *matching bias* (Evans & Lynch, 1973), might be considered a variation of the availability heuristic and assumes that subjects have a bias to select those cards that are named in the conditional rule (that is, "A" and "2"). This interpretation has received some support but has the weakness of not explaining performance in the conditional argument problems.

An alternative explanation is that subjects interpret the conditional statement as a biconditional (that is, "If 2 then A." as well as "If A then 2."). Thus, it is understandable that the "2" card is selected, because the biconditional interpretation would lead to the expectation that the other side should have an "A." But the failure to select the "7" or "D" card demands further consideration. To do this we need to make a distinction between how subjects interpret the "if . . . then" statement and how they test the hypothesis represented by their interpretation.

One strategy, *verification,* attempts to find evidence that supports the hypothesis; the other, *falsification,* seeks information that would refute the hypothesis. To illustrate, suppose the interpretation is biconditional and the strategy is verification. Which cards would confirm that "All 'As' are '2.' " and that "All '2s' are 'A' "? A "2" on the back of the "A" card verifies, as does an "A" on the back of a "2" card. What of the "D" and "7" cards? Nothing that could be on the back of either of those cards could confirm the

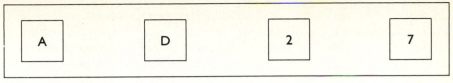

▶ **FIGURE 8-11** *Wason's Hypothesis-Testing Task. Hypothesis: "If a card has an 'A' on one side, then it has a '2' on the other side."* (Modified from Wason & Johnson-Laird, 1972.)

hypothesis (that is, neither a "2" or "7" on the back of "D" or an "A" or "D" on the back of "7" would confirm the biconditional interpretation of the hypothesis). Suppose now that the strategy is falsification. Each card has the potential for information that would falsify the hypothesis (that is, "7" on the back of "A," "D" on the back of "2," "2" on the back of "D," and "A" on the back of "7" would all serve to refute the biconditional interpretation).

What happens when the interpretation is conditional? One card, "A," has the potential to verify this interpretation. The "2" and "D" cards are not relevant to this interpretation, and whatever is on the back of "7" would not verify the hypothesis. If, however, the falsification strategy is used to test the hypothesis, the "A" and "7" cards both have the potential for disconfirming evidence. Thus, from this analysis approximately half the students in the Wason and Johnson-Laird study had a biconditional interpretation, instead of the conditional interpretation. But no matter what their interpretation, the majority used the verification strategy to test their hypothesis. A scant four percent had both a conditional interpretation and the falsification strategy.

Hoch and Tschirgi (1985) have demonstrated, however, that college students are more likely to make the correct selections if it is made explicit that a consonant may have either an odd or even number on the reverse side. This suggests that students make invited inferences in the hypothesis testing task as well as the task that requires evaluation of conditional arguments. When these invited inferences are countermanded, performance improves in both tasks.

Logical performance on the card selection task not only requires the conditional interpretation but also the falsification strategy. As was the case with testing the conclusions of syllogisms, many students do not understand the need to test the conditional hypothesis by attempting to falsify it. That is, they fail to realize that evidence consistent with the hypothesis does not necessarily prove it (for example, a "2" on the other side of the "A" does not establish that the rule holds for the other cards), but only one contradictory piece of evidence necessarily refutes the hypothesis (see Popper, 1959, for the relevance of falsification in science).

CONTENT AND CONDITIONAL REASONING   Although adults do not readily solve the hypothesis testing task and make errors on the conditional arguments, particularly those without a valid conclusion, there is extensive evidence that variations in the content of the conditional statement can affect performance. Thus, as with syllogisms, conditional reasoning is not a simple matching of form to inference rule. The problem, then, is to specify how content influences conditional reasoning and what we can infer about logical knowledge.

The early British research (for example, Wason & Shapiro, 1971) suggested that the abstractness of the conditional statements affected performance on the hypothesis-testing task. Antecedent-consequent relations of concrete statements (for example, "Every time I go to Manchester, I travel by train.") were easier than abstract ones (for example, "If a vowel, then an even number.").

Attempts, however, to replicate these findings were not always successful with American students (see, for example, Griggs & Cox, 1982). Indeed, Cox and Griggs (1982) argued that it is not abstractness that is relevant but the familiarity of the content. American college students were given the hypothesis-testing task with the conditional statement, "If a person is drinking beer, then the person must be over 19." The students readily interpreted this statement as a conditional and tested with the falsification strategy. Familiarity with this situation may serve to do two things. First, it may block the biconditional interpretation since they know that the biconditional is not true; it is not true that beer is drunk if and only if one is over 19. Second, knowing that people under age do but should *not* drink beer may lead to the falsification strategy (that is, check "drinking beer" to be sure *not* "under 19," check "under 19" to be sure *not* "drinking beer").

When the conditional was in the abstract form ("If 'A' is on one side then '2' is on the other."), however, few used the falsification strategy. A third problem was expressed as, "If a person is wearing blue, then the person must be over 19." When this problem was presented first, performance was superior to that for the abstract problems, but performance varied when it was presented second. If the abstract problem occurred first, performance on the color problem was poor and comparable to that of the abstract problem; if the drinking problem occurred first, performance on the color problem improved. These findings suggest that both familiarity and concreteness influenced reasoning.

Cox and Griggs (1982) propose a *memory-cueing/reasoning-by-analogy hypothesis* which specifies that if the task at hand results in the individual remembering past experiences with similar structure, then these analogous experiences will be used to solve the problem. The drinking problem is very familiar for most American college students and brings to mind situations in which a similar type of conditional relationship was tested with the falsification strategy. When the color problem is presented first, it is similar enough to past experiences that the student recognizes the analogy and uses the strategies of the familiar situation. If the color problem follows the drinking problem, this is even more likely to happen. But when the color problem follows the abstract one, the students are less likely to recognize the analogous past experiences. The premise interpretation and solution of the prior problem are readily accessible and likely to be applied to the next problem. Indeed, this is even true for the drinking problem. Performance on this problem was poorer when it followed the abstract problem.

As with syllogistic reasoning, some researchers have taken the position that conditional reasoning does not reflect the use of general logical rules; rather, it depends upon access to relevant and analogous domain-specific knowledge (for example, Cox & Griggs, 1982; Pollard, 1982). Others, however, have argued that form and content interact in the reasoning process (for example, Hoch & Tschirgi, 1983; 1985; Clement & Falmagne, 1986). These researchers assert that adults do rely upon general knowledge to reason with conditional statements, and there is some evidence to support this position. For example, as we have seen, adults do solve the hypothesis-testing task with an abstract conditional if there is implicit or explicit information that clarifies the antecedent-consequent relation and thus suppresses invited inferences that distort the interpretation of the conditional (Hoch & Tschirgi, 1983; 1985).

Recently, Overton and his colleagues (Overton, Ward, Noveck, Black & O'Brien, 1987) have demonstrated in a set of three experiments that, even when the content of the hypothesis-testing task is familiar, there is a developmental improvement in children's ability to solve the problem. Students in fourth, sixth, eighth, tenth, and twelfth grades were presented with familiar-content problems (for example, "If a person is driving a motor vehicle, then the person must be over 16.") and abstract-content problems. At all ages performance was enhanced in the familiar-content problems. Nevertheless, with age there was a steady increase in performance. Such findings suggest that both content and the development of logical competence affect conditional reasoning.

Although we are far from a comprehensive model of conditional reasoning (compare, Johnson-Laird, 1986) it is clear that such a model will have to consider the importance of proposition comprehension, the construction of mental models in working memory, and task demands on working memory (see; for example, Clement & Falmagne, 1986), as well as domain-specific knowledge and the nature of our logical knowledge.

THE DEVELOPMENT OF LOGICAL COMPETENCE

What can we say about the development of logical competence? As is often the case, what we can say depends on what we mean by the term. *Logical competence* has had three types of interpretations (Falmagne, 1975). At one extreme is an operational definition in which performance in logical tasks is logical competence. As we have seen, there are substantial changes in children's performance in these tasks. This use of the term, however, is not particularly useful since it makes competence synonymous with performance and, thus, does nothing to further our understanding about what underlies changes in performance.

Alternatively, logical competence can mean a set of statements that describe the knowledge of logic that can be inferred from performance (see the discussion of knowledge representative and the competence-performance distinction on page 12 in Chapter 1). It is an abstraction of concepts and relations that are represented in performance. Logical competence of this type may or may not have the form of the mental representations that underlie behavior. To offer an analogy, I know the song "The Stars and Stripes Forever." My knowledge of the tune and even specific renditions of it could be represented in the form of a musical staff with appropriately placed notes. Even though this representation could, in principle, delineate all that I know of the tune, it does not necessarily follow that this need be the form of my mental representation.

As will be described later in this chapter when we discuss formal operations, Piaget offered a developmental theory of logical competence in this second sense. In general, however, models of logical competence of this type have focused on adult behavior and have attempted to specify the subset of inference rules that best summarize adult performance. The few attempts, in this tradition, to understand developmental changes have focused on premise comprehension and changes in encoding, rather than on developmental changes in the deductive rule system itself.

The third use of the term logical competence refers to models of those knowledge structures and processes that operate in real time as an individual engages in deductive reasoning. The Johnson-Laird model (for example, Johnson-Laird & Bara, 1984; Johnson-Laird & Steedman, 1978) exemplifies such a use. Although the model emphasizes the process side of reasoning, there are also assumptions, often implicit, about logical knowledge. The model does not assume the knowledge of specific inferential rules. Rather, it assumes more fundamental principles of logic. For example, the process of evaluating a conclusion depends on our knowledge of the implications of "contradiction" (compare, Johnson-Laird, 1982; Macnamara, 1986). That is, we would have no reason to look for a contradiction to our conclusion unless we knew the logical implications of finding such a contradiction.

The Johnson-Laird model is not a developmental model, but it highlights some of the matters we must consider in attempts to model the development of deductive reasoning. That is, at the least we need to consider the representation of logical knowledge, the representation of information in working memory, and the operations on the representations of working memory. The Johnson-Laird model emphasizes the latter two aspects of the reasoning process, but developmentalists cannot avoid the question of logical knowledge, knowledge which may affect the reasoning process from the beginning.

We have seen that often there is more than one way to interpret a premise. On what basis do we select one interpretation instead of another? If I construct a prototype representation of a proposition, what knowledge guides that abstraction process (Falmagne, 1975)? This issue, of course, is analogous to the one we confronted with conceptual knowledge. There the problem was to determine the nature of the knowledge that determines concept membership. Here the problem is to determine the nature of the knowledge that underlies our comprehension of function words (Braine & Rumain, 1983; Macnamara, 1986) and our representation of propositional relations in working memory. We can make the conceptual distinction between premise interpretation and deductive processes (see, for example, Henle, 1962), but it may be unrealistic to do so psychologically (Falmagne, 1980).

Furthermore, we have enough evidence from college students to know that, logicians aside, propositional reasoning is influenced by the content (for example, Cox & Griggs, 1982; Oakhill & Johnson-Laird, 1985) and/or context (for example, Pollard, 1982) of the propositions. Although theorists do not agree on how this information affects reasoning (for example, Cheng & Holyoak, 1985; Oakhill & Johnson-Laird, 1985; Pollard, 1982), such findings indicate that we will not learn enough about the development of propositional reasoning if we restrict our efforts to abstract materials. We have seen that, with supportive context, even preschoolers reason deductively (Hawkins *et al.*, 1984).

Indeed, the research emphasis on the logical forms of conditional and syllogistic arguments probably underestimates the deductive reasoning skills of children. Reasoning about the traditional forms of these arguments is difficult, even for adults. Logicians do not always agree about the valid forms of the syllogism (see Adams, 1984, for a discussion). Besides the often extensive information-processing demands of these tasks, reasoning about these arguments also requires the ability to suspend beliefs. Although preschoolers can do this in a make-believe context, cross-cultural research suggests that formal schooling promotes this ability and thus broadens the contexts in which students recognize that this strategy is appropriate. As children acquire language, they are acquiring the ability to determine the intent of a communication. As we have seen, communication is seldom completely explicit. Rather, inductive processes are usually necessary to draw an appropriate interpretation. Yet propositional reasoning requires the suspension of inductive, empirical assumptions. In school, children are taught to analyze propositional content, suppressing inductive inferences that go beyond what is explicitly stated in a proposition (Donaldson, 1978).

As we have seen, young children can reason deductively and this may be more prevalent in young children's reasoning than we realize. To illustrate, my daughter recently stopped on her drive across country to stay with a former high school friend, who now is the mother of a three-year-old, Nicholas. On the evening of her arrival, Nicholas was fascinated with the contents of my daughter's purse. He sat on the floor and quietly inventoried its contents, pulling out each object and naming it. The next morning my daughter said goodbye and walked out to her car, purse in hand. She soon returned, saying she couldn't find her sunglasses. Nicholas announced that they were in the car, but my daughter had already searched the car for the glasses. Nicholas persisted that the glasses were in the car, but it was not until he announced that they were in the purse that everyone realized what Nicholas was trying to say. Nicholas had seen the glasses in the purse the night before; the next morning he saw the purse go to the car with my daughter and when she returned without the purse he drew the inference that the glasses were in the car. Such events remind us that young children reason about what is prominent in their experiences—namely, people, objects, and events. As psychologists develop tasks that are more appropriate for young children, tasks like that of Hawkins and his colleagues, we might expect to find that deductive reasoning, like inductive reasoning, plays an important role in children's thinking, even at an early age.

The effect of content on reasoning reminds us that the deductive process is just one potential tool we bring to reasoning; we do not limit ourselves to deductive processes. To put it another way, except in a few situations, the goal of our reasoning is not to derive valid inferences but to acquire, modify, and test our beliefs about the world. Psychologists need to explore how the development of deductive reasoning relates to children's early deductive and inductive processes (compare, Colberg, Nester & Trattner, 1985; Wood, 1983). We need to determine how the principles of induction and deduction are differentiated and coordinated in the development of children's reasoning.

Finally, we can make a distinction between reasoning logically and *knowing* that something is necessarily true or necessarily false. Moshman and Timmons (1982) have proposed a three-stage model of the development of logical necessity. In each subsequent stage, knowledge that was implicit in the preceding stage becomes explicit. In stage 1, children may act in accord with logical norms, but they do not distinguish logically necessary conclusions from other types of conclusions. In the second stage, children distinguish logically necessary conclusions from empirical or conventional conclusions. It is not until the third stage that children have an explicit awareness of the concept of logical necessity, and can think explicitly about the form of an argument.

Evidence we have already considered supports the developmental sequence of the first two stages. Preschoolers can reason deductively (for example, Hawkins *et al.*, 1984) but it is not until the later school years that they can explicitly distinguish between necessary propositions and, for example, enabling propositions (for example, Hildyard & Olson, 1978; Russell, 1982). Moshman and Franks (1986) investigated the development of the third stage. Although fourth graders were in stage 2, as evidenced by their ability to distinguish between valid and invalid conclusions, it was not until seventh grade that children could reflect on the form of the argument and recognize that valid conclusions had to follow from some of these arguments. These findings are suggestive of an implicit to explicit development of logical knowledge, but we will need systematic investigations to determine the nature of young children's implicit knowledge and how explicit knowledge develops.

Formal-operational reasoning, the last stage in Piaget's theory of cognitive development, is assumed to begin at 11 or 12 years of age and to be established by about 15. Piaget characterizes formal-operational reasoning as hypothetico-deductive. The first stage of *hypothetico-deductive reasoning,* generation of hypotheses, is an inductive one in which we generate alternative possibilities from our prior knowledge. The second stage is a deductive one in which we derive conclusions from these hypotheses, that is, we deduce predictions from these hypotheses. The third stage involves testing the predictions (Kitchener & Kitchener, 1981).

Hypothetico-deductive reasoning is the method of reasoning used in science, and Piaget uses tasks with scientific content to assess the development of formal operations. There are 15 of these tasks, which vary in content from determining the variables that affect the speed of the oscillation of a pendulum to determining those factors that affect the flexibility of rods. A brief description and illustration of eleven of Piaget's formal operations tasks are presented in Figure 8-12.

To illustrate, consider the flexibility of rods test in Figure 8-12 in which the experimenter presents the following (Inhelder & Piaget, 1958, pp. 46–47):

> . . . the subject [is presented] with a large basin of water and a set of rods differing in composition (steel, brass, etc.), length, thickness, and cross-section form (round, square, rectangular). Three different weights can be screwed to the ends of the rods. In addition, the rods can be attached to the edge of the basin in a horizontal position, in which case the weights exert a force perpendicular to the surface of the water. The subject is asked to determine whether or not the rod is flexible enough to reach the water level. His methods are observed and his comments on the variables he believes influence flexibility are noted and, finally, proof is demanded for the assertions he makes.

In this task there are five distinct variables that might affect flexibility (composition, length, thickness, cross-section form, and weight), and Piaget is interested in the child's ability to vary each factor independently while holding the others constant.

Formal-operational children systematically control and manipulate the variables that *might* affect flexibility. For instance, suppose they hypothesize that length affects flexibility. To test this possibility, they select two rods that differ in length but have the same value for all the other variables that might also affect flexibility. Similarly, as they test each of the other variables for its effect on flexibility, they control all of the other variables. Concrete-operational children, however, do not systematically test variables by controlling all variables except the one being tested. These children may have their own hypotheses, but they fail to recognize other possibilities and their relevance for adequately testing their hypotheses.

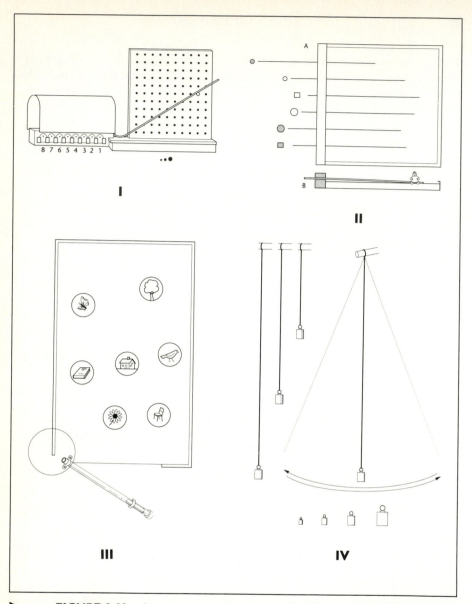

▶ **FIGURE 8-12** *Diagrams of the apparatus and instructions for 11 of Piaget's formal operations tasks.*

I. Falling Bodies on Inclined Plane. The Inclined plane can be raised or lowered by moving the peg on which it rests to different holes in the board. These also serve as an index for measuring height. Marbles of varying sizes are released at different heights on this plane, hit a springboard at the bottom, bound in parabolic curves, and come to rest in one of the compartments (numbered 1 to 8). These are the subject's index to the length of the bound.   **II. Flexibility of Rods.** Diagram A illustrates the variables used in the flexibility experiment. The rods can be shortened or lengthened by varying the point at which they are clamped (see B for apparatus used). Cross-section forms are shown at the left of each rod; shaded forms represent brass rods, unshaded forms represent non-brass rods. Dolls are used for the weight variable (see B). These are placed at the end of the rod. Maximum flexibility is indicated when the end of the rod touches the water.   **III. Angles of Incidence and Reflection.** The principle of the billiard game is used to demonstrate the angles of incidence and reflection. The tubular spring plunger can be pivoted and aimed. Balls are launched from this plunger against the projection wall and rebound to the interior of the apparatus. The circled drawings represent targets which are placed

(Continued)

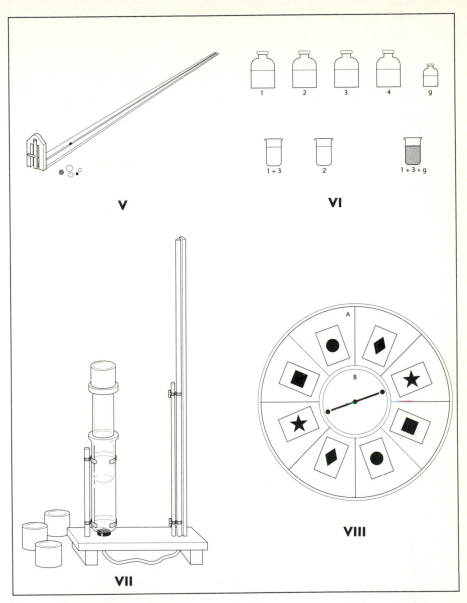

V

VI

VII

VIII

► **FIGURE 8-12** *(Cont.)*

successively at different points.   **IV. Pendulum.** The pendulum problem utilizes a simple apparatus consisting of a string which can be shortened or lengthened, and a set of varying weights. The other variables which at first might be considered relevant are the height of the release point and the force of the push given by the subject.

V. Motion in a Horizontal Plane. Conservation of motion in a horizontal plane is demonstrated with a spring device which launches balls of varying sizes. These roll on a horizontal plane, and the subjects are asked to predict their stopping points. **VI. Chemicals.** This diagram illustrates Experiment I in the problem of colored and colorless chemicals. Four similar flasks contain colorless, odorless liquids: (1) diluted sulphuric acid; (2) water; (3) oxygenated water; (4) thiosulphate. The smaller flask, labeled g, contains potassium iodide. Two glasses are presented to the subject; one contains 1 + 3, the other contains 2. While the subject watches, the experimenter adds several drops of g to each of these glasses. The liquid in the glass containing 1 + 3 turns yellow. The subject is then asked to reproduce the color, using all or any of the five flasks as he wishes.   **VII. Hydraulic Press.** The equipment used for this problem in equilibrium involves two communicating "vessels" of different sizes and shape. Vessel A is

(Continued)

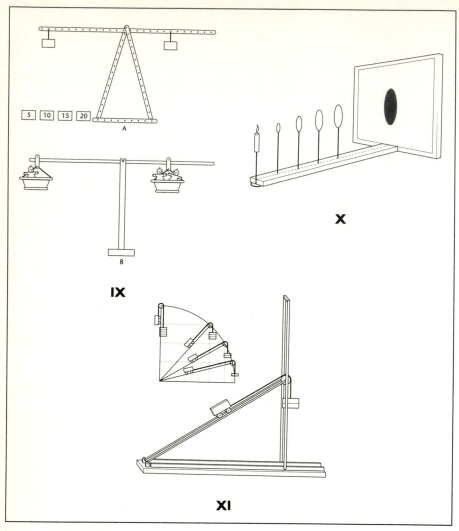

► FIGURE 8-12 (Cont.)

provided with a piston that can be loaded with varying weights. The amount of pressure exerted by the piston (which is dropped into the vessel by the subject) is varied by adding weights.   **VIII. Magnetization.** One pair of boxes (the starred ones) contains concealed magnets, whereas the other pairs contain only wax. The large board (A) is divided into sectors of different colors and equal surfaces, with opposite sectors matching in color. A metal bar is attached to a nonmetallic rotating disk (B); the disk always stops with the bar pointing to one pair of boxes. The boxes (which are matched pairs as to color and design) can be moved to different sectors, but they are always placed with one of a pair opposite the other. The boxes are unequal in weight, providing another variable.

IX. Balance. The balance scale is here shown in two forms: (A) a conventional balance with varying weights which can be hung at different points along the crossbar; (B) a balance equipped with baskets which can be moved along the crossbar to different points and in which dolls are used as weights.   **X. Shadows.** The projection of shadows involves a baseboard, a screen attached to one end of this, a light source, and four rings of varying diameters. The light source and the rings can be moved along the baseboard. The subject is asked to produce two shadows of the same size, using different-sized rings.   **XI. Hauling Weight.** A toy dumping wagon, suspended by a cable, is hauled up the inclined plane by the counterweights at the other end of the cable. The counterweights can be varied and the angle of the plane is adjustable; weights placed in the wagon provide the third variable.

When confronted with a problem, adolescents with formal operations begin by considering the possibilities of the situation; the reality of the situation is subordinated to the possibilities. Children with concrete operations, however, are rooted in the tangible and when confronted with a problem work within the reality of the situation, without systematic consideration of the alternative possibilities. Unlike concrete-operational children, adolescents are not tied to reasoning about what is, but can reason about the alternatives, what might be (Flavell, 1963). As a consequence, adolescents reason with symbols rather than with the concrete specifics of a situation; unlike younger children, adolescents can reason with the form of the propositions, independent of the content of the propositions. Thinking becomes abstract because the truth value of a statement is determined by the truth value of other propositions, rather than by experience (Neimark, 1975).

This type of reasoning also involves the coordination of logical operations. Concrete-operational children can carry out single logical operations on tangible materials; formal-operational adolescents can coordinate two or more logical operations, such as reversibility and negation, and use these operations on propositions.

If individuals perform with evidence of systematic hypothetico-deductive reasoning on these tasks, Piaget infers that they have a complete logical structure of propositional reasoning that encompasses such logical operations as conjunction ("and"), disjunction ("or"), implication or conditional ("if . . . then"), and negation ("not"). As noted earlier, Piaget's theory of cognitive development is a theory of logical competence in the second sense of the term (see page 342). He is concerned with establishing a description of knowledge structures that can be inferred from children's reasoning (Piaget, 1953). Thus, in concrete operations, as we discussed in Chapter 6, Piaget characterized children's logical competence in terms of logico-mathematical operations on objects. In formal operations, the adolescents' logical competence has developed into a system of propositional logic.

Critics of Piaget's theory of formal operations have focused on two issues. First, logicians have criticized Piaget's system of propositional logic (Ennis, 1975; Parsons, 1960). Ennis (1975) argues that Piaget's propositional logic differs from the standard propositional logic of the logician and is flawed by several paradoxes and discrepancies. Considerable background knowledge in symbolic logic is required to understand Piaget's logical system or Ennis's and Parson's criticisms of it. For our purposes it is enough to note that the discrepancies between standard logic and Piaget's logic have led some investigators to conclude that Piaget's logical competence may not be testable (for example, Ennis, 1975).

Second, Piaget inferred the logical competence of formal-operational thinkers on the basis of their performance in the formal operations tasks. Yet, analyses of Piaget's own data fail to confirm that the protocols of adolescents reveal the system of logical skills he attributed to them (for example, Bynum, Thomas & Weitz, 1972; Weitz, Bynum, Thomas & Steger, 1973). Indeed, one study

(Weitz *et al.*, 1973) tested nine-, twelve-, and sixteen-year-olds and found evidence in their protocols for only one-third of the logical operations posited by Piaget. Furthermore, there were no age differences in which operations were used; the older children, however, used them in a more complex and sophisticated manner. Piaget argued that a system of propositional logic best represented the reasoning of those who succeed in the formal operations problems, but it has proven difficult to provide more than fragmentary evidence for this system in formal thinking. Further, we have seen that research on deductive reasoning, which focuses directly on propositional reasoning, has raised many questions about the extent to which formal logic describes adult reasoning. We also have seen that task demands affect performance on these reasoning tasks. Similarly, we will see that task demands affect performance on Piaget's tasks.

THE FORMAL OPERATIONS TASKS AND ADOLESCENT REASONING

Most of the research on formal operations has focused on the generality of Inhelder and Piaget's findings that, by the age of 14 or 15, adolescents reason systematically in the formal operations tasks. Essentially, the evidence indicates that American students are not at the level of Inhelder and Piaget's subjects; most high school students do not perform at the upper level of formal operations (Blasi & Hoeffel, 1974; Keating, 1979; Neimark, 1975). This conclusion is based on the results of a number of studies that investigated performance on a few of Piaget's 15 tasks. No one study has attempted to replicate Piaget's work using all of his tasks. Indeed, six of the tasks (equality of angles of incidence and reflection, centrifugal force, law of floating bodies, communicating vessels, falling bodies on an inclined plane, and equilibrium in the hydraulic press) are seldom used at all (Neimark, 1975). In fact, although it is assumed by most researchers, Piaget does not explicitly state that the same subjects received all the tasks in his original research.

Martorano (1977), however, did use ten of the tasks to assess the development of formal thought in sixth, eighth, tenth, and twelfth grade students. Each of the tasks was scored for the substages of preoperations, early and late concrete operations, and early and late formal operations. Her results indicate that formal thinking begins to emerge between 12 and 15 years of age. But even the oldest students were not consistently at the level of formal operations across all 10 tasks; indeed, the tasks differed considerably in difficulty (see Table 8-3). For example, 90 percent of the twelfth graders performed at a formal operations level on the colored tokens task. In this task, "children are given 5 or 6 cups containing various colored tokens with explicit instructions to make up all possible pairs with tokens taken from the cups" (Inhelder & Piaget, 1958, p. 310). Only 15 percent performed at a formal operations level on the hydraulic press problem. Nor did the tasks intercorrelate very well.

TABLE 8-3 *Proportion of Subjects Passing Each Task at Level Four or Five (Formal Operations)*

		Grade			
		6th	**8th**	**10th**	**12th**
Task	**Approx. Age**	**11.5**	**13.5**	**15.5**	**17.5**
Colored Tokens		.60	.85	.95	.90
Correlations		.30	.45	.70	.95
Chemicals		.30	.40	.75	.85
Permutations		.20	.30	.70	.60
Pendulum		.25	.20	.50	.55
Rods		.25	.20	.65	.60
Shadows		.00	.05	.30	.55
Balance		.10	.00	.40	.50
Communicating Vessels		.05	.25	.20	.45
Hydraulic Press		.00	.00	.05	.15
$\overline{X}$		.205	.27	.52	.61

Source: Martorano, 1977. Copyright 1977 by the American Psychological Association. Reprinted by permission.

Thus, if all or most of Piaget's tasks are not used in a research program, the level of performance will depend upon which tasks are selected. These tasks appear to be measuring different skills. This means that further analyses of task demands will be necessary to determine how propositional logic affects performance on the formal-operational tasks.

Several factors have been suggested as causes for this failure to replicate Piaget's findings. First, the clinical interview method itself has been criticized. Piaget's instructions to the subject are not very specific and may be ambiguous enough to lead to inappropriate expectations on the part of the subject about the demands of the task. To test this possibility, Danner and Day (1977) presented students ages 10, 13, and 17 with three tasks that required the controlling-variables strategy. In each task there were four variables to consider; for example, in a pendulum task, the length of the string, the amount of weight, the height from which the weights were released, and the force with which the weights were released could be varied. In the presentations of the first and second tasks, the children were initially given Piaget's open-ended instructions. If the child did not solve the problem at the formal operations level, additional prompts were given that progressively structured the demands of the task. For example, on the first prompt the experimenter named any variable that the subject had not tested and asked the child to test it. If necessary, the final prompt had the experimenter conduct all four tests while the child watched. These prompts were used only on the first two tasks presented to the children. The performance of the children on the third task, without any prompts, was compared to their initial performance on the first task to determine whether experience with the structured prompts faciliated performance on another task that required the same strategy.

Danner and Day found that approximately 50 percent of the 13- and 17-year-olds performed at the formal operations level on the unprompted first task; none of the 10-year-olds did. After experience with the more structured tasks, 85 percent of the 13-year-olds and 95 percent of the 17-year-olds were at the formal operations level on the unprompted third task. Although the 10-year-olds showed some improvement, it was not as great. Danner and Day argue that the prompts clarified the demands of the tasks and that this served to elicit formal operations in the older children. A comparison of the 17-year-olds' performance with a control group that simply experienced the three tasks without prompts indicated that the control group did not improve. The specification of task demands that occurs with the prompts appears to be the crucial factor in the improvement over tasks. The fact that the older children benefited more from the prompts than the younger children raises questions, of course, about differences in what knowledge the children bring to the situation, what they learn during the training, and how they transfer what is learned to a new situation.

A second concern about the clinical method is that it is a very flexible one in which the questions directed to the subject are likely to vary from one subject to another and one experimenter to another. Nor are there clear or standard rules for deciding when an individual possesses formal operations (Blasi & Hoeffel, 1974). To alleviate the problem of inter-rater reliability, several researchers have modified Piaget's tests or developed new ones (for example, Levine & Linn, 1977; Linn & Rice, 1979), including standardized paper-and-pencil tests of formal operations. Unfortunately, the validity of these new versions is in question, and they often differ in content and complexity from the problem used by Piaget (see Nagy & Griffiths, 1982, for a review of this problem).

The formal operations tasks also require a variety of skills that may not be related to reasoning processes (for example, Kuhn & Brannock, 1977; Tschirgi, 1980). As we have seen with deductive reasoning, the content of the tasks can have a profound effect on performance. In Piaget's tasks, students must work both with logical relations and factual information. Thus, the prior knowledge of a student may influence reasoning in formal operations tasks (Falmagne, 1975). Indeed, Pulos and Linn (1981) demonstrated the effect of prior knowledge on seventh graders' performance in tasks testing the controlling-variables strategy. One group of students was from an upper-middle-class school system that provided extensive laboratory science training; the other group was from a rural area where fishing was a common pastime of the children. A version of Piaget's bending rods task was used as a task with a science content; a fishing task investigated the variables that affected catching a fish; and a presumably neutral content task was about space people on a fictitious planet. The three tasks were presented to each students in a comparable manner. The data indicate that the children from the river delta area performed best on the fishing problem, that the science students performed best on the rods task, and that there was no difference between the groups on the neutral task.

A comparison of these children on seven tasks that required the controlling-variables strategy indicated that 92 percent systematically used the strategy on at least one of the tasks, but only three percent did so on all seven tasks. The authors reason that "differing preconceptions about the operant variables in the task may result in a controlled experiment from the subject's point of view but an uncontrolled experiment according to the experimenter's view of the world" (Pulos & Linn, 1981, p. 34). Failure in a controlling-variable task may reflect biases in the inductive process of generating hypotheses about relevant variables (see, for example, Linn & Swiney, 1981), rather than a failure to comprehend the logic of manipulating one variable at a time.

Finally, there is evidence that performance in a formal operations task is affected by the capacity limitations of working memory. Scardamalia (1977) demonstrated this effect with a variation of the combination (chemicals) task. In this task subjects are asked to determine which combination of several possible chemicals produces a given result (see Figure 8-12). Using independent measures of working-memory capacity, she found that children could systematically combine variables if the number of dimensions in the task was such that the demands on working memory were within the capacity of the child. If, however, the demands were beyond the working-memory capacity, the same child's performance was unsystematic.

Piaget's goal was to specify at the highest, most abstract level, those knowledge structures that are the foundations of behavior. As we have seen, however, the performance of children in Piaget's tasks does not always correspond to the structures that Piaget assumed. Also, the research on formal operations indicates that, contrary to Piaget's original contention, formal-operational thinking does not occur universally in all content domains. More recently, influenced by contemporary research, Piaget (1972) asserted that, unlike the three earlier stages, the occurrence of formal thinking in a given situation will depend upon the past experiences and training of individuals and their familiarity with the content of the task (for example, lawyers solving physics problems, and vice versa).

Taken together, these studies indicate that a number of factors related to the demands of the task, other than logical competence, can affect performance on formal operations problems. These factors include understanding the instructions of a task, familiarity with the content of the task, expectations about which variables are relevant in the task, and the functional capacity of working memory. As was the case with the deductive reasoning tasks and the concrete operations tasks, a variety of variables can affect performance and we still have the challenge of specifying the nature of the structures and processes that determine performance.

Although Piaget's model of adolescent/adult reasoning emphasized deductive, propositional logic, he portrayed mature reasoning as a combination of deductive and inductive processes. As researchers have investigated the development of these processes, both in isolation and in the formal operations problems, it has become apparent that adequate models of children's reasoning will have to incorporate the knowledge structures and processes of both deduction and induction.

▶ ## SUMMARY

This chapter focused on the development of reasoning. Philosophers make a distinction between two types of reasoning: deductive and inductive. In deductive reasoning the form of an argument, the relations between propositions, determine whether a conclusion is valid or not. World knowledge, not the form of the argument, determines the probability that an inductive conclusion is appropriate.

Two types of inductive reasoning were considered: analogical reasoning and the use of availability and representativeness heuristics. Analogical reasoning requires the discovery of higher-order relations that relate the lower-order relations of two domains. Young children have difficulty discovering the higher-order relations of analogies. However, preschoolers can solve analogical problems if the materials are familiar, concrete, and similar in the two domains. Information-processing models indicate that analogical reasoning involves several processes and that there are developmental changes in how these processes are executed.

College students often use two general heuristics—availability and representativeness—to solve inductive problems. Further, they tend to rely on these heuristics even when the use of available statistical information would lead to a more appropriate conclusion. Although there is no research exploring the development of the availability and representativeness heuristics, they seem to be relevant to inductive processes such as concept acquisition that occur early in development. We know little about the acquisition of statistical principles such as the law of large numbers. We do know, however, that college students' application of these principles is influenced by problem content.

Two forms of deductive reasoning were considered: categorical syllogism and conditional reasoning. In the abstract form categorical syllogisms are difficult for college students. This difficulty is, in part, explained by their failure to interpret appropriately the function words that relate the categories of the syllogistic argument. Children have even more difficulty interpreting these words. Johnson-Laird has proposed a processing model of syllogistic reasoning that involves both induction and deduction. Experimental tests lend support to the model and suggest that the performance of nine-year-olds as well as college students is influenced by the same variables.

Although the validity of a syllogistic conclusion is determined by the form of the argument, not the content, the syllogistic reasoning of college students is influenced by the content of the premises. When, for example, conclusions are believable college students are more likely to accept them as valid whether they are or not. Preschoolers are able to solve syllogistic problems if the premises are stated in everyday terms and the content or context of the premises is fanciful. When they are encouraged to suspend their knowledge about the world, they appear able to reason about the relations between categories.

There are four basic forms of the conditional argument. Two of these (affirming the antecedent and denying the consequence) are valid. The other two (asserting the consequence and denying the antecedent) are not. Although college students generally recognize the validity of the two arguments that have valid conclusions, they also tend to accept the two invalid conclusions as valid. Children have comparable difficulties. Although young children solve the affirming the antecedent form, it is not until eighth grade that children solve both valid arguments. As in the case of syllogistic reasoning, interpretation of the function words (that is, "if . . . then") and content of the premises influences reasoning with the conditional statement. Both content and the development of logical competence appear to affect children's performance when testing conditional statements.

Piaget assumed that formal operations begin to develop around 12 years of age. Subsequent work indicates that performance on the several formal operations tasks is not comparable. Performance is not simply a function of propositional reasoning. Rather, several factors, including domain-specific knowledge and working-memory capacity, influence performance.

9

The Development of
Problem-Solving
Skills

Every day children and adults alike are confronted with problems, problems that they actively seek to solve. In fact, some theorists consider problem solving to be the fundamental cognitive activity (for example, Anderson, 1982; Newell, 1980). The issue for cognitive psychology is to specify how, in our efforts to solve problems, we organize the subsystems of cognition that have been the focus of previous chapters. Each of us comes to a problem with a variety of cognitive resources. How is it that we select, regulate, and coordinate resources such as domain-specific knowledge, reasoning skills, and attention in our attempts to reach desired goals?

Problems come in many forms and vary in complexity, but psychologists generally agree that all problems have a few characteristics in common. For any problem there is a discrepancy between the present situation (*initial state*) and a desired state of affairs (*goal state*). Further, there is no immediately obvious way to get from the initial state to the goal state. Thus, whether there are problems or not depends upon the perspectives of the individuals, that is, whether they recognize the problem (desire to achieve the goal state) and whether the means for goal achievements are available. A final characteristic of problems is that they involve the execution of *operations* on the initial state. Whether explicit or implicit, there may be *constraints* on these operations. For example, when doctors make a diagnosis in preparation for treatment, they have a number of techniques available to them, but one of these is not an autopsy.

Even a limited consideration of the problems we face in our daily affairs (for example, planning and preparing dinner, writing a term paper, or selecting a satisfying career) readily illustrates that there are many types of problems.

Problems have different structures, make different information-processing demands, and require different strategies for solution (Reitman, 1965). For the most part researchers have focused on a few specific problems to explore the nature of problem-solving skills (compare, Greeno, 1978). It should be noted, however, that these problems typically are well-defined problems and many of our daily problems are not. *Well-defined problems* are those for which the initial state and the goal state are clearly defined. For example, getting from your house to your 9:00 a.m. English class is a well-defined problem. You know where you are now and what time it is (initial state) and you know where you want to be and at what time (goal state). But problems can be *ill-defined* with either the initial state, the goal state, or both not clearly specified. Writing a term paper certainly qualifies as an ill-defined problem. What is the initial state? What is the goal state? Indeed, in this case one of the difficulties is recognizing when the goal state has been reached. The distinction between well-defined and ill-defined problems does not imply a dichotomy. Rather, problems vary along a continuum of specificity. As is evident later in this chapter, the domain-specific knowledge an individual brings to a problem can determine where a given problem lies on this continuum.

▶ ## REPRESENTATION

One of the first and most important steps in problem solving is *representation* of the problem. That is, solvers must interpret the problems; they must understand the nature of the initial state, the goal state, and the potential operations. The representation of the problem delineates the *problem space* in which a solution is sought (Newell & Simon, 1972). We do not seek willy-nilly for solutions to problems. Rather, on the basis of the representation of the problem, we constrain where we seek a solution. If my problem is to design a new perennial garden, I may consult friends and professionals, read gardening books, and even seek ideas in paintings, but I am unlikely to read developmental psychology books or consult the cashier in the supermarket. Clearly, whether a goal is reached depends upon the problem space in which a solution is sought.

Representation does not just happen. When we construct problem representations, we attend selectively to the information presented to us and we make use of prior knowledge. As we read a problem statement, we must determine which information is relevant to the solution and which is not. Sometimes this is easy (Hayes, Waterman & Robinson, 1977); at other times it is not. Indeed, some problems are difficult because the relevant information is not readily obvious. Consider the following problem.

> Water lilies double in area every 24 hours. At the beginning of the summer there is one water lily on a lake. It takes 60 days for the lake to become covered with water lilies. On what day is the lake half covered?

Can you distinguish the relevant information from the irrelevant information?

Essentially, we bring three types of knowledge to problem representations: knowledge of the language, knowledge of the world, and knowledge about specific problem types (Hayes, 1978). Of course, the importance of linguistic knowledge is obvious, but we cannot take for granted that children always will bring appropriate linguistic knowledge to a problem. Consider the young child whose mother says, "Bring your blue sweaters." The desired goal cannot be attained unless the child understands both the possessive and the plural forms. But this knowledge is not enough. The goal is not completely represented unless the child also uses the knowledge that he or she possesses three blue sweaters. The importance of world knowledge for problem representation is particularly obvious when the content of algebra word problems is modified. For example, consider how your world knowledge affects your interpretation of the following problems (Hayes, 1978, p. 200):

Modified: In a medical exam, a man weighs 150 pounds on a scale which goes from 0 to 300 pounds. What would he weigh on a scale which goes from 0 to 240 pounds?

Original: In a psychology test, a man scored 150 points on a scale which goes from 0 to 300. What would he score on a scale which goes from 0 to 240?

Of course, problem representations are also affected by knowledge we have about specific types of problems. Undoubtedly, my representation of a physics problem will differ from that of a physicist. We return to this issue in a later section of this chapter.

Representation is not a straightforward process. As we attempt to construct a mental model of a problem, we seek internal and external information that will clarify the problem. We bring our knowledge and expectations to any situation and these will interact with problem information in our representation of a given problem. In previous chapters we considered many factors that can affect our mental representations. Any of these might lead to problem representations that delay or prevent us from reaching a goal. For example, the misinterpretation of premises can lead to fallacious conclusions in deductive-reasoning problems and failure to consider relevant probability information can affect the adequacy of our inductive conclusions. At times, our problem representations may have constraints that are not specified by the problem. Consider, for example, the following puzzle.

In a small town, the local baker is the son of the miller from whom he buys flour. The miller's father is the farmer who supplies all the grain to the mill. The miller is not the father of the baker. How can this be?

Many people have difficulty with this puzzle because they represent the miller as a male. We still have stereotypes about occupations. When, however, the representation is not constrained in this way, the solution is obvious.

Similarly, we may come to a problem with a *response set* (see, for example, Luchins, 1942) that limits our responses to those that have worked in the past or with a *perceptual set* (functional fixedness) (Duncker, 1945) that limits our perceptions of a problem to only one perspective. Thus, if the representation imposes inappropriate constraints, the problem space may be restricted in a way that excludes the solution to the problem. These unnecessary constraints can occur in our representation of the initial state, the goal state, or the potential operations.

At other times, our representations of a problem may not include the constraints that would maximize the search for a solution. This may be the case for some of the problems psychologists present to children. In the last chapter, we saw that the level of performance in formal operations problems depends upon the constraints that are imposed with the instructions. For example, with open-ended instructions, students are less likely to exhibit systematic use of the controlling-variables strategy. The fact that they do use the strategy when the goal is made explicit suggests that, initially, their representation of the goal is different than that of the experimenter (Danner & Day, 1977). For instance, children's goals may be to find possible solutions, rather than to demonstrate how to test variables systematically. Thus, children may delineate problem spaces that are not the ones assumed by the experimenter. As a result the children's solutions may be appropriate for their problem spaces, but not for the problem space as the experimenter defines it.

Problem representation can be complex enough that it is difficult to maintain a representation in working memory. Thus, it is often beneficial to use external, explicit representations of the problem space (see, for example, Greeno, 1983). To illustrate, there are many factors to consider as I design my perennial garden; these include color, size, texture, height, time of bloom, and spatial arrangement. All these variables must be considered as specific plants are selected for a given location and this information makes excessive demands on my information-processing skills. In this case, using drawings to develop the garden design would be beneficial. Similarly, recent research indicates that students profit from the use of explicit problem representations. For example, diagrams help children with arithmetic word problems (Lindvall, Tamburino & Robinson, 1982). Thus, the adequacy of our problem representations will be influenced by the strategies we use in the representation process.

Problem representation involves the interaction of top-down and bottom-up processes. The bottom-up processes involve the interpretation of the literal terms or objects of the problem, as they are presented. We also have ideas, hypotheses, or theories that we bring to a problem, and these influence how we represent it. Consider the rather simple problem of running errands in town. Your needs (for example, pick up cleaning, shop for dinner, buy a birthday card) will determine where you go, but you bring to the situation a need to be efficient. Thus, the particular needs of the moment and your general need to be efficient will jointly determine how you represent the problem of running errands.

Karmiloff-Smith (1984) has proposed a three-phase developmental model of how top-down and bottom-up processes affect problem representation. She argues that, no matter what the age or the domain, children pass through three phases as they make progress in a given domain.

In Phase 1 children use procedures that are determined by bottom-up or data-driven processes. Their representations of the problem are dominated by stimulus information. Problem-solving procedures are *success-oriented* with the purpose of narrowing the difference between the goal state and the initial state of the external stimuli. The child uses positive and negative feedback to adapt to the environmental situation. Each adaptation is an individual behavioral unit, determined by the external situation; there is no overall organization.

Phase 2 is characterized by a predominance of top-down processes. In an attempt to unify and control the behavioral components of Phase 1, children develop a *theory-in-action,* an internal representation of the problem that controls their problem-solving behavior. In this phase children impose a top-down representation of the problem, focusing on their internal representation of the problem rather than the external situation and environmental feedback. As a consequence, children may have less success in this phase than in Phase 1.

Thus, in the first phase of problem solving, bottom-up, data-driven processes predominate. In the second phase, however, the situation is reversed; top-down processes predominate. In the final phase of problem solving, Phase 3, a control mechanism "modulates the interaction between data-driven and top-down processes. Neither the environmental feedback nor the top-down process predominates. Phase 3 children are now in control both of external stimuli and of internal representations that guide their behavior" (Karmiloff-Smith, 1984, p. 44).

Karmiloff-Smith presents data from several problem domains, including language acquisition, to support her model. Here we concentrate on one of these—block-balancing. Children between four and nine years of age were presented with the three types of blocks depicted in Figure 9-1 and were asked to balance each block on a narrow metal bar. Children in Phase 1 randomly selected blocks and were successful in balancing each block by moving each block back and forth on the bar until proprioceptive feedback indicated that the block was balanced. Older children in Phase 2 were not as successful, however. They balanced the Type A blocks by putting them on the bar at their geometric center. But when the other blocks did not balance at their geometric center, they put them aside. These children did not use proprioceptive feedback to balance the blocks that did not conform to the geometric center principle. In Phase 3 the children started by putting blocks on the bar at their geometric center. Proprioceptive feedback was used to adjust the position of those blocks that did not balance at the geometric center. Unlike Phase 1 children, these children initially used a top-down process; when this was not successful, they used data-driven proprioceptive feedback to adjust the balance of the other blocks. Furthermore, unlike Phase 1 children, Phase 3 children did not randomly select blocks, but sought similar blocks after balancing one type of block. Thus, both top-down and bottom-up processes interacted as these children sought to represent and solve the problem.

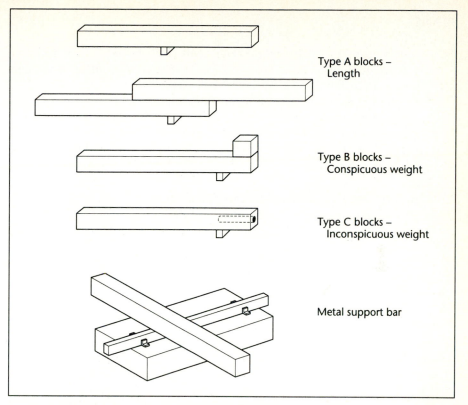

Type A blocks –
Length

Type B blocks –
Conspicuous weight

Type C blocks –
Inconspicuous weight

Metal support bar

▶ **FIGURE 9-1** *Type A blocks balanced at their center. Type B blocks contained conspicuous weights and balanced off center. Type C contained inconspicuous lead weights and also balanced off center. (From Karmiloff-Smith, 1984.)*

▶ ## HEURISTICS

As adults attempt to solve problems, they often use heuristic strategies that are general and independent of the particular content of a problem. Although heuristic strategies are helpful, they do not guarantee a solution. In contrast, for some problems there are algorithms that always lead to a solution. Once the algorithm is learned and correctly applied to a given class of problems, a solution is assured. For example, most of us have acquired an algorithm for the addition of numbers. If we follow the algorithm and make no mistakes in its application, we can correctly solve any problem of addition. But many problems do not have algorithmic solutions. Nevertheless, adults do not behave randomly in these situations. Rather, they use a variety of heuristics to direct their search for solutions. Here we concentrate on three heuristics for which we have relevant developmental research: plans, generating-and-testing hypotheses, and analogies.

PLANS

Every day we construct plans to meet our goals (Miller, Galanter & Pribram, 1960). As we attempt to move from the initial state of a problem to the goal state, we not only construct a representation of the problem space, but also a representation of the activities we intend to execute to achieve the goal. Once we have represented a problem, we do not engage in random actions while hoping to chance on the sought-after goal. Rather, we devise a plan for attaining the goal by symbolically representing possible goal-directed actions. These plans are then used to direct our actions in a systematic attempt to achieve our goals.

Considerable experimental and theoretical effort has sought to determine the nature of planning (for example, Hayes-Roth & Hayes-Roth, 1979; Stefik, 1981; Wilensky, 1981). Although plans have diverse forms, they generally entail the formulation of some goal or intention in advance and the formulation of strategies designed to bring about the goal (Forbes & Greenberg, 1982). Planning involves top-down processes that symbolize hierarchical organization of a goal and its subgoals. That is, many problems are complex enough that breaking them into subproblems, each of which has a subgoal, may aid solution. If we think of problem solving as a search through a problem space for the goal, then subgoals can reduce the size of the problem space that must be searched. Of course, subgoals are only useful if those selected are on the path to the goal. As a consequence, much of the adult research on general problem-solving skills has concentrated on the hierarchical nature of our plans and how we set subgoals in a problem (for example, Newell & Simon, 1972).

ESTABLISHING SUBGOALS   Developmental researchers have demonstrated that young children establish subgoals for problem solving (for example, Klahr & Robinson, 1981; Wellman, Fabricius & Sophian, 1985). For example, Sophian and Wellman (1987) devised a search problem in which search strategies would be overt. Children were presented with three houses each of which had five doors, one large and four small. The task was to find either a grown-up animal or a baby animal; grown-ups were behind large doors and babies behind small doors.

There were three search conditions; one grown-up and one baby were mentioned and hidden in each of these conditions. In the *indirect search condition,* the children were asked to find the baby animal and were told that the baby would never be in a house that did not have a grown-up. Thus, the optimal search strategy would be to search the large doors first until the grown-up was found and then restrict search to the small doors of that house. In the *baby search condition,* the children were asked to find the baby; it could be in any house, regardless of the location of the grown-up. Since the large doors do not supply any information in this condition, a direct search of the 12 small doors is optimal. In the *grown-up search condition,* the children were asked

TABLE 9-1 *Proportion of Houses where the Grown-Up Door was Searched First.*

	Age Group	
Condition	3-Year-Olds	5-Year-Olds
Indirect search	0·38	0·42
Baby search	0·12	0·04
Grown-up search	0·92	0·99

Source: Sophian and Wellman, 1987.

to find the grown-up animal. This is another direct search; in this case, of the three large doors.

As illustrated in Table 9-1, both three- and five-year-olds were likely to establish a subgoal in the indirect search condition. Approximately 40 percent of the time the first door searched was a grown-up door in this condition, which is significantly greater than in the baby search condition. It also, however, was observed significantly less often than in the grown-up search condition. Thus, the children could use problem information to establish a subgoal, but this was not yet a firmly instituted skill.

Given that children this age search for a subgoal, the next question is whether they use the information gained from the subgoal search to constrain their subsequent searches. That is, if a grown-up is present in the indirect search condition, then the next search should be restricted to one of the small doors of that house. If, however, the grown-up is absent, search should switch to another house. Children of both ages used the confirming evidence and were more likely to continue their searches in the same house. There were developmental differences, however, in the use of disconfirming evidence. Although the five-year-olds tended to change houses when no grown-up was present in a house, the three-year-olds continued to search the same house. Taken together, these findings suggest that for the three-year-olds the ability to establish a subgoal exists alongside a direct search strategy and that gradually children acquire the ability to use information derived from attempts to establish a subgoal to constrain their strategies for solving a problem (Sophian & Wellman, 1987). It is important to note that a direct search strategy will lead to the goal in this task, yet during the preschool years children take on a more complex, indirect strategy, one that is more efficient. Thus, by school age, children know something about the logic of disconfirming and confirming evidence and can use this to solve problems. As might be expected, however, during the school years children's strategies for gathering information become more systematic and more sensitive to the logical implications of available information (for example, Neimark & Lewis, 1967).

Problem solving often requires not only the selection of a subgoal, but

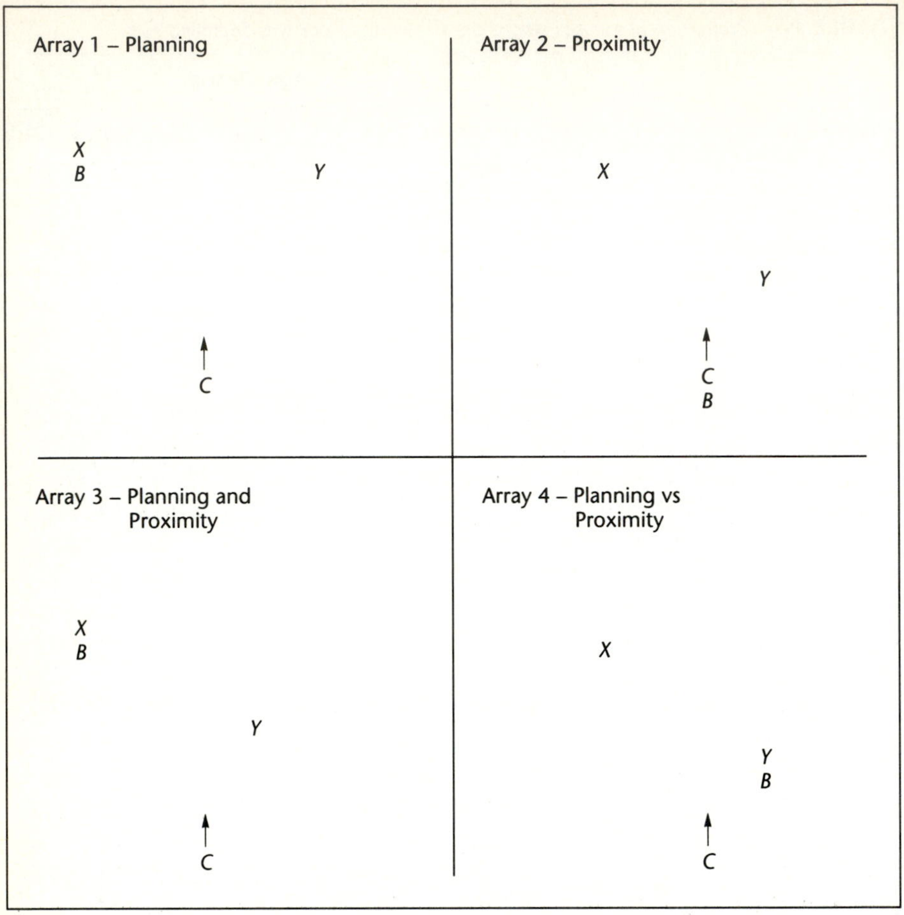

Array 1 – Planning

X
B   Y

                          ↑
                          C

Array 2 – Proximity

              X

                          Y

                          ↑
                          C
                          B

Array 3 – Planning and
          Proximity

X
B

        Y

        ↑
        C

Array 4 – Planning vs
          Proximity

              X

                          Y
                          B

                          ↑
                          C

▶ **FIGURE 9-2**   *Four two-location search arrays used to estimate the independent and joint effects of sighting and planning. (From Wellman, Fabricius & Sophian, 1985.)*

also a plan for sequencing subgoals. Wellman, Fabricius, and Sophian (1985) have sought to trace the early development of planning in problem solving. This research program indicates that planning is evident early in the preschool years and becomes more pervasive during this period. In one study, preschoolers were asked to collect eggs at two locations in a large space (18 feet between locations) and to put them in a basket. This task had four conditions, as illustrated in Figure 9-2, that were designed to assess planning independent of a tendency to go to the nearest location (sighting) and to assess how planning and sighting interact to affect search behavior. For example, in Array 1, the two eggs (X and Y) are equally distant from the child (C). Since the eggs are to be deposited at the basket (B), the most efficient strategy, the one that does not include backtracking, would be to go first to Y and then to X since B is next to X location. The second array assesses sighting, searching at the nearest

	Arrays			
Age	**Planning**	**Proximity**	**Planning and Proximity**	**Planning vs Proximity**
3.0	.50 .50	.42 .58	.47 .53	.47 .53
3.6	.42 .58	.42 .58	.30 .70	.52 .48
4.6	.27 .73	.27 .73	.17 .83	.47 .53
5.6	.08 .92	.62 .38	.08 .92	.88 .12

▶ **FIGURE 9-3** *As is evident above, the first sign of planning occurs at three- and one-half years of age. Planning also increases with age. (From Wellman, Fabricius & Sophian, 1985.)*

location first. The other two combine planning and sighting (Array 3) or put the two in conflict (Array 4).

As is evident in Figure 9-3 , the first sign of planning occurs at three and one-half years of age. The three-year-olds were equally likely to choose either location in the planning array (Array 1), whereas the three-and-one-half-year-olds were more likely to go to the location that precluded backtracking. Planning also increases with age. The five-and-one-half-year-olds used planning even when it was in conflict with sighting (Array 4). In contrast, the three-and-one-half and four-and-one-half-year-olds were influenced by sighting when it conflicted with planning.

The failure of the three-year-olds to plan in this search problem does not, of course, demonstrate that three-year-olds are incapable of planning. The development of problem-solving skills is sensitive to task demands (Miller, Haynes, DeMarie-Dreblow & Woody-Ramsey, 1986), and such skills develop alongside other competing response tendencies (see, for example, Sophian & Wellman, 1987; Wellman *et al.*, 1985). Furthermore, plans for action are based upon the internal representations of the environment (for example, Anooshian, Pascal & McCreath, 1984). Thus, planning may be evident in some problems and not others. Indeed, we might expect to find developmental changes in the types of plans that are generated and used (Wellman *et al.*, 1985). For example, the indirect search problem (Sophian & Wellman, 1987) and Wellman's egg-gathering problem do not require planning in order for the child to achieve the goal. Rather, the planning strategies they assessed make the problem-solving process more efficient, and by three to four years of age, children use such strategies. Younger children may not have a need to improve efficiency, but may engage in planning if planning is necessary to reach a goal.

STRATEGY FLEXIBILITY   Planning requires the selection of strategies for attaining goals, but different types of problems require different strategies for solution. For this reason, an important development in problem solving is the ability to assess the characteristics of a problem and to select strategies in accordance with these characteristics (In Chapter 7, we considered the development of strategies for memory problems). Not surprisingly, strategy flexibility increases with age (Miller, Haynes, DeMaire-Dreblow & Woody-Ramsey, 1986). To illustrate, Miller and her colleagues investigated the information-gathering strategies of children for three types of problems. The children (6-, 8-, and 10-year-olds) were presented a piece of apparatus with two rows of six doors each. The doors could be opened to reveal a drawing of an object. However, only one door could be open at a time.

The same-different judgment problem required the children to decide whether the two rows of objects behind the doors were exactly the same or different, whether the sequence of objects in the top row matched that of the bottom row. The most effective strategy for acquiring the information necessary for making this judgment would be to open corresponding vertical pairs of doors, in order. This strategy requires a series of simple perceptual comparisons and has less memory load than other possible strategies. In the selective-recall task, the children were required to remember the location of six objects (for example, animals) that were located under six of the twelve doors. The appropriate doors for the animals were designated with the same symbol (for example, a cage). Here the question is whether the children will restrict their search to the doors that contain the relevant information. The third problem, remember-all, required memory for the locations of all twelve objects and served as a comparison condition for the two other tasks.

The children used different strategies for gathering information in the three problems. At all ages, they were most likely to use the optimal strategy of searching vertical pairs of doors in the same-different problem. In the remember-all problem, however, they searched the rows of doors horizontally. Both of these tasks required that each door be opened, but the children adjusted their strategies for gathering this information as a function of the problem goal, and there were no age differences in the selection of the strategies. This was not the case, however, for the selective-recall problem. Although the older children used a selective strategy, searching only the doors marked with the relevant symbol, the six-year-olds were not systematic, also opening irrelevant doors. Thus, the older children had a greater tendency to accommodate their information-gathering strategy to the problem. Nevertheless, the youngest children could be strategic on some problems. The problem now is to determine what factors influence the extended development of problem-solving strategies.

As we execute our plans, we must also assess whether we are reaching our subgoals and are still on a path to the goal. Even with well-developed plans, the specific context in which the plan is put in action may require adjustments of the plans as the actions are executed. Effective planning requires continuous evaluation and regulation of plans, as circumstances arise. Thus, effective planning implies the interaction of top-down and bottom-up processes. Although plans are initially devised prior to action, plans are also modified and organized on the basis of the consequences of our actions. Effective planning is a revisionary process of devising a plan, executing the plan, evaluating the adequacy of the plan, and revising the plan.

We have evidence that children do revise their plans, but, as might be expected, younger children are less effective in their revisions. Pea and Hawkins (1987) presented children with a planning task for an activity that was familiar to them, doing classroom chores. They found that the older children (11- and 12-year-olds), who as a group produced more efficient plans, also used a greater variety of strategies in the revision process than the younger children (8- and 9-year-olds).

We might expect that as children become more adept at planning, they become more sensitive to the constraints of a problem situation. One study demonstrates such a developmental change. Gardner and Rogoff (1985, as cited in Rogoff, Gauvain & Gardner, 1987) asked children ranging in age from 4 to $10\frac{1}{2}$ to draw routes through mazes and were presented with accuracy or speed-and-accuracy instructions. These researchers identified three types of planning. "In advance planning, children determined the entire route through the maze prior to drawing. In planning during action, only a partial route was determined prior to drawing. In trial-and-error planning, children did not look ahead at all, evidencing no planning" (p. 310).

As expected, the older children ($7\frac{1}{2}$ to $10\frac{1}{2}$) exhibited greater adjustment of their planning strategies than the younger children ($4\frac{1}{2}$ to $7\frac{1}{2}$). When accuracy was stressed, the older children were more likely to plan in advance. These instructions were less likely to affect the planning strategies of the younger children. With speed and accuracy stressed, however, both age groups were likely to plan during action. Similarly, the characteristics of the mazes affected the planning of the older, but not the younger, children. When the mazes had long dead ends that were not immediately evident, the older children used more advanced planning than when the dead ends were short and could easily be seen. In this case, planning in action was more likely. The younger children, however, did not adjust their plans to the structure of the mazes. The older children not only can construct advance plans, but also can adjust their planning to the circumstances.

Thus, we have some evidence that preschoolers are capable of establishing subgoals and plans for sequencing subgoals. We also know, however, that planning becomes more effective with age. Older children, for example, are better able to assess the characteristics of a given problem and to select strategies appropriate for that problem.

THE DEVELOPMENT OF SELF-REGULATION   The development of problem solving has much in common with the development of memory; in both cases one major development is the voluntary control that children have of their own cognitive processes (Brown & DeLoache, 1978). We saw in Chapter 7 that, under some circumstances, with a context that provides external support, preschoolers engage in actions that facilitate memory (for example, Istomina, 1975). Similarly, in overt search tasks, when the objects and goal are in sight, preschoolers manifest planning skills. As children mature, however, they are less dependent on external structures for achieving their goals. They can generate internal structures (subgoals, strategies, plans) for guiding their actions. Children become increasingly conscious of strategic choices and the possible outcomes of these choices. They are governed less by the context and more by their awareness of the possibilities of the situation (compare, Piaget). As children develop the abilities to control and coordinate their actions, to monitor and regulate their own goal-directed behaviors, and to ignore the distractions of the context, their problem-solving skills become less context specific and more general.

One form of self-regulation that has been studied developmentally is *delay of gratification*. Problem solving requires the ability to delay gratification. That is, problems are problems because an immediate solution is not possible. Thus, problem solving requires the ability to tolerate delays, often extensive delays, between identification of the problem and attaining the goal. Clearly, many problems go unresolved because the problem solver gives up before reaching the goal or settles for a lesser goal. Achievement of educational or vocational goals may be a good everyday example. Many more college freshmen report a career goal of becoming a medical doctor than actually achieve the goal. In part, at least, this failure to achieve a career goal can reflect an inability to endure the delay between starting on this career path and reaching the goal.

Mischel and his colleagues (see, for example, Mischel, 1983) have demonstrated that young children have difficulty delaying gratification and that they know less than older children about effective strategies for self-regulation during delay. In the delay-of-gratification paradigm, children are asked to wait for the experimenter to return (15–20 minutes), when they will receive a preferred reward (for example, two marshmallows). Further, the children understand that they can call back the experimenter anytime and that they will be given a less-preferred reward (for example, a pretzel) if the experimenter is called back. Thus, the question is whether the children can delay long enough to receive their preferred reward. A number of factors affect children's tolerance of delay. First, children delay longer if neither of the rewards is physically present ($X = 11$ minutes). The presence of both rewards is particularly distracting; the children waited only one minute before calling the experimenter and settling for the less-preferred reward.

A subsequent series of experiments demonstrated that it was thinking about the rewards rather than their physical presence per se that affected children's ability to delay gratification. Mischel, Ebbesen, and Zeiss (1972) compared waiting times in two conditions: rewards present versus rewards absent. In each of these conditions, three- and four-year-olds were instructed to think about the rewards, to think about fun things (for example, swinging on a swing with mommy pushing), or were given no instructions about ideation.

Findings indicate that thoughts which distracted the children's attention from the rewards resulted in longer waiting times. Thus, thinking about fun things was as effective when the reward was present as when it was absent. But thinking about the rewards when they were not physically present resulted in very short waiting times that were equivalent to the delay when the rewards were present with no thought instructions.

Furthermore, subsequent work demonstrated that it was not thinking about rewards in general that was disruptive to delay but thinking about their motivational or consummatory qualities. To illustrate, when instructed to think about the consummatory quality of the relevant, preferred reward (for example, the chewy, sweet, soft taste of the marshmallows), children had shorter waiting times than when instructed to think about the more abstract, nonconsummatory qualities (for example, thinking about the marshmallows as white, puffy clouds or as round, white moons) (Mischel & Baker, 1975).

Taken together, Mischel's (1983) work indicates that how children mentally represent rewards (goals) determines how long they delay gratification. If the representation emphasizes the motivational (consummatory, arousal) qualities of the goal, it is more difficult to wait for the goal. But mental representations of the same goal objects that focus "on their nonconsummatory (more abstract, less arousing) qualities appears to facilitate the maintenance of goal-directed behavior and make delay of gratification achievable even by the young child" (Mischel, 1983, p. 219).

As children mature, they come to know more about factors that can distract them from goal-directed behaviors. Mischel and Mischel (1983) asked preschool, third grade, and sixth grade children to choose between strategies to help them wait in the delay-of-gratification paradigm. As demonstrated in Table 9-2, the preschoolers were less likely to appreciate the distracting effects of the physical presence of the reward. By third grade, however, the children preferred to cover the reward rather than leave it exposed. Similarly, when asked whether they would choose consummatory thoughts ("hot" thoughts, such as the sweetness of the marshmallows) or task-contingent thoughts ("cool" thoughts, such as "I am waiting for the two marshmallows"), third and sixth graders, but not preschoolers, were more likely to select the task-contingent thoughts. Finally, not until sixth grade did most children choose the strategy of thinking about cool, nonconsummatory, abstract properties of the goal rather than the hot consummatory properties. Importantly, children of all ages preferred hot ideation in a nondelay situation. The developmental change in the delay condition does not simply reflect avoidance of hot ideation, but the development of a strategy to self-regulate their behavior in the delay-of-gratification paradigm.

Thus, by five years of age, children in this paradigm understand two rules for effective delay: cover the rewards and think about task-oriented, rather than consummatory, ideas. By the sixth grade, children also understand it is more difficult to resist immediate gratification if they think about the motivational or consummatory aspects of the goal. Furthermore, the beginnings of

TABLE 9-2 *Number at Each Age Level Choosing Each Strategy to Help Delay.*

	Cover vs Expose Rewards		Task-oriented vs Consummatory Ideation		Abstract vs Consummatory Ideation	
Preschool	10	14	10	13	10	11
Grade 3	23	10	26	7	17	16
Grade 6	27	8	28	6	26	6

Note: Numbers do not always add to total N because some children refused to make some choices.
Source: Mischel and Mischel, 1983. © The Society for Research in Child Development, Inc.

self-control are evident in the behavior of young preschoolers. Children as young as two spontaneously engage in behaviors that divert their attention from forbidden goals (Vaughn, Kopp, Krakow, Johnson & Schwartz, 1986). This is not to say that children this age are consciously aware of strategies for self-control. Rather, self-control appears to begin with tacit strategies that later become explicit. We have yet to trace the development of self-control strategies as they progress from implicit to explicit knowledge.

In summary, effective planning requires the integration of a number of cognitive skills. The research on children's planning indicates that, when the context is supportive and tasks are age appropriate, young children demonstrate the rudiments of planning. Although these skills develop during the preschool and elementary school years, we have seen that young children can use subgoal structures to facilitate their overt searches. With development, children are increasingly able to plan and select strategies that are appropriate for the demands of a given task. School-age children are capable of evaluating and revising their plans and become more flexible in the planning process. We know little, however, about the development of children's knowledge of the planning process itself (compare, Wilensky, 1981). That is, we know little about how children represent and use knowledge about planning in problem solving.

As we saw in Chapter 7, during the school years there is substantial growth in children's knowledge and monitoring of their own cognitive skills, skills that are important for effective planning and problem solving. During this period children become increasingly aware of strategies for delaying immediate gratification, strategies that serve to prevent them from giving up on a desired goal. Children not only must maintain a mental representation of a goal, but a representation that does not produce conflicting desires and responses.

Although we know little about how goal representation affects problem solving in general, we might expect that goal representations that focus on the hot qualities of a goal may interfere with achieving a desired goal. For example, the student who thinks about how good it will feel to finish a term paper may be more willing to settle for an inadequate paper than the student who maintains a mental representation of a term paper that has a certain style and content.

GENERATING AND TESTING HYPOTHESES

Some problems have a structure for which generating hypotheses of possible solutions and testing these hypotheses can facilitate the search for a solution. Medical diagnosis, for example, often proceeds in this manner (Chi & Glaser, 1985). The patient has a medical problem with a set of symptoms, some relevant to the problem, some not. The doctor generates an initial diagnosis or hypothesis about the cause of the problem and then seeks further information to test the hypothesis. This new information either serves to confirm or disconfirm the hypothesis. Of course, in this example, generating and testing hypotheses requires extensive prior knowledge, but the heuristic can also be demonstrated in laboratory problems that do not require domain-specific knowledge.

Research with concept identification tasks demonstrates developmental changes in how children test hypotheses. In these tasks the experimenter arbitrarily defines a concept or rule to be identified and provides some form of feedback to specify when an exemplar does or does not belong to the category or fit the rule. In one version of these tasks, children are presented a pair of objects on each trial and instructed to select the object that has a marble under it (indicated in Figure 9-4 by the + sign). That is, the children are asked to learn to identify the objects that belong to the class of objects that covers marbles. When the children consistently select the correct object, it is assumed that they have identified the rule that defines the experimenter's concept. A cognitive interpretation of problem solving in this type of task assumes that individuals generate and test hypotheses about the nature of the rule for the category and then maintain or modify these hypotheses on the basis of confirming or disconfirming feedback (Bruner, Goodnow & Austin, 1956; Levine, 1975; Gholson, 1980).

How can we know when someone is testing hypotheses? One possibility, of course, is to ask them. This approach has been used effectively, particularly with adults, and even young children (for example, Phillips & Levine, 1975). A nonverbal technique, *blank-trial probes,* also has been used effectively with children as young as preschool (Levine, 1966; Gholson, 1980; Cantor & Spiker, 1978). Blank trials differ from the typical feedback trials of a concept identification task in that the children are not told whether their selections are correct or not. Rather, they are instructed to continue selecting the object they think is correct. Children start a concept identification task with a pair of objects, make a choice, and then receive feedback about their choice. This and each feedback trial is followed by a set of blank trials. Hypotheses are inferred from the response patterns evident in the response choices on these blank trials.

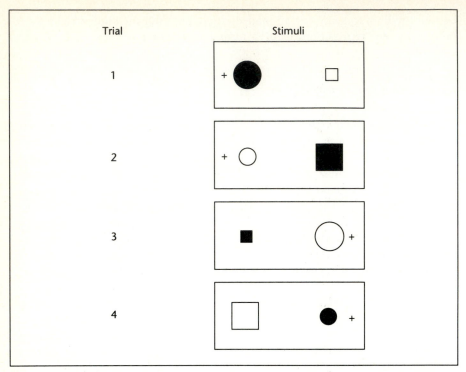

Trial   Stimuli

1

2

3

4

▶ **FIGURE 9-4** *Four trials of a concept identification task in which "circle" is the concept to be identified.* (From Gholson, 1980.)

As depicted in Figure 9-5, there are eight single-feature hypotheses for the concept task illustrated, and the objects are arranged so that each hypothesis has a different response pattern in the blank trials. For example, if a child's hypothesis is square, then the pattern of choices for the four blank trials will be LLRR, and this pattern is different than that for the other seven hypotheses.

Levine (for example, 1963, 1966) makes a distinction between two types of response patterns: response sets and prediction hypotheses. *Response sets* are patterns of responding, such as alternating positions (for example, LRLR) that occur regardless of confirming/disconfirming feedback. The *prediction hypotheses,* however, are sensitive to such feedback. If a prediction hypothesis is disconfirmed, it is rejected and an alternative hypothesis is selected for testing. Response sets are maintained, however, despite disconfirming evidence.

A number of studies have demonstrated that the responses for both children and adults are dictated by prediction hypotheses, but there is a developmental increase in the frequency of these hypotheses (for example, Eimas, 1969; Ingalls & Dickerson, 1969). It is not until second grade that hypothesis testing occurs in a wide variety of conditions (see Tumblin & Gholson, 1981, for a review). Nevertheless, under some circumstances young children can generate and test simple hypotheses. Unlike adults and older children, however,

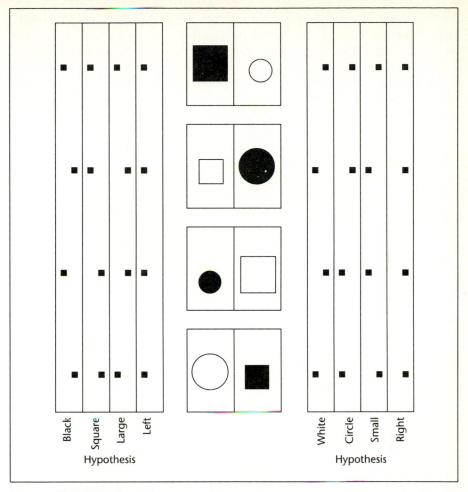

▶ **FIGURE 9-5** *Eight patterns of choice responses that uniquely correspond to the eight hypotheses when the four stimulus pairs are presented on consecutive blank trials. (From Gholson, 1980.)*

preschoolers do not have strategies for systematically testing these hypotheses (Tumblin & Gholson, 1981).

Adults not only generate and test hypotheses, but they also have strategies for testing a sequence of hypotheses (for example, Bruner, Goodnow & Austin, 1956; Johnson, 1978; Laughlin, Lange & Adamopoulos, 1982) and some strategies are more powerful than others for solving a given problem. To give a simple example, consider the concept identification problem in Figure 9-4. One strategy would be to generate a hypothesis (for example, black), select a figure, keep the hypothesis if feedback is positive, and change the hypothesis if feedback is negative. Assuming that the solver remembers which hypotheses he or she has rejected and does not retest these, the process continues until a hypothesis is consistently confirmed. At the other extreme is a *focusing* strategy in which a set of hypotheses is generated (for example, the eight values of the objects in Figure 9-4), an object is selected, and on the basis of feedback all the hypotheses that are disconfirmed are eliminated from the set of hypotheses. This process continues until one hypothesis remains. For example, suppose the first selection is the block on the right. The consequent negative feedback means that four hypotheses (that is, right, square, white, and small) can be eliminated from the original set of hypotheses. Similarly, feedback after selection on the second trial eliminates half the remaining hypotheses; after the third trial only one hypothesis has not been disconfirmed.

With age, hypothesis-testing strategies become more sophisticated (see, for example, Tumblin & Gholson, 1981) and more widely applied (see, for example, Cantor & Spiker, 1984). For example, although Kemler (1978) found that kindergarteners were testing hypotheses (that is, using current feedback to select new hypotheses), the children were not using information from previous trials (that is, remembering all the disconfirmed hypotheses) to select these hypotheses. Cantor and Spiker (1984), however, demonstrated that, if the objects were toy animals rather than the multidimensional objects used in the Kemler study, kindergarteners could use the long-term strategy of testing only those hypotheses that had not been tested and disconfirmed. The kindergarteners used this strategy on 64 percent of the trials; this percentage increased to 93 percent for third graders.

Multidimensional stimuli require a child to discover the value of a dimension that is relevant for solution. This, of course, means that the child must abstract each of the dimensions of these stimuli. We have seen, however, that young children do not readily do this (see Chapter 5). Thus, such stimuli make it difficult for a young child to keep track of the individual dimensions, the several possible hypotheses, much less the outcome of the hypotheses that had been tested. In contrast, the Cantor and Spiker task required the children to discover which toy out of eight was the correct one. Under these circumstances, with a lighter cognitive load, kindergarteners could maintain information from previous trials, although this skill was far from perfected.

We have evidence that young children do test relatively simple hypotheses, but it is also clear that they are not always sensitive to disconfirming evidence. Indeed, Karmiloff-Smith and Inhelder (1974) have argued that young children do not recognize the implications of disconfirming evidence until a hypothesis is well established. In this study, children between the ages of $4\frac{1}{2}$ and $9\frac{1}{2}$ were presented with a variety of blocks and asked to balance each on a metal bar, as depicted in Figure 9-1. The youngest children typically began with behavior patterns and verbalizations that indicated the implicit hypothesis, "put the block on the bar and push down hard." Of course, this was seldom successful. Gradually, these children discovered that if the length blocks (Type A in Figure 9-1) were centered on the bar, they would balance. This led to the geometric center hypothesis, in which all blocks were centered on the bar. This hypothesis persisted even in the face of counterexamples, for example, failure of the conspicuous weight blocks (Type B) to balance. Karmiloff-Smith and Inhelder argue that it is only when the hypothesis is well established that children begin to recognize the implications of the counterexamples and then develop a principle for the conspicuous weight counterexamples. That is, a weight hypothesis was used for the conspicuous weight blocks, but the children persisted with the geometric center hypothesis in their attempts to balance the inconspicuous weight blocks. Length and weight were considered independently. Eventually, the children created a new hypothesis that was general enough to account for all types of blocks. Thus, children appear to persist in their hypotheses until they have enough experience to find the relations between the counterexamples. Then they generate a new hypothesis for the counterexamples; only later do they incorporate all events into a more comprehensive theory.

This is not to say, however, that hypothesis testing is simple and faultless for college students. Adults, for example, do not always use the optimal strategy in concept identification tasks (Johnson, 1978; Levine, 1966). Use of the focusing strategy, for instance, requires that subjects recognize that, in this task with a limited, prescribed set of hypotheses (the eight value hypotheses of Figure 9-4), a special and efficient strategy is possible (that is, the focusing strategy is not possible if the potential hypotheses are unlimited in number). In addition, the focusing strategy requires considerable mental effort to maintain the relevant information in working memory (Klayman & Ha, 1987). More powerful strategies optimize the use of available information and maximize the speed of problem solution, but they also make more demands on memory. For this reason, a more powerful strategy may not optimize performance in some problems (for example, Laughlin, Lange & Adamopoulos, 1982).

Furthermore, we presented indirect evidence in the last chapter that college students often do not use the logically correct falsification strategy to test a hypothesis in the Wason hypothesis-testing task. More direct investigation of college students' hypothesis-testing strategies is possible in the Wason 2-4-6 problem (Wason, 1960). In this task, subjects are told that the experimenter has a rule in mind that generated the numerical series, 2-4-6. Subjects are asked to discover this rule by generating new triples of numbers. After each triple is generated, the experimenter tells the subject whether or not the triple is consistent with the experimenter's rule. Subjects continue to generate triples until they are certain that they know the correct rule. Thus, the task requires subjects to generate hypotheses about the rule, to generate a triple to test the hypothesis, and to use the feedback to modify the hypothesis, if necessary.

In the 2-4-6 problem the experimenter's rule has often been "any three numbers that occur in ascending order." Suppose a subject thinks that the correct rule is "numbers increasing by two." A subject who uses a verification strategy to test this hypothesis produces a test triple that is consistent with this hypothesis. Since this triple and any triple produced by this subject's verification strategy will be consistent with the experimenter's rule, the subject will never determine that his hypothesis is incorrect. A subject who uses falsification strategy to test the same hypothesis will produce a triple that does not increase by increments of two, such as 8-11-14. Since this triple is consistent with the experimenter's rule but not with the subject's hypothesis, the subject can know that the hypothesis, numbers increasing by two, can be rejected.

Wason (1960, 1968) has found that college students are more likely to use the verification strategy in this task, and, as a consequence, they fail to solve the problem. More recently, however, theoretical analyses (Klayman & Ha, 1987) and experimental data (Turner, 1985) have demonstrated that the appropriate strategy for testing a hypothesis depends upon the structure of the problem. To give a brief illustration of this point, consider Figure 9-6. The rectangle in each drawing represents the set of all possible number triples. The circle represents the set of triples that are covered by the experimenter's rule; the triangle represents the set of triples covered by the subject's hypothesis. When the experimenter's rule is ascending numbers, as is the case in most of the research, it is a very general one; a large percentage of all possible triples fits the rule, as represented by the size of the circle in Figure 9-6(a). The hypothesis, numbers increasing by two, is a more specific rule and is related to the experimenter's rule as drawn. In this situation, only the falsification strategy will produce the disconfirming evidence that will lead the subject to reject the incorrect hypothesis. That is, a triple that is outside the triangle and inside the circle will fit the experimenter's rule, but not the subject's hypothesis.

Now consider a different problem structure (Figure 9-6[b]) in which the experimenter's rule is narrower (for example, even numbers increasing by two) and the subject's hypothesis is increasing by two. If the subject uses the *verification* strategy and tests with the triple, 7-9-11, the triple is inconsistent with the experimenter's rule and this disconfirms the subject's hypothesis. Thus, the falsification strategy is not the only strategy for disconfirming a hypothesis. Rather, the problem structure and the strategy for generating a test interact to determine whether confirming or disconfirming evidence is produced.

Of course, subjects cannot know the structure of a problem beforehand, but there is some evidence that patterns of feedback produced by different problem structures lead college students to adjust their test strategies in variations of the 2-4-6 problem (Turner, 1985). We need to further explore how the nature of problems influences strategies for testing hypotheses.

One study (Tschirgi, 1980) suggests that the hypothesis-testing strategies of adults as well as children are influenced by the goal they set for themselves. In this study second, fourth, and sixth grade students as well as college-level students were given eight stories about familiar events. These stories included baking a cake, making a paper airplane, making clay pots, sewing a dress, feeding a cat, planting tomato seeds, washing clothes, and going fishing.

> The stories all followed the same format. First, a character was introduced into a multivariate event in which she or he attempted to do something. The event consisted of either three elements (e.g., cake elements = shortening, sweetening, and flour type) or two elements (e.g., cake

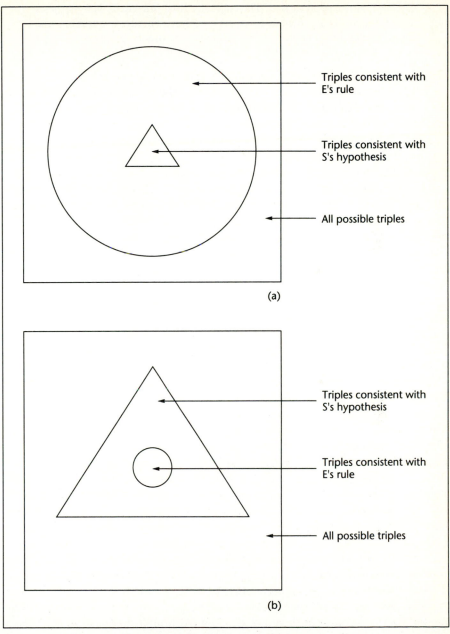

Triples consistent with
E's rule

Triples consistent with
S's hypothesis

All possible triples

(a)

Triples consistent with
S's hypothesis

Triples consistent with
E's rule

All possible triples

(b)

▶ *FIGURE 9-6* *The rectangles represent the sets of all possible number triples, the circles represent the sets of triples covered by the experimenter's (E's) rules, and the triangles represent the sets of triples covered by the subject's (S's) hypothesis.*

elements = shortening and sweetening). Then there was some outcome of the event, either good or bad. The character then proposed his hypothesis concerning which element caused the outcome. Finally, a question was posed, asking the reader to help the character choose the best way to prove the hypothesis. (Tschirgi, 1980, p. 3)

An example of a three-element good-outcome story is presented in Figure 9-7. "The bad outcome cake story changed only the outcome sentence (e.g., to 'The cake turned out just terrible, it was so runny') and a single adjective (e.g., 'great' to 'terrible') in the hypothesis paragraph" (p. 3).

The three response choices represent three possible strategies for testing the hypothesis. The first answer, "a," is a vary-one-thing-at-a-time (VOTAT) strategy. The hypothesized element, honey, is varied. The second answer, "b," is a hold-one-thing-at-a-time (HOTAT) strategy. In this case the hypothesized variable (honey) is the only one held constant and the other two are varied. The third answer, "c," is a change-all-variables (CA) strategy.

With age there was a decrease in the CA strategy, which is an inadequate strategy for testing a hypothesis. At all ages the students were more likely to use the VOTAT strategy for the bad outcome stories and this became more likely with age. The HOTAT strategy was more likely, however, for the good outcome stories; this was equally true at all ages. Thus, the hypothesis-testing strategies improved with age, but at all ages the strategy used was influenced by the nature of the story outcome rather than the logic of hypothesis testing. That is, we have seen, the logically appropriate strategy is to try to disconfirm a hypothesis. In the Tschirgi paradigm this would mean changing the variable that is hypothesized to influence the outcome and holding the other variables constant (VOTAT). The students used this strategy when they were trying to determine the cause of a bad outcome. The students changed the variable they thought was the cause of the bad outcome. When they were testing for the cause of a good outcome, however, they did not vary the hypothesized cause. Rather, they sought to confirm the hypothesis by holding constant the presumed cause of the good outcome and changing the other variables simultaneously (HOTAT). Their strategies appear driven by the goal of eliminating the cause of a bad outcome and maintaining the cause of a good outcome. Although these goals do not conform to the logic of hypothesis testing, they do seem appropriate for the everyday situations in which we seek to preserve positive results and eliminate negative ones. This is probably another case in which the subjects' goals (for example, having a good cake/not having a bad cake) are different than those of the experimenter (that is, testing hypotheses logically).

For the most part, the research on the generate-and-test heuristic has focused on the testing aspect of the strategy. Although there are some data to indicate that hypotheses are affected by how information is presented (Hagafors, 1983), we know little about the process of hypothesis generation. Yet, as we saw in Chapter 8, generation of alternative variables in the controlling variables task influenced how children tested the variables they generated (Pulos & Linn, 1981). Similarly, young children's failure to heed disconfirming evi-

John decided to bake a cake. But he ran out of some ingredients. So:
- he used margarine instead of butter for the shortening
- he used honey instead of sugar for the sweetening and
- he used brown wholewheat flour instead of regular white flour.

The cake turned out great, it was so moist.

John thought that the reason the cake was so great was the honey. He thought that the type of shortening (butter or margarine) or the type of flour really didn't matter.

What should he do to prove this point?

a. He can bake the cake again but use sugar instead of honey, and still use margarine and brown wholewheat flour.

b. He can bake the cake again but this time use sugar, butter and regular white flour.

c. He can bake the cake again still using honey, but this time using butter and regular white flour.

▶ **FIGURE 9-7** *An example of a three-element good-outcome story.* (From Tschirgi, 1980.)

dence may reflect their inability to generate an alternative hypothesis. That is, with some materials young children may fixate on a salient, but incorrect, aspect of the materials, fail to generate alternative hypotheses about the less salient aspects, and thus persevere with an incorrect hypothesis (Small, 1970). Failure to modify a hypothesis after disconfirming evidence may, however, have beneficial consequences for young children. In the real world rules are not as tidy as in the laboratory. Rather, rules often have exceptions (for example, exceptions to language rules). Young children frequently need to formulate rules that handle the majority of cases. In these circumstances it would be maladaptive to give too much weight to disconfirming evidence.

ANALOGIES

The history of science is replete with examples of the use of analogies to solve and/or clarify problems (see, for example, Dreistadt, 1968). Darwin, for instance, used a living tree analogy to conceptualize the development and classification of species. Helmholtz's (1930) theory of hearing specified that the fibers of the basal membrane in the inner ear resonate to frequencies in the way that the strings of harps and pianos resonate. Piaget used group theory of mathematics to model the cognitive structures of concrete operations and a system of propositional logic for the structures of formal operations.

When confronted with a problem, we are influenced by our previous attempts to solve problems, and one type of information that can facilitate solution is previous experience with analogous tasks. We do not automatically use such knowledge, however. Some investigators report transfer between analogous problems (for example, Hayes & Simon, 1974), others do not (for example, Reed, Ernst & Banerji, 1974). To illustrate, Reed and his colleagues gave college students two problems—Missionary-Cannibal and Jealous Husbands—that have comparable problem spaces. The Missionary-Cannibal problem reads as follows (Reed, Ernst & Banerji, 1974):

> Three missionaries and three cannibals having to cross a river at a ferry, find a boat but the boat is so small that it can contain no more than two persons. If the missionaries on either bank of the river or in the boat, are outnumbered at any time by cannibals, the cannibals will eat the missionaries. Find the simplest schedule of crossings that will permit all the missionaries and cannibals to cross the river safely. It is assumed that all passengers on the boat unboard before the next trip and at least one person has to be in the boat for each crossing.

The Jealous Husbands problem reads as follows (Reed, Ernst & Banerji, 1974):

> Three jealous husbands and their wives having to cross a river at a ferry, find a boat but the boat is so small that it can contain no more than two persons. Find the simplest schedule of crossings that will permit all six people to cross the river so that none of the women shall be left in company with any of the men, unless her husband is present. It is assumed that all

passengers on the boat unboard before the next trip, and at least one person has to be in the boat for each crossing.

These two problems can be solved with the same series of legal moves. There was no transfer between the problems, however, unless the students were instructed in the relationship between the two problems. But even in this situation the transfer occurred only from the more difficult Jealous Husbands problem to the Missionary-Cannibal problem, not in the opposite direction.

Yet, Hayes and Simon (1974) reported transfer for analogous versions of The Tower of Hanoi problem (illustrated in Figure 9-8). This problem, of course, has a different structure than the Missionary-Cannibal problem. Solution to the M-C problem is a series of 13 legal moves. Representation of this solution would place excessive demands on working memory. If the students do not represent the solution of the first problem encountered as this idealized sequence of moves, they may not have the information available that would promote positive transfer. The fact that only 7 of 56 students in the Reed *et al.* study reported remembering all or most of the moves of the first problem lends some support to this possibility. Indeed, the rest of the students reported trying to solve the second problem independently of the first problem.

The solution path for the Tower of Hanoi problem can be segmented into a few subgoals (for example, first, get the largest disc to the final position) that are within the capacity of working memory. Then, a few specific moves can be associated with each subgoal. The representation of the solution is hierarchically organized, making fewer cognitive demands (compare, Luger & Bauer, 1978).

If we consider for a moment the process involved, it becomes obvious why transfer from analogous problems may not be straightforward. First, the current problem must be represented with the relevant structured relations that are analogous to a previous problem. As we have seen in Chapter 8, it is not the details of the objects, but the relations between them that are relevant for analogical reasoning. Second, some previous problem and its solution must be mentally represented with a comparable system of relations. Third, this mental representation must be accessed and then mapped to the particulars of the current problem. Thus, problem solving by analogy raises questions about the process of a problem representation (what information is acquired and stored), how previous problems are accessed, and how the initial state and operations of an analogous problem are mapped onto a current problem.

Early investigations of analogical transfer focused on well-defined problems (for example, Tower of Hanoi, Missionary-Cannibal). More recently, Gick and Holyoak (1980, 1983) have sought to identify those factors that influence analogical transfer in an ill-defined problem. They used Duncker's (1945) radiation problem and analogous problems. Table 9-3 presents one of these analogies (attack-dispersion) with its solution and the radiation problem (the analogous solution is in italics). These two problems have very different contents, yet a comparison of the propositions for the two problems demonstrates that the propositions can be matched for analogical relations. For ex-

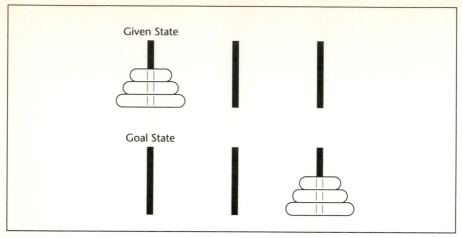

Given State

Goal State

▶ **FIGURE 9-8** *The Tower of Hanoi problem. Move only one disc at a time, take only the top disc on a peg, and never place a larger disc on top of a smaller one. (From Mayer, 1983.)*

ample, in the attack-dispersion story the goal (fortress) has a centered location; similarly, the goal (tumor) of the radiation is centrally located. The problems are not isomorphic, however. There is no relation in the radiation problem that is comparable to the relation expressed in proposition 2a of the attack-dispersion problem. Nor are all the semantic relations analogous. Generally, the role of the army corresponds to the role of the rays. But in propositions 5 and 5′ the two do not have the same semantic relations. "The army is the *object* of the process of destruction in 5, while the rays are the *instrument* of the destruction in 5′ " (Gick & Holyoak, 1980, p. 314).

In a series of experiments, Gick and Holyoak (1980) have demonstrated that the prior presentation of analogous stories, such as the attack-dispersion story, can affect solution of the radiation problem. Further, even stories that have less correspondence between the propositions can lead to analogous solutions. Transfer, however, is relatively weak unless the relevance of the analogous story is made explicit to the student. That is, even when they are capable of mapping the analogical relations and producing an analogous solution for the radiation problem, few students spontaneously notice the significance of the analogous story. This failure to access potential analogies reflects, in part at least, the influence of context on access (see, for example, Spencer & Weisberg, 1986). When the context of the analogous story differs from that of the problem, transfer can be negligible, especially after a few minutes' delay (Spencer & Weisberg, 1986).

Gick and Holyoak (1983) found that analogical transfer is more likely when subjects are familiar with two, rather than one, analogous stories prior to their attempts to solve the radiation problem. They proposed that when subjects have enough experience with comparable analogous problems they are more likely to induce a more general *convergence schema* that is an abstract representation of the set of relations that are common to the several analogies.

TABLE 9-3 *A Summary of Attack-Dispersion Story and of Corresponding Solution to Radiation Problem*

Proposition number	
	Attack-Dispersion story
1–2	A fortress was located in the center of the country.
2a	Many roads radiated out from the fortress.
3–4	A general wanted to capture the fortress with his army.
5–7	The general wanted to prevent mines on the roads from destroying his army and neighboring villages.
8	As a result the entire army could not attack the fortress along one road.
9–10	However, the entire army was needed to capture the fortress.
11	So an attack by one small group would not succeed.
12	The general therefore divided his army into several small groups.
13	He positioned the small groups at the heads of different roads.
14–15	The small groups simultaneously converged on the fortress.
16	In this way the army captured the fortress.
	Radiation problem and dispersion solution
1'–2'	A tumor was located in the interior of a patient's body.
3'–4'	A doctor wanted to destroy the tumor with rays.
5'–7'	The doctor wanted to prevent the rays from destroying healthy tissue.
8'	As a result the high-intensity rays could not be applied to the tumor along one path.
9'–10'	However, high-intensity rays were needed to destroy the tumor.
11'	So applying one low-intensity ray would not succeed.
12'	*The doctor therefore divided the rays into several low-intensity rays.*
13'	*He positioned the low-intensity rays at multiple locations around the patient's body.*
14'–15'	*The low-intensity rays simultaneously converged on the tumor.*
16'	*In this way the rays destroyed the tumor.*

[a]Italicized propositions summarize the target dispersion solution.
Source: Gick and Holyoak, 1980.

That is, this more abstract representation does not include details that are specific to the particular problems, but more general propositions. To illustrate, the goals, constraints, and convergence solutions of the military and radiation problems can be stated more generally as follows (Gick & Holyoak, 1983):

> Military problem
>> Initial state
>>> Goal: Use army to capture forces.
>>> Resources: Sufficiently large army.
>>> Constraint: Unable to send entire army along one road.
>> Solution plan: Send small groups along multiple roads simultaneously.
>> Outcome: Fortress captured by army.

Radiation problem
    Initial state
        Goal: Use rays to destroy tumor.
        Resources: Sufficiently powerful rays.
        Constraint: Unable to administer high-intensity from one direction.
    Solution plan: Administer low-intensity rays from multiple directions
        simultaneously.
    Outcome: Tumor destroyed by rays.

Convergence schema
    Initial state
        Goal: Use force to overcome a central target.
        Resources: Sufficiently great force.
        Constraint: Unable to apply full force along one path.
    Solution plan: Apply weak forces along multiple paths simultaneously.
    Outcome: Central target overcome by force.

Thus, the goal of the radiation problem is "use rays to destroy the tumor"; that of the attack-dispersion story is "the general's army must reach the fortress." These can be more generally stated as "A large force must be delivered to a central location."

Two recent sets of experiments (Catrambone & Holyoak, in press; Spencer & Weisberg, 1986) indicate that experience with multiple analogs does improve analogical transfer to another problem, but only if students are encouraged and directed to discover the similarities and relevant aspects of the multiple analogs. It does not appear that college students readily discover these "underlying regulations on their own" (Catrambone & Holyoak, in press, p. 24). Furthermore, several other factors influence analogical transfer. First, transfer from one problem to another is most likely if the problems share salient surface properties. Second, without such surface similarity between problems, transfer is unlikely if there is a delay between the problems or a change in the encoding context. Finally, under these conditions, a hint about the relevance of a prior problem does facilitate transfer. Taken together, the experimental evidence indicates that college students do not spontaneously induce an abstract schema to represent multiple experiences with analogous problems and their solutions. Although the experimental evidence suggests that analogical transfer is limited, we do know that in the real world such transfer does occur. Our challenge is to identify those conditions that promote analogical transfer. One possibility is that under some circumstances looking for analogies becomes an explicit strategy for solving a problem.

THE DEVELOPMENT OF ANALOGICAL TRANSFER   Under some circumstances, as demonstrated in Chapter 8, preschoolers can reason analogically. The question then is whether, and under what circumstances, young children can apply this skill to goal-directed problem solving. The data are very limited but demonstrate that preschoolers are capable of using analogies to solve problems (Crisafi & Brown, 1986; Holyoak, Junn & Billman, 1984). In three different experiments, Holyoak, Junn, and Billman (1984) asked preschoolers and fifth and sixth graders to solve a problem that had multiple solutions (Holyoak *et al.,* 1984, p. 2043):

> Two bowls were set on a table, one within the child's reach and one farther away. One bowl (the near one) contained a number of small gumballs, and the other was empty. Also on the table were an aluminum walking cane, a large rectangular sheet of heavy paper (posterboard), a hollow cardboard tube, long enough to reach the farther bowl, child-safe scissors, string, tape, paper clips, and rubber bands. The subjects' task was to devise as many ways as possible, using the materials provided, of transferring the balls from the filled to the empty bowl without leaving their seat.

Prior to this problem, the children heard story analogies that emphasized one type of solution, for example, rolling paper into a tube. The older children, like adults, frequently failed to notice the analogous relation, but when given a hint about the relevance of the analogous story they readily carried out the mapping that was necessary for solving the ball problem. Together, three studies indicated that preschoolers can use analogies to solve problems. The performance of these children, however, was highly variable. Furthermore, the correspondence (for example, functional and perceptual) between the analogical story and the ball problem had to be close for transfer to occur. Even with a hint, preschoolers had difficulty mapping the relations of the analogous story to the ball problem. These results indicate that young children can use analogies to solve problems, but that they are limited in their ability to map analogous relations.

Although we know relatively little about the development of analogical problem solving, we do know that, like adults (Gick & Holyoak, 1983), the more experience with analogous problems, the more likely children are to produce analogous solutions (Gholson, Eymard, Morgan & Kamhi, 1987). Gholson and his colleagues gave third and sixth graders a simplified version of the Missionary-Cannibal problem, with either none, one, or two analogous stories learned prior to the transfer problem. One version of the problems is presented in Figure 9-9. In this story there are three objects (fox, goose, corn), a barrier (river), and a means of transport (boat). In the other two stories, the goal structure was the same, but the objects (wolf, rabbit, carrots and lion, pony, bucket of oats), barriers (mountain, canyon), and means of transport (wagon, walking, bridge) changed.

In the experimental conditions, the children were given repeated presentations of the analog story (stories) and recall tests of the eleven propositions until they could act out the solution in the seven moves of propositions 1, 3, 4, 5, 7, 8 and 10. Immediately after reaching this criterion, they were given the background information of the transfer problem and asked to act out the solution. As illustrated in Table 9-4, transfer performance was a function of the number of prior analog stories, with the average number of moves in the two analog condition (9) near optimal performance (7 moves). In fact, 24 of

The Farmer's Dilemma

Background information

Once a man bought a fox, a goose, and some corn at the market. He wanted to take them to his house, but his house was on the other side of a river that he had to cross. He had a boat, but it would only carry the man and one other thing over to his house at a time. He knew that if he left the fox alone with the goose, the fox would eat it. He also knew that if he left the goose alone with the corn, the goose would eat it. So he had to figure out how to get them all across the river to his house without anything being eaten.

Recall Instruction

"Now here is what I want you to try to remember so that you can repeat it back to me."

Relevant and irrelevant propositions:
1. The man took the goose across the river to his house.
2. The goose had some food and water.
3. The man then went back across the river.
4. The man took the fox across the river to his house.
5. Now the man took the goose back across the river with him.
6. The goose waited near the river bank.
7. The man took the corn across the river to his house.
8. The man then went back across the river.
9. The goose was waiting on the river bank.
10. The man took the goose across the river to his house.
11. Now he had the fox, goose, and corn at his house.

▶ **FIGURE 9-9** *A representative story (Analog) including background information, recall instructions, propositions relevant to solution of the task (no. 1, 3, 4, 5, 7, 8, 10), and irrelevant propositions (no. 2, 6, 9, 11). (From Gholson, Eymard, Morgan & Kamhi, 1987.)*

40 children in this condition solved the problem in seven moves. Furthermore, there were no developmental differences in transfer performance. This, taken together with the fact that the sixth graders recalled more of the relevant propositions than the third graders, suggests that transfer performance reflects some knowledge of problem structure, not simply recall of specific moves.

Thus, Gholson and his colleagues found analogical transfer with a variation of the Missionary-Cannibal problem; yet Reed *et al.* found no transfer with the original M-C problem. The two studies differ in many ways, differences that raise several questions about the acquisition of analogous problem structures and the mapping of these structures to the structure of a current problem. For example, the M-C problem and Gholson's variation differ in the number of moves required for solution. Thus, the M-C problem places greater demands on working memory than does the Gholson variation. Furthermore the two problems appear to have different structures. The M-C problem structure is a series of moves, with two choice points in the series. The farmer's

TABLE 9-4 *The Number of Moves in Transfer and the Total Amount of Time in Transfer[a] for Third and Sixth Graders in the Two-Analog, One-Analog, and Control Conditions*

	Condition		
	Two Analog	**One Analog**	**Control**
Grade 3	8.80 (51)	14.05 (161)	27.65 (499)
Grade 6	9.40 (66)	12.90 (169)	25.80 (488)

[a]*Time in seconds is given in parentheses.*
Source: Gholson et al., 1987. Copyright 1987 by the American Psychological Association. Reprinted by permission.

dilemma and the analogous problems appear to have a subgoal structure, that is, "move first the object mentioned in the middle," and even a rule, "always keep the middle object separate from the others." At this point, we know little about how problem structure relates to analogical transfer. There are some data to suggest, however, that positive transfer is more likely if a specific rule has been acquired in a previous problem (for example, Sweller, 1983).

The two studies also differed in how well the subjects knew the solution to the analog problem. The children in the Gholson study could perform the solution perfectly before they were given the transfer problem. This was not the case in the Reed *et al.* study; the college students averaged 3.8 errors on their one attempt to solve the analogous problem. Thus, the children may have had a more complete representation of the analogous solution than the college students.

Finally, the Gholson study makes clear that transfer benefits from more experience with analogous problems. This, of course, replicates the findings of Gick and Holyoak (1983) and lends support to their assertion that more abstract problem structures are derived from analogies when experience with variations in specific details serves to highlight the common relations and to diminish the importance of the details (compare, Karmiloff-Smith, 1984). The children in the two-analog conditions also, however, had more time in a context that was similar to the context of the transfer problem. Further research is necessary to determine the relative roles of context and changes in the mental representation of problem structure in the development of analogical problem solving.

Finally, we have evidence that even young preschoolers can benefit from solving analogous problems, if the task is age appropriate. Crisafi and Brown (1986) used variations of an inference problem developed by Kendler and Kendler (1967). The Kendlers used apparatus similar to that pictured at the top of Figure 9-10. The box was automated, with three colored panels that could be covered. In the first stage of training, the two outer panels were uncovered. The children learned to press the lever (X) on the red panel to obtain a marble (Y) and the lever (A) on the blue panel to get a steel ball (B). When these responses were learned, these panels were covered and the center

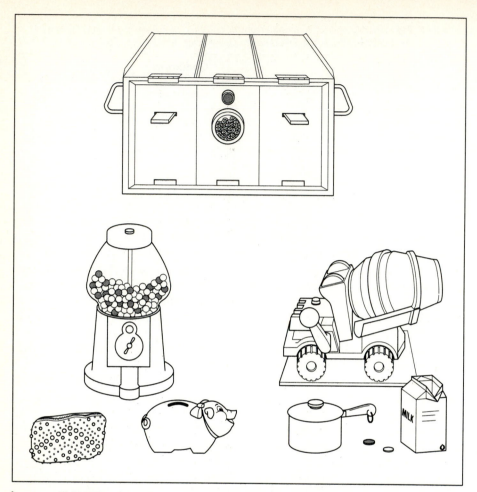

▶ **FIGURE 9-10** *These three versions of the A-B-G problems used the following: automated box (top), familiar objects in familiar relations (bottom left), and familiar objects in unfamiliar relations (bottom right). (From Crisafi & Brown, 1986.)*

panel exposed. The children were trained to put one type object (B) (for example, either marbles or steel balls) in the opening of the outer panel to receive a toy charm (G). This was followed by the inference test in which all the panels were uncovered, and the child was asked to get a toy charm from the center panel. Thus, to perform correctly, the child had to push the lever (A) that produced the appropriate object (B) for getting the toy (G) from the center panel. Kendler and Kendler (1967) found that only six percent of the kindergarteners tested could solve the problem. However, variations, in the apparatus that make the situation more familiar and reduce task-irrelevant information make the task easier for young children.

In their first study, Crisafi and Brown (1986) tested three variations of the Kendlers' task. The problem structure was the same for all variations. That is, there was subgoal training (A-B and X-Y), followed by a subgoal-goal phase (B-G), and then a test phase (A-B-G), in which the two separate responses (A-B and B-G) had to be combined. As pictured at the bottom left of Figure 9-10, one version involved familiar objects in familiar relations; a second version, shown bottom right, used familiar objects in unfamiliar relations. For example, the truck dumped a gumball (G); the pan (A) and the carton (X) held a dime (B) and a penny (Y), respectively. A third version, not shown, consisted of three drawers. A red drawer (A) held nuts (B) and the yellow drawer (X) held copper tubes (Y). When a nut (B) was placed in a center hole, the child received a gumball (G) from the center drawer. These three versions and their object relations are described in Table 9-5.

In the first study, two-year-olds learned each of the three variations. Performance was clearly a function of the familiarity of the objects and the relations. With familiar objects and familiar relations (gumball task), 89 percent of the children made a correct response during the combination test. This percentage was 67 percent for the dump truck task, which had familiar objects in unfamiliar relations. Only 17 percent of the children solved the drawer version of the task. Thus, if the objects and their relations are familiar enough, two-year-olds can learn the arbitrary relations of the subgoal (A-B) and goal (B-G) phases and make the appropriate inference to combine them in the test phase.

In a series of subsequent studies, Crisafi and Brown sought to determine the conditions that would promote transfer from the easier task to the analogous, but more difficult, Kendler version of the task. In a second study, two- and three-year-olds were given the three tasks described in Table 9-5, always in the same order, easy to most difficult. Half the children were given hints before each task about the similarity of the games; the rest of the children had no such hint. Results indicate the hint greatly facilitated the performance of these children, but even 42 percent of the children in the no-hint condition solved the Kendler task. This was significantly greater than the control condition that received only the Kendler task. A third study using the dump truck task rather than the drawer version confirmed that three-year-olds can benefit from a hint about the relevance and similarity of a prior problem.

In a fourth study, the three tasks of the third study were presented and efforts made to encourage transfer without giving an explicit hint. The children were asked to state with the experimenter the rule for solving each problem. Although two-year-olds were unable to do this, the three-year-olds were able to give the rule to a puppet, if they had aid from the experimenter. The experimenter told the rule to the child; the child then told it to the puppet. Three-year-olds benefited from stating the rule in two separate studies. Four-year-olds, however, demonstrated significant transfer even without stating a rule.

Taken together, this series of studies demonstrates several aspects of preschool problem solving. First, in a familiar setting, preschoolers as young as

TABLE 9-5 *Three Variations on Analogous Inference Problems*

A. Study 1

Task Structure	Container-Subgoal Relation (A-B, X-Y)	Subgoal-Goal (B-G)	Combining Test (A-B-G)
Task variant:			
Familiar objects:			
1. Known relations (gumball) machine.........	Bank-penny Purse-dime	Penny—gumball machine→gumball	Bank→penny Penny→gumball
2. New relations (truck).........	Carton-penny Pan-dime	Dime—truck→gumball	Pan→dime Dime→gumball
Unfamiliar objects:			
1. New relations (box drawer).....	Yellow drawer-nut Red drawer-tube	Nut—center drawer→gumball	Yellow drawer→nut Nut→gumball

B. Study 2

Task Structure	Container-Subgoal Relation (A-B, X-Y)	Subgoal-Goal (B-G)	Combining Test (A-B-G)
Task variant:			
1. Easy (gumball machine).........	Bank-penny Purse-dime	Penny—gumball machine→gumball	Bank→penny Penny→gumball
2. Intermediate (box-drawer).........	Yellow drawer-nut Red drawer-tube	Nut—center panel→jelly	Yellow drawer→nut Nut→jelly
3. Hard (box-automated).........	Red panel-marble Blue panel-ball bearing	Marble—center panel→M&M	Red panel→marble Marble→M&M

C. STUDY 3

Task Structure	Container-Subgoal Relation (A-B, X-Y)	Subgoal-Goal (B-G)	Combining Test (A-B-G)
Task variant:			
1. Easy (gumball machine)	Bank-penny Purse-dime	Penny→gumball machine→gumball	Bank→penny Penny→gumball
2. Intermediate (truck).	Carton-white button Pan-grey button	White button-truck→candy bean	Carton→white button White button→candy
3. Hard (box-automated).	Red panel-marble Blue-panel-ball bearing	Marble-center panel→M&M	Red panel→marble Marble→M&M

Source: Crisafi and Brown, 1986. © The Society for Research in Child Development, Inc.

two can combine information to achieve a goal. They were not able, however, to solve analogous problems with unfamiliar operations and objects. By four years of age, children could solve the more difficult Kendler task if it came at the end of an easy-to-hard sequence of analogous tasks. Under these conditions, there was spontaneous transfer from the easier task to the most difficult task. Although transfer was not spontaneous for three-year-olds, they did benefit from knowing the similarity between the tasks or from learning to state explicitly a rule for solving the easier versions of the problem.

In summary, we find that, when the circumstances are supportive (for example, analogs well learned, little delay between problems, context unchanged, similar surface details), young children are capable of using information about analogous solutions to solve problems. The limited developmental work, however, raises many questions about the development of analogical transfer as a heuristic for problem solving. Furthermore, the work with college students raises important questions about the role of prior experience in problem solving.

These data suggest that college students do not spontaneously discover abstract similarities between multiple analogs or readily retrieve relevant analogous relations when solving problems. Yet, many accomplished problem solvers report the importance of analogies in their attempts to solve problems (compare, Hoffman, 1980). Consider two examples: Barbara McClintock, Nobel Prize winner for her research in genetics, reports that, when she tried to understand the genetic structure of the corn she was working with, she imagined herself as a gene in the structure (Keller, 1983). Alexander Graham Bell used his knowledge of the auditory system to design his telephone: "It struck me that the bones of the human ear were very massive indeed, as compared with the delicate thin membrane that operated them, and the thought occurred that if a membrane so delicate could move bones relatively so massive, why should not a thicker and stouter piece of membrane move my piece of steel. And the telephone was conceived" (Gordon, 1961, p. 41).

It is difficult to dismiss the importance of analogies in problem solving. We know that analogies are common (Collins & Gentner, 1987) and that experts use analogies to represent problems (Clement, 1985). Yet we know relatively little about how and when knowledge of analogies spontaneously facilitates problem solving. Furthermore, the research on analogies raises important questions about transfer in general.

▶ TRANSFER

Although there is no doubt that problem solving can benefit from the availability of previously acquired relevant knowledge, we also know that performance in a problem-solving task does not automatically benefit from the acquisition of knowledge that is relevant to the problem (see, for example, Weisberg,

DiCamillo & Phillips, 1978). For example, we saw that college students did not spontaneously access analogous solutions when solving the radiation problem. Rather, they had to be informed of the relevance of the analogous stories (Gick & Holyoak, 1983). Yet, if we never benefited from solving a similar problem or never recognized the relevance of prior knowledge, we would be doomed to tackling each problem as a new one, with no transfer of knowledge from prior experiences. The problem then is to determine when and under what circumstances transfer does occur. Since activation of all potential knowledge would be inefficient and, undoubtedly, overburden our information-processing capabilities, the problem is to determine the conditions that constrain the availability of potentially relevant information.

In a series of experiments, Perfetto and his colleagues (Adams, Kasserman, Yearwood, Perfetto, Bransford & Franks, 1988; Perfetto, Bransford & Franks, 1983; Perfetto, Yearwood, Franks & Bransford, 1987) have explored the conditions that do and do not promote transfer in problem solving. In the initial studies, college students were presented insight problems of the type illustrated in Figure 9-11 (Perfetto, Bransford & Franks, 1983). Students who are not familiar with these problems find them difficult. Before reading further, try to solve each of the problems in Figure 9-11.

Prior to solving these problems, two groups of subjects were asked to rate a set of sentences that were clues for problem solutions. For example, the sentence, "A minister marries several people each week," was the clue for the problem, "A man who lived in a small town in the U.S. married 20 different women of the same town. All are still living and he has never divorced one of them. Yet, he has broken no laws. Can you explain?" Before solving the insight problems, one group of students (informed) was told that the sentences were relevant to the problem solutions; the other group (uninformed) were not told of the connection. A third group (control) did not see the relevant sentences.

The first study replicated earlier work (Weisberg et al., 1978) demonstrating that the informed subjects had significantly more correct solutions than the uninformed or control subjects (the proportions correct were .54, .29, and .19, respectively). Furthermore, subsequent studies demonstrated that, if initial attempts to solve a problem were unsuccessful, subsequent attempts were poor even when the relevance of the prior information was known (Perfetto, Bransford & Franks, 1983). That is, when uninformed subjects were informed of the relevance of the sentences and given a second chance to solve the problems, they still performed more poorly than the subjects who were informed on the first trial. This deficit in performance was specific to the unsuccessful attempts on the previous trial since efforts to solve *new* problems on Trial 2 were as successful as the efforts on Trial 1 of the informed group. Thus, failures to access relevant information and consequent generation of inadequate solutions can have detrimental effects on subsequent attempts to solve a problem (Perfetto, Yearwood, Franks & Bransford, 1987).

These findings suggest at least two factors that work against successful everyday problem solving. First, we are usually uninformed about relevant

A. One day a lady in New York City hailed a passing taxicab. On the way to her destination, the lady talked so much that the driver got quite annoyed.

The driver finally said, "I'm sorry, lady, but I can't hear a word you're saying. I'm deaf as a post, and my hearing aid hasn't worked all day."

When she heard this, the lady stopped yakking. But after she left the cab, she suddenly realized that the cabbie had lied to her. How did she know he had lied?

B. Can you make a tennis ball go a short distance, come to a dead stop, then reverse itself, and go in the opposite direction?

Note: Bouncing the ball is not permitted, nor can you hit it with anything, nor tie anything to it.

C. A man who lived in a small town in the U.S. married twenty different women of the same town. All are still living and he has never divorced one of them. Yet he has broken no law. Can you explain?

D. "This myna bird," said the pet shop salesman, "will repeat anything it hears." A week later the lady who bought the bird was back in the shop to complain that she had talked to the bird, but he had not yet said anything. Nevertheless, the salesman told the truth. Explain!

E. One night my uncle was reading an exciting book when his wife turned out the light. Even though the room was pitch dark, he continued to read. How could he do that?

F. Uriah Fuller, the famous superpsychic, can tell you the score of any baseball game before the game starts. What is his secret?

▶ **FIGURE 9-11** *Insight problems presented to college students. (From Adams, et al., 1988.)*

information and, as several studies demonstrate, we do not spontaneously access information that is relevant for problem solution. Second, inadequate attempts to solve a problem actually interfere with later attempts to solve that problem. The generation of inadequate solutions hinders our ability to access previously acquired information.

Despite this seemingly pessimistic outlook, positive transfer does occur under some circumstances. One factor is the amount of time available for solution. If we consider problem solving as a search through a problem space (Newell & Simon, 1972), then being informed of the relevance of specific information should constrain the search. Without such knowledge, however, the problem space is larger and, therefore, takes more time to search. To test this possibility, Bowden (1985) varied the time available to solve puzzles similar to those used by Perfetto *et al.* (1983). As illustrated in Figure 9-12, college students who were informed of the relevance of the clue sentences achieved most of their solutions in the first 40 seconds of trying to solve a puzzle. The uninformed subjects, however, needed more time; but, when two minutes were available they did not differ from the informed subjects in the number of

G. John was driving to Las Vegas for a vacation when his car broke down in a small town. While the car was being fixed, John decided to get a haircut. The town had just two barber shops, Joe's and Bill's. John looked through the window of Bill's shop and was disgusted.

   "What a dirty shop," he said. "The mirror needs cleaning; there's hair all over the floor; the barber needs a shave, and he has a terrible haircut." It's no wonder that John left Bill's shop and went up the street to check on Joe's Barber Shop. John peeked through Joe's window. "What a difference!" John sighed.

   The mirror was clean, the floors were clean, and Joe's hair was neatly trimmed. But John didn't go in. Instead, he walked back to get his hair cut at Bill's dirty shop. Why?

H. Whenever my aunt comes to visit me at the apartment, she always gets off the elevator five floors beneath my floor. She then walks up the stairway to my apartment. Can you tell me why?

I. Last week I turned off the light in my bedroom and managed to get to bed before the room was dark. If the bed was ten feet from the light switch, how did I manage to get to bed while there was still light?

J. The Reverend Sol Loony announced that on a certain day, at a certain time, he would perform a great miracle. He would walk for twenty minutes on the surface of the Hudson River without sinking into the water. A big crowd gathered to witness the event. The Reverend Sol Loony did exactly what he said he would do. How did he manage to walk on the surface of the river without sinking?

puzzles solved. Note also that the control subjects, who did not receive the clue sentences, benefited from the extra time as well. Thus, positive transfer is more likely when uninformed subjects are given enough time or take enough time to search memory for relevant information.

Furthermore, Perfetto and his colleagues (Adams, Kasserman, Yearwood, Perfetto, Bransford & Franks, 1988) have demonstrated that positive transfer is more likely to occur if acquisition of the relevant information requires processes that are similar to those that are required in the problem-solving task. That is, in many transfer studies, including their own, the processes for acquiring the relevant facts are quite different than those of the problem itself. The informational content is similar, but the processes are not. For example, during the acquisition of the relevant sentences, subjects read each sentence and rated it for truthfulness. The transfer task, however, required the generation of problem solutions. Perfetto and his colleagues reasoned that the dissimilarity in the types of processes required for each task may have limited access to the relevant information. Put another way, similarity of content is not always an adequate retrieval cue. Rather, problem-solving processes serve as retrieval cues for relevant information.

To test this possibility, the relevant sentences were presented either as

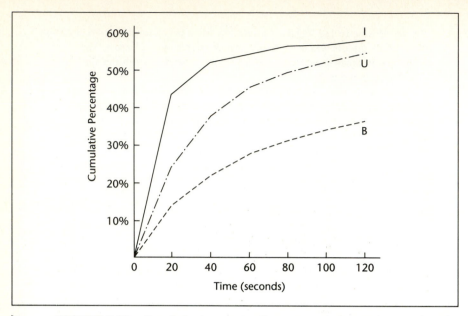

▶ **FIGURE 9-12** *Cumulative percentage of congruent solutions at six intervals within the 2-min solution period. I = informed, U = uninformed, and B = baseline.* (From Bowden, 1985.)

facts as in the Perfetto *et al.* study (1983) (for example, "A person walking on frozen water will not fall through.") or with a problem orientation in which a difficult-to-comprehend, unrealistic statement was presented in the first clause and its solution in the second clause (for example, "A person walking on water will not fall through if it is frozen."). Although none of the subjects were informed about the relevance of the sentences, the students in the problem-oriented condition successfully solved significantly more problems than the students in the fact-oriented condition.

Lockhart, Lamon, and Gick (1988) report findings that complement and confirm those of Adams *et al.* (1988). Prior to the presentation of the insight problems, their subjects were given hint sentences. These hints were either in a declarative or puzzle-like form. For example, a declarative hint was, "It made the clergyman happy to marry several people each week." The same hint in the puzzle form was, "The man married several people each week because it made him happy." followed a few seconds by the word, "clergyman."

In three separate studies Lockhart and his colleagues established that hints in the puzzle form facilitated solution of the insight problems more than hints in the declarative form. Further this occurred despite the fact that there was no difference in memory for the two types of sentences. Thus, the two sets of studies indicate that content alone does not determine the degree of transfer. Even when the content is the same, transfer is more likely if the processing operations for acquiring the information are similar to those necessary for solving the insight problems. Knowledge of relevant facts is not enough.

How might we understand these findings? In Chapter 1 a distinction was made between declarative knowledge and procedural knowledge. Although theorists do not agree how procedural knowledge relates to declarative knowledge (for example, Anderson, 1987; Kolers & Smythe, 1984), they do agree that procedural knowledge is a determinant of our cognitive skills. Solving a problem requires knowledge of how to operate on the available information. For example, solving a linear equation such as $5X + 2 = 3X + 8$ requires several operations to achieve the solution, $X = 3$ (Simon, 1980). Problem solving requires the activation of appropriate operating processes. The insight problems are difficult because it is not clear what mental operations are appropriate for solving these problems. Presumably, when hints are in a puzzle form, they elicit the same operations that are necessary for the problem itself. For instance, the problem orientation of the clue for the marriage problem leads to the operation of "given the goal of understanding why it might be commonplace to marry several times per week, check to see if the interpretation of marry can be 'conduct a marriage ceremony' rather than 'get married' " (Adams *et al.*, 1988, p. 173). Thus, in this puzzle-like hint, the subject is learning to operate on the interpretation of "marry," which is the appropriate operation for the problem itself.

This research on the transfer of procedural knowledge in problem solving indicates the importance of acquiring "knowledge that includes information about the conditions and the constraints of its use" (Bransford, Sherwood, Vye & Rieser, 1986, p. 1081). The competent problem solver is the child who has had experience solving problems and has, therefore, acquired knowledge about how concepts and procedures are applicable for solving problems (Simon, 1980).

▶ DOMAIN-SPECIFIC KNOWLEDGE

To this point the emphasis has been on the development of general problem-solving skills. In their efforts to identify the general cognitive processes of problem solving, researchers have used tasks that, although requiring prior knowledge, do not require extensive prior knowledge. Solution of the problems in Figure 9-11, for example, do require world knowledge, but not the type of knowledge structures that are required for physics problems. Much of our problem solving occurs in knowledge-rich domains, domains in which our knowledge base is intricate and relevant for solving problems. Indeed, children spend a good portion of their time in school attempting to solve domain-specific problems. As children acquire knowledge in, for example, mathematics and science, they become more proficient at solving problems in these domains. Undoubtedly, some of the developmental changes we observe in problem solving represent changes in domain-specific knowledge. We saw hints of this in Chapter 7. Children with knowledge of chess outperformed novice adults in a task requiring memory for the spatial layout of chess pieces. Thus, as children have more experience with a domain we might expect that they acquire specific knowledge structures and processes that will facilitate problem solving in that domain.

Recognizing the importance of domain-specific knowledge, many researchers have focused on problem solving in specific domains such as mathematics (for example, Owen & Sweller, 1985), physics, (for example, Larkin, 1980; Larkin, McDermott, Simon & Simon, 1980) and computer programming (for example, Pennington, 1987). The primary goal of this research has been to characterize the knowledge structures of experts in a given domain and to contrast these with the knowledge structures of novices. This has been done with two ultimate goals in mind: one is to determine how different types of knowledge structures influence the problem-solving process; the other is to determine how a novice becomes an expert.

EXPERT-NOVICE DIFFERENCES

Converging sets of experimental data indicate that experts and novices do not represent problems in the same way. One important difference has been demonstrated in such diverse domains as chess (Chase & Simon, 1973), baseball (Voss, Vesonder & Spilich, 1980), physics (Chi, Feltovich & Glaser, 1981), and the films *Star Wars* and *The Empire Strikes Back* (Means & Voss, 1985). Experts represent problems in terms of categories that are more abstract than those of novices (Honeck, Firment & Case, 1987). When, for example, experts (Ph.D. students in physics) and novices (undergraduates who had just completed a semester course in mechanics) were asked to sort physics problems into categories, the novices sorted the problems on the basis of surface similarities. Novices categorized together problems that had objects (for example, springs) or key words (for example, friction) in common. The experts, however, sorted the problems on the basis of the major physics principle (for example, the Law of Conservation of Energy) that governed solution of the problem (Chi, Feltovich & Glaser, 1981). Thus, experts represent problems in terms of the physical laws that are relevant to solution. Novices represent problems in terms of the literal components stated in the problem. This is the case even when verbal protocols indicate that novices know the physical laws or principles that are relevant for problem solution.

Experts and novices also differ in which features of a problem they consider relevant for solving that problem. When asked to read problems and to specify the features of a problem that would influence their basic approach to the problem, experts were more likely to mention second-order features (for example, statics). These are features that are not mentioned in the problem statement, but can be derived from the literal features of the problem statement.

Novices, however, were more likely to mention literal features of the problem (for example, springs) (see also Schoenfeld & Herrmann, 1982). Furthermore, although think-aloud protocols indicate that both experts and novices bring tacit knowledge to physics problems, novices are more likely to generate wrong inferences or fail to generate inferences that are necessary for problem solution. These data suggest "that experts perceive more in a problem statement than do novices" (Chi, Feltovich & Glaser, 1981, p. 147).

These differences in problem representation appear to reflect differences in the organization of the knowledge that experts and novices bring to a problem. Expert knowledge is organized as schemas of principles. When a schema is activated by the data available in a problem statement, the knowledge contained in the schema provides the information that leads to appropriate inferences and the procedural knowledge for using specific equations. Thus, in the process of representing a problem, experts "classify a problem as an instance of a known category of problems" (Holyoak, 1984b, p. 205). These findings suggest that when subjects have extensive knowledge in a given domain they do recognize problems that are analogous. Novices, however, have more fragmentary knowledge of the domain; they do not have the schematic knowledge base of experts.

Two sets of data support the assumption of such a difference in knowledge organization. Chi and her colleagues (Chi, Feltovich & Glaser, 1981) asked subjects to elaborate on 20 concepts that had been mentioned by experts and novices in the problem-sorting task. Novices and experts were given three minutes to tell everything they could about each of the concepts. These elaboration protocols were then analyzed and conceptual networks derived; these networks represent how concepts were related in the protocol. Figure 9-13 depicts the conceptual network of a novice and an expert for the concept, inclined plane. As the expert network indicates, the principles of mechanics (for example, Conservation of Energy) were immediately linked to the inclined plane concept. Furthermore procedural knowledge for applying the principles is predominant in the conceptual network. This contrasts with the conceptual network of the novice. Although this network is rich with associations, mention of the Conservation of Energy principle is casual and the procedures for problem solution are not mentioned at all. Unlike the experts, the novices did not have representations that contained explicit procedures for problem solution (Chi, Glaser & Rees, 1982).

The richness of expert knowledge structures is further evident in their hierarchical organization of problem categories. Experts not only have more abstract problem schemas, they also have a hierarchical organization of problem subschemas. Subjects were asked to sort 40 physics problems into categories (represented by circles in Figure 9-13; the numerals indicate the number of problems in each category). After this initial sorting, the subjects were given the opportunity to subdivide each of these categories, if they wished (represented by squares and hexagons). Following this they were asked to combine their initial categories in whatever way they wished (represented by triangles).

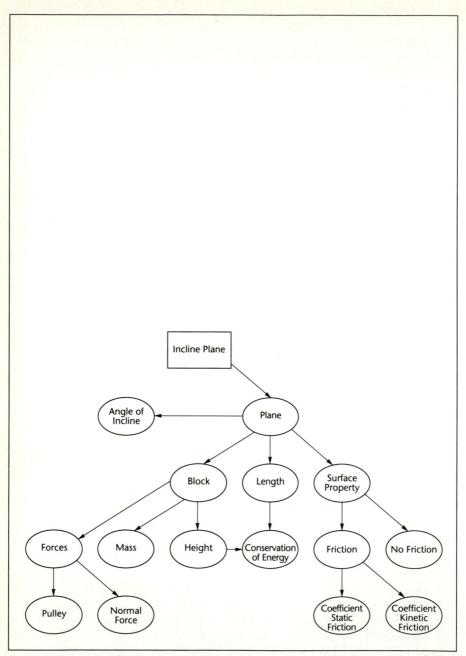

▶ **FIGURE 9-13** *Network representation of a novice schema of an inclined plane (left). Network representation of an expert schema of an inclined plane (right).* (From Chi, Feltovich & Glaser, 1981.)

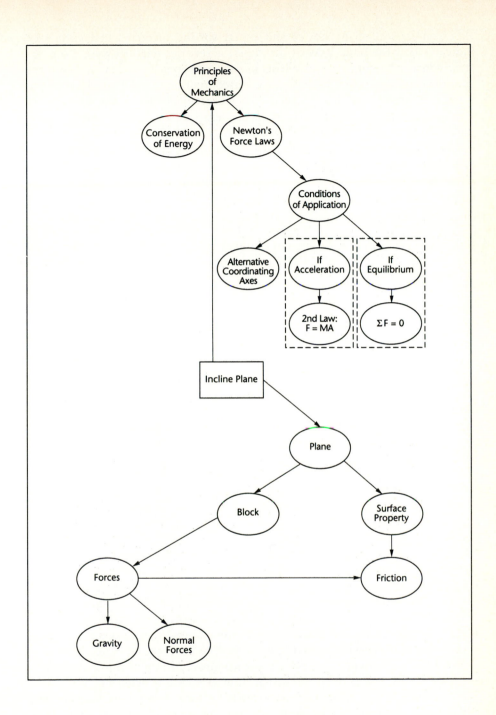

Comparison of the novice and expert sortings depicted in Figure 9-14 indicates that the basic level of the expert categories (circles) were more abstract, incorporating more problems in each category, and that two or three superordinate categories (triangles) were used to organize all 40 problems. One novice, however, had no evidence of a hierarchical knowledge of problem types, and the other had an incomplete hierarchical organization that only included 24 of the 40 problems (Chi, Glaser & Rees, 1982). Thus, converging evidence indicates that even when experts and novices have knowledge of the same physics principles, the knowledge is embedded in very different knowledge structures. Similar effects have been demonstrated as college students acquire knowledge of mathematics (Schoenfeld & Herrmann, 1982).

STRATEGIES   We have evidence that different knowledge structures lead to different problem-solving strategies. Think-aloud protocols indicate that when experts solve a physics problem they use a working-forward strategy. They start with equations that involve the known variables of the problem and work forward to the desired unknown variable. Novices use a working-backward strategy that starts with an equation that involves the desired unknown and they then work back towards the known variables.

To illustrate, assume that two equations are available:

1. $e = f(a,b)$
2. $d = f(c,e)$

Suppose that in a given problem a, b, and c are givens (knowns), and the d is the desired goal (the unknown). The forward-working strategy chooses Equation 1 because the a and b are known. After e is calculated the e and c are knowns and the second equation is selected. The working-backward strategy starts with Equation 2 since it includes the desired unknown, d. Since the e is unknown, the first equation is then selected to determine e (Chi, Glaser & Rees, 1982).

Why this difference? Some models assume that novices are driven by the literal data of the problem statement. That is, as illustrated earlier, novices are particularly attentive to the literal terms of the problem. Since the goal is to determine d, novices start with an equation that contains the desired goal. Expert problem solvers, however, are driven by schemas. Solving a problem begins with identifying the appropriate schema. Since such schemas include solution procedures, it is assumed that experts work with these procedures. Other models assume that as experts acquire knowledge in a domain their initial use of the backward-working procedure becomes so automated that they can work forward through the procedures. Although this issue is not resolved, it does raise questions about how expertise is acquired. We return to this issue in a later section of this chapter. Further, if we accept that solution procedures can become automatic, it raises important questions about how representative verbal protocols are of the actual processes of problem solving.

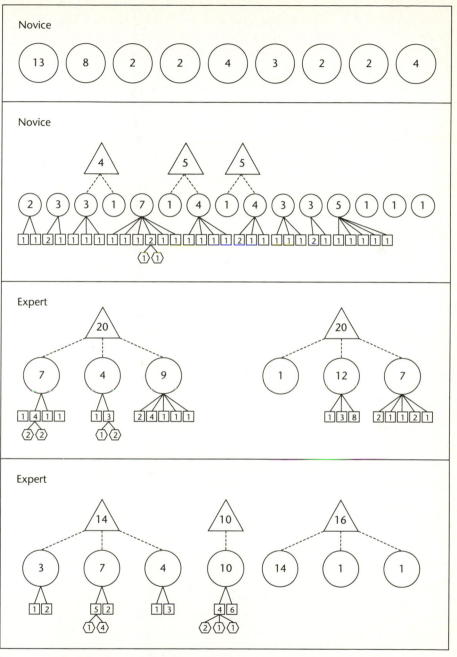

FIGURE 9-14 *Groupings made by novices and experts on a hierarchical sorting task. Circular nodes are the preliminary groups, squares and hexagons are subsequent discriminations, and triangles are the combinations. (From Chi, Glaser & Rees, 1982.)*

Although verbal protocols have proven to be valuable, we should be sensitive to their limitations. These limitations are obvious for children, but even adults are not always able to consciously access and verbalize their thinking processes. Indeed, if we could accurately describe our thinking processes cognitive psychology would be an easy enterprise.

In an effort to assess the development of children's scientific knowledge without relying on verbal protocols, Siegler (1978) introduced a rule assessment methodology that used variations of Piaget's formal operations problems. For example, in the balance scale problem the experimenter put weights of various amounts at different locations on the apparatus pictured in Figure 9-15. The children were asked to predict what would happen when a lever was released that held the balance scale in a horizontal position.

Siegler reasoned that there were four types of rules that children might use to solve this problem; the decision trees for these rules are illustrated in Figure 9-16. The simplest rule, Rule 1, is one in which only weight is considered; if the weights are the same the child predicts that the scale will balance, if the weights are not the same the child predicts that the arm with the greater weight will go down. Rule 2 considers distance as well as weight, but only if the weight is the same on each side. Rules 3 and 4 are progressively more sophisticated in the consideration of weight and distance dimensions.

The children were given the variations of the problem illustrated in Figure 9-15. These variations made it possible to predict different types of behavior patterns for each type of rule. For example, if children used Rule 1 to solve the problems, then they should be correct on the balance, weight, and conflict-weight problems, but make the indicated errors on the other three problem types. If children's problem-solving strategies conformed to the rules proposed by Siegler there should be four different patterns of performance, one for each type of rule.

Of the 120 5-, 9-, 13-, and 17-year-olds tested by Siegler, over 80 percent of them had performance patterns that fit one of the rule types. As might be expected, there were developmental changes in the rules underlying performance. Rule 1 described the behavior of the 5-year-olds. Between 9 and 17 there was a shift from Rule 2 to Rule 3. Even the 17-year-olds were unlikely to use Rule 4, the most sophisticated rule.

DEVELOPMENTAL DIFFERENCES IN EXPERTISE   Most studies of expert-novice differences have assessed these differences at one age, most often with college students. Means and Voss (1985), however, have sought to determine whether young experts have the same knowledge organization of a domain as older experts. This is not an easy question to address since there are very few domains in which young children are experts. Clearly, such domains as physics, mathematics, and computer programming, which have been the focus of many studies, do not qualify. Means and Voss (1985) identified, however, one domain that was familiar to young children as well as college students, the subject matter of the movies *Star Wars* and *The Empire Strikes Back*.

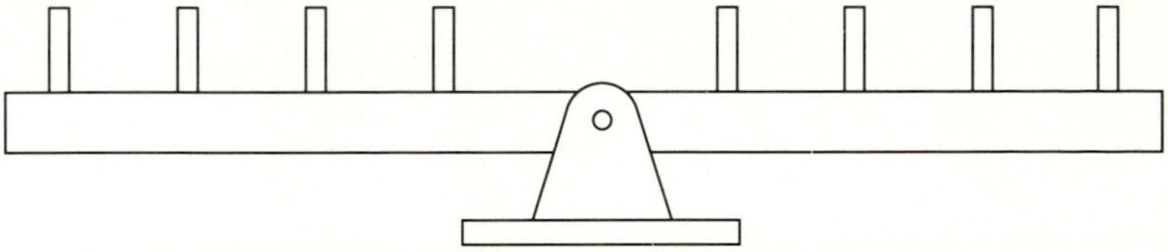

Balance Scale Apparatus

Problem-Type	Rule			
	I	II	III	IV
Balance 	100	100	100	100
Weight 	100	100	100	100
Distance 	0 (Should say "Balance")	100	100	100
Conflict–Weight 	100	100	33 (Chance Responding)	100
Conflict–Distance 	0 (Should say "Right Down")	0 (Should say "Right Down")	33 (Chance Responding)	100
Conflict–Balance 	0 (Should say "Right Down")	0 (Should say "Right Down")	33 (Chance Responding)	100

▶ **FIGURE 9-15** *Predictions for percentage of correct answers and error patterns for children using different rules. (From Siegler, 1978.)*

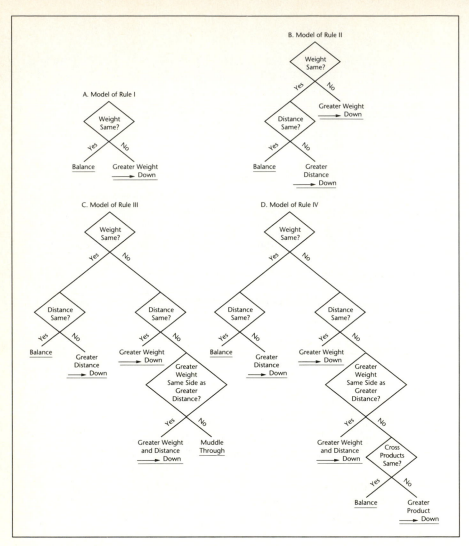

FIGURE 9-16 *Decision tree model of rules for performing balance scale task.* (From Siegler, 1978.)

To assess children's knowledge of these movies, Means and Voss first constructed an idealized hierarchical structure of the combined contents of these movies. The researchers used "a stepwise procedure in which high-level goals were determined, the basic activities were delineated, and the subgoal structure linking the high-level goals and the basic activities was derived" (p. 747). This hierarchy consisted of 43 basic actions (for example, Luke goes to Yoda); several levels of subgoals; and high-level political, military, and ethical goals.

Students in grades two, three, five, seven, nine, and college were designated either novices or experts on the basis of their knowledge of ten basic actions (for example, "What important information did R2 D2 have?") in the idealized hierarchial structure. Experts were those subjects who correctly identified five or more of the ten actions. Novices correctly identified one to four of the actions. The experts averaged 6.70 combined viewings of the two films; the novices averaged 2.78 viewings.

The primary task was a question-and-answer task in which subjects were asked to identify ten basic actions. If the subjects correctly identified a basic action, they were then given a why question (Means & Voss, 1985, p. 748):

> The question began with the phrase, "Why was it important to the Rebel Alliance (Empire) . . . ?" and concluded with insertion of the prior response of the subject. If the subject's response correctly identified a subgoal, another "Why" question was then asked which involved use of the same format as the preceding "Why" question. However, in this case the previously stated correct subgoal response was inserted rather than the correct basic action response. This procedure continued until the subject did not produce an appropriate response or until the subject stated a goal of the highest level.

The data indicate that representation of the *Star Wars* movies was hierarchical for both younger and older experts. The older experts, however, had more information in their hierarchies. They could identify more basic actions, their subgoal structures were fuller, and they identified more high-level goals. There also were qualitative differences in the high-level goals mentioned. The expert college students were more likely to state political and ethical goals, in addition to military goals. The younger experts tended only to state military goals. Further, older experts interpreted *Star Wars* in terms of international conflict; the younger experts had a military-oriented good guy–bad guy schema for the story. Novice differences indicate that older novices, who did not differ significantly from the younger novices in their knowledge of the basic actions, were more likely to state high-level goals that were influenced by an international conflict schema.

Taken together, the data suggest that older subjects came to *Star Wars* with an international conflict schema which affected their interpretation of the films. Older experts differed from older novices in the amount of information they had about the actions and subgoals of the story, not in their knowledge of the theme or higher-level goals of the films. Further, if we assume that younger subjects in general come to the films with a good guy–bad guy schema, then the data indicate that the younger novices were not able to use this schema to interpret the story. It is only when the younger subjects have extensive familiarity with the films that they go beyond the bottom-up representation of the actions and develop the military-oriented representation of good guys–bad guys.

This study raises important questions about the acquisition of expertise. As we attempt to determine how expertise is acquired, we will need to consider such factors as the nature of the prior knowledge that students of different ages bring to a situation as well as their ability to use their schematic knowledge to organize new information. Although these complexities are far from being worked out, we do have the beginnings of some understanding of how a novice becomes an expert.

THE ACQUISITION OF EXPERTISE

As researchers have identified the differences between experts and novices, they have become increasingly concerned with how knowledge states change as an individual becomes an expert (for example, Karat, 1982). Many attempts to describe this process have used specific computer programs to model the change. Larkin (1981, 1985), for example, incorporated a learning mechanism into a program for solving physics problems. Although these programs have their limitations and do not fully capture the ability of experts to recognize the common, but abstract, features of problems, these efforts serve to emphasize the importance of the acquisition of procedural knowledge and the usefulness of characterizing procedural knowledge as production systems.

Expert problem solvers not only have a large body of declarative knowledge, but also a wealth of procedural knowledge. Problem solving is the art of *using* knowledge to achieve a goal. Experts have acquired procedures for operating in a problem domain. They enlist mental operations or procedures as they attempt to solve problems. Further, it is not enough to have knowledge of procedures; we must know when a given procedure is appropriate. How might we think about such procedural knowledge? Many theorists have found it useful to represent procedural knowledge by production systems. These are sets of production rules. Each production rule consists of a condition-action or if-then pair. That is, the condition specifies a particular situation. If that situation occurs, then a certain action is taken. Such rule-based representations have been used in many computer models of problem solving.

Obviously, production systems become very complex when they are used to model expert rule-based representations in such domains as medical diagnosis (Shortliffe, 1976). Production systems have the advantage, however, that despite complexity they can be specific enough to be written as computer programs. Thus, these programs can be run to determine if they accurately simulate human problem solving. Furthermore, these programs can incorporate the general information-processing principles (for example, limited capacity of working memory) that appear to have psychological importance (see, for example, Klahr, Langley & Neches, 1987).

Some theorists have likened the acquisition of cognitive skills in a given domain to the acquisition of motor skills (for example, Carey, 1979). This analogy serves to highlight the importance of learning condition-action pairs, of learning which actions are appropriate for which conditions. A basketball player not only knows many facts about the game, but also has an extensive production system. At any given moment the conditions of the game determine whether the player passes, drives for the basket, or pulls up for a jump shot. After years of play, he can quickly recognize a situation and carry out the action that best fits a condition. Similarly, as we have seen, physics experts readily recognize specific types of problems (that is, certain conditions) and readily use certain procedures (that is, actions) in these conditions.

An expert has learned to recognize thousands of different situations (Chase & Simon, 1973; Simon, 1978), to execute many types of actions, and to associate the many different conditions with appropriate actions. With practice these condition-action pairs become automatic. Most skilled adult readers, for example, can pronounce approximately 50,000 words, without special efforts to sound out the words; the pronunciation is automatic.

Several theorists have attempted to characterize the types of changes that occur as a skill is acquired (for example, Fitts, 1964; Anderson, 1982). These efforts suggest three stages in the acquisition of skills (Stillings, Feinstein, Garfield, Rissland, Rosenbaum, Weisler & Baker-Ward, 1987). These stages are meant to represent the often slow transition from a dominance of controlled processes to a dominance of automatic processes.

The first stage, the *interpretive stage,* is dominated by efforts to learn what is relevant in the task, by acquiring declarative knowledge and by using general processes, often verbalized, for executing the actions specified in declarative knowledge. For example, when beginning tennis players learn to serve, they consciously think about the several parts of the serve. They have to remember how and where to throw the ball, to drop the racquet head behind their backs, to bring the racquet up as the ball reaches the top of the toss, to hit the ball, and to step forward as they do so, and then to follow through after they hit the ball. The instruction they receive is encoded as a set of facts about the skill. These facts can be interpreted to generate behavior (Anderson, 1982, p. 370). Each of the parts of the serve requires controlled processes (that is, attention) for execution. Often in this stage working memory is overloaded, because much of the action requires controlled processes (attention) for interpreting the declarative knowledge (compare, Britton & Tesser, 1982).

In the second stage of acquisition, the *compiled stage,* the parts of the skill are chunked or compiled into a procedure that is specific to the skill. Thus, in this stage the tennis players have organized the parts of the serve into a single procedure. The voluntary awareness of initiating the serve leads to the entire procedure being run off without attention to the parts of the serve. This stage is characterized by speedup of the procedure, the dropout of verbal rehearsal, and the elimination of part-by-part execution of the skill. The load on working memory is reduced, and a production rule is created that collapses a sequence of productions (Anderson, 1982, 1987).

In the final stage, the *automatic stage,* the skill continues to improve and becomes more automatic. Anderson (1982) argues that discrimination and generalization processes induce more refined production rules. Thus, new production rules are created that capture the commonalities of two or more production rules. Furthermore, discrimination processes result in production rules that restrict the range of applications of production to appropriate situations. Although there are differences of opinion about what changes in this stage and how much attention this stage requires, it is clear that complex skills are not completely automatic. Rather, "optimal skilled performance seems to balance the speed and high capacity of automatic processes with the goal-directedness and flexibility of controlled processes" (Stillings *et al.*, 1987, p. 59). Thus, production system models indicate a qualitative change in how controlled and automatic processes interact in skilled performance. Driving a car may best make this point. After years of experience, much of the skill is automatic unless circumstances (for example, icy roads) bring them into awareness.

CONDITIONS THAT PROMOTE THE ACQUISITION OF KNOWLEDGE   One important problem that faces cognitive psychologists is to specify the conditions that promote the acquisition of knowledge and problem-solving skills. In their efforts to explore this issue, researchers (for example, Sherwood, Kinzer, Bransford & Franks, 1987; Campione & Brown, in press) have been influenced by the work of Vygotsky, a Soviet psychologist. Vygotsky (1978) made a distinction between what children can do on their own and what they can do with adult scaffolding (help). Those problems that children cannot solve alone but can solve with prompts define the children's *zone of proximal development*, or "the distance between the actual development level as determined by independent problem solving and the level of potential development as determined through problem solving under adult guidance or in collaboration with more capable peers" (Vygotsky, 1978, p. 86). Thus, the zone of proximal development defines those cognitive functions that are in the process of developing.

Vygotsky believed that much of children's learning is socially mediated (Campione & Brown, in press, p. 8):

> Children experience cognitive activities in social situations and come to internalize them gradually over time. At the outset, the child and adult work together, with the adult doing most of the cognitive work while simultaneously serving as a model. As the child acquires some degree of skill, the adult cedes the child responsibility for part of the job and does correspondingly less of the work. Gradually, the child takes more of the initiative, and the adult serves primarily to provide support and help when the child experiences problems. Finally, the child becomes able to take over complete responsibility for the task and carries it out independently.

To illustrate, consider the exchange between a mother and her six-year-old son. The mother has been asked to assist her child in sorting and learning the organization of a set of pictures of common household objects. The pictures have been sorted into boxes and the mother and child are reviewing where the objects are placed (Rogoff & Gardner, 1984, p. 108):

► *Mother:* Just look at it again, and see if we can see any similarities that'll help you remember. Maybe—first you—oh, first you get up in the morning. *(Points at the box containing grooming items and looks at child.)* Then you get ready—

Child (interrupting): Brush your teeth.

Mother: Yeah, brush your teeth. *(Touches items in the box containing grooming items.)* So we'll remember those things go there. Then you eat your breakfast. *(Touches items in the box containing tableware items and looks at child.)* Then maybe after breakfast, maybe *(gesturing toward child)* you went to mow the lawn or something like—we'll make a little story. *(Touches items in grooming box.)* Like you got up in the morning *(looking at child)*, and got ready. *(Touches items in the tableware box.)* Then we ate our breakfast. *(Touches the items in the box containing cutting items.)* Then we went and mowed the lawn. *(Looks at child.)*

Child (nodding): And then we. . . .

Mother: And then we *(pauses, touching items in the box containing cooking items)* went and cooked something *(pauses and looks at child).*

Child: For lunch. And *(points in the box containing cleaning items).*

Mother: And after lunch we *(pauses, pointing in the cleaning box).*

Child: Cleaned up. *(Rocks forward in chair.)*

Mother: We cleaned up, and then we *(pauses, pointing in the box containing mechanical items, and looks at child).* Maybe we went to the store to look at *(pauses, looking at the child and smiling).*

Child: To look at things that have electricity in them. *(Looks at mother.)*

Mother: Okay. *(Gestures to all boxes, then sits back in chair.)* See if you can tell me the story. *(Touches child.)* Again, how did we do it? *(Points at grooming box.)*

The mother has related the sorting task to daily activities that are familiar to the child. She provides scaffolding by making her messages redundant (for example, labels and points to a box). As she withdraws the scaffolding, she pauses and gives the child a chance to contribute. If the child needs help, she supplies hints (for example, points at the appropriate box). At the beginning the mother is providing the structure, but by the end the child is taking responsibility for the task. Thus, in this view children acquire cognitive skills with scaffolding that is gradually withdrawn as the children acquire expertise (see also Heckhausen, 1987).

Furthermore, we have experimental evidence that, as expected by Vygotsky's position, collaborative problem solving is more beneficial to the acquisition of problem-solving skills than the experience of solving problems alone (for example, Amigues, 1988; Azmita, 1988; Damon & Killen, 1982). Azmita (1988) assessed the model-building skills of five-year-olds and identified a group of experts and a group of novices. The children then worked in one of three conditions for two sessions in which they built copies of Legos models. The children either worked alone, in same-ability dyads (expert and novice dyads), or in mixed-ability dyads in which one child was a novice and the other an expert. After these sessions the children were tested alone on another Legos model and the block design subtest of the Wechsler Preschool and Primary Mental Intelligence Scale.

Only the novices who worked with experts improved across sessions and this improvement generalized to the last session when they worked alone. This was even the case for the block design test. Thus, from an early age children can benefit more from working with an expert partner than from working alone. And, importantly, the strategies they acquire during collaborative problem solving generalize to new problems and to working alone.

Sherwood and his colleagues (Sherwood, Kinzer, Bransford & Franks, 1987; Sherwood, Kinzer, Hasselbring & Bransford, 1987) have argued that the natural scaffolding that occurs in everyday learning is effective because it occurs in the "context of meaningful, ongoing activities" (p. 94). In these everyday activities parents, friends, and peers play an important role as mediators of children's cognitive activities. They monitor performance, supply feedback, help children connect events, and help separate relevant from irrelevant information. That is, effective mediators are sensitive to a child's zone of proximal development and, thus, their hints and prompts promote learning.

Sherwood and his colleagues further argue that one of the advantages of everyday or informal learning is that children have a better understanding of new information because they are more likely to learn the functions of the information. Children learn not only what a screwdriver looks like, they also learn how to use it. Thus, Sherwood and his colleagues argue that everyday learning is effective because children learn how to use concepts and procedures to solve problems. Further, they argue that often this is not the case in more formal, school learning situations. Children acquire facts and procedures with little appreciation of how this knowledge can simplify problem solving.

In a series of experiments, Sherwood and his colleagues demonstrate the importance of learning in a problem-solving context. To illustrate, college students were given 13 factual passages on topics that occur in middle school and high school science classes (for example, the kinds of high-carbohydrate foods that are healthy versus less healthy). Half the students simply read the passages with the intent to remember them; the other half read the same passage in the context of the problems that Indiana Jones might encounter during a trip to South America. For example, the students were asked to consider what kinds of foods should be taken on the trip and then read the passage on high-carbohydrate foods.

The students received either a recall test or a problem-solving task. The recall task required them to name the topics of the passages they had read. The problem-solving task asked them to imagine that they were planning a trip to the desert area of the western United States in search of relics in Pueblo caves. They were to suggest 10 areas of information that were important for planning, being as explicit as possible. The results of both tests confirmed that the problem-solving context enhanced performance. Furthermore, it was clear that the students who acquired information in the problem-solving context spontaneously used this information to make a new set of plans.

These findings confirm the importance of a problem-oriented context during acquisition and support the transfer research reported earlier in which problem-oriented presentation of relevant information facilitated the solution of insight problems. Taken together, the research indicates that problem-solving skills are-enhanced when students acquire knowledge in a context that introduces facts and procedures as tools for solving problems. Sherwood and his colleagues have demonstrated that formal learning situations can be arranged to provide such a context. We might expect, further, that the development of problem-solving skills in everyday, informal settings will be influenced by how effectively social mediators monitor a child's zone of proximal development. That is, to be effective, mediators must be aware of the experiences of the learner that can provide a context for new learning (Sherwood, Kinzer, Hasselbring & Bransford, 1987). Both in and out of school the development of problem-solving skills will depend upon the extent to which a child has the opportunity to solve problems in a context that provides appropriate scaffolding (compare, White, 1971).

▶ SUMMARY

In this chapter we considered the development of problem-solving skills. Critical to problem solving is representation of the problem. From an early age both top-down and bottom-up processes contribute to problem representation. Three heuristic strategies for solving problems were considered. One, plans are used to mentally represent subgoals and strategies for solving a problem. Although young children are capable of simple plans that establish subgoals, with development they engage in more advanced planning, become more sophisticated in their sequencing of subgoals, and more selective in matching strategies to the task demands of a given problem. Furthermore, older children have better strategies for regulating their behavior when a goal is not immediately attainable.

Two, some problems can be solved by generating and testing hypotheses. Preschoolers do test simple hypotheses but have limited abilities for testing hypotheses systematically. Even college students, however, do not always use optimal strategies for testing hypotheses. To some extent, like young children, their strategies are influenced by problem content rather than the logic of hypothesis testing. Three, familiarity with analogous problems can facilitate the problem solving of young children as well as college students. The process is not automatic, however. Several factors, including the extent of experience with analogous problems, contribute to the transfer of solutions from one problem to another. Problem solving in general appears to be facilitated by experience that stresses procedures for solving problems.

Domain-specific knowledge affects our representations of problems and the strategies we use to solve them. Comparisons of experts and novices in a domain indicate that expert knowledge is organized as abstract schemas that incorporate the basic principles of the domain and procedures for solving specific categories of problems. Novices, however, appear to have knowledge structures that are less hierarchical and emphasize the concrete terms of problems. Models of the acquisition of expertise assume that the first stage is an interpretative one in which the novice learns what is relevant to the task. This is followed by a stage in which the parts of the task are compiled; the several parts of the task are integrated into a single routine. In the final stage the routine becomes more automatic. Finally, Vygotsky and others have argued that acquisition of knowledge and problem-solving skills is maximized when a novice is guided by a more knowledgeable individual who initially models problem solution but yields responsibility for problem solution as the novice acquires knowledge and skills.

10

Social Cognition

Children develop in a social context. From birth infants are immersed in a social environment. Initially, this social environment is limited to parents or a few caretakers. "It is an environment in which other persons are perceptually salient, an environment that places social demands on the infant, and one that responds to the infant's actions in predictable ways" (Ostrom, 1984, p. 25). In daily rituals, such as feeding and bathing, infants not only acquire behaviors that facilitate the routine, but also acquire expectations about the behavior of others. Thus, we saw in Chapter 5 that, early in development, children acquire scripts or general event representations for familiar events, scripts that have slots for actors and their actions.

As children mature, their social world expands and each social context makes its own demands on the child. Thus, in this country, by preschool age most children spend some part of each week outside the home in a day-care or nursery-school setting. As children enter each new social context, they must acquire knowledge about that situation, knowledge that will make it possible for them to behave in ways that are appropriate for the situation. Preschoolers at home alone with their mothers do not need to know anything about sharing toys. Those same children in a day-care setting, however, must learn to negotiate the use of toys with their peers. As children enter more and more social contexts, they acquire considerable knowledge about their social world, knowledge that is critical for establishing and maintaining social relations.

In the 1980s a new subdiscipline, social cognition, developed as two disciplines, social psychology and cognitive psychology, interacted. Each of these disciplines brings to the interchange its own distinctive features. We have seen that cognitive psychology focuses on the mental processes and contents of individuals' minds as they work on tasks, often in social isolation. Typically these tasks are circumscribed with well-defined goals. Social psychology, however, focuses on behavior, with an emphasis on interactions between persons. Furthermore, social psychology is concerned with noncognitive processes (for example, emotions, motivation), as well as cognition. Thus, social cognition is not simply a subarea of cognition, but an interdisciplinary area that brings together the assumptions and methods of two disciplines (Holyoak & Gordon, 1984).

Social cognition is a young subdiscipline and, as such, is still establishing how the emphases of the two disciplines will be integrated. Indeed, there is no agreed-upon definition of social cognition (Ostrom, 1984) but, for our purposes, one offered by Shantz (1982) should serve to highlight the potential breadth of the field. "The term refers usually to conceptions and reasoning about people, the self, relations between people, social groups, roles and rules, and the relation of such conceptions to social behavior" (p. 376). In contrast with some models of social behavior (for example, Bijou & Baer, 1961), social cognition "attributes an active, constructive role to the child. It begins with the assumption that the child does not simply receive social input, but is a thinking and reasoning actor in the social world" (Sherrod & Lamb, 1981, pp. 2–3). Social knowledge is constructed through social interaction.

In previous chapters, the emphasis has been on the development of children's knowledge about the object world. Here the focus is on the development of children's knowledge about the social world. Although Piaget assumed that knowledge of the social world parallels knowledge of the physical world (Piaget, 1963), some researchers have questioned this position (for example, Glick, 1978; Hoffman, 1981). These psychologists recognize that, in many ways, people differ from things. Clearly, what children come to know about people is different than what they know about tables and chairs. Thus, we can ask "when and how children develop the capacities to identify, remember, and recognize people as distinct from inanimate objects; make inferences about the behavioral propensities, motivations and emotions of other people; attribute meaning to their own social experiences; remain aware of and open to influences by the social environment; and identify themselves as similar to, yet distinct from others" (Sherrod & Lamb, 1981, p. 2).

We might also ask whether knowledge of the social world in some way entails cognitive structures and processes that are distinct from the more general cognitive structures and processes that have been the focus of this book. Since we have no evidence that this is the case, the emphasis in this chapter is on the development of children's domain-specific knowledge about the social world. No attempt will be made to provide a comprehensive review of the development of social cognition (see Shantz, 1983, for a review). Rather, this chapter will focus on a few key issues, the relevant developmental research, and how social cognition relates to cognition in general.

▶   ## INFANT RESPONSIVENESS TO PEOPLE

From an early age infants are responsive to people. Here we consider the nature of this responsiveness and the early development of social relations. In their daily routines infants have innumerable opportunities to learn about people in general and their caregivers in particular. During the first year they come to have expectations about the behavior of others, to imitate the actions of others, and to use others as sources of information.

DISTINGUISHING PEOPLE FROM NONPEOPLE

Although the lists vary, researchers agree that there are important differences between social and nonsocial objects (see, for example, Ostrom, 1984). Critical to an understanding of the social world is the ability to distinguish social objects from nonsocial objects. A basic question is when and how children make this distinction. To address this question, we must specify how social objects and nonsocial objects differ. We will begin by defining social objects as *conspecifics,* members of the same species. Thus for humans, people are social objects. At some point in our development, we all come to distinguish conspecifics from nonconspecifics. This distinction has obvious adaptive value and is made by many species.

Let us consider some of the possible ways that people differ from nonsocial objects. People are animate. The movements of people are self-initiated. An important difference between people and things is the animate-inanimate distinction. Three-year-olds are sensitive to this distinction (Massey & Gelman, 1988). But some nonsocial objects, nonhuman animals, also are animate. People have faces and bodies with certain configurations. We can, however, make inanimate objects (for example, dolls, holograms) with human facial and body configurations. People talk, but so do radio and television. People have intentions. Some animals have intentions. My dogs have intentions when they ask for water. People make contingent responses, dogs make contingent responses, and we can make inanimate objects respond contingently. The movement of the mobile in the Rovee-Collier research paradigm (see page 88) is contingent on the infants' leg movements.

People do not differ from all other nonsocial objects on any one dimension; rather, the category "people" is specified by a set of correlated attributes (see Chapters 3 and 5 for the discussions of categorization). Animals have some of these attributes; inanimate objects also have some of the attributes.

Most developmentalists have not asked when children distinguish people from nonsocial objects but rather when infants distinguish people from inanimate objects. Two-year-olds distinguish between things and people. They know that things (for example, toys) can be manipulated and that one communicates with people. If they want a toy to move, they manipulate it. Although they talk to their dolls, they are not surprised or upset when a doll does not respond. They can be very persistent, however, if a parent does not respond to their communicative overtures. By two years of age children clearly know that people and things "have different functions and require different ways of interacting" (Legerstee, Pomerleau, Malcuit & Feider, 1987, p. 82).

Some psychologists (for example, Schaffer, 1971) have taken the position that infants are asocial at birth. These psychologists assert that, although people have characteristics that are of interest to neonates, they do not constitute a distinct class. Other psychologists have argued that infants distinguish the category of people from the category of things within the first few weeks of life (for example, Bruner, 1975). How can we resolve this issue? Are people a distinct category for young infants? In Chapter 2 we confronted a similar question about infants' perception of the human face. Although we did not find evidence of an innate ability to discriminate the facial configuration, we did find that the human face has many of the perceptual characteristics that attract infant attention.

Similarly, there is little evidence that young infants distinguish people as a class from classes of things. Rather, people have many of the characteristics that attract infant attention, characteristics such as movement (see, for example, Kaufmann, 1987), familiarity (for example, a mother's voice; see, for example, DeCasper & Fifer, 1980), and contingent responding (Watson, 1972). In order to argue that people are a distinct category for infants, we must be able to rule out the possibility that differential responding to people and objects is a function of one or more of these differences rather than a categorical discrimination between objects and people per se.

In an attempt to control for the factors that distinguish between people and objects, Frye and his colleagues (Frye, Rawling, Moore & Myers, 1983) videotaped the reactions of three- and ten-month-old infants when they were alone, with a familiar toy that was either passive or manipulated (by the mothers, although the mothers were not visible) to be actively interactive with the infants, and with their mothers who were either passive or active and interacting with the infants. Undergraduates and parents of young children were asked to make the following judgments about the responses of the infants: (a) whether the infant was alone or not; (b) if not alone, whether the mother or the object was present; and (c) whether the object or mother was active or passive.

Both sets of judges were able to determine whether the three- and ten-month-olds were alone or not and, if not, whether they were with something that was active or passive. Furthermore, the judges could tell whether the ten-month-olds were with their mothers or the object. They could not, however, make this discrimination for the three-month-olds. When familiarity, movement, and contingent responding are controlled, three-month-old infants do not differentially respond to mothers and objects.

Taken together, the data do not support the position that infants have an inborn capacity to distinguish people from things (see also Sylvester-Bradley, 1985). To determine when infants distinguish people as a category from other categories of nonsocial objects is really to ask when infants recognize the correlation of the attributes that distinguish the category "people" from nonsocial categories such as "doll" and "dog." We have seen in earlier chapters that young infants are sensitive to some of the attributes (for example, faceness, speech) that specify "people." Thus, people have many of the attributes that attract infant attention and responses, but such responsiveness does not necessarily imply that young infants perceive people categorically (see, for example, Legerstee, Pomerleau, Malcuit & Feider, 1987). Such discriminations do not indicate that young infants perceive "people" as a category of objects, distinct from all other nonsocial categories. Indeed, the Younger and Cohen (1985) research cited in Chapter 3 indicates that ten-month-olds but not seven-month-olds are capable of acquiring categories that have correlated attribute structure. The available evidence suggests that people become a distinct category for infants around nine to ten months of age.

KNOWLEDGE OF SPECIFIC PERSONS

As infants acquire knowledge about people in general they also are learning the characteristics of specific individuals (for example, the mother). We have seen that infants as young as three months recognize as familiar some visual aspect of their mothers' face. This does not mean, however, that infants this age distinguish their mothers as individuals separate from other persons. The available research indicates that prior to three months of age, infants do not visually discriminate their mothers from strangers (see Olson, 1981, for a review). Between three months and five months, however, infants do begin to differentiate their mothers from others on the basis of visual cues. Not surprisingly, considering the voice preference data (see Chapter 2), discrimination on the basis of auditory cues occurs earlier.

Important to social development is not only the perceptual recognition of the mother, but also the acquisition of knowledge about the dispositional characteristics of the mother. Mothers interact extensively with their infants and in these interactions we might expect that mothers have some consistency in how they respond to their infants (Snow, 1979). Thus, as infants learn to discriminate their mothers from others they will come to expect certain behaviors from their mothers. For example, they may come to expect a smiling face, a certain type of greeting, and so on.

In Chapter 2 evidence was presented that infants as young as three to four months acquire expectations about the regularities of perceptual events. One study (Stenberg, Campos & Emde, 1983) is suggestive that by seven months of age infants have different expectations for their mothers than for strangers. In this study the facial expressions of infants were evaluated as "a Gerber teething biscuit was given to the baby and then taken away. The infant was allowed to hold the biscuit, put it in his or her mouth, and suck on it for approximately 1–3 sec. Once this had occurred, the biscuit was slowly but deliberately removed and held just beyond the child's reach" (Stenberg et al., 1983, p. 179). This was repeated several times, first by the mother and then by a stranger in one condition and in the opposite order for a second group of infants.

Not surprisingly, the infants showed facial expressions of anger when the biscuit was removed. Further, there was more anger to the mother than the stranger, but only when the mother was second. No such order effect occurred for the stranger. It would appear that the infants were particularly angry with their mothers if they had a negative experience with a stranger and then the mothers did the same negative thing to them. We might speculate that these infants expected their mothers to comfort them after the negative experience with the stranger and were, therefore, particularly angry when this did not occur. Although these data are only suggestive, they do raise important questions about the development of children's conceptual knowledge of specific others. Our social relations are not simply governed by our ability to distinguish one person from another, but by our knowledge of specific individuals and the consequent expectations we have for social interactions with each individual.

THE DEVELOPMENT OF SOCIAL EXPECTATIONS

During their first few months of life, infants have thousands of opportunities to learn that "human beings are always the agents of certain kinds of intervention and to learn that different behaviors bring different responses" (Snow, 1979, p. 167). Snow (1979), for example, observed that maternal responses to smiles, burps, yawns, and other such behaviors were usually predictable. Consider, for instance, infants' cries, which are a frequent behavior in the early months. Adults experience physiological and emotional arousal when they hear infants cry (Lamb, 1981). This arousal usually translates into an attempt to relieve the infants' distresses. Typically, the first step in this effort is to pick up the infants and hold them, an activity which calms them and puts them in a state of quiet alertness. Thus, through the caregivers' efforts the infants go from distress to relief and alertness. Through such regularities in the behavior of caregivers, infants develop specific expectations about the behavior of others. In the distress-relief sequence the infants have the opportunity to "1) learn that distress predictably elicits an intervention that brings relief; 2) recognize the person responsible for facilitating the transition from displeasure to pleasure; 3) develop an integrated, multimodal concept of the caretaker; 4) associate the person's features with the pleasurable outcome he or she produces" (Lamb, 1981, p. 159).

Infants are not only learning the perceptual characteristics of their caregivers, but also to have expectations for the behaviors of others. For example, infants between two and six months of age will quiet at the approach of a caregiver, before there is any physical contact (Gekoski, Rovee-Collier & Carulli-Rabinowitz, 1983). One important type of expectation is that others will be responsive to the infants' behaviors. Infants are learning that specific others can be relied upon and also that they are effective individuals who have at least partial control over their own experiences. In Chapter 3 we presented evidence that, with rather limited training, two-month-olds can learn to control the action of a mobile and maintain the association between their behavior and the contingent movement of the mobile for at least three days. Although inanimate objects do not usually respond as the mobile did, young infants do have innumerable opportunities with social others to learn contingencies (Symons & Moran, 1987). We have no direct evidence, but some theorists (for example, Seligman, 1975; for a review, see Fincham & Cain, 1986) have speculated that infants raised in environments in which they lack control of important stimuli may develop cognitive and motivation deficits.

Furthermore, there is some sugestive evidence that young infants enjoy controlling events (compare, Millar, 1988). Watson and his colleague (Watson, 1972, 1979; Watson & Ramey, 1972) found that four-month-olds were more likely to smile when mobile movement was contingent on their behavior than when movement was independent of behavior. Gunnar-Vongnechten (1978) observed the affective responses of one-year-olds who either could or could not control an active and novel toy. In the experimental condition, infants could touch a panel that activated a toy monkey that banged cymbals. Infants in the control condition could not control the toy but saw it activated in a way that matched that of an experimental infant. Infants who controlled the toy were more likely to smile and laugh. Noncontrolling infants looked more to their mothers; in general, their responses indicated fear or wariness (see also Lutkenhaus, 1984).

According to Watson (1972), people are not initially a special category for infants; what is special for infants is the perception of contingency relations. Watson has hypothesized that people become important to infants because they provide contingency relations. That is, Watson assumes that young infants are sensitive to contingency relations, that contingency relations elicit pleasure in infants and that, since people are most likely to provide contingency relations, people arouse positive emotions and, thus, become important as sources of pleasure. Although we have evidence suggesting that even newborns are sensitive to contingency relations and that their attentional and affective responses are influenced by the perception of such relations (DeCasper & Carstens, 1981), we have little direct evidence of the role of contingency relations in the development of social relations. Levitt (1980), however, has demonstrated that nine- to ten-month-olds who controlled the initial appearance of a stranger (the appearance of the stranger was contingent on the infant touching a specific object) were more positive to the approach of the stranger than infants who initially experienced a noncontingent relation between their behavior and the appearance of the stranger. Taken together, we might speculate that social interactions that establish contingent relations not only foster social expectations but also feelings of pleasure. As young infants are interacting with their caregivers, they are developing social expectations, learning to control others, and experiencing pleasurable feelings in the presence of others. In this process infants are not only learning about others, but also about the self and relations between self and others. We turn to the development of the self concept in a later section of this chapter.

IMITATION

Imitation is an important means of cultural transmission. Through imitation children acquire behaviors, skills, customs, and traditions that are passed from one generation to another. Imitation is evident in newborns' facial expressions, and by the preschool years, imitation is prevalent in a wide variety of behaviors (Masur, 1988; Meltzoff, 1988b). Contrary to Piaget's position on imitation (see Chapter 2), young infants appear capable of imitating others (for discussions of early imitative behavior, see Bjorklund, 1987a; Lewis & Sullivan, 1985). Indeed, evidence suggests that humans are more imitative than any other animals (Meltzoff, 1988a). Although we have little relevant evidence, there are some data to suggest that infant imitation is not limited to the imitation of people. In a classic study, the Kelloggs (1933) raised an infant chimpanzee with their infant son, treating each equally. The chimpanzee never became human-like, but their son did engage in behaviors, such as making food barks and grunts when he saw the chimp's favorite food, that were imitative of the chimpanzee.

Not only do infants imitate the behaviors of others, but they are also capable of deferring imitative behaviors. To illustrate, Meltzoff (1988c) tested nine-month-olds with three different actions on three different objects: (a) shaking a small, plastic egg-shaped object, (b) closing a vertically mounted flap of wood that was hinged to a baseplate, and (c) pushing a small button mounted on the face of a black rectangular box. The button activated a beeper housed inside the box. Infants in the experimental condition saw each action executed three times. The control conditions varied in whether and how the adult interacted with the objects. The infants were tested for imitation either immediately after the modeling or 24 hours later.

Thus, from an early age, infants are capable of imitating the novel actions of others, and, importantly, young infants have the ability to maintain representations of these actions over a delay period. Further, there is some evidence that infants are more likely to imitate the behavior of others when the behavior serves a specific need or goal for the infant (Killen & Uzgiris, 1981). Through observations of others, infants are capable of acquiring behavior that they later use for their own purposes. One observational study in the home indicates that between 16 and 29 months immediate imitation declines and deferred imitation increases in frequency (Kuczynski, Zahn-Waxler & Radke-Yarrow, 1987). Such findings raise important questions about the relevance of imitation for the development of problem-solving skills. For example, Wishart (1986) has presented evidence that the performance of six- and twelve-month-olds on the object permanence tasks is influenced by preschool siblings who model the appropriate behaviors.

Morrison and Kuhn (1983) have demonstrated that older children are most attentive to and most likely to imitate problem-solving behaviors that are moderately different from and improvements on their own efforts. In this study four- to six-year-olds were observed as they worked with a construction set. Initially, the children worked alone with the materials, and seven levels of performance were identified. Children whose performance was low enough that improvement was a possibility were assigned to groups of four. They played at a table with the construction materials in three 10-minute sessions, each two weeks apart. Two weeks after the last group session, each child worked alone with the construction set.

Observations of others increased with age. Further, those children who showed a gain from the first to second individual test were more likely to observe the constructions of others and particularly to observe constructions that were one level above their own constructions. Thus, the children did not attend to and imitate any models available to them. Rather they focused on models that were more advanced than their own constructions, but not too advanced.

These findings suggest an important relation between imitation and cognitive skills. Children do not imitate automatically. Whether imitation occurs depends on how the characteristics of the model and the observer relate to each other. When children have models that are challenging, but not too challenging, they are most likely to imitate and enhance their own performance.

Imitation may serve more than one function. Uzgiris (1981) has argued that imitation has two functions during infancy. One, as we have seen, is cognitive and serves to facilitate understanding of puzzling events. The other is interpersonal and serves as a communicative act to express mutuality. Uzgiris (1984) found that, during the first year, mothers and infants regularly match each other's behaviors and that such matching increased during the first year. Further, interactions that feature mutual imitation typically are longer in duration than those that do not involve imitation (Field, 1978). Imitation may prolong interaction because parents' imitative responses are contingent responses that attract infant attention (Goldberg, 1977).

Young preschoolers also use imitation for communication purposes. Nadel-Brulfert and Baudonniere (1982) found that two-year-olds engaged in reciprocal imitation. Children this age readily switched between the role of model and the role of imitator. The spontaneous imitations of the children appeared to take the form of a dialogue as they explored an experimental setting with several different types of objects. Imitation appears to be an effective strategy for initiating and sustaining interaction. Lubin and Field (1981) found that, except for vocalizations, imitation was used by preschoolers most often to initiate peer interactions. As children mature and their cognitive and interpersonal skills develop, we might expect that the functions and expressions of imitation will also change (see, for example, Yando, Seitz & Zigler, 1978).

Young children not only learn through imitation of others, but also by executing the commands of others. As children acquire verbal skills, adults and siblings can direct their behavior through verbal commands. Rheingold and her colleagues (Rheingold, Cook & Kolowitz, 1987) present evidence that 18- and 24-month-olds actually enjoy carrying out the verbal commands of adults. As in the case of imitation, their behavior is influenced by these commands even after delays. Thus, from an early age, infants are inclined to learn from others, either through imitation or instruction (McLaughlin, 1983).

THE DEVELOPMENT OF SOCIAL REFERENCING

People change from one occasion to another. One important change is affective state. We feel joy, sorrow, and pain. We express these affective states in our facial expressions, vocal patterns, and gestures. Adults are receptive to these expressions of affect; we use affective perceptual information to appraise situations and to regulate our behavior. This process of appraising the affective state of others is called *social referencing* (Campos & Stenberg, 1981, p. 295). We engage in social referencing when a situation is ambiguous and we need further information to interpret the situation. For example, we all have had the experience of hearing an ambiguous remark and searching the speaker's face to determine whether the remark was serious or lighthearted.

What of children? When and how does social reference develop? Before addressing this question, consider for a moment what social referencing entails. First, the child must be able to distinguish between the different patterns of facial, vocal, and gestural behaviors that signify different affective states. Second, the different affective states of another must have different meanings for the child. Third, the child must seek such information from others. Finally, the actions of the child must be influenced by the information garnered from the affective states of others (Feinman, 1985; Klinnert, Campos, Sorce, Emde & Svejda, 1983).

By 10 weeks of age, infants are differentially responsive to the affective expressions of their mothers (Haviland & Lelwica, 1987). The infants not only discriminated between maternal affective expressions, but also made different affective responses to the expressions. In this study mothers were trained to make happy, sad, and angry facial expressions as they said "You make me so happy (sad, mad)" in a voice that matched the facial expression.

The infants' responses to these affective expressions differed. For example, the infants made responses that matched the joy and anger expressions of the mother. The responses were more than imitation. Rather, there appeared to be a change in the infant's own affective state. The response to joy, for example, was one of interest or excitement. The anger presentation was noxious enough that several infants cried and were unable to complete the condition; this did not happen in the other two conditions. Thus, the infant responses suggested that the maternal emotional expression contained meaningful information for the infants, information that induced affective states in the infants (Haviland & Lelwica, 1987).

Although this study does not tell us the relative importance of facial versus vocal expression (compare, Walker-Andrews, 1986) or how general infant emotional responsiveness is, it does demonstrate that by an early age infants are responsive to the behaviors that signal the affective states of at least one important other, the mother (compare, Diskin & Heinicke, 1986). Indeed, we might speculate that young infants learn something about events through their parents' affective responses to these events (Campos & Stenberg, 1981). Such vicarious learning may, for example, lead some children, and not others, to fear thunderstorms or snakes. That is, some events may be initially neutral or ambiguous for young children, but through their parents' affective appraisal of these events, children may acquire positive or negative emotional responses to the events.

Social referencing occurs when infants use the affective expressions of another to gain information about an environmental event. We have evidence that social referencing occurs by 10 to 12 months of age (Dickstein & Parke, 1988; Feinman & Lewis, 1983; Klinnert, 1984; Sorce, Emde, Campos & Klinnert, 1985; Walden & Ogan, 1988). To illustrate, Sorce and his colleagues (Sorce, Emde, Campos & Klinnert, 1985) put 12-month-old infants in an ambigious situation in which the infants were placed on the shallow side of a visual cliff (see Figure 10-1). "The cliff is a large (8 ft × 6 ft) safety glass-covered table divided into two halves, a 'shallow' and a 'deep' side. On the shallow side, a patterned surface is placed underneath the glass so that there is no apparent dropoff. On the deep side, the same surface is placed at a (deeper) distance under the glass to appear as if there is a 'cliff' there" (Campos, 1984, p. 154). The mothers were positioned at the far (deep) side of the cliff with an attractive toy in front of them on the glass. Thus, visual cues provided conflicting information indicating both that there was a drop-off and that the surface was supportive. When infants crawled toward the deep side, looked down at the drop off, and then looked at their mothers, mothers made either a happy or fearful facial expression in one study and either an interest or anger expression in a second study.

None of the 17 infants who looked at their mothers and observed a fearful expression moved across the deep side; 14 of 19 infants made the crossing when the expression was happy. Similarly, infants were less likely to cross when observing an angry expression than an expression of interest. When, however, the apparatus was shallow on both sides the infants were less likely to look to their mothers or to be influenced by the facial expressions. Taken together, the data indicate that infants this age do make social reference by looking for emotional information and that they are more likely to seek such information when a situation is uncertain (see also Gunnar & Stone, 1984; Hornik, Risenhoover & Gunnar, 1987).

Furthermore, children this age also reference the emotional expressions of familiarized strangers. Klinnert and her colleagues (Klinnert, Emde, Butterfield & Campos, 1986) had 12- and 13-month-olds play with an experimenter in the presence of their mothers. After 10 minutes of familiarization, a robot toy emerged, beeping, from under a table. When the child looked at the experimenter, the experimenter responded with either a fearful or smiling expression. The mothers maintained a neutral expression throughout the procedure.

Eighty-three percent of the infants did reference the experimenter. Those infants who received the smiling response were more likely to approach the robot toy and tended to make positive responses such as patting or kissing the toy. When infants receiving the fearful expression did approach the toy, they

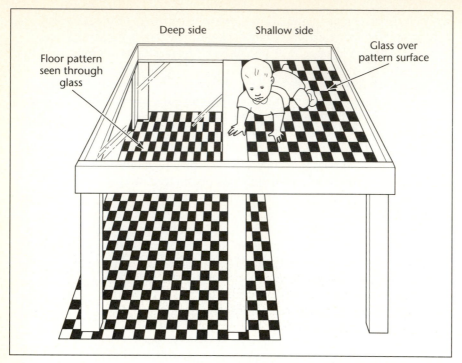

► *FIGURE 10-1* The visual cliff. The infant crawled across a heavy sheet of glass toward the mother. Under the glass was a textured piece of checkered linoleum. For half the distance, it was about a meter below the surface of the glass. At the midpoint, the infant was faced with a visual cliff.

were "more likely to swat it or knock it over" (p. 430). Furthermore, the infants receiving the fearful expression were more likely to approach and touch their mothers. Finally, the expressive states of the infants were influenced by the emotional signals of the experimenter. Positive states in the infants were more likely in the smiling condition than the fearful condition. Thus, from an early age, infants are capable of using the emotional responses of others to regulate their behavior.

There is some evidence, however, that the social referencing of infants is selective (Zarbatany & Lamb, 1985). When 14-month-olds were alone with a stranger, the expression of the stranger was less likely to influence their behavior than when the same expressions were made by their mothers. The unfamiliarity of the stranger, the absence of their mothers, and the unfamiliarity of the room may have contributed to this effect. Further research is necessary to determine the factors that affect the selectivity of infants' social referencing.

Feinman (1982) has offered a broader conception of social referencing, one in which the meaning conveyed can be instrumental (how to behave in a situation) as well as affective (how to feel about an event). Further, Feinman assumes that such information can be actively sought, casually observed, or acquired through instruction. Thus, social referencing is seen as the process of using the interpretations of others to understand a situation. This broader conception raises questions about the relation of imitation of instrumental responses to the social referencing of emotional responses. As we have seen, both types of responses are evident around the same age, nine to ten months of age. Interestingly, this is also the age when infants begin to communicate and follow the gaze and point of others (see Chapter 4). Taken together, the data on communication, instrumental imitation, and social referencing suggests that during the last quarter of the first year infants begin to know, implicitly at least, that others have knowledge, knowledge that infants this age begin to seek and use to interpret and solve problems (Bretherton, 1984).

Feinman's broader conception of social referencing implies that, as children acquire verbal skills, they will use verbal as well as nonverbal information in their attempts to interpret situations. Although we know little about the continuing development of children's social referencing skills, we might expect important changes as children are exposed more frequently to novel situations and acquire the verbal and cognitive skills that make possible more sophisticated interpretations of others' opinions (Feinman, 1982). Further, since children's knowledge of affective states develops through the school years (see, for example, Zahn-Waxler, Cummings & Cooperman, 1984), we might expect developmental differences in the breadth of the affective cues that are used for social referencing.

In summary, the development of social referencing during the first year raises questions about the development of social referencing in the preschool years. In the last chapter we considered the development of children's problem-solving skills. Clearly, an important strategy for solving problems, for reducing uncertainty, is to seek the advice and opinion of others. We know little about the effect of uncertainty on social referencing (Feinman, 1985). Nor do we know anything about the development of selectivity in social referencing. The problem now is to confront these and similar issues to derive developmental models of children's social referencing, models that eventually will incorporate related aspects of social development such as affiliation, conformity, obedience, and social modeling (Feinman, 1982; 1983).

▶ THE COMMUNICATION GAME

Communication is critical to interpersonal relations. Interpersonal relations are established and maintained through communication. Through communication we become aware of the thoughts, beliefs, and desires of others. We do not have direct access to the thoughts of others; we often rely on communication to discover the mental states of others. But communication is only sustained if both the communicator and the listener adhere to the rules and conventions of communication. Recognizing the give and take of interpersonal communication and the relevance of cultural conventions, several theorists have characterized interpersonal communication as a "game" (for example, Goffman 1959; Garfinkle, 1967; Wittgenstein, 1953). Communication is seen as a purposeful social interaction in which the participants have interdependent rules, strategies, and tactics for jointly making decisions and obtaining goals.

In general, we adhere to several rules of conversation (Grice, 1975; Norman & Rumelhart, 1975); as speakers and listeners, we make common assumptions that advance conversation. Basic to communication are the following rules (Norman & Rumelhart, 1975):

1. Be sincere.
2. Be relevant.

Imagine if you did not assume the sincerity of the other. This would raise the possibility that each person is trying to mislead you. Extensive effort and research would be necessary to determine the true meaning of each communication. Imagine not assuming the sincerity of your physics professor. How would you decide what information to accept, what to reject?

The assumption of sincerity is so basic to our communication that we are usually surprised when we discover that this principle has not been followed. After many years I still have vivid memories of two such incidents in my life. We do not always adhere to the principle, however. At some time we all have told at least one "white" lie. Nevertheless, the principle is so fundamental to our culture that our justice system assumes that a defendant is telling the truth unless other evidence convincingly indicates otherwise.

The second principle, be relevant, leads to two related principles:

3. Do not say to others that which they already know.
4. Do not be superfluous.

Imagine somebody talking about what you already know. Why would you remain in the conversation? Boredom would soon set in. If you didn't leave the conversation, you would change the topic. Communication is about the exchange of information. At the same time, we expect a conversation to be relevant to a given topic. We do not hop from one topic to another. Thus, the speaker must make a balance between what is relevant to a given topic and what the listener does and does not know. In order to adhere to these rules the speaker must consider how much the listener knows and tailor his or her communication to the knowledge structure of the listener. Effective communication requires the ability to understand how the other construes a given situation and the ability to fit the message to the listener's frame of reference.

In an elaboration of these basic principles, Higgins (1981) has identified 13 general rules of adult communication. This is not to imply that adults are consciously aware of the communication rules, or that the rules are explicit or well-defined; rather, which rules are followed will depend upon the structure and purpose of the communicative interaction.

Adult research has explored the relevance of several of these communication rules (see Higgins, 1981, for a review). The developmental research has focused on a few of the rules, with particular emphasis on the use of communication rules during referential communication.

THE DEVELOPMENT OF REFERENTIAL COMMUNICATION

Communication has many functions, such as persuasion, establishing a social relationship, and entertaining. For the most part, developmental research has focused on *referential communication,* on communication that makes reference to objects, events, and ideas. Such communication is common in our daily and educational activities. Teachers make numerous references to objects, events, and concepts as they attempt to convey information about a subject. Children refer to real and imaginary objects and events as they engage in play activities. Family conversations are full of references to future and past events. One of the basic functions of communication is to inform other people about particular referents. We make reference to physical objects in the world as well as concepts in our memories. When making reference we must specify the referent in such a way that it will be distinguished from possible alternative referents. How the referent is described will depend upon the set of alternatives and what the speaker thinks the listener knows. The speaker needs to specify the intended referent in such a way that it is neither ambiguous to the listener nor interpreted with a referent different than the one intended. Referential communication has received extensive research, probably because of its pervasiveness and its relative simplicity. Furthermore, the referential function is a component of other, more complex types of communication (Asher, 1979).

Studies of referential communication indicate that effective referential communication increases with age (Krauss & Glucksberg, 1969), and that the developmental change is influenced by children's topics of conversation and their audiences (Martlew, 1979). Consider the referential communication task devised by Glucksberg and his colleagues (Glucksberg, Krauss & Weisberg, 1966). Two children are sitting opposite each other with a screen separating them (see Figure 10-2). The speaker's task is to tell the listener which block he is placing on a spindle. The blocks are distinguished by six novel shapes. The listener's task is to use the information to put blocks on her spindle, in an order that matches that of the speaker. To accomplish his task the speaker must consider the characteristics of the listener, that the listener cannot see the speaker's blocks. He must also describe a given block (the referent) in such a way that it can be distinguished from the other blocks (the nonreferents). The listener must not only interpret the speaker's message, but also provide feedback to the speaker about the adequacy of the message.

In their analysis of referential communications, Whitehurst and Sonnenschein (1985) make a distinction between three components that contribute to referential communication: substantive knowledge, enabling skills, and procedural rules. *Substantive knowledge* is domain-specific knowledge about the

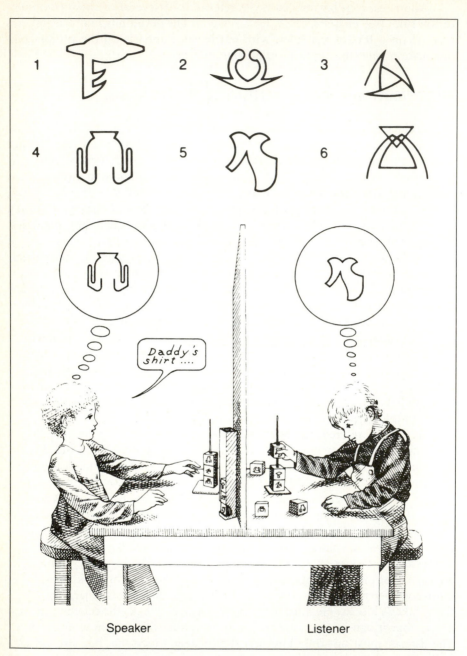

▶ **FIGURE 10-2**   *In this experiment, the speaker describes to the listener which block (top) he is placing on the spindle. The listener attempts to stack her blocks in the same order. (From Krauss & Glucksberg, 1969.)*

referents of communication. *Enabling skills* are information-processing skills such as attention and memory that make communication possible. *Procedural rules* are the rules of communication that are specific to reference, for example, "communicators should produce a message that is appropriate to the context and circumstances" (Higgins, 1981, p. 348).

Clearly the quality of referential communication will depend upon the substantive knowledge of the speaker and the listener (compare, Kahan & Richards, 1985). Several years ago I called the power company and asked them to cut down a decaying Lombardy poplar that was near the power lines. When I returned home the poplar was still standing but a tamarack in the front yard was down. Communication had failed and I had lost a fine tree because the people who did the cutting could not distinguish between a Lombardy poplar and a tamarack. We can expect that developmental changes in substantive knowledge, as well as differences between experts and novices in domain-specific knowledge, will affect the quality of referential communication. We saw in Chapter 5, for example, that young children's conversations are quite effective if the children each have knowledge of a script that underlies the topic of the conversation.

Enabling skills are domain-general skills that are not specific to communication. These are information-processing skills that nevertheless can affect referential communication. Perceptual and memory skills can influence the quality of children's referential communication. Longhurst and Turnure (1971) found, for example, that preschoolers had difficulty in perceptually discriminating between the novel figures used by Glucksberg and his colleagues. Subsequent research has used stimuli that differ on dimensions that young children can readily discriminate and label (for example, Whitehurst & Sonnenschein, 1978). Similarly, failure to remember the characteristics of a referent will interfere with referential communication. Indeed, attention, memory, perception, and decision-making skills all influence the development of referential communication (for example, Sonnenschein, 1982).

Although both the development of domain-specific knowledge and information-processing skills can have effects on referential communication, the emphasis here is on the development of the procedural rules of referential communication. These rules presumably develop out of more general communicative skills. Thus, we have seen that infants and young children adhere to general rules such as turn-taking. Indeed, the communicative efforts of preschoolers are often impressive (see, for example, Garvey & Hogan, 1973; Mueller, 1972; Wellman & Lempers, 1977). Nevertheless, experimental investigations of referential communication demonstrate that young children have difficulties with the procedural rules that are specific to referential communication (see Whitehurst & Sonnenschein, 1985, for a review).

THE DEVELOPMENT OF SPEAKER SKILLS   Two rules are important to the development of speaker skills: the listener rule and the difference rule. The *listener rule* specifies that speakers should produce messages that take into consideration the status, knowledge, and ability of the listener. Several lines of study indicate that preschoolers are sensitive to the listener rule. For example, four-year-olds modify their speech to accommodate the listener's age. When talking to younger children, their topics of conversation are appropriate for the child and their conversational style is modified to have simpler syntax and more repetitions (Sachs & Devin, 1976; Shatz & Gelman, 1973; Tomasello & Mannle, 1985). Maratsos (1973) has shown that three- and four-year-olds will use fewer gestures when communicating with a blindfolded listener. Furthermore, young children produce messages that reflect the past experience and, thus, knowledge state of a listener (see, for example, Menig-Peterson, 1975; Perner & Leeham, 1986; Sonnenschein, 1986b). Perner and Leeham (1986), for example, had three-year-olds communicate with four-year-old partners in two different conditions. In each condition, the three-year-olds were shown two actions that a toy (for example, a bee) could make. In one condition (partial ignorance) the partner saw one of the actions, but not the other. In the other condition (full ignorance) the partner did not see either action. In both conditions the partner then asked the subject what the toy could do.

Answers that took into consideration the past experience of the partner would describe both actions in the full ignorance condition and the action that was not seen in the partial ignorance condition. One-fourth of the younger three-year-olds ($X = 3; 4$) and three-fourths of the older three-year-olds ($X = 3; 9$) made these responses. At both ages the children restricted their answer in the partial ignorance condition to the action that was not seen. However, the younger children, unlike the older children, underinformed their partners in the full ignorance condition; they only described one of the actions. This tendency to underinform was not the result of memory failure, since the children could answer a memory question (for example, "Can the bee do anything else?"). Thus, the older three-year-olds were better able to assess the mental states of their partners and to use this knowledge in their communications.

Although there has not been any systematic exploration of the limitations of preschoolers' use of the listener rule, we might expect that, as young children acquire more domain-specific knowledge about the social cues that signify the various characteristics of the listener, especially mental states, the rule will be more generally applied (compare, Sonnenschein, 1986b).

The *difference rule* specifies that the speaker should "describe how the referent is different from other things with which it might be confused" (Whitehurst & Sonnenschein, 1985, p. 12). To do this, the speaker must consider the context of the message and produce a message that discriminates the referent from all possible nonreferents that the listener might confuse with the referent. In the developmental research, both nonreferents and referents are present in a stimulus array. In everyday conversation, however, the potentially confusable nonreferents may not be present. For example, on occasion my husband breaks the difference rule when he comes home and says, "I saw Roy today and he said . . ." My husband has two colleagues named Roy and he does not give me the information necessary to determine which one is his referent. Sometimes if I am patient and listen to what Roy said, I can figure out which Roy would have made that particular comment. More often, however, I interrupt my husband and ask, "Which Roy?"

Most of the research on the development of speaker skills has concentrated on the difference rule. In a series of studies Whitehurst and Sonnenschein have demonstrated that five-year-olds do not always use the difference rule to produce a message that distinguishes between a referent and the nonreferents. For example, when presented with a stimulus array that has two red objects the young child refers to "the red one," giving a message that is ambiguous since it does not differentiate the "red" referent from the "red" nonreferent in the array. Whitehurst and Sonnenschein (1978) sought to determine the nature of young children's failure to contrast referents with nonreferents. Five-year-olds were asked to describe multi-dimensional triangles for a listener. In the simple condition the attribute (for example, color) that distinguished the referent triangle from the nonreferent triangle was constant across trials. In the complex condition, however, any one of three attributes (size, color, stripes vs spots) could be the attribute that distinguished the referent from the nonreferent.

Children in the simple condition produced contrasting unambigious messages on 56 percent of the trials. However, in the complex condition this percentage dropped to 22 percent. Thus, even when the task is a simple one, children this age have difficulty applying the difference rule to produce an unambiguous message; and, when information-processing demands increase, children have even more difficulty honoring the difference rule.

THE DEVELOPMENT OF LISTENER SKILLS   As children are acquiring knowledge of the rules for speaking, they also are acquiring the rules that guide listening. These listening rules include the comprehension monitoring rule and the feedback rule. The *comprehension monitoring rule* requires that listeners monitor their comprehension of a message. In Chapter 7 we saw that comprehension monitoring skills develop with age. The referential communication research indicates comparable developmental changes. When preschoolers receive ambiguous messages, they respond as if the messages are informative and do not indicate the ambiguity of the message. Further, even when five- and six-year-olds are aware that an ambiguous message has two or more potential referents, they are confident in their guesses; the uncertainty of the message does not affect their judgments about the quality of the message (Robinson & Robinson, 1983a, b).

The *feedback rule* specifies that listeners should indicate when they do not comprehend a message. Thus, listeners must not only monitor their comprehension of a message, but also indicate to the speaker when the message is unclear. When I ask my husband, "Which Roy?", I am telling him that I do not understand who the referent is. Several lines of evidence indicate that young children are unlikely to give appropriate feedback about their comprehension of a message. Flavell, Speer, Green, and August (1981), for example, videotaped children as they attempted to follow instructions for building towers with blocks that varied on several dimensions. Although young children's behavior (for example, pauses, facial expressions, replaying of the instructions) indicated that they had difficulty comprehending the inadequate messages, the younger children were less likely than older children to indicate that the speaker did a "bad job" of telling how to build the towers. Thus, nonverbal indicants suggest that children experience noncomprehension but fail to express verbally the failure of comprehension. Indeed, these nonverbal expressions of confusion probably are not social in nature; they are not intended to convey information to another (Whitehurst & Sonnenschein, 1985). In Chapter 7 we saw a similar type of effect for children's reading of texts.

MESSAGE EVALUATION   Critical to the development of communicative skills is *message evaluation,* the ability to assess the quality of the message. Young children have difficulty assessing the quality of ambiguous messages. They correctly identify unambiguous messages as adequate but fail to recognize the inadequacy of ambiguous messages. Young children usually accept messages as adequate. It is not until seven years of age that children recognize the importance of the message. Robinson and Robinson (1976) had children ranging in age from two-and-one-half to eight years of age participate in a communication game in which they had to indicate the fault for communication failure. When a message was inadequate and communication failed, the older children blamed the speaker; the younger children, however, blamed the listener. Furthermore, young children's assessments were influenced by the status of the speaker. When asked to judge the quality of a speaker's message, younger children were influenced more by the age of the speaker than the quality of the message itself (for example, Ackerman, 1983; Sonnenschein, 1984; Sonnenschein & Whitehurst, 1980). For example, when judging the ambiguous message of an adult speaker, first graders were less likely to judge correctly than when the same message was given by a peer (Sonnenschein, 1986a). The judgments of fourth graders, however, were unaffected by the speaker's age. This effect of the speaker's age appears to reflect young children's assessment of a speaker's intelligence. When first graders listened to a "smart" peer they were less likely to judge an ambiguous message correctly. Conversely, young children were more critical of the ambiguous messages of "stupid" adults (Sonnenschein, 1988). Thus, young children conflate the quality of a message with the abilities of the speaker. Young children have difficulty distinguishing the status of the speaker from the quality of the message. This is not to say that adults do not also have this difficulty on occasion, but it appears to be more prevalent in young children.

Why do young children fail to assess the quality of the message and proceed to behave as if the message is clear? Speer (1984) argues that young children assume the cooperative principle (Grice, 1975), which is the assumption that "speakers seek to be informative, relevant, truthful, and clear" (Speer, 1984, p. 1812). Imagine if young children did not assume this principle as they attempted to acquire language. When would they accept the label given to a novel object and when would they reject it? It would be difficult, if not impossible, for young children to acquire a language if they did not assume the cooperative principle.

Such a strategy would help to explain why young children blame the listener rather than the speaker for communication failure. That is, young children assume that the speaker has followed the cooperative principle; therefore, any failure in communication is the fault of the listener. The fact that young children are more critical of a peer's message than an adult's suggests that young children are more likely to assume the cooperative principle for adults than peers. When, however, children had to evaluate the messages of peers who were described as deceptive they were more likely to detect inconsistencies in the message than children who did not have such an expectation of the speaker (McDevitt & Carroll, 1988).

Central to the development of referential communication skills is an understanding of the distinction between what is actually said (the message) and what the speakers intended to say (what the speakers are thinking—their internal representation). This distinction requires the representation and coordination of two codes. We have seen that preschoolers have difficulty with the appearance/reality distinction, which requires dual codes. Similarly, several lines of research (for example, Robinson, Goelman & Olson, 1983; Robinson & Whittaker, 1986) indicate that young children do not understand the distinction between the speaker's intention and the literal message. Adults are aware of the difference between the intention and the message and we have learned conventions for when to focus on the intention of the speaker and when the message should be treated literally. For example, when you meet a person and they say "How are you?", you know the intention of the speaker is a social greeting. You are not expected to take the message literally and respond with gory details of the state of your health.

If young children do not make the distinction between the literal meaning of a message and the speaker's intended message, the problem is to discover how children learn the distinction, how they come to understand that sometimes there is not a single interpretation of a message and that the message is better treated as a "clue" to the speaker's intended meaning. Several theorists (for example, Robinson & Robinson, 1982; Robinson & Whittaker, 1985) have argued that formal schooling produces the kinds of experiences that emphasize the distinction between the literal message and the speaker's meaning. For example, in school, children learn to read, which requires that they respond to the message as it is given, without consideration of a nonverbal context (Olson & Torrance, 1983). Indeed, the message comes to be seen as a set of clues to the thoughts of the writer. Children must learn to attend to other people's possible meanings. Thus, experiences in school may contribute to children's eventual understanding of the difference between a speaker's intended meaning and the message used to convey that meaning to a listener (Robinson & Whittaker, 1985). If this is the case, we need to learn more about children's conceptions of internal representations and how children relate these mental representations to the verbal messages that are used to express them (Robinson & Whittaker, 1987).

In summary, the referential communication research indicates substantial developmental change during the preschool and elementary school years. Since the developmental research has focused on this age range, we know little about the development of referential communication during the junior and senior high school years. We might expect, however, developmental as well as individual differences during these years that reflect differences in domain-specific knowledge and information-processing skills. Indeed, we know little about how domain-specific knowledge and information-processing skills interact with the procedural rules to influence referential communication (compare, Robinson & Whittaker, 1985).

During the elementary school years, children acquire knowledge about procedural rules for speaking and listening in situations that demand referential communication. The limited data that are available do not indicate that parents give feedback to their children about their communicative efforts. We have speculated, however, that, in school, children learn the importance of the message and the need to formulate messages that fit the characteristics of the listener and the context of the message.

It may be, however, that we acquire two types of knowledge about messages. One is to understand explicitly that what is said may not be what is meant. The other is to understand that the message can be treated as an abstract object, independent of the nonverbal context. We saw in Chapter 8 that, when reasoning about deductive arguments, even college students have difficulty separating the message from the nonverbal context, that is, their beliefs. We might speculate that the second type of knowledge is particularly dependent on formal schooling.

The research on referential communication tells us something about the development of one communicative function in an experimental setting. Communication, however, is multidimensional. To fully understand the development of communicative skills we must appreciate that, for children in a natural setting, communication requires several skills (Schmidt & Paris, 1984). For example, children must not only adapt the messages to the listeners and, as listeners, provide feedback, but also gain and hold the attention of the listeners, and adapt the messages to the social context. The many communicative skills must be coordinated as children engage in conversation. Furthermore, reference is only one of several possible communicative functions. Indeed, reference often serves to advance other communicative functions such as persuasion and entertainment.

▶ THE DEVELOPMENT OF ROLE-TAKING SKILLS

A basic assumption of social cognition is that "the way in which one conceptualizes and reasons about others has a major effect on how one interacts with them" (Shantz, 1983, p. 495). Important in the development of children's social understanding is the ability to take the role of another. Our understanding of others and our consequent responses to others are influenced by our ability to infer the psychological perspectives of others *and* to coordinate this perspective with our own. Others seldom think and feel exactly as we do. Our social relations are facilitated when we recognize these differences, try to understand how others think and feel, and then coordinate this knowledge with our own thoughts and feelings. A mother who is angry with her young son's dangerous behavior may inhibit her expression of anger if she realizes that the child's own behavior and its potential consequences have badly frightened the child.

Piaget (1926) took the position that young children are egocentric, that they do not differentiate between self and others. Piaget assumed that young children attribute their own thoughts, feelings, and so on to other people. Piaget's work has stimulated several theorists to examine the development of social role-taking skills (for example, Feffer & Gourevitch, 1960; Flavell, Botkin, Fry, Wright, & Jarvis, 1968; Chandler, 1972; Selman & Byrne, 1974). These research programs have used different measures of role taking and focused on either affective (for example, Kohlberg, 1969), cognitive (for example, Piaget & Inhelder, 1969), or social-interactional (for example, Selman & Bryne, 1974) aspects of role taking. As a consequence, different models of role taking have been advanced. They have in common, however, an attempt to describe sequential stages of the development of role taking (see Enright & Lapsley, 1980). The several measures of role taking vary, however, in their reliability and validity (Enright & Lapsley, 1980). Here we focus on Selman's task since it focuses on social interaction and appears applicable to a broad age range (Enright & Lapsely, 1980). We do this with the understanding that the measures of role taking do not appear to measure the same thing and that descriptions of the developmental change in role-taking skills will depend upon the measure used.

In general *role taking* can be understood as "the ability to understand the self and others as subjects, to react to others as like the self, and to react to the self's behavior from the other's point of view" (Selman & Byrne, 1974; p. 803). Selman's task is a set of stories in which two individuals are in conflict. The experimenter uses an interview format to ask the child a series of probe questions about the story. For example, one story is as follows (Selman & Byrne, 1974, p. 805):

> Holly is an 8-year-old girl who likes to climb trees. She is the best tree climber in the neighborhood. One day while climbing down from a tall tree she falls off the bottom branch but does not hurt herself. Her father sees her fall. He is upset and asks her to promise not to climb trees any more. Holly promises.
>
> Later that day, Holly and her friends meet Sean. Sean's kitten is caught up in a tree and cannot get down. Something has to be done right away or the kitten may fall. Holly is the only one who climbs trees well enough to reach the kitten and get it down, but she remembers her promise to her father.

Selman (1976; Selman & Byrne, 1974) defines four levels of role-taking skills. Each level is defined by the child's ability to distinguish perspectives and ability to relate different perspectives. Level 0 occurs around four to six years to age. The child "can differentiate self and others as entities, but he does not differentiate their points of view" (1974, p. 804). Nor does he relate perspectives. At this stage, children do not realize that others have different psychological perspectives. At level 1 (six to eight years) the child realizes that there can be different perspectives. "He realizes that people feel differently or think differently because they are in different situations or have different information" (p. 804). Children in this stage do not, however, relate the two perspectives. One or the other perspective is seen as correct, but children do not realize that one person might consider the point of view of the other. Thus, in answer to the question, "Do you think Holly's father would get angry if he found out she climbed the tree" one child answers, "If he didn't know why she climbed the tree, he would be angry. But if Holly tells him why she did it, he would realize she has a good reason" (Selman, 1976, p. 304). This child does not assume that the father can consider Holly's point of view unless he is explicitly informed by Holly.

By Level 2 (eight to ten years) the child is "aware that people think or feel differently because each person has his own uniquely ordered set of values or purposes." Further, the child can reflect on his own "behavior and motivation as seen from outside the self, from the other's point of view. The child recognizes that the other, too, can put himself in the child's shoes, so the child is able to anticipate other's reactions to his own motives or purposes. However, these reflections do not occur simultaneously or naturally. The child cannot 'get outside' the two person perspective" (p. 804). Thus, two perspectives cannot be considered at the same time. For example, consider the following exchange (Selman, 1976, p. 305):

▶ Q: Do you think Holly would climb the tree?
A: Yes, she knows her father will understand why she did it.
Q: What do you think Holly's father would want Holly to do? In this situation would he want her to go up and get the kitten or not?
A: No.
Q: Why not?
A: Because he would be changing his order, and he wouldn't be a good father if he changed his mind. The father may think breaking a promise is worse, but he'd understand that Holly thinks saving the kitten's life is more important.
Q: Would all fathers think this way?
A: No, it all depends on what they think is more important.

This child credits the father with the ability to have two perspectives, his own and Holly's; the two perspectives, however, are not coordinated. The child switches back and forth between the two. Finally at Level 3 (10 to 12 years) the following occurs:

> The child can now differentiate the self's perspective from the generalized perspective, the point of view taken by some average member of a group. In a situation he distinguishes each party's point of view from that of a third person. He can conceive of the concept of "spectator" and maintain a disinterested point of view. The child . . . discovers that both self and other can consider each party's point of view simultaneously and mutually. . . . [He knows that each person] can put himself in the other's place and [can] view himself from that vantage point before "deciding" how to react (pp. 804–805).

In a longitudinal study of boys' responses to two dilemmas during a five-year period, Gurucharri and Selman (1982) found support for developmental progression through the levels of social role taking assumed by Selman. Further, LeMare and Rubin (1987) have demonstrated a relation between children's role-taking performance and peer sociability. For example, third grade children who tended to be social isolates with their peers had poorer role-taking skills than average or sociable children. Of course, this correlation does not establish a causal relation between role taking and sociability. "It may be that a lack of social experience impedes the development of perspective-taking skills; however, it is equally plausible that poor perspective takers are handicapped in their efforts to be sociable" (LeMare & Rubin, 1987, p. 314).

The relation between role taking and social interaction receives further support in a study by Hudson and her colleagues (Hudson, Forman & Brion-Meisels, 1982). In this study, second grade boys and girls were identified as high and low role takers and then were taught how to make caterpillars from construction paper and glue. After this instruction each second grader was videotaped as he or she taught two kindergartners to make the caterpillars. Analyses of the prosocial behavior of the second graders indicated that the high and low role takers were significantly different on eight dimensions of prosocial behavior. These included lending a hand when a child needed help and social problem solving. For example, if a kindergartener was struggling with the scissors, making groans and giving pleading looks the good role takers were more likely to help. Similarly, when the younger children were not attentive, the good role takers used behaviors to regain their attention and to proceed with teaching them the tasks.

In summary, several lines of research indicate developmental changes in the ability of young children to put themselves in the place of another, to appreciate the psychological perspective of another, and to coordinate that perspective with their own. Although the several approaches to role taking are yet to be integrated, they all do indicate developmental changes. They differ, however, in the dimensions that are measured (Ford, 1979; Waters & Tinsley, 1985). We might expect that in the future researchers will analyze the several dimensions that are relevant to role taking and that an integrative model will emerge that includes cognitive, social, and affective dimensions. Furthermore, the reliance on measures that require highly verbal skills probably leads to underestimations of young children's ability to take the perspective of another (Denham, 1986; Iannotti, 1985). Young children's social cognitions are more mature when the situation or person is familiar (for example, Graziano, Moore & Collins, 1988) and when the task is a practical one rather than a hypothetical one (for example, Bearison & Gass, 1979). We need to develop research tools for exploring the development of implicit as well as explicit role-taking skills.

Further, the development of role taking may not be as general as the developmental models suggest (Mandell, 1984). That is, role taking may be influenced by the situation and its familiarity. I may be proficient at taking the role of a student since I spent many years as one. My ability to take the role of a college president may be more limited, however. In a later section of this chapter we see that children's social competence is influenced by what they know about a specific social situation. Thus, we should be concerned not only with the development of general skills for role taking, but also with the development of children's knowledge of specific situations and the related roles. Children, for example, are acquiring knowledge about parental roles, occupational roles, and gender roles (see Huston, 1983, for a review of the research on sex typing). Finally, we must consider how role-taking knowledge translates into social behavior.

▶ CAUSAL REASONING ABOUT INTENTION

In Chapter Six we considered the development of causal reasoning about physical objects. There we saw that even preschoolers have some understanding of causality. Here we consider children's understanding of the causes of behavior, an understanding that is critical to social interaction. People have desires, beliefs, and intentions that influence their behavior. In our daily affairs we all function as naive psychologists. We seldom accept behavior at face value; rather we attempt to understand the causes of behavior. To illustrate with a simple example, last summer I was walking on a rural road of an offshore island. A strange woman stopped her car and asked me if I was walking for exercise. I replied, "Yes, thank you." "Yes" would have answered her question. Why the "thank you"? Given the circumstances I inferred that, despite the indirect nature of her query, her intention was to offer me a ride. I had never before been offered a ride with such a question. Nevertheless, within a few seconds I considered the context and her behavior and inferred an intention that then influenced my own behavior.

Considerable adult research has sought to understand how adults attribute mental states to others and how they make causal inferences (see, for example, Fiske & Taylor, 1984). What do children know about mental states? How do they use such knowledge to reason about the causes of behavior? Just as children are acquiring biological knowledge and theories during the preschool and elementary school years (see Chapter 5), so they also are acquiring psychological knowledge and theories about the mind (see, for example, Astington, Harris & Olson, 1988; Johnson, 1982; Wellman, 1985). Here the focus is on children's understanding of intention and how they reason about intentions.

Basic to our interpretation of behavior is a determination whether a behavior is intended or not. Intention refers "to a mental state that guides and organizes behavior. It is essentially a determination to act in a certain way or to bring about a certain state of affairs" (Shultz, 1980, p. 131). Intention is a critical concept for our explanation of human behavior. For example, in their attempts to understand problem solving, psychologists assume that plans (intentions) play an important role in the process of solving problems (see Chapter 9). Intention is so important in our judgments of behavior that it is codified in our laws. It is one thing to cause accidentally the death of another, but quite another thing if the death was intended. Every day we make judgments about the intentionality of others' actions, and these judgments influence our own behavior. When children complain to the teacher that another child has pushed them, the teacher's response will depend upon a judgment of the intentionality of the push. Similarly, young children who can distinguish between an accidental shove and an intentional shove have the type of information that is necessary for choosing an appropriate response.

By three years of age, the concept of intention influences children's understanding of behavior (see Shultz, 1980, for a review). Three-year-olds distinguish intended acts from mistakes and accidents, both their own and others (see, for example, Shultz, Wells & Sarda, 1980). By five years of age children begin to have recursive awareness of intention. They are aware not only that others have intentions, but also that others are aware of intentions. In a card game situation, Shultz and Cloghesy (1981) found that children aged five years and older displayed strategic acts that indicated they were aware that the experimenter was aware of their intentional state. As might be expected, children's actions in the game indicated recursive awareness of intention before they could verbalize it. It was not until the age of nine that the children made comments, such as "I know which one you think I'm going to point to," that made explicit mention of recursion.

The development of recursive awareness of intention is important to social interaction because it means that children are aware of their similarity to other people and are aware that social knowledge can be reciprocal. For example, knowing that other people will make inferences about my intentions, I may choose, in some situations, to make my intentions explicit so that there are no confusions about my intentions. At other times I may attempt to disguise my intentions. For the last few days I have been trying to get information from my husband and I have tried to do it in such a way that he will not realize my intention, which is to get necessary information from him for a gift.

How do we come to know that an action is intended? Several rules or heuristics for judging intentions have been identified (see, for example, Heider,

1958; Shultz, 1980, 1988). Most of the developmental work, however, has focused on the discounting principle (Kelley, 1973). Although this principle is relevant to nonsocial causal reasoning as well as social causal reasoning (compare, Surber, 1985), the emphasis has been on social reasoning. The principle specifies that "the perceived role of a given cause in producing a given effect is diminished if other plausible causes are also present" (Kassin & Ellis, 1988, p. 950). To illustrate, if I see a young child playing with a puzzle, I am likely to attribute the child's behavior to an intrinsic interest in the puzzle, an intrinsic motivation to play with the materials. If, however, I know that the child was offered a treat for finishing the puzzle, I am likely to discount the influence of intrinsic motivation on the child's behavior and to give more weight to extrinsic motivation.

The developmental research indicates that the discounting principle is evident in young children's behavior (for example, Lepper, Greene & Nisbett, 1973) before it is evident in their causal judgments (Smith, 1975). For example, Wells and Shultz (1980) invited four- and five-year-olds to play with a pair of toys. The children were offered a candy reward for playing with one of the toys, but not the other. After playing with each toy, these toys plus three others were placed before the children and they were asked to judge which toy they preferred to play with. After a series of preference judgments, the five toys were placed in front of the children and they were encouraged to play with them as the experimenter observed how much time was spent with each toy. The children's judgments did not indicate discounting; they did not judge that the nonrewarded toy would be preferred. The children's play behavior did, however, indicate discounting; they were more likely to play with the nonrewarded toy than with the rewarded toy.

Taken together, the research on the development of the discounting principle indicates that several factors determine whether there is evidence of discounting (see Kassin & Lepper, 1984, for a review). One, as evident in the Wells and Shultz (1980) study, is the nature of the task, which determines the type of demands placed on the child. Age is also a factor. Smith (1975), for example, presented kindergarten, second grade, fourth grade, and college level students with a task in which they were presented six pairs of illustrated stories. The main character in each story had a choice between two toys or activities. In one of the stories, however, a second character in some way placed an external constraint on the character's choice. After each pair of stories the students were asked to judge the preferences of the story characters. Although the judgments of the fourth graders and college students indicated use of the discounting principle, the kindergarteners did not use the discounting principle, and the second graders were in transition in their use of the principle.

Thus, young children do not consistently make judgments that suggest discounting, but older children do. The picture is not clear-cut, however. Under some circumstances, even preschoolers make judgments that indicate the use of the discounting principle (for example, Kassin, Lowe & Gibbons, 1980; Lepper, Sagotsky, Dafoe & Greene, 1982).

Two types of explanations have been offered to account for the effect of age on the use of the discounting principle. The cognitive-stage approach assumes that the use of the discounting principle is tied to a particular stage of cognitive development (for example, Morgan, 1981). For example, Kelley (1973) assumed that underlying the discounting principle is the multiple sufficient cause schema. The schema represents causal relationships in which two or more causes are sufficient for producing an effect. In this schema, for a given effect, changes in the strength of one sufficient cause are inversely compensated by changes in the strength of the other sufficient cause. For instance, suppose that two students have equivalent performances on a task and you know that one student made less effort than the other. You are likely to compensate for this difference in effort by attributing more ability to the student who made less effort.

For Piaget, an understanding that a change in one variable can compensate for a change in another variable requires reversibility of mental operations (Inhelder & Piaget, 1958). As we saw in Chapter 6 such reversibility develops during the period of concrete operations. Thus, the cognitive-stage approach assumes that the development of the discounting principle reflects the development of concrete operations (compare, Surber, 1985).

The social-learning explanation essentially takes a bottom-up approach. It argues that children learn to discount in specific contexts and that gradually children acquire a general script for events that involve discounting. Lepper, Sagotsky, Dafoe, and Greene (1982, p. 53) assert:

> From this viewpoint, relatively hypothetical or categorical scripts embodying a "discounting" principle (e.g., "When someone uses powerful incentives or sanctions to induce me to do something, the chances are that it is boring or unpleasant.") are evidenced through the abstraction of common features from sets of relatively more concrete and episodic social scripts (e.g., "When mom tells me I can't have my dessert until I clean my plate, what's left on my plate is usually yucky," or "When dad says I have to finish some task before I can go out to play, that task is probably something I don't want to do.").

Kassin and Lepper (1984) offer a model that incorporates these two accounts of the age effect. In addition it assumes that knowledge of the discounting principle initially is implicit and that later in development the principle becomes explicit. Thus, whether the principle is evident will depend on task demands, whether the task requires implicit (that is, behavioral) or explicit (this is, explanation) knowledge. Table 10-1 illustrates their analysis and includes predictions as to when the discounting effect should be evident. For example, according to the model preschoolers should evidence discounting in their behavior and judgments if the situation is concrete, highly familiar, and scripted. However, if the situation is very novel it is unclear whether even their behavior will indicate the discounting effect. Similarly, adults may be unable to give adequate explanations if the situation is novel.

TABLE 10-1 *A Social-Developmental Analysis of Children's Use of a Discounting Schema as a Function of Age of Child, Response Mode, and Stimulus Situation.*

Subjects	Stimulus Situation		
	Highly familiar, concrete, scripted situations		Novel situations, requiring generalization and abstraction
Preschoolers (pre-operational)	behavior judgment explanation (?)	behavior judgment (?) —	behavior (?) — —
Elementary-school children (concrete operations)	behavior judgment explanation	behavior judgment explanation (?)	behavior judgment (?) —
Adults (formal operations)	behavior judgment explanation	behavior judgment explanation	behavior judgment explanation (?)

Note: Entries in this matrix indicate cases in which evidence of a discounting effect is to be expected.
Source: Kassin and Lepper, 1984. Advances in Motivation and Achievement, Vol. 3, JAI Press, Inc. Greenwich, Connecticut. Reprinted by permission.

In support of the model, Kassin and Ellis (1988) have shown that elementary school children's use of the discounting principle is influenced by situation familiarity. In this study familiarity was manipulated experimentally and it was demonstrated that if children had prior experience in a situation that was similar to the discounting task they were more likely to discount in that task. These findings support the assumption that situation-specific induction processes affect the use of the discounting principle for causal reasoning. Further research will be necessary to determine whether developmental changes in the discounting effect simply reflect increasing familiarity with specific discounting scenarios or whether, as assumed by the model, top-down processes dependent upon general causal schemas also develop and influence the discounting effect. In Chapter 8 we confronted a similar issue when we considered the effects of domain-specific knowledge and general reasoning schemas on deductive and inductive reasoning.

▶ THE DEVELOPMENT OF SELF-UNDERSTANDING

As children acquire knowledge about others they also acquire knowledge about themselves. Indeed, some theorists (for example, Baldwin, 1899; Mead, 1934; Piaget 1932/1965) have argued that the sense of self develops through our interactions with others. In our social interactions we make inferences about ourselves as well as others. We perceive how others react to us and incorporate these perceptions into our concept of self. Although there are some data to support the parallel, there are also data to suggest that our concepts of self and others have at least different emphases (see Damon & Hart, 1982).

THE DEVELOPMENT OF VISUAL SELF-RECOGNITION

Because of methodological limitations, the work tracing the development of self-concept in infancy has concentrated on the development of the infants' ability to recognize the visual self (see Brooks-Gunn & Lewis, 1984, for a review). Essentially, in this research infants are shown images (for example, pictures, mirrors, videotapes) to determine if they make differential responses to themselves and others. For example, Lewis and Brooks-Gunn (1979) compared the tendencies of infants to play with and imitate three types of video-taped images: (a) live images of themselves, (b) images of themselves that were made a week earlier, and (c) images of another infant. At nine months infants discriminated themselves on the basis of contingent movement. They responded more to their own live images than the other two images. Recognition on the basis of contingency increased through the second year. Around 15 months of age infants began to distinguish themselves on the basis of physical features. At this time the infants distinguished the images of themselves that were made a week earlier from the images of another child. Thus, between 9 and 15 months of age infants are beginning to construct "the self as a permanent object with enduring qualities" (Damon & Hart, 1982, p. 848).

Further, there is suggestive evidence that by 24 months infants have a self-awareness that goes beyond physical characteristics. Kagan (1981) assessed the imitation of an experimenter's actions with various toys and determined that around 23–25 months of age 31 percent of the infants cried. Such crying did not occur at 20 months and dropped out by 29 months. Kagan asserts that the infants cried when they were not capable of imitating the actions. That is, infants do not cry when they do not have the self-awareness to recognize their limitations (20 months) or when they are capable of imitating the actions (29 months). Further, at around 24 months of age infants begin to make self-descriptive statements ("I play," "I can do this"). Such statements are meaningful because they do appropriately reflect the qualities of the self.

KNOWLEDGE OF SELF AND OTHERS

Although theorists typically have assumed that knowledge of the self derives from the mother–infant relation (for example, Mead, 1934; Stern, 1985), they do not agree how development of self-knowledge relates to the development of knowledge of the mother. Some have argued that infants' sense of themselves and others develop simultaneously (for example, Lewis & Brooks-Gunn, 1979).

TABLE 10-2 *Infant and Mother Versions of the Agency Tasks*

Infant Version	Mother Version
Task 1: Actor	
Infant acts upon self by feeding self a Cheerio.	Infant acts upon the mother by feeding the mother a Cheerio.
Task 2: Passive Agent	
Infant acts as an agent by passively pretending to feed self with a spoon or pretending to give self a drink with a cup.	Infant acts as an agent by passively pretending to feed the mother with a spoon or pretending to give the mother a drink with a cup.
Task 3: Active Other Agent	
Infant pretends to have a doll walk to a toy table and drink with a cup or eat with a spoon.	Infant asks (verbally or by action) the mother to come to the table and drink with a cup or eat with a spoon.
Task 4: Baby Behavior Role[a]	
Infant treats a doll as a baby by calling it a baby, giving it a drink with a baby bottle, giving it a rattle to play with, or having the doll kiss a toy teddy bear.	Infant treats the mother as a baby by calling her a baby, giving her a drink with a baby bottle, giving her a rattle to play with, or having her kiss a toy teddy bear.
Task 5: Two Interactive Agents	
Infant pretends that one doll feeds the second doll with spoon or gives the second doll a drink with a cup.	Infant pretends that one doll feeds the mother with a spoon or gives the mother a drink with a cup.
Task 6: Mother Behavioral Role[b]	
Infant pretends that the mother doll gives the baby doll a baby bottle, a rattle to play with, or the teddy bear to kiss, or the infant calls the mother doll a "mother" or the baby doll a "baby."	Infant asks (gesturally or verbally) the mother to give the baby doll a baby bottle, a rattle to play with, or the teddy bear to kiss, or the infant calls the mother a "mother" or the baby doll a "baby."

[a]*Two out of the four actions are required for a pass.*
[b]*Two out of the five actions are required for a pass.*
Source: *Pipp, Fischer, and Jennings, 1987. Copyright 1987 by the American Psychological Association. Reprinted by permission.*

Others have proposed a horizontal decalage with either the infants knowing themselves first (for example, Piaget 1962) or other knowledge preceeding self-knowledge (for example, Mead, 1934).

In a recent study, Pipp, Fischer, and Jennings (1987) made initial steps to address this issue and found a complex relationship. They assessed the development of self and mother knowledge in two domains: acting as an agent and recognizing features of a person. As illustrated in Tables 10-2 and 10-3 the agency tasks required the children to act either upon the themselves (infants versions) or upon the mothers (mothers versions). Based upon skill theory

TABLE 10-3 *Infant and Mother Versions of the Feature Tasks*

Task	Infant Version	Mother Version
	Visual Recognition	
Ia	Sticker-nose: Infant pulls sticker off own nose.	Sticker-nose: Infant pulls sticker off mother's nose.
Ib	Sticker-hand: Infant pulls sticker off own hand.	Sticker-hand: Infant pulls sticker off mother's hand.
2	Rouge task: Infant touches own nose after detecting rouge in the mirror.	Rouge task: Infant touches mother's nose after detecting rouge in the mirror.
	Spatial Location	
3	"Where's [Child's Name]?" Infant responds by pointing to self or by stating "Here" or "There."	"Where's Mommy?" Infant responds by pointing to mother or by stating "Here" or "There."
	Verbal Label	
4	"Who's that?" When experimenter points to infant, infant responds by stating his or her own proper name or by stating "me."	"Who's that?" When experimenter points to mother, infant responds by stating some variant of "mother" or by stating mother's proper name.
	Identification of Actor	
5	"Who did that?" After child claps, infant responds by stating his or her own proper name or by stating "me."	"Who did that?" After mother claps, infant responds by stating some variant of "mother" or by stating mother's proper name.
	Featural Possession	
6	"Whose shoe is that?" When experimenter points to infant's shoe, infant responds by stating his or her own proper name or by stating "mine."	"Whose shoe is that?" When experimenter points to mother's shoe, infant responds by stating some variant of "mother" or by stating mother's proper name.
	Familial Possession	
7	"Who do you belong to? Whose baby are you?" Infant responds by stating some family member.	"Who does your mommy belong to?" Infant responds by stating his or her own proper name, by "me" or by referring to some family member.
	Identification of Gender	
8	"Are you a boy? Are you a girl?" Infant responds correctly to both questions.	"Is Mommy a boy? Is Mommy a girl?" Infant responds correctly to both questions.

Source: Pipp, Fischer, and Jennings, 1987. Copyright 1987 by the American Psychological Association. Reprinted by permission.

(Fischer, 1980) the six tasks increased in complexity, starting with the sensorimotor act of eating a Cheerio and ending with the representation of the behavioral role of the mothers. The feature recognition tasks (see Table 10-3) ranged in difficulty from visual recognition to identification of gender.

Infant–mother dyads were tested at monthly intervals from 6 to 41 months of age. Overall, acquisition of self and mother knowledge was similar. Prior to 18 months, however, horizontal decalage was evident. Agency knowledge of self preceeded such knowledge of mother and the reverse was true of feature knowledge. Thus, not surprisingly, infants usually recognize their mothers before they recognize themselves in a mirror, but after 18 months of age featural knowledge of self and mother developed in synchrony. In the agency domain, however, knowledge of self tended to precede knowledge of the mother even at the later ages. In general, then, these findings indicate important similarities in the development of self and mother knowledge. They also indicate, however, that specific domains differ in their developmental patterns. Thus, in everyday life infants may learn first about themselves in some domains and about others first in different domains.

A MODEL OF THE DEVELOPMENT OF THE SELF-CONCEPT

Several theorists (for example, James, 1892/1961; Mead, 1934) make a distinction between two constitutents of the self: the "I" and the "me." The "I" is the subject who does the knowing or thinking. It is the constituent of the self that interprets events, people, and things. "It determines the very meaning of life events, providing itself even with a perspective to itself" (Damon & Hart, 1982; p. 845). Thus, "I" can reflect upon itself, is aware of its own awareness, and can organize and interpret experience. The "me" is the object of thought; it is what is known of the self. The "I" reflects upon the "me," just as it does for other objects of thought. In their review of the literature, Damon and Hart (1982) find many consistent findings in the research, even though a variety of methodologies were used. To organize this research literature they offer a tentative model of how the concept of self changes with age. In this model (see Figure 10-3) they distinguish four constituents of the "me": physical, active, social, and psychological self. At any age children know something about each of these components, but as the child develops, one constituent is emphasized over the others (see the emphasized diagonal boxes in Figure 10-3). Thus, for example, in early childhood, when asked to describe themselves, children are most likely to mention physical characteristics ("I have blond hair"). In middle and late childhood the emphasis is on the active self— the capabilities that the child has and how they compare to others. During development the emphasis changes, as does the nature of each constituent, with the constituent becoming more abstract and systematic. To illustrate, consider the psychological self. When young children refer to this constituent of the self they mention "momentary moods, feelings, preferences and aver-

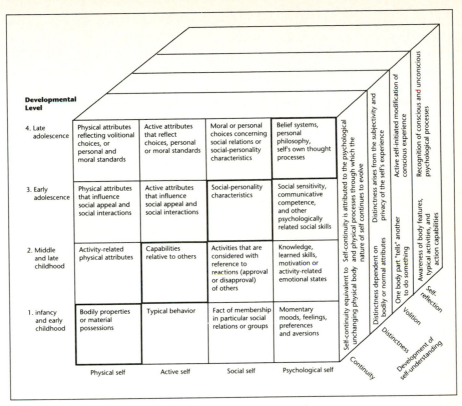

Developmental Level

	Physical self	Active self	Social self	Psychological self
4. Late adolescence	Physical attributes reflecting volitional choices, or personal and moral standards	Active attributes that reflect choices, personal or moral standards	Moral or personal choices concerning social relations or social-personality characteristics	Belief systems, personal philosophy, self's own thought processes
3. Early adolescence	Physical attributes that influence social appeal and social interactions	Active attributes that influence social appeal and social interactions	Social-personality characteristics	Social sensitivity, communicative competence, and other psychologically related social skills
2. Middle and late childhood	Activity-related physical attributes	Capabilities relative to others	Activities that are considered with reference to reactions (approval or disapproval) of others	Knowledge, learned skills, motivation or activity-related emotional states
1. infancy and early childhood	Bodily properties or material possessions	Typical behavior	Fact of membership in particular social relations or groups	Momentary moods, feelings, preferences and aversions

Continuity: Self-continuity equivalent to unchanging physical body / Self-continuity is attributed to the psychological and physical processes through which the nature of self continues to evolve

Distinctness: Distinctness dependent on bodily or normal attributes / Distinctness arises from the subjectivity and privacy of the self's experience

Volition: One body part "tells" another to do something / Active self-initiated modification of conscious experience

Self-reflection: Awareness of body features, typical activities, and action capabilities / Recognition of conscious and unconscious psychological processes

Development of self-understanding

▶ **FIGURE 10-3** *Conceptual foundations of the "Me" (physical, active, social, and psychological self-constituents) and the "I" (continuity, distinctness, volition, and self-reflection) at four developmental levels during childhood and adolescence. (From Damon & Hart, 1982.)*

sions" (Damon & Hart, 1982, p. 860). By late adolescence the psychological constituent is represented by belief systems and personal philosophies.

The side face of the model in Figure 10-3 represents developmental changes in the "I." An individual "is aware of the I through three types of experiences: continuity, distinctiveness, volition" (Damon & Hart, 1982, p. 844). Despite developmental changes, we experience the self in the past as the same self in the present. According to the model this sense of *self-continuity* initially is equivalent to the unchanging physical body but matures to the attribution of self-continuity on the basis of "psychological and physical processes through which the nature of self continues to evolve" (p. 860). We also perceive ourselves as distinct from others. Initially, this *distinctiveness* is evident in bodily characteristics, but by late adolescence this perception rests on our understanding that our experiences are subjective and private. Others cannot directly know our experiences. We also know that we exert *volition*, or control, over ourselves. The young child expresses this as one body part "telling" another something. At the mature end of the continium is recognition that we exert control over and modify our own experiences. Finally, these three types of experiences result in self-reflection. The self can think about the self. Initially these are reflections about actions, capabilities, and body features. Eventually, the self thinks about its own thinking, about conscious and unconscious processes.

Although this model is speculative, it does raise important questions about the development of children's concept of self. For instance, it raises the issue of the relationships between the development of the "I" and "me." The available data do not indicate distinct levels of development for the "I" constituents. The model assumes a gradual emergence of new notions about these constituents. Further research will be necessary to trace how the development of "I" relates to the development of "me" and how the development of self-understanding relates to other aspects of social cognition. We do know, however, that children's conception of others and social relations, such as friendship, appear to follow the same development course as the self-concept. Initially such concepts are characterized by physical attributes and overt activities. With age, these concepts become more abstract and psychological in nature (see, for example, Selman, 1981). In Chapter 5 we considered the characteristic-to-criterial shift of children's concepts. The development of self-concept appears to follow a comparable course, changing from a concrete to a more abstract conception. Unlike most other concepts, however, the self is changing as the child's conception of it changes.

▶ ## PROBLEM SOLVING

Children regularly face social problems, problems such as initiating a friendship, seeking or offering help, and preventing the action of another. Most of the research on children's social problem solving has focused on individual differences rather than developmental change (for example, Shure & Spivak, 1972; Spivak & Shure, 1974). This research sought to identify children whose social problem-solving deficits placed them at risk for the development of normal mental health (Rubin & Krasnor, 1986) and to intervene with training programs (see Urbain & Kendall, 1980, for a review of the training research).

As a consequence of this research focus, we know relatively little about the development of social problem-solving skills. Further, much of this research used hypothetical-reflective tasks to assess problem-solving skills. In these tasks a hypothetical social goal was specified (for example, a child seeks to obtain a toy that is in the possession of another) and the child had to reflect upon how that goal might be achieved. Unfortunately, this type of task tends to underestimate the skills of young children (see Rubin & Krasnor 1986, for a discussion). In addition, there is little evidence that performance on these tasks correlates significantly with social behavior.

Recently, Rubin and Krasnor (1986) have proposed an information-pro-

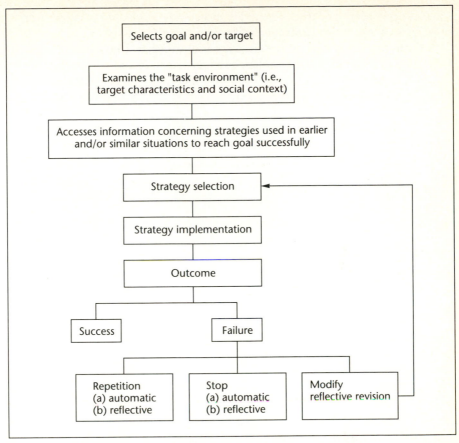

┌─────────────────────────┐
│ Selects goal and/or target │
└─────────────────────────┘

┌──────────────────────────────────────┐
│ Examines the "task environment" (i.e., │
│ target characteristics and social context) │
└──────────────────────────────────────┘

┌──┐
│ Accesses information concerning strategies used in earlier │
│ and/or similar situations to reach goal successfully │
└──┘

┌─────────────────┐
│ Strategy selection │ ◄──────
└─────────────────┘

┌──────────────────────┐
│ Strategy implementation │
└──────────────────────┘

┌──────────┐
│ Outcome │
└──────────┘

┌─────────┐   ┌─────────┐
│ Success │   │ Failure │
└─────────┘   └─────────┘

┌──────────────┐ ┌──────────────┐ ┌──────────────────┐
│ Repetition   │ │ Stop   │ │ Modify   │
│ (a) automatic │ │ (a) automatic │ │ reflective revision │
│ (b) reflective│ │ (b) reflective│ │   │
└──────────────┘ └──────────────┘ └──────────────────┘

▶ **FIGURE 10-4** *There are five component processes involved in this model of social problem solving: selecting a social goal, examining the task environment, accessing and selecting strategies, strategy implementation, and strategy outcome.* (From Rubin & Krasnor, 1986.)

cessing model of social problem solving, which is congruous with the discussion of problem solving in Chapter 9. As pictured in Figure 10-4 there are five component processes in this model: (a) selecting a social goal, (b) examining the task environment, (c) accessing and selecting strategies, (d) strategy implementation, (e) strategy outcome. Although there is relatively little research directly addressing this model, the model is a useful framework for considering developmental issues.

SELECTING A SOCIAL GOAL   Although children have many social needs and often face obstacles in meeting these needs, little research has focused on children's selections of social goals. The hypothetical-reflective tasks, for example, set the goals for the child. In this case it is not always clear that the child's goal is the experimenter's or that the child is sufficiently motivated to supply verbal responses. We saw this problem earlier with other tasks.

Natural observation of preschoolers indicate that a good proportion of their time is spent in social problem solving. Krasnor and Rubin (1983) observed 15 children for five hours each and identified over 6,000 attempts to solve social problems. They identified the following eight types of goals:

1) stop-action (prevent or stop other's action);
2) self-action (obtain permission to engage in activities);
3) object acquisition (acquire sole use of object);
4) attention (direct other's attention to specific object, event, or person);
5) affection (elicit or give prosocial contact);
6) information (elicit specific information or clarification);
7) nonspecific initiation (initiate conversational interaction after at least 10 sec. of noninteraction); and
8) other-action (elicit a specific active response from other not otherwise coded. (p. 1547)

In the preschool setting the other-action goal was the most frequent. Nonspecific initiations, information-seeking and attention goals, were also frequent. Object acquisition, which is the goal most often set for the child in the hypothetical-reflective tasks, was relatively infrequent. Affection goals were the least frequent of all. Thus, in this setting we know something about the goals of young children. We might expect, however, that children's goals will be influenced by the situation. Further, we might expect developmental changes in the social goals that children set for themselves.

Renshaw and Asher (1983) have demonstrated a developmental change in children's social goals. These researchers presented third through sixth graders with hypothetical social situations that were based on story grammar (see Chapter 7) but were incomplete. The children were asked to complete four situations. The experimenter asked them what they would do or say in each situation and then elicited the underlying goal by asking, "Why would you do (or say) those things?" Goals were inferred from the children's responses to this question.

The older children were more likely to produce positive outgoing goals that involved direct and friendly responses (for example, "I'd say, 'Can you play with me?' "). The younger children produced more hostile goals (for example, "I'd tell that child to get lost"). The developmental differences suggest that "older children were oriented to enhancing and maintaining positive peer relationships, whereas the younger children were oriented to preserving their own rights in social situations" (Renshaw & Asher, 1983, p. 364). Why do children set such different social goals? One possibility is that the older children are more likely to take the perspective of the other and to coordinate this perspective with their own perspective. Another possibility is that goal selection is influenced by children's assessment of the task environment. For example, three of the four situations in the study began with negative initiating events. Young children may be more likely to select negative goals after a negative event.

EXAMINING THE TASK ENVIRONMENT   There are social and nonsocial aspects of any situation that might influence the goal set by a child or the strategy selected to achieve that goal. For example, children appear to consider adults and older children as sources of information (Lewis & Feiring, 1979). French (1984) asked first and third graders about the social roles of older, younger, and same-age peers and found similar results for males and females and children of both ages. The children preferred to establish friendships with same-age peers. Older children were preferred as sources of instruction, leadership, help, and sympathy. The children preferred to direct instruction and sympathy to younger children (see also Edwards & Lewis, 1979). Preschoolers in the Krasnor and Rubin (1983) study were more likely to address their problem-solving attempts to same-sex peers than teachers or opposite-sex peers (see also Jacklin & Maccoby, 1978).

ACCESSING AND SELECTING STRATEGIES   The strategies accessed for a given situation will, of course, depend upon the strategies a child has acquired. Retrieval of some strategies may be fairly automatic. That is, a child may have scripts for certain types of social problems. If the task environment activates a given script the retrieval of a relevant strategy will be automatic. Whether strategies are accessed automatically or with deliberate effort, if more than one strategy is accessed, the child must in some way select one strategy for implementation.

STRATEGY IMPLEMENTATION   Once a strategy is selected the child must be able to implement the strategy. We might expect developmental changes in the ability of children to implement certain strategies. Indeed, strategy selection may depend, in part at least, on the children's assessment of their abilities to implement a given strategy. Thus performance factors can influence the selection process.

STRATEGY OUTCOME   Finally, after a strategy has been implemented children must assess whether their goals have been achieved or even partially achieved. On the basis of this assessment they may set new goals if the original goals have been achieved or decide what to do if an attempted strategy has failed. In this case the problem solver has three options: (a) stop attempting to achieve the goal, (b) repeat the same strategy, or (c) modify the previous strategy and try again.

In their preschool study, Krasnor and Rubin (1983) determined that 57 percent of the attempts to solve social problems were successful. Success for specific types of goals ranged from 72 percent for directing attention to 46 percent for eliciting other-action and self-action. "Goals that appeared to involve a higher cost (e.g., stopping an action already in progress, initiating a new activity) tended to fail more often" (p. 1556). Further, some individuals were more successful than others. Approximately 59 percent of the failed attempts were reattempted and most of these involved some modification in the strategy. Although few of these second attempts were successful, the data suggest some strategy flexibility on the part of preschoolers. Other data suggest increased flexibility beyond the preschool years which conforms to the findings cited in the preceeding chapter. Levin and Rubin (1983) found that, following failed requests, third graders were less likely than first graders and preschoolers to make rigid rerequests (this is, verbatim repetitions of the original request) and more likely to make flexible rerequests that rephrased the original request.

Further, there is suggestive evidence that children's attributions for the cause of failure affect their reactions to failure. For example, if children attribute a social failure to an external source rather than their own efforts they are less likely to make another attempt after an initial failure (Rubin & Krasnor, 1986). Thus, we need to consider the nature of children's social causal reasoning as we attempt to model the development of social problem solving.

AN INFORMATION-PROCESSING MODEL OF SOCIAL COMPETENCE

In the real social world children must function "on line." They must be responsive to the actions of others. They cannot completely control the actions of others, but must interpret others' actions and make appropriate responses. Recently, Dodge and his colleagues (Dodge, Pettit, McClaskey & Brown, 1986) have offered an information-processing model of social competence that specifies five separable sequential steps, as depicted in Figure 10-5, and appears compatible with the Rubin and Krasnor model of social problem solving. This model is intended to specify how cognitive skills relate to effective social behavior. The model proposes five components of social interaction: "(1) social cues or stimuli; (2) social information processing of these cues by a child; (3) social behaviors by a child that occur as a function of the child's processing of cues; (4) judgments by peers about the child's behavior; and (5) peers' behavior toward the child" (Dodge, Pettit, McClasky & Brown, 1986, pp. 2–3).

Thus, when social tasks confront children, they must encode the social cues, interpret the cues, generate one or more possible responses, evaluate and decide on a response, and then enact the response. The peer in turn goes through the same process and this can occur over and over in a given social transaction. Inherent in the peer's social information processing is a judgment of a child's social competence. In two experiments, Dodge and his colleagues assessed the social competence of children in two social tasks: entry into a peer group and response to a provocation by a peer. Both of these social tasks have been judged to be important ones for children's daily social interactions.

It was hypothesized that children's patterns of information processing of

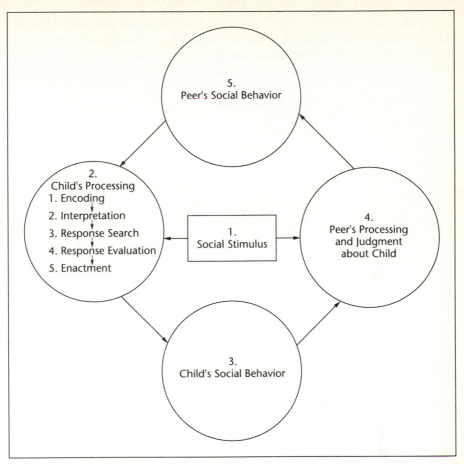

► **FIGURE 10-5** *A model of social exchange in children.* (From Dodge, Pettit, McClasky & Brown, 1986.)

a given situation would relate to how competently they actually behaved in that situation. Further, it was hypothesized that peers' judgments of children's behavior would be related to the quality of the children's behavior. To test these possibilities, children (first, second, and third graders), who were judged by their peers and teachers to be low and high in social competence, were presented a set of five videotape scenarios and a number of questions that were designed to assess the stages of information processing assumed for component two of the model. For the entry task, the first scene of each scenario was the same. Two children were seated at a table taking turns playing a board game. After several turns the scene ended and the subject was asked how much the two children would want him or her to join in play. The subject was then asked to think of as many ways as possible to join the group. Following this, each subject saw five different scenarios; each started with the first scene followed by the arrival of a third child (the entry child) who attempted to join the two children at play and acted out one of five strategies (competent, aggressive, self-centered, passive, and authority intervention). The scene was then stopped and the subject was asked to assess the quality of the entry child's strategy. After viewing the five scenarios, the subject was asked to act out with the experimenter how to ask to join other children in play.

Thus, the procedure assessed each subject's ability to encode and interpret (these two were not separated) a social situation, to search for responses to reach the given goal, to evaluate possible responses, and to enact a competent response.

One to two weeks after this task, each subject was asked to enter a situation in which two peers were engaged in play. Adult ratings of entry behavior and interviews with the peers and the subjects were used to assess the competence of each subject in this situation.

As expected, it was found that information-processing skills that were assessed in the videotape scenarios predicted behavior in the group entry task. Children "who generated competent and nonaggressive strategies in response to a hypothetical entry situation . . . , who evaluated incompetent responses negatively . . . , and who demonstrated high skill in enactment of responses were (more) likely to perform competently and successfuly in actual group entry behavior" (p. 24). Further, each of the processing steps contributed to the adequacy of the group entry behavior. Thus, it would appear that, as the model predicts, there are multiple components of social information processing, and each component contributes uniquely to social competence. In addition, social information appears to be domain specific. Group entry behavior was predicted from the entry processing patterns, but not from the processing patterns in the task in which the child responded to provocation by a peer. Similarly, the information pattern of provocation predicted behavioral responses to provocations, but not group entry behavior.

Taken together, the studies support the assumption that how children process the information of a social situation will predict their behaviors in that situation. Further, these behaviors lead peers to judge the children as competent or incompetent and to respond to the children according to this evaluation. To illustrate this last point, consider the response to Mark's above average entry behavior (Dodge *et al.*, 1986, p. 52):

▶ *Mark enters, pauses for a moment, and moves forward to the proximity of the two peer hosts, who are playing a board game.*
Mark: Can I play?
Host 1: Okay
Host 2: Okay
Host 1: Get yourself a seat.
Mark seats himself.
Host 2: What grade are you in?

Mark: Fourth. What grade are you in?

Host 2: Third

Host 1: Third. I'm eight.

Mark: I'm nine.

Host 2: I'm eight.

Host 1: This—if I were—today was my birthday and if I—if I was nine, I'd be as old as you. (p. 52)

The peers gave Mark the highest rating possible, and, as is evident, their behavior toward him was positive with a connected exchange of information. Contrast this with the entry of David.

▶ *David enters, hovers, motionless, while looking down at the table. Hosts are seated. Host 1 motions Host 2 to spin the dial for the game they are playing.*

Host 2: Line

Host 1: I get to go again.

Host 2: I know.

Host 2 looks at David, who is still standing. After a long pause, Host 2 speaks.

Host 2: What are you staring at?

David: Just watching . . . (inaudible mumble).

Host 2 giggles under his breath. The hosts continue playing the game.

Later in the episode, David moves around the table, looks up at the microphones, and makes several verbalizations that are not coherent . . . and are ignored by the hosts, except for mutual giggling. David never gets to play the game. (p. 53)

When asked to assess David's behavior the hosts rated David at 1.5, with 4 the highest possible rating.

The Dodge *et al.* model emphasizes the importance of children's processing of social information for understanding social behavior. In so doing, it raises several questions. For example, we might wonder if there are differences in the processing of social information as opposed to nonsocial information. Although there is no work directly addressing this issue, we might expect that the primary cognitive processes of encoding, storage, and retreival are comparable. Nevertheless, we might discover strategies and/or processes that are peculiar to social cognition. For example, affect may play a major role in the processing of social information (Shapiro & Weber, 1981). We saw in the delay of gratification research (Chapter 9) that children developed strategies for dealing with the distracting effects of the "hot" properties of rewards. Similarly, we might expect that as children develop they acquire strategies for controlling the affective aspects of social cognition.

Further, Dodge and his colleagues set specific goals for the children in their studies (for example, entry into a peer group). But in the real social world, children often must establish their own social goals. Thus, we need to consider how children set their goals in social situations.

The model is not a developmental one, but it does specify the components of social interaction that may be influenced by developmental changes. For instance, it raises questions about the nature of the social cues that are important to children's processing. That is, we need to determine what social information is encoded and interpreted by children. These cues can range from explicit verbal statements to facial expression. Further, there may be developmental changes in how peers judge another's behavior. What is considered acceptable or appropriate behavior by a young child may not be considered appropriate by an older child.

▶ ## SUMMARY

In this chapter we considered the nature of social cognition and several related developmental topics. Several lines of evidence indicate that young infants are responsive to their social environment. Infants, for instance, engage in reciprocal imitation with their caregivers. Further, they acquire expectations for the behavior of others and enjoy the contingent relations that are prevalent in social interactions. By the last quarter of the first year, infants are making social reference to familiar adults and imitating novel actions, even after a 24-hour delay. Infants this age are using others as sources of information.

During the preschool and elementary school years children acquire speaker and listener communication skills that enhance their referential communication. These skills include: (a) tailoring a message to the characteristics of the listener, (b) producing unambiguous messages that distinguish the referent from the nonreferents, (c) monitoring their comprehension of messages, and (d) providing feedback to the speaker. As children are acquiring communication skills they are learning to evaluate the quality of messages, to distinguish between the literal message and the intention of the speaker. Younger children are less likely to recognize that the speaker is responsible for the quality of a message and more likely to be influenced by the status of a speaker when evaluating a message. We speculated that schooling may teach children the skills necessary for evaluating messages.

Several lines of research indicate developmental changes in children's ability to take the perspective of another. During the school years, children become increasingly sophisticated in their ability to reason about another's perspective and in their ability to relate that perspective to their own. Although we do not have an integrated model of perspective taking, we do have some evidence that level of perspective is related to how children interact socially.

Critical to the understanding of another's behavior and the causes of behavior is the ability to make the distinction between intended and unintended acts. We have evidence that even young preschoolers have some understanding of intention since they can distinguish between intended acts and mistakes or accidents. By the age of five children are able to think recursively about intentions. We use several heuristic principles to determine whether acts are intended or not. Research on the discounting principle indicates that this principle is evident in the behavior of three-year-olds. It is not until the age of five, however, that the principle is evident in their judgments of behavior. Thus, as was the case with nonsocial causal reasoning, social causal reasoning is evident by the preschool years and becomes more sophisticated during this period.

As children acquire the many concepts that organize their world, they also acquire a concept of the self. Infants begin to know something of themselves in terms of contingent movements and visual features. As they acquire knowledge of themselves they also acquire comparable knowledge about a significant other, their mother. During childhood and adolescence the self-concept changes in the aspects emphasized and becomes more abstract.

Although we have little developmental research on social problem solving, we do have general, heuristic models that indicate where we might look for developmental changes. For instance, one model proposes five component processes that contribute to social problem solving: (a) selecting a goal, (b) examining the task environment, (c) accessing and selecting strategies, (d) implementation of a strategy, and (e) evaluations of the outcome. Further, we have data indicating that children's domain-specific knowledge of strategies for social tasks does influence their social behavior and how peers evaluate their behavior.

Bibliography

Abelson, R. P. (1981). Psychological status of the script concept. *American Psychologist, 36,* 715–729.

Abramson, A. S., & Lisker, L. (1970). Discriminability along the voicing continuum: Cross language tests. In B. Hala, M. Romportl, & P. Janota (Eds.), *Proceedings of the Sixth International Congress of Phonetic Sciences* (pp. 569–573). Prague: Academia.

Achenbach, T. M. (1970). Standardization of a research instrument for identifying associative responding in children. *Developmental Psychology, 2,* 283–291.

Ackerman, B. P. (1983). Speaker bias in children's evaluation of the external consistency of statements. *Journal of Experimental Child Psychology, 35,* 111–127.

Ackerman, B. P. (1984a). Storage and processing constraints on integrating story information in children and adults. *Journal of Experimental Child Psychology, 38,* 64–92.

Ackerman, B. P. (1984b). The effects of storage and processing complexity on comprehension repair in children and adults. *Journal of Experimental Child Psychology, 37,* 303–334.

Ackerman, B. P. (1986). The relation between attention to the incidental context and memory for words in children and adults. *Journal of Experimental Child Psychology, 41,* 149–183.

Adams, J. L. (1974). *Conceptual blockbusting: A guide to better ideas.* San Francisco: Freeman.

Adams, L. T., Kasserman, J. E., Yearwood, A. A., Perfetto, G. A., Bransford, J. D., & Franks, J. J. (1988). Memory access: The effects of fact-oriented versus problem-oriented acquisition. *Memory & Cognition, 16,* 167–175.

Adams, L. T., & Worden, P. E. (1986). Script development and memory organization in preschool and elementary school children. *Discourse Processes, 9,* 149–166.

Adams, M. J. (1984). Aristotle's logic. In G. H. Bower (Ed.), *The psychology of learning and motivation* (Vol. 18, pp. 255–311). New York: Academic Press.

Adams, R. J., & Maurer, P. (1983, April). *A demonstration of color perception in the newborn.* Paper presented at the biennial meeting of the Society for Research in Child Development, Detroit.

Aitchison, J. (1977). *The articulate animal: An introduction to psycholinguistics.* New York: Universe Books.

Alexander, P. A., Willson, V. L., White, C. S., & Fuqua, J. D. (1987). Analogical reasoning in young children. *Journal of Educational Psychology, 79,* 401–408.

Ames, E. W., & Silfen, C. K. (1965, March). *Methodological issues in the study of age differences in infants' attention to stimuli varying in movement and complexity.* Paper presented at the biennial meeting of the Society for Research in Child Development, Minneapolis.

Amigues, R. (1988). Peer interaction in solving physics problems: Sociocognitive confrontation and metacognitive aspects. *Journal of Experimental Child Psychology, 45,* 141–158.

Anderson, J. R. (1976). *Language, memory and thought.* Hillsdale, NJ: Erlbaum.

Anderson, J. R. (1982). Acquisition of cognitive skills. *Psychological Review, 89,* 369–406.

Anderson, J. R. (1985). *Cognitive psychology and its implications* (2nd ed.). New York: Freeman.

Anderson, J. R. (1987). Skill acquisition: Compilation of weak-method problem solutions. *Psychological Review, 94,* 192–210.

Anderson, R. C. (1984). Role of the reader's schema in comprehension, learning, and memory. In R. C. Anderson, J. Osborn & R. J. Tierney (Eds.), *Learning to read in American schools: Basal readers and content texts* (pp. 243–257). Hillsdale, NJ: Erlbaum.

Andrews, J. K. (1988). *Can we get from perception to categories without theories? An analysis of current conflicts in the study of categorization.* Paper presented at the meeting of the Society for Philosophy and Psychology, Poughkeepsie, New York.

Anooshian, L. J. (1987, April). *Implicit and explicit remembering by children and adults.* Paper presented at the biennial meeting of the Society for Research in Child Development, Baltimore, MD.

Anooshian, L. J., Pascal, V. U., & McCreath, H. (1984). Problem mapping before problem solving: Young children's cognitive maps and search strategies in large-scale environments. *Child Development, 55,* 1820–1834.

Antell, S. E., Caron, A. J., & Myers, R. S. (1985). Perception of relational invariants by newborns. *Developmental Psychology, 21,* 942–948.

Armstrong, S. L., Gleitman, L. R., & Gleitman, H. (1983). What some concepts might not be. *Cognition, 13,* 263–308.

Asher, S. R. (1979). Referential communication. In G. J. Whitehurst, & B. J. Whitehurst (Eds.), *The functions of language and cognition* (pp. 175–197). New York: Academic Press.

Ashmead, D. H., & Perlmutter, M. (1980). Infant memory in everyday life. In M. Perlmutter (Ed.), *New directions for child development: Vol. 10. Children's memory* (pp. 1–16). San Francisco: Jossey-Bass.

Aslin, R. N. (1987). Visual and auditory development in infancy. In J. D. Osofsky (Ed.), *Handbook of infant development* (2nd ed.) (pp. 5–97). New York: Wiley.

Aslin, R. N., & Jackson, R. W. (1979). Accommodative-convergence in young infants: Development of a synergistic sensory-motor system. *Canadian Journal of Psychology, 33,* 222–231.

Aslin, R. N., & Pisoni, D. B. (1980). Some developmental processes in speech perception. In G. H. Yeni-Komshian, J. F. Kavanagh, & C. A. Ferguson (Eds.), *Child phonology: Vol. 2. Perception* (pp. 67–96). New York: Academic Press.

Aslin, R. N., Pisoni, D. B., Hennessy, B., & Perey, A. J. (1981). Discrimination of VOT by human infants: New findings and implications for the effects of early experience. *Child Development, 52,* 1135–1145.

Aslin, R. N., Pisoni, D. B., & Jusczyk, P. W. (1983). Auditory development and speech perception in infancy. In P. H. Mussen, (Ed.) *Handbook of child psychology* (Vol. 2, pp. 573–687). New York: Wiley.

Aslin, R. N., Shea, S. L., Dumais, S. T., & Fox, R. (1979, March). *Stereoscopic depth perception in young infants.* Paper presented at the biennial meeting of the Society for Research in Child Development, San Fransisco.

Astington, J. W., Harris, P. L., & Olson, D. R. (1988). *Developing theories of mind.* Cambridge, England: Cambridge University Press.

Austin, J. L. (1962). *How to do things with words.* Oxford: Oxford University Press.

Azmitia, M. (1988). Peer interaction and problem solving: When are two heads better than one? *Child Development, 59,* 87–96.

Baddeley, A. D. (1982). Domains of recollection. *Psychological Review, 89,* 708–729.

Baddeley, A. D., & Hitch, G. (1974). Working memory. In G. H. Bower (Ed.), *The psychology of learning and motivation* (Vol. 8, pp. 47–89). New York: Academic Press.

Bahrick, H. P., Bahrick, P. O., & Wittlinger, R. P. (1975). Fifty years of memory for names and faces: A cross-sectional approach. *Journal of Experimental Psychology: General, 104,* 54–75.

Bahrick, L. E. (1983). Infants' perception of substance and temporal synchrony in multimodal events. *Infant Behavior and Development, 6,* 429–451.

Bahrick, L. E., & Watson, J. S. (1985). Detection of intermodal proprioceptive-visual contingency as a potential basis of self-perception in infancy. *Developmental Psychology, 21,* 963–973.

Baillargeon, R. (1986). Representing the existence and the location of hidden objects: Object permanence in 6- and 8-month-old infants. *Cognition, 23,* 21–41.

Baillargeon, R., Gelman, R., & Meck, E. (1981) *Are preschoolers truly indifferent to casual reasoning?* Paper presented at the biennial meeting of the Society for Research in Child Development, Boston.

Baillargeon, R., & Graber, M. (1988). Evidence of location memory in 8-month-old infants in a nonsearch AB task. *Developmental Psychology, 24,* 502–511.

Baillargeon, R., Spelke, E. S., & Wasserman, S. (1985). Object permanence in five-month-old infants. *Cognition, 20,* 191–208.

Baker, L. (1984a). Children's effective use of multiple standards for evaluating their comprehension. *Journal of Educational Psychology, 76,* 588–597.

Baker, L. (1984b). Spontaneous versus instructed use of multiple standards for evaluating comprehension: Effects of age, reading proficiency, and type of standard. *Journal of Experimental Child Psychology, 38,* 289–311.

Baker, L. (1985). How do we know when we don't understand? Standards for evaluating text comprehension. In D. L. Forrest-Pressley, G. E. Mackinnon, & T. G. Waller (Eds.), *Metacognition, cognition, and human performance: Theoretical perspectives* (Vol. 1, pp. 155–205). New York: Academic Press.

Baldwin, J. M. (1899) *Social and ethical interpretations in mental development.* New York: Macmillan.

Banks, M. S. (1980). The development of visual accommodation during early infancy. *Child Development, 51,* 646–666.

Banks, M. S., & Salapatek, P. (1981). Infant pattern vision: A new approach based on the contrast sensitivity function. *Journal of Experimental Child Psychology, 31,* 1–45.

Banks, M. S., & Salapatek, P. (1983). Infant visual perception. In P. H. Mussen (Ed.), *Handbook of child psychology* (4th ed., Vol. 2, pp. 435–571). New York: Wiley.

Barclay, L. K. (1985). *Infant development.* New York: Holt, Rinehart & Winston.

Bar-Hillel, M. (1980). The base-rate fallacy in probability judgments. *Acta Psychologica, 44,* 211–233.

Bar-Hillel, M., & Falk, R. (1982). Some teasers concerning conditional probabilities. *Cognition, 11,* 109–122.

Baroody, A. J. (1984). More precisely defining and measuring the order-irrelevance principle. *Journal of Experimental Child Psychology, 38,* 33–41.

Barrera, M. E., & Maurer, D. (1981). Recognition of mother's photographed face by the three-month-old infant. *Child Development, 52,* 714–716.

Barsalou, L. W., & Sewell, D. R. (1985). Contrasting the representation of scripts and categories. *Journal of Memory and Language, 24,* 646–665.

Bartlett, F. C. (1932). *Remembering: A study in experimental and social psychology.* Cambridge, England: Cambridge University Press.

Bartley, S. H. (1969). *Principles of perception* (2nd ed.). New York: Harper & Row.

Bartoshuk, A. K. (1962). Response decrement with repeated elicitation of human neonatal cardiac acceleration to sound. *Journal of Comparative and Physiological Psychology, 55,* 9–13.

Bates, E. (1979). Intention, convention, and symbols. In E. Bates, L. Benigni, I. Bretherton, L. Camaioni, & V. Volterra (Eds.), *The emergence of symbols: Cognition and communication in infancy* (pp. 33–68). New York: Academic Press.

Bates, E., Bretherton, I., Shore, C. & McNew, S. (1983). Names, gestures, and objects: Symbolization in infancy and aphasia. In K. E. Nelson (Ed.), *Children's language* (Vol. 4, pp. 59–123). Hillsdale, NJ: Erlbaum.

Bauer, P. J., & Mandler, J. M. (1987). Factors affecting very young children's recall of events. *Cognitive Development, 2,* 327–338.

Bauer, P. J., & Shore, C. M. (1987). Making a memorable event: Effects of familarity and organization on young children's recall of action sequences. *Cognitive Development, 2,* 327–338.

Bearison, D. J., & Gass, S. T. (1979). Hypothetical and practical reasoning: Children's persuasive appeals in different social contexts. *Child Development, 50,* 901–903.

Begg, I., & Denny, J. P. (1969). Empirical reconciliation of atmosphere and conversion interpretations of syllogistic reasoning errors. *Journal of Experimental Psychology, 81,* 351–354.

Benedict, H. (1979). Early lexical development: Comprehension and production. *Child Development, 6,* 183–200.

Benson, K. A., & Anderson-Beckman, J. (1981, April). *The "U-Shaped" Development of Sound Localization in Infants: Maturational and Experiential Explanations.* Paper presented at the biennial meeting of the Society for Research in Child Development, Boston.

Bereiter, C., Hidi, S., & Dimitroff, G. (1979). Qualitative changes in verbal reasoning during middle and late childhood. *Child Development, 50,* 142–151.

Berg, K. M., & Smith, M. C. (1983). Behavioral thresholds for tones during infancy. *Journal of Experimental Child Psychology, 35,* 409–425.

Berko, J. (1958). The child's learning of English morphology. *Word, 14,* 150–177.

Berko, J., & Brown, R. (1960). Psycholinguistic research methods. In P. H. Mussen (Ed.), *Handbook of research methods in child development* (pp. 517–557). New York: Wiley.

Berlyne, D. E. (1958). The influence of the albedo and complexity of stimuli on visual fixation in the human infant. *British Journal of Psychology, 49,* 315–318.

Bertenthal, B. I., Campos, J. J., & Haith, M. M. (1980). Development of visual organization: The perception of subjective contours. *Child Development, 51,* 1072–1080.

Best, D. L., & Ornstein, P. A. (1986). Children's generation and communication of mnemonic organizational strategies. *Developmental Psychology, 22,* 845–853.

Bethell-Fox, C. E., Lohman, D. F., & Snow, R. E. (1984). Adaptive reasoning: Componential and eye movement analysis of geometric analogy performance. *Intelligence, 8,* 205–238.

Bijou, S. W., & Baer, D. M. (1961). *Child development: A systematic and empirical theory* (Vol. 1). New York: Appleton-Century-Crofts.

Bindra, D., Clarke, K. A., & Shultz, T. R. (1980). Understanding predictive relations of necessity and sufficiency in formally equivalent "causal" and "logical" problems. *Journal of Experimental Psychology: General, 109,* 423–443.

Bivens, J. A., & Berk, L. E. (1988, April). *A longitudinal study of the development of children's private speech.* Paper presented at the meeting of the American Educational Research Association, New Orleans.

Bjorklund, D. F. (1985). The role of conceptual knowledge in the development of organization in children's memory. In C. J. Brainerd & M. Pressley (Eds.), *Basic processes in memory development: Progress in cognitive development research* (pp. 103–142). New York: Springer-Verlag Press.

Bjorklund, D. F. (1987a). A note on neonatal imitation. *Developmental Review, 7,* 86–92.

Bjorkland, D. F. (1987b). How age changes in knowledge base contribute to the development of children's memory: An interpretive review. *Developmental Review, 7,* 93–130.

Bjorklund, D. F., & Bjorklund, B. R. (1985). Organization versus item effects of an elaborated knowledge base on children's memory. *Developmental Psychology, 21,* 1120–1131.

Bjorklund, D. F., & Jacobs, J. W., III. (1985). Associative and categorical processes in children's memory: The role of automaticity in the development of organization in free recall. *Journal of Experimental Child Psychology, 39,* 599–617.

Black, M. (1946). *Critical thinking.* New York: Prentice-Hall.

Blasi, A., & Hoeffel, E. C. (1974). Adolescence and formal operations. *Human Development, 17,* 344–363.

Blewitt, P. (1982). Word meaning acquisition in young children: A review of theory and research. In H. W. Reese (Ed.), *Advances in child development and behavior* (pp. 139–195). New York: Academic Press.

Bloom, K. (1988). Quality of adult vocalizations affects the quality of infant vocalizations. *Journal of Child Language, 45,* 469–480.

Bloom, K., Russell, A., & Wassenberg, K. (1987). Turn taking affects the quality of infant vocalizations. *Journal of Child Language, 14,* 211–227.

Bloom, L. (1970). *Language development: Form and function in emerging grammars.* Cambridge, MA: MIT Press.

Bloom, L., & Lahey, M. (1978). *Language development and language disorders* (pp. 3–23). New York: Wiley.

Bloom, L., Lahey, M., Hood, L., Lifter, K., & Fiess, K. (1980). Complex sentences: Acquisition of synactic connectives and the semantic relations they encode. *Journal of Child Language, 2,* 235–261.

Bolles, R. C. (1976). Some relationships between learning and memory. In D. L. Medin, W. A. Roberts, & R. T. Davis (Eds.), *Processes of animal memory* (pp. 21–48). Hillsdale, NJ: Erlbaum.

Bomba, P. C., & Siqueland, E. R. (1983). The nature and structure of infant form categories. *Journal of Experimental Child Psychology, 35,* 294–328.

Boole, G. (1854). *An investigation into the laws of thought.* London: Walton & Maberly.

Borkowski, J. G., Levers, S., & Gruenenfelder, T. M. (1976). Transfer of mediational strategies in children: The role of activity and awareness during strategy acquisition. *Child Development, 47,* 779–786.

Bornstein, M. H. (1973). Color vision and color naming: A psychophysiological hypothesis of cultural difference. *Psychological Bulletin, 80,* 257–285.

Bornstein, M. H. (1976). Infants' recognition memory for hue. *Developmental Psychology, 12,* 185–191.

Bornstein, M. H. (1984). A descriptive taxonomy of psychological categories used by infants. In C. Sophian (Ed.), *Origins of cognitive skills* (pp. 313–338). Hillsdale, NJ: Erlbaum.

Bornstein, M. H. (1985). Habituation of attention as a measure of visual information processing in human infants: Summary, systemization, and synthesis. In G. Gottlieb & N. A. Krasnegor (Eds.), *Measurement of audition and vision in the first year of postnatal life: A methodological overview* (pp. 253–300). Norwood, NJ: Ablex.

Bornstein, M. H., Ferdinandsen, K., & Gross, C. G. (1981). Perception of symmetry in infancy. *Developmental Psychology, 17,* 82–86.

Bornstein, M. H., Kessen, W., & Weiskopf, S. (1976a). Color vision and hue categorization in young human infants. *Journal of Experimental Psychology: Human Perception and Performance, 2,* 115–129.

Bornstein, M. H., Kessen, W., & Weiskopf, S. (1976b). The categories of hue in infancy. *Science, 191,* 201–202.

Bornstein, M. H., & Korda, N. O. (1984). Discrimination and matching within and between hues as measured by reaction times: Some implications for categorical perception and levels of information processing. *Psychological Research, 46,* 207–222.

Bornstein, M. H., & Korda, N. O. (1985). Identification and adaptation of hue: Parallels in the operation of mechanisms that underlie categorical perception in vision and audition. *Psychological Research, 47,* 1–17.

Bornstein, M. H., & Krinsky, S. J. (1985). Perception of symmetry in infancy: The salience of vertical symmetry and the perception of pattern wholes. *Journal of Experimental Child Psychology, 39,* 1–19.

Bornstein, M. H., Krinsky, S. J., & Benasich, A. A. (1986). Fine orientation discrimination and shape constancy in young infants. *Journal of Experimental Child Psychology, 41,* 49–60.

Boswell, D. A., & Green, H. F. (1982). The abstraction and recognition of prototypes by children and adults. *Child Development, 53,* 1028–1037.

Bowden, E. M. (1985). Accessing relevant information during problem solving: Time constraints on search in the problem space. *Memory & Cognition, 13,* 280–286.

Bower, T. G. R. (1966a). Slant perception and shape constancy in infants. *Science, 151,* 832–834.

Bower, T. G. R. (1966b). The visual world of infants. *Scientific American, 215*(6), 80–92.

Bower, T. G. R. (1974). *Development in infancy* (lst ed.). San Francisco: Freeman.

Bower, T. G. R., Broughton, J. M., & Moore, M. K. (1970). The coordination of visual and tactual input in infants. *Perception and Psychophysics, 8,* 51–53.

Bower, T. G. R., & Wishart, J. G. (1972). The effects of motor skill on object permanence. *Cognition, 1,* 165–171.

Bowerman, M. (1978). Systematizing semantic knowledge: Changes over time in the child's organization of word meaning. *Child Development, 49,* 977–987.

Bowerman, M. (1979). The acquisition of complex sentences. In P. Fletcher & M. Garman (Eds.), *Language acquisition: Studies in first language development* (pp. 285–305). Cambridge, England: Cambridge University Press.

Bowerman, M. (1982). Reorganizational processes in lexical and syntactic development. In E. Wanner & L. R. Gleitman (Eds.), *Language acquisition: The state of the art* (pp. 51–77). Cambridge, England: Cambridge University Press.

Braine, M. D. S. (1959). The ontogeny of certain logical operations: Piaget's formulation examined by nonverbal methods. *Psychological Monographs, 73*(5, Whole No. 475).

Braine, M. D. S. (1962). Piaget on reasoning: A methodological critique and alternative proposals. In W. Kessen & C. Kuhlman (Eds.), Thought in the young child. *Monographs of the Society for Research in Child Development, 27*(2, Whole No. 83).

Braine, M. D. S. (1976) Children's first word combinations. *Society for Research in Child Development Monographs, 41*(1, Serial No. 164).

Braine, M. D. S. (1978). On the relation between the natural logic of reasoning and standard logic. *Psychological Review, 85,* 1–21.

Braine, M. D. S. (1987). What is learned in acquiring word classes: A step toward an acquisition theory. In M. B. MacWhinney (Ed.), *Mechanism of language acquisition* (pp. 65–87). Hillsdale, NJ: Erlbaum.

Braine, M. D. S., & Rumain, B. (1983). Logical reasoning. In P. H. Mussen (Ed.), *Handbook of child psychology* (4th Ed., Vol. 3, pp. 263–340). New York: Wiley.

Braine, M. D. S., & Shanks, B. L. (1965a). The conservation of a shape property and a proposal about the origin of the conservations. *Canadian Journal of Psychology, 19,* 197–207.

Braine, M. D. S., & Shanks, B. L. (1965b). The development of conservation of size. *Journal of Verbal Learning and Verbal Behavior, 4,* 227–242.

Brainerd, C. J. (1978). *Piaget's theory of intelligence.* Englewood Cliffs, NJ: Prentice-Hall.

Brainerd, C. J. & Kingma, J. (1984). Development of transitivity: A fuzzy-trace theory. *Developmental Review, 4,* 311–377.

Bransford, J. D. (1979). *Human cognition: Learning, understanding and remembering.* Belmont, CA: Wadsworth.

Bransford, J. D., & Franks, J. J. (1971). The abstraction of linguistic ideas. *Cognitive Psychology, 2,* 331–350.

Bransford, J., Sherwood, R., Vye, N., & Rieser, J. (1986). Teaching thinking and problem solving. *American Psychologist, 41,* 1078–1089.

Bredberg, T. (1985). The anatomy of the developing ear. In S. Trehub & B. Schneider (Eds.), *Auditory development in infancy* (pp. 3–20). New York: Plenum Press.

Breen, S. (1987). *Investigation into the effect of familiarity of topic material and number of sentences on comprehension monitoring ability.* Unpublished B.A. honor's thesis, Bowdoin College, Brunswick, ME.

Brennan, W. M., Ames, E. V., & Moore, R. W. (1966). Age differences in infants' attention to patterns of different complexities. *Science, 151,* 354–356.

Breslow, L. (1981). Re-evaluation of the literature on the development of transitive inference. *Psychological Bulletin, 89,* 325–351.

Bretherton, I. (1984). Social referencing and the interfacing of minds: A commentary on the views of Feinman and Campos. *Merrill-Palmer Quarterly, 30,* 419–427.

Brewer, W. F., & Lichtenstein, E. H. (1981). Event schemas, story schemas, and story grammars. In J. Long & A. Baddeley (Eds.), *Attention and performance IX* (pp. 363–379). Hillsdale, NJ: Erlbaum.

Bridges, A. (1980). SVO comprehension strategies reconsidered: The evidence of individual patterns of response. *Child Language, 7,* 89–104.

Bridges, A., Sinha, C., & Walkerdine, V. (1981). The development of comprehension. In G. Wells (Ed.), *Learning through interaction* (pp. 116–156). Cambridge, England: Cambridge University Press.

Bringuier, J. C. (1980). *Conversations with Jean Piaget.* Chicago: University of Chicago Press.

Britton, B. K., & Tesser, A. (1982). Effects of prior knowledge on use of cognitive capacity in three complex cognitive tasks. *Journal of Verbal Learning and Verbal Behavior, 21,* 421–436.

Britton, J. (1970). *Language and learning.* London: Penguin Books.

Broadbent, D. E. (1958). *Perception and communication.* New York: Pergamon Press.

Bronson, G. W. (1974). The postnatal growth of visual capacity. *Child Development, 45,* 873–890.

Bronson, G. W. (1982). *The scanning patterns of human infants: Implications for visual learning.* Norwood, NJ: Ablex.

Brooks, L. R. (1978). Nonanalytic concept formation and memory for instances. In E. Rosch & B. B. Lloyd (Eds.), *Cognition and categorization* (pp. 169–211). Hillsdale, NJ: Erlbaum.

Brooks-Gunn, J. & Lewis, M. (1984) The development of early visual self-recognition. *Developmental Review, 4,* 215–239.

Brown, A. L. (1975). The development of memory: Knowing, knowing about knowing, and knowing how to know. In H. W. Reese (Ed.), *Advances in child development and behavior* (Vol. 10, pp. 103–151). New York: Academic Press.

Brown, A. L . (1976). The construction of temporal succession by preoperational children. In A. D. Pick (Ed.), *Minnesota Symposium on Child Psychology* (Vol. 10, pp. 28–83). Minneapolis: University of Minnesota Press.

Brown, A. L. (1979). Theories of memory and the problems of development: Activity, growth, and knowledge. In L. S. Cermak & F. I. M. Craik (Eds.), *Levels of processing in human memory* (pp. 225–258). Hillsdale, NJ: Erlbaum.

Brown, A. L. (1982). Learning and development: The problem of compatibility, access, and induction. *Human Development, 25,* 89–115.

Brown, A. L., Bransford, J. D., Ferrara, R. A., & Campione, J. C. (1983). Learning, remembering, and understanding. In P. H. Mussen (Ed.), *Handbook of child psychology* (Vol. 3, 4th ed., pp. 77–166). New York: Wiley.

Brown, A. L., & Campione, J. C. (1972). Recognition memory for perceptually similar pictures in preschool children. *Journal of Experimental Psychology, 95,* 55–62.

Brown, A. L., & DeLoache, J. S. (1978). Skills, plans, and self-regulation. In R. S. Siegler (Ed.), *Children's thinking: What develops?* (pp. 3–35). Hillsdale, NJ: Erlbaum.

Brown, A. L., & Scott, M. S. (1971). Recognition memory for pictures in preschool children. *Journal of Experimental Child Psychology, 11,* 401–412.

Brown, A. L., Smiley, S. S., Day, J. D., Townsend, M. A. R., & Lawton, S. C. (1977). Intrusion of a thematic idea in children's comprehension and retention of stories. *Child Development, 48,* 1454–1466.

Brown, J. (1958). Some tests of the decay theory of immediate memory. *Quarterly Journal of Experimental Psychology, 10,* 12–21.

Brown, R. W. (1957). Linguistic determinism and the part of speech. *Journal of Abnormal & Social Psychology, 55,* 1–5.

Brown, R. W. (1973). *A first language: The early stages*. Cambridge, MA: Harvard University Press.

Brown, R. W., Cazden, C., & Bellugi-Klima, U. (1969). The child's grammar from I to III. In J. P. Hill (Ed.), *Minnesota symposia on child psychology* (Vol. 2, pp. 28–73). Minneapolis: University of Minnesota Press.

Bruner, J. S. (1975). The ontogenesis of speech acts. *Journal of Child Language, 2,* 1–19.

Bruner, J. (1983). *Child's talk: Learning to use language*. New York: Norton.

Bruner, J. S., Goodnow, J. J., & Austin, G. A. (1956). *A study of thinking*. New York: Wiley.

Bruner, J. S., Olver, R. O. & Greenfield, P. M. (1966). *Studies in cognitive growth*. New York: Wiley.

Brunswik, E. (1956). *Perception and the representative design of psychological experiments*. Berkeley: University of California Press.

Bullock, M. (1985). Causal reasoning and developmental change over the preschool years. *Human Development, 28,* 169–191.

Bullock, M., & Gelman, R. (1979). Preschool children's assumptions about cause and effect: Temporal ordering. *Child Development, 50,* 89–96.

Bullock, M., Gelman, R., & Baillargeon, R. (1982). The development of causal reasoning. In W. J. Friedman (Ed.), *The developmental psychology of time* (pp. 209–254). New York: Academic Press.

Bundy, R. S., Colombo, J., & Singer, J. (1982). Pitch perception in young infants. *Developmental Psychology, 18,* 10–14.

Burnham, D. K., Earnshaw, L. S., & Quinn, M. C. (1987). The development of the categorical identification of speech. In B. E. McKenzie and R. W. Day (Eds.), *Perceptual development in early infancy: Problems and issues.* (pp. 237–275) Hillsdale, NJ: Erlbaum.

Bushnell, E. W. (1981). The ontogeny of intermodal relations: Vision and touch in infancy. In R. Walk & H. Pick (Eds.), *Intersensory perception and sensory integration* (pp. 5–36). New York: Plenum Press.

Bushnell, E. W., & Roder, B. J. (1985). Recognition of color-form compounds by 4-month-old infants. *Infant Behavior and Development, 8,* 255–268.

Bushnell, I. W. R. (1979). Modification of the externality effect in young infants. *Journal of Experimental Child Psychology, 28,* 211–229.

Bushnell, I. W. R., Gerry, G., & Burt, K. (1983). The externality effect in neonates. *Infant Behavior and Development, 6,* 151–156.

Butterworth, G. (1981). The origins of auditory-visual perception and visual proprioception in human development. In R. D. Walk & H. L. Pick, Jr. (Eds.), *Intersensory perception and sensory integration* (pp. 37–70). New York: Plenum Press.

Butterworth, G. (1983). Structure of the mind in human infancy. In L. P. Lipsitt (Ed.), *Advances in Infancy Research* (Vol. 2, pp. 1–29). Norwood, NJ.: Ablex.

Bynum, T. W., Thomas, J. A., & Weitz, L. J. (1972). Truth-functional logic in formal operational thinking: Inhelder and Piaget's evidence. *Developmental Psychology, 7,* 129–132.

Callanan, M. A. (1985). How parents label objects for young children: The role of input in the acquisition of category hierarchies. *Child Development, 56,* 508–523.

Callanan, M. A., & Markman, E. M. (1982). Principles of organization in young children's natural language hierarchies. *Child Development, 53,* 1093–1101.

Campbell, B. A., & Jaynes, J. (1966). Reinstatement. *Psychological Review, 73,* 478–480.

Campione, J. C., & Brown, A. L. (in press). Guided learning and transfer: Implications for approaches to assessment. In N. Fredericksen, R. Glaser, A. Lesgold, & M. Shafto (Eds.), *Monitoring of skill acquisition*. Hillsdale, NJ: Erlbaum.

Campos, J. J. (1984). A new perspective on emotions. *Child Abuse & Neglect, 8,* 147–156.

Campos, J. J., & Stenberg, C. (1981). Perception, appraisal, and emotion: The onset of social referencing. In M. E. Lamb & L. R. Sherrod (Eds.), *Infant social cognition: Empirical and theoretical considerations* (pp. 273–314). Hillsdale, NJ: Erlbaum.

Cantor, J. H., & Spiker, C. C. (1978). The problem-solving strategies of kindergarten and first-grade children during discrimination learning. *Journal of Experimental Child Psychology, 26,* 341–358.

Cantor, J. H., & Spiker, C. C. (1984). Evidence for long-term planning in children's hypothesis testing. *Bulletin of the Psychonomic Society, 22,* 493–496.

Caplan, J. S. (1981, April). *Children's interpretation of abstract premises: Don't go with what you know*. Paper presented at the biennial meeting of the Society for Research in Child Development, Boston.

Capp G. R., & Capp, T. R. (1965). *Principles of argumentation and debate*. Englewood Cliffs, NJ: Prentice-Hall.

Carey, S. (1979). Cognitive competence. In A. Floyd (Ed.), *Cognitive development in school years* (pp. 45–66). New York: Wiley.

Carey, S. (1985a). Are children fundamentally different kind of thinkers and learners than adults? In S. Chapman, J. Segal, & R. Glaser (Eds.), *Thinking and learning skills* (Vol. 2, pp. 485–517). Hillsdale, NJ: Erlbaum.

Carey, S. (1985b). *Conceptual change in childhood*. Cambridge, MA: MIT Press.

Carney, J. D., & Scheer, R. K. (1974). *Fundamentals of logic* (2nd ed.). New York: Macmillan.

Carni, E., & French, L. A. (1984). The acquisition of before and after reconsidered: What develops? *Journal of Experimental Child Psychology, 37,* 394–403.

Caron, A. J., Caron, R. F., Caldwell, R. C., & Weiss, S. J. (1973). Infant perception of the structural properties of the face. *Developmental Psychology, 9,* 385–399.

Caron, A. J., Caron, R. F., & Carlson, V. R. (1979). Infant perception of the invariant shape of objects varying in slant. *Child Development, 50,* 716–721.

Carson, M. T., & Abrahamson, A. (1976). Some members are more equal than others: The effect of semantic typicality on class-inclusion performance. *Child Development, 47,* 1186–1190.

Case, R. (1972). Validation of neo-Piagetian mental capacity construct. *Journal of Experimental Child Psychology, 14,* 287–302.

Case, R. (1974). Structures and strictures: Some functional limitations on the course of cognitive growth. *Cognitive Psychology, 6,* 544–573.

Case, R. (1985). *Intellectual development: Birth to adulthood*. New York: Academic Press.

Case, R., Kurland, M., & Goldberg, J. (1982). Operational efficiency and the growth of short-term memory span. *Journal of Experimental Child Psychology, 33,* 386–404.

Catrambone, R., & Holyoak, K. J. (In press). Overcoming contextual limitations on problem-solving transfer. *Journal of Experimental Psychology: Learning, Memory and Cognition.*

Cavanaugh, J. C., & Perlmutter, M. (1982). Metamemory: A critical examination. *Child Development, 53,* 11–28.

Chaffin, R., & Herrmann, D. J. (1984). The similarity and diversity of semantic relations. *Memory & Cognition, 12,* 134–141.

Chalkley, M. A. (1982). The emergence of language as a social skill. In S. A. Kuczaj, II (Ed.), *Language development: Vol. 2. Language, thought and culture* (pp. 75–111). Hillsdale, NJ: Erlbaum.

Chandler, M. (1972). Egocentrism in normal and pathological childhood development. In W. Hartup & J. DeWitt (Eds.), *Determinants of behavioral development* (pp. 569–576). New York: Academic Press.

Chapman, L. J., & Chapman, J. P. (1959). Atmosphere effect re-examined. *Journal of Experimental Psychology, 58,* 220–226.

Chapman, M., & Lindenberger, U. (1988). Functions, operations, and decalage in the development of transitivity. *Developmental Psychology, 24,* 542–551.

Chapman, R. S., & Kohn, L. L. (1978). Comprehension strategies in two and three year olds: Animate agents or probable events? *Journal of Speech and Hearing Research, 21,* 746–761.

Chase, W. G., Simon, H. A. (1973). Perception in chess. *Cognitive Psychology, 4,* 55–81.

Chechile, R. A., & Richman, C. L. (1982). The interaction of semantic memory with storage and retrieval processes. *Developmental Review, 2,* 237–250.

Cheng, P. W., & Holyoak, K. J. (1985). Pragmatic reasoning schemas. *Cognitive Psychology, 17,* 391–416.

Chi, M. T. H. (1976). Short-term memory limitations in children: Capacity or processing deficits? *Memory & Cognition, 4,* 559–572.

Chi, M. T. H. (1978). Knowledge structures and memory development. In R. S. Siegler (Ed.), *Children's thinking: What develops?* (pp. 73–96). Hillsdale, NJ: Erlbaum.

Chi, M. T. H. (1979). Knowledge development and memory performance. In M. P. Fridman, J. P. Das, & N. O'Connor (Eds.), *Intelligence and learning* (pp. 221–229). New York: Plenum Press.

Chi, M. T. H. (1985). Interactive roles of knowledge and strategies in the development of organized sorting and recall. In S. Chipman, J. Segal, & R. Glaser (Eds.), *Thinking and learning skills* (Vol. 2, pp. 457–483). Hillsdale, NJ: Erlbaum.

Chi, M. T. H., Feltovich, P. J, & Glaser, R. (1981). Categorization and representation of physics problems by experts and novices. *Cognitive Science, 5,* 121–152.

Chi, M. T. H., & Gallagher, J. D. (1982). Speed of processing: Source of limitation. *Topics in Learning and Learning Disabilities, 2,* 23–32.

Chi, M. T. H., & Glaser, R. (1985). Problem-solving ability. In R. J. Sternberg (ed.), *Human abilities: An information-processing approach* (pp. 227–250). New York: Freeman.

Chi, M. T. H., Glaser, R., & Rees, E. (1982). Expertise in problem solving. In R. J. Sternberg (Ed.), *Advances in the psychology of human intelligence* (Vol. 1, pp. 7–75). Hillsdale, NJ: Erlbaum.

Chomsky, N. (1957). *Syntactic structures.* The Hague: Norton.

Chomsky, N. (1959). Review of Skinner's "Verbal behavior." *Language, 35,* 26–58.

Chomsky, N. (1965). *Aspects of the theory of syntax.* Cambridge, MA: MIT Press.

Chomsky, N. (1980). On cognitive structures and their development: A reply to Piaget. In M. Piatelli-Palmarini (Ed.), *Language and learning: The debate between Jean Piaget and Noam Chomsky* (pp. 35–54). Cambridge, MA: Harvard University Press.

Clark, E. V. (1973). Non-linguistic strategies and the acquisition of word meanings. *Cognition, 2,* 161–182.

Clark, E. V. (1977). Strategies and the mapping problem in first language. In J. Macnamara (Ed.), *Language learning and thought* (pp. 147–168). New York: Academic Press.

Clark, E. V. (1980). Here's the top: Nonlinguistic strategies in the acquisition of orientational terms. *Child Development, 51,* 329–338.

Clark, E. V. (1982) Language change during language acquisition. In M. E. Lamb & A. L. Brown (Eds.), *Advances in developmental psychology* (Vol. 2, pp. 171–195). Hillsdale, NJ: Erlbaum.

Clark, E. V. (1983). Meanings and concepts. In P. H. Mussen (Ed.), *Carmichael's manual of Child psychology: Vol. 3: Cognitive Development* (pp. 787–889). New York: Wiley.

Clark, E. V. (1987). The principle of contrast: A constraint on language acquisition. In B. MacWhinney (Ed.), *Mechanisms of language acquisition* (pp. 1–33). New York: Erlbaum.

Clark, E. V. (1988). On the logic of contrast. *Journal of Child Language, 15,* 317–335.

Clark, E. V., & Hecht, B. F. (1983). Comprehension, production, and language acquisition. *Annual Review of Psychology, 34,* 325–349.

Clark, H. H. (1983). Making sense of nonce sence. In G. B. Flores d'Arcais, & R. J. Jarvella (Eds.), *The process of language understanding* (pp. 297–331). New York: Wiley.

Clark, H. H. & Clark, E. V. (1977). *Psychology and Language.* New York: Harcourt Brace Jovanovich.

Clarkson, M. G., & Clifton, R. K. (1985). Infant pitch perception: Evidence for responding to pitch categories and the missing fundamental. *Journal of the Acoustical Society of America, 77,* 1521–1528.

Clement, C. A., & Falmagne, R. J. (1986). Logical reasoning, world knowledge, and mental imagery: Interconnections in cognitive processes. *Memory & Cognition, 14,* 299–307.

Clement, J. (1985, April). *A method experts use to evaluate the validity of models used as problem representations in science and mathematics.* Paper presented at the meeting of the American Educational Research Association, Chicago.

Clifton, R. K., Morrongiello, B. A., Kulig, J. W., & Dowd, J. M. (1981). Developmental changes in auditory localization in infancy. In R. N. Aslin, J. R. Alberts, & M. R. Petersen (Eds.), *Development of perception* (Vol. 1, pp. 141–160). New York: Academic Press.

Clifton, R. K., & Nelson, M. N. (1976). Developmental study of habituation in infants. The importance of paradigm, response system, and state. In T. J. Tighe & R. W. Leaton (Eds.), *Habituation: Perspectives from child development, animal behavior, and neurophysiology* (pp. 159–206). Hillsdale, NJ: Erlbaum.

Cohen, L. B., & Caputo, N. (1978, May). *Instructing infants to respond to perceptual categories.* Paper presented at the Midwestern Psychological Association Convention, Chicago.

Cohen, L. B., & Gelber, E. R. (1975). Infant visual memory. In L. B. Cohen & P. Salapatek (Eds.), *Infant perception: From sensation to cognition: Vol. 1. Basic Visual processes* (pp. 347–403). New York: Academic Press.

Cohen, L. B., & Strauss, M. S. (1979). Concept acquisition in the human infant. *Child Development, 50,* 419–424.

Colberg, M., Nester, M. A., & Trattner, M. H. (1985). Convergence of the inductive and deductive models in the measurement of reasoning abilities. *Journal of Applied Psychology, 70,* 681–694.

Collins, A., & Gentner, D. (1987). How people construct mental models. In D. Holland & N. Quinn (Eds.), *Cultural models in language and thought* (pp. 243–265). Cambridge, England: Cambridge University Press.

Collins, A. M., & Quillan, M. R. (1969). Retrieval time from semantic memory. *Journal of Verbal Learning & Verbal Behavior, 8*, 407–428.

Cook, M. (1987). The origins of form perception. In B. E. McKenzie & R. H. Day (Eds.), *Perceptual development in early infancy: Problems and issues* (pp. 93–123). Hillsdale, NJ: Erlbaum.

Copi, I. M. (1972). *Introduction to logic* (4th ed.). New York: Macmillan.

Cornell, E. H. (1979). Infants' recognition memory, forgetting, and savings. *Journal of Experimental Child Psychology, 28*, 359–374.

Cornell, E. H. (1980). Distributed study facilitates infants' delayed recognition memory. *Memory & Cognition, 8*, 539–542.

Cornell, E. H., & Bergstrom, L. I. (1983). Serial-position effects in infants' recognition memory. *Memory & Cognition, 11*, 494–499.

Cornell, E. H., & McDonnell, P. M. (1986). Infants' acuity at twenty feet. *Investigative Ophthamology & Visual Science, 27*, 1417–1420.

Cox, J. R., & Griggs, R. A. (1982). The effects of experience on performance in Wason's selection task. *Memory & Cognition, 10*, 496–502.

Craik, F. I. M., & Lockhart, R. S. (1972). Levels of processing: A framework for memory research. *Journal of Verbal Learning and Verbal Behavior, 11*, 671–684.

Craik, F. I. M., & Watkins, M. J. (1973). The role of rehearsal in short-term memory. *Journal of Verbal Learning & Verbal Behavior, 12*, 599–607.

Crassini, B., & Broerse, J. (1980). Auditory-visual integration in neonates: A signal detection analysis. *Journal of Experimental Child Psychology, 29*, 144–155.

Crider, C. (1981). Children's conceptions of the body interior. In R. Bibace & M. Walsh (Eds.), *New directions for child development: Children's conceptions of health, illness, and bodily functions* (pp. 49–65). San Francisco: Jossey-Bass.

Crisafi, M. A., & Brown, A. L. (1986). Analogical transfer in very young children: Combining two separately learned solutions to reach a goal. *Child Development, 57*, 953–968.

Cromer, R. (1979). The strengths of the weak form of the cognition hypothesis for language acquisition. In V. Lee (Ed.), *Language development* (pp. 102–130). New York: Wiley.

Daehler, M. W., Horowitz, A. B., Wynns, F. C., & Flavell, J. H. (1969). Verbal and nonverbal rehearsal in children's recall. *Child Development, 40*, 443–452.

Dale, P. S. (1976). *Language development: Structure and function* (2nd ed.). New York: Holt, Rinehart & Winston.

Damon, W., & Hart, D. (1982). The development of self-understanding from infancy through adolescence. *Child Development, 53*, 841–864.

Damon, W., & Killen, M. (1982). Peer interaction and the process of change in children's moral reasoning. *Merrill-Palmer Quarterly, 28*, 347–367.

Dannemiller, J. L., & Stephens, B. R. (1988). A critical test of infant pattern preference models. *Child Development, 59*, 210–216.

Danner, F. W., & Day, M. C. (1977). Eliciting formal operations. *Child Development, 48*, 1600–1606.

Davis, J. M., & Rovee-Collier, C K. (1983). Alleviated forgetting of a learned contingency in 8-week-old infants. *Developmental Psychology, 19*, 353–365.

Day, M. C. (1980). Selective attention by children and adults to pictures specified by color. *Journal of Experimental Child Psychology, 30*, 277–289.

Day, R. H. (1987). Visual size constancy in infancy. In R. H. Day and B. E. McKenzie (Eds.), *Perceptual development in early infancy: Problems and issues* (pp. 67–91). Hillsdale, NJ: Erlbaum.

Day, R. H., & McKenzie, B. E. (1977). Constancies in the perceptual world of the infant. In W. Epstein (Ed.), *Stability and constancy in visual perception* (pp. 285–320). New York: Wiley.

Day, R. H., & McKenzie, B. E. (1981). Infant perception of the invariant size of approaching and receding objects. *Developmental Psychology, 17*, 670–677.

DeBaryshe, B. D. & Whitehurst, G. J. (1986). Intraverbal acquisition of semantic concepts by preschoolers. *Journal of Experimental Child Psychology, 42*, 169–186.

DeCasper, A. J., & Carstens, A. A. (1981). Contingencies of stimulation: Effects on learning and emotion in neonates. *Infant Behavior and Development, 4*, 19–35.

DeCasper, A. J., & Fifer, W. P. (1980). Of human bonding: Newborns prefer their mothers' voices. *Science, 208*, 1174–1176.

DeCasper, A. J. & Prescott, P. A. (1984). Human newborns' perception of male voices: Preference, discrimination, and reinforcing value. *Developmental Psychobiology, 17*, 481–491.

DeCasper, A. J., & Spence, M. J. (1986). Prenatal maternal speech influences newborns' perceptions of speech sounds. *Infant Behavior and Development, 9,* 133–150.

Dempster, F. N. (1985). Short-term memory development in childhood and adolescence. In C. J. Brainerd & M. Pressley (Eds.), *Basic processes in memory development: Progress in cognitive development research* (pp. 209–248). New York: Springer-Verlag.

Denham, S. A. (1986). Social cognition, prosocial behavior, and emotion in preschoolers: Contextual validation. *Child Development, 57,* 194–201.

de Schonen, S., McKenzie, B., Maury, L., & Bresson, F. (1978). Central and peripheral object distances as determinants of the effective visual field in early infancy. *Perception, 7,* 499–506.

deVilliers, J. G. & deVilliers, P. A. (1978). *Language Acquisition.* Cambridge, MA: Harvard University Press.

deVilliers, J. G. & deVilliers, P. A. (1982). Language development. In R. Vasta (Ed.), *Strategies and techniques of child study* (pp. 117–159). New York: Academic Press.

deVilliers, P. A., & deVilliers, J. G. (1979). *Early language.* Cambridge, MA: Harvard University Press.

Diamond, A. (1985). Development of the ability to use recall to guide action, as indicated by infants' performance on AB̄. *Child Development, 56,* 868–883.

Dias, M. G., & Harris, P. L. (1987, September). *The effect of make-believe play on deductive reasoning.* Paper presented at the Annual Conference of the Developmental Section of the British Psychological Society, University of York, England.

Dickstein, S., & Parke, R. D. (1988). Social referencing in infancy: A glance at fathers and marriage. *Child Development, 59,* 506–511.

Diskin, S. D. & Heinicke, C. M. (1986). Maternal style of emotional expression. *Infant Behavior and Development, 9,* 167–187.

Dockrell, J. E. (1981). *The child's acquisition of unfamiliar words: An experimental study.* Unpublished doctoral dissertation, University of Stirling, Scotland.

Dodd, B. (1975). Children's understanding of their own phonological forms. *Quarterly Journal of Experimental Psychology, 27,* 165–172.

Dodd, D. H., & White, R. M., Jr. (1980). *Cognition: Mental structures and processes.* Boston: Allyn & Bacon.

Dodge, K. A., Pettit, G. S., McClaskey, C. L., & Brown, M. M. (1986). Social competence in children. *Monographs of the Society for Research in Child Development, 56* (2, Serial No. 213).

Donaldson, M. (1978). *Children's minds.* New York: Norton.

Donaldson, M. (1982). Conservation: What is the question? *British Journal of Psychology, 73,* 199–207.

Donaldson, M. & Wales, R. J. (1970). On the acquisition of some relational terms. In J. R. Hayes (Ed.), *Cognition and the development of language* (pp. 235–268). New York: Wiley.

Dooling, D. J., & Lachman, R. (1971). Effects of comprehension on retention of prose. *Journal of Experimental Psychology, 88,* 216–222.

Doyle, A. B. (1973). Listening to distraction: A developmental study of selective attention. *Journal of Experimental Child Psychology, 15,* 100–115.

Dreistadt, R. (1968). An analysis of the use of analogies and metaphors in science. *The Journal of Psychology, 68,* 97–116.

Dromi, E. (1987). *Early lexical development.* Cambridge, England: Cambridge University Press.

Duncker, K. (1945). On problem solving. *Psychological Monographs, 58* (Whole No. 270).

Early, L., Griesler, P., & Rovee-Collier, C. (1985, April). *Ontogenetic changes in retention in early infancy.* Paper presented at the biennial meeting of the Society for Research in Child Development, Toronto, Canada.

Edwards, C. P., & Lewis, M. (1979). Young children's concepts of social relations: Social functions and social objects. In M. Lewis & L. Rosenblum, (Eds.), *The child and its family* (pp. 245–266). New York: Plenum Press.

Eilers, R. E., & Oller, D. K. (1985). Infant speech perception: Environmental contributions. In S. E. Trehub & B. Schneider, *Auditory development in infancy* (pp. 197–213). New York: Plenum Press.

Eimas, P. D. (1969). A developmental study of hypothesis behavior and focusing. *Journal of Experimental Child Psychology, 8,* 160–172.

Eimas, P. D. (1974). Auditory and linguistic processing of cues for place of articulation by infants. *Perception and Psychophysics, 16,* 513–521.

Eimas, P. D. (1975). Auditory and phonetic coding of the cues for speech: Discrimination of the (r - l) distinction by young infants. *Perception and Psychophysics, 18,* 341–347.

Eimas, P. D. (1985). The equivalence of cues in the perception of speech by infants. *Infant Behavior and Development, 8,* 125–138.

Eimas, P. D., & Miller, J. L. (1978). Effects of selective adaptation on the perception of speech and visual patterns: Evidence for feature detectors. In R. D. Walk & H. L. Pick, Jr. (Eds.), *Perception and experience* (pp. 307–345) New York: Plenum.

Eimas, P. D., Siqueland, E., Jusczyk, P., & Vigorito, J. (1971). Speech perception in infants. *Science, 171,* 303–306.

Einhorn, H. J., & Hogarth, R. M. (1986). Judging probable cause. *Psychological Bulletin, 99,* 3–19.

Elliot, A. J. (1981). *Child language.* Cambridge, England: Cambridge University Press.

Engen, T., & Lipsitt, L. P. (1965). Olfactory responses and adaptation in the human neonate. *Journal of Comparative and Physiological Psychology, 59,* 312–316.

Ennis, R. H. (1975). Children's ability to handle Piaget's propositional logic: A conceptual critique. *Review of Educational Research, 45,* 1–41.

Enright, R. D., & Lapsley, D. K. (1980). Social role-taking: A review of the constructs, measures, and measurement properties. *Review of Educational Research, 50,* 647–674.

Entwisle, D. R., & Huggins, W. H. (1973). Iconic memory in children. *Child Development, 44,* 392–394.

Epstein, W., Glenberg, A. M., & Bradley, M. M. (1984). Coactivation and comprehension: Contribution of text variables to the illusion of knowing. *Memory & Cognition, 12,* 355–360.

Erickson, J. R. (1978). Research on syllogistic reasoning. In R. Revlin, & R. E. Mayer (Eds.), *Human reasoning* (pp. 39–50). Washington, DC: Winston.

Erreich, A., Valian, V., & Winzemer, J. (1980). Aspects of a theory of language acquisition. *Journal of Child Language, 7,* 157–179.

Evans, J. St. B., Barston, J. L., & Pollard, P. (1983). On the conflict between logic and belief in syllogistic reasoning. *Memory & Cognition, 11,* 295–306.

Evans, J. St. B., Brooks, P. G., & Pollard, P. (1985). Prior beliefs and statistical inference. *British Journal of Psychology, 76,* 469–477.

Evans, J. St. B., & Lynch, J. S. (1973). Matching bias in the selection task. *British Journal of Psychology, 64,* 391–397.

Fagan, J. F., III. (1972). Infants' recognition memory for faces. *Journal of Experimental Child Psychology, 14,* 453–476.

Fagan, J. F., III. (1973). Infants' delayed recognition memory and forgetting. *Journal of Experimental Child Psychology, 16,* 424–450.

Fagan, J. F., III. (1974). Infant recognition memory: The effects of length of familiarization and type of discrimination task. *Child Development, 45,* 351–356.

Fagan, J. F., III. (1978). Facilitation of infants' recognition memory. *Child Development, 49,* 1066–1075.

Fagen, J. W., & Rovee-Collier, C. K. (1982). A conditioning analysis of infant memory. In R. L. Isaacson & N. E. Spear (Eds.), *The expression of knowledge* (pp. 67–111). New York: Plenum Press.

Fagen, J. W., & Rovee-Collier, C. K. (1983). Memory retrieval: A time-locked process in infancy. *Science, 222,* 1349–1351.

Fagen, J. W., Yengo, L. A., Rovee-Collier, C. K., & Enright, M. K. (1981). Reactivation of a visual discrimination in early infancy. *Developmental Psychology, 17,* 266–274.

Falmagne, R. J. (1975). Overview: Reasoning, representation, process, and related issues. In R. J. Falmagne (Ed.), *Reasoning: Representation and process* (pp. 247–264). Hillsdale, NJ: Erlbaum.

Falmagne, R. J. (1980). The development of logical competence: A psycholinguistic perspective. In R. H. Kluwe, & H. Spada (Eds.), *Developmental models of thinking* (pp. 171–197). New York: Academic Press.

Fantz, R. L. (1958). Pattern vision in young infants. *Psychological Record, 8,* 43–47.

Fantz, R. L. (1961). The origin of form perception. *Scientific American, 204*(5), 66–72.

Fantz, R. L. (1963). Pattern vision in newborn infants. *Science, 140,* 296–297.

Fantz, R. L. (1965). Visual perception from birth as shown by pattern selectivity. *Annals of the New York Academy of Sciences, 118,* 793–814.

Fantz, R. L., Fagan, J. F., & Miranda, S. B. (1975). Early visual selectivity as a function of pattern variables, previous exposure, age from birth and conception, and expected cognitive deficit. In L. B. Cohen & P. Salapatek (Eds.), *Infant perception: From sensation to cognition* (Vol. 1, pp. 249–345). New York: Academic Press.

Farah, M. J., & Kosslyn, S. M. (1982). Concept development. In H. W. Reese & L. P. Lipsett (Eds.), *Advances in child development and behavior* (Vol. 12, pp. 125–167). New York: Academic Press.

Feffer, N., & Gourevitch, V. (1960). Cognitive aspects of role-taking in children. *Journal of Personality, 28,* 383–396.

Feinman, S. (1982). Social referencing in infancy. *Merrill-Palmer Quarterly, 28,* 445–470.

Feinman, S. (1983). How does baby socially refer? Two views of social referencing: A reply to Campos. *Merrill-Palmer Quarterly, 29,* 467–471.

Feinman, S. (1985). Emotional expression, social referencing, and preparedness for learning in infancy: Mother knows best, but sometimes I know better. In G. Zivin (Ed.), *The development of expressive behavior: Biology-environment interactions* (pp. 291–318). Orlando, FL: Academic Press.

Feinman, S. & Lewis, M. (1983). Social referencing at ten months: A second-order effect on infants' responses to strangers. *Child Development, 54,* 878–887.

Field, J., Muir, D., Pilon, R., Sinclair, M., & Dodwell, P. (1980). Infants' orientation to lateral sounds from birth to three months. *Child Development, 51,* 295–298.

Field, T. (1978). Interaction behaviors of primary versus secondary caretaker fathers. *Developmental Psychology, 14,* 183–184.

Fillmore, C. J. (1968). The case for case. In E. Bach & R. T. Harms (Eds.), *Universals of linguistic theory* (pp. 1–90). New York: Holt, Rinehart & Winston.

Fincham, F. D., & Cain, K. M. (1986). Learned helplessness in humans: A developmental analysis. *Developmental Review, 6,* 301–333.

Fischbein, E., Pampu, I., & Minzat, I. (1970). Comparison of ratios and the chance concept in children. *Child Development, 41,* 377–389.

Fischer, K. W. (1980). A theory of cognitive development: The control and construction of hierarchies of skills. *Psychological Review, 87,* 477–531.

Fisher, C. B., Ferdinandsen, K., & Bornstein, M. T. (1981). The role of symmetry in infant form discrimination. *Child Development, 52,* 457–462.

Fiske, S. T., & Taylor, S. E. (1984). *Social cognition.* Reading, MA: Addison-Wesley.

Fitts, P. M. (1964). Perceptual-motor skill learning. In A. W. Melton (Ed.), *Categories of human learning* (pp. 243–285). New York: Academic Press.

Fivush, R. (1984). Learning about school: The development of kindergarteners' school scripts. *Child Development, 55,* 1697–1709.

Fivush, R. (1987). Scripts and categories: Interrelationships in development. In U. Neisser (Ed.), *Concepts and concept development: Ecological and intellectual factors in categorization* (pp. 234–254). Cambridge, England: Cambridge University Press.

Fivush, R., & Slackman, E. A. (1986). The acquisition and development of scripts. In K. Nelson (Ed.), *Event knowledge: Structure and function in development* (pp. 71–96). Hillsdale, NJ: Erlbaum.

Flavell, J. H. (1963). *The developmental psychology of Jean Piaget.* Princeton, NJ: Van Nostrand.

Flavell, J. H. (1971). First discussant's comments: What is memory development the development of? *Human Development, 14,* 272–278.

Flavell, J. H. (1981). Cognitive monitoring. In W. P. Dickson (Ed.), *Children's oral communication skills* (pp. 35–60). New York: Academic Press.

Flavell, J. H. (1982). On cognitive development. *Child Development, 53,* 1–10.

Flavell, J. H. (1985). *Cognitive development* (2nd ed.). Englewood Cliffs, NJ: Prentice-Hall.

Flavell, J. H. (1986). The development of children's knowledge about the appearance-reality distinction. *American Psychologist, 41,* 418–424.

Flavell, J. H., Botkin, P., Fry, C., Wright, J., & Jarvis. P. (1968). *The development of role-taking and communication skills in children.* New York: Wiley.

Flavell, J. H., Flavell, E. R., & Green, F. L. (1983). Development of the appearence-reality distinction. *Cognitive Psychology, 15,* 95–120.

Flavell, J. H., Flavell, E. R., & Green, F. L. (1987). Young children's knowledge about the apparent-real and pretend-real distinctions. *Developmental Psychology, 23,* 816–822.

Flavell, J. H., Green, F. L., & Flavell, E. R. (1986). Development of knowledge about the appearence-reality distinction. *Monographs of the Society for Research in Child Development, 51*(1, Serial No. 212).

Flavell, J. H., Speer, J. R., Green, F. L. & August, D. L. (1981). The development of comprehension monitoring and knowledge about communication. *Monographs of the Society for Research in Child Development, 46*(5, Serial No., 192).

Flavell, J. H., & Wellman, H. M. (1977). Metamemory. In R. V. Kail & J. W. Hagen, *Perspectives on the development of memory and cognition* (pp. 3–33). Hillsdale, NJ: Erlbaum.

Flavell, J. H., & Wohlwill, J. F. (1969). Formal and functional aspects of cognitive development. In D. Elkind & J. H. Flavell (Eds.), *Studies in cognitive development* (pp. 67–120). New York: Oxford University Press.

Flavell, J. H., Zhang, X. D., Zou, H., Dong, Q., & Qi, S. (1983). A comparison between the development of the appearance-reality distinction in the People's Republic of China and the United States. *Cognitive Psychology, 15,* 459–486.

Flores d'Arcais, G. B., & Schreuder, R. (1983). The process of language understanding: A few issues in contemporary psycholinguistics. In G. B. Flores d'Arcais and R. J. Jarvella (Eds.), *The process of language understanding* (pp. 1–41). New York: Wiley.

Fong, G. T., Krantz, D. H., & Nisbett, R. E. (1986). The effects of statistical training on thinking about everyday problems. *Cognitive Psychology, 18,* 253–292.

Foorman, B. R., Sadowski, B. R., & Basen, J. A. (1985). Children's solutions for figural matrices: Developmental differences in strategies and effects of matrix characteristics. *Journal of Experimental Child Psychology, 39,* 107–130.

Forbes, D. L. & Greenberg, M. T. (1982). Editors' notes. *Children's planning strategies* (pp. 1–4). San Francisco: Jossey-Bass.

Ford, M. (1985). Review of *Mental models: Towards a cognitive science of language, inference, and consciousness. Language, 61,* 897–903.

Ford, M. E. (1979). The construct validity of egocentrism. *Psychological Bulletin, 86,* 1169–1188.

Fox, R., Aslin, R. N., Shea, S. L., & Dumais, S. T. (1980). Stereopsis in human infants. *Science, 207,* 323–324.

Fraisse, P. (1963). *The psychology of time.* New York: Harper & Row.

Frankel, M. T., & Rollins, H. A. (1982). Age-related differences in clustering: A new approach. *Journal of Experimental Psychology, 34,* 113–122.

Frauenglass, M., & Diaz, R. (1985). Self-regulatory functions of children's private speech: A critical analysis of recent challenges to Vygotsky's theory. *Developmental Psychology, 21,* 357–364.

Freeley, A. J. (1966). *Argumentation and debate: Rational decision making* (2nd ed.). Belmont, CA: Wadsworth.

French, D. C. (1984). Children's knowledge of the social functions of younger, older, and same-age peers. *Child Development, 55,* 1429–1433.

French, L. A. (1986). The language of events. In K. Nelson (Ed.), *Event knowledge: Structure and function in development* (pp. 119–136). Hillsdale, NJ: Erlbaum.

French, L. A., & Nelson, K. (1985). *Young children's knowledge of relational terms: Some ifs, ors, and buts.* New York: Springer-Verlag.

Friedman, A. (1979). Framing pictures: The role of knowledge in automatized encoding and memory for gist. *Journal of Experimental Psychology: General, 108,* 316–355.

Friedman, S. (1972). Habituation and recovery of visual response in the alert human newborn. *Journal of Experimental Child Psychology, 13,* 339–349.

Frye, C., Rawling, P., Moore, C., & Myers, I. (1983). Object-person discrimination and communication at 3 and 10 months. *Developmental Psychology, 19,* 303–309.

Furrow, D. (1984). Social and private speech at two years. *Child Development, 55,* 355–362.

Furth, H. (1974). Two aspects of experience in ontogeny: Development and learning. In H. W. Reese (Ed.), *Advances in child development and behavior* (Vol. 9, pp. 47–67). New York: Academic Press.

Fuson, K. C. (1979) The development of self-regulating aspects of speech: A review. In G. Zivin (Ed.), *The development of self-regulation through private speech* (pp. 135–217). New York: Wiley.

Gallagher, J. M., & Wright, R. J. (October, 1977). A structural analysis of analogy items used in adolescent studies. Paper presented at the meeting of the Northeastern Educational Research Association, Ellenville, New York.

Ganon, E. C., & Swartz, K. B. (1980). Perception of internal elements of compound figures by one-month-olds. *Journal of Experimental Child Psychology, 30,* 159–170.

Gardner, H. (1980). Cognition comes of age. In M. Piatelli-Palmarini (Ed.), *Language and learning:*

The debate between Jean Piaget and Noam Chomsky (pp. XIX-XXXVI). Cambridge, MA: Harvard University Press.

Gardner, W., & Rogoff, B. (1985, September). *Children's improvisational and advance planning.* Paper presented at the meeting of the American Psychological Association, Los Angeles.

Garfinkel, H. (1967). *Studies in ethnomethodology.* Englewoods Cliffs, Hillsdale, NJ: Prentice-Hall.

Garner, W. R. (1974). The processing of information and structure. Potomac, MD: Erlbaum.

Garnham, A., Oakhill, J., & Johnson-Laird, P. N. (1982). Referential continuity and the coherence of discourse. *Cognition, 11,* 29–46.

Garvey, C. (1977). *Play.* Cambridge, MA: Harvard University Press.

Garvey, C. & Hogan, R. (1973). Social speech and social interaction. *Child Development, 44,* 562–568.

Gathercole, V. C. (1987). The contrastive hypothesis for the acquisition of word meaning: A reconsideration of the theory. *Journal of Child Language, 14,* 493–531.

Gayl, I. E., Roberts, J. D., & Werner, J. S. (1983). Linear systems analysis of infant visual pattern preferences. *Journal of Experimental Child Psychology, 35,* 30–45.

Geis, M. F., & Hall, D. M. (1976). Encoding and incidental memory in children. *Journal of Experimental Child Psychology, 22,* 58–66.

Gekoski, M. J., Rovee-Collier, C. K., & Carulli-Rabinowitz, V. (1983). A longitudinal analysis of inhibition of infant distress: The origins of social expectations? *Infant Behavior and Development, 6,* 339–351.

Gelman, R. (1972). Logical capacity of very young children: Number invariance rules. *Child Development, 43,* 75–90.

Gelman, R. (1979). Preschool thought. *American Psychologist, 34,* 900–905.

Gelman, R. (1982). Accessing one-to-one correspondence: Still another paper about conservation. *British Journal of Psychology, 73,* 209–220.

Gelman, R. (1987, August). *Cognitive development: Principles guide learning and contribute to conceptual coherence.* Paper presented at the meeting of the American Psychological Association, New York.

Gelman, R., & Gallistel, C. R. (1978). *The child's understanding of number.* Cambridge, MA: Harvard University Press.

Gelman, R., & Meck, E. (1983). Preschooler's counting: Principles before skill. *Cognition, 13,* 343–359.

Gelman, R., Meck, E., & Merkin, S. (1986). Young children's numerical competence. *Cognitive Development, 1,* 1–29.

Gelman, S. A. (1988). The development of induction within natural kind and artifact categories. *Cognitive psychology, 20,* 65–95.

Gelman, S. A., Collman, P., & Maccoby, E. E. (1986). Inferring properties from categories versus inferring categories from properties: The case of gender. *Child Development, 57,* 396–404.

Gelman, S. A., & Markman, E. M. (1986a). Categories and induction in young children. *Cognition, 23,* 183–209.

Gelman, S. A., & Markman, E. M. (1986b). Understanding natural kinds: A developmental comparison. *Papers and Reports on Child Language Development, 25,* 41–48.

Gelman, S. A., & Markman, E. M. (1987). Young children's inductions from natural kinds: The roles of categories and appearences. *Child Development, 58,* 1532–1541.

Gelman, S. A., & Taylor, M. (1984). How two-year-old children interpret proper and common names for unfamiliar objects. *Child Development, 55,* 1535–1540.

Gentile, R. J., Kessler, D. K., & Gentile, P. K. (1969). Process of solving analogy items. *Journal of Experimental Psychology, 60,* 494–502.

Gentner, D. (1977). Children's performance on a spatial analogies task. *Child Development, 48,* 1034–1039.

Gentner, D. (1983). Structure-mapping: A theoretical framework for analogy. *Cognitive Science, 7,* 155–170.

Gentner, D., & Toupin, C. (1986). Systematicity and surface similarity in the development of analogy. *Cognitive Science, 10,* 277–300.

Gholson, B. (1980). *The cognitive-developmental basis of human learning: Studies in hypothesis testing.* New York: Academic Press.

Gholson, B., Eymard, L. A., Morgan, D., & Kamhi, A. G. (1987). Problem solving, recall, and isomorphic transfer among third-grade and sixth-grade children. *Journal of Experimental Psychology, 43,* 227–243.

Gibson, E. J. (1969). *Principles of perceptual learning and perceptual development*. New York: Appleton-Century-Crofts.

Gibson, E. J., Owsley, C. J., & Johnston, J. (1978). Perception of invariants by five-month-old infants: Differentiation of two types of motion. *Developmental Psychology, 14,* 407–415.

Gibson, E. J., & Walker, A. S. (1984). Development of knowledge of visual-tactual affordances of substance. *Child Development, 55,* 453–460.

Gibson, J. J. (1950). *The perception of the visual world*. Boston: Houghton Mifflin.

Gibson, J. J. (1966). *The senses considered as perceptual systems*. Boston: Houghton Mifflin.

Gibson, J. J. (1979). *The ecological approach to visual perception. Boston: Houghton Mifflin.*

Gick, M., & Holyoak, K. (1980). Analogical problem solving. *Cognitive Psychology, 12,* 306–355.

Gick, M., & Holyoak, K. (1983). Schema induction and analogical transfer. *Cognitive Psychology, 15,* 1–38.

Ginsburg, H. P. (1983). *The development of mathematical thinking*. New York: Academic Press.

Ginsburg, H. P., & Opper, S. (1988). *Piaget's theory of intellectual development* (3rd ed.). Englewood Cliffs, NJ: Prentice-Hall.

Girle, R. A. (1983). A top-down approach to the teaching of reasoning skills. In W. Maxwell (Ed.), *Thinking: The expanding frontier* (pp. 139–147). Philadelphia: Franklin Institute Press.

Gitomer, D. H., & Curtis, M. E. (1983, March). *Individual differences in verbal analogy problem solving*. Paper presented at the annual meeting of the American Educational Research Association, Montreal, Canada.

Gleason, H. A. (1961). *An introduction to descriptive linguistics*. New York: Wiley.

Gleitman, L. R., & Gleitman, H. (1987). Language and language development. In H. Gleitman, *Basic Psychology* (2nd ed.) (pp. 239–262). New York: Norton.

Glenberg, A. M., Wilkinson, A. C., & Epstein, W. (1982). The illusion of knowing: Failure in the self-assessment of comprehension. *Memory & Cognition, 10,* 597–602.

Glick, J. (1978). Cognition and social cognition: An introduction. In J. Glick & K. A. Clarke-Stewart (Eds.), *The development of social understanding* (pp. 1–9). New York: Gardner Press.

Glucksberg, S., Krauss, R. M., & Weisberg, R. (1966). Referential communication in nursery school children: Method and some preliminary findings. *Journal of Experimental Child Psychology, 3,* 333–342.

Godden, D. R., & Baddeley, A. D. (1975). Context-dependent memory in two natural environments: On land and underwater. *British Journal of Psychology, 66,* 325–331.

Goffman, E. (1959). *The presentation of self in everyday life*. Garden City, New York: Doubleday.

Goldberg, S. (1977). Social competence in infancy: A model of parent-infant interaction. *Merrill-Palmer Quarterly, 23,* 163–177.

Goldberg, S., Perlmutter, M., & Myers, N. (1974). Recall of related and unrelated lists by 2-year-olds. *Journal of Experimental Child Psychology, 18,* 1–8.

Goldin-Meadow, S. (1985). Language development under atypical learning conditions: Replication and implications of a study of deaf children of hearing parents. In K. E. Nelsen (Ed.), *Children's language* (Vol. 5, pp. 197–245). Hillsdale, NJ: Erlbaum.

Goldman, S. R., & Pellegrino, J. W. (1984). Deductions about induction: Analyses of developmental and individual differences. In R. J. Sternberg (Ed.), *Advances in the psychology of human intelligence* (Vol. 2, pp. 149–197). Hillsdale, NJ: Erlbaum.

Goldman, S. R., Pellegrino, J. W., Parseghian, P., & Sallis, R. (1982). Developmental and individual differences in verbal analogical reasoning. *Child Development, 53,* 550–559.

Goldstein, B. E. (1984). *Sensations and perceptions* (2nd ed.). Belmont, CA: Wadsworth.

Golinkoff, R. M. (1983). The preverbal negotiation of failed messages: Insights into the transition period. In R. M. Golinkoff (Ed.), *The transition from prelinguistic to linguistic communication* (pp. 57–78). Hillsdale, NJ: Erlbaum.

Golinkoff, R. M., Hirsh-Pasek, K., Baduini, C., & Lavallee, A. (1985, October). *What's in a word?: The young child's predisposition to use lexical contrast*. Paper presented at the meeting of Boston Child Language Conference, Boston.

Goodman, G. S., & Golding, J. (1983, April). Effects of real world knowledge on memory development. In K. Nelson (Chair), *Memory and representation of the real world*. Symposium presented at the biennial meeting of the Society for Research in Child Development, Detroit.

Goodman, S. (1981). The integration of verbal and motor behavior in preschool children. *Child Development, 52,* 280–289.

Gopnik, A. (1982). Words and plans: Early language and the development of intelligent action. *Journal of Child Language, 9,* 303–318.

Gopnik, A., & Meltzoff, A. N. (1984). Semantic and cognitive development in 15- to 21-month-old children. *Journal of Child Language, 11,* 495–513.

Gopnik, A., & Meltzoff, A. N. (1986a). Relations between semantic and cognitive development in the one-word stage: The specificity hypothesis. *Child Development, 57,* 1040–1053.

Gopnik, A., & Meltzoff, A. N. (1986b). Words, plans, things, and locations: Interactions between semantic and cognitive development in the one-word stage. In S. A. Kuczaj & M. S. Barrett (Eds.) *The development of word meaning: Progress in cognitive development research* (pp. 199–223). New York: Springer-Verlag.

Gordon, W. J. J. (1961). *Synetics.* New York: Harper & Row.

Gottlieb, G. (1981). Roles of early experience in species-specific perceptual development. In R. N. Aslin, J. R. Alberts, & M. R. Petersen (Eds.), *Development of perception: Psychobiological perspectives* (Vol. 1, pp. 5–44). New York: Academic Press.

Graesser, A. C., Gordon, S. E., & Sawyer, J. D. (1979). Recognition memory for typical and atypical actions in scripted activities: Tests of a script pointer + tag hypothesis. *Journal of Verbal Learning and Verbal Behavior, 18,* 319–332.

Granrud, C. E. (1986). Binocular vision and spatial perception in 4- and 5-month-old infants. *Journal of Experimental Psychology: Human Perception and Performance, 12,* 36–49.

Granrud, C. E., Haake, R. J., & Yonas, A. (1985). Infants' sensitivity to familiar size: The effect of memory on spatial perception. *Perception and Psychophysics, 37,* 459–466.

Gray, H. (1978). Learning to take an object from the mother. In A. Lock (Ed.), *Action, gesture and symbol: The emergence of language* (pp. 159–182). New York: Academic Press.

Graziano, W. G., Moore, J. S., & Collins, J. E. (1988). Social cognition as segmentation of the stream of behavior. *Developmental Psychology, 24,* 568–573.

Greeno, J. G. (1978). Natures of problem-solving abilities. In W. K. Estes (Ed.), *Handbook of learning and cognitive processes* (Vol. 5, pp. 239–270). Hillsdale, NJ: Erlbaum.

Greeno, J. G. (1983, May). *Skills for representing problems.* Paper presented at the annual meeting of the American Educational Research Association, Montreal, Canada.

Greeno, J. G., Riley, M. S., & Gelman, R. (1984). Conceptual competence and children's counting. *Cognitive Psychology, 16,* 94–143.

Grice, H. P. (1975). Logic and conversation. In P. Cole and J. L. Morgan (Eds.), *Syntax and semantics* (Vol. 3, pp. 41–58). New York: Academic Press.

Griggs, R. A., & Cox, J. R. (1982). The elusive thematic-materials effect in Wason's selection task. *British Journal of Psychology, 73,* 407–420.

Grudin, J. (1980). Processes in verbal analogy solution. *Journal of Experimental Psychology: Human Perception and Performance, 6,* 67–74.

Gunnar, M. R. & Stone, C. (1984). The effects of positive maternal affect on infant responses to pleasant, ambiguous, and fear-provoking toys. *Child Development, 55,* 1231–1236.

Gunnar-Vongnechten, M. R. (1978). Changing a frightening toy into a pleasant toy by allowing the infant to control its actions. *Developmental Psychology, 14,* 157–162.

Gurucharri, C., & Selman, R. L. (1982). The development of interpersonal understanding during childhood, preadolescence, and adolescence: A longitudinal follow-up study. *Child Development, 53,* 924–927.

Guttentag, R. E. (1984). The mental effort requirement of cumulative rehearsal: A developmental study. *Journal of Experimental Child Psychology, 37,* 92–106.

Haaf, R. A. (1977). Visual response to complex face-like patterns by 15- and 20-week-old infants. *Developmental Psychology, 13,* 77–78.

Haaf, R. A., & Bell, R. Q. (1967). A facial dimension in visual discrimination by human infants. *Child Development, 38,* 893–899.

Haaf, R. A., & Brown, C. J. (1976). Infants' response to face-like patterns: Developmental changes between 10 and 15 weeks of age. *Journal of Experimental Child Psychology, 22,* 155–160.

Hagafors, R. (1983). Effects of information presentation mode on subjects' hypotheses in a probabilistic inference task. *Acta Psychologica, 53,* 195–204.

Hagen, J. W., & Hale, G. H. (1973). The development of attention in children. In A. D. Pick (Ed.), *Minnesota symposia on child psychology* (Vol. 7, pp. 117–140). Minneapolis: University of Minnesota Press.

Hagen, J. W., Jongeward, R. H. Jr., & Kail, R. V. (1975). Cognitive perspectives on the development of memory. In H. W. Reese (Ed.), *Advances in child development and behavior* (Vol. 10, pp. 129–161). New York: Academic Press.

Hagen, J. W., & Wilson, K. P. (1982). Some selected thoughts on attention: A reply to Lane and Pearson. *Merrill-Palmer Quarterly, 28,* 529–532.

Hagert, G., & Waern, Y. (1986). On implicit assumptions in reasoning. In T. Myers, K. Brown, & B. McGonigle (Eds.), *Reasoning and discourse processes* (pp. 93–115). London: Academic Press.

Haith, M. M. (1978). Visual competence in infancy. In R. Held, H. Leibowitz, & H. L. Teuber, (Eds.), *Handbook of Sensory Physiology* (Vol. 8, pp. 319–356). Berlin: Springer-Verlag.

Haith, M. M. (1980). *Rules that babies look by: The organization of newborn visual activity.* Hillsdale, NJ: Erlbaum.

Haith, M. M. (1988, March). *Visual expectations in early infancy.* Paper presented at the Southwestern Society for Research in Human Development Meetings, New Orleans.

Hale, G. A. (1979). Development of children's attention to stimulus components. In G. A. Hale & M. Lewis (Eds.), *Attention and cognitive development* (pp. 43–64). New York: Plenum Press.

Hale, G. A., & Taweel, S. S. (1974). Age differences in children's performance on measures of component selection and incidental learning. *Journal of Experimental Child Psychology, 18,* 107–116.

Hale, G. A., Taweel, S. S., Green, R. Z., & Flaugher, J. (1978). Effects of instructions on children's attention to stimulus components. *Developmental Psychology, 14,* 499–506.

Halford, G. S., & Kelly, M. E. (1984). On the basis of early transitivity judgements. *Journal of Experimental Child Psychology, 38,* 42–63.

Hampton, J. A. (1981). An investigation of the nature of abstract concepts. *Memory & Cognition, 9,* 149–156.

Hannigan, M. L., Shelton, T. S., Franks, J. J., & Bransford, J.D. (1980). The effects of episodic and semantic memory on the identification of sentences masked by white noise. *Memory & Cognition, 8,* 278–284.

Harding, C. G. (1983). Setting the stage for language acquisition: Communication development in the first year. In R. M. Golinkoff (Ed.), *The transition from prelinguistic to linguistic communication* (pp. 93–113). Hillsdale, NJ: Erlbaum.

Harding, C. G. (1984). Acting with intention: A framework for examining the development of the intention to communicate. In L. Feagans, C. Garvey & R. Golinkoff (Ed.), *The origins and growth of communication* (pp. 123–135). Norwood, NJ: Ablex.

Harding, C. G., & Golinkoff, R. M. (1979). The origins of intentional vocalizations in prelinguistic infants. *Child Development, 50,* 33–40.

Harman, G. (1986). *Change in view: Principles of reasoning.* Cambridge, MA: MIT Press.

Harris, P. L. (1983). Infant cognition. In P. H. Mussen (Ed.), *Handbook of child psychology* (4th ed. Vol. 2), (pp. 689–782). New York: Wiley.

Harris, P. L. (1985). The origins of search and number skills. In H. M. Wellman (Ed.), *Children's searching: The development of search skills and spatial representation* (pp. 105–122). Hillsdale, NJ: Erlbaum.

Harris, P. L., Kruithof, A., Terwogt, M. M., & Visser, T. (1981). Children's awareness and detection of textual anomaly. *Journal of Experimental Child Psychology, 31,* 212–230.

Harris, P. L., & MacFarlane, A. (1974). The growth of the effective visual field from birth to seven weeks. *Journal of Experimental Child Psychology, 18,* 340–348.

Hary, J. M., & Massaro, D. W. (1982). Categorical results do not imply categorical perception. *Perception & Psychophysics, 32,* 409–418.

Hasher, L., & Griffin, M. (1978). Reconstructive and reproductive processes in memory. *Journal of Experimental Psychology: Human Learning and Memory, 4,* 318–330.

Hasher, L., & Zacks, R. T. (1979). Automatic and effortful processes in memory. *Journal of Experimental Psychology: General, 108,* 356–388.

Hashtroudi, S., Mutter, S. A., Cole, E. A., & Green, S. K. (1984). Schema-consistent and schema-inconsistent information: Processing demands. *Personality and Social Psychology Bulletin, 10,* 269–278.

Haviland, J. M., & Lelwica, M. (1987). The induced affect response: 10-week-old infants' responses to three emotion expressions. *Developmental Psychology, 23,* 97–104.

Hawkins, J., Pea, R. D., Glick, J., & Scribner, S. (1984). "Merds that laugh don't like mushrooms": Evidence for deductive reasoning by preschoolers. *Developmental Psychology, 20,* 584–594.

Hayes, D. S., Scott, L. C., Chemelski, B. E., & Johnson, J. (1987). Physical and emotional states as memory-relevant factors: Cognitive monitoring by young children. *Merrill-Palmer Quarterly, 33*, 473–487.

Hayes, J. R. (1978). *Cognitive psychology: Thinking and creating.* Homewood, IL: Dorsey Press.

Hayes, J. R., & Simon, H. A. (1974). Understanding written problem instructions. In L. W. Gregg (Ed.), *Knowledge and cognition* (pp. 167–200). Hillsdale, NJ: Erlbaum.

Hayes, J. R., Waterman, D. A., & Robinson, C. S. (1977). Identifying the relevant aspects of a problem text. *Cognitive Science, 1*, 297–313.

Hayes, L. A., & Watson, J. S. (1981). Neonatal imitation: Fact or artifact? *Developmental Psychology, 17*, 655–660.

Hayes-Roth, B., & Hayes-Roth, F. (1979). A cognitive model of planning. *Cognitive Science, 3*, 275–310.

Hayne, H., & Rovee-Collier, C. (1985, April). *Contextual determinants of reactivated memories in infants.* Paper presented at the biennial meeting of the Society for Research in Child Development, Toronto, Canada.

Hayne, H., Rovee-Collier, C., & Perris, E. E. (1987). Categorization and memory retrieval by three-month-olds. *Child Development, 58*, 750–767.

Hebb, D. O. (1958). *A textbook of psychology.* Philadelphia: Saunders.

Heckhausen, J. (1987). Balancing for weaknesses and challenging developmental potential: A longitudinal study of mother-infant dyads in apprenticeship interactions. *Developmental Psychology, 23*, 762–770.

Heibeck, T. H., & Markman, E. M. (1987). Word learning in children: An examination of fast mapping. *Child Development, 58*, 1021–1034.

Heider, E. R. (1972). Universals in color naming and memory. *Journal of Experimental Psychology, 93*, 10–20.

Heider, E.R., & Oliver, D.C. (1972). The structure of the color space in naming and memory for two languages. *Cognitive Psychology, 3*, 337–354.

Heider, F. (1958). *The psychology of interpersonal relations.* New York: Wiley.

Heider, K. G. (1970). *The Dugum Dani: A Papuan culture in the Highlands of West New Guinea.* Chicago: Aldine.

Held, R., Birch, E. E., & Gwiazda, J. (1980). Stereoacuity of human infants. *Proceedings of the National Academy of Science USA, 77*, 5572–5574.

Helmholtz, H. L. F. von. (1962). *A Treatise on Physiological Optics.* (J. P. C. Southall, Ed. & Trans.). New York: Dover. (Original work published 1890.)

Helmholtz, H. L. F. von. (1930). *Sensations of tone.* (A. J. Ellis, Trans.). New York: Longmans & Green.

Helson, H. (1933). The fundamental propositions of Gestalt psychology. *Psychological Review, 40*, 13–32.

Henle, M. (1962). On the relation between logic and thinking. *Psychological Review, 69*, 366–378.

Hershenson, M. (1964). Visual discrimination in the human newborn. *Journal of Comparative and Physiological Psychology, 58*, 270–276.

Hershenson, M. (1967). Development of the perception of form. *Psychological Bulletin, 67*, 326–336.

Higgins, E. T. (1981). The 'communication game': Implications for social cognition. In E. T. Higgins, C. P. Herman, & M. P. Zanna (Eds.), *Social Cognition: The Ontario Symposium* (Vol. 1, pp. 343–392). Hillsdale, NJ: Erlbaum.

Hildyard, A., & Olson, D. R. (1978). Memory and inference in the comprehension of oral and written discourse. *Discourse Processes, 1*, 91–117.

Hintzman, D. L. (1976). Repetition and memory. In G. H. Bower (ed.), *The psychology of learning and motivation* (Vol. 10, pp. 47–91). New York: Academic Press.

Hoch, S. J., & Tschirgi, J. E. (1983). Cue redundancy and extra logical inferences in a deductive reasoning task. *Memory & Cognition, 11*, 200–209.

Hoch, S. J., & Tschirgi, J. E. (1985). Logical knowledge and cue redundancy in deductive reasoning. *Memory & Cognition, 13*, 453–462.

Hochberg, J. E. (1981). Levels of perceptual organization. In M. Kuborg & J. R. Pomerantz (Eds.), *Perceptual Organization* (pp. 255–278). Hillsdale, NJ: Erlbaum.

Hockett, C. D. (1960). The origin of speech. *Scientific American, 203*(3), 89–96.

Hoffman, M. L. (1981). Perspectives on the difference between understanding people and understanding things: The role of affect. In J. Flavell and L. Ross (Eds.) *Social cognitive development: Frontiers and possible futures* (pp. 67–81). Cambridge, England: Cambridge University Press.

Hoffman, R. R. (1980). Metaphor in science. In R. P. Honeck & R. R. Hoffman, *Cognition and figurative language* (pp. 393–423). Hillsdale, NJ: Erlbaum.

Holyoak, K. J. (1984a). Analogical thinking and human intelligence. In R. J. Sternberg (Ed.), *Advances in the psychology of human intelligence* (Vol. 2, pp. 199–230). Hillsdale, NJ: Erlbaum.

Holyoak, K. J. (1984b). Mental models in problem solving. In J. R. Anderson, & S. M. Kosslyn (Eds.), *Tutorials in learning and memory: Essays in honor of Gordon Bower* (pp. 193–218). San Francisco: Freeman.

Holyoak, K. J., & Gordon, P. C. (1984). Information processing and social cognition. In R. S. Wyer, Jr., & T. K. Srull (Eds.), *Handbook of social cognition* (Vol. 1, pp. 39–70). Hillsdale, NJ: Erlbaum.

Holyoak, K. J., Junn, E. N., & Billman, D. O. (1984). Development of analogical problem-solving skill. *Child Development, 55*, 2042–2055.

Holzman, T. G., Pellegrino, J. W., & Glaser, R. (1982). Cognitive dimensions of numerical rule induction. *Journal of Educational Psychology, 74*, 360–373.

Honeck, R. P., Firment, M., & Case, T. J. S. (1987). Expertise and categorization. *Bulletin of the Psychonomic Society, 25*, 431–434.

Honeck, R. P., Kibler, C. T., & Sugar, J. (1985). The conceptual base view of categorization. *Journal of Psycholinguistic Research, 14*, 155–174.

Hornik, R., Risenhoover, N., & Gunnar, M. (1987). The effects of maternal positive, neutral, and negative affective communications on infant responses to new toys. *Child Development, 58*, 937–944.

Horowitz, F. D. (1974). Infant attention and discrimination: Methodological and substantive issues. *Monographs of the Society for Research in Child Development, 39*(Serial No. 158, Nos. 5–6).

Horton, M. S., & Markman, E. M. (1980). Developmental differences in the acquisition of basic and superordinate categories. *Child Development, 51*, 708–719.

Howard, D. V. (1983). *Cognitive psychology: Memory, language, and thought.* New York: Macmillan.

Howe, C. (1981). *Acquiring language in a conversational context.* New York: Academic Press.

Hudson, J. A. (1986). Memories are made of this: General event knowledge and development of autobiographic memory. In K. Nelson (Ed.), *Event knowledge: Structure and function in development* (pp. 97–118). Hillsdale, NJ: Erlbaum.

Hudson, J. A., & Nelson, K. (1983). Effects of script structure on children's story recall. *Developmental Psychology, 19*, 625–635.

Hudson, L. M., Forman, E. A., & Brion-Meisels, S. (1982). Role taking as a predictor of prosocial behavior in cross-age tutors. *Child Development, 53*, 1320–1329.

Hume, D. (1963). *Enquiries concerning the human understanding and concerning the principles of morals.* Oxford, England: The Clarendon Press. Reprinted from posthumous edition of 1777.

Humphrey, G. K., Humphrey, D. E, Muir, D. W., & Dodwell, P.C. (1986). Pattern perception in infants: Effect of structure and transformation. *Journal of Experimental Child Psychology, 41*, 128–148.

Hunt, J. M. (1961). *Intelligence and experience.* New York: Ronald Press.

Hunt, J. M. (1963). Motivation inherent in information processing. In O. J. Harvey (Ed.). *Motivation and Social Interaction* (pp. 35–94). New York: Ronald Press.

Hunter, M. A., Ames, E. W., & Koopman, R. (1983). Effects of stimulus complexity and familiarization time on infant preferences for novel and familiar stimuli. *Developmental Psychology, 19*, 338–352.

Huston, A. C. (1983). Sex-typing. In P. H. Mussen (Ed.), *Handbook of child psychology* (4th ed. Vol. 4, pp. 387–467). New York: Wiley.

Huttenlocher, J. (1974). The origins of language comprehension. In R. L. Solso (Ed.), *Theories in cognitive psychology* (pp. 331–368). Potomac, MD: Erlbaum.

Huttenlocher, J., & Lui, F. (1979). The semantic organization of some simple nouns and verbs. *Journal of Verbal Learning and Verbal Behavior, 18*, 141–162.

Huttenlocher, J., & Smiley, P. (1987). Early word meanings: The case of object names. *Cognitive Psychology, 19*, 63–89.

Iannotti, R. J. (1985). Naturalistic and structured assessments of prosocial behavior in preschool children: The influence of empathy and perspective taking. *Developmental Psychology, 21,* 46–55.

Inhelder, B., & Piaget, J. (1958). *The growth of logical thinking from childhood to adolescence.* New York: Basic Books.

Inhelder, B., & Piaget, J. (1964). *The early growth of logic in the child.* New York: Norton.

Ingalls, R. P., & Dickerson, D. J. (1969). Development of hypothesis behavior in human concept identification. *Developmental Psychology, 1,* 707–716.

Istomina, Z. M. (1975). The development of voluntary memory in preschool-age children. *Soviet Psychology, 13,* 5–64.

Jacklin, C. N., & Maccoby, E. E. (1978). Social behavior at thirty-three months in same-sex and mixed-sex dyads. *Child Development, 49,* 557–569.

Jacoby, L. L., & Witherspoon, D. (1982). Remembering without awareness. *Canadian Journal of Psychology, 36,* 300–324.

James, W. (1890). *Principles of psychology* (Vol. 1). New York: Holt.

James, W. (1961). *Psychology: The briefer course.* New York: Harper & Brothers. (Original work published in 1892)

Jeffrey, W. E. (1982). Selective attention: Response inhibition or stimulus differentiation? A reply to Lane and Pearson. *Merrill-Palmer Quarterly, 28,* 523–528.

Jenkins, J. J. (1979). Four points to remember: A tetrahedral model of memory experiments. In L. S. Cermak & F. I. M. Craik (Eds.), *Levels of processing in human memory* (pp. 429–446). Hillsdale, NJ: Erlbaum.

Johnson, C. N. (1982). Acquisition of mental verbs and the concept of mind. In S. A. Kuczaj (Ed.), *Language development* (Vol. 1, pp. 445–478). Hillsdale, NJ: Erlbaum.

Johnson, E. S. (1978). Validation of concept-learning strategies. *Journal of Experimental Psychology: General, 107,* 237–266.

Johnson, H., & Smith, L. B. (1981). Children's inferential abilities in the context of reading to understand. *Child Development, 52,* 1216–1223.

Johnson, J., & Newport, E. (1989). Critical period effects in second language learning: The influence of maturational state on the acquisition of English as a second language. *Cognitive Psychology, 21,* 60–99.

Johnson, N. S. (1981, August). *The role of schemata in comprehension and memory: A developmental perspective.* In A. C. Graesser (Chair), *The use of schemata in human information processing.* Symposium presented at the meeting of American Psychological Association, Los Angeles.

Johnson, N. S. (1983a, June). *There's more to a story than meets the eye: The role of story structure and story schemata in reading.* Paper presented at the University of Wisconsin Symposium on Factors Related to Reading Performance, Milwaukee.

Johnson, N. S. (1983b). What do you do if you can't tell the whole story? The development of summarization skills. In K. E. Nelson (Ed.), *Children's language* (Vol. 4, pp. 315–383). Hillsdale, NJ: Erlbaum.

Johnson, N. S., & Mandler, J. M. (1980). A tale of two structures: Underlying and surface forms in stories. *Poetics, 9,* 51–86.

Johnson-Laird, P. N. (1975). Models of deduction. In R. J. Falmagne (Ed.), *Reasoning: Representation and process in children and adults* (pp. 7–54). Hillsdale, NJ: Erlbaum.

Johnson-Laird, P. N. (1982). Ninth Bartlett memorial lecture. Thinking as a skill. *Quarterly Journal of Experimental Psychology, 34A,* 1–29.

Johnson-Laird, P. N. (1983). *Mental models.* Cambridge, MA: Harvard University Press.

Johnson-Laird, P. N. (1986). Conditionals and mental models. In E. C. Traugott, A. ter Meulen, J. S. Reilly, & C. A. Ferguson (Eds.), *On Conditionals* (pp. 55–75). Cambridge, England: Cambridge University Press.

Johnson-Laird, P. N., & Bara, B. G. (1984). Syllogistic inference. *Cognition, 16,* 1–61.

Johnson-Laird, P. N., Oakhill, J., & Bull, D. (1986). Children's syllogistic reasoning. *Quarterly Journal of Experimental Psychology, 38A,* 35–58.

Johnson-Laird, P. N., & Steedman, M. (1978). The psychology of syllogisms. *Cognitive Psychology, 10,* 64–99.

Johnson-Laird, P. N., & Wason, P. C. (1970). A theoretical analysis of insight into a reasoning task. *Cognitive Psychology, 1,* 134–148.

Jusczyk, P. W. (1981). The processing of speech and nonspeech sounds by infants: Some implications. In R. N. Aslin, J. R. Alberts, & M. R. Peterson (Eds.), *Development of perception* (Vol. 1, pp. 191–229). New York: Academic Press.

Kagan, J. (1971). *Change and continuity in infancy.* New York: Wiley.

Kagan, J. (1981). *The second year: The emergence of self awareness.* Cambridge, MA: Harvard University Press.

Kahan, L. D., & Richards, D. D. (1985). Effects of two types of familiarity on children's referential communication abilities. *Communication Monographs, 52,* 280–287.

Kahneman, D., Slovic, P., & Tversky, A. (Eds.). (1982). *Judgment under uncertainty: Heuristics and biases.* Cambridge, England: Cambridge University Press.

Kahneman, D., & Tversky, A. (1972). Subjective probability: A judgment of representativeness. *Cognitive Psychology, 3,* 430–454.

Kahneman, D. & Tversky, A. (1973). On the psychology of prediction. *Psychological Review, 80,* 237–251.

Kail, R. V., Jr. (1984). *The development of memory in children* (2nd ed. pp. 57–101). New York: Freeman.

Kaplan, P. S., & Werner, J. S. (1986). Habituation, response to novelty, and dishabituation in human infants: Tests of a dual-process theory of visual attention. *Journal of Experimental Child Psychology, 42,* 199–217.

Karat, J. (1982). A model of problem solving with incomplete constraint knowledge. *Cognitive Psychology, 14,* 538–559.

Kareev, Y. (1982). A priming study of developmental changes in the associative strength of class relations. *Child Development, 53,* 1038–1045.

Karmiloff-Smith, A. (1984). Children's problem solving. In M.E. Lamb, A. L. Brown, & B. Rogoff (Eds.), *Advances in developmental psychology* (Vol. 3, pp. 39–90). Hillsdale, NJ: Erlbaum.

Karmiloff-Smith, A. & Inhelder, B. (1974) "If you want to get ahead, get a theory." *Cognition, 3,* 195–212.

Kassin, S. M., & Ellis, S. A. (1988). On the acquisition of the discounting principle: An experimental test of a social-developmental model. *Child Development, 59,* 950–960.

Kassin, S. M., & Lepper, M. R. (1984). Oversufficient and insufficient justification effects: Cognitive and behavioral development. In J. Nicholls (Ed.), *The development of achievement motivation* (pp. 73–106). Greenwich, CT: JAI.

Kassin, S. M., Lowe, C. A., & Gibbons, F. X. (1980). Children's use of the discounting principle: A perceptual approach. *Journal of Personality and Social Psychology, 39,* 719–728.

Katz, N., Baker, E., & Macnamara, J. (1974). What's in a name? A study of how children learn common and proper names. *Child Development, 45,* 469–473.

Kaufmann, F. (1987). Aspects of motion perception in infancy. In H. Rauh, & H.C. Skinhauser (Eds.), *Psychobiology and early development* (pp. 101–115). Amsterdam: Elsevier Science Publishers.

Keating, D. P. (1979). Thinking processes in adolescence. In J. Adelson (Ed.), *Handbook of adolescent psychology* (pp. 211–246). New York: Wiley.

Keeny, I. J., Cannizzio, S. R., & Flavell, J. H. (1967). Spontaneous and induced verbal rehearsal in a recall task. *Child Development, 38,* 953–966.

Keil, F. C. (1983). On the emergence of semantic and conceptual distinctions. *Journal of Experimental Psychology: General, 112,* 357–385.

Keil, F. C. (1986). The nonrepresentative nature of representational change: Some possible morals to draw from Nelson's *Making Sense. Cognitive Development, 1,* 281–291.

Keil, F. C. (1987). Conceptual development and category structure. In U. Neisser (Ed.), *Concepts and conceptual development: Ecological and intellectual factors in categorization* (pp. 175–200). Cambridge, England: Cambridge University Press.

Keil, F. C., & Batterman, N. (1984). A characteristic-to-defining shift in the development of word meaning. *Journal of Verbal Learning and Verbal Behavior, 23,* 221–236.

Keller, E. F. (1983). *A feeling for the organism: The life and work of Barbara McClintock.* New York: Freeman.

Kelley, H. H. (1973). The process of causal attribution. *American Psychologist,* 107–128.

Kellman, P. J. (1984). Perception of three-dimensional form by human infants. *Perception and Psychophysics, 36,* 353–358.

Kellman, P. J., Gleitman, H., & Spelke, E. S. (1987). Object and observer motion in the perception of objects by infants. *Journal of Experimental Psychology: Human Perception and Performance, 13,* 586–593.

Kellman, P. J., & Short, K.R. (1987). Development of three-dimensional form perception. *Journal of Experimental Psychology: Human Perception and Performance, 13,* 545–557.

Kellman, P. J., & Spelke, E. S. (1981, April). *Infants' perception of partly occluded objects:*

Sensitivity to movement and configuration. Paper presented at the biennial meeting of the Society for Research in Child Development, Boston.

Kellman, P. J., & Spelke, E. S. (1983). Perception of partly occluded objects in infancy. *Cognitive Psychology, 15,* 483–524.

Kellogg, W., & Kellogg, L. A. (1933). *The ape and the child.* New York: McGraw Hill.

Kemler, D. G. (1978). Patterns of hypothesis testing in children's discriminative learning: A study of the development of problem-solving strategies. *Developmental Psychology, 14,* 653–673.

Kemler, D. G. (1983). Holistic and analytic modes in perceptual and cognitive development. In T. Tighe, & B. E. Shepp (Eds.), *Perception, cognition and development* (pp. 77–102). Hillsdale, NJ: Erlbaum.

Kemler, D. G., & Smith, L. B. (1979). Accessing similarity and dimensional relations: Effects of integrality and separablity on the discovery of complex concepts. *Journal of Experimental Psychology: General, 108,* 133–150.

Kemler Nelson, D. G. (1984). The effect of intention on what concepts are acquired. *Journal of Verbal Learning and Verbal Behavior, 23,* 734–759.

Kemler Nelson, D. G. (1988). When category learning is holistic: A reply to Ward and Scott. *Memory & Cognition, 16,* 79–84.

Kendall, P. C., & Braswell, L. (1985). *Cognitive-behavioral therapy for impulsive children.* New York: Guilford Press.

Kendler, T. (1960). Learning, development, and thinking. *Annals of the New York Academy of Science, 91,* 52–63.

Kendler, T. S., & Kendler, H. H. (1967). Experimental analysis of inferential behavior of children. In L. P. Lipsitt & C. C. Spiker (Eds.), *Advances in child development and behavior* (Vol. 3, pp. 157–190). New York: Academic Press.

Kessen, W. (1960). Research design in the study of developmental problems. In P. Mussen (Ed.), *Handbook of research methods in child development* (pp. 36–70). New York: Wiley.

Kessen, W., Salapatek, P., & Haith, M. (1972). The visual response of the human newborn to linear contour. *Journal of Experimental Child Psychology, 13,* 9–20.

Killen, M., & Uzgiris, I. C. (1981). Imitation of actions with objects: The role of social meaning. *Journal of Genetic Psychology, 138,* 219–229.

Kimble, G. A., Garmezy, N., & Zigler, E. (1974). *Principles of general psychology* (4th ed.). New York: Ronald Press.

Kintsch, W. (1970). Models for free-recall and recognition. In D. A. Norman (Ed.), *Models of human memory* (pp. 333–374). New York: Academic Press.

Kintsch, W., & van Dijk, T. A. (1978). Toward a model of text comprehension and production. *Psychological Review, 85,* 363–394.

Kitchener, K. S., & Kitchener, R. F. (1981). The development of natural rationality: Can formal operations account for it? *Contributions to human development, 5,* 160–181.

Klahr, D., Langley, P., & Neches, R. (1987). *Production system models of learning and development.* Cambridge, MA: MIT Press.

Klahr, D., & Robinson, M. (1981). Formal assessment of problem-solving and planning processes in preschool children. *Cognitive Psychology, 13,* 113–148.

Klahr, D. & Wallace, J. G. (1972). Class-inclusion processes. In S. Farnham-Diggory (Ed.) *Information processing in children* (pp. 143–172). New York: Academic Press.

Klayman, J., & Ha, Y. W. (1987). Confirmation, disconfirmation, and information in hypothesis testing. *Psychological Review, 94,* 211–228.

Klee, T., & Fitzgerald, M. D. (1985). The relation between grammatical development and mean length of utterance in morphemes. *Journal of Child Language, 2,* 251–269.

Kleiner, K. A. (1987). Amplitude and phase spectra as indices of infants' pattern preferences. *Infant Behavior and Development, 10,* 49–59.

Kleiner, K. A., & Banks, M. S. (1987). Stimulus energy does not account for 2-month-olds' face preferences. *Journal of Experimental Psychology: Human Perception and Performance, 13,* 594–600.

Klinnert, M. D. (1984). The regulation of infant behavior by maternal facial expression. *Infant Behavior and Development, 7,* 447–465.

Klinnert, M. D., Campos, J. J., Sorce, J. F., Emde, R. N., & Svejda, M. (1983). Emotions as behavior regulators: Social referencing in infancy. In R. Plutchik & H. Kellerman (Eds.), *Emotion: Theory, research, and experience* (Vol. 2, pp. 57–86). New York: Academic Press.

Klinnert, M. D., Emde, R. N., Butterfield, P., and Campos, J. J. (1986). Social referencing: The infant's use of emotional signals from a friendly adult with mother present. *Developmental Psychology, 22,* 427–432.

Koblinsky, S. A., & Cruse, D. F. (1981). The role of frameworks in children's retention of sex-related story content. *Journal of Experimental Child Psychology, 31,* 321–331.

Kodroff, J. K., & Roberge, J. J. (1975). Developmental analysis of the conditional reasoning abilities of primary-grade children. *Developmental Psychology, 11,* 21–28.

Koffka, K. (1935). *Principles of Gestalt Psychology.* New York: Harcourt, Brace & World.

Kohlberg, L. (1969). Stage and sequence: The cognitive developmental approach to socialization. In D. A. Goslin (Ed.), *Handbook of socialization: Theory of research* (pp. 347–480). Chicago: Rand McNally.

Kohlberg, L., Yaeger, J., & Hjertholm, E. (1968). Private speech: Four studies and a review of theories. *Child Development, 39,* 691–736.

Kohler, W. (1947). *Gestalt Psychology.* New York: Liveright.

Kolers, P. A., & Smythe, W. E. (1984). Symbol manipulation: Alternatives to the computational view of mind. *Journal of Verbal Learning and Verbal Behavior, 23,* 289–314.

Koslowski, B., & Okagaki, L. (1986). Non-Human indices of causation in problem-solving situations: Causal mechanism, analogous effects, and the status of rival alternative accounts. *Child Development, 57,* 1100–1108.

Kosslyn, S. M. (1978). The representational-development hypothesis. In P. A. Ornsetin (Ed.), *Memory development in children* (pp. 157–189). Hillsdale, NJ: Erlbaum.

Kosslyn, S. M. (1980). *Image and mind.* Cambridge, MA: Harvard University Press.

Krasnor, L. R., & Rubin, K. H. (1983). Preschool social problem solving: Attempts and outcomes in naturalistic interaction. *Child Development, 54,* 1545–1558.

Krauss, R. M. and Glucksberg, S. (1969). The development of communication: Competence as a function of age. *Child Development, 40,* 255–266.

Kreutzer, M. A., Leonard, C. T., & Flavell, J. H. (1975). An interview study of children's knowledge about memory. *Monographs of the Society for Research in Child Development, 40*(1, Serial No. 159).

Kuczaj, S. (1983). *Crib speech and language play.* New York: Springer-Verlag.

Kuczynski, L., Zahn-Waxler, C., & Radke-Yarrow, M. (1987). Development and content of imitation in the second and third years of life: A socialization perspective. *Developmental Psychology, 23,* 276–282.

Kuhl, P. K. (1979). The perception of speech in early infancy. In N. J. Lass (Ed.), *Speech and language: Advances in basic research and practice* (pp. 1–47). New York: Academic Press.

Kuhl, P. K. (1985). Methods in the study of infant speech perception. In G. Gottlieb & N. Krasnegor (Eds.), *Measurement of Audition and Vision in the First Week of Postnatal Life: A Methodological Overview* (pp. 223–251). Norwood, NJ: Ablex.

Kuhl, P. K., & Meltzoff, A. N. (1982). The bimodal perception of speech in infancy. *Science, 218,* 1138–1141.

Kuhn, D., & Brannock, J. (1977). Development of the isolation of variables scheme in experimental and "Natural Experiment" contexts. *Developmental Psychology, 13,* 9–14.

Kuhn, T. S. (1970). *The structure of scientific revolution* (2nd ed). Chicago: University of Chicago Press.

Kurtz, B. E., Reid, M. K., Borkowski, J. G., & Cavanaugh, J. C. (1982). On the reliability and validity of children's metamemory. *Bulletin of the Psychonomic Society, 19,* 137–140.

Kuzmak, S. D., & Gelman, R. (1986). Young children's understanding of random phenomena. *Child Development, 57,* 599–566.

Lamb, M. E. (1981). The development of social expectations in the first year of life. In M. E. Lamb & L. R. Sherrod (Eds.), *Infant social cognition: Empirical and theoretical considerations* (pp. 155–175). Hillsdale, NJ: Erlbaum.

Landau, B. (1982). Will the real grandmother please stand up? The psychological reality of dual meaning representations. *Journal of Psycholinguistic Research, 11,* 47–62.

Landis, T. Y. (1982). Interactions between text and prior knowledge in children's memory for prose. *Child Development, 53,* 811–814.

Lane, D. M. (1979). Developmental changes in attention-deployment skills. *Journal of Experimental Child Psychology, 28,* 16–29.

Lane, D. M., & Pearson, D. A. (1982). The development of selective attention. *Merrill-Palmer Quarterly, 28,* 317–337.

Lane, D. M., & Pearson, D. A. (1983). Can stimulus differentiation and salience explain developmental changes in attention? A reply to Hagen and Wilson, Jeffrey, and Odom. *Merrill-Palmer Quarterly, 29,* 227–233.

Larkin, J. H. (1980). Skilled problem solving in physics: A hierarchical planning model. *Journal of Structural Learning, 6,* 271–297.

Larkin, J. H. (1981). Enriching formal knowledge: A model for learning to solve textbook physics problems. In J. R. Anderson (Ed.), *Cognitive skills and their acquisition* (pp. 311–334). Hillsdale, NJ: Erlbaum.

Larkin, J. H. (1985). Understanding, problem representations, and skill in physics. In S. Chipman, J. Segal, & R. Glaser (Eds.), *Thinking and learning skills* (Vol. 2, pp. 141–159). Hillsdale, NJ: Erlbaum.

Larkin, J., McDermott, J., Simon, D. P., & Simon, H. A. (1980). Expert and novice performance in solving physics problems. *Science, 208,* 1335–1342.

Lasky, R. E., Syrdal-Lasky, A., & Klein, R. E. (1975). VOT discrimination by 4- to 6-month-old infants from Spanish environments. *Journal of Experimental Child Psychology, 20,* 215–225.

Laughlin, P. R., Lange, R., & Adamopoulos, J. (1982). Selection strategies for "mastermind" problems. *Journal of Experimental Psychology: Learning, Memory, and Cognition, 8,* 475–483.

Legerstee, M., Pomerleau, S., Malcuit, G., and Feider, H. (1987). The development of infants' responses to people and a doll: Implications for research in communication. *Infant Behavior and Development, 10,* 81–95.

LeMare, L. J., & Rubin, K. H. (1987). Perspective taking and peer interaction: Structural and developmental analyses. *Child Development, 58,* 306–315.

Lempert, H., & Kinsbourne, M. (1983). Perceptual constraints on the use of language by young children. In K. E. Nelson (Ed.), *Children's language* (Vol. 4, pp. 125–156). Hillsdale, NJ: Erlbaum.

Lenneberg, E. H. (1967). *Biological foundations of language.* New York: Wiley.

Lepper, M. R., Greene, D., & Nisbett, R. E. (1973). Undermining children's intrinsic interest with extrinsic rewards: A test of the "overjustification" hypothesis. *Journal of Personality and Social Psychology, 28,* 129–137.

Lepper, M. R., Sagotsky, G., Dafoe, J. L., & Greene, D. (1982). Consequences of superfluous social constraints: Effects on young children's social inferences and subsequent intrinsic interest. *Journal of Personality and Social Psychology, 42,* 51–65.

Leslie, A. M., & Keeble, S. (1987). Do six-month-old infants perceive causality? *Cognition, 25,* 265–288.

Levin, E. A., & Rubin, K. H. (1983). Getting others to do what you want them to do: The development of children's requestive strategies. In K. E. Nelson (Ed.), *Children's language* (Vol. 4, pp. 157–186). Hillsdale, NJ: Erlbaum.

Levine, D. I., & Linn, M. C. (1977). Scientific reasoning ability in adolescence: Theoretical viewpoints and educational implications. *Journal of Research in Science Teaching, 14,* 371–384.

Levine, M. (1963). Mediating processes in humans at the outset of discrimination learning. *Journal of Experimental Child Psychology, 26,* 341–358.

Levine, M. (1966). Hypothesis behavior by humans during discrimination learning. *Journal of Experimental Psychology, 71,* 331–338.

Levine, M. (1975). *A cognitive theory of learning: Research on hypothesis testing.* Hillsdale, NJ: Erlbaum.

Levinson, P. J., & Carpenter, R. L. (1974). An analysis of analogical reasoning in children. *Child Development, 45,* 857–861.

Levitt, M. J. (1980). Contingent feedback, familiarization, and infant affect: How a stranger becomes a friend. *Developmental Psychology, 16,* 425–432.

Lewis, M., & Brooks-Gunn, J. (1979). *Social cognition and the acquisition of self.* New York: Plenum Press.

Lewis, M., & Feiring, C. (1979). The child's social network: Social object, social functions, and their relationship. In M. Lewis & L. A. Rosenblum (Eds.), *The child and its family* (pp. 9–27). New York: Plenum Press.

Lewis, M., & Sullivan, M. W. (1985). Imitation in the first six months of life. *Merrill-Palmer Quarterly, 31,* 315–333.

Lewis, T. L., Maurer, D., & Kay, D. (1978). Newborns' central vision: Whole or hole? *Journal of Experimental Child Psychology, 26,* 193–203.

Liberman, A. M. (1970) The grammars of speech and language. *Cognitive Psychology, 1,* 301–323.

Liberman, A. M., Cooper, F., Shankweiler, D., & Studdert-Kennedy, M. (1967). Perception of the speech code. *Psychological Review, 74,* 431–461.

Lichtenstein, S., Slovic, P., Fischhoff, B., Layman, M., & Combs, B. (1978). Judged frequency of lethal events. *Journal of Experimental Psychology: Human Learning and Memory, 4,* 551–578.

Lieven, E. V. M. (1982). Context, process and progress in young children's speech. In M. Beveridge (Ed.), *Children thinking through language* (pp. 7–26). London: Edward Arnold Press.

Light, L. L., Kayra-Stuart, F., & Hollander, S. (1979). Recognition memory for typical and unusual faces. *Journal of Experimental Psychology: Human Learning and Memory, 5,* 212–228.

Limber, J. (1976). Unravelling competence, performance and pragmatics in the speech of young children. *Journal of Child Language, 3,* 309–318.

Lindberg, M. A. (1980). Is knowledge base development a necessary and sufficient condition for memory development? *Journal of Experimental Child Psychology, 30,* 401–410.

Lindvall, C. M., Tamburino, J. L., & Robinson, L. (1982, March). *An exploratory investigation of the effects of teaching primary grade children to use specific problem solving strategies in solving simple arithmetic story problems.* Paper presented at the meeting of the American Educational Research Association, New York.

Linn, M. C., & Rice, M. (1979). A measure of scientific reasoning: The springs task. *Journal of Educational Measurement, 16,* 55–58.

Linn, M. C., & Swiney, J. F., Jr. (1981). Individual differences in formal thought: Role of expectations and aptitudes. *Journal of Educational Psychology, 73,* 274–286.

Lisker, L., & Abramson, A. S. (1970). The voicing dimensions: Some experiments in comparative phonetics. In B. Hela, M. Romportl & P. Janota (Eds.), *Proceedings of the Sixth International Congress of Phonetic Sciences* (pp. 563–567). Prague: Academia.

Lockhart, R. S. (1984). What do infants remember? In M. Moscowitch, (Ed.), *Infant memory: Its relation to normal and pathological memory in humans and other animals* (pp. 131–143). New York: Plenum Press.

Lockhart, R. S., Lamon, M., & Gick, M. L. (1988). Conceptual transfer in simple insight problems. *Memory & Cognition, 16,* 36–44.

Longhurst, T. M. and Turnure, J. E. (1971). Perceptual inadequacy and communicative ineffectiveness in interpersonal communication. *Child Development, 42,* 2084–2088.

Lorenz, K. Z. (1974). Analogy as a source of knowledge. *Science, 185,* 229–234.

Lovett, S. B. (1985). Children's understanding of random generating devices. *Dissertation Abstracts International, 46,* 1357B. (University Microfilms No. 85-11329, 128)

Lubin, L., & Field, T. (1981). Imitation during preschool peer interaction. *International Journal of Behavioral Development, 4,* 443–453.

Lucariello, J. (1983, April). *Is the basic level always basic?* Paper presented at the biennial meeting of the Society for Research in Child Development, Detroit.

Lucariello, J., & Nelson, K. (1985). Slot-filler categories as memory organizers for young children. *Developmental Psychology, 21,* 272–282.

Lucariello, J. & Rifkin, A. (1986). Event representations as the basis for categorical knowledge. In K. Nelson (Ed.), *Event knowledge: Structure and function in development* (pp. 189–204). Hillsdale, NJ: Erlbaum.

Lucas, D. A. (1979, April). *Alleviated forgetting in 3-month-old infants.* Paper presented at the meeting of the Eastern Psychological Association, Boston.

Luchins, A. S. (1942). Mechanization in problem solving. *Psychological Monographs, 54*(Serial No. 248).

Luger, G. F., Wishart, J. G., & Bower, T. G. R. (1984). Modelling the stages of the identity theory of object concept development in infancy. *Perception, 13,* 97–115.

Lunzer, E. A. (1965). Problems of formal reasoning in test situations. In P. H. Mussen (Ed.), European research in cognitive development. *Monographs of the Society for Research in Child Development, 30*(2, Serial No. 100), pp. 19–46.

Lutkenhaus, P. (1984). Pleasure derived from mastery in three-year olds: Its function for persistence and the influence of maternal behavior. *International Journal of Behavioral Development, 7,* 343–358.

Macnamara, J. (1982). *Names for things: A study of human learning.* Cambridge, MA: MIT Press.

Macnamara, J. (1986). *A border dispute: The place of logic in psychology.* Cambridge, MA: MIT Press.

MacFarlane, A., Harris, P., & Barnes, I. (1976). Central and peripheral vision in early infancy. *Journal of Experimental Child Psychology, 21,* 532–538.

Mandell, N. (1984). Children's negotiation of meaning. *Symbolic Interaction, 7,* 191–211.

Mandler, J. M. (1978). A code in the node: The use of a story schema in retrieval. *Discourse Processes, 1,* 14–35.

Mandler, J. M. (1983). Representation. In P. H. Mussen (Ed.), *Handbook of child psychology* (4th ed., Vol. 3, pp. 420–494). New York: Wiley.

Mandler, J. M. (1984a). Representation and recall in infancy. In M. Moscovitch (Ed.), *Infant memory: Its relation to normal and pathological memory in humans and other animals* (pp. 75–101). New York: Plenum Press.

Mandler, J. M. (1984b). *Stories, scripts, and scenes: Aspects of schema theory.* Hillsdale, NJ: Erlbaum.

Mandler, J. M., & Bauer, P. J. (1988). The cradle of categorization: Is the basic-level basic? *Cognitive Development, 3,* 247–264.

Mandler, J. M., & DeForest, M. (1979). Is there more than one way to recall a story? *Child Development, 50,* 886–889.

Mandler, J. M., Fivush, R., & Reznick, J. S. (1987). The development of contextual categories. *Cognitive Development, 2,* 339–354.

Mandler, J. M., & Johnson, N. S. (1977). Remembrance of things parsed: Story structure and recall. *Cognitive Psychology, 9,* 111–151.

Mandler, J. M., & Robinson, C. A. (1978). Developmental changes in picture recognition. *Journal of Experimental Child Psychology, 26,* 122–136.

Mandler, J. M., Scribner, S., Cole, M., & DeForest, M. (1980). Cross-cultural invariance in story recall. *Child Development, 51,* 19–26.

Maratsos, M. P. (1973). Nonegocentric communication abilities in preschool children. *Child Development, 44,* 697–700.

Maratsos, M. P. (1983). Some current issues in the study of the acquisition of grammar. In P. H. Mussen (Ed.), *Handbook of child psychology* (Vol. 3, pp. 707–786). New York: Wiley.

Markman, E. M. (1977). Realizing that you don't understand: A preliminary investigation. *Child Development, 48,* 986–992.

Markman, E. M. (1979). Realizing that you don't understand: Elementary school children's awareness of inconsistencies. *Child Development, 50,* 643–655.

Markman, E. M. (1981) Two different principles of conceptual organization. In M. E. Lamb & A. L. Brown (Eds.), *Advances in Developmental Psychology* (Vol. 1, pp. 199–236). Hillsdale, NJ: Erlbaum.

Markman, E. M. (1984). The acquisition and hierarchical organization of categories by children. In C. Sophian (Ed.), *Origins of cognitive skills: The eighteenth annual Carnegie symposium on cognition* (pp. 371–406). Hillsdale, NJ: Erlbaum.

Markman, E. M. (1987). How children constrain the possible meanings of words. In U. Neisser, (Ed.), *Concepts and conceptual development: Ecological and intellectual factors in categorization* (pp. 255–287). Cambridge, England: Cambridge University Press.

Markman, E. M. & Callanan, M. A. (1984). An analysis of hierarchical classification. In R. J. Sternberg (Ed.), *Advances in the psychology of human intelligence* (Vol. 2, pp. 325–365). Hillsdale, NJ: Erlbaum.

Markman, E. M., & Gorin, L. (1981). Children's ability to adjust their standards for evaluating comprehension. *Journal of Educational Psychology, 73,* 320–325.

Markman, E. M., & Hutchinson, J. E. (1984). Children's sensitivity to constaints on word meaning: Taxonomic versus thematic relations. *Cognitive Psychology, 16,* 1–27.

Markman, E. M. & Seibert, J. (1976). Classes and collections: Internal organization and resulting holistic properties. *Cognitive Psychology, 8,* 561–577.

Marler, P., Zoloth, S., & Dooling, R. (1981). Innate programs for perceptual development: An ethological view. In E. S. Gollin (Ed.), *Development Plasticity* (pp. 135–172). New York: Academic Press.

Martlew, M. (1979). Young children's capacity to communicate. In K. Connolly (Ed.), *Psychological Survey* (Vol. 2, pp. 110–127). Boston: George Allen Unwin.

Martorano, S. C. (1977). A developmental analysis of performance on Piaget's formal operations task. *Developmental Psychology, 13,* 666–672.

Massey, C. M., & Gelman, R. (1988). Preschooler's ability to decide whether a photographed unfamiliar object can move itself. *Developmental Psychology, 24*(3), 307–313.

Masur, E. F. (1981). Mothers' responses to infants' object-related gestures: Influences on lexical development. *Journal of Child Language, 9,* 23–30.

Masur, E. F. (1988). Infants' imitation of novel and familiar behaviors. In T. R. Zentall and B. G. Galef, Jr. (Eds.), *Social learning: Psychological and biological perspectives* (pp. 301–318). Hillsdale, NJ: Erlbaum.

Matlin, M. (1983). *Cognition.* New York: Holt, Reinhart & Winston.

Maurer, D. (1975). Infant visual perception: Methods of study. In L. B. Cohen & P. Salapatek (Eds.), *Infant perception: From sensation to cognition* (Vol. 1, pp. 1–76). New York: Academic Press.

Maurer, D. (1983). The scanning of compound figures by young infants. *Journal of Experimental Child Psychology, 35,* 437–448.

Maurer, D., & Lewis, T. L. (1979). Peripheral discrimination by three-month-old infants. *Child Development, 50,* 276–279.

Mayer, R. E. (1983). *Thinking, problem solving, cognition.* New York: Freeman.

McBurney, P. H., & Collings, V. B. (1984). *Introduction to sensation/perception* (2nd ed.). Englewood Cliffs, NJ: Prentice-Hall.

McCall, B. B., & Kagan, J. (1967). Stimulus schema discrepancy and attention in the infant. *Journal of Experimental Psychology, 5,* 381–390.

McCartney, K. A., & Nelson, K. (1981). Children's use of scripts in story recall. *Discourse Processes, 4,* 59–70.

McClusky, K. & Linn, P. (1977, March). *Habituation and dishabituation of visual attention to familiar, similar, and novel categories in 10- and 16-week old infants.* Paper presented at the biennial meeting of the Society of Research in Child Development, New Orleans.

McDevitt, T. M., & Carroll, M. (1988). Are you trying to trick me? Some social influences on children's responses to problematic messages. *Merrill-Palmer Quarterly, 34,* 131–145.

McGarrigle, J., & Donaldson, M. (1975). Conservation accidents. *Cognition, 3,* 341–350.

McGarrigle, J., Grieve, R., & Hughes, M. (1978). Interpreting inclusion: A contribution to the study of the child's cognitive and linguistic development. *Journal of Experimental Child-Psychology, 26,* 528–550.

McKoon, G., & Ratcliff, R. (1979). Priming in episodic and semantic memory. *Journal of Verbal Learning and Verbal Behavior, 18,* 463–480.

McLaughlin, B. (1983). Child compliance to parental control techniques. *Developmental Psychology, 19,* 667–673.

McNeill, D. (1966). Developmental psycholinguistics. In F. Smith & G. A. Miller (Eds.) *The genesis of language* (pp. 15–84). Cambridge, MA: MIT Press.

Meacham, J. A. (1979). The role of verbal activity in remembering the goals of actions. In G. Zivin (Ed.), *Development of self-regulation through private speech* (pp. 237–263) New York: Wiley.

Mead, G. H. (1934). *Mind, self and society.* Chicago: University of Chicago Press.

Means, M. L., & Voss, J. F. (1985). Star wars: A developmental study of expert and novice knowledge structures. *Journal of Memory and Language, 24,* 746–757.

Medin, D. L. (1983). Structural principles in categorization. In T. Tighe & B. E. Shepp (Eds.), *Perception, cognition, and development* (pp. 203–230). Hillsdale, NJ: Erlbaum.

Mehler, J., Bertoncini, J., Barriere, M., & Jassik-Gerschenfeld, D. (1978). Infant recognition of mother's voice. *Perception, 7,* 491–497.

Meier, R. P. (1987). Elicited imitation of verb agreement in American sign language: Iconically or morphologically determined? *Journal of Memory and Language, 26,* 362–376.

Melkman, R., Tversky, B., & Baratz, D. (1981). Developmental trends in the use of perceptual and conceptual attributes in grouping, clustering, and retrieval. *Journal of Experimental Child Psychology, 31,* 470–486.

Melton, A. W. (1970). The situation with respect to the spacing of repetitions and memory. *Journal of Verbal Learning and Verbal Behavior, 9,* 596–606.

Meltzoff, A. N. (1981). Imitation, intermodal coordination and representation in early infancy. In G. Butterworth (Ed.), *Infancy and Epistemology* (pp. 85–114). Brighton, England: Harvester Press.

Meltzoff, A. N. (1988a). The human infant as *Homo imitans.* In T. R. Zentall & B. G. Galef, Jr. (Eds.), *Social learning: Psychological and biological perspectives* (pp. 319–341). Hillsdale, NJ: Erlbaum.

Meltzoff, A. N. (1988b). Imitation of televised models by infants. *Child Development, 59,* 1221–1229.

Meltzoff, A. N. (1988c). Infant imitation and memory: Nine-month-olds in immediate and deferred tests. *Child Development, 59,* 217–225.

Meltzoff, A. N., & Borton, R. W. (1979). Intermodal matching by human neonates. *Nature, 282,* 403–404.

Meltzoff, A. N., & Moore, M. K. (1977). Imitation of facial and manual gestures by human neonates. *Science, 198,* 75–78.

Meltzoff, A. N., & Moore, M. K. (1983a). Newborn infants imitate adult facial gestures. *Child Development, 54,* 702–709.

Meltzoff, A. N., & Moore, M. K. (1983b). The origins of imitation in infancy: Paradigm, phenomena, and theories. In L. P. Lipsitt & Rovee, C. K. (Eds.), *Advances in infancy research* (Vol. 2, pp. 265–301). Norwood, NJ: Ablex.

Mendelson, M. J. (1979). Acoustic-optical correspondences and auditory-visual coordination in infancy. *Canadian Journal of Psychology, 33,* 334–346.

Mendelson, M. J., & Ferland, M. B. (1982). Auditory-visual transfer in four-month-old infants. *Child Development, 53,* 1022–1027.

Mendelson, M., & Haith, M. M. (1976). The relation between audition and vision in the human newborn. *Monographs of the Society for Research in Child Development, 41*(4, Serial No. 167).

Menig-Peterson, C. L. (1975). The modification of communicative behavior in preschool-aged children as a function of the listener's perspective. *Child Development, 46,* 1015–1018.

Mervis, C. B. (1985). On the existence of prelinguistic categories: A case study. *Infant Behavior and Development, 8,* 293–300.

Messer, D. J. (1983). The redundancy between adult speech and nonverbal interaction: A contribution to acquisition? In R. M. Golinkoff (Ed.), *The transition from prelinguistic to linguistic communication* (pp. 147–165). Hillsdale, NJ: Erlbaum.

Meyer, D. E. (1970). On the representation and retrieval of stored semantic information. *Cognitive Psychology, 1,* 242–300.

Milewski, A. E. (1976). Infants' discrimination of internal and external pattern elements. *Journal of Experimental Child Psychology, 22,* 229–246.

Millar, W. S. (1988). Smiling, vocal, and attentive behavior during social contingency learning in seven- and ten-month-old infants. *Merrill-Palmer Quarterly, 34,* 301–325.

Miller, G. A. (1956). The magical number seven, plus or minus two: Some limits on our capacity for processing information. *Psychological Review, 63,* 81–97.

Miller, G. A. (1977). *Spontaneous apprenticies: Children and language.* New York: Seabury Press.

Miller, G. A. (1978). The acquisition of word meaning. *Child Development, 49,* 999–1004.

Miller, G. A., Galanter, E., & Pribram, K. H. (1960). *Plans and the structure of behavior.* New York: Holt.

Miller, P. H., & Bigi, L. (1979). The development of children's understanding of attention. *Merrill-Palmer Quarterly, 25,* 235–250.

Miller, P. H., Haynes, V. F., DeMarie-Dreblow, D., & Woody-Ramsey, J. (1986). Children's strategies for gathering information in three tasks. *Child Development, 57,* 1429–1439.

Mischel, H. N., & Mischel, W. (1983). The development of children's knowledge of self-control strategies. *Child Development, 54,* 603–619.

Mischel, W. (1983). The role of knowledge and ideation in the development of delay capacity. In L. S. Liben (Ed.), *Piaget and the foundations of knowledge* (pp. 201–229). Hillsdale, NJ: Erlbaum.

Mischel, W., & Baker, N. (1975). Cognitive appraisals and transformations in delay behavior. *Journal of Personality and Social Psychology, 31,* 254–261.

Mischel, W., Ebbesen, E. B., & Zeiss, A. R. (1972). Cognitive and attentional mechanisms in delay of gratification. *Journal of Personality and Social Psychology, 21,* 204–218.

Mistry, J. J., & Lange, G. W. (1985). Children's organization and recall of information in scripted narratives. *Child Development, 56,* 953–961.

Mistry, J. J., & Rogoff, B. (1987, April). *Influence of purpose and parental assistance on preschool children's remembering.* Paper presented at the biennial meeting of the Society for Research in Child Development, Baltimore.

Moore, D., Benenson, J, Reznick, J. S., Peterson, M., & Kagan, J.(1987). Effect of auditory numerical information on infants' looking behavior: Contradictory evidence. *Developmental Psychology, 23,* 665–670.

Moore, T. (1986). Reasoning and inference in logic and in language. In T. Myers, K. Brown, & B. McGonigle (Eds.), *Reasoning and discourse processes* (pp. 51–66). London: Academic Press.

Moray, N. (1959). Attention in dichotic listening: Affective cues and the influence of instructions. *Quarterly Journal of Experimental Psychology, 11,* 56–60.

Morgan, M. (1981). The over-justification effect: A developmental test of self-perception interpretations. *Journal of Personality and Social Psychology, 40,* 809–821.

Morrison, H., & Kuhn, D. (1983). Cognitive aspects of preschoolers' peer imitation in play situation. *Child Development, 54,* 1041–1053.

Morse, P. A. (1972). The discrimination of speech and nonspeech stimuli in early infancy. *Journal of Experimental Child Psychology, 14,* 477–492.

Mosenthal, P. (1979). Children's strategy preferences for resolving contradictory story information under two social conditions. *Journal of Experimental Child Psychology, 28,* 323–343.

Moshman, D., & Franks, B. A. (1986). Development of the concept of inferential validity. *Child Development, 57,* 153–165.

Moshman, D., & Timmons, M. (1982). The construction of logical necessity. *Human Development, 25,* 309–323.

Moulton, E. R. (1966). *The dynamics of debate.* New York: Harcourt, Brace & World.

Mueller, E. (1972). The maintenance of verbal exchanges between young children. *Child Development, 43,* 930–938.

Muir, D. W. (1985). Infants' auditory spatial sensitivity. In S. Trehub & B. Schneider (Eds.), *Auditory development in infancy* (pp. 51–83). New York: Plenum Press.

Muir, D. W., Abraham, W., Forbes, B., & Harris, L. (1979). The ontogenesis of an auditory localization response from birth to four months of age. *Canadian Journal of Psychology, 33,* 320–333.

Muir, D. W., & Field, J. (1979). Newborn infants orient to sounds. *Child Development, 50,* 431–436.

Mulholland, T. M., Pellegrino, J. W., & Glaser, R. (1980). Components of geometric analogy solution. *Cognitive Psychology, 12,* 252–284.

Murray, F. B., & Armstrong, S. L. (1978). Adult nonconservation of numerical equivalence. *Merrill-Palmer Quarterly, 24,* 255–263.

Nadel-Brulfert, J., & Baudonniere, P. M. (1982). The social function of reciprocal imitation in 2-year-old peers. *International Journal of Behavioral Development, 5,* 95–109.

Nagy, P., & Griffiths, A. K. (1982). Limitations of recent research relating Piaget's theory to adolescent thought. *Review of Educational Research, 52,* 513–556.

Naus, M. J., & Ornstein, P. A. (1983). Development of memory strategies: Analysis, questions, and issues. In M. T. H. Chi (Ed.), *Trends in memory development research: Contributions to human development series* (Vol. 9, pp. 1–30). Basel: Karger.

Neimark, E. D. (1975). Intellectual development during adolescence. In F. D. Horowitz (Ed.), *Review of child development research* (Vol. 4, pp. 541–594). Chicago: University of Chicago Press.

Neimark, E. D., & Chapman, R. H. (1975). Development of the comprehension of logical quantifiers. In R. J. Falmagne (Ed.), *Reasoning: Representation and process in children and adults* (pp. 135–151). Hillsdale, NJ: Erlbaum.

Neimark, E. D., & Lewis, N. (1967). The development of logical problem-solving strategies. *Child Development, 38,* 107–117.

Neimark, E. D., & Slotnick, N. S. (1970). Development of the understanding of logical connectives. *Journal of Educational Psychology, 61,* 451–460.

Neisser, U., & Becklen, R. (1975). Selective looking: Attending to visually specified events. *Cognitive Psychology, 7,* 480–494.

Nelson, K. (1973) Structure and strategy in learning to talk. *Monographs of the Society for Research in Child Development, 38*(Serial No. 149).

Nelson, K. (1977). The syntagmatic-paradigmatic shift revisited: A review of research and theory. *Psychological Bulletin, 84,* 93–116.

Nelson, K. (1981). Individual differences in language development: Implications for development and language. *Developmental Psychology, 7,* 170–187.

Nelson, K. (1984). The transition from infant to child memory. In M. Moscovitch (Ed.), *Advances in the study of communication and affect: Vol 9. Infant memory: Its relation to normal and pathological memory in humans and other animals* (pp. 103–130). New York: Plenum Press.

Nelson, K. (1985). *Making sense: The acquisition of shared meaning*. New York: Academic Press.

Nelson, K. (1986). *Event knowledge: Structure and function in development*. Hillsdale, NJ: Erlbaum.

Nelson, K., & Brown, A. L. (1978). The semantic-episodic distinction in memory development. In P. A. Ornstein (Ed.), *Memory development in children* (pp. 233–241). Hillsdale, NJ: Erlbaum.

Nelson, K., & Gruendel, J. M. (1979). At morning it's lunchtime: A scriptal view of children's dialogues. *Discourse Processes, 2,* 73–94.

Nelson, K., & Gruendel, J. M. (1981). Generalized event representations: Basic building blocks of cognitive development. In M. E. Lamb & A. L. Brown (Eds.), *Advances in developmental psychology* (Vol. 1, pp. 131–158). Hillsdale, NJ: Erlbaum.

Nelson, K., & Gruendel, J. M. (1986). Children's scripts. In K. Nelson (ed.), Event knowledge: and function in development, (pp. 21–46). Hillsdale, NJ: Erlbaum.

Nelson, K., & Seidman, S. (1984). Playing with scripts. In I. Bretherton (Ed.). *Symbolic play* (pp. 45–71). Orlando, FL: Academic Press.

Newell, A. (1972). A note on process-structure distinctions in developmental psychology. In S. Farnharm-Diggory (Ed.), *Information processing in children* (pp. 126–139). New York: Academic Press.

Newell, A. (1980). Citation classic—Human problem solving. *Current contents/social and behavioral sciences, 34,* 14.

Newell, A., & Simon, H. A. (1972). *Human problem solving*. Englewood Cliffs, N.J: Prentice-Hall.

Newport, E. L. (1986, November). *Maturational constraints on language learning*. Paper presented at the meeting of the Psychonomic Society, New Orleans.

Newport, E. L., Gleitman, H., & Gleitman, L. R. (1977). Mother, I'd rather do it myself: Some effects and non-effects of maternal speech style. In C. E. Snow, & C. A. Ferguson (Eds.), *Talking to children: Language input and acquisition* (pp. 109–149). Cambridge, England: Cambridge University Press.

Newport, E. L., & Supalla, T. (In press). A critical period effect in the acquisition of a primary language. *Science*.

Newstead, S. E., & Griggs, R. A. (1983). Drawing inferences from quantified statements: A study of the square of opposition. *Journal of Verbal Learning and Verbal Behavior, 22,* 535–546.

Nicholas, D. W., & Trabasso, T. (1980). Toward a taxonomy of inferences for story comprehension. In F. Wilkening, J. Becker & T. Trabasso (Eds.), *Information integration by children* (pp. 243–265). Hillsdale, NJ: Erlbaum.

Nickerson, R. S. (1986). *Reflections on reasoning*. Hillsdale, NJ: Erlbaum.

Nisbett, R. E., Krantz, D. H., Jepson, C., & Kunda, Z. (1983). The use of statistical heuristics in everyday inductive reasoning. *Psychological Review, 90,* 339–363.

Nissen, M. J., & Bullemer, P. (1987). Attentional requirements of learning: Evidence from performance measures. *Cognitive Psychology, 19,* 1–32.

Norman, D. A., & Bobrow, D. G. (1975). On data-limited and resource-limited processes. *Cognitive Psychology, 7,* 44–64.

Norman, D. A., & Rumelhart, D. E. (1975). *Explorations incognition*. San Francisco: Freeman.

Nosbush, L., Oakes, L., & Breslow, L. (1983, April). *Development and representation in transitive inferences*. Paper presented at the biennial meeting of the Society for Research and Child Development, Detroit.

Oakhill, J. V., & Johnson-Laird, P. N. (1985). The effects of belief on the spontaneous production of syllogistic conclusions. *The Quarterly Journal of Experimental Psychology, 37A,* 553–569.

O'Connell, B., & Gerard, A. (1985). Scripts and scraps: The development of sequential understanding. *Child Development, 56,* 671–681.

Odom, R. C. (1982). Lane and Pearson's inattention to relevant information: A need for the theoretical specification of task information in developmental research. *Merrill-Palmer Quarterly, 28,* 339–345.

Olson, D. R. (1977). From utterance to text: The bias of language in speech and writing. *Harvard Educational Review, 47,* 257–281.

Olson, D. R. & Torrance, N. G. (1983). Literacy and cognitive development: A conceptual transformation in the early school years. In S. Meadows (Ed.), *Developing thinking* (pp. 142–160). London: Methuen.

Olson, G. M. (1976). An information processing analysis of visual memory and habituation in infants. In T. J. Tighe & R. N. Leaton (Eds.), *Habituation: Perspectives from child development, animal behavior, and neurophysiology* (pp. 239–277). Hillsdale, NJ: Erlbaum.

Olson, G. M. (1981). The recognition of specific persons. In M. E. Lamb & L. R. Sherrod (Eds.), *Infant social cognition: Empirical and theoretical considerations* (pp. 37–59). Hillsdale, NJ: Erlbaum.

Olson, G.M. (1984). Learning and memory in infants. In J. R. Anderson & S. M. Kosslyn (Eds.), *Tutorials in learning and memory: Essays in honor of Gordon Bower* (pp. 1–29). San Francisco: Freeman.

Olson, G. M., & Sherman, T. (1983). Attention, learning, and memory in infants. In P. H. Mussen (Ed.), *Handbook of child psychology* (4th ed., Vol. 2, pp. 1001–1080). New York: Wiley.

Olson, G. M., & Strauss, M. C. (1984). The development of infant memory. In M. Moscovitch (Ed.), *Infant memory: Its relation to normal and pathological memory in human and other animals* (pp. 29–48). New York: Plenum Press.

Oppenheimer, R. (1956). Analogy in science. *American Psychologist, 11,* 127–135.

Ornstein, P. A., & Baker-Ward, L. (1983, April). *The development of mnemonic skill.* Paper presented at the Biennial Meeting of the Society for Research in Child Development, Detroit.

Ornstein, P. A., & Naus, M. J. (1978). Rehearsal processes in children's memory. In P. A. Ornstein (Ed.), *Memory development in children* (pp. 69–99). Hillsdale, NJ: Erlbaum.

Ornstein, P. A., Naus, M. J., & Liberty, C. (1975). Rehearsal and organization processes in children's memory. *Child Development, 46,* 818–830.

Oster, H. S. (April, 1975). *Color perceptions in ten-week-old infants.* Paper presented at the biennial meeting of the Society for Research in Child Development, Denver.

Ostrom, T. M. (1984). The sovereignty of social cognition. In R. S. Wyer, Jr., & T. K. Srull (Eds.), *Handbook of social cognition* (Vol. 1, pp. 1–37). Hillsdale, NJ: Erlbaum.

Over, R. (1987). Can human neonates imitate facial gestures? In B. E. McKenzie & B. H. Day (Eds.), *Perceptual development in early infancy: Problems and issues* (pp. 219–233). Hillsdale, NJ: Erlbaum.

Overton, W. F., Ward, S. L., Noveck, I. A., Black, J. & O'Brien, D. P. (1987). Form and content in the development of deductive reasoning. *Developmental Psychology, 23,* 22–30.

Owen, E., & Sweller, J. (1985). What do students learn while solving mathematics problems? *Journal of Educational Psychology, 77,* 272–284.

Pace, A. J., (1979, September). *Children's awareness of script-inconsistent story information.* Paper presented at the annual meeting of the American Psychological Association, New York.

Pace, A. J., (1981, April). *Comprehension monitoring by elementary students: When does it occur?* Paper presented at the annual meeting of the American Educational Research Association, Los Angeles.

Pace, A. J., & Feagans, L. (1984). Knowledge and language: Children's ability to use and communicate what they know about everyday experiences. In L. Feagans, (Ed.), *The origins and growth of communication* (pp. 268–280). Norwood, NJ: Ablex.

Paris, S. G. (1973). Comprehension of language connectives and propositional logical relationships. *Journal of Experimental Child Psychology, 16,* 278–291.

Paris, S. G., & Carter, A. Y. (1973). Semantic and constructive aspects of sentence memory in children. *Developmental Psychology, 9,* 109–113.

Paris, S. G., & Lindauer, B. K. (1976). The role of inference in children's comprehension and memory for sentences. *Cognitive Psychology, 8,* 217–227.

Paris, S. G., & Lindauer, B. K. (1977). Constructive aspects of children's comprehension and memory. In R. V. Kail, Jr., & J. W. Hagen (Eds.), *Perspectives on the development of memory and cognition* (pp. 35–60). Hillsdale, NJ: Erlbaum.

Paris, S. J., Newman, D. & Jacobs, J. (1985). Social contexts and functions of children's remembering. In M. Pressley & C. Brainerd (Eds.), *Cognitive learning and memory in children: Progress in cognitive development research* (pp. 81–115). New York: Springer-Verlag.

Paris, S. G., Newman, R. S., & McVey, K. A. (1982). Learning the functional significance of mnemonic actions: A microgenetic study of strategy acquisition. *Journal of Experimental Child Psychology, 34,* 490–509.

Parsons, C. (1960). Inhelder and Piaget's The growth of logical thinking. II. A logician's viewpoint. *British Journal of Psychology, 51,* 75–84.

Pascual-Leone, J. (1970). A mathematical model for the transition rule in Piaget's developmental stages. *Acta Psychologica, 32,* 301–345.

Pascual-Leone, J. (1978). Compounds, confounds, and models in developmental psychology: A reply to Trabasso and Foellinger. *Journal of Experimental Child Psychology*, 26, 18–40.

Pasnak, R., Kurkjian, M., & Triana, E. (1988). Assessment of stage 6 object permanence. *Bulletin of the Psychonomic Society*, 4, 368–370.

Pea, R. D., & Hawkins, J. (1987). Planning in a chore-scheduling task. In S. L. Friedman, E. K. Scholnick, & R. R. Cocking (Eds.), *Blueprints for thinking: The role of planning in cognitive development* (pp. 273–302). Cambridge, England: Cambridge University Press.

Peeck, J., Van Den Bosch, A. B., & Kreupeling, W. J. (1982). Effect of mobilizing prior knowledge on learning from text. *Journal of Educational Psychology*, 74, 771–777.

Pennington, N. (1987). Stimulus structures and mental representations in expert comprehension of computer programs. *Cognitive Psychology*, 19, 295–341.

Perfetto, G. A., Bransford, J. D., & Franks, J. J. (1983). Constraints on access in a problem solving context. *Memory & Cognition*, 11, 24–31.

Perfetto, G. A., Yearwood, A. A., Franks, J. J., & Bransford, J. D. (1987). Effects of generation on memory access. *Bulletin of the Psychonomic Society*, 25, 151–154.

Perner, J. and Leeham, S. (1986). Belief and quantity: Three-year olds' adaptation to listener's knowledge. *Journal of Child Language*, 13, 305–315.

Peters, A. M. (1986). Early syntax. In P. Fletcher & M. Gorman (Eds.), *Language acquisition* (2nd ed., pp. 307–325). Cambridge, England: Cambridge University Press.

Peterson, L. R., & Peterson, M. J. (1959). Short-term retention of individual verbal items. *Journal of Experimental Psychology*, 58, 193–198.

Phillips, S., & Levine, M. (1975). Probing for hypotheses with adults and children: Blank trials and introtacts. *Journal of Experimental Psychology: General*, 104, 327–354.

Piaget, J. (1926). *The language and thought of the child*. New York: Harcourt, Brace, & World.

Piaget, J. (1952a). *The child's conception of number*. London: Routledge & Kegan Paul.

Piaget, J. (1952b). *The origins of intelligence*. New York: International University Press.

Piaget, J. (1953). *Logic and psychology*. Manchester, England: Manchester University Press.

Piaget, J. (1954). *The construction of reality in the child*. New York: Basic Books.

Piaget, J. (1962). *Play, dreams and imitation in childhood*. New York: W.W. Norton & Co.

Piaget, J. (1963). *The psychology of intelligence*. New York: International Universities Press.

Piaget, J. (1965). *The moral judgement of the child*. New York: Free Press. (Originally published 1932)

Piaget, J. (1969). *The child's conception of time*. London: Routledge & Kegan Paul.

Piaget, J. (1970). Piaget's theory. In P. H. Mussen (Ed.), *Carmichael's Manual of Child Psychology* (3rd ed, pp. 703–732). New York: Wiley.

Piaget, J. (1972). Intellectual evolution from adolescence to adulthood. *Human Development*, 15, 1–12.

Piaget, J., & Inhelder, B. (1956). *The child's conception of space*. London: Routledge & Kegan Paul.

Piaget, J., & Inhelder, B. (1969). *The psychology of the child*. New York: Basic Books.

Piaget, J., & Inhelder, B. (1971). *Mental imagery in the child*. New York: Basic Books.

Piaget, J., & Inhelder, B. (1975). *The origin of the idea of chance in children*. New York: Norton.

Piaget, J., Montangero, J., & Billeter, J. B. (1977). La formation des correlats. In J. Piaget (Ed.), *Recherches sur l'abstraction reflechissante: L'abstraction des relations logico-arithmetiques*, (pp. 115–129). Paris, France: Presses Universitaires de France.

Piatelli-Palmarini, M. (1980). *Language and learning: The debate between Jean Piaget and Noam Chomsky*. Cambridge, MA: Harvard University Press.

Pillow, B. H. (1988). Young children's understanding of attentional limits. *Child Development*, 59, 38–46.

Pipp, S., & Haith, M. M. (1984). Infant visual responses to pattern: Which metric predicts best? *Journal of Experimental Child Psychology*, 38, 373–399.

Pipp, S., Fischer, K. W. & Jennings, S. (1987). Acquisition of self- and mother knowledge in infancy. *Developmental Psychology*, 23, 86–96.

Pisoni, D. B. (1977). Identification and discrimination of the relative onset time of two component tones: Implications for voicing perception in stops. *Journal of the Acoustic Society of America*, 61, 1352–1361.

Pollard, P. (1982). Human reasoning: Some possible effects of availability. *Cognition*, 12, 65–96.

Popper, K. R. (1959). *The logic of scientific discovery*. New York: Basic Books.

Posnansky, C. J., & Neumann, P. G. (1976). The abstraction of visual prototypes by children. *Journal of Experimental Child Psychology, 21,* 367–379.

Posner, M. I. (1973). *Cognition: An introduction.* Glenview, Ill.: Scott, Foresman.

Posner, M. I., & Keele, S. W. (1968). On the genesis of abstract ideas. *Journal of Experimental Psychology, 77,* 353–363.

Posner, M. I., & Keele, S. W. (1970). Retention of abstract ideas. *Journal of Experimental Psychology, 83,* 304–308.

Potter, M. C., & Levy, E. I. (1969). Recognition memory for a rapid sequence of pictures. *Journal of Experimental Psychology, 8,* 10–15.

Pressley, M., Borkowski, J. G., & O'Sullivan, J. (1985). Children's metamemory and the teaching of memory strategies. In D. L. Forrest-Pressley, G. E. MacKinnon, & T. G. Waller (Eds.), *Metacognition, cognition, and human performance* (pp. 111–153). New York: Academic Press.

Pressley, M., Forrest-Pressley, D. L., Elliott-Faust, D., & Miller, G. E. (1985). Children's use of cognitive strategies, how to teach strategies, and what to do if they can't be taught. In M. Pressley & C. J. Brainerd (Eds.), *Cognitive learning and memory in children: Progress in cognitive development research* (pp. 1–47). New York: Springer-Verlag.

Pressley, M., Heisel, B. E., McCormick, C. B., & Nakamura, G. V. (1982). Memory strategy instruction with children. In C. J. Brainerd & M. Pressley (Eds.), *Verbal processes in children* (pp. 125–159). New York: Springer-Verlag.

Pressley, M., Levin, J. R., & Ghatala, E. S. (1984). Memory strategy monitoring in adults and children. *Journal of Verbal Learning and Verbal Behavior, 23,* 270–288.

Pressley, M., Ross, K. A., Levin, J. R., & Ghatala, E. S. (1984). The role of strategy utility knowledge in children's strategy decision making. *Journal of Experimental Child Psychology, 38,* 491–504.

Pulos, S., & Linn, M. C. (1981). Generality of the controlling variables scheme in early adolescence. *Journal of Early Adolescence, 1,* 26–37.

Quinn, P. C., & Eimas, P. D. (1986). On categorization in early infancy. *Merrill-Palmer Quarterly, 32,* 331–363.

Rabinowitz, J. C., Craik, F. I. M., & Ackerman, B. P. (1982). A processing resource account of age differences in recall. *Canadian Journal of Psychology, 36,* 325–344.

Rea, C. P., & Modigliani, V. (1987). The spacing effect in 4- to 9-year-old children. *Memory & Cognition, 15,* 436–443.

Reed, S. K. (1972). Pattern recognition and categorization. *Cognitive Psychology, 3,* 382–407.

Reed, S. K., Ernst, G. W., & Banerji, R. (1974). The role of analogy in transfer between similar problem states. *Cognitive Psychology, 6,* 436–450.

Reich, P. A. (1976). The early acquisition of word meaning. *Journal of Child Language, 3,* 117–123.

Reich, P. A. (1986). *Language development.* Englewood Cliffs, NJ: Prentice-Hall.

Reissland, N. (1988). Neonatal imitation in the first hour of life: Observations in rural Nepal. *Developmental Psychology, 23,* 464–469.

Reitman, W. R. (1965). *Cognition and thought: An information-processing approach.* New York: Wiley.

Renshaw, P. D., & Asher, S. R. (1983). Children's goals and strategies for social interaction. *Merrill-Palmer Quarterly, 29,* 353–374.

Repp, B. H. (1982). Phonetic trading relations and context effects: New experimental evidence for a speech mode of perception. *Psychological Bulletin, 92,* 81–110.

Revelle, G. L., Wellman, H. M., & Karabenick, J. D. (1985). Comprehension monitoring in preschool children. *Child Development, 56,* 654–663.

Revlis, R. (1975). Syllogistic reasoning: Logical decisions from a complex data base. In R. J. Falmagne (Ed.), *Reasoning: Representation and process in children and adults* (pp. 93–133). Hillsdale, NJ: Erlbaum.

Rheingold, H. L., Cook, K. V., Kolowitz, V. (1987). Commands activate the behavior and pleasure of 2-year-old children. *Developmental Psychology, 23,* 146–151.

Rice, M. L. (1980). *Cognition to language: Categories, word meanings, and training.* Baltimore: University Park Press.

Rice, M. L., & Kemper, S. (1984). *Child language and cognition: Contemporary issues.* Baltimore: University Park Press.

Richards, D. D. (1988). Dynamic concepts and functionality: The influence of multiple representations and environmental constraints on categorizations. *Human development, 31,* 11–19.

Richards, D. D., & Goldfarb, J. (1986). The episodic memory model of conceptual development: An integrative viewpoint. *Cognitive Development, 1,* 183–219.

Riley, C. A. (1976). The representations of comparative relations and the transitive inference task. *Journal of Experimental Child Psychology, 22,* 1–22.

Riley, C. A., & Trabasso, T. (1974) Comparatives, logical structures, and encoding in a transitive inference task. *Journal of Experimental Child Psychology, 17,* 187–203.

Robbins, D., Barresi, J., Compton, P., Furst, A., Russo, M., & Smith, M. (1978). The genesis and use of exemplar vs. prototype knowledge in abstract category learning. *Memory & Cognition, 6,* 473–480.

Roberge, J. J. (1970). A study of children's abilities to reason with basic principles of deductive reasoning. *American Educational Research Journal, 7,* 583–596.

Robinson, E., Goelman, H., & Olson, D. R. (1983). Children's understanding of the relation between expressions (what is said) and intentions (what was meant). *British Journal of Developmental Psychology, 1,* 75–86.

Robinson, E. J., & Robinson, W. P. (1976). The young children's understanding of communication. *Developmental Psychology, 12,* 328–333.

Robinson, E. J., & Robinson, W. P. (1982). The advancement of children's verbal referential communication skills: The role of metacognitive guidance. *International Journal of Behavioral Development, 5,* 329–355.

Robinson, E. J., & Robinson, W. P. (1983a). Children's uncertainty about the interpretation of ambiguous messages. *Journal of Experimental Child Psychology, 36,* 81–96.

Robinson, E. J., & Robinson, W. P. (1983b). Communications and metacommunication: Quality of children's instructions in relation to judgements about the adequacy of instructions and the locus of responsibility for communication failure. *Journal of Experimental Child Psychology, 36,* 305–320.

Robinson, E. J., & Whittaker, S. J. (1985). Children's responses to ambiguous messages and their understanding of ambiguity. *Developmental Psychology, 21,* 446–454.

Robinson, E. J., & Whittaker, S. J. (1986). Learning about verbal referential communication in the early school years. In K. Durkin (Ed.), *Language development in the school years* (pp. 155–171). Cambridge, MA: Brookline Books.

Robinson, E. J., & Whittaker, S. J. (1987). Children's conception of relations between messages, meanings, and reality. *British Journal of Developmental Psychology, 5,* 81–90.

Roche, A. F., Siervogel, R. M., & Himes, J. H. (1978). Longitudinal study of hearing in children: Baseline data concerning auditory thresholds, noise exposure, and biological factors. *Journal of the Acoustical Society of America, 64,* 1593–1601.

Rock, I. (1977). In defense of unconscious inference. In W. Epstein (Ed.), *Stability and Constancy in Visual Perception* (pp. 321–373). New York: Wiley.

Rogoff, B. (1981). Schooling and the development of cognitive skills. In H. C. Triandis & A. Heron (Eds.), *Handbook of cross-cultural psychology: Developmental psychology* (Vol. 4, pp. 233–294). Boston: Allyn & Bacon.

Rogoff, B., & Gardner, W. (1984). Adult guidance of cognitive development. In B. Rogoff & J. Lave (Eds.), *Everyday cognition: Its development in social context* (pp. 95–116). Cambridge, MA: Harvard University Press.

Rogoff, B., Gauvain, M., & Gardner, W. (1987). The development of children's skills in adjusting plans to circumstances. In S. Friedman, E. K. Scholnick, & R. R. Cocking (Eds.), *Blueprints for thinking: The role of planning in cognitive development* (pp. 303–320). Cambridge, England: Cambridge University Press.

Rosch, E. H. (1975). Cognitive representations of semantic categories. *Journal of Experimental Psychology: General, 104,* 192–233.

Rosch, E. H., & Mervis, C. B. (1975). Family resemblances studies in the internal structure of categories. *Cognitive Psychology, 7,* 573–605.

Rosch, E., Mervis, C. B., Gray, W. D., Johnson, D. M., & Boyes-Braem, P. (1976). Basic objects in natural categories. *Cognitive Psychology, 8,* 382–439.

Rose, S. A. (1981). Developmental changes in infants' retention of visual stimuli. *Child Development, 52,* 227–233.

Rose, S. A., & Blank, M. (1974). The potency of context in children's cognition: An illustration through conservation. *Child Development, 45,* 499–502.

Rose, S. A., Gottfried, A. W., & Bridger, W. H. (1981). Cross-modal transfer and information processing by the sense of touch in infancy. *Developmental Psychology, 17,* 90–98.

Rose, S. A., Gottfried, A. W., Melloy-Carminar, P., & Bridger, W. H. (1982). Familiarity and novelty preferences in infant recognition memory: Implications for information processing. *Developmental Psychology, 18,* 704–713.

Rose, S. A., & Ruff, H. A. (1987). Cross-modal abilities in human infants. In J. D. Osotsky (Ed.), *Handbook of infant development* (2nd ed., pp. 318–362). New York: Wiley.

Rosenblith, J. F., & Sims-Knight, J. E. (1985). *In the beginning: Development in the first two years.* Belmont, C. A.: Brooks-Cole.

Rossi, S., & Wittrock, M. C. (1971). Developmental shifts in verbal recall between mental ages two and five. *Child Development, 42,* 333–338.

Roth, C. (1983). Factors affecting developmental changes in the speed of processing. *Journal of Experimental Child Psychology, 35,* 509–528.

Rovee, C. K., & Rovee, D. T. (1969). Conjugate reinforcement of infant exploratory behavior. *Journal of Experimental Child Psychology, 8,* 33–39.

Rovee-Collier, C. K. (1979, March). *Reactivation of infant memory.* Paper presented at the biennial meeting of the Society for Research in Child Development, San Francisco.

Rovee-Collier, C. K., & Fagen, J. W. (1981). The retrieval of memory in early infancy. In L. P. Lipsitt (Ed.), *Advances in infancy research* (Vol. 1, pp. 225–254). Norwood, NJ: Ablex.

Rovee-Collier, C. K., Griesler, P. C., & Earley, L.A. (1985). Contextual determinants of retrieval in three-month-old infants. *Learning and Motivation, 16,* 139–157.

Rovee-Collier, C. K., Patterson, J., & Hayne, H. (1985). Specificity in the reactivation of infant memory. *Developmental Psychobiology, 18,* 559–574.

Rovee-Collier, C. K., Sullivan, M. W., Enright, M., Lucas, D., & Fagen, J. W. (1980). Reactivation of infant memory. *Science, 208,* 1159–1161.

Rozin, P. (1976). The evolution of intelligence and access to the cognitive unconscious. In J. M. Sprague & A. D. Epstein (Eds.), *Progress in psychobiology and physiological psychology* (Vol. 6, pp. 245–280), New York: Academic Press.

Rubin, K. H. & Krasnor, L. R. (1986). Social-cognitive and social behavioral perspectives on problem solving. In M. Perlmutter (Ed.), *Cognitive perspectives on children's social and behavioral development: The Minnesota symposia on child psychology* (Vol. 18, pp. 1–68). Hillsdale, NJ: Erlbaum.

Ruff, H. A. (1978). Infant recognition of the invariant form of objects. *Child Development, 49,* 293–306.

Ruff, H. A. (1984). An ecological approach to infant memory. In M. Moscovitch (Ed.), *Infant memory: Its relation to normal and pathological memory in humans and other animals* (pp. 49–73). New York: Plenum Press.

Rumain, B., Connell, J., & Braine, M. D. S. (1983). Conversational comprehension processes are responsible for reasoning fallacies in children as well as adults: If is not the biconditional. *Developmental Psychology, 19,* 471–481.

Rumelhart, D. E. (1975). Notes on a schema for stories. In D. G. Bobrow & A. Collins (Eds.), *Representation and understanding* (pp. 211–236). New York: Academic Press.

Rumelhart, D. E., & Abrahamson, A. A. (1973). A model for analogical reasoning. *Cognitive Psychology, 5,* 1–28.

Russell, J. (1982). The child's appreciation of the necessary truth and the necessary falseness of propositions. *British Journal of Psychology, 73,* 253–266.

Sachs, J. S. (1967). Recognition memory for syntactic and semantic aspects of connected discourse. *Perception and Psychophysics, 2,* 437–442.

Sachs, J. S., & Devin, J. (1976). Young children's use of age-appropriate speech styles in social interaction and role-playing. *Journal of Child Language, 3,* 81–98.

Sachs, J. S., & Truswell, L. (1978). Comprehension of two-word instructions by children in the one-word stage. *Journal of Child Language, 5,* 17–24.

Salapatek, P. (1975). Pattern perception in early infancy. In L. B. Cohen & P. Salapatek (Eds.), *Infant perception: From sensation to cognition* (Vol. 1, pp. 133–248). New York: Academic Press.

Salapatek, P., & Kessen, W. (1966). Visual scanning of triangles by the human newborn. *Journal of Experimental Psychology, 3,* 155–167.

Salapatek, P., & Kessen, W. (1973). Prolonged investigation of a plane geometric triangle by the human newborn. *Journal of Experimental Child Psychology, 15,* 22–29.

Scardamalia, M. (1977). Information processing capacity and the problem of horizontal decalage: A demonstration using combinatorial reasoning tasks. *Child Development, 48,* 28–37.

Schacter, D. L., & Moscovitch, M. (1984). Infants, amnesia, and dissociable memory systems. In

M. Moscovitch (Ed.), *Infant memory: Its relation to normal and pathological memory in human and other animals* (pp. 173–216). New York: Plenum Press.

Schaffer, H. R. (1971). *The growth of sociability.* Harmondworth, England: Penguin.

Schaller, M. J. (1975). Chromatic vision in human infants. *Bulletin of the Psychonomic Society, 6,* 39–42.

Schank, R. C., & Abelson, R. (1977). *Scripts, plans, goals and understanding.* Hillsdale, NJ: Erlbaum.

Schiff, A. R., & Knopf, I. J. (1985). The effect of task demands on attention allocation in children of different ages. *Child Development, 56,* 621–630.

Schlesinger, I. M. (1977). *Production and comprehension of utterances.* Hillsdale, NJ: Erlbaum.

Schmidt, C. R., & Paris, S. G. (1983). Children's use of successive clues to generate and monitor inferences. *Child Development, 54,* 742–759.

Schmidt, C. R., & Paris, S. G. (1984). The development of verbal communicative skills in children. *Advances in child development and behavior* (Vol. 18, pp. 1–47). Orlando, FL: Academic Press.

Schmidt, C. R., Schmidt, S. R., & Tomalis, S. M. (1984). Children's constructive processing and monitoring of stories containing anomalous information. *Child Development, 55,* 2056–2071.

Schmidt, H., & Spelke, E. S. (1984, April). *Gestalt relations and object perception in infancy.* Paper presented at the International Conference on Infant Studies, New York.

Schneider, B. A., Trehub, S. E., & Bull, D. (1979). The development of basic auditory processes in infants. *Canadian Journal of Psychology, 33,* 306–319.

Schneider, W. (1985). Developmental trends in the metamemory-memory behavior relationship: An integrative review. In D. L. Forrest-Pressley, G. E. MacKinnon, & T. G. Waller (Eds.), *Metacognition, cognition, and human performance* (Vol. 1, pp. 57–109). New York: Academic Press.

Schneider, W., & Shiffrin, R. M. (1977). Controlled and automatic human information processing: I. Direction, search, and attention. *Psychological Review, 84,* 1–66.

Schoenfeld, A. H., & Herrmann, D. J. (1982). Problem perception and knowledge structure in expert and novice mathematical problem solvers. *Journal of Experimental Psychology: Learning, Memory, and Cognition, 8,* 484–494.

Schuberth, R. E. (1983). The infant's search for objects: Alternatives to Piaget's theory of object concept development. In L. P. Lipsitt & C. K. Rovee-Collier (Eds.), *Advances in infancy research* (Vol. 2, pp. 137–182). Norwood, NJ: Ablex.

Scott, M. S., Greenfield, D. B., & Urbano, R. C. (1985). A comparison of complementary and taxonomic utilization: Significance of the dependent measure. *International Journal of Behavioral Development, 8,* 241–256.

Scoville, R. (1984). Development of the intention to communicate: The eye of the beholder. In L. Feagans, G. Garvey & R. Golinkoff (Eds.), *The origins and growth of communication* (pp. 109–122). Norwood, NJ: Ablex.

Seligman, M. E. P. (1975). *Helplessness: On depression, death, and development.* San Francisco: Freeman.

Selman, R. L. (1976). Social-cognitive understanding: A guide to educational and clinical practice. In T. Lickona (Ed.), *Moral development and behavior: Theory, research, and social issues* (pp. 299–316). New York: Holt, Rinehart, & Winston.

Selman, R. L. (1981). The child as friendship philosopher. In S. R. Asher & J. M. Grottman (Eds.), *The development of children's friendships* (pp. 242–272). Cambridge, England: Cambridge University Press.

Selman, R. L., & Byrne, D. F. (1974). A structural-development analysis of levels of role taking in middle childhood. *Child Development, 45,* 803–806.

Shaffer, W. O., & LaBerge, D. (1979). Automatic semantic processing of unattended words. *Journal of Verbal Learning and Verbal Behavior, 18,* 413–426.

Shantz, C. U. (1982). Thinking about people thinking about people. *Contemporary Psychology, 27,* 376–377.

Shantz, C. U. (1983). Social cognition. In P. H. Mussen (Ed.), *Handbook of child psychology* (4th ed., Vol. 3, pp. 495–555). New York: Wiley.

Shapiro, E. K., & Weber, E. (1981). *Cognitive and affective growth: Developmental Interaction.* Hillsdale, NJ: Erlbaum.

Sharp, D. W., Cole, M., & Lave, C. (1979). Education and cognitive development: The evidence from experimental research. *Monograph of the Society for Research in Child Development, 44*(Serial No. 178).

Sharps, M. J., & Gollin, E. S. (1985). Memory and the syntagmatic-paradigmatic shift: A developmental study of priming effects. *Bulletin of the Psychonomic Society, 23*, 95–97.

Shatz, M. (1985). An evolutionary perspective on plasticity in language development: A commentary. *Merrill-Palmer Quarterly, 31*, 211–223.

Shatz, M., & Gelman, R. (1973). The development of communication skills: Modification in the speech of young children as a function of listener. *Monographs of the Society for Research in Child Development, 38*(5, Serial No. 152).

Shephard, R. N., & Metzler, J. (1971). Mental rotation of three-dimensional objects. *Science, 171*, 701–703.

Shepp, B. E., Barrett, S. E., & Kolbet, L. L. (1987). The development of selective attention: Holistic perception versus resource allocation. *Journal of Experimental Child Psychology, 43*, 159–180.

Sherman, S. J., & Corty, E. (1984). Cognitive heuristics. In R. S. Wyer Jr., & T. K. Srull (Eds.), *Handbook of social cognition* (Vol. 1, pp. 189–286). Hillsdale, NJ: Erlbaum.

Sherman, T. (1985). Categorization skills in infants. *Child Development, 56*, 1561–1573.

Sherrod, L. R., & Lamb, M. E. (1981). Infant social cognition: An introduction. In M. E. Lamb & L. R. Sherrod (Eds.) *Infant social cognition: Empirical and theoretical consideration* (pp. 1–10). Hillsdale, NJ: Erlbaum.

Sherwood, R. D., Kinzer, C. K., Bransford, J. D., & Franks, J. J.(1987). Some benefits of creating macro-contexts for science instruction: Initial findings. *Journal of Research in Science Teaching, 24*, 417–435.

Sherwood, R. D., Kinzer, C. K., Hasselbring, T. S., & Bransford, J. D. (1987). Macro-contexts for learning: Initial findings and issues. *Applied Cognitive Psychology, 1*, 93–108.

Shiffrin, R. M., & Schneider, W. (1977). Controlled and automatic human information processing: II. Perceptual learning, automatic attending, and a general theory. *Psychological Review, 84*, 127–190.

Shortliffe, E. H. (1976). *Computer-based medical consultations: MYCIN*. New York: Elsevier.

Shultz, T. R. (1980). Development of the concept of intention. In W. A. Collins (Ed.), *Development of cognition, affect, and social relations: The Minnesota symposia on child psychology* (Vol. 13, pp. 131–164). Hillsdale, NJ: Erlbaum.

Shultz, T. R. (1982). Rules of causal attribution. *Monographs of the Society for Research in Child Development, 47*(1, Serial No. 194).

Shultz, T. R. (1988). Assessing intention: A computational model. In J. W. Astington, P. L. Harris, & D. R. Olson (Eds.), *Developing theories of mind* (pp. 341–367). Cambridge, England: Cambridge University Press.

Shultz, T. R., & Cloghesy, K. (1981). Development of recursive awareness of intention. *Developmental Psychology, 17*, 465–471.

Shultz, T. R., Fisher, G. W., Pratt, C. C., & Rulf, S. (1986). Selection of causal rules. *Child Development, 57*, 141–152.

Shultz, T. R., & Kestenbaum, N. R. (1985). Causal reasoning in children. *Annals of Child Development, 2*, 195–249.

Shultz, T. R., & Mendelson, R. (1975). The use of covariation as a principle of causal analysis. *Child Development, 46*, 394–399.

Shultz, T. R., & Ravinsky, F. B. (1977). Similarity as a principle of causal inference. *Child Development, 48*, 1552–1558.

Shultz, T. R., Wells, D., & Sarda, M. (1980). Development of the ability to distinguish intended actions from mistakes, reflexes, and passive movements. *British Journal of Social and Clinical Psychology, 19*, 301–310.

Shure, M. B., & Spivak, G. (1972). Means-ends thinking, adjustment, and social class among elementary school-aged children. *Journal of Consulting and Clinical Psychology, 38*, 348–353.

Siegal, M., Waters, L. J., & Dinwiddy, L. S. (1988). Misleading children: Causal attributions for inconsistency under repeated questioning. *Journal of Experimental Child Psychology, 45*, 438–456.

Siegel, L. S. (1971a). The development of the understanding of certain number concepts. *Developmental Psychology, 5*, 362–362.

Siegel, L. S. (1971b). The sequence of development of certain number concepts in preschool children. *Developmental Psychology, 5*, 357–361.

Siegel, L. S., McCabe, A. E., Brand, J., & Matthews, J. (1978). Evidence for the understanding of class inclusion in preschool children: Linguistic factors and training effects. *Child Development, 49,* 688–693.

Siegler, R. S. (1976). The effect of simple necessity and sufficiency relationships on children's causal inferences. *Child Development, 47,* 1058–1063.

Siegler, R. S. (1978) The origins of scientific thinking. In R.S. Siegler (Ed.), *Children's thinking: What develops?* (pp. 109–149). Hillsdale, NJ: Erlbaum.

Siegler, R. S. & Robinson, M. (1982) The development of numerical understanding. In H. W. Reese & L. P. Lipsitt (Eds.), *Advances in child development and behavior* (Vol. 16, pp. 241–312). New York: Academic Press.

Simon, H. A. (1978). Information-processing theory of human problem solving. In W. K. Estes (Ed.), *Handbook of Learning and Cognitive Processes* (Vol. 5, pp. 271–295). Hillsdale, NJ: Erlbaum.

Simon, H. A. (1980). Problem solving and education. In D. T. Tuma & F. Reif (Eds.), *Problem solving and education: Issues in teaching and research* (pp. 81–96). New York: Wiley.

Sinnott, J. M., Pisoni, D. B., & Aslin, R. N. (1983). A comparison of pure auditory thresholds in human infants and adults. *Infant Behavior and Development, 6,* 3–17.

Siqueland, E. R., & DeLucia, C. A. (1969). Visual reinforcement of nonnutritive sucking in human infants. *Science, 165,* 1144–1146.

Skinner, B. F. (1957). *Verbal behavior.* New York: Appleton-Century-Crofts.

Skyrms, B. (1975). *Choice and chance* (2nd ed.). Belmont, CA: Wadsworth.

Slackman, E. A., Hudson, J. A., & Fivush, R. (1986). Actions, actors, links, and goals: The structure of children's event representations. In K. Nelson (Ed.), *Event knowledge: Structure and function in development* (pp. 47–70). Hillsdale, NJ: Erlbaum.

Slater, A., Earle, D. C., Morison, V., & Rose, D. (1985). Pattern preferences at birth and their interaction with habituation-induced novelty preferences. *Journal of Experimental Child Psychology, 39,* 37–54.

Slater, A., Morison, V., & Rose, D. (1983). Perception of shape by the newborn baby. *British Journal of Developmental Psychology, 1,* 135–142.

Slater, A., Morison, V., & Rose, D. (1984). Habituation in the newborn. *Infant Behavior and Development, 7,* 183–200.

Slobin, D. I. (1979). *Psycholinguistics* (2nd. ed.). Glenview, IL: Scott, Foresman.

Small, M. Y. (1970). Children's performance on an oddity problem as a function of the number of values on the relevant dimension. *Journal of Experimental Child Psychology, 9,* 336–341.

Small, M. Y., & Butterworth, J. (1981). Semantic integration and the development of memory for logical inferences. *Child Development, 52,* 732–735.

Smiley, S. S., & Brown, A. L. (1979). Conceptual preference for thematic or taxonomic relations: A nonmonotonic age trend from preschool to old age. *Journal of Experimental Child Psychology, 28,* 249–257.

Smith, E. E., & Medin, D. L. (1981). *Categories and concepts.* Cambridge, MA: Harvard University Press.

Smith E. E., Shoben, E. J., & Rips, L. J. (1974). Structure and process in semantic memory: A feature model of semantic decisions. *Psychological Review, 81,* 214–241.

Smith, L. (1982). Class inclusion and conclusions about Piaget's theory. *British Journal of Psychology, 73,* 267–276.

Smith, L. B. (1979). Perceptual development and category generalization. *Child Development, 50,* 705–715.

Smith, L. B. (1983). Development of classification: The use of similarity and dimensional relations. *Journal of Experimental Child Psychology, 36,* 150–178.

Smith, L. B. (1984). Young children's understanding of attributes and dimension: A comparison of conceptual and linguistic measures. *Child Development, 55,* 363–380.

Smith, L. B., & Kemler, D. G. (1977). Developmental trends in free classification: Evidence for a new conceptualization of perceptual development. *Journal of Experimental Child Psychology, 24,* 279–298.

Smith, L. B., & Kemler, D. G. (1978). Levels of experienced dimensionality in children and adults. *Cognitive Psychology, 10,* 502–532.

Smith, M. C. (1975). Children's use of the multiple sufficient cause schema in social perception. *Journal of Personality and Social Psychology, 32,* 737–747.

Smith, N. V. (1973). *The acquisition of phonology: A case study.* Cambridge, England: Cambridge University Press.

Smith, S. M., Glenberg, A., & Bjork, R. A. (1978). Environmental context and human memory. *Memory & Cognition, 6*, 342–353.

Snow, C. E. (1979). The role of social interaction in language acquisition. In A. Collins (Ed.), *Minnesota Symposia on Child Development* (pp. 157–182). Hillsdale, NJ: Erlbaum.

Snow, C. E. (1987). Children's narrative skills. *Science, 24*, 471–472.

Soja, N. N. (1986). Color word acquisition: Conceptual or linguistic challenge. *Papers and reports on child language development, 25*, 104–113.

Sokolov, E. N. (1960). Neuronal attention as affected by medication during labor. In M. A. B. Brazier (Ed.), *The central nervous system and behavior* (pp. 187–276). New York: Josiah Macy Jr. Foundation.

Sokolov, E. N. (1963). *Perception and the conditioned reflex*. New York: Macmillan.

Sonnenschein, S. (1982). The effect of redundant communications on listeners: When more is less. *Child Development, 53*, 717–729.

Sonnenschein, S. (1984). The effect of redundant communications on listeners: Why different types may have different effects. *Journal of Psycholinguistic Research, 13*, 147–166.

Sonnenschein, S. (1986a). Development of referential communication: Deciding that a message is uninformative. *Developmental Psychology, 22*, 164–168.

Sonnenschein, S. (1986b). Development of referential communication skills: How familiarity with a listener affects a speaker's production of redundant messages. *Developmental Psychology, 22*, 549–552.

Sonnenschein, S. (1988). The development of referential communication: Speaking to different listeners. *Child Development, 59*, 694–702.

Sonnenschein, S., & Whitehurst, G. J. (1980). The development of communication: When a bad model makes a good teacher. *Journal of Experimental Child Psychology, 3*, 371–390.

Sophian, C. (1980). Habituation is not enough: Novelty preferences, search, and memory in infancy. *Merrill-Palmer Quarterly, 26*, 239–257.

Sophian, C., & Huber A. (1984). Early developments in children's causal judgments. *Child Development, 55*, 512–526.

Sophian, C., & Wellman, H. (1987). The development of indirect search strategies. *British Journal of Developmental Psychology, 5*, 9–18.

Sorce, J. F., Emde, R. N., Campos, J., & Klinnert, M. D. (1985). Maternal emotional signaling: Its effect on the visual cliff behavior of 1-year-olds. *Developmental Psychology, 21*, 195–200.

Spear, N. E. (1976). Retrieval of memories. In W. K. Estes (Ed.), *Handbook of learning and cognitive processes. Vol. 4: Attention and memory* (pp. 17–90). Hillsdale, NJ: Erlbaum.

Spear, N. E. (1978). *The processing of memories: Forgetting and retention*. Hillsdale, NJ: Erlbaum.

Spears, W. C., & Hohle, R. H. (1967). Sensory and perceptual processes in infants. In Y. Brackbill (Ed.), *Infancy and early childhood* (pp. 51–121). New York: Free Press.

Speer, J. R. (1984). Two practical strategies young children use to interpret vague instructions. *Child Development, 55*, 1811–1819.

Spelke, E. S. (1976). Infants' intermodal perception of events. *Cognitive Psychology, 8*, 553–560.

Spelke, E. S. (1979). Perceiving bimodally specified events in infancy. *Developmental Psychology, 15*, 626–636.

Spelke, E. S. (1985). Perception of unity, persistence, and identity: Thoughts on infants' conception of objects. In J.Mehler and R. Fox (Eds.), *Neonate cognition* (pp. 89–113). Hillsdale, NJ: Erlbaum.

Spelke, E. S. (1986, November). *Mechanisms for perceiving objects*. Paper presented at the meeting of the Psychonomic Society, New Orleans.

Spelke, E. S. (1988). Where perceiving ends and thinking begins: The apprehension of objects in infancy. In A. Yonas (Ed.), *Perceptual Development in Infancy: Minnesota Symposia on Child Psychology* (Vol. 20, pp. 197–234). Hillsdale, NJ: Erlbaum.

Spence, M. J., & DeCasper, A. J. (1987). Prenatal experience with low-frequency maternal-voice sounds influences neonatal perception of maternal voice samples. *Infant Behavior and Development, 10*, 133–142.

Spencer, R. M., & Weisberg, R. W. (1986). Context-dependent effects on analogical transfer. *Memory & Cognition, 4*, 442–449.

Spiker, C. C. (1963). The hypothesis of stimulus interaction and an explanation of stimulus compounding. In L. P. Lipsitt, & C. C. Spiker (Eds.), *Advances in child development and behavior* (Vol. 1, pp. 233–264). New York: Academic Press.

Spivak, G., & Shure, M. B. (1974). *Social adjustment of young children*. San Francisco: Jossey-Bass.

Standing, L., Conezio, J., & Haber, R. N. (1970). Perception and memory for pictures: Single-trial learning of 2500 visual stimuli. *Bulletin of the Psychonomic Science, 19*, 73–74.

Starkey, P., Spelke, Q. S., & Gelman, R. (1983). Detection of intermodal numerical correspondences by human infants. *Science, 222*, 179–181.

Stechler, G. (1964). Newborn attention as affected by medication during labor. *Science, 144*, 315–317.

Stefik, M. (1981). Planning and meta-planning (MOLGEN: Part 2). *Artificial Intelligence, 16*, 141–169.

Stein, N. L. (1982). What's in a story: Interpreting the interpretations of story grammars. *Discourse Processes, 5*, 319–335.

Stein, N. L., & Glenn, C. G. (1979). An analysis of story comprehension in elementary school children. In R. O. Freedle (Ed.), *Advances in discourse processes, Vol. 2: New directions in discourse processing* (pp. 53–120). Norwood, NJ: Ablex.

Stenberg, C. R., Campos, J. J. & Emde, R. N. (1983). The facial expression of anger in seven-month-old infants. *Child Development, 54*, 178–184.

Stern, D. N. (1985). *The interpersonal world of the infant*. New York: Basic Books.

Stern, D. N., Spieker, S., & MacKain, K. (1982). Intonation contours as signals in maternal speech to prelinguistic infants. *Developmental Psychology, 18*, 727–735.

Sternberg, R. J. (1977). Component processes in analogical reasoning. *Psychological Review, 84*, 353–378.

Sternberg, R. J. (1979). Developmental patterns in the encoding and combination of logical connectives. *Journal of Experimental Child Psychology, 28*, 469–498.

Sternberg, R. J. (1980). Development of linear syllogistic reasoning. *Journal of Experimental Child Psychology, 29*, 340–350.

Sternberg, R. J. (1986). Toward a unified theory of human reasoning. *Intelligence, 10*, 281–314.

Sternberg, R. J., Conway, B. E., Ketron, J. L., & Bernstein, M. (1981). People's conceptions of intelligence. *Journal of Personality and Social Psychology, 41*, 37–55.

Sternberg, R. J., & Nigro, G. (1980). Developmental patterns in the solution of verbal analogies. *Child Development, 51*, 27–38.

Sternberg, R. J., & Rifkin, B. (1979). The development of analogical reasoning processes. *Journal of Experimental Child Psychology, 27*, 195–232.

Stillings, N. A., Feinstein, M. H., Garfield, J. L., Rissland, E. L., Rosenbaum, D. A., Weisler, S. E., & Baker-Ward, L. (1987). *Cognitive science: An introduction*. Cambridge, MA: MIT Press.

Stone, B., & Day, M. C. (1981). A developmental study of the processes underlying solution of figural matrices. *Child Development, 52*, 359–362.

Strange, W., & Jenkins, J. J. (1978). Role of linguistic experience in the perception of speech. In R. D. Walk & H. L. Pick (Eds.), *Perception and experience* (pp. 125–169). New York: Plenum Press.

Strauss, M. S. (1979). Abstraction of prototypical information by adults and 10-month-old infants. *Journal of Experimental Psychology: Human Learning and Memory, 5*, 618–632.

Strauss, M. S., & Curtis, L. E. (1981). Infant perception of numerosity. *Child Development, 52*, 1146–1152.

Streeter, L. A. (1976). Language perception of two-month-old infants shows effects of both innate mechanism and experience. *Nature, 259*, 39–41.

Streri, A., & Spelke, E. S. (1988). Haptic perception of objects in infancy. *Cognitive Psychology, 20*, 1–23.

Strohner, H., & Nelson, K. E. (1974). The young child's development of sentence comprehension: Influence of event probability, nonverbal context, syntactic form, and strategies. *Child Development, 45*, 567–576.

Stroop, J. R. (1935). Studies of interference in serial verbal reactions. *Journal of Experimental Psychology, 18*, 643–662.

Strutt, G. F., Anderson, D. R., & Well, A. D. (1975). A developmental study of the effects of irrelevant information on speeded classification. *Journal of Experimental Child Psychology, 20*, 127–135.

Sugarman, S. (1981). The cognitive basis of classification in very young children: An analysis of object-ordering trends. *Child Development, 52*, 1172–1178.

Sugarman, S. (1984). The development of preverbal communication: Its contribution and limits in promoting the development of language. In R. L. Schiefelbusch & J. Pickar (Eds.), *The acquisition of communicative competence* (pp. 23–67). Baltimore: University Park Press.

Sugarman-Bell, S. (1978) Some organizational aspects of pre-verbal communication. In I. Markova (Ed.), *The social context of language* (pp. 49–66). New York: Wiley.

Sullivan, M. W. (1982). Reactivation: Priming forgotten memories in human infants. *Child Development, 53,* 516–523.

Sullivan M. W., Rovee-Collier, C. K., & Tynes, P. M. (1979). A conditioning analysis of infant long-term memory. *Child Development, 50,* 152–162.

Summers, W. V., Horton, D. L., & Diehl, V. A. (1985). Contextual knowledge during encoding influences sentence recognition. *Journal of Experimental Psychology: Learning, Memory and Cognition, 11,* 771–779.

Surber, C. F. (1985). Developmental changes in inverse compensation in social and nonsocial attributions. In S. R. Yussen (Ed.), *The growth of reflection in children* (pp. 149–166). New York: Academic Press.

Sweller, J. (1983). Control mechanisms in problem solving. *Memory & Cognition, 11,* 32–40.

Sylvester-Bradley, B. (1985). Failure to distinguish between people and things in early infancy. *British Journal of Developmental Psychology, 3,* 281–292.

Symons, D. K., & Moran, G. (1987). The behavioral dynamics of mutual responsiveness in early face-to-face mother-infant interactions. *Child Development, 58,* 1488–1495.

Taplin, J. E. (1971). Reasoning with conditional sentences. *Journal of Verbal Learning and Verbal Behavior, 10,* 219–225.

Taplin, J. E., Staudenmayer, H., & Taddonio, J. L. (1974). Developmental changes in conditional reasoning: Linguistic or logical? *Journal of Experimental Child Psychology, 17,* 360–373.

Tartter, V. C. (1986). *Language processes.* New York: Holt, Rinehart & Winston.

Templin, M. C. (1957). *Certain language skills in children: Their development and interrelationships.* Minneapolis: University of Minnesota Press.

Terrace, H. S. (1985). In the beginning was the "Name." *American Psychologist, 40,* 1011–1028.

Thompson, B. R., & Spencer, W. A. (1966). Habituation: A model phenomenon for the study of neuronal substrates of behavior. *Psychological Review, 73,* 16–43.

Thorndyke, P. W. (1977). Cognitive structures in comprehension and memory of narrative discourse. *Cognitive Psychology, 9,* 77–110.

Tomasello, M., & Farrar, M. J. (1986). Joint attention and early language. *Child Development, 57,* 1454–1463.

Tomasello, M., & Mannle, S. (1985). Pragmatics of sibling speech to one-year-olds. *Child Development, 56,* 911–917.

Trabasso, T. (1975). Representation, memory, and reasoning: How do we make transitive inferences? In A. D. Pick (Ed.), *Minnesota Symposia on Child Psychology* (Vol. 9, pp. 135–172). Minneapolis: University of Minnesota Press.

Trabasso, T., Isen, A. M., Dolecki, P., McLanahan, A. G., Riley, C. A., & Tucker, T. (1978). How do children solve class-inclusion problems? In R. S. Siegler (Ed.), *Children's thinking: What develops?* (pp. 151–180). Hillsdale, NJ: Erlbaum.

Trabasso, T., & Riley, C. A. (1975). The construction and use of representations involving linear order. In R. L. Solso (Ed.), *Information processing and cognition: The Loyola Symposium* (pp. 381–410). Hillsdale, NJ: Erlbaum.

Trabasso, T., Riley, C. A. & Wilson, E. G. (1975). The representation of linear order and spatial strategies in reasoning: A developmental study. In R. J. Falmagne (Ed.), *Reasoning: Representation and process in children and adults* (pp. 201–229). Hillsdale, NJ: Erlbaum.

Trabasso, T., Secco, T., & Van den Broek, P. (1984). Causal cohesion and story coherence. In H. Mandl, N. L. Stein, & T. Trabasso (Eds.), *Learning and comprehension of text* (pp. 83–111). Hillsdale, NJ: Erlbaum.

Trabasso, T., & Sperry, L. L. (1985). Causal relatedness and importance of story events. *Journal of Memory and Language, 24,* 595–611.

Trehub, S. E. (1979) Reflections on the development of speech perception. *Canadian Journal of Psychology, 33,* 368–381.

Trehub, S. E. (1987). Infants' perception of musical patterns. *Perception and Psychophysics, 41,* 635–641.

Trehub, S. E., Schneider, B. A., & Endman, M. (1980). Developmental changes in infants sensitivity to octave-band noises. *Journal of Experimental Child Psychology, 29,* 282–293.

Trehub, S. E., Thorpe, L. A., & Morrongiello, B. A. (1987). Organizational processes in infants' perception of auditory patterns. *Child Development, 58,* 741–749.

Tschirgi, J. E. (1980). Sensible reasoning: A hypothesis about hypotheses. *Child Development, 51,* 1–10.

Tulving, E. (1972). Episodic and semantic memory. In E. Tulving & W. Donaldson (Eds.), *Organization of memory* (pp. 381–403). New York: Academic Press.

Tulving, E. (1984). Precis of *Elements of episodic memory. The Behavioral and Brain Sciences, 7,* 223–268.

Tulving, E. (1985). How many memory systems are there? *American Psychologist, 40,* 385–398.

Tulving, E., & Thomson, D. M. (1973). Encoding specificity and retrieval processes in episodic memory. *Psychological Review, 80,* 352–373.

Tumblin, A., & Gholson, B. (1981). Hypothesis theory and the development of conceptual learning. *Psychological Bulletin, 90,* 102–124.

Tunmer, W. E., Nesdale, A. R., & Pratt, C. (1983). The development of young children's awareness of logical inconsistencies. *Journal of Experimental Child Psychology, 36,* 97–108.

Turner, N. R. (1985). *The effects of rule feedback and rule generality on hypothesis testing strategies.* Unpublished BA honor's thesis, Bowdoin College, Brunswick, Maine.

Tversky, A., & Kahneman, D. (1974). Judgments under uncertainty: Heuristics and biases. *Science, 185,* 1124–1131.

Tversky, A., & Kahneman, D. (1980). Causal schemata in judgments under uncertainity. In M. Fishbein (Ed.), *Progress in social psychology* (Vol. 1, pp. 49–72). Hillsdale, NJ: Erlbaum.

Underwood, B. J., & Schulz, R. W. (1960). *Meaningfulness and verbal learning.* Chicago: Lippincott.

Urbain, E. S., & Kendall, P. C. (1980). Review of social-cognitive problem-solving interventions with children. *Psychological Bulletin, 88,* 109–143.

Uzgiris, I. C. (1964). Situational generality of conservation. *Child Development, 35,* 831–841.

Uzgiris, I. C. (1981). Two functions of imitation during infancy. *International Journal of Behavioral Development, 4,* 1–12.

Uzgiris, I. C. (1984). Imitation during infancy: Its interpersonal aspects. In M. Perlmutter (Ed.), *Parent-child interaction and parent-child relations in child development* (pp. 1–32). Hillsdale, NJ: Erlbaum.

Uzgiris, I. C., & Hunt, J. McV. (1975). *Assessment in infancy. Ordinal scales of psychological development.* Urbana, IL: University Press.

van Dijk, T. A. (1980). Story comprehension: An introduction. *Poetics, 9,* 1–21.

Vaughn, R., Kopp, C. B., Krakow, J. B., Johnson, K., & Schwartz, S. (1986). Process analyses of the behavior of very young children in delay tasks. *Developmental Psychology, 22,* 752–759.

Vedeler, D. (1987). Infant intentionality and the attribution of intentions to infants. *Human Development, 30,* 1–17.

von Hofsten, C. (1982). Eye-hand coordination in the newborn. *Developmental Psychology, 18,* 450–461.

von Hofsten, C. (1986). Early spatial perception taken in reference to manual action. *Acta Psychologica, 63,* 323–335.

von Hofsten, C., & Spelke, E. S. (1985). Object perception and object-directed reaching in infancy. *Journal of Experimental Psychology: General, 114,* 198–212.

von Wright, J. M. (1973). Relation between recall and visual recognition of the same stimuli in young children. *Journal of Experimental Child Psychology, 15,* 481–487.

Voss, J. F., Vesonder, G. T., & Spilich, G. J. (1980). Text generation and recall by high-knowledge and low-knowledge individuals. *Journal of Verbal Learning and Verbal Behavior, 19,* 651–667.

Vygotsky, L. S. (1962). *Thought and language.* New York: Wiley. (Original work published 1934)

Vygotsky, L. S. (1978). *Mind in society.* Cambridge, MA: Harvard University Press.

Wagner, D. A. (1981). Culture and memory development. In H. C. Triandis & A. Heron (Eds.), *Handbook of cross-cultural psychology: Developmental psychology* (Vol. 4, pp. 187–232). Boston: Allyn & Bacon.

Walden, T. A., & Ogan, T. A. (1988). The development of social referencing. *Child Development, 59,* 1230–1240.

Waldrop, M. M. (1988a). Soar: A unified theory of cognition? *Science, 241,* 296–298.

Waldrop, M. M. (1988b). Toward a unified theory of cognition. *Science, 241,* 27–29.

Walker, A. S., Owsley, C. J., Megaw-Nyce, J., Gibson, E. J., & Bahrick, L. E. (1980). Detection of elasticity as an invariant property of objects by young infants. *Perception, 9,* 713–718.

Walker, C. H., & Meyer, B. J. F. (1980). Integrating different types of information in text. *Journal of Verbal Learning and Verbal Behavior, 19*, 263–275.

Walker-Andrews, A. S. (1986). Intermodal perception of expressive behaviors: Relation of eye and voice? *Developmental Psychology, 22*, 373–377.

Ward, T. B. (1988). When is category learning holistic? A reply to Kemler Nelson. *Memory & Cognition, 16*, 85–89.

Ward, T. B., & Scott, J. (1987). Analytic and holistic modes of learning family-resemblance concepts. *Memory & Cognition, 15*, 42–54.

Wason, P. C. (1960). "On the failure to eliminate hypotheses in a conceptual task." *Quarterly Journal of Experimental Psychology, 12*, 129–140.

Wason, P. C. (1968). 'On the failure to eliminate hypotheses in aconceptual task'—A second look. In P. N. Johnson–Laird & P. C. Wason (Eds.), *Thinking: Readings in a cognitive science* (pp. 307–313). Cambridge, England: Cambridge University Press.

Wason, P. C., & Johnson-Laird, P. N. (1970). A conflict between selecting and evaluating information in an inferential task. *British Journal of Psychology, 61*, 509–515.

Wason, P. C., & Johnson-Laird, P. N. (1972). *Psychology of reasoning: Structure and content.* Cambridge, MA: Harvard University Press.

Wason, P. C., & Shapiro, D. (1971). Natural and contrived experience in a reasoning problem. *Quarterly Journal of Experimental Psychology, 23*, 63–71.

Waters, H. S., & Tinsley, V. S. (1985). Evaluating the discriminant and convergent validity of developmental constructs: Another look at the concept of egocentrism. *Psychological Bulletin, 97*, 483–496.

Watson, J. S. (1972). Smiling, cooing, and 'the game.' *Merrill-Palmer Quarterly, 18*, 323–339.

Watson, J. S. (1979). Perception of contiguity as a determinant of social responsiveness. In E. B. Thoman (Ed.), *The origin of the infant's social responsiveness* (pp. 33–64). Hillsdale, NJ: Erlbaum.

Watson, J., & Ramey, C. (1972). Reactions to response-contingent stimulation in early infancy. *Merrill-Palmer Quarterly, 18*, 219–288.

Weir, R. H. (1962). *Language in the crib.* The Hague: Mouton Publishers.

Weisberg, R., DiCamillo, M., & Phillips, D. (1978). Transferring old associations to new situations: A nonautomatic process. *Journal of Verbal Learning and Verbal Behavior, 17*, 219–228.

Weissberg, J. A., & Paris, S. G. (1986). Young children's remembering in different contexts: A reinterpretation of Istomina's study. *Child Development, 57*, 1123–1129.

Weitz, L. J., Bynum, T. W., Thomas, J. A., & Steger, J. A. (1973). Piaget's system of 16 binary operations: An empirical investigation. *The Journal of Genetic Psychology, 123*, 279–284.

Well, A. D., Lorch, E. P., & Anderson, D. R. (1980). Developmental trends in distractability: Is absolute or proportional decrement the appropriate measure of interference? *Journal of Experimental Child Psychology, 30*, 109–124.

Wellman, H. M. (1977). Tip of the tongue and feeling of knowing experiences: A developmental study of memory monitoring. *Child Development, 48*, 13–21.

Wellman, H. M. (1983). Metamemory revisited. In M. T. H. Chi (Ed.), *Trends in memory development research: Contributions to human development series* (Vol. 9, pp. 31–51). Basel: Karger.

Wellman, H. M. (1985). The child's theory of mind: The development of conceptions of cognition. In S. R. Yussen (Ed.), *The growth of reflection in children* (pp. 169–206). New York: Academic Press.

Wellman, H. M., Collins, J., & Glieberman, J. (1981). Understanding the combination of memory variables: Developing conceptions of memory limitations. *Child Development, 52*, 1313–1317.

Wellman, H. M., Fabricius, W. V., & Sophian, C. (1985). The early development of planning. In H. M. Wellman (Ed.), *Children's searching and the development of search skill and spatial representation* (pp. 123–149). Hillsdale, NJ: Erlbaum.

Wellman, H. M., & Lempers, J. D. (1977). The naturalistic communicative abilities of two-year-olds. *Child Development, 48*, 1052–1057.

Wells, D., & Shultz, T. R. (1980). Developmental distinctions between behavior and judgment in the operation of the discounting principle. *Child Development, 51*, 1307–1310.

Werker, J. F., Gilbert, J. H. V., Humphrey, K., & Tees, R. C. (1981). Developmental aspects of cross-language speech perception. *Child Development, 52,* 349–355.

Werker, J. F., & Lalonde, C. E. (1988). Cross-language speech perception: Initial capabilities and developmental change. *Developmental Psychology, 24,* 672–683.

Werker, J. F., & Tees, R. C. (1984). Cross-language speech perception: Evidence for perceptual reorganization during the first year of life. *Infant Behavior and Development, 7,* 49–63.

Werner, H. (1948). *Comparative psychology of mental development.* New York: International University Press.

Werner, J. S., & Perlmutter, M. (1979). Development of visual memory in infants. In H. W. Reese & L. P. Lipsitt (Eds.), *Advances in child development and behavior* (Vol. 14, pp. 1–56). New York: Academic Press.

Whaley, J. F. (1981). Readers' expectations for story structures. *Reading Research Quarterly, 17,* 90–114.

Wheldall, K., & Poborca, B. (1980). Conservation without conversation? An alternative, non-verbal paradigm for assessing conservation of liquid quantity. *British Journal of Psychology, 71,* 117–134.

White, B. L. (1971). *Human infants: Experience and psychological development.* Englewood Cliffs, NJ: Prentice-Hall.

White, C. S., & Alexander, P. A. (1986). Effects of training on four-year olds' ability to solve geometric analogy problems. *Cognition and Instruction, 3,* 261–268.

Whitehurst, G. J., Falco, F. L., Lonigan, C. J., Fischel, J. E., DeBaryshe, B. D., Valdez-Menchaca, M. C., & Caulfield, M. (1988). Accelerating language development through picture book reading. *Developmental Psychology, 24,* 552–559.

Whitehurst, G. J., & Sonnenschein, S. (1978). The development of communication: Attribute variation leads to contrast failure. *Journal of Experimental Child Psychology, 25,* 490–504.

Whitehurst, G. J., & Sonnenschein, S. (1985). The development of communication: A functional analysis. *Annals of Child Development, 2,* 1–48.

Wilcox, M. J., & Webster, E. J. (1980). Early discourse behavior: An analysis of children's responses to listener feedback. *Child Development, 51,* 1120–1125.

Wilensky, R. (1981). Meta-planning: Representing and using knowledge about planning in problem solving and natural language understanding. *Cognitive Science, 5,* 197–233.

Wimmer, H. (1979). Processing of script deviations by young children. *Discourse Processes, 2,* 301–310.

Winer, G. A. (1980). Class-inclusion reasoning in children: A review of the empirical literature. *Child Development, 51,* 309–328.

Wiser, M., & Carey, S. (1983). When heat and temperature wereone. In D. Gentner & A. Stevens (Eds.), *Mental models* (pp. 267–297). Hillsdale, NJ: Erlbaum.

Wishart, J. G. (1986). Siblings as models in early infant learning. *Child Development, 57,* 1232–1240.

Wishart, J. G., & Bower, T. G. R. (1984). Spatial relation and the object concept: A normative study. In L. P. Lipsitt & C. Rovee-Collier (Eds.), *Advances in infancy research* (Vol. 3, pp. 57–125). Norwood, NJ: Ablex.

Wittgenstein, L. (1953). *Philosophical investigations.* New York: MacMillan.

Wohlwill, J. F. (1973). *The study of behavioral development.* New York: Academic Press.

Wood, P. K. (1983). Inquiring systems and problem structures: Implications for cognitive development. *Human Development, 26,* 249–265.

Woodward, R. S., & Sells, S. B. (1935). An atmosphere effect informal syllogistic reasoning. *Journal of Experimental Psychology, 18,* 451–460.

Yando, R., Seitz, V., & Zigler, E. (1978). *Imitation: A developmental perspective.* Hillsdale, NJ: Erlbaum.

Yin, R. K. (1978). Face perception: A review of experiments with infants, normal adults, and brain-injured persons. In R. Held, W. H. Leibowitz, & H. L. Tueker (Eds.), *Handbook of sensory physiology* (Vol. 8, pp. 594–608). Berlin: Springer-Verlag.

Younger, B. A., & Cohen, L. B. (1985). How infants form categories. In G. H. Bower (Ed.), *The Psychology of Learning and Motivation* (Vol. 19, pp. 211–247). Orlando, FL: Academic Press.

Younger, B. A., & Cohen, L. B. (1986). Developmental change in infants' perception of correlations among attributes. *Child Development, 57,* 803–815.

Zabrucky, K., & Ratner, H. H. (1986). Children's comprehension monitoring and recall of inconsistent stories. *Child Development, 57,* 1401–1418.

Zahn-Waxler, C., Cummings, E. M., & Cooperman, G. (1984). Emotional development in childhood. *Annals of Child Development, 1,* 45–106.

Zaporozhets, A. V., & Elkonin, D. B. (Eds.). (1971). *The psychology of preschool children* (pp. 89–110). Cambridge, MA: MIT Press.

Zarbatany, L., & Lamb, M. E. (1985). Social referencing as a function of information source: Mothers versus strangers. *Infant Behavior and Development, 8,* 25–33.

Zivian, M. T., & Darjes, R. W. (1983). Free recall by in-school and out-of-school adults: Performance and metamemory. *Developmental Psychology, 4,* 513–520.

Name Index

Craik, F. I. M., 264, 265, 268, 283
Crassini, B., 70
Crider, C., 217
Crisafi, M. A., 384, 387, 388, 389
Cromer, R., 160, 161, 164
Cruse, D. F., 297
Cummings, E. M., 427
Curtis, L. E., 235
Curtis, M. E., 310, 311

D
Daehler, M. W., 268
Dafoe, J. L., 442, 443
Dale, P. S., 132, 143
Damon, W., 411, 445, 448, 449
Dannemiller, J. L., 37, 38, 49
Danner, F. W., 351, 352, 359
Darjes, R. W., 274
Davis, J. M., 91
Day, J. D., 284
Day, M. C., 260, 306, 351, 352, 359
Day, R. H., 54, 55, 56, 112
DeBaryshe, B. D., 141, 206
DeCasper, A. J., 66, 418, 421
DeForest, M., 294
DeLoache, J. S., 367
DeLucia, C. A., 62
DeMarie-Dreblow, D., 365, 366
Dempster, F. N., 264, 280
Denham, S. A., 440
Denny, J. P., 323
de Schonen, S., 31
deVilliers, J. G., 158, 159
deVilliers, P. A., 158, 159
Devin, J., 432
Diamond, A., 3, 114, 115, 116, 117,
    120
Dias, M. G., 333
Diaz, R., 170
DiCamillo, M., 393
Dickerson, D. J., 372
Dickstein, S., 425
Diehl, V. A., 284
Dimitroff, G., 336
Dinwiddy, L. S., 227
Diskin, S. D., 424
Dockrell, J. E., 154
Dodd, B., 147
Dodd, D. H., 9
Dodge, K. A., 454, 455, 456
Dodwell, P. C., 45, 66
Dolecki, P., 236
Donaldson, M., 224, 227, 343
Dong, Q., 242, 243
Dooling, D. J., 284
Dooling, R., 97
Dowd, J. M., 66
Doyle, A. B., 258
Dreistadt, R., 380
Dromi, E., 150
Dumais, S. T., 33, 34
Duncker, K., 359, 381

E
Earle, D. C., 37
Earley, L. A., 88, 90, 91, 93, 94

Earnshaw, L. S., 103, 104
Ebbesen, E. B., 368
Edwards, C. P., 453
Eilers, R. E., 103, 105
Eimas, P. D., 62, 99, 101, 102, 103, 104, 105, 108,
    111, 372
Einhorn, H. J., 254
Elkonin, D. B., 259, 268
Elliot, A. J., 161
Elliott-Faust, D., 267
Ellis, S. A., 442, 444
Emde, R. N., 419, 424, 425
Endman, M., 64
Engen, T., 22
Ennis, R. H., 349
Enright, M., 92
Enright, R. D., 437
Entwisle, D. R., 86
Epstein, W., 297
Erickson, J. R., 324
Ernst, G. W., 380
Erreich, A., 161
Evans, J. St. B., 316, 324, 330, 338
Eymard, L. A., 385, 386

F
Fabricius, W. V., 362, 364, 365
Fagan, J. F., III, 37, 51, 84, 86
Fagen, J. W., 79, 88, 90, 92, 93, 94
Falco, F. L., 141
Falk, R., 316
Falmagne, R. J., 320, 341, 343, 352
Fantz, R. L., 25, 26, 36, 37, 48, 49
Farah, M. J., 181, 182, 192, 228
Farrar, M. J., 140, 141
Feagans, L., 296
Feffer, N., 437
Feider, H., 417, 419
Feinman, S., 424, 425, 426, 427
Feinstein, M. H., 409
Feiring, C., 453
Feltovich, P. J., 398, 399, 400
Ferdinandsen, K., 44, 45
Ferland, M. B., 70
Ferrara, R. A., 261
Field, J., 66
Field, T., 423
Fiess, K., 159
Fifer, W. P., 66, 418
Fillmore, C. J., 156
Fincham, F. D., 421
Firment, M., 398
Fischbein, E., 318
Fischel, J. E., 141
Fischer, K. W., 446, 447, 448
Fischhoff, B., 316
Fisher, C. B., 45
Fisher, G. W., 246, 254
Fiske, S. T., 440
Fitts, P. M., 409
Fitzgerald, M. D., 132
Fivush, R., 183, 185, 186, 191
Flaegher, J., 260
Flaugher, J., 259
Flavell, E. R., 241, 242, 243, 244,
    245

Flavell, J. H., 4, 6, 7, 12, 17, 241, 242, 243, 244,
	245, 268, 269, 270, 271, 273, 349, 433, 437
Flores d'Arcais, G. B., 165
Fong, G. T., 317
Foorman, B. R., 309
Forbes, B., 66
Forbes, D. L., 362
Ford, M., 327
Ford, M. E., 439
Forman, E. A., 439
Forrest-Pressley, D. L., 267
Fox, R., 33, 34
Fraisse, P., 183
Frankel, M. T., 268
Franks, B. A., 344
Franks, J. J., 263, 285, 393, 395, 410, 412
Frauenglass, M., 170
Freeley, A. J., 304
French, D. C., 453
French, L. A., 186, 187, 188
Friedman, A., 296
Friedman, S., 83
Fry, C. L., Jr., 437
Frye, D., 418
Fugua, J. D., 306
Furrow, D., 173
Furst, A., 200
Furth, H., 16
Fuson, K. C., 171

G
Galanter, E., 362
Gallagher, J. D., 278, 280
Gallagher, J. M., 305
Gallistel, C. R., 229, 230
Ganon, E. C., 42
Gardner, H., 2
Gardner, W., 367, 410
Garfield, J. L., 409
Garfinkel, H., 428
Garmezy, N., 64
Garner, W. R., 201
Garnham, A., 295
Garvey, C., 314, 431
Gass, S. T., 440
Gathercole, V. C., 152
Gauvain, M., 367
Gayl, I. E., 37
Geis, M. F., 274
Gekoski, M. J., 420
Gelber, E. R., 82
Gelman, R., 70, 71, 220, 226, 227, 229, 230, 231,
	232, 233, 234, 235, 246, 247, 248, 249,
	250, 251, 318, 417, 432
Gelman, S. A., 168, 208, 209, 210, 304
Gentile, P. K., 305
Gentile, R. J., 305
Gentner, D., 306, 311, 312, 313, 392
Gerard, A., 190
Gerry, G., 43
Ghatala, E. S., 273, 274
Gholson, B., 193, 371, 372, 373, 374, 385, 386,
	387
Gibbons, F. X., 442
Gibson, E. J., 58, 60, 74, 201
Gibson, J. J., 54, 55, 57, 58, 62, 69, 77

Gick, M., 314, 381, 382, 383, 385, 387, 393
Gick, M. L., 396
Gilbert, J. H. V., 104
Ginsburg, H. P., 20, 234, 238
Girle, R. A., 319
Gitomer, D. H., 310, 311
Glaser, R., 306, 309, 371, 398, 399, 400, 402, 403
Gleason, H. A., 100
Gleitman, H., 47, 48, 62, 126, 127, 130, 141, 193
Gleitman, L. R., 126, 127, 130, 141, 193, 194, 195,
	196
Glenberg, A. M., 92, 297
Glenn, C. G., 291, 294
Glick, J., 332, 333, 416
Glieberman, J., 271
Glucksberg, S., 429, 430, 431
Godden, R., 93, 282
Goelman, H., 435
Goffman, E., 428
Goldberg, J., 278
Goldberg, S., 212, 423
Goldfarb, J., 211
Golding, J., 296
Goldin-Meadow, S., 138, 141
Goldman, S. R., 307, 309
Goldstein, B. E., 27, 30, 44, 48
Golinkoff, R. M., 139, 141, 154
Gollin, E. S., 213
Goodman, G. S., 296
Goodman, S., 175
Goodnow, J. J., 371, 373
Gopnik, A., 144, 145, 169
Gordon, P. C., 314, 416
Gordon, S. E., 296
Gordon, W. J. J., 392
Gorin, L., 298
Gottfried, A. W., 38, 75, 83
Gottlieb, G., 14, 15
Gourevitch, V., 437
Graber, M., 119, 120, 122
Graesser, A. C., 296
Granrud, C. E., 35, 57
Gray, H., 140
Gray, W. D., 197
Graziano, W. G., 440
Green, F. L., 241, 242, 243, 244, 245, 433
Green, H. F., 200
Green, R. Z., 259, 260
Green, S. K., 296
Greenberg, M. T., 362
Greene, D., 442, 443
Greenfield, D. B., 213
Greenfield, P. M., 179
Greeno, J. G., 234, 235, 357, 359
Grice, H. P., 286, 336, 428, 434
Griesler, P. C., 88, 90, 91, 93, 94
Grieve, R., 236
Griffin, M., 93
Griffiths, A. K., 352
Griggs, R. A., 329, 340, 341, 343
Gross, C. G., 44, 45
Grudin, J., 310
Gruendel, J. M., 183, 188, 189, 190
Gruenenfelder, T. M., 276
Gunnar, M. R., 425
Gunnar-Vongnechten, M. R., 421

Lifter, K., 159
Light, L. L., 296
Limber, J., 132
Lindauer, B. K., 285, 288
Lindberg, M. A., 274, 275
Lindenberger, U., 241
Lindvall, C. M., 127, 359
Linn, M. C., 352, 353, 378
Linn, P., 106
Lipsitt, L. P., 22
Lisker, L., 102, 104
Lockhart, R. S., 80, 264, 268, 396
Lohman, D. F., 310
Longhurst, T. M., 431
Lonigan, C. J., 141
Lorch, E. P., 257
Lorenz, K. Z., 304
Lovett, S. B., 318
Lowe, C. A., 442
Lubin, L., 423
Lucariello, J., 189, 191, 198
Lucas, D. A., 92
Luchins, A. S., 358
Luger, G. F., 114, 381
Lui, F., 212
Lunzer, E. A., 305
Lutkenhaus, P., 421
Lynch, J. S., 338

M
McBurney, P. H., 31
McCabe, A. E., 226, 236
McCall, B. B., 36
McCartney, K. A., 189
McClaskey, C. L., 454, 455, 456
McClusky, K., 106
Maccoby, E. E., 208, 453
McCormick, C. B., 269
McCreath, H., 365
McDermott, J., 398
McDevitt, T. M., 435
McDonnell, P. M., 29
MacFarlane, A., 31
McGarrigle, J., 227, 236, 237
McKain, K., 136
McKenzie, B., 31
McKenzie, B. C., 54, 56, 112
McKoon, G., 263
McLanahan, A. G., 236
McLaughlin, B., 423
Macnamara, J., 141, 167, 168, 320, 342, 343
McNeill, D., 98
McNew, S., 142
McVey, K. A., 273
Malcuit, G., 417, 419
Mandell, N., 440
Mandler, J. M., 12, 20, 80, 122, 190, 191, 198, 199, 234, 261, 290, 291, 293, 294, 295, 296
Mannle, S., 432
Maratsos, M., 159, 432
Markman, E. M., 150, 151, 152, 153, 204, 205, 206, 208, 209, 211, 212, 214, 215, 238, 298, 304
Marler, P., 97
Martlew, M., 429

Martorano, S. C., 350, 351
Massaro, D. W., 101
Massey, C. M., 417
Masur, E. F., 140, 422
Matlin, M., 335
Matthews, J., 226, 236
Maurer, D., 25, 28, 31, 33, 35, 43, 53, 101
Maurer, P., 31
Mayer, R. E., 382
Meacham, J. A., 176
Mead, G. H., 444, 445, 446, 448
Means, M. L., 398, 404, 406, 407
Meck, E., 230, 235, 250
Medin, D. L., 111, 193, 194, 211
Megaw-Nyce, J., 58, 60
Mehler, J., 66
Meier, R. P., 164
Melkman, R., 204
Melloy-Carminar, P., 38, 83
Melton, A. W., 85
Meltzoff, A. N., 70, 74, 75, 76, 144, 169, 422
Mendelson, M. J., 69, 70
Mendelson, R., 251
Menig-Peterson, C. L., 432
Merkin, S., 234
Mervis, C. B., 149, 194, 195, 196, 197
Messer, D. J., 141
Metzler, J., 11
Meyer, B. J. F., 289
Meyer, D. E., 41, 42
Millar, W. S., 421
Miller, G. A., 147, 148, 226, 264, 362
Miller, G. E., 267
Miller, J. L., 103
Miller, P. H., 259, 365, 366
Minzat, I., 318
Miranda, S. B., 37
Mischel, H. N., 369, 370
Mischel, W., 368, 369, 370
Mistry, J. J., 189, 270
Modigliani, V., 85
Montanegro, J., 305
Moore, C., 418
Moore, D., 72
Moore, J. S., 440
Moore, M. K., 72, 75, 76
Moore, R. W., 37
Moore, T., 302, 303, 320
Moran, G., 421
Moray, N., 257
Morgan, D., 385, 386
Morgan, M., 443
Morison, V., 37
Morrison, H., 84, 422
Morrongiello, B. A., 66, 68
Morse, P. A., 80
Mosenthal, P., 299
Moshman, D., 344
Mueller, E. E., 431
Muir, D. W., 45, 66
Mulholland, T. M., 306, 307
Murray, F. B., 227
Mutter, S. A., 296
Myers, I., 418
Myers, N., 212
Myers, R. S., 43, 58, 59, 84, 85

Renshaw, P. D., 452
Repp, B. H., 101
Revelle, G. L., 298
Revlis, R., 321, 324
Reznick, J. S., 72, 191
Rheingold, H. L., 423
Rice, M., 148, 149, 164
Richards, D. D., 209, 211, 431
Richman, C. L., 280
Rieser, J., 397
Rifkin, A., 189, 191, 307, 308, 309, 310
Riley, C. A., 236, 239, 240
Riley, M. S., 234, 235
Rips, L. J., 11
Risenhoover, N., 425
Rissland, E. L., 409
Robbins, D., 200
Roberge, J. J., 336, 337
Roberts, J. D., 37
Robinson, C. A., 261, 290
Robinson, C. S., 357
Robinson, E. J., 433, 434, 435, 436
Robinson, L., 127, 359
Robinson, M., 231, 362
Robinson, W. P., 433, 434, 435
Roche, A. F., 65
Rock, I., 44
Roder, B. J., 85
Rogoff, B., 270, 273, 367, 410
Rollins, H. A., 268
Rosch, E. H., 194, 195, 196, 197
Rose, D., 37, 84
Rose, S. A., 38, 70, 72, 73, 75, 83, 86, 226
Rosenbaum, D. A., 409
Rossi, S., 212
Ross, K. A., 273
Roth, C., 87, 110
Rovee, D. T., 87
Rovee-Collier, C. K., 79, 87, 88, 89, 90, 91, 92, 93,
   94, 95, 107, 417, 420
Rozin, P., 231, 233
Rubin, K. H., 439, 450, 451, 452, 453
Ruff, H. A., 70, 72, 73, 84, 87, 106
Rulf, S., 246, 254
Rumain, B., 323, 336, 337, 343
Rumelhart, D. E., 291, 307, 428
Russell, A., 135, 136
Russell, J., 344
Russo, M., 200

S
Sachs, J. S., 145, 146, 283, 432
Sadowski, B. R., 309
Sagotsky, G., 442, 443
Salapatek, P., 29, 30, 32, 35, 36, 37, 38, 39, 40, 45,
   49, 97
Sallis, R., 309
Sarda, M., 441
Sawyer, J. D., 296
Scardamalia, M., 353
Schacter, D. L., 80
Schaffer, H. R., 417
Schaller, M. J., 32
Schank, R. C., 182, 290
Scheer, R. K., 322, 323
Schiff, A. R., 258
Schlesinger, I. M., 160

Schmidt, C. R., 288, 299, 436
Schmidt, H., 46
Schmidt, S. R., 299
Schneider, B. A., 63, 64
Schneider, W., 272, 277
Schoenfeld, A. H., 399, 402
Schreuder, R., 165
Schuberth, R. E., 114
Schulz, R. W., 262
Schwartz, S., 370
Scott, J., 202
Scott, L. C., 270
Scott, M. S., 82, 213
Scoville, R., 132
Scribner, S., 294, 332, 333
Secco, T., 292, 294
Seibert, J., 215
Seidman, S., 189
Seitz, V., 423
Seligman, M. E. P., 421
Sells, S. B., 323
Selman, R. L., 437, 438, 439, 450
Sewell, D. R., 190
Shaffer, W. O., 277
Shanks, B. L., 245
Shankweiler, D., 98
Shantz, C. U., 416, 436
Shapiro, E. K., 340, 457
Sharp, D. W., 273
Sharps, M. J., 213
Shatz, M., 141, 432
Shea, S. L., 33, 34
Shelton, T. S., 263
Shephard, R. N., 11
Shepp, B. E., 281
Sherman, S. J., 316, 317
Sherman, T., 82, 84, 111
Sherrod, L., 416
Sherwood, R. D., 397, 410, 412, 413
Shiffrin, R. M., 277
Shoben, E. J., 11
Shore, C. M., 142, 190
Short, K. R., 62
Shortliffe, E. H., 408
Shultz, T. R., 246, 247, 249, 251, 252, 253, 254,
   441, 442
Shure, M. B., 450
Siegal, M., 227
Siegel, L. S., 226, 236, 239
Siegler, R. S., 4, 231, 252, 404, 405, 406
Siervogel, R. M., 65
Silfen, C. K., 36
Simon, D. P., 398
Simon, H. A., 357, 362, 380, 381, 394, 397, 398,
   409
Sinclair, M., 66
Singer, J., 68
Sinha, C., 167
Sinnott, J. M., 65
Siqueland, E. R., 62, 99, 102, 108
Skinner, B. F., 7, 11
Skyrms, B., 251, 302, 303, 314
Slackman, E. A., 183, 186
Slater, A., 37, 84
Slobin, D. I., 126, 155, 156, 157
Slotnick, N. S., 330
Slovic, P., 314, 316

Vye, N., 397
Vygotsky, L. S., 170, 171, 173, 175, 410, 414

W

Waern, Y., 323
Wagner, D. A., 273
Walden, T. A., 425
Waldrop, M. M., 256
Wales, R. J., 226
Walker, A. S., 58, 60, 74
Walker, C. H., 289
Walker-Andrews, A. S., 424
Walkerdine, V., 167
Wallace, J. G., 236
Ward, S. L., 341
Ward, T. B., 202
Wason, P. C., 335, 338, 339, 340, 375, 376
Wassenberg, K., 135, 136
Wasserman, S., 117, 118
Waterman, D. A., 357
Waters, L. J., 227, 439
Watkins, M. J., 265, 268
Watson, J. S., 2, 75, 76, 418, 421
Weber, E., 457
Webster, E. J., 139
Weir, R. H., 171
Weisberg, R. W., 382, 384, 392, 393, 429
Weiskopf, S., 97
Weisler, S. E., 409
Weiss, S. J., 51, 52
Weissberg, J. A., 270
Weitz, L. J., 349, 350
Well, A. D., 257, 258
Wellman, H., 269, 270, 271, 272, 298, 362, 363,
    364, 365, 431, 441
Wells, D., 441, 442
Werker, J. F., 104, 105
Werner, H., 179, 201
Werner, J. S., 37, 38, 82, 83, 84, 86
Whaley, J. R., 292
Wheldall, K., 226
White, B. L., 413
White, C. S., 306
White, R. M., Jr., 9
Whitehurst, G. J., 141, 206, 429, 431, 432, 433,
    434

Whittaker, S. J., 435, 436
Wilcox, M. J., 139
Wilensky, R., 362, 370
Wilkinson, A. C., 297
Willson, V. L., 306
Wilson, E. G., 239, 240
Wilson, K. P., 257, 260
Wimmer, H., 189
Winer, G. A., 235, 236
Winzemer, J., 161
Wiser, M., 220
Wishart, J. G., 113, 114, 115, 422
Witherspoon, D., 263
Wittgenstein, L., 428
Wittlinger, R. P., 86
Wittrock, M. C., 212
Wohlwill, J. F., 2, 12, 17, 18
Wood, P. K., 344
Woodward, R. S., 323
Woody-Ramsey, J., 365, 366
Worden, P. E., 297
Wright, J., 437
Wright, R. J., 305
Wynns, F. C., 268

Y

Yaeger, J., 174, 188
Yando, R., 423
Yearwood, A. A., 393, 395
Yearwood, J. E., 393, 395
Yengo, L. A., 92
Yin, R. K., 48
Yonas, A., 57
Younger, B. A., 109, 110, 111, 419

Z

Zabrucky, K., 299
Zacks, R. T., 277
Zahn-Waxler, C., 422, 427
Zaporozhets, A. V., 259, 268
Zarbatany, L., 426
Zeiss, A. R., 368
Zhang, X. D., 241, 243
Zigler, E., 64, 423
Zivian, M. T., 274
Zoloth, S., 97
Zou, H., 242, 243

Subject Index

Compiled stage, in skills acquisition, 409
Complexity, visual fixation and, 37
Component selection tasks, 258–59
Comprehension
  cognitive skills and, 186–88
  context and, 192, 284
  evaluation process in, 299
  factors affecting, 165–67, 283–99
  failure of, 299
  feedback rule, 433–34
  inferences and, 285–90
  memory and, 283–99
  methods of studying, 131–32
  monitoring of, 297–99, 433
  nonlinguistic knowledge and, 164–67
  prelinguistic, 145–47
  process of described, 283
  repair process in, 299
  schemas and, 290–97
Comprehension monitoring rule, 433
Comprehension task, 152
Computer models, for problem solving, 408
Computer science, 7, 11, 304
Concept acquisition
  inductive reasoning and, 303–4
  perceptual development and, 201–3
  of superordinate concepts, 204–7
Concept identification, hypothesis testing and, 371–72
Concept relations, 211–16
  reversibility in, 239–41
Concepts
  abstract vs., perceptually based, 192
  nature of, 179
Conceptual development, 192–211
  appearance-reality distinction and, 241–45
  categorical inferences in, 208–11
  causality, 245–54
  characteristic-to-criterial shift in, 207
  class inclusion, 235–38, 241
  in concrete operations stage, 222–54
  conservation concepts, 223–29
  criterial feature model of, 193–94, 202, 204
  domain-specific knowledge and, 216–20
  family resemblance models of, 194–202, 204
  information-processing skills and, 223
  number concepts, 229–35
  perceptual development and, 201–3
  of self-concept, 444–50
  superordinate concept acquisition, 204–7
  transitive inference, 235, 238–41
  word meaning acquisition and, 149
Conceptual knowledge, 178–79
  semantic knowledge vs., 148–49
Conceptual organization
  part-whole relations, 214–16
  syntagmatic vs. paradigmatic responding, 213
Conceptual representation, 179–81
Concrete operations stage, 6, 222–54. *See also*
    Developmental stages; Middle childhood
  appearance-reality distinction and, 241–45
  causality in, 245–54
  class inclusions and, 212
  conservation concepts in, 223–29
  logical operations and, 349
  transitive inference in, 238–39
Condition-action pairs, 408–9

Conditional reasoning, 334–41
  content and, 339–41
  hypothesis testing and, 337–39
Conditional statements, 186
Conditioned responses, 87–96
Conditioning methodology
  in auditory discrimination studies, 64–65
  in object perception studies, 57
Cones, color discrimination and, 32
Congruent content, 332–33
Conjugate foot-kick response, 88–92, 93–95
Conjugate reinforcement paradigm, 87
Conservation concepts, 223–26
  attention and, 259
  methodology concerns, 226–29, 232
Conspecifics, 417
Constancies
  identity-existence, 112
  perceptual, 54–58
Constants, objects as, 54
Constraints
  on problem representation, 358–59
  on problem solving, 356
Constructive theories, 69
Content, reasoning and, 339–41, 343
Content knowledge, 274–77
Content words
  effects of knowledge about, 330–34
  function words and, 319–20
Context
  causality and, 254
  communication and, 127
  comprehension and, 127, 165–67
  conservation concepts and, 226–27
  learning and, 412–13
  principle of contrast and, 152
  in psycholinguistics, 131–32
  reasoning and, 343
Contingency relations, 421, 445
Contingent condition, in parent-child interaction, 135–36
Contrast, principle of, 206
  in word meaning acquisition, 150, 152–54
Contrast relations, 211
Contrast sensitivity function (CSF), 29–30
Controlling variables task, 352–53, 378
Convergence
  accommodation and, 32
  analogical transfer and, 382–84
  in knowledge representation studies, 181–82
Conversation, rules of, 286, 428
  assumption of, 434–35
  enabling inferences and, 286
Conversion error, 328
Core concepts, 220
Correlated attributes, 109, 197–98
Counting, 229–31
Covariation, principle of, 246–47, 251–54
Criterial feature model, 193–94, 202
  characteristic-to-criterial shift, 207
  superordinate concept acquisition and, 204
Critical period, for language acquisition, 162–63
Cross-sectional method of study, 3
Crying, as intentional communication, 133
CSF (contrast sensitivity function), 29–30
Culture
  appearance-reality distinctions and, 243

formal operations performance and, 352–53
language and, 127
metamemory development and, 273
perception and, 23
speech perception and, 103–4
statistical heuristics and, 317
story schemas and, 294

D

Deaf children, 138, 141, 162
Decision-making skills, 431
Declarative knowledge
memory and, 9, 80
nature of, 11
procedural knowledge vs., 9, 234
in sensorimotor stage, 20–22
in skills acquisition, 409
Deductive inferences, 285, 287–88
Deductive reasoning, 301–2, 319–44
categorical syllogisms, 320–34
developmental stages and, 343–44
logical competence and, 341–44
Delay of gratification, 368–71
Deprivation studies, with animals, 16
Depth perception, 33–35
Descriptive approach, to causality, 246
Detection threshold, 63–65
Determinism, 246–48
Developmental psycholinguists, 130–31
Developmental stages. *See also specific stages*
age norms vs., 20
concept relations and, 212
conditional reasoning and, 335–37, 341
discounting principle and, 442–44
expertise and, 404–8
hypothesis testing and, 371, 378
knowledge acquisition and, 410
logical competence and, 342–44
in problem representation, 359–60
problem solving and, 363, 365, 367, 372–73, 404
referential communication and, 429, 436
role taking and, 438
self-concept and, 448–50
self-regulation and, 368–70
social referencing and, 427
syllogistic reasoning and, 327, 329–30
syntagmatic-paradigmatic shift and, 213
Developmental theories, 14–15. *See also* Theories
competence-performance issue in, 117
Difference rule, speaker skills and, 432–33
Differential visual tracking paradigm, 42–43
Differentiation hypothesis, 201
Digit-span test, 275
Discounting principle, 442–44
Discrimination
auditory, 64–65
color, 32–33, 35
pattern, 39–53, 41–43
Discrimination learning, 27
Discriminative stimulus, 92
Dishabituation, 26. *See also* Habituation-dishabituation paradigm
Disjunction, in scripts, 186
Displacement, as language capacity, 126–27
Distance effect, in transitive inference, 240
Distinctiveness, 449
Distributed study, recognition memory and, 85

Domain-specific knowledge
analogies and, 304
appearance-reality distinctions and, 245
concepts and, 216–20
about memory. *See* Metamemory
problem solving and, 397–413
about referential communication, 429, 431
referential communication and, 431
about social world. *See* Social cognition

E

Ear, anatomy of, 62–63
Early childhood. *See also* Developmental stages;
Preoperations stage
analogical transfer in, 384–85, 387–92
appearance-reality confusion in, 241–45
basic-level vs. superordinate categorization in, 198–99
causality concepts in, 246–54
class inclusion concepts in, 235–38
communication in, 432
concept relations in, 211–16
conceptual development in, 149, 192–211
cooperative principle assumed in, 434–35
deductive reasoning in, 332–34, 343, 344
hypothesis testing in, 372–74, 378, 380
imitation in, 423
inductive reasoning in, 304, 306, 314, 318, 343–44
intention concept in, 441
knowledge acquisition in, 178–220
language acquisition in, 124
listener skills in, 433–34
logical competence in, 332–33
memory in, 82, 86, 267–68, 270
metamemory in, 270
number concepts in, 230–36
one-word period, 142–47
prelinguistic communication in, 132–47
private speech in, 170–76
problem solving in, 362–65, 368, 372–74, 378, 380, 384–85
psycholinguistic methodology for, 131–32
reasoning in, 332–33
recognition memory in, 82, 86
referential communication in, 431
scripts in, 182–92
social environment in, 415
social problem solving in, 453–54
speaker skills in, 432
story schemas in, 294–95
syllogistic reasoning in, 332–34
syntax acquisition in, 155–69
transitive inference in, 239–41
word meaning acquisition in, 147–54
Education
message evaluation and, 435–36
metamemory development and, 273–74
story schemas and, 294
Egocentricity, role taking vs., 437
Egocentric speech, 188
The Empire Strikes Back, studies using, 404–8
Enabling inferences, 286, 288–89
Enabling skills, 431
Enactive or motoric knowledge, 179–80
Encoding
in analogical reasoning, 307–10

Encoding (*cont.*)
  categorization and, 107
  conditional reasoning and, 335
  processes of, 260
  in reasoning model, 325
  retrieval and, 282–83
  of social information, 454–58
  in syllogistic reasoning, 329
Encoding-specificity hypothesis, 282, 284
Ending, in story grammar, 291
Enhancement, in speech perception, 105
Enrichment studies, 16–17
Environmentalist theories, 14–16
Episode, in story grammar, 290–91
Episodic memory, 263
  general event representations vs., 184–85
Evaluation process, in comprehension, 299
Event representations, 179
  development of, 190–92
  scripts and, 182–92
Exemplar matching, availability heuristic and,
    317–18
Exemplar models, 199–201
  superordinate concept acquisition and, 204
Exercise Hypothesis, 162–63
Exhaustive encoding, 307, 309
Expectations
  in infancy, 419–20
  perceptual, 53–54
  problem representation and, 358
  schemas and, 292–94
  social, 419–21
Experience
  analogical problem solving and, 380–81, 385
  collaboration vs., 411–12
  conditional reasoning and, 335–36
  in developmental theory, 5, 14–17
  role-taking skills and, 440
  speech perception and, 104–5
Experimental method of study, 3. *See also* Scientific
    thought
Expertise
  acquisition of, 407–13
  developmental differences in, 404–8
Expert systems, 408
Expert vs. novice problem solving, 398–408
Explicit knowledge
  implicit knowledge vs., 231–35, 237, 241
  logical competence and, 237, 241, 344
  number concepts and, 231
Eye, anatomy of, 27–28
Eye fixation, analogical reasoning and, 310, 311

F
Face schemas, 290
Facial expressions, infant responsiveness to, 75–76,
    424–25
Facial perception, in infancy, 48–53
  categorization in, 106–7
  social cognition and, 418
Failure to communicate, prelinguistic, 138–39
Failure to comprehend, monitoring and, 299
Failure of inductive inference, 303–4
Failure to remember, 282
Falsification strategy, 338–39, 375–76
Family resemblance models, 194–202
Fantasy, syllogistic reasoning and, 332–33
Farmer's Dilemma problem, 385–87

Features
  characteristic, 194–201
  criterial, 193–94
  in infant categorization, 107
Feedback rule, 433–34
Figurative knowledge, 222
Flexibility of rods test, 345, 346
Focusing strategy, 374
Foot-kick paradigm, for infant retention, 88–95
Forgetting, 8
Formal operations stage, 6. *See also* Adolescence;
    Developmental stages
  analogical reasoning and, 305
  hypothetico-deductive reasoning in, 303
  knowledge representation in, 12
  performance factors in, 350–54
  probability concept in, 318
  reasoning in, 345–54
  tasks in, 345–48
Formants, in speech sounds, 98
Frequency, 63–65
Freudian theory, cognitive theory vs., 1–2
Fricative sounds, 101
Friendship, self-concept development and, 450
Function, in artifact categories, 209
Functional categories, 191
Functional models of development, vision and, 36
Function words, 319–20, 328–30

G
General event representations (GERs), 183–92
Generalization test, 27
Gestalt theory
  object perception and, 62
  visual perception and, 44–48
Gestures, in prelinguistic communication, 137–38
Gholson analogical transfer study, 385–87
Goal-oriented behavior
  delay of gratification and, 368–71
  hypothesis testing strategies, 376–77
  in language development, 129, 132–38
  in prelinguistic communication, 137–38, 140
  problem-solving plans, 362–71
  in social problem solving, 451–52, 457–58
Goal state, in problem solving, 356
Good continuation, principle of, 44–47
Grammars
  children's, 157–60
  story, 291–95
  structure in, 155–56
  transformational, 156
Gratification, delay of, 368–71

H
Habituation, 25, 82
Habituation-dishabituation paradigm, 25–26
  in categorization studies, 106, 109–11
  for memory studies, 82–84
  in object perception studies, 57–59
  in object permanence studies, 117–18
  paired-comparison variation on, 83
  with pattern discrimination, 41, 46–47, 51
  with visual-tactile coordination, 73
HAS (high-amplitude sucking) paradigm, 62
Heuristics
  availability, 315–19, 338
  causality and, 254

generating and testing hypotheses, 371–80
in inductive reasoning, 314–19
planning, 362–71
in problem solving, 361–92
representative, 314–15, 317–19
statistical, 317, 319
Hierarchy
in children's scripts, 186
class inclusions, 212–14, 235–38
expert vs. novice problem solving and, 399–403
in languages, 126, 157–60
in problem-solving plans, 362–65
in story grammars, 291
High-amplitude sucking (HAS) paradigm, 62
Higher-order concepts, 223
Holistic perception, 201–2
Horizontal decalage, 226, 448
"How-to" knowledge, 9
Hyponym test, 152, 153
Hypothesis testing
conditional reasoning and, 337–41
in experimental method of study, 3
in language acquisition, 161
in problem solving, 371–80
Hypothetical-reflective tasks, 450–51
Hypothetico-deductive reasoning, 303, 345

I
Identity-existence constancy, 112
Identity interpretation, in syllogistic reasoning, 329
Idiomorphs, 143
Ikonic mode of knowledge representation, 180
Ikonic representation, 180. *See also* Imaginal
representation
Ill-defined problems, 357, 381–84
Illicit conversion, 335
Imagery, as mnemonic strategy, 267
Imaginal representation, 178, 180–82
"I" and "me," 448–50
Imitation
proprioceptive-visual coordination and, 75–76
self-recognition and, 445
social cognition and, 422–23
Implicit knowledge
of causality principles, 247
explicit knowledge vs., 231–35, 237, 241
logical competence and, 344
number concepts and, 231–35
Incidental learning tasks, 274
effort to learn and, 281
Incongruent content, syllogistic reasoning and,
332–33
Inconsistencies, detection of, 298–99
Inductive inferences, 286–88, 303–4
Inductive reasoning, 302–19
analogical reasoning, 304–14
cognitive development and, 303, 318
defined, 302
developmental stages and, 343–44
probability and heuristics in, 314–19
suppression of, 343
Infancy. *See also* Developmental stages;
Sensorimotor stage
attention studies in, 36–38
auditory development in, 62–68
categorical perception in, 97–101, 106–11
categorization in, 148, 417–19
causality concepts in, 254

color discrimination in, 32–33, 35, 97
contingency relations in, 417
defined, 19
depth perception in, 33–35
expectations in, 419–21
facial perception in, 48–53
imitation in, 422–23
intentional communication in, 133–37
intersensory relations in, 68–77
memory in, 79–96, 115–16, 119–22
object perception in, 54–62
object permanence concept in, 111–21
oculomotor system in, 31–32
pattern perception in, 27–30, 39–53
perception in, 22–27, 48–62
perceptual expectations in, 53–54
prelinguistic communication in, 133–41
problem solving in, 427
proprioceptive-visual coordination in, 75–77
recognition memory in, 82–87
responsiveness to people in, 416–27
self-concept development in, 445–47
sensorimotor development in, 19–22
shape categorization in, 106
social environment in, 415
social referencing in, 424–27
speech perception in, 97–105
vision development in, 27–62
visual-auditory coordination in, 69–72
visual capacities summarized, 35–36
visual-tactile coordination in, 72–75, 77
Inferences, 285–90
in analogical reasoning, 307–9
analogous inference problems, 387–92
causal, 440–44
deductive, 285, 287–88
failures, 303–4
inductive, 286–88, 303–4
as reasoning, 301
transitive, 235, 238–41, 301
Information-processing approach, 4, 7–10
to class inclusion studies, 236–37
to conceptual development, 202
to knowledge representation, 11, 181–82, 256–57
to learning, 256–57, 260
memory in, 8–10, 79, 256
in nativist theory, 69
to problem representation, 359
in production systems, 408
to scripts, 190
to social problem solving, 450–58
to transitive inference, 240
Information-processing skills, 223, 431
Initial state, in problem solving, 356
Inner speech, 170–76
Insight problems, 393–97, 413
Integral dimensions, analogical reasoning and,
308–9
Intelligence testing, analogies for, 304–5
Intention
causal reasoning about, 440–44
defined, 441
discounting principle and, 442–44
Intentional communication, 133–36
Interactionist theory, 15–16
Internal inconsistencies, 298–99
Interpersonal vs. intrapersonal language use, 127
Interpretive stage, in skills acquisition, 409

tetrahedral model of, 261–62
Learning theory, 17–18
Lexical inconsistencies, 298
Linguistic categories, 156–60
Linguistic grammars, story grammars vs., 291, 292
Linguistic knowledge, 358
Linguistic theory
  cognitive theory and, 7
  knowledge representation in, 11
  story grammars and, 292
Linguistics, 320
Linguists, 130
Listener rule, 431–32
Listener skills, 433–34
Logic. *See also* Reasoningcategorical syllogisms, 320–24
  linguistics and, 320
  psychology and, 320, 349
Logical competence
  class inclusion and, 237–38
  conditional reasoning and, 341
  defined, 341–42
  development of, 332–33, 341–44, 349–50
  as reasoning model, 323
  transitive inference and, 238–41
Longitudinal method of study, 3
Long-term memory. *See also* Permanent memory
  declarative and procedural knowledge in, 9
  infant retention studies, 88–90
  in information processing, 8–10
  knowledge stored in, 9–10
  organization of knowledge in, 9–10

M

Manual visual-tactile coordination, 72–74
Mapping
  in analogical reasoning, 307, 309–10, 314
  in analogous problem solving, 382, 385–86
Mapping problem, in language development, 148
Matching bias, reasoning errors and, 338
Maturation
  in developmental theory, 14–17
  language learning and, 163–64
  memory development and, 280–81
  speech perception and, 104
Maturational State Hypothesis, 163
Mean length of utterance (MLU), 132, 139
Mechanism, principle of, 246, 249–51, 253
Mediators, role of, 410–13
"Me" and "I," 448–50
Memory, 79–96. *See also* Long-term memory;
     Memory development; Permanent memory;
     Working memory
  availability heuristic and, 315–16
  in broad vs. narrow sense, 80–81
  characteristics affecting, 261–62
  cognitive theory and, 79–81
  comprehension and, 283–99
  for conditioned responses, 87–96
  defined, 79
  developmental change and, 81
  in early childhood, 82, 86, 267–68, 270
  as enabling skill, 431
  episodic, 263
  general event representations vs., 184–85
  general vs. specific, 93–95, 96
  in infancy, 79–96, 115–16, 119–22

inferences and, 285–90
in information-processing system, 8–10, 79, 256
  knowing vs. remembering, 263
  learning and, 79–80, 256–57, 260–83
  mental representation and, 121–22
  methods of studying, 263–64
  object permanence and, 115–16
  as reconstructive, 283–84
  referential communication and, 431
  retention factors, 86–87
  retrieval failures, 282
  schemas and, 285–90, 292, 296–97
  semantic vs. episodic, 263–64
  shared scripts and, 189
  for stories, 294–95
  tetrahedral model of, 261–62
  variables determining, 261
  visual recognition, 81–87
Memory cueing/reasoning-by-analogy hypothesis, 340
Memory development, 256–57, 260–83. *See also*
    Memory
  automatic processes in, 277–80
  content knowledge and, 274–77
  maturational changes and, 280–81
  metamemory in, 269–74, 276
  methods of studying, 263–64
  mnemonic strategies and, 267–69
  permanent memory retrieval, 281–83
  problem solving and, 367–68
Mental representations
  appearance-reality distinctions and, 243–44
  concepts as, 148
  deductive inferences and, 285
  development of, 122
  infant memory and, 121–22
  logical competence and, 342
  message evaluation and, 435
  problem representation and, 358–59
  schemas as, 290
  self-regulation and, 369–71
  in syllogistic reasoning model, 324–27
Message evaluation, 434–36
Metacognitive experiences, 273–74
Metamemory
  acquisition of, 273–74
  content knowledge and, 275–77
  defined, 269
  development of, 269–74
  performance and, 271–73
Metaphor, comprehension of, 165
Methodology, 2–3. *See also specific subjects of
    study*
  analogical reasoning testing, 305–10, 312
  analogical transfer studies, 380–92
  appearance-reality studies, 242–43
  attention studies, 257–59
  causality studies, 248–50, 252–53
  class inclusion studies, 235, 237–38
  comprehension studies, 284, 298–99
  concept relations studies, 213
  conceptual development studies, 193–94, 198–201, 207–208
  conservation concept studies, 225–29
  content knowledge testing, 274–75
  delayed-gratification studies, 368–69

Methodology (*cont.*)
  difference rule study, 433
  domain-specific concept studies, 217–19
  environmental manipulation problems, 16–17
  expertise studies, 406–8
  hypothesis-testing studies, 371–78
  imitative behavior studies, 422–23
  inference testing, 285–86, 288–89
  knowledge representation studies, 180–82
  knowledge transfer studies, 393–97
  memory studies, 81–83, 121–22, 261, 263–64,
    278–79, 283
  message evaluation study, 434
  metamemory studies, 272–73, 276
  number concept studies, 232
  object permanence studies and, 113–20
  for problem-solving rule assessment, 404–6
  problem-solving studies, 362–67, 412–13
  in psycholinguistics, 130–32, 135–36, 139,
    150–54, 167–68
  referential communication study, 429–30
  with representational-development hypothesis,
    180
  role-taking studies, 438–39
  schema use testing, 296–97
  in sensorimotor stage, 25–27
  social cognition studies, 418–19
  social problem-solving studies, 450, 455–57
  speaker skills testing, 432
  syllogistic reasoning studies, 327, 329, 332–33
  task demands and performance, 226–29
  theory and, 4
  transitive inference studies, 238–39
  voice preference studies, 67
Middle childhood. *See also* Concrete operations
    stage; Developmental stages
  analogical transfer in, 385–87
  attention in, 257–60
  causality concepts in, 252–53
  class inclusion concepts in, 235–36
  comprehension and memory in, 256–57
  conservation concepts in, 223–29
  GERs and memory in, 189
  learning and memory in, 256–57, 260–83
  Piagetian theory on, 222–23
  private speech decline in, 171, 174–75
  problem solving in, 363, 366, 367
Miller's Analogies Test, 304
Mismatches, in language development, 142, 146–47
Missionary-Cannibal problem, 380–81, 385–86
MLU. *See* Mean length of utterance
Mnemonic strategies
  content knowledge and, 275–77
  development of, 267–69
  mental effort and, 279–80
Monocular cues, depth perception studies and,
    33
Motor activity, thought and, 20
Motoric mode of knowledge representation, 179–80
Motor skills, 408–10
Movies, problem-solving studies using, 404–8

N
Nasal sounds, 101
Nativist theory, 14
  on intersensory relations, 69, 77
  on language acquisition, 161

perceptual constancy in, 54–55
Nature-nurture issue, 14–15
Necessary condition, 251–52
Necessary and sufficient condition, 252
Negation, reversibility rule of, 225
Negative propositions, 321
Negotiations, of failed communication, 139
Neonates. *See also* Infancy
  pattern discrimination in, 41–43
  perception of people by, 417–18
  recognition memory in, 84
  sensorimotor stage in, 19, 20, 21
  visual scanning by, 39–40
Neurophysiological models of development, vision
    and, 35–36
Non-nomial words, 144–45
Normative approach, to causality, 246
Novices, acquisition of expertise by, 408–13
Novice vs. expert problem solving, 398–408
Null hypothesis, enrichment studies and, 17
Number concepts, 229–35
Number conservation concept, 224–25

O
Object categorization, 97
  paired-comparison paradigm and, 106
  word acquisition and, 150–51
Object concept, 112
Object knowledge, as language prerequisite, 128
Object perception
  development of, 54–62
  proprioceptive-visual coordination, 75–77
  visual-tactile coordination, 72–75
Object permanence
  competence-performance and, 117–21
  development of, 111–21
  in sensorimotor stage, 21–22
  syntax acquisition and, 169
Objects
  categorization of. *See* Object categorization
  part-whole relations of, 214–16
  perception of people vs., 417–19
  social vs. nonsocial, 417
Oculomotor system, development of, 31–32
One-one principle, 229
Operant-conditioning paradigm, 26–27
  recognition memory in, 87–96
  size constancy studies with, 55
Operations, in problem solving, 356
Oral visual-tactile coordination, 72, 74–75
Order-irrelevance principle, 230
Organization
  concept relations, 211–16
  expert vs. novice problem solving and, 399–403
  in long-term memory, 9–10, 281
  part-whole relations, 214–16
  in pattern perception, 43–48
  perception as, 23–25
  in Piagetian theory, 6
  in scripts, 182–83, 186
  syntagmatic vs. paradigmatic responding, 213
Overextension, in language development, 143
Overlaps, in language development, 143

P
Paired-comparison paradigm, 82–84, 86
  in categorization studies, 106

hypothetico-deductive reasoning as, 345
Scripts, 182–83
   causality concepts in, 246
   discounting principle and, 443
   in early childhood, 182–92
   referential communication and, 431
   as schemas, 283, 290
Secondary circular reactions, 20–21
Selective attention, 7
Self-concept, 444–50
Self-continuity, 449
Self-regulation, problem solving and, 367–71
Self-terminating encoding, in analogical reasoning, 307, 309
Self-understanding, 444–50
Selman's task, 437–39
Semantic integration, referential integration and, 288–89
Semantic memory, 263
Semantics, 127, 132, 157–58
Semantic vs. conceptual knowledge, 148–49
Sensation
   methods of studying, 25–27
   perception and cognition vs., 22–23
Senses, 68–77
Sensitivity, as memory knowledge, 270
Sensorimotor knowledge, 178, 180
Sensorimotor stage, 6, 19–22. *See also* Infancy
   knowledge representation in, 12
   methods of studying, 25–27
   sensory capacity in, 22. *See also specific senses*
   syntax acquisition in, 169
Sensory registers, in information processing, 8–10
Separable dimensions, analogical reasoning and, 308–9
Separate entities, perception of objects as, 59–62
Sequencing
   as language prerequisite, 129–30
   in problem solving, 364–65
Sequential relations, in story grammars, 291
Serial position effect, 85, 267
Setting, in story grammar, 290–91
Shape constancy, 56–58
Short-term memory. *See* Working memory
Similarity principle, 253–54
   in causality, 246
Similars, 211
Sincerity, as rule of communication, 428
Sinusoidal contours, in prelinguistic communication, 136
Size constancy, 55–56
Skills acquisition, 408–10
   for social problem solving, 450–58
   stages in, 409–10
Snellen Chart, 27
Sociability, role-taking skills and, 439
Social cognition, 415–58
   causal reasoning about intention, 440–44
   communication and, 427–36
   defined, 416
   as discipline, 415–16
   expectations and, 419–21
   imitation and, 422–23
   object knowledge vs., 416
   problem solving and, 450–58
   role-taking skills, 436–40

self-understanding and, 444–50
   social referencing, 424–27
Socially mediated learning, 410–13
Social psychology, cognitive psychology and, 415
Social referencing, 422–23
Social speech, private speech vs., 173–74
Social vs. nonsocial objects, 417
Sound localization, 66
Sound perception. *See* Auditory development;
      Speech perception
Spatial contiguity, principle of, 246, 254
Spatial frequency, visual acuity and, 27–29
Speaker skills development, 431–33
Spectograms, 98–99
Speech
   egocentric, 188
   language prerequisites for, 129–30
   private, 170–76
   thought and, 170–71
Speech perception, 65, 97–105
Speech production, 131
Speech sounds, 98–101
Speeded classification task, 257
Sports, expert problem solving in, 408–9
Stable-order principle, 229
Stage theory, of Piaget, 6–7. *See also specific stages*
Star Wars, studies using, 404–8
Statistical heuristics, 317, 319
Statistical information, inductive reasoning and, 314–15, 317, 319
Steady-state formants, in speech sounds, 98
Stereopsis, 33–34
Stimulus-response models. *See* Behaviorist theory
Stops, in speech sounds, 101
Storage processes, 260, 282–83
Stories, memory for, 294–95
Story grammars, 291–95
Story schemas, 291–95
Strategies
   defined, 267
   mental effort and, 279–80
   for problem-solving, 366–67
Strategy variables, knowledge of, 270, 271
Stroop task, 277, 278
Structural theory, 5
Structure, 181, 193–211
Subgoals, in problem solving, 362–65
Substantive knowledge, referential communication and, 429, 431
Success-oriented problem solving, 360
Sucking response, to auditory stimuli, 62
Sufficient condition, 252
Superordinate concepts, 204–7
Superordinate vs. basic-level categories, 196–99
Syllogisms, 320–34
Syllogistic reasoning, 320–22, 323–24
   in early childhood, 332–34
   logical competence development and, 343
   models of, 323–28
Symbolic logic, in formal operations stage, 12
Symbol manipulation, language and, 125, 129, 145
Symmetry, pattern discrmination and, 45
Syntagmatic responding, paradigmatic responding vs., 213
Syntax, 127
   acquisition of, 155–69

Syntax (*cont.*)
  in early childhood, 132
  prelinguistic, 146

T

Tactile senses, visual-tactile coordination, 72–75, 77
Task variables, knowledge of, 270, 271
Taxonomic category, principle of, 150–51
Taxonomic relations, developmental stage and, 212, 213–14
Temporal contiguity, principle of, 246, 253–54
Temporal priority, principle of, 246, 248–49, 253
Temporal repairs, in children's scripts, 184, 190
Temporal sequence
  causality in, 245–54
  in scripts, 182–86, 190
  in story schemas, 291
Tennis, expert problem solving in, 409
Tertiary circular reactions, 21–22
Tetrahedral model, 261–62
Thai speakers, categorical perception in, 103–4
Thematic categories, in scripts, 191
Thematic relations, word acquisition and, 150–51
Theories, 4–10. *See also specific theories*
  of conceptual development, 193–211
  construction of, 3–4
  constructive vs. nativist, 69
  defined, 3
  differentiation, 201
  information-processing, 4, 7–10
  of knowledge representation, 179–82
  of language acquisition, 161–62
  in long-term memory, 281
  Piagetian, 4–7
  of self-concept development, 444–46, 448
  stage, 6–7
  structural, 5
Theory-in-action problem solving, 360
Thought
  as arising from action, 20
  language and, 169–76
  schemes and, 5
  about self, 450
Threshold, auditory discrimination and, 63–65
Toddlers. *See* Developmental stages; Early childhood; Sensorimotor stage
Tonic neck reflex, sensory integration with, 68
Top-down processes
  attention to, 36, 38
  in comprehension, 283
  in language comprehension, 165–66
  in perception, 23
  in planning, 362
  in problem representation, 359–60
Tower of Hanoi problem, 381–82
Transfer, in problem solving, 392–97
Transformational grammar, 156
Transitional formants, in speech sounds, 98
Transitive inference, 235, 238–41, 285, 301
Turn taking, by infants, 135–36

U

Underextension, in language development, 142–43
Universal propositions, 321
Universal theories, 14, 104

V

Validity, reasoning and, 331, 336
Variables
  controlling-variables tasks, 352–53, 378
  as memory knowledge, 270–71
Verbal Behavior (Skinner), 7
Verbal commands, 423
Verbal description, for concept acquisition, 204
Verification strategy, in hypothesis testing, 338, 339, 376
Vision
  anatomy of eye, 27–28
  attention and, 36–38
  basic visual capacities, 35–36
  color discrimination, 32–33
  depth perception, 33–35
  development of, 27–62
  object perception, 54–62
  oculomotor system and, 31–32
  pattern perception and, 27–30, 39–53
  perceptual expectations and, 53–54
  proprioceptive-visual coordination, 75–77
Visual acuity, 27–29
Visual-auditory coordination, 69–72, 77
Visual preference paradigm, in attention studies, 36–38
Visual preference test, 25
  paired-comparison variation on, 83
  proprioceptive-visual coordination and, 76–77
Visual recognition memory, 81–87
Visual scanning paradigm, 39
Visual self-recognition, 445
Visual-tactile coordination, 72–75, 77
Voiced vs. voiceless sounds, 100
Voice onset time (VOT), 101–4
Volition, in self-concept, 449–50

W

Wason's hypothesis-testing task, 338–39
Well-defined problems, 357, 381
Word meaning, 147–54, 277
Word order strategy, for language comprehension, 164–65
Working memory, 264–67
  attention and, 278
  defined, 264–65
  formal operations tasks and, 353
  functions of, 265–67
  in information processing, 8–10
  maturational change in, 280–81
  problem representation and, 359
  rehearsal and, 268
  short-term memory vs., 264
  syllogistic reasoning and, 325
World knowledge, problem representation and, 358

Z

Zone of proximal development, 410, 413

A	9
B	0
C	1
D	2
E	3
F	4
G	5
H	6
I	7
J	8